KINGS & QUEENS
OF GREAT BRITAIN

EVERY QUESTION ANSWERED

KINGS & QUEENS
OF GREAT BRITAIN

EVERY QUESTION ANSWERED

DAVID SOUD

METRO BOOKS
New York

METRO BOOKS
New York

An Imprint of Sterling Publishing
387 Park Avenue South
New York, NY 10016

© 2013 Moseley Road Inc.

This 2013 edition published by Metro Books by arrangement with Moseley Road Inc.

Moseley Road Inc, www.moseleyroad.com
Publisher: Sean Moore
General Manager: Karen Prince
Editorial Director: Damien Moore
Art Director: Tina Vaughan
Production Director: Adam Moore

Design Philippa Baile and Duncan Youel, www.oiloften.co.uk
          Dawn Terrey, www.dawnterrey.co.uk

ISBN 978-1-4351-4570-2

For information about custom editions, special sales, and premium and corporate purchases, please contact Sterling Special Sales at 800-805-5489 or specialsales@sterlingpublishing.com.

Manufactured in China

2 4 6 8 10 9 7 5 3 1

www.sterlingpublishing.com

  C O

1

The House of Wessex

N T E N T S ✚

2

The Norman Kings

3

The House of Plantagenet

4

The Houses of Lancaster and York

5

6

7

The House of Tudor

The House of Stuart

The House of Hanover

8

The House of Windsor

9

Royal Edicts

PREFACE

This book is a kind of pageant. It presents a parade of personalities that, to varying degrees, have shaped the history of Britain and the world. While it touches on the larger historical forces in which kings and queens have often been enmeshed, it focuses chiefly on the monarchs of Britain as individual people. While the life stories recounted here are necessarily limited—untold thousands of pages have been devoted to more detailed biographies of Britain's monarchs—this book offers a sense of who these kings and queens were, the situations in which they found themselves, and how they handled the formidable pressures of the crown.

The author F. Scott Fitzgerald famously remarked that the rich are different; he might have done better to say that royalty are different. Though contemporary media culture, with its relentless coverage of the lives and habits of the Windsors, has sometimes made their lives seem almost ordinary, there remains a barrier between them and the rest of us, a sense that they inhabit a separate universe of custom, wealth, duty, and privilege that only occasionally, and in carefully managed ways, overlaps with our own.

Yet at the same time, we know that in the most fundamental sense the kings and queens of Britain have always been very much like us, that they share common human needs and desires and feelings, that they play out their ambitions and personal dramas in the same way the rest of us do in our various arenas. When we look into their personal lives, their triumphs, their errors, we often see in their chronicles our own life stories, written in a script that may be grander and more archaic but which we can still read and comprehend.

That ambiguity, that sense that kings and queens are both like and unlike the rest of us, will always be a source of fascination. In contemplating the enormous personal power of Henry VIII or seeking to understand the far less formidable position of George V, we appreciate how these people can seem at once deeply human and unapproachably distant. And in the dramas of the various British dynasties we encounter, as in the plays of Shakespeare, an astonishing range of personality types and human situations. The more forceful characters have not always made for the most successful reigns, nor have the less charismatic occupants of the British throne always been unsuccessful rulers.

When we think of the kings and queens of England, some storied names come quickly to mind: Henry VIII, Elizabeth I, Henry V, Richard III, George III, Victoria, and Elizabeth II, to take a few, loom larger in our consciousness than most of their predecessors and successors. But some of Britain's most magnificent monarchs—Henry II, Edward I, and Edward III come to mind—have receded somewhat from our collective consciousness; and some of the most compelling life stories, such as those of the unexpectedly decisive Henry I, the narcissistic Richard II, and the hapless Henry VI, tend to go unappreciated. The outsized personalities of William II, Edward II, and George IV stand out all the more sharply against the seeming dullness of Anne, Victoria, and George V.

And many of the tantalizing what-ifs of British history revolve around the island's monarchs. What if the Saxons under Harold Godwinson had not broken their shield wall at the Battle of Hastings? What if Henry V or Edward IV had lived to reign even ten years longer? What if Catherine of Aragon had succeeded in giving birth to a boy? What if the Gunpowder Plot had succeeded? What if Edward VIII had never met Wallis Simpson? The questions go on, and their implications are endlessly discussable.

Whether you read this book chronologically or dip into it whenever you grow curious about a particular British king or queen, you may well find yourself asking similar questions, and wondering about both the larger contexts and the details of these monarchs' reigns. With that in mind, the book includes both feature spreads on interesting historical contexts and a hundred-page appendix of royal documents, ranging from momentous speeches to household inventories. The documents in particular reveal the process of ruling a kingdom—or in the case of more recent history, the business of remaining relevant in a political system that no longer affords the British monarch much political power.

The pageant of the British monarchy is no fairy tale; the lives of the kings and queens of Britain have often been full of intrigue, war, illness, and grief. Sometimes the course of a king or queen's reign has been determined in dark ways—through conspiracy, scandal, and even murder. Loyalties change, victories turn into defeats, defeats become opportunities. But in many cases humanity, decency, and vision have prevailed. Here is the human situation writ large, and decked in royal regalia. Enjoy it.

Above and right
Durham Cathedral. Begun under William I, it remains one of the finest examples of late Romanesque architecture in Europe.

10 Introduction

INTRODUCTION

he history of the British monarchy is, in some ways, a distilled history of Britain. It is the chronicle of how that nation has seen itself, from its earliest beginnings to its current situation as a post-imperial power. British customs, institutions, and even the English language evolved largely in relation to the kings and queens who, as Shakespeare wrote, were "the makers of manners."

England as we know it began to take shape, however hesitantly, in the wake of the withdrawal of Roman legions from the Britannia in the fifth century. For the next several centuries, after a brief clash of Celtic and Germanic cultures that probably gave rise to the legend of King Arthur, "England" meant Angle-land, a collection of Germanic kingdoms dominated by the Angles, the Saxons, and the Jutes. The Old English they spoke in various forms, one of which gave rise to the great epic Beowulf, is a foreign language to nearly all speakers of English as we know it now, but its traces remain in such sturdy, direct words

A statue on Lichfield Cathedral of William the Conqueror, whose successful invasion in 1066 transformed not only England's social structure but also its language.

of Germanic origin as "rock," "love," "what," and even "king." Those words, with their tactile edges, bespeak a sterner culture than the one that would eventually dominate and transform Anglo-Saxon England.

The Anglo-Saxon kings, most famously those of the House of Wessex, were lawgivers, but they also were bound by a more communal sense of legitimacy than later British monarchs would enjoy. Some, such as Alfred the Great and Athelstan, became icons of wise, forthright, and even cultured kingship, but all had to demonstrate prowess as military men. This was partly due to the culture they inhabited, but it also was essential in defending the Anglo-Saxon kingdoms from incursions by the

Norse, especially the Danish, who for generations held control over large swaths of the north and east of what is now England. The city of York, for instance, was once the Viking town of Jorvik.

And it was Norsemen—ones who had settled in the north of France and come to be known as Normans—who eventually wrested control of England from its Anglo-Saxon population. While it is commonplace to say that 1066 was a pivotal date in Western history, it is hard to overstate its importance to Britain. When William the Conqueror defeated Harold Godwinson at the Battle of Hastings and swiftly brought England to heel, he and his successors brought with them a hybrid culture of Norse martial prowess and Carolingian notions of societal structure and nobility. They also brought with them the French language, which, after centuries as a badge of nobility, gradually merged with Old English to form Middle English, the language of Chaucer—an early version of the English you are reading now.

That French cultural infusion had its greatest impact under the Plantagenet dynasty, related to the Normans, which arrived in the person of Henry II and his formidable queen, Eleanor of Aquitaine, in 1189. The Plantagenet rulers brought to England the vibrant, deeply chivalrous culture of Occitan, with its pageantry, romance, and drama. But the Plantagenet kings also tended to England as only one of their hereditary realms, not as the jewel in their crowns. The hankering of English kings for lands in France would reach its pinnacle in the Hundred Years' War, in the fourteenth and fifteenth centuries—a conflict in which such legendary English victories as Crécy, Poitiers, and Agincourt would give way to vicious infighting among noble houses, and the aristocratic bloodletting of the Wars of the Roses.

In the wake of the Wars of the Roses, one monarch was left standing: Henry VII, founder of the storied Tudor dynasty. From 1485 until 1603, the Tudors would reign over an unprecedented and sometimes torturous adolescence for England. Henry VIII would, for complex reasons, break precipitously with the Roman Catholic Church, making England a pariah nation to much of Europe. Despite the efforts of Mary Tudor to wrench England back into the Catholic fold, the nation would remain fundamentally, even oppressively, Protestant. Fortunately, in Elizabeth I England had a monarch capable of navigating the precarious final decades of the sixteenth century and establishing England as something more than just a military power. Under the imperious rule of the Virgin Queen, the age of the poets Shakespeare and Marlowe, the scientist Francis Bacon and the composer John Dowland, England underwent its Renaissance, and came into its own as an arena of lively and sophisticated modern culture.

When Elizabeth died childless, never having married, the Tudor age gave way to that of the Stuart dynasty of Scotland, and England and Scotland began to gravitate toward union. Under the reign of James I, not only did England refine both its Protestant identity and its language with the Authorized (King James) Version of the Bible; it also established its first colonies in America, and began to entertain anew the imperial ambitions that had once given rise to long and intractable conflicts on the European continent.

The English Civil War and the Interregnum, in some ways a relatively modest echo of the Thirty Years' War, ultimately led to a different sort of monarchy. After the de facto dictatorship of Oliver Cromwell, the Restoration brought back a brief period of Stuart-sponsored indulgence and extravagance before politically charged conflicts over religion and the royal prerogative led in 1688 to the so-called Glorious Revolution—in reality a friendly takeover of the British throne by William of Orange. The resulting Bill of Rights, along with other measures, began the gradual process of resolving the long-standing tensions between monarch and Parliament in favor of the latter. From 1689 onward, the British Crown inexorably became less and less the center of political power, and more and more the habitation of a particular kind of symbolic capital, emblematic of patriotism and tradition, and occasionally endowed with significant moral force.

The great virtue of the monarchs of the House of Hanover was that, despite their sometimes operatic family squabbles and episodes of madness, intuitively grasped this transformation, and for the most part did not resist it. Not long after George I's ascension in 1714 onward, it was inescapably clear that political power in Britain was concentrated increasingly in the hands of Parliament, and especially those of the often gifted and fascinating Prime Ministers that would dominate the Hanoverian era: Walpole, the Pitts, Derby, Gladstone, and Disraeli, among others. At the same time, the British Empire began its rise to world dominance, becoming the dominant global presence by the reign of Queen Victoria.

In the twentieth century, the fortunes of the British royal family waxed and waned. Often challenged as an outmoded and fundamentally reactionary institution, the monarchy of the Windsors—who, during the First World War, adopted that quintessentially English name—has nonetheless remained, even gaining popularity in recent years despite the sometimes tawdry, sometimes poignant scandals and misfortunes that have tarnished the family. The Windsor ideal of monarch as a kind of public servant, a custodian of traditional British values, may be ambiguous, but it showed its merits during the Second World War, when George VI and his family became symbols of British steadiness, and Elizabeth II has at times succeeded in assuming that potent role.

As the twenty-first century begins to unfold, a new generation of royals has had to weather an existence increasingly open to public scrutiny, vulnerable to unscrupulous intrusions, and subject to the vagaries of the culture of celebrity. How William, Kate, and Harry will fare going forward will largely depend on their ability to control their public images—to maintain the symbolic capital that has become the stock in trade of the British monarchy. Whatever controversies still surround the continued existence of the monarchy, one hopes they will manage it well.

This book presents the history of the British monarchy as the story of individual kings and queens. All of them remain symbols, albeit with different valences and varying potencies—but each was also, importantly, a human being, subject to the same affections and temptations, joys and griefs, that surround us all. That they often had to face such human situations in an atmosphere of almost alien privilege, subject at the same time to kinds of pressure people of other social ranks seldom if ever encounter, only makes their stories more compelling.

As we range over these brief but revealing biographies, we can judge for ourselves which of these monarchs most successfully occupied the throne. To do so, each of us has to consider our criteria. What of the fierce kings like Henry II, who, with equal parts charisma, force, and guile, held together disparate realms? Or the lawgivers

ENTRY TO THE TRAITORS GATE

like Alfred the Great and Edward I Longshanks, who combined martial prowess with a strong sense of justice? Or the ones who, like Elizabeth I, successfully piloted England through dangerous and unpredictable times? There may be a place for those who, like Henry V, understood how to weld a nation together behind a common cause, or even those who, in the spirit of George VI, understood their place in the scheme of things and set about modeling courage and decency, as best they could, for a nation in need of inspiration.

It is hard to measure the monarchs of one era against those of another, but we can consider how each king or queen responded to his or her time. In doing so, we can also examine ourselves, and come to understand our own time better. Along the way, we can read fascinating stories, and ponder what might have been as well as what was.

The Tower of London, the scene of countless dramatic events in the history of the British monarchy since its construction under William the Conqueror.

edmund lui tint al encountre e desconfit forine

estut edward sen fuy
en hungrie pur le
kuit le traunt. ou il
engendra ceus ke sut
ici escriz. mes la gene
racium de margarete
si ala auant.

Edward sun fiz ke fu ex ille

Edgar etheling sun fiz

seinte margarete sa fille

edmund coun

The House of Wessex

From the time of Roman Britannia
to the Norman invasion of 1066,
England was seldom a unified
country. Rather, it was mostly
divided among petty kingdoms ruled
by Anglo-Saxon kings, and large
swaths of Britain were eventually
held by the Danes and other Vikings.
This was a heroic age, the era that
gave rise to the great epic *Beowulf*,
but it did not lack sophistication.
In time, the kingdom of Wessex
came to dominate the rich culture
of Anglo-Saxon England. Such
towering rulers as Alfred the Great
and Athelstan, along with the
sainted Edward the Confessor, made
the House of Wessex one of the great
dynasties of British history.

THE KINGS WHO BUILT ENGLAND

The House of Wessex, also known as the House of Cerdic, was the first royal line to rule over a kingdom we would recognize today as England. With few interruptions, from the ninth to the eleventh centuries, they held a shifting swath of territory that defined English culture. In doing so, they had to defend their realm against the incursions of land-hungry invaders—most prominently the Vikings, who left their own indelible imprint on British culture. Only with the Norman invasion in 1066 would the last of the Wessex kings fall, and with his death would come a complete transformation of what it meant to be English.

Boudicca, female leader of the Iceni, who put up an impressive resistance to Roman occupiers in the first century CE.

Of course, Britain had kings, or at least chieftains, long before the House of Wessex materialized. The region has been inhabited for millennia; from Orkney to Stonehenge, its early peoples have left relics for us to ponder. For several centuries before the Christian era, the British Isles, like much of Europe, had been home to Celtic peoples, for whom kings largely played a symbolic role. It was only a matter of time before more sturdy organization would come, from within or without. In the first century BCE, it seems that high kings became more dominant, with one Caswallon commanding the allegiance of most Britons.

THE ARRIVAL OF THE ROMANS

But then a different, much more effective organization arrived in the form of the Roman Empire. In 55 BCE, Julius Caesar tentatively invaded Britain. He was more concerned with unrest in Gaul than in conquering Britain, and after an impressive show of force soon withdrew. About a century later, Rome would return with a much more ambitious agenda. At that time, the British high king Cunobelin had proved an able leader, unifying much of what is now England—a mixed blessing, since it was his power, and the

evident mineral resources in his kingdom, that brought Britain to the attention of the Roman emperor Claudius.

ROMAN BRITAIN

Cunobelin died in 40 CE; his successor, Caradoc, had only three years on the throne before facing a full-scale invasion of the Roman legions. At the Battle of the Medway, the Britons were defeated. After a few years of desultory guerrilla campaigning, Caradoc was captured and sent to Rome, where he and his family apparently settled down to enjoy life on the Mediterranean. Meanwhile, the Romans established their base at Londinium, which became London, and the process of Romanizing Britain, or Britannia, began. Though some tribes resisted—most famously the Iceni under the female warrior Boudicca—within a generation the conquest was largely finished.

England would be a realm of the Roman Empire for the next four centuries, during which Roman customs would establish a firm foothold. In 122, Emperor Hadrian ordered the construction of his wall as a fortified northern boundary to the empire. Within those boundaries, Romanized Briton even produced

527

Constantinople's Emperor Justin dies aged 77. His son Justinian begins a 38-year reign.

535

Massive eruption of the volcano Krakatoa in Indonesia spews so much ash into the upper atmosphere that the world's climate is cooled for the next three years.

540

Antioch falls to the Persians who loot the city before retiring to Persia.

603

Battle of Degasaston sees the defeat of Picts and Scots, handing control of what is now northern England to the English.

a handful of emperors in the waning years of the empire. But by the mid-fifth century, Rome itself was under siege. The great migration of Germanic and other tribes on the mainland took its toll, and eventually Britannia was left to fend for itself.

The history here remains murky, but it is clear that with the Roman administrative apparatus gone, all order broke down, as old tribal rivalries and individual ambitions asserted themselves. Some Britons simply reverted to the old ways, while others attempted to sustain a Romanized way of life. The story goes that Vortigern, a high king in the south, turned to the Roman practice of hiring mercenary forces, in this case Germanic warriors under Hengist and Horsa, rewarding them with grants of land and thereby giving them a foothold in Britain. Once the Germanic tribes saw how rich and fertile that land was, and how sparsely defended, they started coming in droves.

THE ANGLES AND SAXONS

The arrival of the Angles, Saxons, and Jutes spelled the end of Romanized Britain. Though from about 450–550 there was inspired resistance to the steady invasion—the legend of King Arthur, who may well have originally been a Romanized British cavalry leader, seems to have originated here—the inexorable strength of the Germanic tribes, both in military prowess and in numbers, eventually won out, as the Britons were pushed back to Wales, Cornwall, and even Breton in France. For the next three centuries, a series of Anglo-Saxon kingdoms were carved out; among them were Kent, Northumbria, Mercia, Essex, Sussex, and Wessex. Christianity arrived on the island from both Rome and Ireland, and many kings converted, a settlement largely in favor of Roman control being reached at the Synod of Whitby in 663. Eventually, one man, Egbert of Wessex, would defeat all his rivals and lay the groundwork for a kingship of England.

King Arthur remains the most iconic image of kingship in British culture. The Arthurian legends have inspired a number of British kings, including Edward III, founder of the Order of the Garter.

Glastonbury in Somerset, the epicenter of many legends about King Arthur. Those legends are widely regarded as being rooted in the resistance of Romanized Britons to the incursions of Germanic tribes in the fifth and sixth centuries.

610	616		654		709	720
According to Islamic belief, Mohammed has his first vision of the Archangel Gabriel who begins the revelation of the Koran.	Traditional date for the founding of a Christian chapel to St. Peter on Thorn Island in the River Thames, now Westminster Abbey.		Arabs invade Rhodes, melting down the famous statue, the Colossus of Rhodes.		King Cenred of Mercia in England abdicates and travels to Rome to become a monk.	The Moors cross the Pyrenees and capture Narbonne.

FROM EGBERT TO ALFRED THE GREAT

Egbert was born in Wessex somewhere around the year 770. As he came of age, one king was dominating much of Britain. Offa of Mercia was a formidable leader and ruthless warrior; he was also powerful enough that even Charlemagne, rather grudgingly, acknowledged him as a lesser but still legitimate European ruler. Offa expanded his influence by demanding fealty from neighboring kingdoms, and he was brilliantly systematic about securing his lands. To this day, the remains of Offa's Dyke, a long line of earthworks that were probably once topped with wooden palisades, extends at least 64 miles (103 km) along much of what is now the border between England and Wales. It was Offa, perhaps along with Beorhtric, then king of Wessex, who seems to have engineered Egbert's exile to the continent, where he was to remain for 13 years, probably under the protection

Egbert of Wessex overcame the dominance of Mercia and made the House of Wessex the most important line of kings in pre-Norman Britain.

of Charlemagne. It may be that he learned something of the business of kingship while staying within Charlemagne's carefully run empire. In any case, on the death of Beorhtric in 802, Egbert was there to claim the throne. More than likely, he had the considerable weight of Charlemagne and Rome behind him, but in any case Offa was long dead and his successors ineffective, so the time was right for Egbert's star to rise.

Egbert seems to have risen to prominence steadily, and his gathering power came to fruition in 825, when his forces defeated a Mercian army at Ellendun, breaking the Mercian hold on the south. Four years later, he invaded and conquered Mercia itself, establishing himself as king over a large portion of the South and the Midlands of England. By 830, he had invaded Northumbria and accepted the fealty of its king, and even extended his reach into Wales. Briefly, Egbert was, in power if not in title, King of England.

Egbert's ascendancy did not last; within a year, he forfeited much of the land he had conquered. But the dominance of Mercia had been overcome, and the House of Wessex had established itself as a major force in England. This new prominence was made clear in 838, when the Archbishop of Canterbury acknowledged Egbert and his son Aethelwulf as protectors of the monasteries and churches over a sizable chunk of the south. When Egbert died the next year, Aethelwulf was affirmed as King of Wessex.

KING AETHELWULF

Aethelwulf had already distinguished himself in Egbert's early military campaigns, and his father had rewarded him with the kingship of Kent. Aethelwulf himself would follow that precedent, giving his son Aethelstan control of the eastern portion of his domains. At this point, Aethelwulf enjoyed sufficient stature

The kingdoms of England around 825, showing the position of Wessex relative to the other major Saxon realms.

778	793	810	814
King Charles of the Franks invades Spain to fight the Muslims. His rearguard is defeated by Basques at Roncesvalles, an incident made famous by the epic poem *The Song of Roland*.	Vikings sack the Abbey of Lindisfarne, their first major raid on England. 	*The Book of Kells*, an illuminated manuscript of the four gospels in Latin, is completed in Ireland.	 Death of Emperor Charlemagne, also known as King Charles of the Franks.

to be recognized as a worthy king on the continent. He seems to have been quite religious, and in 855 undertook a trip to Rome to meet the pope. If period accounts are to be believed, he took with him on that journey two of his five sons, Aethelred and Alfred. But there was another reason for Aethelwulf's trip: Viking raiders, who had begun plundering British monasteries in the late eighth century, were marauding in greater numbers and terrorizing more and more of the south, and Aethelwulf sought divine aid against them. Period chronicles indicate that a good portion of the business of kingship in the ninth century was fending off Vikings, which Aethelwulf did with mixed success. And he had troubles at home as well. By the time he returned to Wessex, Aethelstan had died, and his eldest remaining son Aethelbald had conspired to take the throne. To keep the peace, Aethelwulf gave Aethelbald a portion of the kingdom to rule. Then, recognizing that his four remaining sons were likely to contend for control of Wessex, he drew up a will passing the throne among his sons according to age.

Aethelbald was thus the first to inherit the throne, but he died in 860 after only two years of rule, leaving it to his brother Aethelbehrt. Aethelbehrt ruled for five years, unifying the lands of the House of Wessex rather than delegating his brothers to rule satellite kingdoms. When he died in 865, his brother Aethelred became king, only to face the most dangerous Viking invasion yet. That year, a large force of Norsemen destroyed the kingdoms of East Anglia and Northumberland, and threatened Mercia. The Mercians and Wessexmen joined forces, and for the rest of Aethelred's reign managed a stiff enough resistance to hold off the invaders despite some stinging defeats.

In 871, Aethelred died, and the throne passed to Aethelwulf's youngest son Alfred. Given his place in the family, it is remarkable that Alfred lived to wear the crown of Wessex. But his ascension was a watershed in English history. It is not for nothing that Alfred is the only British monarch to have the epithet, "the Great."

Aethelbert ruled Wessex for only five years, but within that span he did much to unify Wessex as a kingdom.

VIKING RAIDERS

The popular depiction of Vikings as tall, violent warriors with horned helmets may contain traces of the truth—they were formidable sailors and soldiers with a taste for fighting and looting—but it hardly suggests the complexity of Viking culture. In reality, they were as interested in trade as anything else and sailed all over the known world—even to North America—in search of land and resources. Viking soldiers served Byzantine emperors, and Viking relics have been found in India. They showed a remarkable ability to adapt to the cultures of the lands where they settled, and in the case of England, eventually even integrated with the people there. And their helmets did not have horns.

The arrival of Viking raiders in England in the late eighth century signaled the start of a long, bitter struggle in which Wessex kings would lead resistance against the powerful Danes and, eventually, the Norse.

840	847		851	855
The Holy Roman Emperor Louis the Pious dies, aged 62. His 45-year-old son Lothair succeeds him as emperor.	Pope Leo IV builds the Leonine Wall to protect St. Peter's.		Canterbury Cathedral is sacked by Danish forces who navigate the Thames estuary. The Vikings are defeated at Ockley by King Aethelwulf.	The Holy Roman emperor Lothair dies, aged 60, after dividing his lands between his three sons. He is succeeded as emperor by his 33-year-old son, who will reign for 20 years as Louis II.

Aethelred (right), one of Alfred the Great's three brothers and his immediate predecessor on the throne of Wessex. With Alfred at his side, he managed to fend off major Viking aggression.

THE EARLY REIGN OF ALFRED THE GREAT

We do not know much for certain about Alfred's early life; the chronicles closest to his reign are often unreliable, and as the youngest of Aethelwulf's sons he was probably never expected to take the throne of Wessex, and so was never the subject of careful record-keeping. He seems to have been born around 847, and his devout father probably intended him, and perhaps his brother Aethelred, for careers in the Church, which might explain why they reportedly accompanied Aethelwulf on his 855 journey to Rome. By

A statue of Alfred the Great in Winchester, erected on the thousandth anniversary of his death. This martial depiction only captures one side, and that a relatively reluctant one, of Alfred, who was by temperament more scholar than warrior.

868, he was fighting alongside Aethelred in the resistance against Viking raiders.

The year 871 was a seemingly endless succession of battles—at least nine, one of which was an impressive victory at Ashdown in January, for which Alfred has traditionally been given credit. But there were more defeats than victories, and it seems that in one of them, at some point in the spring, Aethelred was mortally wounded. By the succession arrangement, Alfred took the throne rather than either of Aethelred's two young sons. There was no time for festivities; the Kingdom of Wessex was fighting for its survival against Danish forces known to the Saxons as the Great Heathen Army. Toward the summer, Alfred's forces suffered a major setback at Wilton, and it was clear that, if he wanted to neutralize the Danish threat for any length of time, Alfred would have to buy time to build and reorganize his defenses.

So buy time he did—literally. Late that year, Alfred arrived at terms with the Danes, paying them a considerable sum of money to leave Wessex alone. For the next five years, the agreement held, and Alfred could attend to the business of organizing and strengthening his kingdom. In addition to beefing up his army, he began to build a navy, the better to attack the Vikings on the water, where they had hitherto held an undisputed advantage.

ALFRED'S DEFEAT AND RESURGENCE

But Alfred's preparations did not prepare Wessex for the next Viking onslaught, which came in 876 under a new and enterprising Danish leader, Guthrum. Over the previous two years, Guthrum had succeeded in bringing under his control both Northumbria and Mercia, and when he turned his attention to Wessex his forces enjoyed immediate success. After a series of raids and probing attacks in which the Wessexmen were driven back, Alfred was forced to negotiate peace settlements more than once, but it was clear that Guthrum wanted all of Wessex for himself. In effect, Alfred had

863	871	872	874	874
The Battle of Lalakaon is a significant victory for the Byzantines over the Arabs that starts a period of resurgence for the Byzantine Empire.	Holy Roman Emperor Louis II defeats the Saracens at the Muslim stronghold of Bari in 871.	The first hospital to be opened in the Muslim world is founded in Cairo.	Start of the ten year Huang Chao Rebellion in China that would lead to millions of deaths and fatally undermine the already weakened Tang Dynasty	Iceland is discovered by Viking Norsemen who begin almost immediate colonization.

become the last Anglo-Saxon king standing in the way of Danish rule of all England.

On January 6, 878, the feast of Epiphany, Guthrum made his decisive move. While Alfred and most of his Wessexmen celebrated the feast at Chippenham in Wiltshire, Guthrum's forces launched a surprise night attack. Whether he had assistance from someone within Alfred's ranks is an open question; certainly the Danish forces failed to set off any alarms as they approached. It was a complete rout: Alfred and a small group of followers barely escaped, making their way into the fens where they could evade any pursuers.

GUERRILLA TACTICS

It was a crushing defeat for Alfred. Had a less gifted and determined leader been in his place, the raid at Chippenham might have spelled the end of Anglo-Saxon England as a viable nation. But, with his extraordinary combination of charisma, skill, willpower, and humility, Alfred kept the hopes of Wessex alive, even as he was forced to retreat into hiding. One famous story relates that, during his flight from Chippenham, Alfred rested incognito in the hut of a peasant woman. When she asked him to tend to some loaves of bread in her oven while she was out, he was so absorbed in his troubles that he let them burn. When the woman returned and found he had been negligent, she gave him a sharp scolding, which he accepted meekly, feeling that he deserved it.

For the next few months, Alfred and a small force engaged in a guerrilla resistance against the Vikings. It seems that they were able to maintain good contacts with the larger Wessex community, but regardless, the situation was precarious. That May, however, Alfred emerged from his hideout in Somerset, issued a general call for warriors, and marched on the Danes. Sometime in mid-May, the two armies met at a place called Ethandun, which has since been identified as Edington in Wiltshire. Forming a stout shield-wall, Alfred's forces not only

EDMUND THE MARTYR

Other English kingdoms did not fare as well against the Vikings as Wessex. Nearby East Anglia was overrun by the Great Heathen Army, and in the process one of its kings, Edmund (d. 869), became a martyr and saint. Though we have no reliable information on his life or death—what little existed was likely destroyed by the Danes—the story goes that, after his army's defeat at the hands of the Danes, Edmund was captured and ordered to renounce Christ. When he refused, he was beaten, used for target practice by Viking archers, and beheaded. Some accounts relate how a wolf led searchers to Edmund's discarded head. He went on to become the patron saint of England until Edward III replaced him with St. George, and his final resting place, Bury St. Edmunds in Suffolk, became a place of pilgrimage and a major monastic center.

withstood the Great Heathen Army; they decisively defeated them, driving them back to the fortifications at Chippenham, where for the next two weeks Alfred starved them out in a siege.

THE CONVERSION OF GUTHRUM

Guthrum seems to have realized that, in Alfred, he had met a Saxon king capable of defying and defeating him. Accordingly, when the Danes sued for peace, this time they kept it. Guthrum even offered to convert to Christianity; when he was baptized, Alfred stood as his godfather. It was a fascinating turn of events. On the one hand, it demonstrated the pragmatism of Guthrum and the Vikings, who were prepared to adapt in order to settle the

875	877	878	881
The Holy Roman emperor Louis II dies having named his cousin Carloman as his successor.	The Vikings capture Exeter, England.	Battle of Ethandun. Alfred the Great of Wessex decisively defeats the Vikings under Guthrum.	Battle of Saucourt-en-Vimeu. Louis III decisively defeats Vikings near the River Somme, an event later commemorated in the poem "Ludwigslied."

A coin from Alfred's reign, done in the Roman style and naming him "King of the Saxons."

lands they had already conquered; on the other, it suggests something about the powerful impression Alfred must have made in the victory at Edington and after. In any case, Guthrum, under his new Christian name of Aethelstan, settled in to rule his extensive lands to the north and east of Wessex, which would eventually be known as the Danelaw. Though other Vikings would continue to make forays into Wessex and the surrounding lands, for the next several years Alfred was free to refashion Wessex to suit his vision of a Christian kingdom.

ALFRED'S VISION OF KING AND COUNTRY

Alfred was a devout Christian, and from the start of his reign he regularly sent gifts to Rome. In recognition of that constancy—and probably also of his status as a bastion of the faith against the largely non-Christian Vikings—in about 883 Pope Marinus sent him an assortment of gifts, reportedly including what was believed to be a piece of the True Cross. It was a powerful statement, and enhanced Alfred's status as an iconic Christian king.

Alfred had always been more inclined toward faith and scholarship than toward bloodshed and tactics; he became a formidable military leader because war was an unavoidable aspect of kingship, and it was essential to keeping his faith from being driven out of Britain. When peace prevailed, he pursued learning. Well into his thirties, he learned Latin, and gained enough proficiency to translate what he considered the most valuable texts for distribution around his kingdom. Perhaps in emulation of what he had encountered in his childhood travels through the Frankish empire to Rome, he encouraged widespread education in Wessex. Years of disruptive attacks by the Danes had undermined existing educational traditions, and the monasteries had been depopulated. Alfred recruited trained scholars, mostly churchmen, from all over Britain and abroad, establishing schools in which talented children of all social backgrounds could be taught. It seems that Alfred saw literacy as essential both to the efficient administration of his kingdom and to the sense of community he hoped to build in Wessex; for him, literacy was inseparable from individual and collective strength of character.

THE RESTORATION OF LONDON

In 886, Alfred undertook a restoration and refortification of London—another symbolic act that led to his being acknowledged as king of all the Anglo-Saxon peoples of Britain, though he never formally took such a title. But refortifying London was only a small part

The Alfred Jewel, held in the Ashmolean Museum in Oxford. A piece of very fine workmanship, it appears to have been intended as a pointer for reading.

884	885	887	891	892	893
France's Carloman is succeeded by Holy Roman Emperor Charles III, son of the late Louis the German.	Vikings lay siege to Paris but are driven off.	Death of Abu ibn Majah, Muslim scholar who compiled the official hadiths of the Sunni branch of Islam.	The king of Italy Guy of Spoleto is crowned Holy Roman emperor by Pope Stephen V.	England is invaded by the Danes who arrive from the mainland in 330 ships accompanied by their wives and children.	King Alfonso III of Leon captures Zamora from the Muslims.

of a general defensive strategy that Alfred had formulated specifically to repel Viking attacks. The Vikings had traditionally held the advantage of mobility: they traveled swiftly by sea and land, struck without warning, and often withdrew as quickly as they attacked. The only way to defend his kingdom against them, Alfred reasoned, was to have a standing army, significant numbers of mounted units, and a perimeter of fortified bases close enough to each other that troops could respond quickly and decisively to any incursions. It was a grand strategy for its day, and Alfred had to work hard to drum up enthusiasm for it. After all, it required rotations of troops, most of whom would be drawn away from their fields and trades; and building and maintaining the fortifications, which Alfred made a local responsibility, was expensive.

But his strategy proved its worth. In 893, a huge Viking force—over 300 ships—arrived at what is now Hastings from the continent, where they had been harried by the Franks. This was no raid; it was a protracted resettlement effort, and for the next four years Alfred once more had to engage in a long defensive campaign. But the Vikings found that Alfred's 30 forts and highly mobile troops were more than a match for them, and eventually gave up.

When King Alfred the Great eventually died in 899, it was a gigantic loss for the Anglo-

An image illustrating a famous legend in which Alfred is chastised by a peasant woman for allowing her cakes to burn. The woman had given Alfred refuge following his flight from the Viking raid at Chippenham.

Saxon cause, but he had left his kingdom in excellent shape to defend and develop itself. His vision of a Christian realm, in which learning and skilled craftsmanship were valued and the king had a deep responsibility for the well-being of his subjects on every level, did much to inspire an emerging sense of English nationhood.

ALFRED THE LAWGIVER

Alfred the Great was not merely a warrior and scholar; he also synthesized and documented a new code of laws. Drawing on earlier codes in different English kingdoms, he added his own regulations and adapted others to suit his idea of an orderly kingdom. Though the resulting code is often self-contradictory, it was primarily a symbolic document, not so much establishing a set of binding legal strictures as signaling Alfred's intention to enforce order and fairness. In addition to his legal code and other documents, Alfred ordered the writing of the Anglo-Saxon Chronicle, our main source for the history of those distant times. It was still being updated centuries after his death.

893

The Battle of Benfleet, Essex. The English under Aethelred of Mercia defeat a large Viking army, clearing the Thames Estuary for trade, and build a church on the battlefield to celebrate the victory.

896

Traditional date for the arrival of the Magyar tribes in the Hungarian Plain, the start of the Kingdom of Hungary.

Edward was the eldest son of King Alfred the Great and Queen Elswith. He was active in his father's campaigns against the Vikings and was more of a warrior than a scholar by temperament.

EDWARD THE ELDER

Fortunately for the kingdom of Wessex, Alfred's son Edward, known as Edward the Elder, proved a capable successor to his illustrious father. He was around 25 years old when he took the throne after Alfred's death, and what few records we have suggest he was well educated and highly regarded. He came of age during his father's long campaigns to keep the Danes at bay, and seems to have been, unlike his father, more a warrior than a scholar by temperament. But he was not a sure successor to the throne. Egbert had made arrangements for an orderly succession among his sons but not his grandsons, and Edward's cousins Aethelwold and Aethelhelm, the sons of Alfred's older brother and kingly predecessor Aethelred, theoretically had at least as good a claim on the throne.

BATTLE FOR SUCCESSION

Those tensions erupted into conflict as soon as Alfred was buried. Aethelwold immediately contested the succession. When his protests went unheeded, he briefly occupied the town of Winborne before going over to the Danes, securing their allegiance as King of Northumberland before attempting to take the throne of Wessex from Edward. In 901, he launched his offensive, and in 902, in a battle near a place called Holme, the rivalry ended. Tactically, the fight seems to have been something of a draw, with the Danes holding the field, but Aethelwold was killed in the fighting, ending any uncertainty about who was monarch in Wessex and allowing Edward to negotiate a new peace with the Danes of East Anglia.

Like most such truces, the peace did not last, and for the next several years Edward, like Alfred, remained locked in a struggle with Danish expansionism and raiding. But Edward was both as steady a leader as his father and more offensively minded. Taking the fight to the

900	904	912	914	927
Greenland is discovered by the Norseman Gunbjorn, who is blown off course while sailing from Norway to Iceland.	Thessalonika, the second largest city in the Byzantine Empire, is captured by a Muslim army and utterly destroyed.	King Ordono of Galicia and Leon conquers Evora from the Muslims in Spain.	Viking settlers found Waterford, now recognized as being the oldest city in Ireland.	King Athelstan of Wessex and Mercia is accepted as overlord by all rulers in England, creating a unified Kingdom of England.

Danes, he ventured even into Northumberland to assert his might, assisted by allied Mercian forces. In 910, a Danish army retaliated by sailing up the River Severn into Mercia and wreaking destruction. In an impressive display of responsiveness, Edward and his armies managed to trap the Vikings, and in the Battle of Tettenhall decimated them, killing two of their kings. Though lesser raids continued, Tettenhall signaled the end of major Danish incursions into the south.

AETHELSTAN, "FIRST KING OF THE ENGLISH"

After that victory, Edward wasted no time extending Alfred's line of fortifications along the whole border with the Danelaw. In 918, his sister Aethelflaed, Queen of Mercia, died, leaving only a young daughter to inherit the throne. Edward stepped in, uniting Mercia with Wessex under his rule. By 920, all the Danes living south of the Humber had acknowledged him as king. The more northern Viking lands around Jorvik (York) seem to have defied him; this was partly because numbers of Norsemen, expelled from Ireland and in many cases from Scandinavia itself in the course of Harald Fairhair's campaign to unify the Norse under his rule, had begun to assert their ambitions where Danish territorial expansion had failed.

In 924, the soldierly Edward died while suppressing a revolt in Mercia. His son and successor, Aethelstan, who had been raised in Mercia and had close ties to that kingdom, was proclaimed King of Mercia before even being confirmed as king by the nobles of Wessex. Aethelstan combined the qualities of Alfred and Edward: he was charismatic but also cultured and scholarly, a skilled warrior but also generous and devout. In short, he was as close to the ideal king as the Anglo-Saxons could hope for, and in due course they recognized that.

The Norsemen of York recognized it as well, just as they saw that Aethelstan was in too strong and secure a position to challenge. In 926, he arranged for his sister to marry Sitric, the

An illuminated manuscript image of Aethelstan giving a book to St. Cuthbert. The earliest extant period portrait of an Anglo-Saxon king, it also reveals the wealth and sophistication of Aethelstan's court.

Norse king of York, and when Sitric died the next year Aethelstan simply moved in and proclaimed himself king. When Sitric's brother Guthfrith, ruler of Dublin, challenged Aethelstan's annexation of York (and by extension Northumbria), it seems that Aethelstan had little trouble defending his position; there may not even have been a fight.

SCOTTISH REBELLION

Aethelstan soon had undisputed control of all England. He set the River Wye as the border with Wales, and accepted the fealty of the Scots and the Welsh as well as the Norse of Northumbria. The rest of his reign was almost idyllic: there were only problems in 934 and 937, when he crushed rebellions by Scottish and Norse malcontents. Not only in effect but also in title, Aethelstan became the first "King of the English." He presided over a learned and esteemed court, and he formed alliances with rulers throughout Europe, including Harald Fairhair, who had managed to become the first King of Norway. But when he died in 939, in his mid-forties, he left no children to inherit the throne, for he had never married.

KING EDMUND

Edmund, the half-brother of Aethelstan, was only about 18 when he took the throne, but he had already served alongside Aethelstan in campaigns against the Danes and Norsemen. As a young king, he could expect to be tested, and a challenge soon came from Olaf Guthfrithson, the Norse ruler of Dublin, who decided to make good on his father's onetime claim to sovereignty over York. Olaf swiftly

930		931	936	940
Founding of the Althing, the Parliament of Iceland, the oldest Parliament in the world.		The largest basalt flow in recorded history takes place when the volcano Eldgja erupts in southern Iceland.	Otto I is crowned king of Germany at Aachen. He is later recognized as the founder of the Holy Roman Empire in its medieval form.	Gorm the Old unites the various Danish tribes into a single kingdom of Denmark.

took York and, meeting little resistance, kept going, driving his forces into Mercia.

Edmund finally checked Olaf's advance, laying siege to his army at Leicester, but Olaf managed to withdraw, and a peace was hammered out in which he was allowed control not only over York but also over some Danish lands to the south. After Olaf's death the next year, his successor, Olaf Sihtricson, found himself facing a challenge from Edmund. The young Saxon king wrested back all of Mercia almost immediately, and Olaf Sihtricson was run out of York by his cousin, Ragnall Guthfrithson, precipitating a divisive conflict within the Norse ranks that made both men's forces easy pickings for Edmund. In 944, he swept into the north once more, killing Ragnall in the Battle of York and forcing Olaf to flee all the way back to Dublin.

It was a restoration and extension of the order that had flourished under Aethelstan, and at only 24 years old, Edmund seemed set for a long and prosperous rule. But it was not to be. The story goes that in 946, during a feast, Edmund spotted among the revelers a thief he had exiled from the kingdom and ordered the man arrested. In the ensuing scuffle, Edmund was stabbed, and he died of his wound shortly afterward.

KING EADRED

Once more, the King of the Anglo-Saxons had died without an heir. Fortunately, this time there was no one to contest the succession of Edmund's brother Eadred. Though Eadred was chronically ill—period accounts depict him as incapable of chewing and swallowing meat—his rule was no less dramatic than his brother's,

Ripon Cathedral in Yorkshire, as it looks today. In 948, the original structure was put to the torch on the orders of Eadred, who wanted to punish Wulfstan, Archbishop of York, for supporting Eric Bloodaxe.

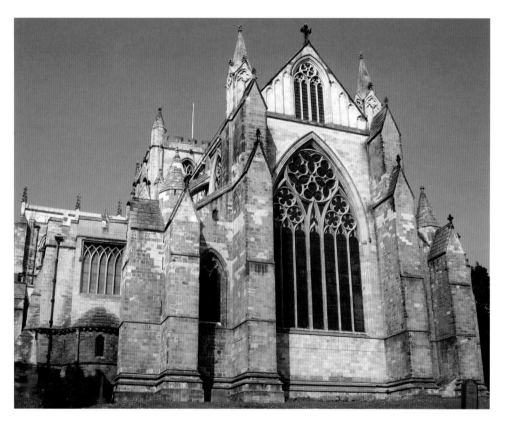

942	943	944	945	946
Death of Prince Idwal Foel of Gwynedd in battle against the English allows Hywell Dda of Deheubarth to annex Gwynedd and Powys, making him ruler of all of Wales.	Ergotism strikes Limoges in France, killing an estimated 40,000 who have eaten bread made from diseased rye.	A great storm hits England causing immense damage, including the collapse of 1,500 houses and churches in London alone.	St. Dunstan becomes Abbot of Glastonbury, England.	The Battle of Baghdad, which saw the almost total destruction of the city, marks the end of the long war between the Emir of Iraq and the Emir of Mosul, with victory going to the Iraqis.

and for much the same reason: problems with the Norsemen of York and Northumbria.

Once more, two warlords were vying for control of Norse lands. One was Olaf Sihtricson, newly returned from Dublin to try his fortune once more in York. The other was a more dangerous character altogether: Eric Haraldson, known to his contemporaries and to history as Eric Bloodaxe. Eric literally became a legend, his embroidered story appearing in Norse sagas and other tales, which often depict him as deserving his epithet. He seems to have been one of the sons of Harald Fairhair, but Norse noblemen either rejected or removed him as successor in favor of his brother Haakon, who had been raised in Aethelstan's court. If accounts of Eric's behavior are at all suggestive, he was violent and ruthless even by Norse standards. Once he was run out of Norway, he resolved to dominate Orkney and then set himself up as king of Northumbria.

ENGLAND AND THE NORSE SAGAS

Aethelstan and Eric Bloodaxe were such towering figures that they found their way into Norse sagas. Aethelstan is depicted in Egil's Saga as an ideal warrior king. When Egil's brother dies in an otherwise triumphant battle, Aethelstan consoles Egil at the victory feast, giving him a priceless gold armband by extending it to him on the tip of a sword. Eric Bloodaxe figures in that saga as well, but not so favorably. He is depicted as a great but cruel and reckless warrior, an embodiment of the lawless violence that so often undoes characters in the sagas. These appearances in the sagas of figures so famous in England serves as a reminder of the rich Nordic history of England, and of the depth of Nordic influence in English culture.

ERIC BLOODAXE

A key player in these Norse power games was Wulfstan, Archbishop of York, who supported Eric Bloodaxe, and it seems that Eadred held him personally accountable for much of the conflict. Accordingly, when Eadred first swept into Norse territory in 948, he burned the cathedral at Ripon, though he avoided a direct assault on York. When Norse troops attacked as he withdrew, he turned on them, drove them back to York, and threatened to lay waste to the entire kingdom if they did not expel Eric. They complied, but in 952 Wulfstan apparently invited him back and once more placed him on the throne of York. Eadred, his patience exhausted, invaded two years later, arresting and imprisoning Wulfstan and sending Eric into flight, where he was apparently killed at a place called Stainmore.

Once more, a member of the House of Wessex could call himself King of the English. But, again, that king would die young—in Eadred's case, at the age of 32, of an illness

that historians have speculated may have been a chronic inflammatory disorder such as Crohn's Disease, which likely afflicted many in the Wessex line, going back at least as far as Alfred the Great.

Like both his immediate predecessors, Eadred had no children, so on his death in 955 Edmund's son Eadwig inherited the throne at the age of 14. Actually, he inherited only the throne of Wessex, the kingdom of Mercia passing in theory to his younger brother Edgar, who was too young to assume the mantle of kingship. In a string of otherwise forceful Wessex kings, Eadwig is the exception; he commanded little respect, accomplished almost nothing, and died just four years into his reign at the age of 18. It seems to have been with some relief that the people of Wessex saw the throne pass to Edgar.

EDGAR THE PEACEABLE

After the early death of Eadwig, his younger brother Edgar succeeded to the throne—though during Eadwig's brief reign Edgar was given

Eadwig, one of the weakest of the Wessex kings, took the throne at the age of 14 and held it only until his death four years later.

951

The German king Otto I crosses the Alps with a large army to assert his claim to be king of Italy.

954

Erik Bloodaxe, last independent king of York, is killed by Earl Maccus. Thereafter, all England is permanently united under the Wessex dynasty.

955

The Italian duke of Spoleto's 18-year-old son Octavianus, notorious as a drunken seducer of married women, is elected Pope John XII.

956

An earthquake tumbles the Lighthouse of Alexandria, one of the Seven Wonders of the Ancient World.

Edgar the Peaceable, as depicted on Lichfield Cathedral. He was the first English ruler to be formally crowned and anointed as King of England.

control of Mercia and Northumbria, becoming acknowledged as ruler of those lands. This worked to his eventual advantage, in that he became popular within the lands he inhabited while Eadwig enjoyed little esteem; when Eadwig died, the accession of Edgar to the throne of Wessex probably seemed a return to authentic kingship.

Edgar's nickname does not suggest that he was less of a soldier than some of his warlike predecessors. Though he was reportedly small in stature, he was a strong and savvy leader, and he could not have ruled in peace had he not been capable in war. He was only 16 when he took the throne, but fortunately he had a strong council of nobles. He also had an able and upright ecclesiastical counselor: Dunstan, who had been spurned by the temperamental Eadwig but was made Archbishop of Canterbury by Edgar.

ST. DUNSTAN

It was Dunstan who took the role of father-figure to the young king, who seemed early in his reign more interested in pleasure and romance than in fulfilling his great-grandfather Alfred's vision of lofty Christian kingship. A number of stories about amorous episodes attached themselves to Edgar—including the unsavory implication that he was responsible for the murder of a rival for the attentions of his eventual queen, Elfrida. Dunstan appears to have used his authority as Archbishop of Canterbury to chastise and mentor Edgar; in any case, after marrying, the young king settled down to the business of administering his realm.

Under Edgar, the monasteries of England were largely restored and reformed. Dunstan was in touch with ecclesiastical developments on the continent, and he brought to England the Benedictine reforms that were revitalizing the monastic tradition. The reforms, which imposed stricter discipline, were not popular, but they did bring the English church in line with developments elsewhere. Otherwise, Edgar showed a gift for political theater. In 973, he was formally crowned King of the English—the first monarch to be anointed thus, and therefore technically the first to fully possess that title. The celebrations included impressive military displays by land and sea, and petty kings from all over Britain came to do Edgar homage. It was the spectacle of a united England, but it was not to last.

EDWARD THE MARTYR

It is tempting to suggest that the beginning of the end of Anglo-Saxon England was the marriage of Edgar the Peaceable to Elfrida. It was

An illustration depicting Edward the Martyr being offered a cup of mead by his stepmother Elfrida, unaware that her attendant is about to murder him.

958
Didda, famous for her wisdom, becomes ruler of Kashmir where she will hold power for almost 50 years.

966
Duke Mieszko of Poland is baptized a Christian, marking the start of the process of converting the Poles from paganism to Christianity.

967
At Christmas, Pope John XIII crowned King Otto I of Germany's son, also Otto, as Emperor Otto II to rule jointly with his father.

made possible by a murder, and it led to a murder. When Edgar died in 975, he was succeeded by Edward, his son by an earlier marriage. Edward took the throne at the difficult age of 13—too young to know very little about life or kingship, but old enough to assert his will against his counselors. And he was reportedly given to tantrums. Things went awry.

Much of what happened was beyond the young king's immediate control, but he was unable or unwilling to exert his influence over the kingdom. Widespread famine struck England in 976, and it led to a breakdown in the rule of law; disgruntled, fearful, and opportunistic Anglo-Saxons took to violence, even sacking monasteries, which had grown more rich and powerful with Dunstan's advocacy. Edward himself fell victim: on a visit to his stepmother Elfrida—the second or third wife of King Edgar—and her son Aethelred in 978, he was murdered on arrival; later chronicles suggest that the killing was done at Elfrida's behest.

The memorial statue of Byrhtnoth, doomed leader of the Saxon forces at Maldon in 991. The battle partly led to Aethelred the Unready's acceptance of the Danegeld.

Aethelred the Unready—his name really translates "ill-counseled"—became king at a young age. His reign was a cascade of poor decisions.

AETHELRED THE UNREADY

Aethelred was at most 13 years old, but he nonetheless had sufficient support to be named king. In effect, the witan, or royal council, had control of the kingdom, at least until the influential Aelfhere's death in 983. But recent events had not gone unnoticed. The Danes and the Norse, long held under control by a series of strong Saxon kings, realized that all was not well in the House of Wessex, and around 980 they began renewing their raiding and pillaging. In 991, a Saxon force was obliterated at Maldon in Essex, a disaster immortalized in the poem *The Battle of Maldon*.

It was here that Aethelred earned his epithet "the Unready," which is really a rather inaccurate translation of a phrase meaning "ill counseled." On the advice of the witan and others, Aethelred agreed to begin paying the Danegeld (literally Dane Money)—in effect, to accept the terms of a protection racket run by marauding Danes. And, as is the case with all protection rackets, the cost of protection—which was, of course, protection from the so-called protectors—increased considerably over time, nearly bankrupting the kingdom.

974 Pope Benedict VI is seized by men acting on the instructions of the future antipope Boniface VII. He is imprisoned in the Castel Sant'Angelo (right) in Rome where he is later strangled to death.

979 The Belgian city of Brussels is founded as a fortress on an island in the River Senne.

981 Viking Eric the Red discovers Greenland, then enjoying a much warmer climate than it does today, and leads settlers to the new land.

984 Chinese engineer Qiao Wei builds the first pound lock on the Grand Canal, allowing boats to move between different water levels more safely.

Misstep followed misstep. Aethelred failed to exercise any leadership in the field. He pointlessly financed the building of a navy without skilled sailors to man it, and then did nothing as it was destroyed. In 1002, he ordered the slaughter of every Dane in England who was not of the Anglo-Danish population that respected his sovereignty. In the wake of the massacres, old allegiances crumbled, and for the next several years England was a war zone, riven by raids and conflicts, its kingship very nearly up for grabs. In December 1013, the Danish adventurer Sweyn Forkbeard drove Aethelred into exile and actually claimed the throne, only to be killed in a fall from his horse three months later. Aethelred returned from exile, but found himself fighting against Sweyn's capable son Canute. In the spring of 1016, Aethelred died, having ruled over an astonishing collapse in Saxon power and morale.

EDMUND IRONSIDE

Aethelred's son Edmund, known as Ironside, was made of far sterner stuff than his father, and on his accession he immediately engaged

Sweyn Forkbeard, the Danish king who drove Aethelred the Unready into exile and began a Danish interregnum.

Medieval illustration depicting a scene from the Battle of Ashingdon (1016), in which Sweyn Forkbeard's son Canute (right) defeated the forces of Wessex led by Edmund Ironside (left) and became the unrivaled king of all England, which he ruled for almost 20 years.

Canute's forces in a series of battles. The campaign lasted for several months of 1016, and was mostly a stalemate. In October of that year, at Ashingdon in Essex, Canute managed a victory, and Edmund had to negotiate a peace in which Canute was ceded Mercia and Northumbria. On his return to Wessex, Edmund died suddenly; there are strong indications he was murdered, though for unknown reasons. Apparently by prior arrangement, Canute became King of England in November 1016. The glory years of the House of Wessex had

THE RELIQUARIES OF WINCHESTER

The royal seat of Wessex was Winchester. In a symbolic gesture, Canute's body was interred there alongside the remains of previous, Saxon kings of Wessex. When William the Conqueror and his immediate descendents adopted Winchester as the home of the royal treasury, they also built a cathedral there, and re-interred the remains of former kings in reliquary boxes. During the English civil war, Roundhead troops pried open the boxes and dumped out their contents. Canute's remains, along with those of several other kings, were scattered and mingled. When they were later replaced in the boxes, the bones remained unsorted. Four skulls were even put in one box.

1000	1005	1010	1020
Viking explorer Leif Ericson becomes the first European to land in North America, though the site of his landing is now uncertain.	Brian Boru, high king of Ireland, recognizes the bishop of Armagh as the successor to St. Patrick and grants Armagh supremacy over all other bishops in Ireland.	Monk Elmer of Malmesbury, England, built a wooden and cloth glider in which he leapt from the monastery tower and glided over 200 metres before crashing and breaking both his legs.	Construction of the Kandariya Mahadeva Temple is completed in India, at the time it is the largest Hindu temple in the world.

ended; it would be more than a quarter-century before one of its members ruled again.

THE DANISH INTERREGNUM

Canute was perhaps 20 years old when he took the English throne, but he was nothing if not enterprising. A product of the dynastic struggles in Denmark—he actually took a break from his campaigning in England in 1014 to make a play for the Danish throne—he would eventually become the most powerful monarch in Northern Europe.

The records regarding Canute's kingship are spotty, and since most were written by Saxon monks they can hardly be expected to paint a flattering portrait of the Danish king. It seems that early in his reign Canute established himself by ruthlessly bringing the Saxon earls to heel. Some were very likely killed, others exiled. But he also married Aethelred's widow, Emma of Normandy. Canute proved a capable administrator, and under his rule England at least regained the stability that had been lost under Edward and Aethelred. Furthermore, Canute became a generous patron of the Church, rebuilding and financing monasteries, and even journeying to Rome in 1027.

In short, Canute was the most effective King of England since Aethelstan. Though capable of being ruthless, he preferred to cultivate loyalty rather than enforce it, and he encouraged a sense of common nationhood among the English and the Danes. A famous story depicts him sitting on his throne by the ocean, demonstrating his power over the northern seas by commanding the tide to turn; in fact, he was demonstrating the limits of his power. Canute was as sagacious as he was powerful, which is why, under his rule, England and much of Scandinavia became one realm. The administration of that realm required him to give over the management of Wessex to Earl Godwin, a decision that would have major ramifications until the Norman invasion in 1066.

When Canute died in 1035, his son and heir Hardicanute was in Denmark, fighting the Norse, so he named his half-brother Harold

A later depiction of Canute commanding the tide to turn. The story, though often misinterpreted, remained popular as a metaphor for both the pride and the limits of kingship.

Harefoot regent in England. When events kept Hardicanute abroad, Harold was elected king. It seems that Earl Godwin, the powerful lord of Wessex, threw his considerable weight behind this decision. In his short spell as king, Harold became infamous for one crime. Around 1037, Alfred, the son of Aethelred the Unready and therefore, through Canute's marriage to Aethelred's widow, half-brother to Harold and Hardicanute, visited England. He had a claim to the throne and may have even been testing the waters, but Harold went too far in having him arrested and blinded so brutally that he died from the wounds. Harold lost significant Saxon support, and when Hardicanute, secure in Denmark, decided to return to England in 1040 and claim the throne, Harold conveniently died

Hardicanute was invited to take the throne, but he nonetheless arrived in force, and immediately levied a tax to finance his expedition. It was a characteristically clumsy and autocratic move that would make him an unpopular king. In 1042, while drinking at a feast, he suffered some sort of seizure and died. Poison may have been involved.

Medieval manuscript portrait of Canute the Great. Canute may have been a Dane, but he proved a highly capable and popular king among the English.

1024	1026	1032	1040
The Holy Roman emperor Henry II dies, aged 51. He is succeeded by his son Conrad II.	King Canute of England, Denmark, and Norway begins a pilgrimage to Rome.	Fear throughout Christendom of the approaching apocalypse based on a reading of the Book of Revelations that seemed to promise the Second Coming of Christ would take place a thousand years after His Crucifixion—an event dated to the year 33. The savage winter of 1032/33 only adds to the panic.	The Weihenstephan Brewery first brews beer—as it has done ever since, making this the oldest brewery in the world.

EDWARD THE CONFESSOR

The sudden death of Hardicanute left England without a king. Since Hardicanute had no children, the throne went to an unexpected candidate: Edward, the lone surviving son of Aethelred the Unready. Edward had spent most of his life in exile in Normandy, never expecting to become King of England. Even his own mother had married Canute and thrown in her lot with the Danes rather than the Saxons. Though about 40 years old when crowned, he was still unprepared, and he had to learn the hard way how to deal with the convoluted politics of a kingdom divided among Saxons, Danes, and Norsemen and dominated by powerful lords who could undermine his rule at will.

Edward the Confessor was the last of the Wessex kings.

None of the nobles of England was as strong as Earl Godwin. Since his appointment by Canute as lord of Wessex, he and his sons had become the most illustrious and influential family in England; only Leofric of Mercia and Siward of Northumbria even approached Godwin in stature. King Edward could ill afford to anger the Godwins. This was a problem, since Edward likely held Earl Godwin partly responsible for the death by blinding of Alfred under Harold Harefoot—not a surprising grudge, given that Godwin had apparently arrested Alfred and turned him over to Harold. Regardless, Edward married Godwin's daughter Edith in 1045.

Soon enough tensions arose between Edward and the Godwins, mainly because he denied them and their allies the influence they desired and doubtless felt they deserved. Having spent most of his life in Normandy, Edward was, by custom and inclination, Norman, and appointed Normans to some key posts, including bishoprics, which further alienated the Godwins. Things came to a head in 1051, when the Godwins were accused of plotting against the king. Edward took the opportunity to exile Godwin and his sons. It was a bad move. The Godwins were as popular among the Saxons as they were powerful, and Edward was something of an import, an alien king.

WILLIAM THE BASTARD

It was while the Godwins were out of the picture that, apparently, William the Bastard, ruler of Normandy, visited England. William would later claim that during his visit Edward had promised him the English throne—a story more plausible than it may at first sound, given that

Westminster Abbey as it appears now, long after the newer, massive Gothic cathedral was ordered built by Henry III. The original, Romanesque structure, built by Edward the Confessor as an expansion of an existing abbey, is long gone.

1045

King Edward the Confessor of England begins the building of Westminster Abbey on an island in marshes beside the Thames to the west of London.

1045

Moveable type printing is developed by Chinese printer Bi Sheng, who used porcelain squares for his type.

1045

Death of Count Radbot of Habsburg, founder of the Habsburg Dynasty that would later come to dominate European politics.

the Saxon alternative was likely Earl Godwin's impressive son Harold, and Edward clearly felt more comfortable with Normans. But Edward also began casting around for other alternatives to Godwins, and found one in his nephew Edward, currently living in Hungary. King Edward recalled his nephew to England, only for the young man to be slain shortly after arrival, probably by agents of the Godwins.

In 1052, the Godwins returned from exile and immediately garnered enough support that Edward had no choice but to restore them to their former positions. It was a huge loss of face, and after it Edward seems to have taken a less active role as king, devoting himself to Christianity. It was here that he left his most lasting impact on England: Westminster Abbey. He intended the church as a royal burial chapel, and it has remained so, off and on, ever since. The original Romanesque structure was an impressive edifice, and enough of it was built by 1065 that it could be consecrated that year.

But that year also saw Edward's health decline. Earl Godwin had died in 1053, and his son Harold had gradually taken over most of the responsibilities of rule as Edward increasingly withdrew into the devotional way of life that would eventually get him canonized. In the first week of January, 1066, Edward died. His successor was a foregone conclusion.

THE END OF ANGLO-SAXON ENGLAND

Harold Godwinson was a fierce warrior, having proved himself in ruthless campaigns against the Welsh. He was also immensely popular. He had only one weakness: the enmity of his brother Tostig, who had been removed, at Harold's insistence, from his position as Earl of Northumbria for his failure to maintain unity and order in the region. No sooner did Harold take the throne than Tostig conspired with the Norse king, Harald Hardrada, to invade the north of England. He could not have chosen a worse time for Harold, who rightly expected an invasion from William of Normandy at any time. In September, Harald Hardrada, along with the treacherous Tostig and some 200 ships, invaded. Harold marched his troops north and crushed the invaders at Stamford Bridge in Yorkshire. Tostig was killed.

However, no sooner did Harold claim victory at Stamford Bridge in the north than he and his army were obliged to race south, for William's invasion force had arrived. The two armies met near Hastings on October 14, 1066. Harold's death in that battle spelled the end of Anglo-Saxon England. A new, hybrid, Anglo-Norman England would emerge, giving birth to a different language and culture. But that is another story.

Edward the Confessor on his throne, the opening image of the Bayeux Tapestry, which chronicles the momentous events of 1066.

1046	1047	1053	1066
The German king is crowned Holy Roman Emperor Henry III on Christmas Day at Rome by the bishop of Bemberg who he has installed as Pope Clement II.	Harald Hardrada becomes king of Norway. He founds the city of Oslo a year later.	Master Japanese sculptor Jocho Busshi creates his masterpiece, the Amida Buddha.	King Harold Godwinson of England is killed at the Battle of Hastings, which is won by Duke William of Normandy who thus becomes King William I of England.

The Norman Kings

No single event transformed British history more than the invasion of William the Conqueror in 1066. William and his Norman descendants completely transformed how the nobility related to commoners, how England connected with the continent, and even how the English language evolved. The Normans brought to Britain a powerful sense of privilege and ruthless efficiency in conquest and administration. Though they remained very much Normans, often concerned more with events across the Channel than with developments in England, they left an indelible imprint on the British idea of kingship, and forged a bond between England and France that would prove both rewarding and disastrous in the succeeding generations.

WILLIAM I ✠ Conqueror and Reshaper of a Nation

House Normandy
Born 1028
Reigned 1066–1087
Consort Matilda of Flanders
Children Ten, including William II, Henry I, and Robert Curthose, Duke of Normandy
Successor William II

HE TRULY REIGNED OVER ENGLAND

THE ANGLO-SAXON CHRONICLE

Matilda of Flanders, William's queen. who sometimes served as regent during his sojourns on the continent.

William I, the Conqueror, was not merely the warlike Norman who made 1066 the most famous date in British history. He was also, by all accounts, a strong king, an able administrator, and a faithful husband. His rule forever transformed what it means to be English.

Before he was William the Conqueror, he was William the Bastard. The illegitimate son of Robert I, Duke of Normandy, William was nonetheless heir to his father's realm. Robert died young, leaving William to inherit Normandy as a child and spend his formative years amid discord, conspiracy, and battle. The young duke became a prize among feuding landowners; though he was housed by a number of patrons and protected by his maternal uncle Walter of Falaise, at least three of his guardians were assassinated. Stories would later circulate of William having to hide among peasants. Such a precarious existence, in which trust was rare and precious, doubtless contributed to the style of leadership, at once ruthless and principled, that William displayed throughout his life.

A LEADER COMES OF AGE

He was in danger through most of his childhood, but William was relatively safe from open challenges, because he was supported by Henry I of France and, more importantly, his great-uncle Robert, Archbishop of Rouen. But the Archbishop's death in 1037 led to ten years of tumult in Normandy. William grew to be a tall, sturdy teenager, trained in combat, with the watchfulness of someone accustomed to sudden threats. At around the age of 16, he established his own court at Valognes.

A rival soon emerged to challenge him for control of Normandy. His cousin, Guy of Burgundy, won the support of powerful barons, and William was forced to seek the protection of Henry I. In 1047, William and Henry's forces defeated those of Guy in a brutal fight at Val-es-Dunes. The young William distinguished himself as a ferocious fighter. All that remained was to consolidate his control over Normandy. That effort took over a decade, during which William not only suppressed rebellious Normans but also fended off an invasion by Henry himself, who had perhaps become wary of his former protégé.

In the course of subduing Normandy, William mastered the techniques of land acquisition that would characterize his eventual conquest of England: deliberate advance, ruthless intimidation, and construction of castles to secure recently conquered areas. He made a formidable impression as a leader, with commanding physical stature and extraordinary self-possession, and was anything but impulsive. His marriage to Matilda of Flanders, though it secured a valuable alliance, seems to have been a happy one, and William was reportedly a constant husband. He also became known for his piety.

With Normandy firmly in hand, William began to extend his reach. He had betrothed his eldest son Robert to the sister of Herbert II of Maine; in 1062, when Herbert died childless, William used that pretext to take over Maine, in northwest France. The same rationale—that an aging, childless ruler had given William rights to his kingdom—took on much more weight in January of 1066, when Edward the Confessor of England died.

1028
William is born in Falaise, Normandy.

1035
Canute the Great dies, and his large kingdom, which includes England, is divided up among rival successors.

Opposite A 17th-century portrayal of William the Conqueror. Though we have no images of William from life or living memory, he has remained a speculative subject for portrait painters.

Harold Godwinson, the last Anglo-Saxon king. He might have withstood William's invasion but for exhaustion and tactical errors, which may have been made against his orders.

THE INVASION OF ENGLAND

William had long been expected to stake his claim to the English throne. He openly asserted that Edward had promised it to him, and that Edward's successor, Harold Godwinson, during a brief sojourn in Normandy, had agreed to support William in taking it. We cannot know that Edward and Harold had in fact given such assurances, but even if they had, William would have been foolish to take them at face value or to believe that the Saxon landowners of England would accept Norman rule. His years of preparation for a full-scale invasion, including building a sizeable fleet, indicate that he had no illusions about what lay ahead. When Harold Godwinson was crowned shortly after Edward's death, everyone concerned knew that it was only a matter of time.

But William waited. Methodical as ever, he would not sail for England until he was fully ready. For most of 1066, Harold's forces were guarding the southern coast against the expected invasion. William stockpiled supplies, and supplemented his Norman forces with soldiers from his territories and alliances in Brittany and Flanders as well as hired mercenaries from throughout Europe. The arrival in the fall of favorable winds provided the opening he needed. The shift in weather was not the only thing favoring William; Harold had marched his forces north to confront another invasion, this one by the Norwegian king, Harald Hardrada. Three days after Harold defeated Harald Hardrada at Stamford Bridge in Yorkshire, William's forces landed at Pevensey.

FROM HASTINGS TO LONDON

William wasted no time establishing a beachhead in England, marching on Hastings, and occupying and fortifying its keep. By the time he heard about Harold's triumph at Stamford Bridge, the Saxon king had already reached London and begun marching toward Hastings.

As William readied himself in Hastings, Harold's forces occupied the crest of Senlac hill. On the morning of October 14, battle was joined. At first, William's troops took heavy losses; the Saxon army had formed an impenetrable shield wall atop the hill. But at some point Harold's soldiers broke the shield wall to advance on retreating Normans. Accounts differ as to whether the Norman retreat was a ruse designed to bait the Saxons into advancing; regardless, breaking the shield wall was a disastrous decision. Norman cavalry were able to ride down and slaughter Harold's footsoldiers, and in the resulting melee Harold himself was killed. Their king slain, the Saxon army surrendered.

Victory at Hastings, however, did not pave a smooth road to kingship. William encountered both dysentery among his forces and stubborn resistance from the Saxons, and moved methodically to secure the territory between the coast and London. Over the next two months, he burned Dover, subjugated Canterbury and most of Surrey, and secured the royal treasury at Winchester before marching directly on London. Turned back at the Thames, he marched clockwise around the city, pillaging as he went. Soon, most of the Saxon leaders submitted, and on Christmas Day, 1066, William was crowned in Westminster Cathedral. At the coronation, Norman guards outside the cathedral confused a celebratory outburst in the nave with an uprising, and set fire to nearby houses as a means of subduing the Londoners. That hair-trigger response was indicative of the tensions that accompanied the crowning of a Norman king. They would not abate easily, or soon.

CONSOLIDATING NORMAN RULE

After his coronation, William moved quickly to achieve stability. He allowed some powerful Saxon earls to retain their positions, though the families of many who fought at Hastings were stripped of their lands. This bought William valuable time; he only controlled the south, and the powerful Saxon earls of Mercia and Northumbria were content to leave things as they stood.

1054	1066	
The Great Schism, in which the Eastern Orthodox and Roman Catholic churches separate, begins.	In the Battle of Hastings, William defeats Harold Godwinson, who is killed in the fighting along with many of the Anglo-Saxon nobility.	

In early 1067, William returned to Normandy, taking with him several prominent Saxons as hostages; it was the first of many trips across the Channel he would make over the course of his reign. In his stead, his half-brother Odo, Bishop of Bayeux, and another Norman ally were left to manage what had become an occupation. Revolts flared across the kingdom, and late that year William was forced to return and reassert his authority. He besieged Exeter, where Harold's mother had established herself, and built the first of scores of castles he ordered constructed during his rule. From that point on, the ruthlessly efficient Norman method of pacification spread across England, with fortified towers serving as both bases and symbols of unimpeachable power.

Such campaigns to keep the king's peace came at a price, and William imposed stiff taxes to finance them, enriching himself in the process. Rather than keep one base, he traveled throughout England when he was there, a practice that placed even more strain on the populace. Often, he had to bring his own barons to heel, as their arrogant and arbitrary exertion of power only stoked anti-Norman feeling. In 1068, Saxon earls in the north revolted, and with their defeat any hope of home rule by Saxons disappeared. William began a program of systematic dispossession, installing Norman and French barons across the kingdom. Any resistance was crushed.

A year later, when Saxon rebels took York, William embarked on a punitive campaign that

The death of Harold Godwinson at Hastings, from the Bayeux Tapestry. Though legend has it that Harold died from an arrow to the eye, he is more likely the figure being cut down by a mounted Norman.

1071	1073	1077
The Seljuk Turks defeat Byzantine forces in the Battle of Manzikert. Though the Byzantines suffer minor losses, their emperor is captured, and the Turks begin the conquest of the Holy Land that will eventually spur calls for a crusade.	A reorganization of the English Church makes York subordinate to Canterbury. 	Holy Roman Emperor Henry IV stands in the snow for three days to have Pope Gregory welcome him back into the Church after his excommunication.

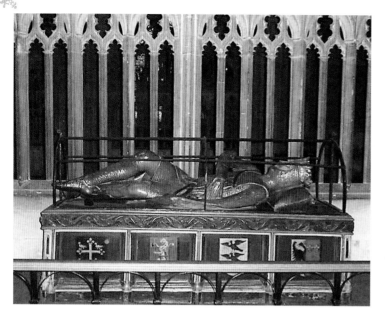

The Burial Effigy of Robert Curthose, eldest son of William I, in Gloucester Cathedral. Called Curthose ("short boots") by his disdainful father, Robert caused William, and eventually his brothers William and Henry, no end of trouble. Despite his rebelliousness, he inherited Normandy on William's death.

land was worked by villeins (peasants), who were completely subject to the rule of their local landowners.

The plight of the villein under such feudalism was often dire. Villeins owned no land, were heavily taxed on what goods they possessed, and could make almost no major life decisions without the consent of the local lord. Leaving the manor was almost unthinkable; it would cost the lord valuable labor, and would offer no guarantee of habitation elsewhere. Abuses of power were rampant.

But the old hierarchies of Anglo-Saxon society, based more on collective decision-making, remained, undergirding the Norman system, and over time the two systems merged. With relatively few variations, this hybrid form of feudalism would remain the template for English rule for centuries.

became known as the Harrying of the North. It was the single most brutal episode in William's violent career. Untold thousands of people were killed, estates laid waste, and farmlands salted. Whole villages were wiped off the map. When the carnage was past, William was effectively master of England. The devastation doubtless encouraged Malcolm III of Scotland to make peace with William in 1072. That treaty concluded, William returned to Normandy, where he largely remained for over a decade, once more leaving his vassals to manage England.

NORMAN FEUDALISM

William's control of England meant the arrival of a Norman brand of feudalism, in which the entire kingdom was the property of the Crown. William treated a portion of it as his own; the rest was divided among manors, which were allotted to barons who swore allegiance to the Crown. The barons owed not only taxes but military and sometimes civilian service to the king. In the feudal hierarchy of grants and obligations, barons distributed stretches of their manors to knights in their service. The

THE TROUBLED CROWN

Between 1072 and 1085, William spent most of his time in Normandy, but problems persisted both there and in England. William's sons were proving less than helpful at managing Normandy. Robert, the eldest, was charismatic and brave, but also impulsive and vain. Richard, the second son, died in a hunting accident in the New Forest, William's great hunting preserve in England. William, the third son, was a stout warrior but lacked Robert's personal magnetism. The youngest, Henry, was probably meant to become a bishop. As William dealt with a range of adversaries—rebellious Saxons, Danish raiders, French and Angevin rivals—he found himself increasingly embattled. He grew fat as he aged, and no longer seemed the terrifying campaigner of earlier years.

In 1075, two of his own Norman earls rebelled, but this time William remained in Normandy, letting his other vassals subdue the revolt. When one of the conspirators took refuge in a castle in Brittany, William laid siege to it, but a relief mission from King Philip of France forced him to withdraw. Whether this minor setback made William appear weak is

---

1077

The Byzantine emperor Michael VII abdicates and is succeeded by Nicephorus III Botaniates.

1080

King Alfonso VI of Castille accepts Roman liturgy in his kingdom, replacing the ancient Spanish forms of service.

1081

The Norman Robert Guiscard invades the Balkans, laying siege to the Byzantine city of Durazzo.

1083

Henry IV takes over Rome, to be driven back eventually by Robert Guiscard.

HEREWARD THE WAKE

Of the many Saxons to resist Norman rule, the most colorful was Hereward the Wake, a nobleman based in what is now Cambridgeshire. Around 1070 he returned from abroad and took up arms against William. Establishing his base in the Isle of Ely, Hereward proceeded to harry the Normans, even managing to sack Peterborough Abbey. His reputation grew so troublesome that he became a marked man. Norman forces eventually managed to attack his well-defended base in the Isle of Ely, but Hereward escaped. Accounts differ about his later days, some suggesting that William eventually pardoned him. Hereward's deeds were widely celebrated and embellished, and collected in a text called the Gesta Herewardi.

open to question, but in 1078 William's son Robert launched his own revolt in Normandy, supported by Philip. Robert even managed to unhorse his father in a battle outside the walls of the castle of Gerberoi. By 1080 the affair had been smoothed over, but now William appeared even more vulnerable. In the north of England, the Scots and the Danes began to raid with more audacity.

In 1082, William placed under arrest his half-brother Odo, who had been one of his most trusted lieutenants in England. The reasons remain unclear, but it may have been that Odo had outsize ambitions of his own, perhaps even for the papacy, and had attempted to woo some of William's barons into his own schemes.

The Domesday Book, now held in the National Archives in London.

William revered and supported the Church, but he tolerated no ecclesiastical interference in his rule, and Odo proved no exception. The following year, Robert rebelled yet again, and William's queen, Matilda, died. She had been a valuable partner in many ways, often ruling Normandy in her husband's absences, and the double blow must have grieved William. Controlling his kingdoms was proving increasingly difficult.

THE DOMESDAY BOOK

In 1085, rumors of an imminent invasion of England by the Danes prompted William to bring a large army across the Channel. The invasion never came—Canute IV of Denmark was overtaken by domestic unrest—but the logistics of moving and maintaining such a large force strained the kingdom's resources. In the aftermath, William decided to make a thorough accounting of all English assets, measuring them against population and wealth of the kingdom when he first took the throne. Part of his motivation was revenue, but he may also have wanted a record of the vast network of feudal obligations that formed the scaffolding of his government. He ordered the survey conducted that Christmas.

The result was an astonishing feat of information-gathering. Over the next several months, William's agents spread to every corner of the kingdom, recording assets ranging from tracts of land, to livestock, to ploughs. Over 13,000 locales were detailed, and every investigation was double-checked before being committed to record. This massive undertaking distressed most of the English, who knew it was intended to lay the groundwork for increased taxation. William's auditors were so meticulous that the document they were preparing became known as the Domesday Book—in other words, the book of judgment, in which all Englishmen's deeds would be entered into account.

The Domesday Book actually consists of two texts: the Little Domesday and the Great Domesday, each documenting the assets in

1083 King Alfonso VI of Castile captures Talavera from the Emirate of Cordoba.

1084 St. Bruno of Cologne founds the Carthusian Order of Monks, later also to include nuns, with a set of rules distinct from those of St. Benedict.

1086 The Domesday Book surveys are taken throughout England.

a different part of the kingdom. Ironically, the Little Domesday is the longer document, as it goes into much greater detail than its companion. William himself never seems to have made use of it; scribes may not have completed the texts until after his death.

The Domesday Book is now kept in the National Archives in London, where it remains the most ambitious administrative undertaking of any medieval monarch. It is riddled with errors, but it remains a revealing portrait of Norman England.

THE DEATH OF WILLIAM

A year after ordering the compilation of the Domesday Book, William was back in Normandy, facing down yet another rebellion. He arranged for the marriage of his daughter Constance to the Count of Brittany, forging another alliance against France. But he was now some 60 years old, doubtless worn down by years of campaigning and kingship, and the loss of Matilda and the rebelliousness of Robert may have left him feeling increasingly isolated. After sacking the town of Mantes, he was mortally injured in a riding accident whilst surveying the devastastion wrought by his army. Most probably he developed an infection from the injury. He was taken to Rouen, where he lay dying for over a month.

On his deathbed, William settled his

The Abbey of St-Étienne, established by William and Matilda. William was buried here, but his bones were later scattered when Calvinists sought to strip the church of Catholic elements.

accounts. Despite Robert's rebelliousness, and doubtless with some misgivings, he named his eldest son his successor as Duke of Normandy. To William, his second remaining son, he gave the crown and scepter of England. In what was likely a symbolic move, he also gave William his sword. Henry, the youngest, was given a large sum of money. William also ordered the release after his death of all his prisoners, including his half-brother Odo.

Accounts of his death conflict, but it is clear that, as soon as William expired, his family scattered to look after their various interests. The body, stripped of its valuables, was left in Rouen, and afterward transported to Caen for burial. At his interment in the Abbey of St. Stephen, it was discovered that the grave was too short for William's six-foot frame; in a final indignity, his attendants tried to fit him in nonetheless, and his decaying body burst, filling the room with noxious odors. It was an unbecoming end to a monarch who had forever transformed the island of Britain.

WILLIAM'S LEGACY

William may have been the King of England, but he remained a Norman. He regarded all his territories as separate holdings, and Normandy as his base. England was, above all, a source of revenue and prestige, and he visited it as necessary. Among his fellow Normans and in his court, he spoke French, and his barons regarded their first language as a badge of their supremacy. Though William reportedly attempted to learn Old English, he never managed to.

But his impact on England can scarcely be overstated. One can only imagine how different the history of England might have been if, on that October day in 1066, Harold Godwinson's soldiers had not broken the shield wall atop Senlac hill. The victorious Normans brought with them much—good and bad—that came to define English life in the centuries that followed.

MOTTE-AND-BAILEY

Norman castles established what became known as motte-and-bailey construction. The motte was a high mound, with slopes so steep that it would be impossible to ascend at speed. Atop the motte stood the keep, the wooden tower that served as the main fortification. Around the motte, outside a deep ditch, was the bailey, an area of up to three or so acres (1.5 hectares) surrounded by a wooden palisade. Norman forces were capable of erecting motte-and-bailey castles quickly and efficiently. Over time, many of them were converted into formidable stone fortresses.

1086

Count Roger I of Sicily captures Syracuse, the last major Muslim stronghold on Sicily.

1086

Castile's Alfonso VI is defeated at Zallaka by a Muslim army from Africa under Yusuf ibn Tashfin, leader of the fanatical Berber sect (the Almoravids) that has gained dominance in North Africa.

1087

The Byzantine emperor Alexius I Comnenus is defeated at the Battle of Drystra by heretic Bogomils in Thrace and Bulgaria.

Hastings Castle, which William ordered built on his arrival in England in 1066. Much of the castle has since slipped into the Channel, and centuries of wars have also taken their toll.

William's forebears were Nordic, but as a Norman he had absorbed the attitudes of the French ruling class. William himself was careful to balance the interests of Church and state, even keeping their judicial processes separate, but his rule ultimately brought England closer within the orbit of Rome. And with his French sense of nobility came a disdain not only for the English, but also for commoners

Most fundamentally, William's conquest inaugurated a turn southward in English consciousness; instead of Scandinavia, England became tied to France, and that relationship, more often hostile than amicable, has been a main feature of European history and culture ever since. By the end of William's rule, the Saxon nobility that had hitherto dominated England had been so completely dispossessed as to be nearly extinct; only two Saxon tenants-in-chief are listed in the Domesday Book. That striking change in the ruling culture has reverberated down the centuries.

in general. His view of the kingdom as his personal property led him to establish vast preserves for his own pleasure, most famously the New Forest. Every leaf of the New Forest was considered as belonging to the king. That sense of privilege, combined with the linguistic gulf between Norman rulers and English populace, heightened the sense of distance between landed aristocracy and commoners that, despite the moderating influences of time and reform, persists to this day.

Perhaps most importantly, William's conquest of England permanently transformed its language. The Old English of the Saxons, a Germanic tongue, gradually merged with the Normans' French, becoming the Middle English of Chaucer's Canterbury Tales, and eventually the Early Modern English of Shakespeare. The English language as we know it, and the complex and scintillating culture that uses it, would never have taken shape had William, Duke of Normandy, not bent his will toward the conquest of lands across the Channel.

The Tower of London. The White Tower, the fortress's inner keep, was built by William. William used castles to consolidate his control over England, personally ordering the construction of nearly 80. Many of them still stand, reminders of how well he projected his power as king.

1087
A vast fleet drawn from Genoa and Pisa captures the city of Mahdia in North Africa. The Pisan share of the plunder was used to build the famous Cathedral in Pisa.

1087
Japanese emperor Shirakawa abdicates and retires to a monastery. His successor Emperor Horikawa carries out the arduous ritual duties, while Shirakawa rules Japan from behind the scenes, initiating the "cloistered rule" era of Japanese history.

1087
William the Conqueror dies in Rouen. He has invaded the French Vexin to retaliate for raids on his territory and sacked and burned the town of Mantes. But when he rides out to survey the ruins he is thrown from his horse and fatally injured.

THE BAYEUX TAPESTRY

One of the most widely known works of medieval art is a tapestry—or, more precisely, an embroidery—from Bayeux, France, depicting the events that culminated in the Battle of Hastings. Though its exact origins remain unclear, the Bayeux Tapestry is a meticulously crafted pictorial narrative and a major artifact of British and world history.

The earliest extant record of the Bayeux Tapestry is in a 1476 account of how it was removed from a storage chest each summer to be hung in the nave of Bayeux Cathedral during the Feast of John the Baptist. Though tradition in Bayeux held the tapestry to have been commissioned by Queen Matilda, wife of William the Conqueror, more recent scholarship suggests that it was in fact William's half-brother Odo, the Earl of Essex and Bishop of Bayeux, who had the tapestry made within about 25 years of the Battle of Hastings. Odo was a scheming, disreputable sort—though William seems to have trusted him as a kind of second-in-command, he also had to discipline him for both financial corruption and secret plots—but he was a notable patron of the arts. He even designed the cathedral in which the tapestry was hung. Given that construction of Bayeux Cathedral began in 1070, the tapestry may well have been commissioned at that time. The renown of Anglo-Saxon needlework and the tapestry's accurate use of Old English spellings suggest that the actual embroidery was done in England, either in Winchester or in Kent.

In the 18th century, scholars rediscovered the tapestry, and drawings and engravings of its images circulated widely, making it a tourist attraction. Wear and tear led to some restoration work in the 19th century; other repairs had clearly been done much earlier. As the depiction of a successful invasion of England, the tapestry became a potential piece of propaganda for any continental European power hoping to duplicate William's success. Such it was to Napoleon, who had it brought to Paris in 1803, only to return it to Bayeux after Lord Nelson's victory at Trafalgar put an end to any plans of invading England. Similarly, the Nazi regime tried and failed to get hold of the tapestry during World War II. After

HALLEY'S COMET

Perhaps the most famous image on the Bayeux Tapestry is that of a flaming star with a tail—it represents Halley's comet, which appeared in 1066. The related text on the tapestry reads "isti mirant stella," or "They admired the star." Admiration, in this sense, was certainly tinged with tremendous fear and anxiety. Comets were called "the terror of kings," because they were seen as foretelling disaster, especially upheaval in the human order, and the fall of monarchs. We can only speculate the extent to which recollection of the comet affected Norman and English morale leading up to the Battle of Hastings, but, in the case of Harold Godwinson, its import actually held true.

the war, the tapestry was returned to Bayeux, where it now resides in its own museum.

HISTORY AS WALL HANGING

The Bayeux Tapestry has suitably epic dimensions: it is about 231 feet (70 m) long and 19.5 inches (49.5 cm) wide. It contains over 600 images of people, more than 200 of horses, and well over 500 of other animals, including many in its intricate borders. Its final few feet have been lost, though the narrative it presents is largely complete. Though its colors have darkened with age, it remains vivid, detailed,

A detail from the Bayeux Tapestry illustrating the construction of a Motte-and-bailey fortification, which the Normans used to great effect in securing their conquest of England.

and full of movement. Through a sequence of about 50 images, it progresses from one of Edward the Confessor dispatching Harold Godwinson to Normandy in 1064 through the flight of English warriors after Harold's death in the Battle of Hastings. The events are told from the Norman point of view, but without any evident condescension toward the English; if there is an agenda behind the tapestry, it is simply that William was justified in invading,

and that he defeated admirable enemies who fought well but lost.

The Bayeux Tapestry clearly served as both a commemoration of the Norman invasion and a celebration of Norman power. It probably also functioned, rather like stained glass windows, as a way of communicating a historical narrative to a largely illiterate churchgoing population. It remains an iconic record of perhaps the most pivotal events in English history.

WILLIAM II ✠ Dissolute Warrior

House Normandy
Born c. 1056
Died 1100
Reigned 1087–1100
Consort None
Children None
Successor Henry I

The relatively brief but fascinating reign of William II foreshadowed the virtues and flaws that would characterize British monarchs for centuries. A gifted military leader, William ruled with a firm grip but earned the enmity of the Church. Many regarded his court as a den of royal decadence.

William, the second surviving son of William the Conqueror, had always enjoyed his father's favor. Called Rufus, perhaps because he had a red beard or ruddy complexion, he was a stout man of about 30 when, having been given his father's crown, scepter, and sword, he arrived in England to assume his duties. He carried with him sealed instructions from his father to Archbishop Lanfranc of Canterbury, a trusted advisor. On September 26, 1087, William was anointed and crowned at Westminster, after which he released his father's prisoners and arranged for the distribution of his father's deathbed bequests throughout the kingdom. It was a seamless transition—at first.

THE REBELLION OF 1088

Among the more questionable deathbed decisions of William the Conqueror was his order to liberate his half-brother Odo, Bishop of Bayeux and former Earl of Kent, whom he had imprisoned seemingly for scheming to advance his own position on the continent without consulting William. Odo returned to Kent and wasted no time networking with his other half-brother, Robert of Mortain, and a number of Norman nobles in England.

In fact, the death of the Conqueror had placed quite a few Norman barons in a difficult spot. Normandy was in the hands of Robert Curthose, and William Rufus ruled England. There was no love lost between the two brothers, and barons who held lands in both Normandy

and England feared that allegiance to one lord might cost them their holdings in the other's realm. William II also drew his barons' ire by exerting the same imperious control his father had used to keep his vassals in check. In Normandy, the impulsive and freewheeling Robert had let central authority devolve, and his vassals were beginning to enjoy room to expand their own ambitions. Given the choice, many of the Anglo-Norman barons would rather have a weaker king.

Odo, a man of extraordinary personal wealth and ambition, became the ringleader of a plot to overthrow William and turn the English throne over to Robert. In concert, Odo and his Anglo-Norman allies fortified their castles, ravaged royal lands, and raised armies. Then they waited for reinforcements from Normandy. But the Norman forces proved unable to cross the Channel, and William seized the upper hand. In a politically astute move, William appealed directly to the people of England, promising

Odo of Bayeux, as depicted on the tapestry he probably commissioned to commemorate the Norman Conquest. The ambitious, aggressive Odo waves a club, possibly because, as a clergyman, he was forbidden to wield a sword.

> ## WILLIAM RUFUS HAD A RED FACE ASTONISHING STRENGTH, THOUGH NOT VERY TALL, AND HIS BELLY RATHER PROJECTING...
>
> *WILLIAM OF MALMESBURY*

1087
The Byzantine emperor Alexius I Comnenus is defeated at the Battle of Drystra by heretic Bogomils in Thrace and Bulgaria who have revolted against Constantinople.

1087
Control of the western Mediterranean is wrested from the Arabs by Genoa and Pisa, whose forces capture Mahdiya in Africa.

1088
The University of Bologna is founded, the first institution of its kind in Europe.

Opposite A portrait of William II as he appears in the Stowe manuscripts.

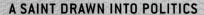

A SAINT DRAWN INTO POLITICS

Saint Anselm of Canterbury, antagonist of William II, began his career in the Church by seeking out Lanfranc, who was at the time prior of the Benedictine Abbey of Bec in Normandy. After Lanfranc's departure, Anselm became prior and then abbot, and under his leadership the abbey became a famed center of learning. When, on Lanfranc's death, Anselm was invited to become Archbishop of Canterbury, he initially expressed reluctance, claiming that he was merely a learned monk unfit for a politically charged post. As Archbishop, he clashed with William before going into voluntary exile. Anselm had enormous influence as a theologian. Among many other accomplishments, he articulated what has become known as the ontological argument for the existence of God.

were the primary rivals, and in 1091 William took the fight across the Channel, taking the eastern portion of Normandy for himself.

William and Robert then set aside their differences and turned their attention to Scotland. In William's absence, Malcolm III of Scotland had invaded the north of England. Though William's vassals had repulsed the invasion, it was an offense that could not go unpunished. William and Robert's army swiftly brought Malcolm to heel, and he swore fealty (loyalty) to William. In 1093, William returned with yet another army, colonizing the region around Carlisle. In response, Malcolm launched another foray into England. In a disastrous turn for Scotland, Malcolm and his heir were killed at Alnwick. After several years of dynastic struggle in Scotland, King Donald III was captured and blinded by William's deputy, Edgar the Atheling, who in 1097 placed his own son on the Scottish throne. Scotland became a vassal state to England.

them wealth and more just laws. These gestures may not even have been necessary, because the rebels were powerful Norman barons, objects of even more English hatred than the king. The English, and the Church, sided with William.

In short order, William brought many of his barons into line, either intimidating them into submission or buying them off. He then cornered Odo in Rochester. Odo agreed to forfeit all his English possessions in return for safe passage to Normandy. Most of the rebellion's leaders consented to the same terms. What might have been an abrupt end to William's reign had turned into a resounding triumph. William seemed invulnerable, and his ruthlessness in putting down the rebellion proved a powerful deterrent to any discontented barons.

EXPANDING HIS RULE

William's decisive victory over the rebels of 1088 did little to resolve the lingering tensions among the sons of William the Conqueror. Henry had ambitions of his own, but William and Robert

ROBERT DE MOWBRAY

In the interim, William had subdued more restive barons in the north. Chief among them was Robert de Mowbray of Northumberland. William laid siege to Mowbray's castle of Bamburgh in 1095, but could not breach it. Then he hit upon the stratagem of building a rival fortress, eventually luring Mowbray into the open and capturing him. But Mowbray's wife continued to hold Bamburgh. In a characteristic display of ruthlessness, William announced that, unless the castle was surrendered, he would blind Mowbray in full view of its walls. Mowbray's wife capitulated, and the north was secure.

In 1096, about to embark on the First Crusade, Robert mortgaged all of Normandy to William for 10,000 marks of silver. William raised the money with a nationwide tax. Though he was nominally only regent, he now effectively ruled both Normandy and England. Two years later, after two campaigns of varying success, he erected a series of castles on the Welsh border. The masters of those castles, operating largely outside the

1089	1091	1093	
Ergotism—the effect of long-term ergot poisoning also known as St. Anthony's Fire—strikes a French village, whose inhabitants run through the streets in fits of madness.	Normans in Italy, originally arrived as mercenaries and now inhabitants, complete their conquest of Sicily.	Work begins on Durham Cathedral, one of the finest examples of Norman architecture. At the time, the Bishop of Durham had both ecclesiastical and military authority.	

Westminster Hall as it appears now, the epicenter of the British government.

An early engraving of Westminster Hall and its environs, when the building was an expression of courtly majesty.

English system, would in time become forces unto themselves, but under William the English border regions became much more secure.

SIMMERING RESENTMENTS
In the first two years of his rule, William had been advised by Archbishop Lanfranc, a man of such experience and gravitas that he was able to check some of William's unsavory tendencies. Lanfranc had even chided the king for disregarding the promises he had made to secure support against the rebel barons in 1088. But in 1089 the venerable churchman died, and William lost a valuable voice of restraint and conciliation.

The brutality William visited upon those who incurred his displeasure was partly a necessity and partly a legacy of his father, but it also reflected a gratuitous streak in William himself. He lavished his favorites with gifts, but he had a fiery temper, and could be shockingly cruel. He was quick to impose dispossessions, imprisonments, mutilations, and executions, and seldom inclined to any sort of leniency. While that approach made William feared, it also made him hated.

The populace, though they had supported his authority against that of the rebel barons, soon came to resent him. Like his father, William often traveled around his kingdom; unlike his father, he resided in England, so such royal

1093
Scotland's Malcolm III MacDuncan and his eldest son Edward are ensnared and killed on November 13 at a place in Northumberland, England, that will be called Malcolm's cross. He is succeeded by his brother Donald Bane who will reign until 1097.

1094
Valencia falls to El Cid after a siege of 9 months. He violates all the conditions of surrender: having the cadi ibn Djahhaff burned alive and slaughtering many citizens.

1094
Spanish Christian hero El Cid captures Valencia from the Muslims and begins his rule of the area that will last to his death in 1099.

1095
Pope Urban II preaches a crusade against the infidel. The pope points out that vast areas of land are available to knights who join the cruscade. The First Crusade raises more than 30,000 men.

The medieval historian William of Malmesbury, as depicted in a modern stained-glass window in Malmesbury Abbey. Born during the reign of William II, he recounted with sharp disapproval the rumored practices of the king and his court.

progresses occurred far more frequently. The arrival of the royal host was a local catastrophe. The members of William's large entourage took what they pleased, often raping and looting as they passed. William's countenancing of such routine brutality and exploitation stoked popular resentment.

And William proved extraordinarily effective at collecting revenue. His chief agent in this was Ranulf Flambard, a Norman priest who had become keeper of the royal seal under William the Conqueror. The name "Flambard" may have referred to Ranulf's flamboyant personality. He was brilliant, manipulative, and ceaselessly inventive in the pursuit of revenue. As the architect of William's fiscal policies, he became the widely reviled symbol of royal exploitation. William entrusted him with a range of responsibilities, to the extent that William of Malmesbury, a historian born during William's reign, described him as "manager of the whole kingdom."

Ranulf supervised extensive development of London. As William's royal seat, the city needed the architectural trappings of a magnificent capital, and the enterprising Ranulf pursued the project with characteristic ingenuity and willpower. London Bridge was rebuilt in stone, and a new wall built around the Tower. His greatest project, the Great Hall at Westminster, was the largest such building in Europe, and remains an iconic setting for government and ceremonial events. Ranulf exacted forced labor to speed up construction, and records indicate that a number of workers lost their lives in the process. William first held court there in May 1099, at which time Ranulf was made Bishop of Durham.

TROUBLES WITH THE CHURCH

Ranulf Flambard's appointment as Bishop of Durham was an unseemly irony. Ranulf was not merely William's most trusted minister; he was also a churchman. Yet he took unscrupulous advantage of the king's disdain for the clergy. William's father had always guarded against ecclesiastical incursions on his power, but he was by all accounts a pious

Christian and maintained good relations with the Church. For Ranulf, the Church was a source of royal revenue and personal wealth, and with William's blessing he treated it as such. Under William's rule, Church assets were absorbed by attrition. The process was simple: if a bishopric or abbacy came open, William appointed no one to fill it, so that its assets could be redirected to the royal coffers—and Ranulf's purse. As far as the clergy were concerned, the policy bordered on desecration.

CRISIS AT CANTERBURY

Matters came to a head after the death of Lanfranc, when William left the Archbishopric of Canterbury open for four years in order to siphon off its wealth. In 1093, a serious illness elicited a spasm of remorse from William, and he promised to pay due respect to the Church. Anselm, a protégé of Lanfranc, was named Archbishop of Canterbury.

History remembers Anselm chiefly as a theologian; he was a profound thinker and an influential apologist for Christianity. But he was also the first Archbishop of Canterbury to become a thorn in an English king's side. Things were bad from the start: the terms of Anselm's appointment remained in dispute, and he openly criticized what many regarded as the decadence of William's court. William took measures to have Anselm removed, even appealing to Pope Urban II, whom William had agreed to support against his rival pope in Avignon on condition that papal legates could not enter England without William's express permission. The tug of war between William and Anselm continued until 1097, when an exhausted and exasperated Anselm withdrew into exile, once more leaving Canterbury's ecclesiastical wealth to the tender mercies of William and Ranulf.

Such brazen disregard for the property and prerogatives of the Church enraged the clergy, and the characterizations of William in clerical documents of the period are damning in the extreme. But those depictions were not simply based on the king's appropriation of Church

1096

The first lectures take place at the University of Oxford, which rapidly becomes a center of learning.

1098

The Battle of Nicaea ends in defeat for a Muslim army by a combined force of crusaders and Byzantine Greeks who take the Seljuk Turks' capital. The French knight Walter the Penniless is killed after having led hordes through Europe and Asia in what will be called the Peasants' Crusade.

1098

The first crusaders lay siege to Antioch, a key city on the approach to Jerusalem. Antioch becomes a bastion of crusader activity in the Holy Land.

wealth. William's court offended ecclesiastical, and English, sensibilities in other ways.

A DEN OF INIQUITY

To his many detractors, William was not just an extortionist with a crown; he was also a decadent Frenchman, and his court was a den of iniquity. According to contemporary reports, fashion, flamboyance, and sex set the tone in William's court. He had a gaggle of male favorites, whom he allegedly encouraged to wear their hair long and curled, to dress themselves in opulent robes that opened at the hip, and to walk like women. According to William of Malmesbury, nights at court were given over to gambling, drinking, and indiscriminate sex in darkened rooms. Whether or not this is entirely true, the perception remained that William had inaugurated an era of pervasive

A medieval depiction of William's death in the New Forest. Though it was termed an accident, suspicion remains that William was in fact assassinated.

moral corruption. Most Englishmen thought of French courts as worldly, aestheticized, and hedonistic, but they were largely appalled that such a culture should be planted in English soil, especially in the extreme manner that William and his retinue seemed to embody.

In all likelihood, both William and Ranulf were sexually attracted to men, and they made no secret of it. William never married and produced no heir. Within the nobility, his sexual orientation was no obstacle to his authority or esteem; what drew the ire of onlookers was the colossal self-indulgence and general lasciviousness William fostered in his court. At one point, Anselm baited the king by asking him to participate in a council on combating homosexuality; William curtly declined.

But whatever criticisms arose from the Church, the barons, and the populace, William remained a strong, intimidating, effective ruler. His aggressive centralization of power and his antagonism with the Church anticipated later conflicts between the Crown and Canterbury that would have much more momentous results.

DEATH IN THE FOREST

The Norman kings were enthusiastic hunters. William the Conqueror established extensive royal preserves, most famously the New Forest, to pursue the pastime. But it was a dangerous sport, and more than one of William II's relations had been killed in the course of the hunt. On August 2, 1100, at the height of his powers, William met a similar fate.

That morning, the king and a large party including his brother Henry and several nobles went into the New Forest to hunt deer. As the huntsmen drove the deer toward the waiting hunting party, arrows flew. One of them, shot by Walter Tirel, the Count of Poix and a superb archer, struck William in the chest killing him instantly. As soon as the party saw the king dead, they scattered. Henry, with astonishing clarity of purpose, rode to Winchester to secure the royal treasury and stake his claim to the throne. Tirel eventually went into exile. William's body was left in the dust until a group of servants took it to Winchester Cathedral, where it was interred.

It may have been an accident, but William's contemporaries and many historians have suggested otherwise. William had no shortage of enemies, and outright rebellion would have been foolhardy. Henry's presence at the hunt, and his swift and decisive maneuvering in the immediate aftermath, has been taken by some to indicate that he was behind an evident murder. He certainly gained a kingdom by it. But what lay behind William's sudden death will probably always remain a mystery. To this day, a small monument, the Rufus Stone, marks a spot in the New Forest where William is said to have fallen. The inscription on the stone describes his death as accidental.

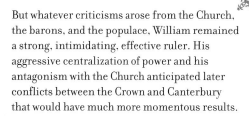

1098	1099		1099	1100
The Orkneys, The Hebrides, and the Isle of Man are seized by Norway's Magnus III.	The crusaders conquer Jerusalem, massacring its Muslim and Jewish inhabitants. Godfrey of Bouillon is named King of Jerusalem.		El Cid dies in July at age 59 after being defeated by the Almoravids at Cuenca. His widow will hold Valencia against the Moors until 1102.	Jerusalem's Godfrey of Bouillon dies in July at age 39 after successful forays against the Seljuk Turks that have taken him as far as Damascus.

HENRY I ✣ A Force for Stability

House Normandy

Born 1068

Died December 1, 1135

Reigned 1100–1135

Consort Matilda of Scotland (died 1118), Adeliza of Louvain

Children Four, including Empress Matilda and William Adelin, and more than 20 illegitimate children

Successor Stephen

Henry crossing the Channel, from a medieval manuscript. Henry spent much of his reign in Normandy, traveling back and forth across the Channel so often that he established a regular ferry system.

Henry I had been the least noteworthy of the sons of William the Conqueror, but as King of England he revealed himself to be savvy, cool-headed, and decisive. His rule, the longest yet of any English king, brought decades of stability to the realm.

When Henry responded to his brother King William's death in the New Forest by riding to Winchester to take control of the royal treasury and then name himself King of England, he certainly brought suspicion on himself. His two brothers, as much as they feuded with each other, had never trusted Henry, and with good reason; he spent years causing trouble, repeatedly changing allegiances. Years earlier, William and Robert had even made a pact that, in the event of either brother's death, the other would inherit, effectively blocking Henry from succession.

William's death could not have come at a more opportune time for Henry: Robert was away collecting accolades in the First Crusade, and few of the Anglo-Norman barons, for all their ambitions, wanted to risk rebellion and anarchy. With characteristic decisiveness, the day after William's death Henry had himself elected king by a hastily gathered council of nobles. Two days later he was crowned in London.

THE POLITICS OF STABILITY

Henry's coronation held clues to his plans for the kingdom. Clearly, he was keenly aware of the sense of injustice and exploitation that had permeated England under William and his financial enforcer, Ranulf Flambard, and he took pains to assure lukewarm supporters that things would be different. He formally renounced the excesses and injustices of his Norman predecessors, promised to respect the holdings of the Church, granted secure inheritance rights to the barons, and even placated the commoners by outlawing collective punishment of villages for unsolved murders. Those promises were then written up as a charter for good measure, and Ranulf was immediately imprisoned in the Tower.

While Henry gained valuable popularity with these measures, especially with the commonfolk, he also alienated many Norman barons by making two decisions with far-reaching implications for England. In his Coronation Charter he promised to revive the principles of Anglo-Saxon law—a move that validated a culture the barons disdained. Then, in November 1100, Henry married Edith, the daughter of Malcolm III of Scotland and a member of the House of Wessex. In marrying Edith, who changed her name as queen to the more Norman Matilda, Henry inaugurated a more distinctly English royal line, but he also earned the scorn of Norman nobles who saw him as having sullied their superior blood.

> HE PREFERRED CONTENDING BY COUNSEL RATHER THAN BY THE SWORD: IF HE COULD, HE CONQUERED WITHOUT BLOODSHED."
>
> *WILLIAM OF MALMESBURY*

1100	1106	1115	1118	
Henry I takes the throne of England.	In the Battle of Tinchebrai, Henry I defeats his brother Robert Curthose, who is then imprisoned in the Tower of London.	St. Bernard founds a Cistercian monastery at Clairvaux, in northeastern France. Bernard will become an influential diplomat as well as a famed mystic and devotee of the Virgin Mary.	The crusaders invade Egypt, but are defeated.	**Opposite** Henry brought decades of stability to England, and also, through his marriage and his laws, infused Anglo-Saxon culture into that of Norman England.

Henry had moved quickly and intelligently to establish himself, but trouble soon arrived from abroad in the return of his brother Robert, who was outraged to find Henry in control not only of England but of Normandy as well, thanks to the mortgage agreement Robert had made with William before departing for the Holy Land. To make matters worse, Ranulf became the first prisoner to succeed in escaping from the Tower, and joined Robert. Predictably, Robert wasted little time in making a play to unseat Henry. In the summer of 1101, he landed with an army at Portsmouth. But Robert then bypassed both Winchester and London to parley with Henry at Alton in Hampshire, where he agreed to terms allowing him to resume control of Normandy and receive an annuity from Henry. The two brothers also agreed to name each other heirs. In the final analysis, it may be that Robert simply didn't have the stomach for a protracted campaign in England.

One of the terms of the Alton agreement was a general amnesty for Anglo-Norman barons who had backed Robert. Henry likely never intended to honor that pledge, and spent the next year compiling charges against some of the participants. One in particular, Robert of Belleme, Earl of Shrewsbury, became the symbolic target of Henry's revenge. In 1102,

Winchester Castle, of which only the Great Hall now remains, was a crucially important stronghold during Norman times. The royal treasury, the Exchequer, and the Domesday Book were all housed here. Today, it houses a magnificent 13th-century replica of King Arthur's legendary Round Table.

Henry sent a forceful message by laying siege to Robert's castle, stripping him of his English lands and exiling him and his followers. Henry had little difficulty controlling his English barons for the rest of his long reign.

ACQUISITIONS AND TROUBLES ABROAD

As might have been expected, Henry's truce with Robert soon gave way to sporadic fighting, and Robert's hold over the perpetually unruly landlords of Normandy began to slip. Sensing advantage, Henry invaded in 1106. During his siege of the castle at Tinchebrai, Robert's forces arrived. After tense negotiations, battle was joined. In little more than an hour, Henry was victorious and Robert his prisoner. Robert, ever a destabilizing force, found himself confined to the Tower of London for the rest of his long life. Normandy would belong to the English Crown for another century.

In the aftermath of Tinchebrai, however, William had made one serious miscalculation: he had imprisoned Robert, but failed to take control of Robert's son William. The young William, known as Clito, Latin for "prince," became a rallying point for Henry's enemies. As William Clito approached manhood, he became an increasingly agitating thorn in Henry's side. Henry had to spend most of his time in Normandy rather than England, suppressing hostile barons and fending off attempts by neighboring rulers to undermine him.

In 1119, the King of France, Louis VI, took up William's cause as a pretext for invading Normandy, and was defeated at Brémule. Afterward, in a distinctly Norman gesture of chivalry, Henry returned the captured horses of Louis and William—but he kept the standard of Louis, which had also fallen into his hands. William Clito continued to pose problems for Henry until his death in another conflict in 1128.

DOMESTIC REFORMS & CONTROVERSIES

Henry's frequent sojourns in Normandy—so frequent that he established a regular ferry service—did not keep him from being an

---

1118

A great fire destroys nearly all of Magdeburg in Germany.

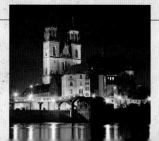

1119

Ilgahzi of Aleppo wipes out the Crusader army of Antioch at Ager before being himself crushed at Hab by King Badlwin II of Jerusalem.

1120

The Knights Templar are founded in Jerusalem by French knight Hugues de Payens with the aim of protecting pilgrims on the roads of the Holy Land.

QUEEN MATILDA

Born Edith, daughter of Malcolm III of Scotland, Matilda was no ordinary queen. While still a young child, she was sent to Romsey Abbey, where she learned English, French, and Latin. She and Henry had known each other for some time before their marriage, and seem to have been fond of each other, though they spent most of their time apart. As queen and regent, Matilda demonstrated considerable culture and administrative ability, initiating a range of construction projects and commissioning manuscripts. She also displayed impressive piety, tending to the sick—especially lepers—and reportedly attending Lent services barefoot. Anglo-Norman barons may have seen Matilda as having inferior blood, but the people adored her.

effective king in England, which enjoyed decades of relative peace and order under his rule. For nearly 20 years, his queen Matilda often governed as his regent. After the birth of two children, Adelaide and William, the king and queen lived separately but amicably. Matilda's role as regent made for excellent public relations; she had a well-deserved reputation for piety and supported a cultured court of her own.

But the person who did most to run the kingdom in Henry's absence was Roger, Bishop of Salisbury. It was claimed that Roger, then a priest in Caen, so impressed Henry with the speed and efficiency with which he performed mass that Henry decided on the spot to retain him. While that may be a stretch, Henry did recruit promising administrators from all over Europe, and not simply from among the uppermost classes.

Roger was a gifted, sophisticated, worldly cleric. A brilliant administrator, he oversaw magnificent building projects, helped reform the legal system, and is credited with creating the finance ministry, the Exchequer.

When Henry entered into a dispute with Anselm of Canterbury, whom he had invited back from self-imposed exile on taking the throne, Roger managed to appease both king

A later manuscript image of the sinking of the White Ship, a dynastic catastrophe that cost the lives of Henry's sons William and Richard, leaving England without a male heir.

and archbishop, at least for a while. Their main conflict involved the principle of investiture: who had the right to appoint bishops. The controversy was part of a burgeoning conflict across Europe between sacred and secular powers. In England it was settled with a compromise that distinguished between the bishops' ecclesiastical and secular rights and obligations. Henry relinquished claim on the power to appoint bishops, but retained his ability to demand secular fealty.

FROM TRIUMPH TO DISORDER

In 1118, Matilda died. Though they had lived apart for many years, she and Henry had formed an effective partnership, and she tolerated his dalliances with a series of mistresses—relationships that produced more than 20 illegitimate children. William doubtless felt his age. He had bested his rivals, instituted reforms, and forged valuable alliances. His daughter Adelaide had wed Heinrich V, Emperor of Germany, becoming an empress at the age of 11; his son William, by marrying the daughter of the ruler of Anjou and Maine, helped secure peace along the Norman borders.

In 1120, disaster struck. William and his younger brother Richard, along with a number of Henry's other children and courtiers, were killed when their ship foundered off the coast of Normandy. Suddenly, an aging Henry was without a male heir. In 1125, he summoned his now widowed daughter, Matilda of Germany, back to England, and arranged for her to marry Geoffrey Plantagenet of Anjou, nearly ten years her junior. It was a desperate move, and none too pleasing to the Anglo-Norman barons. They resented having to swear fealty to a woman, and her marriage to an Angevin was intolerable.

That union, however, would prove remarkably fruitful, although its benefits would not be felt until after a period of wrenching disorder. When Henry died in 1135, probably from food poisoning, Matilda was swept aside by Henry's nephew, Stephen of Blois, inaugurating what became known as The Anarchy.

1120
Henry's son William of Adelin is one of about 300 people drowned in the sinking of the White Ship off Normandy.

1122
The Concordat of Worms resolves the investiture controversy by giving kings the right to invest bishops with secular but not sacred authority.

1123
The Italian city of Bologna elects consuls to run its internal government, continuing a trend among Italian cities to become effectively independent of the king of Italy.

1124
Mael Maedoc ua Morgair (St. Malachy) becomes bishop of Down in Ireland and starts to introduce Cluniac reforms to the Irish Church.

STEPHEN ✠ Splendid Knight, Careless King

House Normandy

Born c. 1096

Died October 25, 1154

Reigned 1135–1141

Consort Matilda of Boulogne

Children Five, including Eustace IV, Count of Boulogne, Marie I, Countess of Boulogne, and William I, Count of Boulogne

Successor Henry II

> BECAUSE OF THE KING'S UNDUE SOFTNESS, PUBLIC DISCIPLINE HAD NO FORCE
>
> *WILLIAM OF NEWBURGH*

Brave and generous, possessed of the common touch, Stephen of Blois seemed a promising king. But, as his nobles and adversaries soon discovered, he was not cut out for the role. As he lost the control that Henry had secured over England, the country was torn apart by rival forces.

On the fateful night of November 25, 1120, when the White Ship foundered off Normandy and some 300 people drowned, including Henry's heir William Adelin, another twist of fate unfolded. Stephen of Blois, Henry's nephew, was among the revelers, but decided to remain ashore rather than cross the Channel with his friends and relatives, perhaps because he was feeling ill. In the aftermath of the disaster, he suddenly had a claim to the throne of England.

Stephen and his brother Henry had become favorites in Henry I's court. Courageous, friendly, and energetic, Stephen had gained reputation and significant land holdings. He seemed the embodiment of the noble knight, even being among the first to swear fealty to his cousin Matilda when Henry established her as his heir. It may be that Stephen, in adapting so well to the role of the noble retainer, never developed the ruthless political instincts necessary for a king. Henry's decision to name Matilda his heir may partly have reflected an awareness of his otherwise promising nephew's weaknesses.

AN UNEXPECTED CORONATION

When Henry died suddenly in 1135, however, Stephen acted with striking swiftness. Hurrying to London, where jubilant crowds celebrated his arrival, he had himself elected king. Then he made for Winchester, where his powerful brother Henry was bishop, and claimed the royal treasury. A campaign of propaganda and payouts helped sway most of the Anglo-Norman

barons in Stephen's favor. They already looked askance at Matilda and her Angevin husband, so their allegiance was not difficult to win. Three weeks after Henry's death, Stephen was crowned.

This lightning-fast seizure of the crown was made possible by Matilda's absence. Pregnant with her third child, she had also sided with her husband Geoffrey in disputes with Henry over land, and had neither been present at Henry's deathbed—a major oversight, given that she would likely have been acclaimed as his successor by the nobles gathered there— nor made her way to England with sufficient dispatch. Stephen may well have already laid

Henry of Blois, Stephen's brother and Bishop of Winchester. Instrumental in Stephen's accession to the throne, he later became one of many supporters the king estranged.

1135	1136	1138		1139	
William takes the English throne on his father's death.	Geoffrey of Monmouth, a Welsh monk living mostly near Oxford, writes his *History of the Kings of Britain*. Though filled with inaccurate and mythologized accounts, including some of King Arthur, it remained a respected chronicle for centuries.	The establishment of Florence as a communally governed city-state is first documented.		Matilda arrives in England to challenge Stephen.	**Opposite** A later image of Stephen, whose inability to maintain control of the kingdom led to civil war.

STEPHANVS   REX:

plans for the takeover, waiting only for the moment to arrive. Certainly his powerful brother Henry's support and political acumen smoothed Stephen's path to the throne.

Once crowned, Stephen seemed secure. Even Matilda's loyal half-brother, Robert of Gloucester, conceded that there was simply nothing to be done, and offered his fealty. Taking a page from his uncle's playbook, Stephen sealed his immense popularity with a new charter of liberties, according new rights and privileges to the Church and promising more just and generous enforcement of laws.

FROM STRENGTH TO WEAKNESS

But cracks quickly appeared in what had seemed a sure foundation. No sooner had Henry died and Stephen assumed the throne than David I of Scotland had launched an invasion. Whether he was seeking revenge for the displacement of Matilda, taking advantage of a strong king's sudden death, or testing the new ruler, his actions necessitated a kingly response. Stephen needed to assert his power, ruthlessly if necessary.

Stephen's nobles and soldiers were supremely confident; after all, Stephen had a well-earned reputation as a formidable warrior himself. But, given the opportunity, he did not take up the fight. Instead, he negotiated a peace in which David was allowed to keep the city of Carlisle for himself. Stephen could hardly have sent a worse message. In the cutthroat world of royal politics, he made the fatal error of not inspiring fear as well as admiration.

Rebellions began springing up across England. Inexplicably, even after intransigent defiance, rebellious barons were given little more than slaps on the wrist. In 1137, when Stephen traveled to assert control over Normandy, he again did not fight but bought off his adversaries, including Matilda's husband, the powerful Geoffrey of Anjou. Stephen's ineffectual responses to those who challenged his authority made him seem a paper tiger, and soon enough his control over England began to dwindle, as the barons of the West Country rose in defiance. Another invasion by the Scots led to their taking possession of Newcastle.

Stephen's attempts to be more ruthless proved too little, too late. He had lost too much credibility with the barons. Then he managed to alienate the clergy as well. In 1138, he passed over his brother Henry for Archbishop of Canterbury. Then he stripped the entire family of Roger of Salisbury—King Henry's able assistant—of their lands and castles. Stephen's brother took his revenge for being passed over by condemning the action.

THE ANARCHY

By 1138, Stephen had managed to weaken himself so much that the way was open for Matilda's faction to make a move. Robert of Gloucester, now in Normandy, publicly switched his allegiance to Matilda, prompting Stephen to revoke his holdings and providing a pretext for Robert to take action. The following year, that action came in the form of an invasion, with Matilda alongside Robert.

Stephen, ever politically obtuse, does not seem to have recognized the significance of Matilda's arrival on English soil. He even escorted her to Robert's stronghold of Bristol—a chivalrous but politically inept move, in that Robert's rebellion was now ennobled by Matilda's claim to the throne. Barons in the west rallied to Robert and Matilda, and while Stephen was campaigning against them with some success, barons in the east and then the midlands rose in rebellions of their own. In February 1141, Stephen was defeated and captured near Lincoln. Matilda gained the upper hand.

Matilda, now known as "Lady of the English," made arrangements to be crowned. But it never happened, partly because the imperious Matilda

THE NORMAN NOBILITY

During the Norman period, which included the reign of Stephen, one factor that contributed to ongoing conflicts was the Norman principle that the nobility, though sworn to serve their king, were considered his peers, and no decent king would order the outright execution of a baron, no matter how badly he behaved. A Norman ruler might strip a resistant baron's title and seize his assets, exile him, or even imprison him, but it would be very bad form to have him hanged or beheaded. Rebellious barons thus had fewer deterrents and longer careers than would have been expected in Anglo-Saxon times.

1141	1142	1143		1144
Stephen is captured by Matilda's allies, then released.	Construction of Krak des Chevaliers, the great castle of the Knights Hospitaller, begins in the Kingdom of Jerusalem, in what is now Syria. At its peak, it would hold a garrison of nearly 2,000.	Roger of Sicily captures Sfax in North Africa and imposes his overlordship on the emirate of Mahdia.		Geoffrey of Anjou, son-in-law of England's late Henry I, becomes duke of Normandy.

Matilda of England, who briefly ruled but was never crowned.

proved to be even more politically ham-fisted than Stephen. No sooner did she assume authority than she raised taxes on the barons, and then annexed for the Crown the municipal taxes London had been allowed for its own maintenance. The people of London refused to accept her. Matilda even managed to lose the support of Henry of Winchester, who refused to come to court after she rejected his counsel.

Stephen's wife, Matilda of Boulogne—no shrinking violet herself—soon arrived in England with her own army, and the unpopular Matilda was forced to flee London for Oxford. In the following campaign, Robert of Gloucester was captured, and Matilda had little choice but to accept a prisoner exchange: Robert for Stephen. Eventually, Stephen's forces were able to capture Matilda herself, but she famously escaped by climbing from a window and wearing a white cloak as camouflage against the snow. The back-and-forth play of advantage never led to victory for either side.

The conflict wore on for years, England divided into warring camps. Stephen held the throne, but could not extend his control very far. He ruled the southeast, Matilda's faction controlled a swath of the west, and powerful barons held sway over much of the midlands and the north. While Stephen and Matilda vied for supremacy, elsewhere barons rode roughshod over the populace, extorting what they wished and settling old scores among themselves. In contested areas, the rule of law completely unraveled. Period accounts suggest widespread violence, hardship, and fear—in a word, anarchy.

In 1148, Matilda returned to the continent, leaving her English campaign in the hands of her ambitious young son Henry Plantagenet. His initial sorties into England proved ineffectual, however. In 1147, Henry ran out of money, and Stephen, in yet another mystifying decision, covered his adversary's debt to his hired troops. When Henry invaded England again in 1153, the long years of attrition had taken such a toll that most of the Anglo-Norman barons were eager for some kind of resolution.

A QUESTION OF SUCCESSION

It took a confluence of events for that resolution to arrive. The first of these occurred not in England but on the continent, where young Henry Plantagenet not only took control of Normandy but married Eleanor of Aquitaine, placing the better part of France, with all its resources, in his hands. Suddenly, he was a mighty ruler.

The second event was a death. In 1153, Stephen laid siege to Wallingford Castle. When Henry arrived with an army to relieve the siege, a decisive battle seemed imminent. But it never happened. Instead, the bishops stepped in to broker a peace, and the barons, fatigued from the long years of tension and unrest, were happy to let the war wind down. The resulting arrangement, the Treaty of Wallingford, allowed Stephen to reign until his death on the condition that he name Henry his heir. This outraged Stephen's son Eustace, who threatened to derail the tenuous peace. But Eustace grew ill and died shortly after, removing a major obstacle to the settlement, and his younger brother William renounced any claim of his own. Stephen would be the last of the Norman kings.

The next year, Stephen died, and Henry assumed the throne. In retrospect, Stephen's death shortly after Wallingford may have ensured stability; had he lived much longer, things might have taken a turn back toward anarchy. As it was, he was little mourned.

1147	1148	1152	1153	1154
Bernard of Clairvaux summons the knights of Europe to the Second Crusade. It ends in demoralizing defeat with the failure to capture Damascus.	Matilda leaves England.	Frederick Barbarossa becomes Holy Roman Emperor. He will prove a tireless campaigner until he drowns in the Saleph River in 1190, on his way to the Holy Land with the Third Crusade.	The Treaty of Wallingford establishes Henry Plantagenet as heir to the throne.	Stephen dies, and Henry II becomes the first Plantagenet king.

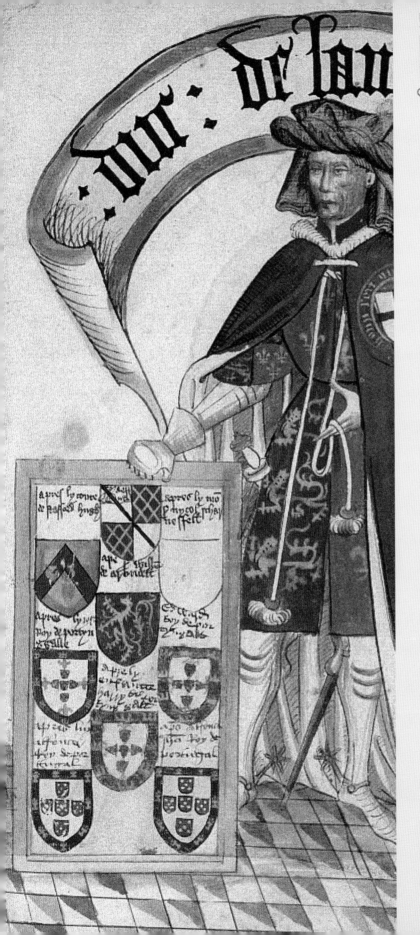

The House of Plantagenet

With the arrival on the English throne of Henry II, member of the House of Plantagenet, England entered the glittering age of its first imperial splendor. The Plantagenets were the most deeply and colorfully French of the British monarchs, and they brought to the English court the sumptuous pageantry, chivalric ideals, and dynastic intrigues of the southern realms of Anjou and Aquitaine. While some Plantagenet kings, such as Richard I, the Lionheart, regarded England as something of a backwater, Edward I and Edward III surely number among Britain's greatest monarchs, and the tragically self-destructive reign of Richard II brought to an end a truly extraordinary dynasty.

HENRY II ✛ The First Imperial King of England

House Plantagenet

Born March 5, 1133

Died July 6, 1189

Reigned 1154–1189

Consort Eleanor of Aquitaine

Children Eight, including Richard I and John

Successor Richard I

When Henry Plantagenet, of the House of Anjou, was crowned King of England at the age of twenty-one, he already possessed vast holdings in France through inheritance and marriage. Those resources, and the force of his character, made him the strongest English monarch in generations—until his sons began to maneuver against him.

When Henry took the throne, he faced the twofold challenge of restoring order and stability in England and retaining control of his many lands on the continent. He embarked on both enterprises with a dynamism that astonished friends and enemies alike. Henry's tireless traveling throughout his lands—he was known to wear out horses with hard riding—reinforced the sense that he was very much the master of his realms.

ESTABLISHING AUTHORITY

Henry was no stranger to the English nobility; even in his teenage years he had campaigned throughout the country, impressing people wherever he went with his bravery, charisma, and force of will. As king, he proved indefatigable, traveling around England at breathtaking speed, making his presence felt everywhere. It is as if he understood that, if he were to recover the peace that had prevailed for so long under his grandfather Henry I, he could not remain an abstraction to the barons and the common people.

His first imperatives were to restore the rule of law and subdue the barons, many of whom had come to regard themselves as rulers unto themselves during the civil war. Extending a blanket amnesty to all who had fought against Matilda, Henry assembled a royal administration of the most qualified men he could find. He also embarked on a campaign of destroying what were known as "adulterine" castles, the fortresses built throughout the countryside without royal consent by barons taking advantage of a weak king. Though this measure had been agreed to as part of the Treaty of Wallingford, only now was it being enforced. Castles were compelling symbols of power, and by demolishing a large number of them Henry sent a resounding message about the new state of affairs. He had troops specially trained in siege warfare, capable of breaching fortifications with intimidating efficiency.

In mid-1155, Henry made a telling example of one baron, Hugh de Mortimer, who dismissed the young king as an overweening child and fortified three of his castles against him. In a potent display of dominance, Henry not only laid siege to the castle in which Hugh was lodged but also erected a wall around it so that no one within could escape. Hugh

During the civil war, barons had built unauthorized castles throughout England. One of Henry's first priorities was to raze them in a show of authority. He was an expert in siegecraft.

> HE IS A GREAT, INDEED THE GREATEST OF MONARCHS, FOR HE HAS NO SUPERIOR OF WHOM HE STANDS IN AWE, NOR SUBJECT WHO MAY RESIST HIM
>
> *ARNULF OF LISIEUX*

1154

Henry II takes the English throne as the first Plantagenet king.

1154

The Almohads capture Grenada, completing their conquest of Muslim Spain.

1155

Pope Adrian IV grants Henry lordship of Ireland.

Opposite Henry II, arguably the most powerful English king before Henry VIII.

HENRICVS . II ,

A medieval manuscript image of Henry II debating with Thomas Becket, Archbishop of Canterbury. The death of Becket at the hands of three of Henry's knights left a stain on his kingship that took years to overcome.

Thomas Becket, first Henry's chancellor and then his nemesis as Archbishop of Canterbury, a formidable administrator and iron-willed opponent.

courtiers learned quickly to get out of the way and wait out his rages. During one debate about Scotland, he reportedly chewed his way through a blanket before recovering his composure.

Once Henry had thoroughly secured England, it was Scotland that beckoned as the next prize. Its king, Malcolm IV, was even younger than Henry, and weak in constitution; given the surname Virgo, "the Maiden," he never married and would die at the age of twenty-four. Henry had little trouble with Malcolm. In 1157, he needed only one meeting to restore all the lands Malcolm's predecessor, David I, had managed to annex during the Anarchy, and he secured the young Scottish king's fealty. After Scotland came Wales, which proved more refractory. In 1158, after a long campaign, the Welsh princes finally submitted. Only when, a year later, Henry proposed an expedition to conquer Ireland did he encounter enough dissent to second-guess his plans, and he left that undertaking for the future.

RESTORATION AND REFORM

Having matured through years of conflict, misrule, and disorder, Henry had seen many times over how not to rule a kingdom. He looked back past Stephen to the reign of Henry I for inspiration, and adopted many policies with roots in that period, often expanding them.

In order to manage such a vast set of territories—historians often refer to Henry's holdings as the Angevin Empire—the king recruited large numbers of "new men," promising members of the minor nobility who could be counted on to keep the machinery of governance running smoothly and efficiently. Among them, the foremost was Thomas Becket, Henry's chancellor. Once a clerk under Archbishop Theobald of Canterbury, Becket had risen to archdeacon, and came to Henry highly recommended. The king and his chancellor formed a remarkably effective partnership.

Though Becket was some fifteen years older than his king, the two men became fast friends. Becket was a brilliant and multifaceted

was forced into a humiliating public ritual of submission. Shortly thereafter, Henry of Winchester, the last power broker of the civil war yet to kneel before his new king, fled England for good. In a matter of months, with a masterful sense of symbolic gestures, Henry had the kingdom firmly within his grasp.

As a king, Henry well knew how to be imperious, but he also had the common touch. He was surrounded by pomp, yet he dressed simply, often in riding clothes, and he was not above dropping in on a local tavern for a few flagons of ale—a practice that further endeared him to the commonfolk. In addition to his favored pastime of hunting—he had lodges and preserves throughout England—Henry was literate and intellectually inclined, a keen student of history who surrounded himself with learned men and enjoyed debating ideas. Some courtiers complained that serving the king could too often feel like attending school. This range of interests, joined with Henry's vast continental holdings and the wealth they provided, led to his ruling over the largest royal court in Europe. For all that majesty, however, Henry famously had a temper as well, and his

1162	1163	1165
Temujin, later to be known as Genghis Khan, is likely born in Mongolia. He will go on to build one of the largest and most ethnically diverse empires in history.	Norman king William of Sicily loses his last toehold in North Africa to the Almohad Muslims.	Leipzig obtains a charter from Emperor Frederick Barbarossa, continuing the trend by which cities in Germany gain self-government in return for cash payments and taxes.

A royal writ, stamped with the king's seal and used to disseminate legal and administrative decisions throughout Henry's kingdom.

administrator, capable of managing nearly every aspect of the government, and he relished his role, savoring the pageantry of the court much more than his relatively restrained sovereign. He even campaigned with Henry on the continent, at one point bringing a force of 700 knights to Henry's campaign against Raymond of Toulouse, and defeating a French champion in single combat. The king even entrusted Becket with the upbringing of his son and heir, Young Henry.

Henry saw administering justice as one of the prime duties of a king, and he set out to transform the English legal system, establishing precedents that formed much of the basis for common law. For all his traveling and campaigning, Henry was detail-oriented, and both he and Becket were skilled lawyers. Many of the king's reforms had to do with

his judges, whom he appointed carefully and held strictly accountable. Henry also generated a large number of writs—formal documents conveying royal decisions and policies—that covered all sorts of legal issues. In an impressive feat of communication, Henry arranged for the Chancery to post his writs throughout the kingdom, so that the law became less about the king's physical person than about the written and interpreted word, backed by the sovereign's will.

As his reign progressed, Henry deepened his centralization and reform of the legal system. He was exceptionally good at delegating authority, and appointed traveling justices to hear cases throughout England. He also largely replaced trials by ordeal or combat with trial by jury. Many of his legal reforms reflected the myriad cases left in the wake of the civil war, which often involved property disputes.

The civil war had also undermined the kingdom's fiscal condition. Henry reformed the currency, streamlining the process of coinage and placing royal officials in charge of a more centralized system of mints. Money flowed out into the realm and back into the Exchequer, refilling royal coffers depleted over the course of Stephen's reign.

CONTINENTAL CONFLICTS

Henry's accomplishments in England only gain luster in light of his long sojourns on the continent. Between 1156 and 1163, he spent six of seven years abroad, an absence so pronounced that his English subjects wondered if he would ever return. Routine management of Anjou, Normandy, and Aquitaine was not the only imperative; also keeping Henry on the continent was rivalry with Louis VII of France, a decades-long chess match of moves and countermoves that, as historians have noted, resembled the Cold War.

It was a difficult situation, fraught with conflicting loyalties. Both Louis and Henry sought alliances to buttress their positions. Henry's efforts were complicated by the fact

Louis VII of France. He and Henry matched resource and wits for decades, locked in an intense rivalry for control of lands on the continent.

1167	1169	1170	1173	1174
Crusader forces invade Egypt, leading to an inconclusive peace agreement that ultimately paves the way for Saladin to seize power.	Saladin become Sultan of Egypt.	Archbishop Thomas Becket is murdered within Canterbury Cathedral by knights in the service of Henry II.	Henry II's sons rise in revolt, spurred on by his estranged wife Eleanor of Aquitaine.	A horse race is held at Newmarket, England, on the first known racetrack in Europe of post-Roman times.

that he and many of his allies were sworn not to raise their swords against Louis, who was technically their feudal lord. Nevertheless, such rulers as the counts of Flanders and Blois formed defensive ties with the English monarch. In 1154, the two kings made a tenuous peace, agreeing on some borders; four years later, it was agreed that Young Henry would be betrothed to Louis's daughter Margaret.

Henry and Louis sought to avoid a head-to-head confrontation, but tensions rose as Henry continued extending his dominions, gradually asserting control over the previously independent Duchy of Brittany, and then setting his sights on Toulouse. Toulouse was nominally part of Aquitaine, yet Count Raymond V ruled as if wholly independent. It may be that Henry's

A BITTERLY IRONIC APPOINTMENT

Henry II enjoyed good relations with the Church for the first few years of his reign, not least because the pope at the time, Adrian IV was the only Englishman ever to sit on the papal throne. It was all the more ironic, then, that when Henry sought to extend control over the English church by appointing Thomas Becket, his friend and trusted advisor, to be Archbishop of Canterbury, the king would find himself facing a far more defiant ecclesia. One can only wonder how Henry's reign would have unfolded had he kept Becket solely as chancellor and appointed a different archbishop.

queen Eleanor urged him to reassert control, but it is unlikely he needed any prompting. His 1159 campaign against Raymond proved frustrating, however. At one point, Henry had to refrain from attacking the city of Toulouse when he discovered that Louis was there, a guest of Raymond, to whom Louis had married one of his daughters.

Tensions further escalated when, by strategic marriages, Louis peeled away Henry's ally Theobald of Blois. Henry responded with a marriage of his own—the promised one between Young Henry and Margaret, though both were small children—and used it as a pretext to annex the territory of Vexin, in northwestern France, which was to go with the arranged marriage. Just as the region seemed about to descend into all-out war, both sides erred on the side of restraint, and in 1162 a peace deal was reached. As both sides knew, however, wars can be fought by proxy, and Louis would prove skillful at finding proxies in dangerous places.

THE DEATH OF BECKET

In 1161, Theobald of Canterbury died. He had served in that position with tremendous gravitas for over two decades, and he and Henry had largely avoided the clashes that had marred previous relations between the Crown and Canterbury. However, tensions remained, and the Church continued to operate largely as a state unto itself.

Those conflicts were surely foremost in Henry's mind when he appointed Thomas Becket to succeed Theobald at Canterbury. On the one hand, the decision made sense: Theobald had favored Becket, and Henry surely presumed that he and Becket would continue to be friends and collaborators. On the other, the English ecclesiasts were less than sanguine about the prospect of a worldly, haughty administrator taking such a vital Church post. Becket himself tried to beg out of the appointment—a customary show of humility, but also an indication that he foresaw the conflicts that might unfold. What did come was disaster.

1176	1176	1178		1178
First known mechanical clock in Europe is installed at Sens Cathedral, France.	The forces of the Holy Roman Emperor Frederick Barbarossa are defeated at Legnano, preserving the autonomy and authority of the Papal States.	The Leaning Tower of Pisa begins to lean.		Chinese documents record the discovery of a land in the Pacific named Mu Lan Pi, possibly California.

The ruins of Clarendon, the royal hunting lodge in Wiltshire where the Constitutions of Clarendon— an assertion of King Henry's authority over areas in which the Church had formerly been free of civil accountability— first took shape.

Becket had been a brilliant chancellor, but he was also a vain, willful and single-minded man. No sooner did he take up his duties as archbishop than, to Henry's surprise and consternation, he resigned the chancellorship. Soon after, it became clear that he was going to take his new position, with all its responsibilities, far more seriously than most had expected. His loyalties shifted entirely to the Church, where he proceeded to become an ongoing source of frustration to Henry. Becket acted less the pious priest than the stern champion, unafraid to brandish his ecclesiastical authority against those who, in his mind, trespassed on the prerogatives of the Church. Henry's own temper, exacerbated by what he saw as a betrayal, only hardened positions on both sides.

In 1163, Henry allowed Becket and his bishops to attend the Council of Tours, a conference organized by Pope Alexander III and dominated by a zealous reaction against worldliness among the clergy. It was an unprecedented grant of license to the English clergy, who had been kept relatively clear of Rome since William the Conqueror. Becket returned with a heightened militancy, and things swiftly came to a head when the issue of criminal trials for churchmen arose again. As Henry correctly saw, clerics were literally getting away with murder, and the only way to curb their impunity was to make them subject to secular criminal law. To Henry's consternation, Becket took up Theobald's old position and refused to budge. The following year, Henry drew up the Constitutions of Clarendon, an epochal document establishing that the Crown had prerogative over the Church in all questions other than those of Church doctrine. He then accused Becket of misconduct during his tenure as chancellor. The writing was on the wall, and Becket fled into exile.

During his six years on the continent, Becket persisted in angering Henry, asserting the authority of the Church and undermining Henry's alliances. When he returned to England

---

1180

France's Louis VII dies, aged 59, after a 43-year reign and is succeeded by his 15-year-old who will rule until 1223 as Philip II Augustus.

1187

Saladin decimates the forces of Christian Jerusalem at Hattin. When he then conquers Jerusalem, he forbids his soldiers to harm its inhabitants—a stark contrast with the Christian conquest of Jerusalem in 1099. Saladin's conduct establishes him as an icon of chivalry.

AN EXTRAORDINARY QUEEN

Eleanor of Aquitaine was one of the most extraordinary women of the middle ages. Born into the court of her father, William X, Duke of Aquitaine, she was given a sophisticated education, but also enjoyed such vigorous activities as hawking and hunting. Highly cultured, Eleanor also patronized troubadours and other artists. She was a brilliant woman with a forceful personality—one that came to trouble her equally strong-willed husband Henry II. During the reign of her son Richard I of England, she served as regent during his years of crusading.

in 1170, he immediately precipitated a crisis by denouncing the coronation of Young Henry by the Archbishop of York. Henry had arranged the early coronation to ensure a smooth succession, and now his efforts were in jeopardy. Becket also began excommunicating bishops who had supported Henry. In a fit of rage, the king infamously declared that his retainers were cowards if they could not summon the courage to rid him of one "turbulent priest." Though it was likely just one of Henry's outbursts, four knights took him at his word, and on December 29 confronted Becket in Canterbury Cathedral. Becket apparently had heard they were coming, but refused to flee, and in the resulting altercation he was cut down on the altar steps.

It was a catastrophic blow for Henry. On hearing the news, he shut himself alone in his chambers for three days in evident shock and grief. He was now, as far as Europe was concerned, the king who had ordered an archbishop murdered in his cathedral. The pope placed England under interdict, so that no sacraments other than baptism and last rites could be performed. Henry was forced to revoke the Constitutions of Clarendon and promise to go on a crusade—a promise he never fulfilled. It would take many years for Henry to recover from the disaster; in the interim, Becket was canonized.

SONS IN REBELLION

Henry, seemingly unassailable before, was staggered by the death of Becket, and in its immediate aftermath his weakness emboldened his adversaries. Though he surely could expect his continental nemesis Louis VII to stir up trouble, Henry found himself confronted with the rebellion of his own family.

Henry had sought to avert such a crisis, but he had four headstrong sons, and an imperious and hostile wife in Eleanor of Aquitaine. Eleanor, now estranged from Henry, did all she could to turn his children against him. Henry had made her task easier by making a mistake common to many great rulers throughout history: he had sought to divide his lands among his children. Young Henry had been crowned King of England and been given Anjou, Richard received Aquitaine, and Geoffrey inherited Brittany. John, the youngest and Henry's favorite, was given castles in Anjou.

The situation proved intolerable for Young Henry, who saw what he regarded as his rightful inheritance being whittled away. King Louis had found the perfect proxy in his cold war against Henry, and he had discovered him within the English royal family. First, he stirred up Young Henry's indignation. Supported by Eleanor, Young Henry and Richard took up arms. Louis was quick to assist, and other neighboring rulers offered their support in exchange for promises of land. The Scots soon joined in. Henry had on his hands what came to be known as the Great Revolt. He had managed to capture and imprison Eleanor in the spring of 1173, but his sons were loose on the continent. Clearly troubled by this familial warmongering, he

1187

The Punjab is conquered by Mohammed of Ghor who rules at Ghazni as governor for his brother Ghiyas-ud-Din Mohammed.

1187

In Italy, Verona Cathedral is completed after 48 years of construction.

1187

Zen Buddhism arrives in Japan.

commissioned a wall painting in Windsor Castle depicting an eagle being attacked by its own young.

For the next year and a half, Henry was faced with the difficult and distasteful task of bringing his own sons to heel. Though weakened by the murder of Becket, he was still in his prime, and his sons were no match for his willpower and experience. In 1174, things turned decisively toward Henry. Forced to return to England to confront invading Scots and other rebels, he made the remarkably astute move of traveling to Canterbury to perform penance for Becket's death, even allowing himself to be flogged, and declaring that the rebellion was punishment for his sins. Soon after, William the Lyon, King of Scotland, was captured. Henry had, against all expectations, gained not only the upper hand in the conflict but the moral high ground as well.

Shortly thereafter, Henry defeated his rebellious sons in a dogged campaign. They were formally reconciled, but tensions remained. Young Henry would die of a fever in 1183 and Geoffrey in a jousting tournament three years later, leaving Richard and John to contend for Henry's inheritance. Richard was granted extensive lands on the continent—but King Henry attempted to transfer to John the Duchy of Aquitaine, where

Eleanor of Aquitaine, Henry's wife and one of the most remarkable women of medieval Europe.

Richard had previously distinguished himself as a ferocious soldier. Richard refused, and John declined to force the issue. In the end, John would receive only Ireland, which Henry's forces had recently subdued. Since Ireland was considered a backwater and its kings were still in power, John became known as Lackland. Richard in particular would remain rebellious, and he eventually proved enough of a commander to match his father.

HENRY'S LEGACY

Having quashed the Great Revolt, Henry was once more the imperious king he had been before the murder of Thomas Becket had thrown his reign into disarray. Eleanor, the queen who had borne him eight children and then turned on him, was kept prisoner, and he was able to rule with a regained sense of security. Henry even succeeded in restoring his reputation to the point that, in 1185, he was asked to be the ruler of the crusader kingdom of Jerusalem. He declined.

Henry spent much of his late reign in France, securing continental holdings and countering the machinations of the new French king, the crafty Philip Augustus. In 1189, worn out, ill, and barely able to stand, Henry finally found himself overmatched by the intransigent Richard, and agreed to terms. To his great sorrow, he found that John, his favorite son, had sided against him as well. On his deathbed at Chinon in Anjou, Henry was every bit the exhausted and embittered sovereign, cursing his rebellious sons. The throne of England would go to Richard, Eleanor's favorite, but also a tireless and charismatic campaigner, much like Henry in his youth.

Henry may have died unsatisfied, but he had ruled England and a large swath of the continent for over three decades, re-establishing order in a troubled kingdom and redefining the kingship. He had made costly mistakes, but he had also established himself as one of the most admired and feared monarchs in Europe. His remaining sons, both of whom would wear the crown themselves, would suffer in comparison.

1188	1188	1189	1189
The advance of Saladin through the Holy Land is halted at the fortress of Krak des Chevaliers by the Knights Hospitallers.	Alfonso IX of Leon convenes in Leon a meeting of nobles, clergy, and town representatives that is later recognized as being the first parliament in Spain.	The crusader fortresses of Montreal and Krak fall to Saladin. The Battle of Acre ends in a costly crusader victory over Saladin. The Christians then lay siege to Acre, which holds out for two years.	Henry II dies, and his son Richard I takes the throne.

RICHARD I ✛ The Crusader King

House Plantagenet

Born September 8, 1157

Died April 6, 1199

Reigned 1189–1199

Consort Berengaria of Navarre

Children None

Successor John

HIS VALOUR COULD NO THRONG OF MIGHTY LABOURS QUELL.

ROGER OF HOWDEN

Few English rulers have been so mythologized as Richard I, the Lionheart, but he was by nature a soldier, not a king, and vainglorious as well. He did little for England, spending only a few months there during his decade as king and draining the kingdom's wealth to finance his military expeditions.

The young Richard Plantagenet lived a life very different from those of his brothers. The second son of Henry II by Eleanor of Aquitaine, he spent many of his formative years in his mother's native court at Poitiers, where he absorbed its culture of troubadours and legends, dreaming of knightly glory. The young Richard, brave and magnetic, distinguished himself from an early age as a warrior.

SON AGAINST FATHER

Henry II never got along with his legitimate sons. To the extent that he paid them attention, he apparently regarded them as political chess pieces and problematic makers of dynastic demands. Even his favorite, John, eventually rebelled against him. But Richard seems to have genuinely hated his father, and with reason.

As the favorite of his mother Eleanor, Richard clearly took her side in the tensions that emerged early between her and the king. It may be that Henry's many infidelities—customary for a medieval king, but surely hurtful to a proud, famously attractive queen—stirred up early resentment in Richard. But over time, Henry angered Richard in more direct and deeper ways. As a child, Richard had been betrothed to Alys, the daughter of King Louis VII of France, but Alys had been raised in England as a result, and rumors circulated that Henry eventually had taken her as a mistress. This was a monstrous affront to Richard's honor, but for political reasons he had little choice but to tolerate the alleged insult.

When Young Henry, heir to the English throne, died in 1183, Richard became his father's nominal heir, but Henry sought to appease John by giving him Aquitaine, which further incensed Richard. When Henry died in 1189, father and son had been at open war on the continent.

FROM CORONATION TO CRUSADE

On Henry's death, Richard wasted no time getting himself crowned in London. His coronation was marred by violence. Apparently, Richard had banned Jews from the ceremony, and some who sought to attend were flogged. Londoners, stirred up by that event and rumors that followed it, began massacring the city's Jewish population. Similar atrocities followed in York and elsewhere. Richard did punish some of the perpetrators and issued a writ barring violence against Jews, but it was an inauspicious start.

In any event, Richard's attention was elsewhere. Two years earlier, the great Muslim warrior Saladin had decimated the Christian forces of Jerusalem at the Horns of Hattin and then captured the city itself, and calls for a new crusade reverberated through Europe. Richard became the first northern European monarch to pledge his participation.

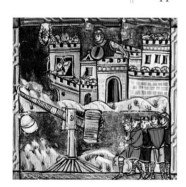

At the Siege of Acre (1189–1191) during the Third Crusade, Richard cemented his reputation as a great soldier and general—but he also made enemies who later exacted a costly retribution.

1189

Richard inherits the throne from his father, Henry II, and promptly departs on the Third Crusade.

1191

On his march from Acre to Jerusalem, Richard defeats Saladin at the Battle of Arsuf, but he is unable to follow up his victory and must leave the Holy Land without entering Jerusalem.

1191

Two magnificent ancient tombs, claimed to be those of King Arthur and Queen Guinevere, are found at Glastonbury Abbey, England.

Opposite Richard I in stained glass—an iconic portrait of Richard as heroic Crusader. The reality of his reign was more ambiguous.

The king's first order of business, then, was to raise the resources for such a gigantic enterprise, and England bore a heavy portion of the price. For 10,000 marks, Richard allowed Scotland to buy its independence from England. He then collected taxes, sought loans, and sold off a number of assets and offices. He even put the chancellorship up for sale, though it ended up in the hands of the capable William Longchamp. Richard is even alleged to have said that he would have sold London had he found a buyer. It was an ironic anticipation of the royal motto he would later adopt for himself, and which remains that of the royal family: Dieu et mon droit (God and my right). Richard felt he had the right to sell out his kingdom in order to crusade for his God.

He departed in 1190, with several thousand troops and a fleet of 100 ships. With him was Philip II of France; it may be that the two of them agreed to crusade together so that neither could take advantage of the other's extended absence. It was an eventful voyage to the Holy Land. In Sicily, Richard was offended by his widowed sister Joanna's treatment at the hand of King Tancred, so he captured the city of Messina and successfully demanded her release. Then he offended Philip, who parted ways with him in the course of the journey. Once arrived, however, Richard immediately established himself as a peerless general, leading the successful Siege of Acre. In its aftermath however, his more ruthless and arrogant side asserted itself, as he ordered the massacre of thousands of Muslim prisoners and offended fellow crusader Leopold of Austria by casting down the Austrian's banner as unworthy to stand next to Richard's—a misstep for which he, and England, would later pay dearly.

SALADIN

It was at Acre, and then on Richard's long march down the coast toward Jerusalem, that the king engaged in a long campaign against Saladin. Theirs was one of the great military rivalries of history. Both men were magnificent soldiers and brilliant strategists. They appear never to have met personally, but they accorded each other deep respect and communicated indirectly, negotiations being a key aspect of the conflict. On his march southward, Richard organized his army in a resourceful, well-defended array. When Saladin, after many skirmishes and probing raids that failed to divide the crusaders' ranks, finally attacked at Arsuf, Richard was able to counterattack and drive off the Muslim army with heavy losses. While not decisive, it was a symbolic victory in that it removed some of Saladin's aura of invincibility.

Richard proved unable to advance on Jerusalem, however, and Philip had returned to France, where he wasted no time undermining his erstwhile ally. In 1192, after coming to terms with Saladin—at one point he appears to have proposed to make the city neutral in its sacredness, jointly ruled by Christians and Muslims, only to have his fellow crusaders reject the notion—Richard sailed for home. Though he had been unable to win back Jerusalem, tales of his martial prowess preceded him, and he was hailed as the greatest of Christian champions.

Salah al-Din Yussuf ibn Ayyub, known in the West as Saladin. He and Richard, who engaged in a running campaign in the Holy Land, regarded each other as equals.

A WORTHY ADVERSARY

Saladin, Richard's chief adversary in the Third Crusade, was a Kurdish Muslim who had risen to become sultan of Egypt and Syria. Not only did the crusaders fear his military brilliance; they also admired his famous nobility of character. Though not a Christian, he became an icon of chivalry. When he conquered Jerusalem, he forbade his soldiers to injure its inhabitants. In one famous gesture, at Arsuf, Saladin sent Richard two stallions to replace a horse he had lost in the battle. When he died of a fever shortly after Richard's departure from the Holy Land, it was reportedly discovered that he had given nearly all his fortune to the poor of his sultanate.

1192	1192	1194
On his return from the Crusade, Richard is captured by Leopold of Austria and subsequently held for a ransom that costs England dearly.	Battle of Tarain. Sultan Shahabuddin Muhammad Ghauri of Afghanistan defeats a vast Rajput army, going on to capture Delhi and a vast swath of northern India. The resulting sultanate of Delhi persisted to 1857.	Richard returns to England, to be greeted by jubilant crowds.

Richard's captivity and subsequent ransom during his return from the Third Crusade cost England a staggering sum.

A LONG AND COSTLY JOURNEY

Before departing on the crusade, Richard had extracted a promise from his brother John not to enter England for three years. Richard was surely not so naïve as to believe that John would honor that pledge; it was probably made more to darken John's reputation further should he play for the throne in his brother's absence. But Richard had also named his half-brother Geoffrey's son Arthur of Brittany his heir, so John may have felt he had little to lose by making a move in Richard's absence. Within a year of Richard's departure, John briefly succeeded in taking control, having William of Longchamp acknowledge him as heir over Arthur. But the nobles refused to accept him, and he was forced to turn his schemes, with the help of Philip, to Richard's lands on the continent.

But fortune soon turned against Richard. On his voyage home he was forced ashore in the Adriatic, and with a handful of retainers began a long and perilous overland journey toward France. In late 1192, while traversing the lands of Leopold of Austria, he was recognized and captured. Leopold, who still despised Richard for the insult at Acre, turned the king over to the Holy Roman Emperor Henry VI, who held him ransom for the outrageous sum of 150,000 marks. The pope excommunicated both rulers for imprisoning a crusader, but they held firm.

A campaign began in England to raise the necessary sum, which was far more than the annual revenue of the Crown. A general tax extracted a quarter of both clerical and lay incomes, and Church assets were appropriated. It took well over a year to accumulate the ransom, during which John disgraced himself by attempting, along with Philip, to pay Henry VI to keep Richard captive. In early 1194, Richard was finally released, the ransom delivered by his mother Eleanor. He was received in London with rejoicing, despite his adventures and misadventures abroad having nearly bankrupted the kingdom. John had every reason to expect exile or imprisonment, but Richard, flush with his triumphant return and likely seeking to smooth things over, instead forgave him and named him his heir.

A SOLDIER TO THE END

After his return to England, Richard might have been expected to attend to the precariously depleted royal treasury. Instead, he returned to campaigning. In his absence, Normandy had yet again been left unattended, and Philip had claimed it for himself. Richard set about wresting it back.

In this as in nearly all his military undertakings, Richard was largely successful, and he spared no expense in five years of campaigning. In 1199, while laying siege to the small castle of Chalus in the Limousin, Richard was struck in the shoulder by a crossbow bolt fired from the castle wall. The wound became infected, and within days he died at the relatively young age of 41. His ever-faithful mother Eleanor reached his bedside in time to be with him in his final moments.

Richard had proved a costly king in some ways, but, apart from having drained the royal coffers, he left his lands in surprisingly good shape, with stable governance and secure borders. In his long absences, however, the nobility had found that they could govern the kingdom effectively without the king looking over their shoulders. That discovery would prove costly, in a different sense, to his successor.

1196

Riots in London led by Robert Fitz Osborn attack the houses of the rich, but the rioters disperse rather than fight the king's forces. Fitz Osborn is captured in St Mary le Bow and hanged.

1199

Death of Abu Yusuf Yaqub al-Mansur, probably the greatest of the Almohad caliphs of North Africa and Spain.

1199

Richard I dies when an arrow wound, received at the castle of Chalus, becomes infected. His brother John becomes king.

KINGS ON CRUSADE

The Crusades had an enormous impact on Europe, one that spanned the two centuries from approximately 1100 to 1300 and continues to shape Western culture to this day. England, however, was a relatively small and even marginal nation during this period, and of its kings only two made the perilous voyage to the Holy Land: Richard I and Edward I. Still, the Crusades both directly and indirectly affected the course of British history.

In 1095, Pope Urban II responded to Byzantine Emperor Alexios I's call for aid against the encroaching Seljuk Turks by convening the Council of Clermont and declaring general absolution for those willing to take up arms to defend Christendom and regain Jerusalem. The First Crusade quickly followed, as the prospect of combining holy war with pilgrimage enticed tens of thousands of nobles and warriors to take up the cross (the source of the term crusade) and travel toward the Holy Land.

Among them was Robert Curthose, son of William the Conqueror, who had inherited Normandy on his father's death but not England, which had gone to his brother William Rufus. Robert mortgaged Normandy to William in order to finance his crusading campaign. For the next three years, through the capture of first Antioch in 1098 and then Jerusalem in 1099, Robert remained on crusade, only returning to Normandy in 1100—just in time to see the English throne snatched out of reach by his brother Henry I. The First Crusade had effectively decided an English succession.

THE THIRD CRUSADE

Like most European monarchs, Henry II took the crusader vow, but in his case the oath was largely an act of penance for the murder of Thomas Becket in 1170. Henry also laid up a vast store of wealth to finance an expedition; as was common during the Crusades, the sum was held in trust by the Knights Templar. In 1187, however, when more calls for crusaders came, he begged out; he even declined to go after Saladin's capture of Jerusalem in 1187. Henry's money went to the Holy Land, but Henry did not. Though he had trouble enough at home managing his fractious and rebellious sons and his vast Angevin lands, it seems most likely that Henry simply had little interest in going on crusade.

His least favorite son, Richard the Lionheart, was altogether more enthused. When the Third Crusade was launched after the fall of Jerusalem, Richard used England as a source of money and manpower, selling off lands and offices and levying harsh taxes to finance his expedition. His claim that he would have sold London could he only have found a buyer was probably not in jest.

Whatever his failures as a king, Richard was a magnificent success as a Crusader, at least at covering himself in glory. Not only did he play a key role in the long and successful siege of Acre; he managed to defeat Saladin himself at the Battle of Arsuf in 1191. The rivalry between Richard and Saladin has gone down as one of the most famous in history, not so much for its military brilliance as for the courtliness

The Krak des Chevaliers in Syria, the most formidable and famous of Crusader forts. Edward I studied such fortifications while campaigning in the Ninth Crusade, and later made good use of what he learned.

JOURNEYING TO THE HOLY LAND

Undertaking a crusade was a massive, expensive affair, and the journey from England to the Holy Land was arduous. In the First Crusade, most armies traveled south through the Rhineland and Hungary to the Balkans before eventually reaching the Bosphorus, where they could be ferried across to Asia Minor and resume their march toward Antioch and then Jerusalem. The crusaders faced harsh extremes of weather and often ran dangerously low on provisions, often leading to conflict with local populations. By the time of the Third Crusade, control of more Mediterranean ports meant that sea travel became the preferred mode of transport. Richard I sailed from Marseille to Acre, stopping at Messina along the way.

A 19th century rendering of the surrender of Acre to Philip Augustus of France, Richard I's rival in Europe and compatriot in the Crusades.

displayed by both men, who esteemed each other as worthy opponents and traded gestures of that respect, the most famous of which was Saladin's gift of a fine horse to Richard after Richard's was slain at Arsuf. But though he came within sight of Jerusalem, Richard lacked the resources to mount a siege, and was forced to give up his crusade.

Though Richard's military exploits in the Holy Land earned him great renown, they came at a tremendous cost to England. Not only did Richard nearly empty the treasury and virtually put England on sale to finance his campaign; the ransom required to free him after his imprisonment on the way home stretched the kingdom very nearly to its limit. Richard is a case study in one particular moral hazard of the Crusades: warlike kings thirsting for glory could bankrupt their kingdoms to finance crusades, all the while claiming they were doing God's will.

EDWARD I

While still a prince and heir-apparent to his father Henry III, Edward Longshanks took part in the rather desultory Ninth Crusade, launched in 1270. Its nominal leader was Louis IX of France, and Edward brought only a small force of a few hundred men, so when Louis peeled off from the expedition to join a different campaign in Tunis, Edward was left to linger bravely but ineffectively in Acre before returning home to claim his throne. While there, he survived a Muslim assassination attempt. More importantly, he studied the advanced fortifications of the Crusader castles, learning principles of design and construction he would put to good use in his own castles, particularly those in Wales.

JOHN ✠ His Own Worst Enemy

House Plantagenet

Born c. December 24, 1166

Died October 18, 1216

Reigned 1199–1216

Consort Isabel of Gloucester (divorced 1199), Isabella of Angouleme

Children Five, including Henry III of England

Successor Henry III

While his brother Richard has been mythologized as a brave and honorable soldier-king, John has been vilified in popular imagination as a scoundrel and a tyrant. The reality is more complicated, but only slightly. John had some ability, but he forfeited far too much trust, and undermined his own rule.

Born to Eleanor of Aquitaine when she was well into her forties, John was the youngest son of Henry II. Having been left little in the way of inheritance, he became known by the surname Lackland, but that did not keep him from nursing ambitions about the throne.

John led something of an itinerant childhood and youth. As the legitimate son of Henry least likely ever to assume the kingship, he was sent at a young age to Fontevrault Abbey in Anjou, where he received the sort of education that might befit a future bishop. Stories would later circulate of his being an arrogant, unruly child, even hitting another student over the head with a chessboard when about to lose a game. For a while John lived as part of the household of his older brother, Young Henry. In his teens, John lived with Ranulf de Glanville, his father's justiciar, and it was likely there that he developed a lasting interest in the machinery of governance. He was also fond of reading, and became a sharp, often cuttingly witty conversationalist.

John was only seven at the onset of the Great

Revolt, and likely had only a faint idea at best that his father's granting him castles in Young Henry's lands triggered the conflict. Henry kept John with him during the rebellion, and it was likely at this time that John became his favorite. The king was clearly concerned about how to shape the future of a son who stood to inherit little in the way of traditional princely assets. John's brothers, on the other hand, had little to do with him, and he gained a reputation for sharp mood swings and unpredictable behavior.

In 1185, Richard sent John to take possession of Ireland. Since he could not be called king there with the Irish kings still in place, he took the title Lord of Ireland. But John acquitted himself poorly there, insulting the Irish rulers and spending his time hunting while Norman gains were eroded. In a telling indication of his character, he refused to take any blame for the outcome.

But owing to the early deaths of Young Henry and Geoffrey, John found himself one step from the throne when his brother Richard was crowned in 1189. That same year, John married Isabel of Gloucester. But even though Richard was unmarried and had no children, he opted to name as heir to the English throne his young nephew, Arthur of Brittany, son of Geoffrey. It was a pointed rejection of John, whom Richard neither liked nor trusted. Before leaving on the Third Crusade, Richard placated John with lands and castles in England, but made him promise not to enter the country for three years.

King John meeting with Philip II of France. The two men had conspired together against Richard the Lionheart, but became enemies on John's accession to the English throne.

WHY, AMONG THESE UNJUST DEMANDS, DID THE BARONS NOT ASK FOR MY KINGDOM ALSO?"

KING JOHN

1199	1200	1204	1206	
John takes the throne of England.	The University of Paris is chartered, affirming Paris as a center of learning and culture, and an arena for theological disputes.	Normandy falls under French rule.	St. Francis of Assisi founds the Order of the Friars Minor.	**Opposite** King John, whose poor judgment led to conflict with his nobles and eventually to the Magna Carta.

It was the move of a king who knew all too well that his brother was capable of trying to usurp the throne.

AMBITIONS AND SCHEMES

Richard's misgivings about John were prescient. Within a year, John had managed to return to England, where he exploited the divisions created by justiciar William Longchamp's high-handed conduct. John began referring to himself as "Highest Governor of the Realm," and even assembled his own shadow court. In little time, he managed to take control of London and leverage Longchamp into announcing him as heir to Richard, but he lacked genuine support, and when Walter of Coutances, the popular Archbishop of Rouen, arrived in England to shore things up for Richard, John was obliged to withdraw.

In 1193, when Richard was being held hostage, John decided to angle for Richard's lands on the

continent, and to that end he pledged his loyalty to Philip II of France. It was an audacious and dishonorable move, and John earned lasting scorn for his attempt, with Philip, to pay Henry VI to keep Richard imprisoned. While he was not without allies, John did not have the charisma or the warlike credentials of his brother, and when Richard returned from captivity John was left at his mercy. Combining magnanimity and condescension, Richard forgave John, saying that he was, at the age of 27, merely a child who had been led astray by Philip, and stripped him of all his lands save Ireland, that nominal holding. For the rest of Richard's reign, John was tightly controlled, and served with apparent loyalty.

RESISTANCE IN FRANCE

Given John's reputation, when he finally did take the throne in 1199 he immediately confronted dissent among the nobles. John was in the difficult position of succeeding Richard, who was still revered as a fearless crusader king, when he himself had done little to earn any reputation as a soldier or leader of men. Richard may have cost the country dearly with his campaigns, but they were honorable, and he had won himself and England glory. Though John had gained credibility in the final years of his brother's reign, he still faced a rival for the throne: Arthur of Brittany. While the English nobles largely supported John, many on the continent flocked to Arthur, encouraged by the relentless Philip of France.

John had no alternative but to campaign to preserve his French lands. Assembling an army, he waded into Normandy; once he had arrived, allies in Flanders and elsewhere confirmed their support, and the movement in favor of Arthur unraveled without a battle. In the ensuing Treaty of Le Goulet (1200), John made a tentative peace with Philip, agreeing to accept the French king as his feudal lord in return for Philip's acknowledgement that John was the rightful heir to the Angevin lands. It was a satisfactory outcome—John was only affirming what had been in principle true for

KING JOHN AND ROBIN HOOD

John's reputation as an avaricious villain has been cemented by the legends of Robin Hood. However, though Robin Hood's name appears in official records as early as 1228, and ballads about his exploits were widely known by the 15th century, if the yeoman outlaw existed at all it was likely not during John's reign. Only in the 16th century did Robin Hood become positioned as a loyal subject of Richard the Lionheart, resisting the greedy usurper John and his tax hungry lieutenant, the Sheriff of Nottingham—a fact that reveals how vilified John remained, and remains, in common memory.

1206	1207	1209
The various Merkits, Naimans, Mongols, Keraits, Tatars and Uyghurs tribes of eastern Asia are united under the rule of Temujin, better known by his title of Genghis Khan.	Leeds and Liverpool are officially founded. John sold such charters as a way of generating revenue.	The Albigensian Crusade against the Cathars begins in the south of France. After a number of atrocities, the Cathars are effectively wiped out.

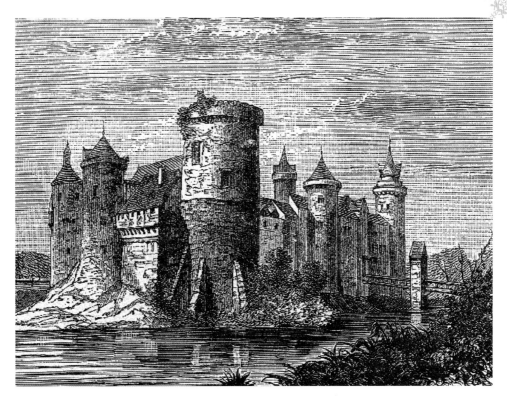

Rouen Castle, where John had his nephew and rival Arthur of Brittany imprisoned, and very probably killed. The incident permanently blackened John's reputation.

generations—but he looked weak in comparison to the warlike Richard, and began to be known as "John Softsword" as a result.

Two years later, John managed to undo that peace. For reasons that remain unclear, he abandoned his wife, Isabel, and married the young and beautiful Isabella of Angouleme. This would not have posed a serious problem had Isabella not already been betrothed to another French nobleman, who appealed to Philip for support. Philip, as John's feudal lord, summoned him to the French court in Paris. John refused—giving Philip a pretext to launch a punitive campaign and once more declare his support for Arthur.

Over the next two years, John would continue to snatch defeat from the jaws of victory. In a bold surprise attack at Mirebeau in 1202, John's forces won what might have been a decisive victory; in the battle, a number of French nobles, including Arthur himself, were captured. But rather than build on that success to enhance his reputation with the barons, John mistreated the prisoners. According to some accounts, a number were left to starve—an unforgivable offense in a dispute among nobles who were, in many cases, related to one another. Worse yet by far, the following year the teenaged Arthur, imprisoned in Rouen Castle, was dead. Rumors spread rapidly that John had killed his nephew in a fit of impious rage and thrown his body in the Seine. Whatever the truth, it is likely that John ordered the killing.

Already mistrusted, John was now a pariah. His allies fell away, and he proved unable to hold his ground in Normandy. In late 1203, he was forced to return to England. His mother Eleanor's death the following spring removed the last figurehead of the Angevin Empire, and by 1206 John had been forced to give up all his lands north of Aquitaine. He was now the King of England, and little more.

1209

Old London Bridge (actually probably the 6th bridge over the Thames on the site) is completed. It will stand until 1831.

1209

The Mongols under Genghis Khan conquer the Xia state of northern China.

Pope Innocent III clashed with John over the king's refusal to accept Stephen Langton as Archbishop of Canterbury.

TROUBLE AT HOME

Both John's prestige and his tax base were now sharply diminished. This led to his being much more personally involved in the governance of England. On the one hand, he engaged himself in professionalizing and enforcing the system of justice, such that freemen could expect their grievances—especially those against the barons—to be treated more credibly. On the other, even this was a means to generate revenue by levying steep financial penalties on those who had the means to pay them. John's attentive record-keeping appears to have served a similar purpose; he kept detailed accounts so as to know where revenue was owed or could be found.

In short order, the king developed a reputation as avaricious and grasping. Taxes soared, especially those of Jews, and John devised new forms of collection. In addition to regular revenue collection, barons found themselves subject to a "scutage" tax—one paid in lieu of active military service—when no military campaigns were underway. Further, John used taxation as a means of reward and punishment; lords whom he regarded as suspect found themselves taxed far more heavily than those of whom he approved. In all this, the king operated with an imperious scorn for the counsel of his retainers.

CONTINUED ESTRANGEMENT

As if alienating his barons were not enough, John also managed to incite the wrath of the Church. In 1205, the archbishopric of Canterbury came available, and a dispute erupted over who should take the position. The squabbling, much of which actually involved factions within the Church, eventually gained the personal attention of Pope Innocent III. The pope decided to dismiss all the candidates, including John's own, and appointed Stephen Langton. When John refused to comply, Innocent installed Langton anyway.

John reacted with characteristic extremity. He barred Langton from entering England and confiscated a number of Church assets. In this, as with Philip of France, John was overmatched; Innocent was a powerful, sagacious pontiff, who knew how to work the levers of power. When subsequent negotiations broke down, the pope placed England under interdict. John used the interdict as a pretext to annex more of the Church's wealth, and attempted to cajole and bully English clerics into taking his side. In 1209, the pope excommunicated John. Philip, now able to style himself the champion of the Church, was free to invade with impunity. Eventually, John agreed to Innocent's terms, even ceding England to the papacy and thereby making himself less a king than the feudal lord of someone else's lands.

John's ruthless pursuit of royal revenue ultimately involved the same inhuman measures that had cost him so much of his French territories. William de Braose was a favored lieutenant of John; he had been given charge of Arthur during his captivity and granted extensive lands. But anyone close to John was in a precarious position, and at one point the king turned on William, accusing him of owing an outrageous amount to the Crown. When William couldn't produce the sum, John confiscated his lands and exiled him. Worse yet, John pursued him, eventually capturing his wife and eldest son, who then died in prison, allegedly of starvation. The story emerged that John had been outraged when William's wife was heard to remark on the circumstances surrounding Arthur's death.

KING'S CLASH WITH POPE

King John's clash with Pope Innocent III was a classic example of the conflict between sacred and secular power that so often flared up through the Medieval and Renaissance periods. Such a brazen attempt on the part of a weak and unpopular king to defy papal authority was bound to fail against a pontiff as capable and confident as Innocent. Only later, when the threat of excommunication lost its edge, would kings be able to assert their authority against that of the Church with any consistency.

1209	1210	1210	1211
The Franciscan order of monks has its origin at Assisi, where Italian friar Giovanni Francesco Bernardone obtains approval from Pope Innocent III for rules he has drawn up to administer the new order.	The Holy Roman Emperor Otto IV is excommunicated by the pope but proceeds to complete his conquest of southern Italy.	*Tristan und Isolde* by German poet Gottfried von Strassburg, who will die with his epic incomplete.	Portugal's Sancho I dies, aged 57, and is succeeded by his son who will reign until 1223 as Afonso II.

The signing of the Magna Carta quickly became a touchstone of the relations between monarch and nobles.

A surviving copy of the Magna Carta. Though the document changed little in practical terms, it became a symbol of freedom from royal oppression.

Whatever the cause, it was a monstrous course of action by the king, and cost him what little of his credibility remained among the nobility.

That estrangement of the barons would return to haunt John after his failed attempt, in 1214, to recover his French lands. Thanks to his ruthless amassing of wealth, the king had adequate resources to hire plenty of mercenaries when many of the English barons refused to support the venture. Had John succeeded, he might have shored up his position, but his early victories in the campaign came to naught. At Bouvines in Flanders, Philip's army decisively defeated John's allies, and the king returned to England empty-handed.

THE MAGNA CARTA

Shortly after John's return to England, a large group of barons rebelled. In an impressive show of unity, they marched on London,

gathering support among wavering nobles as they advanced. John had little choice but to ask Stephen Langton, the archbishop he had resisted, to broker a deal.

Langton was hardly impartial, but his influence had little to do with the outcome. John was a weak and hated king, and he was facing barons who were not only certain of their cause but also accustomed, after the long absences of Richard, to handling the work of governance without undue influence from the Crown. At Runnymede near Windsor, on June 15, 1215, John signed what came to be known as the Magna Carta, the Great Charter.

The Magna Carta had more symbolic than practical significance. It affirmed baronial rights that had been eroded, but more importantly it was framed in the discourse of freedom: freedom from royal oppression, freedom from arbitrary justice, freedom of the Church, and so forth. John was able to get the agreement voided by the pope, however, which precipitated all-out war between him and the barons.

A KING WITHOUT A CAPITAL

John's evasion of the Magna Carta so enraged his nobles that they did the previously unthinkable and invited Louis, son of Philip of France, to take the English throne. John was forced from London, and began a brief sojourn as a wandering, fading, and reviled king. At one point, some of the Crown Jewels and other valuables were lost when baggage sank into fens during a weary leg of the campaign. In October 1216, exhausted and isolated, John died of dysentery in Nottinghamshire. It was a dismal end, but one he had carved out for himself.

John left England in shaky condition, its finances depleted and its people demoralized. In the event, Louis of France did not take the throne; instead, John's nine-year-old son Henry was hastily crowned in Gloucester, using a diadem belonging to his mother because the coronation regalia had been washed away.

1212	1214	1215	1216
The Children's Crusade, really a set of disorganized movements led by charismatic commoners, rises and then diminishes across Europe.	The Mongols under Genghis Khan conquer the Jin state of northern China, implementing a policy of massacre that sees tens of thousands killed.	John signs the Magna Carta at Runnymede.	John dies, and his nine-year-old son Henry III takes the throne.

HENRY III ✛ The King Who Never Grew Up

House Plantagenet

Born October 1, 1207

Died November 16, 1272

Reigned 1216–1272

Consort Eleanor of Provence

Children Nine, including Edward I and Edward Crouchback

Successor Edward I

Crowned at the age of nine, Henry III spent the first decade of his reign as a figurehead, while able advisors governed England. On coming of age, he continued to rely on the opinions and imperatives of others, allowing the kingdom to slide into disorder over the course of his long reign.

Young Henry III became king at a precarious juncture. His father, King John, had died in a kind of internal exile, and Louis, the French dauphin, was in possession of London. England was in danger of becoming an extension of the burgeoning realm of the Capetians of France. In addition, Henry's older cousin Eleanor, the sister of Arthur of Brittany, had a compelling claim to the throne, though she had been held gently captive for years in Dorset. Only the most politically astute maneuvering would assure a smooth succession for Henry. Fortunately, the young king was guided by men who understood this.

REGENCY AND RESTORATION

From Henry's accession until he declared himself of age in 1227, England was governed by two brilliant men: William Marshal as regent and Hubert de Burgh as justiciar. It was they who arranged for Henry's surprisingly smooth assumption of kingship. Soon after he was crowned, they issued an edict in his name that he would rule in accordance with the Magna Carta—minus the clauses allowing for the use of force against the king. They then turned their attention to Louis of France, who was reluctant to withdraw his claim to the throne and commanded the loyalty of a number of barons. Over the next year, Marshal and de Burgh blocked every attempt by Louis to gain a firmer foothold in England. The defeat of a larger French fleet by de Burgh proved the tipping point in Louis's fading ambitions for the throne of England. After a face-saving bribe, he withdrew his claim.

For the next few years, Henry did as he was told, allowing himself to be guided by his agents. Marshal, a widely respected knight, and de Burgh, a formidable administrator, kept the peace between king and barons, and ensured that while taxes were reduced money still flowed into the royal treasury. In 1219, Marshal died, and de Burgh became de facto regent as well as justiciar. But when Henry, itching to assert his authority, officially came of age, de Burgh was named justiciar for life, and remained the power behind the throne for another five years. It may be that de Burgh was unwilling to surrender power to a king in whom he had no confidence, but in the end he was to have no choice.

FOREIGN INFLUENCES

In 1232, Henry finally asserted himself, removing de Burgh as justiciar, stripping him of his titles and lands, and imprisoning him. It was an abrupt reversal, and Henry

> HE DID NOT KEEP HIS PROMISES,
> HAVING LITTLE REGARD FOR THE
> KEYS OF THE CHURCH AND FOR THE
> CONDITIONS OF THE GREAT CHARTER
> SO MANY TIMES PAID FOR
>
> *MATTHEW PARIS*

1216
Henry is crowned King of England at Gloucester aged nine.

1219
William Marshal, Henry's respected regent, dies.

1220
The building of Salisbury Cathedral begins in England.

1223
Pope Honorius III confirms the Order of Friars Minor, or the Franciscans, who go on to exert a profound influence on the religion of the high medieval period.

Opposite Henry III, whose ineffectual and self-indulgent leadership left the kingship significantly weakened.

was likely prompted by an advisor who had come to exercise a shadowy influence over the impressionable young king: Peter des Roches, Bishop of Winchester, who had once served as justiciar and had designs on power himself.

In this, as in so many cases in his long reign, Henry revealed himself to be weak-willed and easily swayed. It seemed that the young king could not or would not grow up, and let his favored advisors make up his mind. In most cases the decisive voice was that of des Roches. Des Roches was from Poitou in Touraine, which had ceased to be Angevin territory, and when, under his influence, Henry began to fill his administration with Poitevins, the barons took notice. They also recalled that des Roches had been a right-hand man of the hated King John. In 1234, under the leadership of Edmund Rich, Archbishop of Canterbury, and William Marshal's son Richard, they rose in resistance. After a series of tense confrontations, Rich threatened Henry with excommunication if he did not expel des Roches. Henry relented. For the next decade, relative tranquility prevailed.

In 1236, Henry married Eleanor, daughter of Raymond Berenguer of Provence. Theirs apparently proved a happy marriage—there is no record of Henry keeping mistresses, and he apparently valued Eleanor's counsel—but more importantly it led to more foreign influence in

Westminster Abbey, Henry's labor of love and greatest accomplishment.

the English court. Henry again started appointing French relations to important posts, passing much of the wealth of the Crown to favored foreigners. This infusion of French culture also meant that Henry's was a sophisticated, aesthetically minded court, and English arts and literature began to absorb increasingly French notions of literary romance and architectural design. But it also raised tensions with the barons, who once again chafed at the exploitation of England by foreign opportunists.

HENRY AND WESTMINSTER ABBEY

Henry III could lay claim to few real accomplishments, but one was the expansion and renovation of Westminster Abbey. The abbey had been the coronation church since the accession of William the Conqueror, but it was Henry who gave it the magnificent scale and design it now enjoys, largely out of his devotion to Edward the Confessor. After laying the foundation stone for the Lady Chapel in 1220, Henry began construction in earnest in 1245, razing Edward the Confessor's church to make way for the massive Gothic cathedral we now know, on which Henry lavished attention and wealth. The cathedral, though still unfinished, was consecrated in 1269.

THE SECOND BARONS' WAR

As Henry reached his thirties, he increasingly sought to display his authority and ambition. He forged treaties with the Scottish and the Welsh, though neither pact offered any real advantage to England other than a lull in border incursions. In 1250, Henry pledged to go on crusade. The nobles would likely have been glad to see him go, but when he amassed the funds to do so, he misdirected them in a breathtakingly foolish way, using them instead to fund the pope's ongoing campaign against the Hohenstaufen rulers of Sicily. Henry had apparently agreed also to pay the pope's outstanding debts. All this was in return for

1226	1227	1231	1236	1241
Francis of Assisi dies, aged 44.	Henry comes of age and begins his personal rule.	Pope Gregory IX officially establishes the Inquisition, placing it under the management of the Dominican Order. It will come to be one of the most feared institutions in Europe.	Henry marries Eleanor of Provence.	The Mongols invade Hungary, which will mark their farthest advance into Europe. Some historians credit the Mongols with having introduced gunpowder to European warfare.

the empty promise that Henry's second son Edmund would be given the kingdom of Sicily.

Such inexplicable decisions, together with the mounting sense that Henry was allowing the kingdom to be infiltrated and looted by his foreign relatives, turned more and more barons against him. In 1258, matters came to a head.

Simon de Montfort, Henry's brother-in-law, was a former crusader and onetime advisor to the king. Though they had once fallen out, Henry had later relied on de Montfort's military prowess in controlling Gascony, the last portion of France over which the English still had control. In time, however, even de Montfort lost patience with Henry and, along with other powerful barons, presented the king with a catalog of grievances. In what came to be known as the Mad Parliament, the barons met with the king in Oxford and pressured him into signing the Provisions of Oxford, which effectively left him a figurehead once more while a council of barons ran the country.

By 1261, Henry had reneged. De Montfort at first left England, but in 1263 the barons begged him to return, and with his arrival came the Second Barons' War. A year later, at Lewes, de Montfort's forces defeated the royalist army, taking Henry's ambitious son Edward, who had acquitted himself well in the battle, as a hostage.

What de Montfort did with his newfound power was as visionary as it was surprising. Instead of merely setting up his council as rulers of England, he also instituted a much broader idea of Parliament—one that included elected

A medieval depiction of the Battle of Evesham, where the would-be reformer Simon de Montfort's army was ambushed, and its leader's body dismembered. Had Montfort won the day, English history might have unfolded very differently.

representatives from all over the kingdom, and freemen as well as noblemen. Had his fellow barons been as open to such a radical notion, English history might have taken a momentous turn. But they were not. Edward escaped from captivity—probably with baronial help—and raised an army. In August 1265, Edward's forces ambushed an army led by de Montfort's son, and de Montfort and his followers found themselves isolated and outnumbered near Evesham Abbey. De Montfort and his dream of reform died on the field.

A QUIET END

After the victory at Evesham, the rebellion wound down as the ever more impressive Edward reasserted royal authority. From 1267 onward, Edward would in fact rule the kingdom, serving as one last, unacknowledged regent for his ineffectual and rapidly declining father.

In 1269, Westminster Abbey was reconsecrated, and the relics of Edward the Confessor re-interred. Henry had invested years and untold wealth in expanding the cathedral, which now stands as a monument to the cultural flowering that took place under his long if otherwise undistinguished reign.

With his death three years later, Henry left behind largely empty royal coffers and a baronial class far more empowered and largely disenchanted with the kingship. It would be the task of his remarkably capable son, Edward Longshanks, to repair the damage.

1264	1265	1265	1269	1272
At the Battle of Lewes, Simon de Montfort's forces defeat those of Henry, making de Montfort supreme in England.	Thomas Aquinas begins his Summa Theologica, the most influential work of Christian theology in the medieval era.	Simon de Montfort is defeated and dies at the Battle of Evesham.	Westminster Abbey, greatly expanded in Gothic style, is reconsecrated.	Henry III dies, and Edward I takes the throne.

EDWARD I ✦ Lawgiver and Empire-builder

House Plantagenet

Born June 17, 1239

Died July 7, 1307

Reigned 1272–1307

Consort Eleanor of Castile (died 1290), Margaret of France

Children 19 in all, including Edward II

Successor Edward II

dward I is a colossal figure in English history. Called Longshanks, he was indeed tall at over six feet, and every inch a king. He brought to the throne both a warlike spirit and a born administrator's attention to efficiency and fairness. Though flawed, he was undeniably one of the great English kings, and his legacy remains both in England's landscape and its laws.

Edward learned early about the privileges and responsibilities of kingship. He came of age during his father's struggles with the nobles, and clearly thought hard about the positions of both sides, actually siding with de Montfort's initial protests before becoming the royalist champion who finally vanquished the rebels. His support of the Provisions of Oxford indicates that he both recognized his father's failures as a king and believed from a young age in a more consultative style of leadership. In 1254, at the age of 15, he was married to Eleanor, daughter of Alfonso of Castile, two years younger than he. The marriage was dynastic, but it proved to be a love match; Edward and his queen would remain devoted to one another until her death in 1290.

The burial effigy of Eleanor of Castile, first wife of Edward I. Though theirs was a dynastic marriage, by all accounts the king and queen genuinely loved each other. After Eleanor died in 1290, Edward remarried happily, but he spent most of his reign alongside Eleanor.

> WHAT TOUCHES ALL, SHOULD BE APPROVED OF ALL, AND IT IS CLEAR THAT COMMON DANGERS SHOULD BE MET BY MEASURES AGREED UPON IN COMMON."
>
> *EDWARD I*

THE YOUNG LION

When Henry III died, Edward was not at his bedside; he was not even in England, having departed on a crusade in 1270, shortly after securing his father's position in the wake of the baronial rebellion led by Simon de Montfort. Edward had gained something of a reputation in the Second Barons' War for achieving victory through trickery rather than forthright force of arms, and a crusade was an ideal vehicle for burnishing his slightly tarnished image. At this point the crusades were hollow, often cynical imitations of the great expeditions of the past, but Edward earned a reputation there as one of the most brave and skilled warriors in Europe, and even survived an attempted assassination by poisoned blade. He brought home with him the lessons he had learned in tactics and siegecraft.

It speaks to the relative stability of the throne in 1272 that Edward did not, as Richard had before him, need to rush home and secure his inheritance. He had no fraternal rivals, and in his absence the gears of government ran smoothly in the hands of the chancellor, Robert Burnell. Along the way, he stopped to visit the pope and to assert control over his hereditary holding of Gascony. Though he had already been named king, his coronation took place on his return in August 1274. It was a magnificent ceremony, with a sense of political spectacle that had been largely absent from England since the glory days of Henry II.

1274

Edward returns to England and claims the throne.

1275

Marco Polo begins to serve under Kublai Khan. Polo's account of his journey to the East will go on to inspire future explorers, and stimulate interest in trade.

Opposite Edward I Longshanks, certainly one of the greatest administrators and soldiers to occupy the English throne.

Caernarfon Castle, one of the intimidating fortresses Edward ordered built to secure his conquest of Wales.

KING AND LAWGIVER

Though Edward asserted himself early as a military campaigner, his main priority as king was to set in order the administration of the realm. In this, he was ably assisted by Robert Burnell, who as chancellor became Edward's most trusted advisor. Not since the early years of Henry II and Thomas Becket had an English king and his chancellor formed such an effective partnership, and in this case it would only be sundered by Burnell's death in 1292. To begin with, Edward issued a blanket amnesty to all the remaining opponents of his father, allowing them to buy back the lands they had lost.

THE HUNDRED ROLLS

Then Edward embarked on the most ambitious administrative undertaking since the Domesday Book: a vast, nationwide investigation into official corruption. For the king, it served a dual purpose, both establishing himself among the common people as a just ruler and building a basis for the reassertion of royal prerogatives against the relative autonomy of the barons. The resulting documentation, known as the Hundred Rolls, was an exhaustive account of misconduct, grand and petty, throughout England. Edward had managed a brilliant triangulation, simultaneously positioning himself as the champion of the common people against official corruption and taking the high ground of justice and reform from the barons.

Edward's first test as king came in the form of disrespect from Llewelyn ap Gruffydd, the Prince of Wales. Llewelyn failed to appear at the coronation and offer his fealty; when two more commands from Edward were met with indifference, he decided to make an example of the defiant prince. Declaring Llewelyn a traitor to the Crown, in 1277 he stormed into Wales with an army of 15,000 and in short order brought Llewelyn to heel without even having to fight.

In 1282, a more organized rebellion took root in Wales, sparked by Llewelyn's brother Daffydd. This time, Edward responded ruthlessly. Over six years, he aimed for complete dominance, not only defeating the rebels in battle but also establishing a military occupation, constructing a chain of castles from which to enforce his authority and settling English barons in Wales. In a shocking turn, he dispensed with the relatively genteel punitive measures of the Angevin tradition and had Daffydd hanged, drawn, and quartered as a traitor. In 1284, the Statutes of Wales established that country as a Crown colony, effectively part of the realm. It was an imperious display of martial and administrative prowess. The Welsh would bridle often under English rule, but they would never throw it off.

THE MODEL PARLIAMENT

But Edward did not stop with the Hundred Rolls. He was determined to secure both royal authority and a clearly documented sense of precedent and procedure, mainly for the purposes of taxation. Accordingly, the information collected in the Hundred Rolls was used to initiate a steady stream of legal moves called Quo warranto ("by what warrant?") proceedings, in which noblemen and local officials were required to show proof in writing that they actually held viable appointments to their posts or title to their properties. It

1284

The Statutes of Wales subject Wales wholly to English rule. The two countries will henceforth share a common government.

1276

Death of King James the Conqueror of Aragon marks a temporary end to the Christian wars against the Moslems in Spain.

1282

Mongol Invasion of Syria is halted at the Battle of Homs by Sultan Qalawun.

was good law, but in practice it was manifestly unfair, in that many lands and positions had been granted long before documentation of royal rulings had become customary. In the end, Edward and the nobles reached a compromise. In concert with the indefatigable Burnell, Edward continued to issue statutes codifying various aspects of the law, such as maintaining the peace, recovering debts, settling land disputes, and handling church grants. It was not glamorous work, but responsible governance seldom is. Edward's motivations were not entirely unselfish; after all, such systematization provided more consistent revenue, which the Crown sorely needed, and created numerous new mechanisms for the exercise of kingly authority. The lasting legacy of Edward's project, however, was the common law that would henceforth provide the scaffolding for much of English society.

One of the new, far more finely minted English pennies from Edward's reign.

Over the years, especially after Burnell's death in 1292, Edward turned his attention to military campaigns, which required extensive funding. Funding meant taxation, and the imposition of taxes remained a sore point, especially for the middle tier of small landowners and prominent townspeople

for whom taxes were most burdensome. The Magna Carta, which Edward had reissued in 1270, during a spell of protest among the nobles, stipulated that no one could be taxed without their consent. The king's response was to convene Parliament. And it was not just an ordinary Parliament. In a decision that only a king as strong as Edward could have managed, he adopted the ideals of the man he had once vanquished, Simon de Montfort.

In 1295, 49 noblemen and 292 commoners, representing the Church as well as counties and boroughs all over England, gathered for what would later be called the Model Parliament, because it served as the basic template for all future Parliaments. Though its main purpose was to arrive at an agreement on taxation, it quickly developed into a forum for debating other issues, especially grievances against the Crown. Edward, in need of revenue, had little choice but to allow this development, even though it eroded some of the royal authority he had so painstakingly accumulated. A less patient and sagacious king might have attempted to bully his way out of the arrangement, but Edward did not. Yet again, he demonstrated a genius not only for command but also for compromise.

Edward would have need of those skills soon after the Model Parliament. In 1297, while engaged in both suppressing yet another, if minor, Welsh revolt and an ongoing conflict with Scotland, Edward organized a campaign in Flanders. Once more, he sought to levy taxes. Two powerful barons, Roger Bigod and Humphrey de Bohun, raised the legitimate objection that it might not be wise to open a third overseas front, and they protested a tax Edward invoked without due process to finance the expedition. Just as Edward was preparing to depart, the two barons arrived at the Exchequer with what came to be called the Remonstrances, a series of documented objections to Edward's conduct, and to his excessive taxation. It was a case of Edward's own legalistic approach being used against him, and things grew

SUPERB FORTIFICATIONS

Edward was a gifted soldier and commander, and very knowledgeable about castles. When he ordered a series of castles built in Wales, the king had them designed according to principles he had absorbed during his brief crusade. He spared no expense, building concentric castles, with both inner and outer walls, and incorporating crenelations and arrow slits to make possible an active defense. Edward was one of very few monarchs in his day wealthy enough to build such advanced and extensive fortifications. Caernarfon Castle, for instance, begun in 1283, took more than 45 years to build, at the staggering cost of £25,000. It housed a garrison of some 40 soldiers.

1285

Sultan Qalawan captures the supposedly impregnable crusader fortress of Margat – a major blow to the Knights Hospitaller.

1290

The Ottoman Empire that will rule much of the Mediterranean for the next six centuries is founded by the Byitynian king Osman al-Ghazi, aged 31, leader of the Seljuk Turks.

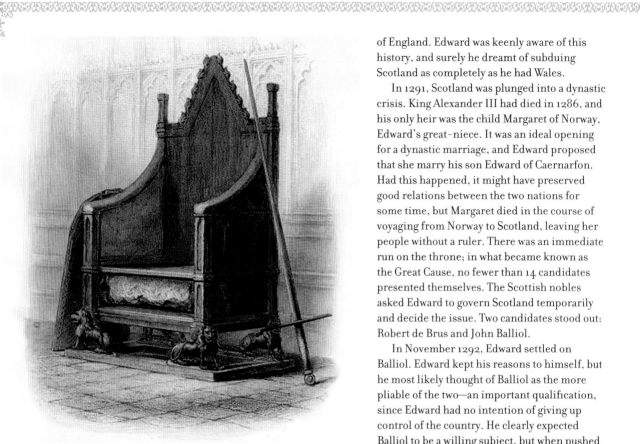

Edward's coronation throne, with the Stone of Destiny, symbol of Scottish kings, set beneath the seat. In 1996, seven centuries after Edward brought it back with him to London, it was returned to Scotland.

tense in a way disquietingly reminiscent of the baronial rebellions under Edward's father. Once more, however, a compromise was reached, this time because a defeat by the Scots at Stirling encouraged the two sides to bury their differences. Still, the entire affair showed a degree of restraint, a sense of process, that had its roots in the Magna Carta and in the willingness of the men involved to seek common cause.

CAMPAIGNS AGAINST SCOTLAND

Early in his reign, Edward had undertaken a decisive conquest of Wales. Though it remained restive, it was now irrevocably joined with England. The situation of Scotland was different. The border with England's northern neighbor had been a perpetual source of strife, even when Scottish kings swore fealty to those

of England. Edward was keenly aware of this history, and surely he dreamt of subduing Scotland as completely as he had Wales.

In 1291, Scotland was plunged into a dynastic crisis. King Alexander III had died in 1286, and his only heir was the child Margaret of Norway, Edward's great-niece. It was an ideal opening for a dynastic marriage, and Edward proposed that she marry his son Edward of Caernarfon. Had this happened, it might have preserved good relations between the two nations for some time, but Margaret died in the course of voyaging from Norway to Scotland, leaving her people without a ruler. There was an immediate run on the throne; in what became known as the Great Cause, no fewer than 14 candidates presented themselves. The Scottish nobles asked Edward to govern Scotland temporarily and decide the issue. Two candidates stood out: Robert de Brus and John Balliol.

In November 1292, Edward settled on Balliol. Edward kept his reasons to himself, but he most likely thought of Balliol as the more pliable of the two—an important qualification, since Edward had no intention of giving up control of the country. He clearly expected Balliol to be a willing subject, but when pushed far enough—Edward ordered Balliol to appear before him at Westminster—the Scottish ruler dug in his heels. Soon, the Scots were in open arms. They saw themselves as fighting in defense of their sovereignty; Edward seemingly regarded them as having already forfeited any sovereignty to defend.

In 1296 he invaded, laying siege to Berwick, which resisted. Incensed, Edward took the city in pitiless assault. Then he took Dunbar. Word of his wrath traveled ahead of his army, and both Edinburgh and Stirling, the two most formidable Scottish castles, fell with little resistance. Balliol was stripped of his title and thrown in the Tower. Edward, like his ancestor Henry II highly sensitive to political symbolism, took back to London the Stone of Destiny, upon which centuries of Scottish kings had stood to be crowned, and had it fitted beneath his coronation

1290	1291	1295	1299	1301
Expulsion of the Jews from England, a dark chapter in the reign of Edward I, and of English history as a whole.	With the Muslim capture of Acre, the last holdout of the Crusaders in the Holy Land, two centuries of Crusader rule in parts of the region, often peaceful, come to an end.	The Model Parliament convenes.	The crusader kingdom of Jerusalem ends with the fall of Acre to the Mamluks.	Dante Alighieri is exiled from Florence. While traveling from court to court in Italy for the next two decades, he will write his great Commedia.

throne. The message was clear: Scotland, like Wales, was now a province of England.

The Scots, however, did not respond to this statement as meekly as Edward might have hoped. More than once, Scotland proved the one arena in which Edward's instincts consistently let him down. In attempting to crush their spirit, he only stoked it. In the first incarnation of what came to be called the Auld Alliance, the Scots made common cause with the French, whose new king, Philip IV, had annexed Gascony. It was at this time that Edward, having heavily taxed his subjects to fund his campaigns, faced the Remonstrances of Roger Bigod and Humphrey de Bohun.

When the Scots, under the charismatic and crafty William Wallace, defeated Edward's forces at Stirling Bridge, the English closed ranks behind their king. Edward charged north with an intimidating force of some 2,000 armored cavalry and 12,000 footsoldiers, including longbowmen. Wallace

William Wallace, in stained glass, at the Wallace Monument near Stirling. Wallace was a formidable guerrilla leader, and Edward only defeated him by tracking down his army near Falkirk. He was betrayed, captured, and executed in 1305.

avoided direct contact with the overwhelming English force but in July 1298, at Falkirk, Edward hunted down the Scottish army and, using the deadly accuracy and penetrating power of his longbows, broke up the Scottish formations and decimated them. It was a crushing victory, but Wallace escaped, and

Scottish guerrilla resistance continued. Even when Wallace was finally captured and executed in 1305, the Scots refused to submit.

DEATH AND LEGACY

In 1307, Scotland boiled over with rebellion yet again, now under the leadership of Robert the Bruce, grandson of the Robert de Brus whom Edward had passed over for the Scottish kingship in 1292. Once more, Edward, now aging and in ill health, headed north with his army. But near Carlisle he fell victim to dysentery, and died in his servants' arms on July 7.

Legends quickly arose about his final wishes: that he wanted his bones carried with his army into Scotland, that he wanted his heart sent to the Holy Land. We cannot be sure what his final utterance was, but when he died England lost one of its greatest kings.

The legacy of Edward I is not unspotted. He was capable of great cruelty, and his persecution and expulsion of the Jews from England in 1290—a course of action no less reprehensible for being typical of his time— must not be overlooked. Yet, judged by the standards of his era and the legacy of law and Parliamentary rule he left behind, he was an enormously successful king. His heir would prove far less than an equal.

THE ENGLISH COINAGE

One of Edward's most far-reaching if less obviously important reforms was an overhaul of English coinage, which had degraded in quality during Henry III's reign. Not only did Edward introduce new coins, including the groat, the halfpenny, and the farthing; he also vastly improved the minting process, so that English coins became the envy of Europe. English subjects were allowed, for a fee, to exchange their old, inferior coins for the new, more valuable ones.

1301

Edward of Caernarfon, son of King Edward I of England, is proclaimed Prince of Wales replacing the native Welsh dynasty. It becomes customary for the eldest son of the English monarch to become Prince of Wales.

1304

Sultan Ala-ud-din Khilji of Delhi conquers Gujarat. His subsequent love affair with Rani Padmini, queen of Chittor, would become legendary and form the basis of the epic poem *Padmavat*.

1307

Edward I dies on campaign against Scotland.

EDWARD II ✢ A Valley Between Two Peaks

House Plantagenet

Born April 25, 1284

Died September 21, 1327

Reigned 1307–1327

Consort Isabella of France

Children Four, including Edward III and Joan, Queen of Scots

Successor Edward III

> HE WAS PASSIONATELY ATTACHED TO ONE PERSON, WHOM HE CHERISHED ABOVE ALL
>
> *RANULF HIGDEN*

Like his grandfather Henry III, Edward II inherited exceptionally large shoes to fill. His father, Edward I, had by nearly unanimous acclaim been a remarkably successful king. But Edward II allowed his affection for two favorites—first Piers Gaveston, and later Hugh Despenser—to override all consideration of responsible kingship.

Edward II was the sole surviving son of Edward I, but by the latter's death in 1307 father and son despised each other. The young Prince of Wales had no interest in the traditional activities of princes, such as jousting and hunting, preferring boating, swimming, and learning trade skills and crafts. Had he become a responsible and responsive monarch, these interests might even have been virtues, linking his life with those of commoners, but that was not to be.

THE KING'S DARLING

The consuming object of Edward's interest was neither his kingdom nor his hobbies, but one

The charter with which Edward II granted his favorite, Piers Gaveston, the title Earl of Cornwall. Such gifts, which flouted rank and decorum, earned Gaveston the enmity of other nobles.

man: Piers Gaveston, a knight of Gascony whom Edward I had appointed to his son's retinue years before. Though speculation swirled, and still does, that they were lovers, we cannot be absolutely certain. Edward was married to Isabella, daughter of Philip IV of France, and their marriage proved stable enough, at least for a while, to produce four children.

What had incensed Edward's father, and then alienated the nobles, was the utterly unseemly favoritism the prince showed Gaveston, and the cavalier disrespect with which both of them, but especially Gaveston, treated the barons. Edward I, wary of the influence the knight had over the his son, exiled Gaveston in 1307, and it was claimed that on his deathbed he insisted that Gaveston be perpetually barred from England.

Soon after his father's death, however, Edward summoned Gaveston back to his side. Trouble began even before the coronation; while Edward traveled to France to retrieve his bride, he had Gaveston serve as regent. At the coronation itself, Edward and his favorite showed a scandalous disregard for protocol. In a shocking breach of decorum, Gaveston was allowed to wear purple robes and pearls, as if he were royalty, and he was given charge of the festivities. Edward ignored his new wife—a princess of France, no less—to dote on Gaveston. He had even passed on to Gaveston a number of wedding presents, including some of his wife's jewels.

1308	1308	1309	1310	
Edward II marries Isabella of France and is officially crowned King of England.	The Muslim Sultanate of Rum breaks up into a number of small Turkish states.	Clement V, in a momentous change, relocates the papacy to Avignon in what becomes known as the Babylonian Captivity. Predominantly French popes will rule from Avignon for nearly 70 years.	Edward II is forced to accept the rule of the Lords Ordainer.	**Opposite** Though just as physically imposing as his father, Edward II was self-indulgent rather than ambitious, willful rather than strong, and capricious rather than disciplined.

EDVARDVS

All this might have been tolerated had Edward proved a responsible king, but he was far more interested in amusing himself and conspiring against the nobles than in managing the realm. Worse still, he and Gaveston ridiculed the barons, assigning them insulting nicknames and dismissing their requests. Perhaps most maddeningly, Gaveston was an accomplished knight who routinely won tournaments and whose manliness was therefore above question. Within months, the nobles had united in contempt and dismay, and in May of 1308 Edward was forced to exile Gaveston. He did so by making him Lord of Ireland. Within a year, after spending far more energy conniving to recover Gaveston than fulfilling the duties of kingship, Edward used promises of reform and a series of bribes to secure his friend's return.

But when Gaveston arrived back at court, Edward simply resumed his former hedonism and disrespect. Thomas of Lancaster, Edward's cousin and the powerful Earl of Lancaster, organized a plot to get rid of Gaveston for good. In 1310, he and a number of other nobles pressured Edward not only into permanently exiling his favorite as an enemy but also into conceding the real governance of England to a committee of noblemen called the Lords Ordainer.

When Gaveston soon returned to court yet again, the nobles faced a dilemma: they could either endure his presence, thereby losing both face and power; or they could administer rough justice, and likely initiate a long and potentially bloody conflict with the king. They chose the latter. Edward and Gaveston fled London, but Gaveston was eventually caught and delivered into the hands of the Earl of Warwick. After a hasty trial in June 1312, Gaveston was taken to a hilltop, run through with a sword, and beheaded.

Edward was grief-stricken and vengeful. For the time being he could do little, but Gaveston's execution cleared a path for another influential favorite to take his place—Hugh Despenser the younger, son of the Earl of Winchester. In the coming years, he and his father would exert increasing influence on Edward, earning the same baronial enmity that had undone Gaveston.

FIASCO IN SCOTLAND

With the death of Gaveston, Edward found himself not only bereft but also weakened; the nobles, led by the self-serving Thomas of Lancaster, had taken control, and he had no response. He would have to campaign for the esteem of his kingdom. Perhaps for this reason, he decided to march on Scotland, where Robert the Bruce's insurgency had gained momentum. Stirling Castle, the last major English stronghold in Scotland, was under siege from Robert's brother, and the English commander Philip de Mowbray had negotiated with the Scots that, if not relieved by June 24, 1314, he would surrender the castle and withdraw to England.

Edward hastily assembled an army but, even though he had campaigned with his father and had some military expertise, he was no strategist. Several of his ablest commanders and most powerful barons, including Thomas of Lancaster, chose not to join the expedition, but Edward would not be deterred. On June 17, joined by Scottish enemies of Robert the Bruce, Edward's army of some 20,000 footsoldiers and 2,000 armored cavalry marched from Berwick toward Stirling. Robert awaited him with an army of well under 10,000 men.

Ignoring the advice of Mowbray and unable to assert control over his unruly army, Edward allowed himself to be lured into fighting on marshy ground near Bannockburn, terrain that gave Robert's more lightly armored troops the advantage. Before the battle properly started, one of Edward's nobles spotted Robert the Bruce, unarmored, riding in front of the woods

EDWARD THE SECOND

The reign of Edward II would eventually inspire a drama of the same name by the Elizabethan playwright Christopher Marlowe. Marlowe was openly homosexual, and clearly fascinated by Edward's relationship with Piers Gaveston. Telescoping years of history, Marlowe's play extends beyond Edward's death, to the execution of Mortimer by Edward III. Marlowe himself met a violent death, and his play was first performed posthumously. It has since been performed countless times. In 1923, the German playwright Bertolt Brecht adapted Marlowe's play to his own revolutionary theatrical style.

1311	1311	1312	1312
The completion of the spire of Lincoln Cathedral, in England. At a height of 525 feet, it is the tallest building in the world, surpassing the Great Pyramid of Giza. The spire collapses in a storm in 1549 and is never rebuilt.	Notre Dame Cathedral at Reims, a masterpiece of Gothic architecture, is completed after 99 years of construction.	Piers Gaveston is executed. In France, the king abolishes the Order of Knights Templar, accusing them of heinous practices.	The Canary Islands are discovered by Genoese mariner Lancelotto Malocello. The islands had been known to the Romans, but knowledge of them was forgotten after the fall of Rome.

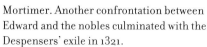

A statue of Robert the Bruce at Bannockburn in 1314, holding the axe he famously wielded in the battle. Edward's disgraceful conduct at that historic defeat left his already stained reputation in tatters.

Isabella, Edward's queen, who proved his most deadly enemy.

where his troops were gathered, and charged the Scottish king with his lance. Robert neatly avoided the lance and split the Englishman's head open with an axe. It was a sign of things to come. Edward and his commanders had blundered into a trap, and Robert's disciplined troops routed the English. Edward disgraced himself further by fleeing the battlefield with his bodyguards. About a third of his army made it back to England alive.

THE DOWNWARD SPIRAL

After the disaster at Bannockburn, Edward had so completely lost credibility as king that he was once more forced to accept rule by the Lords Ordainer. Yet he still schemed to recover his authority and found willing helpers in his new favorite, Hugh Despenser, and his father. Soon enough, even as a severe famine ravaged England, Edward was showering the Despensers with the same attention and favors that he had once given Gaveston. When the Despensers sought to expand their control from lands Edward had granted them in Wales, they ran afoul of powerful barons there, especially Roger

Mortimer. Another confrontation between Edward and the nobles culminated with the Despensers' exile in 1321.

For the next two years, Edward took the offensive, leading armies to defeat first Mortimer and then Thomas of Lancaster. Mortimer was thrown in the Tower and Lancaster beheaded. Edward even managed to invade Scotland and gain some measure of revenge for Bannockburn. In a brutal purge, Edward ordered hundreds of executions and exiled a number of nobles. The Despensers were summoned back to England and resumed lining their pockets.

It was Edward's queen who finally proved his most capable enemy. Isabella, who had endured years of humiliation, returned to the continent after her English lands went to the Despensers. In a colossal error, Edward allowed the young prince, Edward, to join her there. Roger Mortimer escaped from the Tower, and he and Isabella, now lovers, raised a mercenary army. In September 1326, they landed in Essex and within weeks Edward's erstwhile followers had either deserted him or been imprisoned. The Despensers were executed, along with others.

Edward, however, could hardly be executed. In a momentous maneuver, it was determined that Parliament should decide his fate. In January 1327, after hearing the charges against him, Edward agreed to abdicate in favor of his son. He was imprisoned in Berkeley Castle. Later that year, he was apparently murdered. Varying accounts of his killing, some lurid, have circulated since, though some historians have argued that he may actually have escaped to live out his days in Italy. The details of his fate will likely always remain unclear. At the time, a public funeral in 1327 settled the issue.

Edward II had been an indisputably bad king. It may be that, having spent his childhood in the orbit of his powerful and exacting father, he never developed a strong core of his own and remained subject to the stronger personalities around him. Regardless, it was left to his son, Edward III, to restore the power and prestige of a weakened England.

1314	1315	1321	1326	1327
The Scots, under Robert the Bruce, defeat the English at the Battle of Bannockburn. Edward disgraces himself by fleeing the field.	Famine, precipitated by a climatic shift, hits England and parts of the continent, causing widespread hardship and unrest.	The Despensers are exiled, but soon return to England.	Isabella and Roger Mortimer invade England.	Edward II abdicates and is likely murdered while in captivity.

EDWARD III ✠ Conqueror of France

House Plantagenet
Born November 13, 1312
Died June 21, 1377
Reigned 1327–1377
Consort Philippa of Hainault
Children 13, including Edward the Black Prince and John of Gaunt
Successor Richard II

After the disastrous reign of his father, Edward III restored national unity and pride and made England a feared military power. But he also had to rule England in the midst of fiscal crisis and the Black Death. Though ably assisted, he did not always manage as well with the details of domestic governance. Still, much of his long reign was seen as a kind of golden age.

Edward III ascended to the throne in 1327, after the forced abdication of his feckless father, Edward II. He was only 14 at the time, and affairs of state remained in the hands of his mother, Isabella of France, and her lover, Roger Mortimer, the Earl of March. It would take time for Edward to assert himself as king.

HIS LIKE HAD NOT BEEN SEEN SINCE THE DAYS OF KING ARTHUR

FROISSART

A YOUNG KING SEIZES THE REINS
For the first three years of Edward's nominal reign, Mortimer functioned as a de facto dictator and took full advantage of his position, belittling other nobles and according himself lands and titles with seeming impunity. He also regarded Edward as both a valuable asset and a potent threat, and kept him under close control.

Shortly after his coronation, Edward joined Mortimer in an offensive against the Scots, tracking a raiding army to Stanhope, near Durham. After a standoff in which neither side was willing to advance from its chosen ground, Scottish commander James Douglas launched a surprise night raid on the English camp. In the confusion, Edward's tent collapsed on him, and he was nearly captured. The Scots withdrew after killing hundreds of English soldiers. It was a humiliating first campaign for the young prince, and he did not forget it.

The defeat at Stanhope might have been insignificant militarily, but it had huge political consequences. The offensive, which involved large numbers of expensive mercenaries, was money squandered from a straitened treasury. The emboldened Scots negotiated for their independence and won it, the Treaty of Edinburgh-Northampton in 1328 recognizing Scotland as a sovereign state no longer subservient to England. The setback damaged Mortimer's standing and the young king began quietly and patiently laying the groundwork to overthrow him, forging alliances with other nobles. He also married Philippa of Hainault, a match that would prove happy and long-lived.

In 1330, Mortimer became aware of Edward's scheming, and summoned him to Nottingham Castle to face questioning. It was some measure of Mortimer's power and arrogance that he could do so. Edward and a handpicked band

A later manuscript illustration of Roger Mortimer and Isabella of France. After forcing Edward II's abdication and securing control of the throne, Mortimer ruled England as a tyrant until his arrest and execution by Edward III in 1330.

1327	1330	1333	1335	**Opposite** Edward
Edward III is crowned King of England.	Roger Mortimer is arrested by Edward and a band of nobles, and executed shortly after.	At the Battle of Halidon Hill, Edward defeats the Scots, and refines his tactics to include deadlier use of the English longbow.	The Mongol state of Ilkhan, based around Persia, fragments after the death of ruler Abu Said without an heir.	III, who returned England to stability and, in the first half of the Hundred Years' War, secured dazzling victories in France.

EDWARDVS   III·

of allies managed to sneak into the castle by night, surprising and arresting Mortimer, reportedly in the presence of Isabella. In short order, Mortimer was condemned as a traitor and executed at Tyburn. Edward tempered his ruthlessness and spared Mortimer the agony of being drawn and quartered. Isabella would be given an allowance and kept under close watch for the rest of her life.

Edward quickly established himself as a seemingly ideal king. He was charismatic, vigorous, and skilled at arms, combining the regal air of his grandfather with the common touch of Henry II. And he explicitly set out to create the ideal court, one modeled on that of the legendary King Arthur. Edward hosted fabulous tournaments in which he participated with a good-natured willingness to contend with any comers. He worked well, even companionably, with his peers, and decorated his court, literally and figuratively, with the iconography of chivalry: coats of arms, banners, music, and festivities. In lieu of a Round Table, Edward founded the Order of the Garter, and its blue and gold ribbon became the sign of prestige to which countless knights aspired.

But pageantry aside, Edward was also keen to demonstrate his and England's prowess on the battlefield, and he wasted no time in doing so. In 1333, at the age of 21, he personally led his army into Scotland, and met the enemy at Halidon Hill. In a tactic that foreshadowed coming English military dominance, Edward's longbows unleashed wave after devastating wave of finely aimed arrows. The Scots were crushed, and England regained control of Berwick. More importantly, Edward avenged his earlier humiliation at Stanhope, establishing his credentials as a warrior king.

CLAIMING FRANCE

After his victory over the Scots, Edward turned his martial ambitions to a far greater task. Scotland, though restive, had been checked, and the French had made it clear that any offensive against the Scots would invite French hostilities. French ships began raiding towns along the Channel, and in 1337 the French king, Philip VI, annexed Aquitaine.

Edward responded by taking a force across the Channel. He aimed to incite an all-out confrontation, but the French refused to take the bait, and the English army was left to engage in empty maneuvers and minor skirmishes. In 1340, however, Edward's ships destroyed most of the French fleet at Sluys, off the coast of Flanders. It was a momentous turn: not only did it earn England control of the Channel, it also ensured that the French would not be able to invade England in the foreseeable future. Edward was free to fight entirely in France, on the offensive.

His ambition stoked by the victory at Sluys, Edward made an audacious move: he claimed the throne of France. He was, through his mother, the grandson of the great Philip IV, so he regarded his claim as legitimate. The French rejected it, invoking the Salic law of succession, which barred inheritance through the female. Both sides began securing alliances and preparing for a protracted conflict. Edward's claim had launched what eventually would become known as the Hundred Years' War.

But war is expensive, and the French knew that campaigning on French soil would soon drain Edward's royal coffers. They let him pursue his campaigns, never allowing a decisive battle to materialize. By 1341, Edward's expeditions had placed England under huge fiscal strain, and he was so caught up in his ambitions that he was squeezing his nobles for more and dismissing capable administrators from office. At Parliament, lords and commoners alike protested Edward's policies. To his credit, Edward learned. He scaled back his expenses in France, waiting until he could mount a fully financed, major invasion; and by placing a tariff on England's most lucrative export, wool, he shifted much of the tax burden onto foreigners.

In 1346, Edward made his move. Landing in Normandy with a large invasion force, he so terrorized the countryside that Philip VI had no choice but to send forth his own armies

1337	1337	1340	1344	1345
The first good harvest in China for four years ends a famine that is thought to have killed around 6 million people.	With Edward's first invasion of France comes the start of the Hundred Years' War.	Construction of the Doge's Palace in Venice, an icon of the Italian renaissance, is begun.	Three large Florentine banks—Compagnia dei Bardi, the Peruzzi, and the Acciaiuoli—all go bankrupt as economic conditions worsen across Europe.	The Miracle of the Host occurs in Amsterdam—an event that is still commemorated with a civil procession.

The Battle of Crécy, in which Edward's forces inflicted a crushing defeat on the French. The victory inspired a wave of patriotic feeling in England.

or appear impotent. The French and English met at Crécy, on ground chosen by Edward. He employed similar tactics to those that had brought him victory at Halidon Hill: his knights, dismounted, waited with other footsoldiers while longbowmen, behind an array of defenses, waited for the French to come into range. According to some accounts, Edward's forces had early versions of cannon as well.

The French had a far larger army, but they were exhausted, while the English were rested and well provisioned. Sure of victory with his superior numbers, Philip nonetheless insisted on attacking. His mercenary crossbowmen were ineffective, and when the French knights charged they trampled some of their own troops. Crossing a plain toward the bristling English lines they were decimated by English arrows, which not only were aimed with pinpoint accuracy but could also pierce armor. When the fighting ended, the French dead outnumbered the English dead by some ten to one.

1346	1347	1349	1350	1354
At the Battle of Crécy, Edward's troops inflict a momentous defeat on the French.	The Black Death arrives in Europe. Over the next 20 years, it will wipe out between a third and a half of the population of some countries, causing fears of apocalypse, hysteria, and labor shortages.	An earthquake in Rome causes widespread damage, including the partial collapse of the Colosseum—leaving it as it stands today.	Giovanni Boccaccio visits Petrarch in Florence, in a meeting of two great renaissance minds.	The Turks take Gallipoli, conquering their first land across the Dardanelles.

The victory at Crécy marked the ascendancy of England as a major European military power. Edward's popularity skyrocketed and, as a string of victories ensued, wealth streamed into the country. In 1356, Edward's son the Black Prince, so called for the color of his armor, won another crushing victory at Poitiers, even capturing the French king, John II, and a number of his peers.

The sense of national unity galvanized by war against the French now took lasting root. Edward himself spoke English, not French, and great literature in English—or what we now know as Middle English—began to flourish. In addition, much of Edward's army was in fact Welsh, and their role in the war tightened the bonds between England and Wales. England now thought of itself as a great power, the equal of any in Europe. The patriotic spirit that arose in the wake of Crécy and Poitiers would forever transform the nation's vision of itself.

TWILIGHT YEARS

But there was a dark undercurrent to the glittering triumphs of Edward's campaigns in France. In 1348, Edward's daughter Joan suddenly fell ill and died. Others followed. The Black Death had begun to rage through Europe, and England was not spared from this devastating plague. Over the coming decades, nearly a third of its population—some two million people—would fall victim, with the same cataclysmic effects as in the rest of Europe. Labor became scarce and expensive,

revenues declined, and apocalyptic fears took hold. Edward lost some of his most trusted and capable advisors to the plague.

TREATY OF BRÉTIGNY

By 1360, continued campaigning in France was out of the question. With the Treaty of Brétigny, Edward renounced his claim to the French throne in exchange for unchallenged possession of his conquered territories. But even that proved too difficult, as England was overextended and a depopulated France had been reduced to near anarchy. John II, the imprisoned King of France, died in captivity in 1364, the French unable to produce his ransom. His successor, Charles V, fomented unrest in Aquitaine. Edward's most feared commander, his son Edward the Black Prince, fell ill, and the king's other sons proved incapable of holding what Edward and the Black Prince had gained. By 1370, Edward's wife had died. The 1375 Treaty of Bruges reduced England's presence in France to Calais, Bordeaux, and some other coastal holdings.

To his credit, Edward worked hard to secure the stability of the realm. In 1351, he issued the Statute of Labourers, which remedied, insofar as was possible, the shortage of labor due to the Black Death by capping escalating wages and limiting worker migration. Other statutes clarified the definition of treason and limited the control of the papacy over English subjects. Justices of the Peace were given the power not

THE ENGLISH LANGUAGE

Edward's glittering court and his momentous victories overseas not only recalled the legendary exploits of King Arthur; they also nurtured a rising sense of English culture that was inseparable from the English language. The works of Geoffrey Chaucer, most famously The Canterbury Tales, would spawn myriad imitators, as did the poems of William Langland, best known for his visionary work Piers Plowman. The great tradition of English literature as we know it had earlier roots, but the flowering of English vernacular poetry in the time of Edward III was a pivotal stage in its growth.

1356	1359	1363	1367	1371
At the Battle of Poitiers, the Black Prince inflicts another devastating defeat on the French, capturing their king.	Defeat by the Ottoman Turks forces Byzantine emperor John V to cede so much territory that his rule is confined to little more than the city of Constantinople.	The largest naval battle in history takes place at Lake Poyang when the Han fleet of 140 ships and 650,000 men is catastrophically defeated by the Ming fleet of over 100 ships and 200,000 men.	Geoffrey Chaucer becomes a yeoman in the household of Edward III.	Battle of Maritsa. The Ottoman Turks invade Serbia, defeating the Serb army and wiping out nearly all the Serb nobles, after which large areas of the Balkans fall to the Turks.

Edward, Prince of Wales, known as the Black Prince because of his dark armor. A gifted military leader, he never became king, dying of a long illness, perhaps cancer, in 1376. His son succeeded to the throne as Richard II.

only to investigate crimes and make arrests but also to try suspects, ensuring that criminal cases, even felonies, were handled locally from start to finish.

But by 1375, Edward's health was in steep decline, and left power in the less generous and capable hands of his son John of Gaunt. It would be under John of Gaunt's tenure that English government would see its most remarkable changes.

PARLIAMENTARY EVOLUTION

The most important developments in English politics during Edward's long reign involved Parliament. In 1341, Edward presided over the first Parliament to divide into two houses. Though not at first known by their current names, the House of Lords contained the barons and the clergy, while the House of Commons comprised the knights and burgesses representing towns and boroughs across the country. This development opened the door for more striking changes late in Edward's reign.

In 1376, Edward had grown old, and the Black Prince lay dying in London. Edward's son John of Gaunt held the reins of government, and a rising tide of dissent had expressed itself in the perception of widespread corruption. The perception was almost certainly accurate. The House of Commons in particular was proving problematic, in that it had to approve all new taxes, and over the past 30 years had grown more confident and vocal in its demands.

The resulting Parliament, known as the Good Parliament, lasted for nearly three months, and witnessed important changes in the conduct of government business. Both Houses were determined to root out corruption in the regime, especially the Royal Council, but the House of Commons did so with surprising

boldness. They elected the first-ever Speaker of the House of Commons, Peter de la Mare from Hereford. The eloquent de la Mare proceeded to criticize the king for levying excessive taxes and mismanaging the campaigns in France; he also demanded a thorough accounting of royal expenditures. This last demand was not just intended to eliminate waste; it was meant to reveal when, where, and how members of the Royal Council were deliberately misdirecting resources. The House of Commons even established the principle of impeachment and used it against some ministers. Lord Latimer, Chamberlain of the Household and the first English minister to be impeached, was imprisoned. The king's famously conniving mistress, Alice Perrers, was called before Parliament and banished from court. Parliament even forced Edward to accept a new set of advisors.

The work of the Good Parliament would not last. John of Gaunt, outraged, convened another Parliament the following year. Called, suitably enough, the Bad Parliament, it declared unlawful what the previous session had set in place. Gaunt had Peter de la Mare imprisoned, but de la Mare was released on Edward's death and again became Speaker of the House. In the coming century of unrest and dynastic disorder, royal authority would reassert itself. But the principles and procedures of the Good Parliament would not be forgotten, and eventually they would resurface with lasting effect.

DEATH AND LEGACY

In June 1376, the Black Prince died. Before expiring, he summoned the King and John of Gaunt to his bedside and had them agree to name his son Richard the next king. A year later, depressed and largely neglected, Edward III succumbed to a stroke. He had been the last of the great Plantagenet warrior kings, but he had been unable, often for reasons beyond his control, to consolidate his gains and pass them on. His grandson Richard would lose them completely.

1371	1373		1376	1377
Hongwu of the Ming Dynasty begins a census of China that records a population of 59,873,305 people liable for tax. However, some categories of people are excluded, so the total population is thought to have been around 75 million.	The city of Phnom Penh, Cambodia, is founded.		Edward calls what comes to be known as the Good Parliament, though in fact he has little to do with its deliberations or outcomes.	Edward dies.

THE HUNDRED YEARS' WAR

The Hundred Years' War, generally considered as extending from 1337 to 1453, arose from English claims to French lands. In a sense, it was an inevitable, bloody resolution to a conflict that dated back to William the Conqueror: the ambiguous position of English monarchs as kings in Britain but feudal vassals on the continent. In the Hundred Years' War, English power in France reached its height—and then collapsed almost completely.

From 1066 onward, English kings ruled domains on both sides of the Channel, and for the Norman and early Plantagenet kings their holdings in France tended to deserve much more attention than England. Henry II, for instance, was not merely King of England; he was also Count of Anjou and Duke of Aquitaine. He was therefore the ruler of two powerful and wealthy domains that formed part of France, which was less a unified kingdom than a constellation of largely independent fiefdoms. England was something of a hinterland to these glittering realms, with their sophisticated courts.

EDWARD III AND THE EARLY ENGLISH VICTORIES

Though conflicts had erupted sporadically between the kings of England and the French, it was Philip VI's annexation of Aquitaine in 1337 that prompted Edward III to ramp up the conflict by staking an open claim to the throne of France. It was a move designed to drive a wedge between Philip and some of his restive vassals, who might see advantages in supporting a rival king.

Edward's expeditions into France were not systematic conquests, but calculated efforts to undermine French cohesiveness—and they largely worked. When the French did manage to

THE ENGLISH LONGBOW

The iconic image of the English victories at Crécy and Poitiers, and later at Agincourt, is of the longbow. Generations of Englishmen were systematically trained in using the longbow, which was a devastating weapon: not only did it have a range of up to 400 yards (365 m); it could penetrate most kinds of armor, and a good archer could fire as many as six well-aimed shots a minute. At a distance, enemies faced massive barrages of arrows; in closer combat, archers could pick off knights one by one. When, as at Poitiers, French knights wore armor that successfully deflected most arrows, the longbowmen simply killed their horses beneath them.

confront Edward with an army at Crécy in 1346, he won a decisive, morale-crushing victory. At Poitiers ten years later, Edward the Black Prince achieved an even more complete and demoralizing victory, even capturing the French king, John II, who was to be ransomed for the staggering sum of three million crowns. Without its king, defeated, and still suffering from the devastation of the Black Death, which had swept through in 1348, France descended into anarchy. Noble houses fought for supremacy, and peasants rebelled as living conditions grew intolerable.

After a truce was reached with the Treaty of Brétigny in 1360, John II was allowed to return to France to raise his ransom; his son Louis was held hostage in England as insurance. When Louis escaped, John reacted not with joy but with dismay, and insisted, against the wishes of his court, on returning to imprisonment as a matter of honor and good faith. He would eventually die in England, unransomed. Given that his imprisonment involved a princely lifestyle while his French subjects were suffering unbearable hardships, John's gesture reveals the combination of high principle and callous inhumanity that characterized the nobility of the time.

THE WAR AFTER POITIERS

The tenuous peace of Brétigny broke down in 1369, and within a few years the French, under Charles V, had won back control over most of France, leaving the English in possession of lands along the coast from Bordeaux to Bayonne. Nothing much happened for the next quarter-century, but France again unraveled under the reign of Charles VI, whose incapacity due to mental illness—he was known as Charles the Mad—led to vicious, even murderous rivalries among the French noble houses. It was this disarray that made it possible for Henry V to invade France successfully, first with the raid that led to his 1415 victory at Agincourt and then with another, more protracted campaign of land acquisition.

Henry V's untimely death in 1422 was the beginning of the end of English ambitions in France. Though his infant son, Henry VI, was nominally king of both England and France, the English proved unable to extend their reach far south into France. Inspired by Joan of Arc, the French overcame the English siege of Orléans in 1429 and rolled back English gains. In 1444, a truce was negotiated, but the English broke it five years later. Charles VII, anticipating as

Joan of Arc, whose visionary leadership and tactical brilliance inspired French troops to a series of victories in 1429 before she was imprisoned by the English and burned as a heretic.

much, had prepared an army to drive the English from Normandy and Gascony; he succeeded in only two years. When, in a last gasp, English forces under John Talbot recaptured Bordeaux in 1452, they were crushed at Castillon the next year. England's French territories were reduced to the port city of Calais.

The Hundred Years' War was a crucible of French and English national identities, in that the two realms' long enmity provided each with a sense of collective purpose and distinctness. Even today, its residue remains as a kind of lighthearted disdain between many French and English.

RICHARD II ✠ Last of the Plantagenets

House Plantagenet

Born January 6, 1367

Died February 14, 1400

Reigned 1327–1377

Consort Anne of Bohemia (died 1394), Isabella of Valois

Children None

Successor Henry IV

Richard II has been immortalized as a grasping, self-indulgent, and cruel king, and in many cases he was. He was also a patron of the arts and, on occasion, a capable leader and administrator. But he had a gift for humiliating and alienating people whose support he needed, and when the darker undercurrents of his personality came to the fore, he found himself at the mercy of vengeful enemies.

Richard II was only ten years old when he took the throne in 1377, yet another young king thrust into the turmoil and intrigue of royal politics. His father, Edward the Black Prince, had died even before his grandfather the king, and Richard's succession had been carefully scripted. The boy had been adorned with an array of titles, and the previous Christmas, at Windsor Castle, Edward III had required his court to acknowledge Richard as their rightful sovereign. Though no regent was appointed, none was needed, for Richard's uncle John of Gaunt was the most powerful noble in the kingdom, possessed of fabulous wealth, 30 castles, and a sizeable private army, and he acted on his nephew's behalf.

A BRAVE YOUNG KING

Though in his early years Richard did not have control over the government, he was still its figurehead. In 1381, he would have an unlooked-for chance to demonstrate that he knew what that role entailed. Throughout the reign of Edward III, the heavy taxes collected to support wars abroad had given rise to deep resentment. The scourge of the Black Death, which had wiped out about a third of England's population, only aggravated the general sense of dislocation and distress. In the first four years of Richard's reign, three new poll taxes had been imposed, requiring a shilling of every

adult. A rebellion led by a peasant named Wat Tyler suddenly mushroomed into a crisis. Tens of thousands of peasants vented their rage on manors, abbeys, and wealthy establishments of all kinds, demanding lower rents, lower taxes, and amnesty for themselves. John of Gaunt was far from London, bargaining with the Scots, and few forces were available to defend the city. The rebels killed the Archbishop of Canterbury and torched his castle. London began to burn. The treasurer was murdered as well. Richard, along with his mother and his cousin Henry, John of Gaunt's son, took refuge with retainers in the Tower.

But the peasant rebels did not want Richard's blood; they wanted his protection. Over the course of Edward III's reign, the king had begun to be seen as the advocate of the common people in their many grievances against the nobility, and Wat Tyler and his followers believed that if they could speak with the king, they could have their demands met. Richard seems to have recognized the import of this, and three times he rode out of the Tower with a handful of retainers and negotiated with the rebels face to face. Each time, he promised to grant them amnesty and institute reforms. When he met Tyler at Mile End, he once more began to placate the crowd, but the Lord Mayor, incensed at Tyler's gesticulations toward the king, struck him dead. In that tense moment, when the crowd might have turned violent, Richard said, "Sirs, will you kill your king? I

John of Gaunt, third son of Edward III and the most powerful nobleman in England for most of Richard's reign. Richard may never have realized the extent to which his rule relied on John of Gaunt's backing.

> SIRS, WILL YOU KILL YOUR KING?
>
> *RICHARD II*

1377	1378	1378	1381	
Richard II is crowned King of England.	The Holy Roman Emperor Charles IV divides his lands among his three sons and dies at Prague on 29 November, aged 62.	The Western (or Great) Schism begins, resulting in rival popes in Rome and Avignon. Mostly a conflict of political factions rather than a theological dispute, it will only be resolved at the Council of Constance from 1414–1418.	The Peasants' Revolt erupts in England, with Wat Tyler as its most famous leader. At the age of 14, Richard faces down a mob.	**Opposite** Richard II, whose narcissistic and autocratic style led to his overthrow, and the end of the Plantagenet dynasty.

am your leader. Follow me." It was a stunning instance of bravery from a boy of 14, and it worked. The mob followed Richard out of London and dispersed.

Richard kept none of his promises. Many of the rebels were captured and executed, and the peasants' hardships continued unabated. But if Richard's duplicity revealed something of his manipulativeness, his courage and resolve gained him respect among the nobility. The following year, he married Anne of Bohemia, daughter of the Holy Roman Emperor. His success as a king seemed assured, especially with John of Gaunt's wealth and power firmly undergirding Richard's authority.

A DECADENT MONARCH

In the coming years, Richard began to assert his royal prerogatives with a cavalier insensitivity that recalled the rampant corruption of Edward II. Two of his favorites in particular—Robert de Vere, the Earl of Oxford, and Michael de la Pole, a wealthy commoner whom Richard created Earl of Suffolk and named his chancellor—benefited enormously from the king's patronage. They accrued massive wealth, and the court became highly aestheticized, even decadent. Amid

Robert de Vere fleeing his defeat by Henry Bolingbroke at Radcot Bridge in 1387. De Vere was forced to flee into exile. Richard would wait nearly a decade to exact revenge.

costume parties and extravagant feasts, Richard indulged in pleasures and demanded gestures of obeisance while military campaigns in France foundered expensively. He embodied an ideology of kingship in which the sovereign was an icon of absolute power and extravagant pageantry, possessed of divinely ordained, inviolable majesty and authority.

THE LORDS APPELLANT

Most troubling of all, Richard seemed to believe that he, unlike even the storied Edward III, need not answer to anyone. In 1385, his expensive expedition into Scotland did not even manage to engage the Scots. The French, emboldened by Richard and his government's inability to formulate a coherent strategy for the continent, made plans to invade England that were only disrupted by rebellions in the Low Countries. The last straw came a year later, when the king created Robert de Vere, who was of rather undistinguished if noble background, Duke of Ireland—a title reserved for members of the royal family.

In 1386, John of Gaunt left England to advance his right to the throne of Castile. With his protector gone, Richard was more vulnerable than he knew; but both the nobility and Parliament knew it, and they took advantage of the king's exposed position to bring him under control. Richard got his first taste of direct and forthright opposition, and he handled it with shocking incompetence.

First, Richard attempted to bully Parliament. In what came to be known as the Wonderful Parliament of late 1386, he was challenged to remove from positions of power some of his favorites. An enraged Richard was forced to stand aside as Michael de la Pole was impeached for embezzlement, and the royal accounts were opened for review. Though he saw it differently, the king had brought humiliation on himself. He quit London and set off on a royal progress through the country, which was really an effort to gather forces with which he would gain absolute power. One of those forces was

1381

Timur (Tamerlaine) begins his conquest of Persia, which would be completed by 1387. Timur initiated a programme of building towers made from the decapitated heads of those who oppose him. After the fall if Isfahan he has 28 towers made of 1,500 heads each.

1382

The Wycliffe Bible, the first full English translation, is completed. John Wycliffe and his movement, the Lollards, prefigure the Protestant reformation in their rejection of papal authority.

1386

Venice conquers Corfu, beginning an expansion into the eastern Mediterranean.

THE WILTON DIPTYCH

Richard's patronage of the arts contributed to an ongoing cultural flowering in 14th-century England. One work of art that captures the highly aestheticized splendor of Richard's court is the Wilton Diptych, now in the National Gallery in London. The diptych, an expensively and exquisitely made rendering of Richard offering devotion to the Virgin and Child, also reveals something of Richard's religiosity. The angels behind the Virgin and Child wear badges of the white hart, Richard's personal symbol, and one of the saints accompanying him is Edward the Confessor, for whom Richard displayed particular devotion.

several of Richard's favorites of treason. It was a bold power play, and for a time it worked. In the Miraculous Parliament of November 1387, a broadside of accusations were leveled at Richard's inner circle.

Richard summoned the Lords Appellant to the Tower. They refused. The king called his allies to arms, and Richard de Vere marched toward London at the head of an army. In December 1387, at Radcot Bridge, Henry Bolingbroke's forces routed de Vere's and de Vere himself barely managed to survive the melee and make his way into the safety of permanent exile. De la Pole fled the country as well. Richard soon faced another, harsher Parliament.

In the Merciless Parliament of 1388, the accusations of the Lords Appellant were upheld, and Richard's inner circle was decimated by a wave of exiles and executions. Michael de la Pole and Robert de Vere were condemned to death in absentia. Several other favorites were beheaded. Like Edward II, Richard was forced to submit to the governance of a noble council.

REVENGE, AND MORE REVENGE

In 1389, John of Gaunt returned from Spain, and with his tremendous gravitas managed to stabilize the situation. Richard regained traction, and began gathering a new set of admirers. He made a show of forgiving his adversaries, and seemed to have learned his lesson. But inwardly he was nursing his wrath. In 1397, he launched a vicious purge, ordering a steady round of executions in a belated and brutal tit-for-tat. The timing of Richard's vengeful tour de force remains a mystery—he might have moved against his enemies earlier—but the effects were devastating. Even his uncle Thomas of Gloucester was killed, murdered while imprisoned in Calais. When Henry Bolingbroke and another Lord Appellant, Thomas Mowbray, entered into a quarrel that was to be resolved through trial by combat, Richard nullified the trial and exiled them both, Mowbray for life and Bolingbroke for ten years. In a final move to secure his position, he made peace with France to ensure that none

a private army. Richard also convened a council of magistrates in Nottingham who, conveniently, denounced the Wonderful Parliament as treasonous and its decisions void.

But Parliament was not the only opposition; powerful nobles had grievances as well, and their spokesmen became known as the Lords Appellant—not because they appealed to the king or to Parliament in any ordinary sense, but because, in the legal parlance of the time, an appeal was an accusation. Their leader was Richard's uncle Thomas of Gloucester, and among them was his cousin and boyhood companion Henry Bolingbroke, Earl of Derby. The five Lords Appellant formally accused

---

1387

At the Battle of Radcot Bridge, Robert de Vere's forces are scattered by those of Henry Bolingbroke. De Vere escapes into exile, but Richard is forced to accept constraints on his rule.

1387

The Battle of Otterburn sees the Scottish commander James Douglas killed and the English commander Harry Hotspur Percy captured. It is considered a Scottish victory.

1388

At the Merciless Parliament, the charges of the Lords Appellant are upheld. Richard's government is purged.

Henry Bolingbroke, crowned Henry IV. He and Richard grew up together as cousins, but became enemies as adults.

stick until physically restrained. His longtime devotion to Edward the Confessor—curiously, a commitment he shared with his predecessor Henry III—deepened into fixation, and he reportedly aspired to leave what he considered the petty machinations of England behind and be elected Holy Roman Emperor.

In 1399, John of Gaunt died. Richard, out of what combination of vindictiveness and greed we will never know, disinherited Henry Bolingbroke, John of Gaunt's son. The huge assets of John of Gaunt's family, the House of Lancaster, were now Richard's for the taking, and he helped himself. It was a fatal error. Not only had Richard made a mortal enemy of Henry Bolingbroke; he had demonstrated in the starkest terms that no nobleman's lands and titles were safe with such a volatile and utterly untrustworthy monarch on the throne. Richard's hangers-on might see his confiscation of Bolingbroke's inheritance as a potential windfall, but outside his circle it appeared as a threat.

Bolingbroke, already grieving the death of his father, felt the full shock of Richard's arbitrariness. He and Richard had grown up together, even taking the Order of the Garter alongside each other as children. Even after Henry had chastened Richard as one of the Lords Appellant, Richard had granted him the prominent title of Duke of Hereford. John of Gaunt had even concurred with Richard's temporary exile of Bolingbroke. Richard may have been biding his time, concealing his vengeful intentions toward Bolingbroke until John of Gaunt was out of the way. It may also be that, once John of Gaunt was dead, an increasingly grandiose Richard felt he was completely free to do as he pleased, and it pleased him to seize the lands of the wealthiest family in England.

of his exiled enemies could count on French backing. Richard's queen Anne had died in 1394, so he was free to cement his new alliance by marrying the seven-year-old daughter of Charles VI of France.

A COSTLY MISTAKE
By this point, Richard's behavior was becoming increasingly volatile. When his wife Anne died in 1394, he had the building in which she died razed; at her funeral, he became wildly emotional and beat the Earl of Arundel with a

ABDICATION AND SUCCESSION
Regardless, Bolingbroke returned to England, arriving in his hereditary lands in Yorkshire in July 1399. His small cadre of supporters

1391	1392	1394	1396
Earl Henry of Orkney conquers the Shetland and Faroe Islands.	Go Komatsu becomes the 100th Emperor of Japan, reuniting the country after a period of anarchy.	The Sultanate of Delhi enters a 20 year period of civil war after the death of Sultan Mahmud II.	The Cursade of Nicopolis advances along the Danube, pillaging and killing under the leadership of the Hungarian king Sigismund who is supported by both the Roman and the Avignon popes.

swelled as he marched on London. Bolingbroke secured some nobles' support by promising that he was only in England to reclaim his patrimony and nothing more, making his campaign merely one more effort to put the king in his place. At some point, probably sooner than later, Bolingbroke developed grander ambitions to claim the throne.

Richard was in Ireland when Bolingbroke arrived, and it took him nearly three weeks to make it back to Wales; in that time, whatever slim chance Richard had of marshaling support and confronting Bolingbroke evaporated. He and his retinue took up residence at Conwy Castle. On August 19, after negotiations mediated by Henry Percy of Northumberland, Richard agreed to surrender to Bolingbroke at Flint Castle. By now, abdication was likely a foregone conclusion, though Richard would not formally agree to it for another month.

The problem now was succession. As a grandson of Edward III, Bolingbroke had a strong claim to the throne, but one nobleman had more immediate claim: Edmund Mortimer, Earl of March, whose recently deceased father,

another grandson of Edward, had been the heir presumptive under Richard. But Mortimer was only eight years old and incapable of making his own case. Parliament was convened, and made the determination that Bolingbroke was the rightful heir because his descent from Edward III, unlike that of the young Mortimer, was entirely through the male line. It was a decision based more on contingency than on the logic of succession, and it would have violent repercussions.

Henry Bolingbroke of the House of Lancaster took the throne as Henry IV. After his abdication, Richard vanished from sight, eventually being held in Pontefract Castle. As long as he was alive, he remained the focus of plots against Henry. In 1400, he died, apparently of starvation. Whether he was left to starve or, in a final gesture of proud defiance, starved himself, we will never know. The perception at the time was that Henry had ordered Richard killed.

With the death of Richard II, the storied Plantagenet line came to an end. But not entirely. In truth, it continued for another turbulent century in the form of two cadet branches, the Houses of Lancaster and York. Their rivalry would shape English history in the coming century.

Richard II was, by any measure, a bad king. Some historians have even suggested that mental illness, perhaps a pathological narcissism, lay at the root of his conduct. But under his rule, the cultural and literary flowering that began under Edward III continued, as the various strands of English culture began to twine together into an Englishness that remains vividly recognizable today.

Pontefract Castle, where Richard starved to death in prison. It was a bleak end for a monarch who had sought absolute power.

1397	1398	1399	1400
Richard exiles Henry Bolingbroke and Thomas Mowbray. In Florence, the Medici bank is founded. Florence will become the financial center of Europe.	Timur invades northern India, sacking Delhi and massacring an estimated 500,000 Hindus.	Richard abdicates and is succeeded by Bolingbroke as Henry IV.	Richard II dies of starvation in Pontefract Castle.

The Houses of Lancaster and York

The usurpation of the throne by Henry Bolingbroke brought the House of Lancaster, a cadet branch of the Plantagenets, to the pinnacle of English power. But despite the glorious exploits in France of Henry V, the 15th century would see a bloody dynastic clash between the Houses of Lancaster and York, which came to be known as the Wars of the Roses. Replete with heroic exploits, shifting allegiances, and sudden turns of fortune, the Wars of the Roses are one of the most dramatic episodes in British history. From the mentally unbalanced Henry VI of Lancaster and his defiant queen, Margaret of Anjou, to the formidable Edward IV of York and the legendary Richard III, the era boasts a scintillating array of personalities.

HENRY IV: ✠ Troubled Usurper

House Lancaster

Born April 15, 1367

Died March 20, 1413

Reigned 1399–1413

Consort Joan of Navarre

Children Seven, including Henry V, Thomas of Lancaster, John of Lancaster

Successor Henry V

When Henry Bolingbroke of the House of Lancaster accepted the crown after the abdication of his cousin Richard II, he knew he had set a dangerous precedent: the overthrow of an anointed king. Throughout his reign, Henry would have to deal with the consequences of that fateful transition. In spite of them—or perhaps because of them—he proved a resilient and decisive ruler.

Henry's coronation was the culmination of a long, complicated, and ultimately deadly relationship with his cousin and predecessor on the throne. Henry's father, John of Gaunt, was the third son of Edward III and the power behind the throne of Richard II. Richard and Henry had grown up together; in 1377, they had entered the Order of the Garter side by side, admitted by an aging Edward III. However, the two boys drifted apart in their teens for reasons that remain unclear but doubtless had much to do with their obviously different temperaments: Richard was a sophisticate, an aesthete, while Henry became a consummate soldier and man of action.

One story does suggest an early turning point in their relationship. Just after Richard's accession, the mobs of the Peasants' Revolt marched on London, and both boys took refuge in the poorly guarded Tower. According to the story, at one point all was in jeopardy, and some of the nobles around the boys were being killed. Young Henry was in imminent danger from the crowd, but Richard failed to lift a finger in his defense; Henry was only saved from possible murder by a knight who whisked him to safety. Later, Richard would famously ride out and face down the riotous mobs with impressive courage. But Henry stopped residing at court. The story may well be exaggerated, but it does suggest the sort of mutual mistrust one might expect to take root between two very different young men in such a relationship.

Henry built his life away from court around the pursuit of knightly accomplishment. Of middling height but powerful and athletic, with red Plantagenet hair and an outgoing manner, the young Bolingbroke cut an impressive figure,

> ## I, HENRY OF LANCASTER, CHALLENGE THIS REALM OF ENGLAND AND THE CROWN
>
> *HENRY IV*

A period manuscript image of Henry IV taking the throne. The precedent he set in deposing and having killed an anointed king haunted him throughout his reign.

1377

Richard II is crowned King of England.

1378

The Holy Roman emperor Charles IV divides his lands among his three sons and dies at Prague on November 29, aged 62.

1378

The Western (or Great) Schism begins, resulting in rival popes in Rome and Avignon. Mostly a conflict of political factions rather than a theological dispute, it will only be resolved at the Council of Constance from 1414–1418.

Opposite A period portrait of Henry IV, who spent much of his reign successfully securing the throne he seized from Richard II.

Thomas, Earl of Gloucester, whose change of allegiance from Richard II to Henry Bolingbroke did not spare him from the consequences of his apparent complicity in the death of Thomas of Woodstock.

A period illustration of Henry taking the throne from Richard II. Both men proved adept at political theater.

and he constantly sought out martial challenges. In his twenties, he featured as a dominant jouster in contests and tournaments on both sides of the Channel, and from there he tried his hand at military adventures. In 1390 and again in 1392, he led a small force of knights to Lithuania, where the Teutonic Knights were battling to Christianize the country by conquest. Though the fighting proved inconclusive at the time, Henry burnished his reputation as a soldier. When he organized a similar expedition the next year, his travels took him all the way to Jerusalem and back. Not only did he become the only medieval English king to enter Jerusalem; he also made a powerful impression at the many courts he visited in the course of his trip. One is tempted to think that, on returning to England in 1393 and settling down to the business of being John of Gaunt's heir, Henry found his combative spirit stifled.

A SWIFT ASCENT TO POWER

Henry's young adulthood was not all tournaments and campaigns. In 1386, at the age of 20, he was recruited to be one of the five Lords Appellant, the nobles who openly challenged the policies of Richard II and demanded that he cede control, at least for a time, to a ruling council. The other Lords Appellant, especially his uncle Thomas of Gloucester, likely sought Henry not only as an esteemed and wealthy young nobleman and the king's cousin, but also as a kind of symbolic counterweight to the influence of John of Gaunt, who was out of the country when the Lords Appellant made their move. In any case, despite the purges of the Merciless Parliament and Bolingbroke's humiliating defeat of Richard's supporter Robert de Vere at Radcot Bridge, Richard did not appear alienated by his cousin's involvement; he even made him Duke of Hereford shortly after.

But everything changed a decade later. In 1397, for reasons that remain unclear, Richard visited a swift and violent revenge on the Lords Appellant. Two were killed, including Thomas of Gloucester, and one was stripped of lands and titles and imprisoned on the Isle of Man. The two remaining Lords Appellant, Thomas Mowbray and Bolingbroke, received a different, more public form of royal retaliation. Mowbray and Bolingbroke had fallen into a serious quarrel, apparently over remarks about Richard, and a Parliamentary committee decided to let the two men settle the issue through trial by combat.

RIGHTFUL INHERITANCE

Richard, however, had his own designs. At the trial, just as Bolingbroke and Mowbray were about to fight, Richard threw down his ceremonial staff and forbade the trial, instead exiling them both—Bolingbroke for ten years and Mowbray for life. It was a cruel piece of political theater, apparently done with the tacit support of John of Gaunt. It was also the prelude to Richard's fatal error and Bolingbroke's march to the throne.

In 1399, John of Gaunt died. Henry Bolingbroke stood to inherit all his father's vast holdings. Richard, however, summarily stripped Bolingbroke of his right to any inheritance, arrogating it to the Crown. It was a

1381

The Peasants' Revolt erupts in England, with Wat Tyler as its most famous leader. At the age of 14, Richard faces down a mob..

1381

Tamerlaine begins his conquest of Persia, which would be completed by 1387. He initiates a program of building towers made from the decapitated heads of those who oppose him. After the fall of Isfahan he has 28 towers made of 1,500 heads each.

1382

The Wycliffe Bible, the first full English translation, is completed. John Wycliffe and his movement, the Lollards, prefigure the Protestant reformation in their rejection of papal authority.

A statue at Alnwick Castle of Henry "Hotspur" Percy, the most renowned knight of his day. The Percys were instrumental in Henry IV's taking the throne, but later turned on him.

raids and invasions, and very powerful. At this juncture in English history, the Percys were, in effect, kingmakers, and Bolingbroke could not afford to alienate them.

With the Percys on board, Bolingbroke marched on London, gaining followers as he went. Richard had been in Ireland, and lost valuable time waiting for favorable winds to sail back to Wales. When he arrived, he had little choice but to hole up with supporters in Welsh castles; within weeks he was captured, and brought to the Tower of London.

We may never know exactly when Henry Bolingbroke made the decision to drop his earlier assurances and play for the ultimate prize, but at some point he did. Richard was a vain, autocratic, unpopular king who was ripe for a fall; Henry seemed the arm of justice. Henry Percy negotiated Richard's abdication. The king, with characteristic drama, turned his throne over to God rather than any man. The only question was succession, for Bolingbroke did not have the most compelling claim to the throne; priority in succession belonged to the eight-year-old Edmund Mortimer, Earl of March, who was descended from John of Gaunt's older brother Lionel.

Bolingbroke's claim to the throne could only be advanced by leverage or by sophistry; he used both. Arguing, without real precedent, that being descended through the male line gave him the more compelling claim, and adding that he had, with the help of God, saved the realm from the depredations of Richard, Henry simply seized the throne. Bolingbroke's real argument consisted of two hard facts: that he was a 32-year-old man with an army, while Edmund Mortimer was a small boy without a clue. Parliament confirmed Richard's abdication in absentia, and on October 13, 1399, Bolingbroke became Henry IV, anointed with oil allegedly given to Thomas Becket by the Virgin Mary.

A KING UNDER SIEGE

Henry IV's address to Parliament was the first such speech in English since before the Battle of

shocking move, which both enraged the already grieving Bolingbroke and distressed his fellow nobles: it seemed that no one's inheritance was now secure.

After taking counsel with friends in France and eluding Richard's watchful allies abroad, Bolingbroke set sail for England in July 1399, with ten ships and some 300 men. Setting ashore in Yorkshire, his home territory, Bolingbroke swiftly won the allegiance of a series of castles and set about securing the support of other nobles. He took the high ground, affirming that he had only returned to take back his rightful inheritance and no more. That assertion, which may or may not have been true when he first said it, was crucial to winning the support of the powerful Percy family of Northumberland. The Earls of Northumberland, like those of the Welsh Marches, were the first line of defense on hostile borders; they were fiercely proud, battle-tested from guarding against Scottish

1386	1387	1387	
Venice conquers Corfu, beginning an expansion into the eastern Mediterranean.	At the Battle of Radcot Bridge, Robert de Vere's forces are scattered by those of Henry Bolingbroke. De Vere escapes into exile, but Richard is forced to accept constraints on his rule.	The Battle of Otterburn sees the Scottish commander James Douglas killed and the English commander Harry Hotspur Percy captured. It is considered a Scottish victory.	

Hastings. But Henry's mind was hardly on such symbolic beginnings; nor would he ever be able to direct his attention toward administrative reform. He had more immediate, and more dire, concerns. However he might try to obscure the reality with legal disputation or assurances of leadership, he had simply taken the throne, not inherited it, and what he had done unto Richard might also be done unto him.

If Richard's seizure of Bolingbroke's inheritance had dismayed many of England's nobles, Bolingbroke's seizure of the throne frightened Richard's supporters, who expected to be stripped of lands and titles themselves. Henry's decision to place the assets of Richard's circle under attainder, pending investigation of the men's roles in Thomas of Gloucester's death, exacerbated their fears. In a matter of weeks, they rebelled.

The Epiphany Rising, so called because its conspirators hatched the plan before Christmas of 1399 and hoped to overthrow Henry during Epiphany, involved several nobles who had linked their fortunes to those of Richard. Their plan might have worked had not one of them, Edward of Norwich, changed his allegiance and reported the scheme to Henry. The remaining conspirators were rounded up and executed, in diverse places and with varying degrees of cruelty.

THE DARKEST DEED
The lesson was an old one: as long as Richard II remained alive, he gave hope to would-be conspirators. Small wonder, then, that within two months, around February 14, 1400, Richard died while imprisoned in Pontefract Castle. The cause of death remains unclear. We know from later examination of Richard's remains that he did not die violently, but he may well have starved to death. Whether he starved himself in a kind of hunger strike, or whether he was simply left to expire, we may never know. But the blame attached to Henry. It was one thing to force a bad king into abdication; it was something altogether different to kill him. Still different was deposing a king who had himself seized the throne in disregard of customary succession. Soon other, much more daunting challengers arose, and among them were the Percys. Though Henry had taken pains not to antagonize the powerful lords of Northumberland, over the next several years their power would inspire three separate attempts to topple Henry, and it would cost him dearly to fend them off.

SECURING THE THRONE
The first rebellion arose in Wales, led by Owen Glendower (Owain Glyndwr). Glendower was a Welsh lord whose local quarrel with an English neighbor snowballed into a general rebellion. Even worse, the cause attached itself to the Mortimer family of young Edmund; his uncle, also named Edmund, married Glendower's daughter and cemented the alliance.

OWEN GLENDOWER: WELSH LEGEND

Of the many nobles who rebelled against Henry IV, Owen Glendower is perhaps the most intriguing. Though descended from Welsh princes and well positioned to claim the rule of Wales, Glendower spent his first 40 years living a fairly staid life: securing an education, soldiering, and eventually settling down on his estates in Wales. It remains unclear whether, in 1400, he actively sought to lead a rebellion or whether events propelled him into it; regardless, he performed it with gusto, leading guerrilla campaigns when open warfare proved impracticable. Only after the death in 1408 of Henry Percy the elder, his last major English backer, was Glendower forced to go permanently into hiding. His final resting place remains a mystery, ensuring his legendary status as a Welsh champion who seemingly vanished into the mist. All the more fitting that, in Shakespeare's Henry IV, Glendower is depicted as something of a sorcerer.

The tomb effigy of Henry IV and his wife Joan of Navarre. It seems to convey some of the weariness that doubtless weighted on the king.

Glendower's initially sporadic rebellion now centered on a legitimate rival claimant to the throne. The Percys, once Henry's key supporters but now alienated by unfulfilled promises of land and gold, turned against him. Their leader was Henry Percy the younger, aptly nicknamed Hotspur for his vainglorious, ambitious temperament. When he led his forces south to join those of Glendower and Mortimer, Henry moved decisively to cut them off.

On July 21, 1403, the two armies met near Shrewsbury. The battle was long, bloody, and confused. For the first time, English longbowmen made war on each other, with devastating effect, precipitating a rush into hand-to-hand combat that left the kingdom in the balance. Henry was in the thick of the fiercest fighting. Both his son, Prince Hal, and Hotspur Percy were struck in the face by arrows. Prince Hal was saved by surgeons but permanently scarred; Hotspur was slain. The fighting only ended when it became clear that Hotspur was dead, his uncle Thomas Percy captured, and King Henry still standing.

Two years later, Hotspur's father, spared by Henry after his kinsmen's rebellion, conspired with Edmund Mortimer to launch another rebellion, joined by Thomas Mowbray and Richard Scrope, Archbishop of York. After crushing this revolt, Henry went so far as to order the execution of Scrope. Executing an archbishop was well-nigh unthinkable, and for many of Henry's detractors it further tainted his already stained reputation. But Henry had seen how appeasement had only inspired further trouble. Only in 1408, after the elder Henry Percy was defeated and killed at the Battle of Bramham Moor, the elder Edmund Mortimer had died in Wales, and Owen Glendower had been hounded into hiding, did the king feel reasonably secure on his throne.

A LONG, DARK DECLINE

If, by 1408, Henry's throne was secure, his health was anything but. In 1405, he suffered the first of many debilitating illnesses. Over time, he also developed a disfiguring skin condition that may or may not have been leprosy. In pain and clearly terrified for the condition of his soul, he gradually, if reluctantly, ceded power to his council, which included Prince Hal. Though tensions between king and heir flared in the final years, even to the point that some speculated that Hal might simply take the throne for himself, in the end the transition was smooth.

In that accomplishment alone, Henry remains an impressive if somewhat tragic monarch. He took the throne unscrupulously, and he had to defend it more ruthlessly than he clearly would have preferred. Whether or not he ordered the death of Richard, it weighed on him, as did, in all likelihood, the execution of Archbishop Scrope. He died tormented, physically and psychologically; the two may well have been linked. But he passed on to his heir a unified kingdom with a stable regime. His son, Prince Hal, had already fulfilled a long and rigorous apprenticeship, leading campaigns in Wales and serving on Henry's privy council. He would bring that training, along with his native seriousness and confidence, to his own short but storied reign.

1396	1397	1398	1399	1400
The Crusade of Nicopolis advances along the Danube, pillaging and killing under the leadership of the Hungarian king Sigismund who is supported by both the Roman and the Avignon popes.	Richard II exiles Henry Bolingbroke and Thomas Mowbray. In Florence, the Medici bank is founded. Florence will become the financial center of Europe.	Tamerlaine invades northern India, sacking Delhi and massacring an estimated 500,000 Hindus.	Richard II abdicates and is succeeded by Bolingbroke as Henry IV.	Richard II dies of starvation in Pontefract Castle.

HENRY V ✠ Conqueror of France

House Lancaster
Born September 16, 1386
Died August 31, 1422
Reigned 1413–1422
Consort Catherine of Valois
Children Henry VI
Successor Henry VI

Henry V has gone down in history as perhaps the most successful and inspiring of England's warrior kings. Though he died young, he accomplished much in his short reign, and was clearly a man of extraordinary ability and commitment. We can only speculate as to what sort of king he might have proved—and how different English history might be—had he lived to reign in peacetime, until his heir came of age.

Prince Hal, as young Henry was known during his father's reign, came of age early. Born while his father, as one of the five famous Lords Appellant, had risen in dissent against Richard II, he was raised from the start in politically uncertain circumstances. Hal became known as a bright, active, gracious child, and even made an impression at the age of ten, appearing at a tournament on horseback with a sword. He accompanied King Richard on campaign in Ireland, where the two apparently forged something of a bond. Hal also received an impressive education, becoming a lifelong reader and collector of books as well as a competent musician.

Prince Henry depicted receiving a copy of Thomas Hoccleve's Regement of Princes from the author. As beautiful as this image is, it is also consistent with Henry's disciplined, upright temperament.

THE APPRENTICE KING

But Hal's father became Henry IV, an embattled king, and while barely into his teens the young prince would enter combat himself. At only 16, Hal fought at the Battle of Shrewsbury, where he was permanently scarred by an arrow to the face. Afterward, he led the campaign in Wales against Owen Glendower. With precocious insight, Hal combined military offensives with economic blockades, cutting off supplies of weapons and other necessities to Glendower's supporters. It helped that Glendower, beguiled by fantasies of greater conquests, overextended himself, leaving Hal free to lay siege successfully to some of his strongholds.

Hal's campaigns in Wales clearly gave him a keen and even advanced tactical sense; he became expert in such principles as logistics, mobility, and effective choice and use of weapons and terrain. But by 1409 the Welsh conflict had wound down, and Hal found himself receiving an apprenticeship of a different sort: the political maneuvering that surrounded his increasingly debilitated and often disapproving father.

In the last few years of Henry IV's reign, Hal began to take an active role in government. In many cases this meant clashing with King Henry,

OUR KING WENT FORTH TO NORMANDY, / WITH GRACE AND MIGHT OF CHIVALRY; / THERE GOD FOR HIM WROUGHT MARVELLOUSLY, / WHEREFORE ENGLAND MAY CALL, AND CRY DEO GRATIAS: / DEO GRATIAS ANGLIA REDDE PRO VICTORIA

THE AGINCOURT SONG

1413
The University of St. Andrews, the oldest university in Scotland and third-oldest in Britain, is chartered by a Papal Bull.

1415
Jan Hus, the Czech religious reformer whose ideas anticipated those of the Reformation by a century, is burned at the stake.

1416
The first war between Venice and the Ottoman Empire is won by the general Loredan who defeats the Turks at the Dardanelles.

Opposite Henry V, who fit such exploits into his relatively brief reign that he remains one of Britain's most revered kings.

who was often incapacitated but insisted on retaining power. Their most serious clash involved the increasingly unstable situation in France, where King Charles VI had gone insane, and rival factions, the Burgundians and the Armagnacs, were vying for power. The king supported the Armagnacs, the prince the Burgundians. The king was cautious and conservative, the prince decisive and ambitious.

In September 1412, matters came to a head in a public confrontation between Hal and his father. Some nobles had been pressing Hal to seize the throne, and King Henry trusted no one. Appearing before his father, Hal explained his position. Then, in a curious gesture that may have been calculated political theater but may also have been the sincere expression of a serious-minded, deeply religious young man, Hal asked his father to resolve the conflict by killing him on the spot. The king, of course, refused. A few months later, he died, and young Hal became Henry V.

A story goes that, while Henry IV lay on his deathbed, at one point it seemed he had expired. Hal picked up the crown, only to have Henry stir and ask the prince by what right he held the crown, given that his father had had no right to take it in 1399. Hal is said to have replied that he would keep the crown as his father did, by force if necessary. When he was crowned Henry V on March 20, 1413, he wasted no time confirming that he would be king of all the English, and establishing himself as a capable, supremely confident ruler.

St. Anthony, the father of Christian monasticism. Henry V had a strong ascetic streak, and was said to seek out the company of hermits and other holy men.

A DYNAMIC YOUNG KING

Henry V cut an impressive figure as a young king; he was over six feet tall, lean and athletic, with a soldier's haircut and a profound seriousness of character that commanded respect. The popular image of Henry, derived partly from Shakespeare but also from older, apocryphal accounts, is that of a fun-loving, mischievous, even wayward young prince who deliberately transformed himself when the time came. One such narrative says that Hal spent the entire night before his coronation with an anchorite in Westminster Abbey, emerging a completely changed man. While he may well have visited the anchorite—Henry was a deeply religious man—the known facts of his early years do little to support the image of a carousing, mischief-making lad. More likely, he was essentially a serious and disciplined young man from the start, though able to enjoy himself as much as the next person.

ENSURING STABILITY

Once crowned, Henry immediately took a series of shrewd steps to secure his position and ensure stability in England. It was one thing to stabilize the coinage and attend conscientiously to legal proceedings; it was another altogether to heal the ruptures caused, directly or indirectly, by his father's seizure of the throne. In a potent symbolic gesture, he had Richard's body brought to Westminster Abbey and buried amid much pageantry in the tomb Richard had commissioned. By according such dignities to Richard, he not only reminded everyone that the former king was dead and buried; he also established that he was innocent of Richard's death, and felt secure enough in his own rule to set the matter publicly to rest.

Henry also extended an olive branch to his father's enemies, even restoring many of them to lands and titles that had been stripped during Henry IV's reign. Even the Percys, the powerful Northumberland family that had produced the ringleaders of multiple rebellions, were welcomed back into royal favor. Henry had martial prowess and personal gravitas, but also diplomatic skills, and his efforts largely succeeded.

Still, early in his reign he faced one conspiracy against him, and he ended it with the necessary ruthlessness. Three noblemen—Richard, Earl of Cambridge, Henry Scrope,

1417	1418	1418	1419
Pope Benedict XIII, the last Avignon pope, is deposed, ending the Western Schism.	The Portuguese begin the colonization of the Madeira Islands.	Filippo Brunelleschi wins a competition to design the dome of Florence Cathedral. The resulting dome, one of the great achievements of Renaissance architecture, leads to the cathedral simply being referred to as the Duomo, the dome.	Portuguese explorers land in the Madeira Islands in the Atlantic off North Africa.

THE GREATEST MOTIVATIONAL SPEECH EVER?

Accounts agree that, just before the Battle of Agincourt commenced, Henry gave a speech commending his troops and declaring he would sooner die with them than be taken captive and held for ransom. While we cannot be sure what he said, the speech became part of the mythology of Agincourt and of England. Given its most famous rendering in Shakespeare's Henry V, it remains the gold standard of inspiring leadership. Whether Henry would have proved so uplifting a king had he lived to settle down to the administration of a vast English-French empire is uncertain, but on the pivotal day of his reign, he rose to the occasion.

Baron of Masham, and Sir Thomas Grey—plotted to depose Henry and replace him with Edmund Mortimer, who had a legitimate ancestral claim to the throne. When their scheme was revealed to the king he had them beheaded in short order.

In another seemingly insignificant but momentous change, Henry had all government business conducted in English. It was the consummation of a linguistic and cultural flowering that had begun under Edward III and continued under Richard II: the enshrinement of English as a great language, the equal of any other and the common tongue of both rulers and ruled.

But Henry's main agenda, one he had pursued even as prince, was the conquest of France. He asserted his right to the French throne through his descent from both Henry II, ruler of the Angevin Empire, and Isabella of France, daughter of the King of France and wife of Edward II. It was a claim the French would never accept, regardless of their internal disarray under the mentally ill Charles VI. The Armagnac faction in France attempted to appease him with land, money, and the hand in marriage of Charles VI's daughter Catherine, but never enough to dissuade him from invading. Negotiations dragged on, and Henry eventually won the backing of his privy council. He embarked on a typically systematic campaign of financing and preparation, Parliament granting him the right to levy a stiff tax to fund the campaign.

A period depiction of the Battle of Agincourt. While hardly accurate, it captures the popular sense of the battle as a chivalric contest.

FROM HARFLEUR TO AGINCOURT

On August 11, 1415, Henry invaded. His force of some 12,000 men, including a corps of gunners, soon laid siege to the town of Harfleur. He was a vigorous, detail-oriented commander, constantly present to see that his orders were fulfilled to the letter, and occasionally pitching in with his own hands. In a few weeks, Harfleur capitulated, but by then Henry's army had begun to suffer from sickness. Rather than return to England having only conquered one city, and hoping to draw the French into the open, Henry decided to march his remaining troops

1419	1419	1419	1420
The doge's palace in Venice that dates to the 9th century receives a new facade that will endure for more than 550 years.	In the First Defenestration of Prague, rioting Hussites throw over a dozen members of the town council out the windows of the town hall to their deaths.	An army of knights, mercenaries, and adventurers summoned to a crusade against heretics by Pope Martin V is defeated at Prague by a small force of Bohemian peasants and laborers led by the blind veteran John Zizka.	*The Crucifixion* and *The Last Judgment* are painted by Flemish artists Jan and Hubert van Eyck.

A period image of the marriage of Henry V and Catherine of Valois in 1420. Though Henry did not live much longer, their union produced an heir.

muddy from heavy rains and flanked by woods. Though Henry's army was weary and depleted, the terrain favored the English, and Henry knew it. The French knew it as well, and for most of the morning refused to attack the English formation of longbowmen behind arrays of wooden stakes at the flanks, and knights and men at arms holding the center. Eventually, Henry decided to press the issue: he had his forces move forward, just within longbow range, and set their defenses again. Then, with a flight of arrows, the English provoked a French cavalry charge, followed by thousands of knights on foot.

A GLORIOUS VICTORY

The result was a slaughter. Henry had set his line where the forests on either side of the field forced a narrow advance, slowing the charge. The French knights' heavy plate armor protected them from some of the steel-tipped English arrows, but it also weighed the soldiers down, leaving them knee-deep in the muck. Horses struck by arrows threw their riders and caused more chaos among the French soldiers. By the time the French reached the English lines, they were exhausted, and the English men at arms, assisted by the lightly armored bowmen, had the advantage. Thousands of French knights had put themselves in the vanguard, eager to avenge earlier defeats, and they were decimated. Henry himself waded into the melee, at one point protecting his injured brother Humphrey, Duke of Gloucester.

By the time the fighting subsided, the English had taken thousands of French knights prisoner. Amid fears that the French might launch another assault with fresh forces, Henry ordered all of them killed, sparing only those who would fetch the highest ransom. It was a ruthless decision, but a tactically sound one, and it only slightly stained Henry's reputation. When all was done, the English had lost at most a few hundred men, the French several thousand, including the core of their leadership and knighthood. It was a glorious victory for the English.

to lay siege to Calais. The French mustered an army, and the two forces encountered each other on October 24 near Agincourt.

That night, the two camps kept a long vigil. Henry ordered his soldiers to remain silent, and as morning approached gave a speech in which he affirmed the justice of his cause, reminded them of their forefathers' victories over the French, and vowed to die alongside his common troops rather than allow himself to be captured and ransomed. Dawn brought a tense standoff between the armies.

Historians remain unsure about the numbers at Agincourt. Henry's army likely numbered around 8,000 men at this point; the French force, which included many more mounted knights, was at least twice as large. They met at a broad, recently plowed field,

1420	1421	1421
Florence makes vain attempts to put a 20 percent ceiling on interest rates charged by Florentine bankers.	The Portuguese prince Henry the Navigator, aged 27, assembles Europe's greatest pilots, map-makers, astronomers, scholars, and instrument makers at Sagres on the Cape St. Vincent where they will pioneer the science of navigation.	The Ottoman sultan Mohammed I dies, aged 34, after an eight-year reign in which he has consolidated the empire. He s succeeded by his 18-year-old son who will reign until 1451 as Murad II and who will extend the empire into southeastern Europe.

A TRIUMPH CUT SHORT

After Agincourt, Henry returned to England to a hero's welcome. The French played every diplomatic card they could to prevent or defer another English invasion.

When Sigismund of Luxembourg, King of Hungary, came to England to negotiate a peace in which Henry settled for less than he desired, such were Henry's diplomatic skills that, by the time Sigismund left, the two kings had exchanged knighthoods and vowed to go on crusade, and Sigismund supported Henry's claim.

In 1417, Henry invaded again, with a larger army. After two years of campaigning, he had conquered much of Normandy, successfully laid siege to Rouen, and arrived outside Paris. The French, with their leadership largely killed or captured at Agincourt and in complete disarray from intrigues, met Henry's terms. In the Treaty of Troyes, he was named heir and regent of France, and in 1420 he married Catherine, daughter of Charles VI. On their return to England, Henry and his Queen toured the realm.

But Henry had little to do with the jubilation that followed victory in France and a royal marriage. He was growing more grim and purposeful in his demeanor and his judgments, and he was afraid of supernatural threats to his life—a common enough anxiety in his time. In 1419 he requested that the English clergy collectively pray for protection from black magic. He became a frequent visitor to holy sites, and attended mass with dogged devotion. He seemed to believe that he would need extraordinary divine help to sustain his successes and secure himself.

In 1421, Henry returned to France to suppress pockets of resistance. During a long and successful siege of Meaux, northeast of Paris, he became ill, probably with dysentery. He continued campaigning as his condition worsened, even being carried on a litter at times. But he knew he was dying, and made arrangements for his infant son, the future Henry VI, to inherit the throne. As he approached death, Henry lamented that he would never take the throne of France, and that he would not have the chance to lead a crusade to the Holy Land. On August 31, 1422, he died peacefully at the Chateau de Vincennes near Paris. He was 35.

England, so recently elated at the triumphs of its young king, was plunged into grief. His funeral was magnificent, as was the chapel in which he was laid in Westminster Abbey. Once more, the fate of the nation was left to the guardians of a child king, this one still an infant, and all would hinge on how well those protectors handled the grave responsibility with which Henry had entrusted them.

In his early death, Henry avoided the long decline that darkened the later reign of Edward III. If he had lived, he might have found himself not so well equipped for the governance of so vast an empire, with a restive French population and English nobles free once more to bicker among themselves. His intense religious devotion might have led him to neglect his duties. Then again, he might have proved equal to all the challenges before him. Henry V was an extraordinary king; as is so often the case, we are left to wonder what might have been had he been given more time.

Henry's tomb effigy in Westminster Abbey. The tomb, completed in 1431, describes him as "hammer of the Gauls."

1421	1421	1421	1422
The Chinese Ming emperor Yung Lo moves his capital from Nanking to Peking as he continues to reform local government and attempts to establish trade with islands to the south.	Forence buys Livorno and establishes the Consuls of the Sea.	The North Sea engulfs more than 70 Dutch villages and more than 100,000 die as the shallow Zuider Zee spreads over thousands of square miles.	Lisbon becomes Portugal's seat of government.

HENRY VI ✠ Playething of Fate

House Lancaster

Born December 6, 1421

Died May 21, 1471

Reigned 1422–1461, 1470–1471

Consort Margaret of Anjou

Children Edward, Prince of Wales

Successor Edward IV

enry VI inherited the thrones of England and France while still an infant. It would have taken a strong-willed, politically savvy ruler to fill the shoes of his storied father, and Henry was not that man. More interested in faith and learning than in war and governance, and given to bouts of debilitating mental illness, he became little more than a pawn among the machinations that exploded into the Wars of the Roses.

Joan of Arc, the French peasant whose visionary sense of a divine calling to save France inspired fierce and often successful resistance to English rule under Henry.

Though Henry inherited the throne as an infant, he was not crowned King of England until he was almost eight, in 1429, and even then only to assert his inheritance against the claim of Charles of Valois, who as the son of Charles VII had been crowned King of France in an act of defiance some months before. Shortly after his father's death, Henry's two kingdoms had been placed under the regency of his uncle John, Duke of Bedford, who spent most of his time trying to hold English territory against the gradually resurging French. In England, Henry's other surviving uncle, Humphrey, Duke of Gloucester, served as Protector and Defender of the Realm.

It was soon clear that, whatever his virtues, the young king lacked the resolve, the ruthlessness, and perhaps even the desire to rule effectively. When given arms and armor as a child, he set them aside. He preferred quiet study and devotional exercises to the business of governance, and he so deplored bloodshed that he refused even to go hunting. In a gentler

time, amid wise counselors and selfless nobles, that meekness might not matter, but Henry was not born into such a time. His positive legacy as a king would largely consist of the education institutions he founded: Eton College, and King's College, Cambridge.

LOSING FRANCE

The main point of contention was France. Inspired by the heroics of Joan of Arc in 1429, the French had repulsed the English at Orléans and swept to a string of victories, culminating in the defiant coronation of Charles VII in Rheims. On his tenth birthday, Henry was taken to Paris and crowned King of France amid much hostility; it would be his only venture into that country. As the gains of Henry V eroded, the hunt for scapegoats began, and infighting seethed among the young king's advisors. Cardinal Henry Beaufort and William de la Pole, Duke of Suffolk, argued for a negotiated peace; Humphrey of Gloucester and the powerful Richard, Duke of York—next in line to the throne—wanted to prosecute the war further. The pious Henry sided with the former.

In 1435, the Duke of Bedford died. Two years later, Henry officially came of age, but he remained meek and compliant, committed to the peace policy of the Duke of Suffolk. For the next several years, things continued to unravel slowly in France. Infighting around Henry

KINGDOMS ARE BUT CARES, / STATE IS DEVOID OF STAY, / RICHES ARE READY SNARES, / AND HASTEN TO DECAY

HENRY VI

1430

Joan of Arc leads the successful relief of the English siege of Orléans, becoming a national symbol of French resistance of English hegemony.

1430

The Order of the Golden Fleece is founded by Duke Philip III of Burgundy to celebrate his marriage to Isabella of Portugal. It will later become the most coveted order of chivalry in Europe and still exists today.

1431

Joan of Arc is burned at the stake in the Old Market Square of Rouen on May 30.

Opposite Henry VI, who inherited the throne as an infant and proved far too unstable to manage the kingdom.

HENRICVS VI.

Richard Plantagenet, Duke of York. The most powerful nobleman in England, York despised the Dukes of Suffolk and Somerset, suspecting them of collusion with the French. He may have been right.

came to a head in 1447, when Suffolk managed to have Humphrey of Gloucester arraigned for treason; Gloucester died shortly after being imprisoned. In 1449, Richard of York was sent off to Ireland—an exile thinly disguised as an appointment. Suffolk no longer had any real rivals as Henry's chief counselor, but he also took a more warlike turn to France. Within three years, he had managed to lose nearly all of England's territories there.

Even worse, in 1445, Henry had made what may have been the worst dynastic marriage in the history of English royalty: under the guidance of Suffolk, he had wed Margaret of Anjou, of the House of Valois. The union had been devised to ensure peace, but when it was discovered that the arrangement involved England's ceding territory back to the French, Suffolk in particular became the target of general outrage. Evidence emerged of secret communications with the French, and Suffolk was imprisoned for treason. Though Henry managed to commute a certain death sentence to five years' exile, Suffolk was hunted down and killed attempting to cross the Channel.

Henry could no longer escape a general sense that he was completely ineffectual. Margaret of Anjou, however, was anything but; proud and strong-willed, she could easily overcome her husband and steer his opinions in favor of French interests. It was as if Suffolk had

managed to plant a French spy in the royal bedchamber. It did not help matters that the marriage did not prove fruitful; it would be eight years before Margaret conceived, and given Henry's ethereal character—he wore hair shirts, refused to curse, and regarded sex as dirty—speculation would persist, with good reason, that the child was not his.

Suffolk was succeeded as leader of the peace-seeking faction by Edmund Beaufort, Duke of Somerset. Somerset promptly entered into a bitter rivalry with Richard of York, who had succeeded Bedford in France, and who accused Somerset of denying him the resources to campaign with any effectiveness. In 1449, at the urging of Suffolk, Somerset had replaced York as commander of English forces in France, and proceeded to lose Rouen, Normandy, and Gascony with such shocking incompetence that York considered it treasonous. It may have been.

A DOWNWARD SPIRAL

By 1450, most of France was lost, and England, bereft of strong leadership and good governance, had suffered a breakdown in public order. Parliament and the people were outraged at the staggering mismanagement that had lost nearly all of France and bankrupted the Crown. Accusations of treason extended beyond Suffolk to other ministers, some of whom were actually killed by violent mobs. Soldiers home from France, demoralized and penniless but armed and accustomed to violence, turned to brigandage, or served as enforcers in the liveried private armies of powerful lords. French and even English soldiers had taken to piracy along the English coast.

The ambient violence first took organized form among the commoners, and most especially in a rebellion in Kent, headed by Jack Cade. Cade, who declared himself related to the Mortimer family of March Lords, issued a list of grievances against Henry and his government—chiefly against Henry's advisors—and marched on London with an army some 5,000 strong. Once there, Cade declared himself the new Lord Mayor, and he

A TIGER'S HEART

Margaret of Anjou was every bit the imperious monarch her husband was neither able nor willing to be. Whether her militant advancement of the Lancastrian cause was inspired by ambitions for her royal line or by sheer bloody-mindedness, or some combination of the two, we cannot be sure, but her ruthlessness became so legendary that Shakespeare, in his highly embroidered three-part play Henry VI, has the Duke of York call her a "tiger's heart wrapped in a woman's hide." Captured after the Battle of Tewkesbury (1471), in which her son Edward was killed, she was ransomed and returned to France, where she eventually died.

1433	1434	1434	1436	1438
The Ming Dynasty of China decides to abandon ambitions to trade with or colonize distant regions and largely disbands its large warfleet. This creates a naval power vacuum in the Indian Ocean, which will later be filled by European fleets.	Jan van Eyck completes the Arnolfini wedding portrait, a milestone in Northern Renaissance art.	African slaves introduced into Portugal by a caravel returning from the southern continent are the first of millions that will be exported in the next four centuries.	The great dome of Florence Cathedral is completed. Designed by Filippo Brunelleschi it was the largest unsupported octagonal dome in the world.	The position of Holy Roman Emperor becomes the hereditary property of the Habsburg dynasty.

and his followers began looting and killing. The Lord High Treasurer, among other ministers, was captured and beheaded. Henry fled London. But Cade was not content to demand better governance in an abstract sense; he specifically called on Henry to summon Richard of York to set the kingdom's affairs in order. Cade's rebellion subsided after the usual false promises of amnesty, and he was hunted down and killed.

Two years later, Richard of York returned from Ireland with his army and demanded his place on the Royal Council. He also demanded the arrest of Somerset, but Queen Margaret prevented Henry from acceding to that demand. For the first time, it looked as though the palace intrigues might erupt into open war. York, without sufficient backing among the nobility, backed down.

The tense rivalry between York and Somerset took a sharp turn in 1453. Word came from France that the English had lost Bordeaux; of all the gains made by Henry V, only Calais remained. On hearing the news, Henry wept. Then, as if the grim tidings were too much for him, he lost his sanity, lapsing into a nearly catatonic state in which he scarcely communicated and failed to recognize the son to whom Margaret gave birth that year. The condition lasted through 1454, and while Henry was incapacitated, York managed to have himself installed as Protector of the Realm. In this effort, he had the support of the most powerful noble in England: Richard Neville, Earl of Warwick, known to history as the Kingmaker. Apart from his vindictiveness toward the hated Somerset, York governed England with prudence and skill, but he had made implacable enemies, including Queen Margaret.

When Henry recovered his wits late in 1454, he promptly, and disastrously, restored the status quo ante, removing York and replacing him with Somerset. Then, in an uncharacteristic flurry of activity, he ordered a series of inquiries into the actions of York's supporters. York and the Nevilles promptly gathered a formidable army and marched on London. Henry and Somerset, caught out by York's audacity, hastily assembled a smaller army, and the two

Margaret of Anjou, Henry's strong-willed queen. As Henry faltered, Margaret became the leader of the Lancastrian cause, which she pursued ruthlessly.

forces met at St. Albans in Hertfordshire on May 22, 1455. The resulting fight, involving a total of perhaps 5,000 combatants, was a pale foreshadowing of the slaughter that would ensue over the next 30 years, but it was, for the moment, bloody enough. Among the dead was Somerset. Henry had come to St. Albans but then vanished, only to be found after the battle hiding in a local shop, having reportedly relapsed into insanity.

The Wars of the Roses, as they would much later come to be known, had begun. One might almost end the account of Henry's kingship here, for from this point on it effectively ceased to exist. The remainder of Henry's troubled reign, such as it was, involved his being the pawn and the prize of feuding factions: the Yorkists, led at first by Richard of York, and the Lancastrians, led for all intents and purposes by Queen Margaret.

THE PAWN KING

For the next several months, the tables had turned yet again, and Richard of York held power while Henry remained incapacitated. Tensions remained high, and Margaret in particular was determined to keep the throne for her son, Edward, Prince of Wales. When Henry once more recovered in early 1456, he yet again removed York, this time at the urging of Margaret, who would henceforth determine Henry's decisions.

One of the first of those decisions was to remove the royal court from London to Coventry, which was safer territory. The move indicated that for Margaret all other considerations, including the seething popular unrest in London and elsewhere, were at best secondary to the business of consolidating power. In 1459, rightly suspecting they were about to be accused of treason, York and Warwick refused to attend a great council in Coventry. Hunted down by Henry's forces, they fled the country, after which they were attainted: stripped of lands and titles, and exiled on pain of death.

The next year, the Nevilles, along with York's son Edward of March, invaded England, and

1439	1440	1445	1447	1448	1449
Fra Angelica completes the altarpiece of the Dominican friary of San Marco in Florence.	England's Eton School is founded by Henry VI. It will become the largest of the ancient English public schools.	The Portuguese set up their first permanent trading post in Africa, at Arguin, in what is now Mauritania.	The Spanish Inquisition is founded as a separate organization.	King Christopher of Denmark, Norway, and Sweden dies without an heir, after which the three countries separate.	The French capture Rouen from the English, continuing a process of French successes in a grinding war of sieges and attrition that will end with the English being driven from France.

defeated the royal forces at Northampton, once more capturing Henry, who had again lapsed into madness. After some negotiation, the Act of Accord disinherited Henry's son Edward and established York as both heir to the throne and Lord Protector. Once more, Henry was little more than a game piece held by the winning player. But Margaret, outraged at the disinheritance of her son, rallied the Lancastrian forces.

A later rendering of the Battle of Towton (1461), a bloody affair in which Edward IV led the Yorkists to a devastating victory.

York, anxious to put down Lancastrian resistance once and for all, led his forces into Yorkshire in late 1460. At the Battle of Wakefield, an ill-advised assault, he and his son Edmund, Earl of Rutland were killed. Margaret had their heads placed on the gates of York. Then her forces marched south, and defeated the Yorkists in a second battle at St. Albans. After the fighting, Henry was found sitting under a tree. Once more, Henry had changed owners, and the Lancastrians now held sway.

But Margaret and the Lancastrians had overplayed their hand. On their march to St. Albans, and from there to London, they looted the countryside, stirring up such intense anti-Lancastrian sentiment that London refused them entry. And in Edward of March, now the champion of the Yorkist cause, they had gained a formidable enemy. Tall and strong, and a capable military leader, Edward had both a kingly bearing and rightful claim to the throne through the Act of Accord. To general acclaim in London, he was hastily crowned Edward IV.

England now had rival kings, and it was agreed that the issue would be decided on the field of battle. The armies met at Towton in Yorkshire, in March 1461. In the midst of a snowstorm, they conducted the singly bloodiest battle ever to take place on English soil. As many as 20,000 men may have died in the furious fighting. Henry remained with Margaret in York; in stark contrast, the 18-year-old Edward led his troops. In the end, the Yorkists routed the Lancastrians, killing most of their leaders, and Henry and Margaret were forced to flee the country. Henry languished in Scotland, while Margaret went with their son to France.

In 1465, Henry was captured, and imprisoned under degrading conditions in the Tower of London. Edward IV reigned for another four years while Henry, doubtless absorbed in either madness or prayer, lived out a meager existence as a captive. But suddenly, in 1470, he was liberated and hailed as king again. Warwick had turned on Edward and overthrown him; once more Henry was a puppet king. The brief return to the throne lasted only six months, until Edward IV returned, defeated and killed Warwick and Henry's young heir Edward, and locked Henry away once more. On May 21, 1571, Henry was quietly killed, surely on orders of Edward.

SAINTED IN MEMORY

Henry's murder was a sad and brutal end. From the start, he had been far better equipped for a monastic life than a kingship, and his madness—possibly inherited from his grandfather, Charles VI of France—left him completely victim to the intrigues of those around him, including his queen.

After his death, Henry became an object of veneration, an icon of saintliness and purity to the many in England, especially commoners, disenchanted with the amoral intrigues that had so blighted his reign. His grave became a place of pilgrimage, and some visitors, predictably, reported miracles there. It is probably how the meek and troubled Henry would have preferred to be remembered. To this day, each May 21, flowers are delivered to the Tower of London from Eton College and King's College, Cambridge, in memory of their pious, generous founder.

1450

Francesco Sforza is handed control of Milan. It is the beginning of one of Italy's great Renaissance dynasties.

1454

The Gutenberg Bible, the first European text printed with movable type, becomes available for the first time.

The interior of King's College Chapel, Cambridge. The pious Henry's bequest made possible this magnificent church, with some of the most refined and intricate Gothic architecture in England, including the world's largest fan vault.

EDWARD IV ✣ Pinnacle of the House of York

House York

Born April 28, 1442

Died April 9, 1483

Reigned 1461–1470, 1471–1483

Consort Elizabeth Woodville

Children More than ten, including Edward V, Richard, Duke of York, and Elizabeth of York

Successor Edward V

Elizabeth Woodville, Edward's queen and a quietly pivotal figure in English history. She would be instrumental in the downfalls of the Earl of Warwick and, eventually, Richard III.

A cursory look at English royal history might lead one to believe that Edward IV was just another player in the Wars of the Roses, a pawn like his predecessor, Henry VI, or a power broker who had his brief period of supremacy. But Edward IV was much more than that. Altogether, he ruled for more than 20 years, and over the course of his two reigns he emerged as a strong, skilled, and sagacious king.

Edward, the second son of Richard, Duke of York, was born in Rouen in 1442, during the already unsteady reign of the hapless Henry VI. Edward's father was at the center of the conflicts that spiraled into the Wars of the Roses; especially, the enmity between York and the Dukes of Suffolk and then Somerset, both of whom disastrously mismanaged English efforts to keep the lands conquered in France by Henry V, proved the spark that ignited the war.

Edward came of age in a highly cultured but also tense, politically and even physically dangerous environment; he not only watched the intrigues and periodic bloodlettings of the early Wars of the Roses, but also spent some of his formative years fulfilling his duties as Earl of March in Wales, where order largely had to be maintained by military force. He grew into a very tall, charismatic young man with light brown hair and winsome if perhaps a bit broad manners, and was known to have a taste for drink and an eye for women.

DOING BATTLE

In 1459, at the age of 17, Edward became a trusted lieutenant of his father in the struggle against the Lancastrian faction led by Queen Margaret. The following year, while he was gathering forces in Wales, his father and younger brother the Earl of Rutland were killed at the Battle of Wakefield. Suddenly, at the age of 18, Edward was Duke of York, the leader of the Yorkist cause, with a strong claim of his own to the throne of England.

A few weeks after Wakefield, Edward was faced with the task of cutting off a Welsh Lancastrian force led by Owen Tudor, second husband of Catherine, Henry V's widow. With the decisiveness that would prove his hallmark as a commander, Edward marched his army to Mortimer's Cross to await the foe. On the morning of the battle, a perihelion, or "sun dog"—the appearance of two extra suns due to reflections in atmospheric ice crystals—made his troops uneasy. Edward, declaring that the three suns were a sign of the Trinity and therefore of divine favor, rallied his men's spirits for combat. In the ensuing fight, his forces mostly held firm against a Lancastrian assault. Edward held the center of his line, and when the Lancastrian forces finally broke he pursued them hotly. Owen Tudor was captured and executed.

The Battle of Mortimer's Cross signaled that, in Edward, the Yorkists now had a leader who was also a skilled tactician and formidable soldier,

WORDS FAIL ME TO RELATE HOW WELL THE COMMONS LOVE AND ADORE HIM, AS IF HE WERE THEIR GOD

AN ANONYMOUS MILANESE REPRESENTATIVE AT EDWARD'S COURT, IN A LETTER IN THE SFORZA ARCHIVES

	1462	1463	1466	1466
Opposite Edward IV, whose two reigns might have led to a dynasty for the House of York had he not died while his sons were too young to defend themselves.	Cosimo de'Medici, one of the great patrons of the Italian Renaissance, founds a Platonic Academy in Florence.	Bosnia and Herzegovina in the Balkans come under the rule of Sultan Mehmet II of the Ottoman Turks.	The Incas of South America conquer the extensive Chimu State, adding a large area of fertile coastal lands to their empire.	The Kingdom of Georgia, which has been in long-term decline since the Mongol Wars, finally collapses and fragments into a number of petty states.

A fourpence, or groat, from the reign of Edward IV. He was immensely popular among commoners as well as Yorkists.

even at the age of 18. In the spring of 1461, with the support of his powerful cousin Richard Neville, Earl of Warwick, he entered London and, on March 4, was crowned King Edward IV. He was now one of two rival kings, and England would not be big enough for both of them.

The bulk of the Lancastrian forces remained in Yorkshire and had yet to be confronted. It was agreed that the two armies would meet to decide the kingship by combat. In late March, in a blinding snowstorm by the village of Towton in Yorkshire, the two armies clashed. Both sides had issued the order to give no quarter, and the result was the single bloodiest day of fighting ever on English soil. At first, the

Lancastrians held firm on their well-chosen ground, but the wind was behind the Yorkists, and as the snow fell they showered arrows on their enemies from a safe distance until the Lancastrians had had enough and advanced. So began several hours of brutal close combat, in which the Lancastrians, who outnumbered the Yorkists, began driving them back. Edward himself waded to the front to steady the Yorkist left flank. Eventually, Yorkist reinforcements arrived under the leadership of the Duke of Norfolk, and the tide turned. The Lancastrians broke, and were cut down as they fled. Most of the Lancastrian leaders—apart from King Henry, who had remained in York—were killed, and the total number of casualties may have exceeded 20,000. At the day's end, Henry and Margaret would have to flee into exile, and Edward IV was master of England.

A CLASH WITH THE KINGMAKER

Edward's official coronation in June 1461 was greeted by commoners as the start of a new age of order and justice. Unlike his weak and mentally unstable predecessor, Edward looked every inch a young king, and his combination of soldierly credentials, learning, and gracious manners—he soon could greet nearly everyone at court by name—suggested that England might have a ruler to measure against the revered Henry V. But things would not be so simple. The young Edward was not immune to mistakes, and his chief supporter, the Earl of Warwick, who had earned his subsequent nickname of Kingmaker, clearly expected to exercise considerable influence on governance. Having been rewarded by Edward with the Earldom of Northumberland, he immediately embarked on ambitious plans for his royal protégé.

Edward may have been already an accomplished soldier and courtier, but he was also, at least by reputation, a womanizer, and one seeming escapade precipitated a disastrous falling out with Warwick. Warwick and Edward had already disagreed about the diplomatic course to pursue on the continent: Warwick

EDWARD IV: BOOK COLLECTOR

Among Edward's many pursuits were commissioning and collecting fine manuscript books. By the time of his reign, the art of manuscript illumination had become extraordinarily refined, so that many of the books in his library were sumptuous works of visual art. He also enjoyed reading history, especially lives of great rulers. Of Edward's collection, some 50 volumes were passed on; they became the foundation of the "Old Royal Library," which would be donated to the British Museum by King George II in 1757. Significantly, Edward took interest in the printing press, and sponsored William Caxton's first efforts in England.

1467	1468	1469	1469
Charles the Bold (to his friends) or Charles the Terrible (to his enemies) becomes Duke of Burgundy and launches a bid to make his wealthy domains independent of France.	Orkney transfers from Norway to Scotland as the dowry of Princess Margaret who marries King James III of Scotland.	Thomas Malory completes his *Morte d'Arthur*, providing England with a popular and influential reworking of the tales of Arthur and the Round Table.	The expanding Songhai Empire of West Africa annexes the rich trading city of Timbuktu.

Richard Neville, 16th Earl of Warwick. Known as the Kingmaker, the powerful Earl of Warwick both helped Edward IV to the throne and then, after their falling out, removed him. After Warwick's death at the Battle of Barnet (1471), Edward ruled unopposed.

who had died fighting in the Lancastrian cause at the second battle of St. Albans. In short, she was everything Warwick scorned. The revelation that Edward had wed her both deeply humiliated Warwick—he had some explaining to do in France—and offended him; it seemed a shockingly ungrateful act from the king Warwick had essentially placed on the throne.

Certainly, Edward's marriage was a poor decision for a monarch. It offered no advantage to his family or to England, and it even earned censure from the Privy Council as unbecoming a king. But though the marriage may have come as a surprise, Edward's appetite for women was no secret, and it was rumored that he had lured a number of noblewomen into bed with promises of matrimony. Criticisms aside, the marriage proved successful: Edward and Elizabeth had ten children and remained together until his death, though Elizabeth had to put up with his incessant collection of mistresses.

Warwick might have been willing to make his peace with Edward's marriage and the embarrassment that came with it, but he found himself unable to stomach the ensuing advent of Woodvilles through more marriages, titles, and posts at court. Not only did their ascendancy, especially that of Elizabeth's brother Anthony, the second Earl Rivers, begin to erode Warwick's influence; surely Warwick regarded them as parvenus, upstarts, unworthy of the attention Edward gave them. Then, in 1468, Edward had his sister Margaret marry Charles the Bold, Duke of Burgundy; it was clear that he and Warwick had utterly irreconcilable visions of English policy. It may well be that Edward was consciously asserting his own independence from his sponsor.

But Edward probably did not anticipate that Warwick would respond by attempting to remove him as king. Warwick recruited to his cause Edward's flighty and similarly disaffected brother George, Duke of Clarence, whom Edward had forbid to marry Warwick's daughter. The two assembled an army and marched to "support" some rebels in the North. Edward was caught out, and decided to await reinforcements in

favored forging an alliance with France, but Edward preferred an alignment with France's longtime enemy, Burgundy. Dismissing the king's opinion, Warwick had begun negotiating for Edward to make a dynastic marriage with a French princess. In 1464, just when the effort was showing signs of coming to fruition, Edward informed Warwick that he had already been married, secretly, for months.

Edward's hitherto secret bride was Elizabeth Woodville, daughter of Sir Richard Woodville. Though she was considered one of the most beautiful women in England, she was a commoner. Even worse, she was the widow of Sir John Grey,

---

1470

The second phase of the Wars of the Roses in England breaks out when the earl of Warwick rebels against King Edward IV, only to be killed along with most Lancastrian lords in 1471.

1472

Portuguese explorer João Vaz Corte-Real discovers the island of Bacalao in the Atlantic. His description is so vague that later mariners were unable to find it again. It is now thought he may have reached Newfoundland.

1473

Aztec ruler Axayacatl conquers the city of Tlatelolco, converting what had been a tribal alliance into an Aztec autocracy and starting the rise of the Aztec Empire.

Nottingham. In July 1469, near Edgecote Moor in Oxfordshire, Edward's reinforcements encountered both the rebels and Warwick's army, and were defeated. Edward was captured, and Warwick undertook to rule in his name.

It was a transparent power grab by Warwick, and the nobles had none of it. He was soon forced to release Edward, who, with surprising generosity, forgave Warwick and Clarence. He would soon have cause to regret his forbearance, as they rebelled again the following year. This time, they were smartly defeated and fled into exile.

Warwick, desperate to regain power, then did the unthinkable and formed a tenuous alliance with his enemy Margaret of Anjou. Assured of support from France, their combined force invaded in 1470. Edward, his support stripped by some key defections, was forced to flee. So began the so-called Readeption of Henry VI, who was abruptly extracted from his imprisonment in the Tower and set back on the throne to serve as a more tractable puppet for Warwick.

RETURN TO POWER

In defecting to the Lancastrian cause and gaining French support for an invasion of England, Warwick was taking on a calculated risk: the entry of powerful Burgundy on the side of Edward. And it was to Burgundy that Edward fled. At first, he

found only lukewarm support, but when France, along with Warwick, declared war on Burgundy, Charles the Bold gave Edward the army he had been seeking. On his return to England, he and his small force got a skeptical reception at first; the rightful if unsteady king, Henry VI, was back on the throne. Edward at first claimed, like Henry IV before him, that he aimed only to recover his dukedom, but as he marched south he began to gather more support. Clarence, evidently deciding he had not fared so well under the new regime, threw his weight behind his sibling, and Edward's youngest brother, Richard of Gloucester, proved a stout lieutenant.

On April 14, 1471, Edward's relatively modest army met Warwick's much larger force at Barnet, north of London. During the night, Edward quietly crept his forces forward; then he launched his attack early in the morning, in a thick fog. At first, the battle was even, but then confusion set in, and when some of the Lancastrian forces mistakenly attacked their own side, cries of treason went up, and the Lancastrian line collapsed. In the rout, Edward sent troops to hunt down and capture Warwick, but he was dead when they found him, cut down while trying to get to his horse.

Warwick's defeat and death left a massive void at the helm of the Lancastrian cause, but Margaret of Anjou, Henry VI's queen, attempted

A magnificent stained-glass depiction of Edward IV and his family in Canterbury Cathedral. It shows every promise of a thriving royal line. The promise ultimately proved deceptive.

to link up with Welsh forces and make another play for London. Edward pursued, and at Tewkesbury delivered a crushing victory in which many remaining Lancastrian leaders, and more importantly the young prince Edward, son of Henry VI, were killed. On May 21, 1471, Henry VI was killed in the Tower at Edward's command. The Lancastrian cause was effectively over. Edward would rule unopposed for the next 12 years.

A KING OF SUBSTANCE

Edward had proved himself to be a superb military leader—he never lost an engagement—but it remained to be seen how successful a king he could be once stability was restored. To England's surprise, he turned out to be as capable an administrator as he was a general. His royal motto, modus et ordo (method and order), aptly described his effective, streamlined style of management. He also selected officials and advisors wisely, including the former Lancastrian John Fortescue, who helped Edward redefine power relations between himself and the "over-mighty" nobles by making the king the wealthiest person in England.

Though Edward's natural charisma helped, nothing made him more popular as King of England than his extraordinarily effective management of the royal finances. In effect, he turned the monarchy into an investment firm, garnering such returns that the Crown became self-supporting, requiring no taxation. He dreamed of conquering France, but he was a realist, and when his allies failed to provide enough resources during a tentative invasion, he settled for a cash payoff from the French—a decision that disappointed his brothers but was surely wise for England.

And it was one of his brothers who proved the only remaining problem for Edward. Clarence, always restive, eventually began to scheme against Edward, and in 1478 the king had him imprisoned for treason and killed. The story goes that Clarence was drowned in a butt of Malmsey.

As the years went on and England prospered,

A posthumous portrait of Edward IV. Though flattering, it shows signs of the way in which his prodigious appetites took a toll on his health in his later years.

Edward also became a patron of culture. He actively supported William Caxton's invention and popularization of the printing press, and both commissioned and collected fine manuscripts. He also lavished money on his court, which was one of the most magnificent in Europe.

But Edward never outgrew his youthful appetites. Though his marriage to Elizabeth Woodville seems to have been happy, he continued to collect mistresses from all walks of life, his favorite being a commoner named Jane Shore. Over time, that outsize living began to catch up with him.

In 1483, he became deathly ill, perhaps from pneumonia. On his deathbed, he settled his affairs and urged his family and counselors to settle their differences in support of his young son, who would become Edward V. When he died, England mourned. Edward had been far from saintly, but he had been a gracious, brave, shrewd, and effective monarch. Had he curbed his appetites and lived longer, he might have become one of England's greatest kings.

1478	1480	1482	1482
Giuliano de' Medici is murdered by conspirators while at Mass in Florence Cathedral. His brother Lorenzo, known as il Magnifico (the Magnificent), is left sole de facto ruler of Florence.	Ottoman forces besiege the Neapolitan city of Otranto, where they allegedly behead over 800 Christians for refusing to convert to Islam.	Ivan III declares that Russia is independent of the Mongol Empire and refuses to pay the usual tribute.	The Ottoman Turks take over Herzegovina in the Balkans and convert most of the region's inhabitants to Islam.

EDWARD V ✠ Prince in the Tower

House York

Born November 2, 1470

Died 1483?

Reigned April 9, 1483–
June 26, 1483

Consort None

Children None

Successor Richard III

John Everett Millais' painting 'The Princes in the Tower' remains an iconic image of innocence destroyed by palace intrigue.

dward V, son of Edward IV, became king at only 12 years old, and his reign, such as it was, lasted less than three months. Imprisoned with his younger brother in the Tower of London, he was deposed by Parliament at the behest of his uncle, Richard III, and disappeared soon afterward.

Edward was born in the midst of the Wars of the Roses, but most of his short life was spent under the peace and prosperity of his father's later reign. Edward IV attended carefully to the upbringing of his son, who was raised mostly at Ludlow Castle in Wales, under the guardianship of his maternal uncle Anthony Woodville, Earl Rivers, a highly educated man who ensured that Edward's preparation for kingship was sound.

VICTIM OF INTRIGUE

When Edward IV died suddenly in 1483, young Edward was proclaimed king. Richard of Gloucester, Edward IV's brave and loyal youngest brother, had been named regent.

Like many other nobles, Richard hated the Woodvilles, whom he regarded as grasping, unscrupulous upstarts. On the journey into London, Edward's party, which included Earl Rivers, was met by Richard along the way. In short order, Earl Rivers was arrested, and Richard took control of young Edward.

From this point on, the young king became a pawn in the family power struggle. At some point, Richard decided to take the throne for himself and Edward was escorted to the royal residence in the Tower of London, later joined by his younger brother, and his coronation was postponed. At the same time, Richard, who had been confirmed as Lord Protector, either discovered or fabricated a conspiracy against him, and sent to execution Earl Rivers and a number of other Woodville partisans.

In June, a sermon was delivered in London asserting that Edward IV had been subject to a marriage contract with another woman when he married Elizabeth Woodville, voiding the marriage and making Edward and his brother illegitimate. Shortly after, Parliament declared the Lord Protector King Richard III and Edward's fate was sealed. Though he and his brother were seen within the Tower a couple of times afterward, by July's end they had vanished.

The most obvious conclusion was that they had been murdered at Richard's behest. The charge has stuck, not only because the children's continued existence posed a potential threat to Richard, but also because, years later, James Tyrell, a knight in Richard's service, reportedly admitted to having smothered the princes with pillows, though he confessed under torture and could not attest to the location of the bodies. Another prime suspect is King Richard's erstwhile ally the Duke of Buckingham, who was executed in October 1483.

Some maintain that the princes were not killed but were spirited out of the country. However, given the ruthlessness of the times and of Richard, that is unlikely. In 1674, workmen discovered the skeletons of two children buried just by the Tower and reinterred them under a staircase. Though the bones indicate children of the right ages, no positive identification has been made. Other resting places have been suggested, but, for now at least, the mystery of Edward V, shortest-lived of England's monarchs, remains unsolved.

1483

The Sistine Chapel opens in Rome. Gradually adorned with magnificent art, most famously the frescoes of Michelangelo, it will eventually become one of the most visited sacred sites in the world.

1483

The Dominican monk Tomas de Torquemada becomes the first Grand Inquisitor of the Spanish Inquisition.

Opposite Edward V quickly earned a reputation as a bright, thoughtful, gracious boy who showed all the promise his father hoped for.

RICHARD III: ✚ Villain or Man of His Time?

House York

Born October 2, 1452

Died August 22, 1485;

Reigned 1483–1485

Consort Anne Neville

Children Edward
of Middleham, two
illegitimate children

Successor Henry VII

Richard III is easily the most vilified king in English history, largely because of the image drawn of him by Tudor historians, who had a vested interest in his being as awful as possible. But what sort of king, and man, was he really, in the context of his troubled times? In his brief reign, he managed to demonstrate a real capacity for governance, but he also demonstrated extraordinary ruthlessness in his own cause.

According to some of the most outrageous stories vilifying Richard, he was born after a two-year pregnancy, hideously deformed, with his hair and teeth already grown. In reality, he was the product of a difficult birth, but otherwise he was a healthy, strong child, and his only deformity was a severe case of scoliosis that developed in adolescence and left him with one shoulder somewhat higher than the other.

None of this was a major factor in his early life. As the youngest son of Richard, Duke of York, young Richard was born in 1452 into the intrigues of the Wars of the Roses, and grew up moving among castles and great houses. Only eight years old when his father and older brother Edmund were killed in the Battle of Wakefield, he became a ward of no less a personage than Richard Neville, Earl of Warwick, who would come to be known as the Kingmaker. At Warwick's castle in Middleham, Yorkshire, he underwent his aristocratic apprenticeship in the arts of war and diplomacy, and met his eventual wife Anne Neville, Warwick's daughter.

His oldest brother Edward IV's struggle for the throne brought Richard into the thick of combat at an early age. At 17, he was trusted with his own command; at 18, at the battles of Barnet and Tewkesbury, he led it with devastating effectiveness. Like Edward, he was a bold and skillful military commander, perfectly

willing to wade into the thick of combat. At no time did his loyalty to his brother waver, and Edward seems to have regarded Richard as his most redoubtable lieutenant. Accordingly, the rewards heaped up, culminating in Richard being named not only Lord Constable and Lord High Admiral of England, but also Lord President of Edward's Council of the North.

Richard spent most of his time during Edward's reign in the north, which he ruled like a king; his seat at Warwick's former castle of Middleham was a kind of second royal court—fitting enough for a prince wealthier and more powerful than any Englishman but his king. It may be that Richard's business there kept him from London, but it is also clear that there was no love lost between him and the Woodvilles, Edward's in-laws, whom Richard, like Warwick and many others, regarded as grasping and unscrupulous. Richard may also have disliked the more hedonistic excesses of Edward's court, for he himself was very self-contained

MORE DOUBTING THAN TRUSTING IN HIS OWN CAUSE WHENCE HE HAD A MISERABLE LIFE "

FROM A HANDWRITTEN PASSAGE IN RICHARD'S BOOK OF HOURS

Anne Neville, Richard's wife. When she died in 1485, shortly after the loss of their son, Richard was evidently grief-stricken, but that did not stop rumors from circulating that he had poisoned her.

1483	1483	1483	
The General Council of the Inquisition is established in Spain. It will lead to the Expulsion of the Jews in 1492.	France's Louis XI dies, aged 60, after a 22-year reign in which the nation's prosperity has revived despite repressive taxes. He is succeeded by his 13-year-old son, who will reign until 1498 as Charles VIII.	Italian artist Sandro Botticelli paints *The Magnificat*.	Richard III, who served his brother Edward IV loyally but then swiftly seized the throne from Edward's rightful heir, only to die defending it shortly afterward.

and disciplined, and developed a reputation for upstanding conduct. In fact, his governance of the north seems to have been altogether effective and fair, and he enjoyed enormous popularity there. As the guardian of the northern borders, he even took an army into Scotland at one point, capturing the city of Berwick and making it a permanent part of England.

A PATH TO THE THRONE

It came as no surprise—except perhaps to the Woodvilles—that when, in 1483, Edward found himself on an untimely deathbed, he asked his counselors and relations to set aside their differences in support of 12-year-old Edward, Prince of Wales, soon to be Edward V. Once Richard was appointed Lord Protector, or regent, however, any faint hope of reconciliation died. It was at this crucial juncture—a child king, relations contending for control, the powerful regent poised against other ambitious family members, oceans of mutual disdain and suspicion—that Richard's life took a fateful turn.

Much has been written about Richard's character. We cannot be sure what drove his decisions over the next few months. But there were perhaps signs of darker undercurrents in his personality. Two famous portraits, one likely a copy, rather unusually show him fiddling with a ring on one finger. He may be putting it on or taking it off, but he was also reported to have a nervous habit of partially drawing and inserting a dagger in its scabbard. Both images suggest a certain anxiety, or impatience, or barely repressed urge to action. Richard may have been a very tightly wound man. In any case, his steadfast loyalty did not, in the end, extend past his brother.

ROYAL POWER STRUGGLE

Edward IV died on April 9, 1483. His queen Elizabeth Woodville immediately sent for

A contemporary image of Richard III and family. It suggests a happiness they could scarcely have had time to share before a series of disasters struck.

1484	1484	1484	1484
Pope Sixtus IV dies on August 12 after a 13-year papacy marked by nepotism and political intrigue.	Venice acquire Rovigo and reaches the height of its mainland expansion. Venetian territory will remain essentially unchanged for 300 years, but the city's wealth and influence will soon begin to decline.	Pope Innocent VIII issues a bull against witchcraft.	Christopher Columbus asks Portugal's Joao II to back him in a westward voyage to the Indies, but his request is rejected.

Edward V, who died in the Tower after being confined there on Richard's orders. The extent of Richard's responsibility for his fate remains unclear.

young Edward V, who set out from Wales with a retinue of some 2,000 men, accompanied by Earl Rivers. There was apparently a flurry of maneuvering; the Woodvilles secured the royal treasury and took command of the Tower of London, while Richard sent word to his allies and traveled quickly south from Yorkshire.

Richard met up with the young king's traveling party at Stony Stratford in Buckinghamshire. Henry Stafford, the Duke of Buckingham, joined them as well. Buckingham was married to a Woodville, but he shared Richard's contempt for the family, and was more than happy to ensure that Richard and not the Woodvilles gained control of the young monarch. The two of them had a cordial dinner with Rivers—and then arrested him and had him whisked off to Pontefract Castle in Yorkshire. Richard then escorted the unsuspecting Edward to the royal residence in the Tower of London.

Richard had anticipated and outmaneuvered the Woodvilles. He was in London, and the young king was completely under his control. On June 10, Richard's own troops arrived in force. Elizabeth Woodville, who had sought sanctuary in Westminster Abbey with her other children, was compelled to deliver her younger son, Richard, to the Tower as well. Richard was confirmed as Lord Protector, and Edward's coronation, originally scheduled for May, was postponed.

On June 13, Richard convened a meeting of the royal council and declared that the Woodvilles had engaged in a conspiracy against his life. Among those charged were his ally William, Lord Hastings, and Edward IV's mistress Jane Shore. It was a purge. Hastings

and Earl Rivers were executed, and others fled or were arrested.

The problem of legitimate succession remained. But Richard had a trump card, one that his brother Clarence had once attempted to play. Richard knew better than to play it himself; he had allies in the Church do it. On June 22, a sermon was preached in London asserting that, when he married Elizabeth Woodville, King Edward IV was already contracted in marriage to another woman. If that were the case, then his marriage to Elizabeth Woodville was void and their children illegitimate. Three days later, Parliament concurred, and on June 26, Richard became King Richard III.

In a dazzling display of power politics and sheer ruthlessness, Richard had scattered or killed his enemies, seized control of other claimants to the throne, and had himself crowned King of England, all in less than three months. When, later that year, the Duke of Buckingham attempted to marshal a rebellion against his former ally, he was hunted down and killed.

RICHARD AS KING

The popular perception of Richard focuses on his seizure of the crown and his final campaign; it neglects the two years he spent ruling England. In his role as Lord President of the Northern Council, he had functioned as a kind of deputy king, and in that capacity he had not only won widespread acclaim but learned how he believed the business of governance should be conducted. He was comfortable in a leadership role, and in the early part of his reign held a splendid court. If he lacked the easy charisma of his brother Edward IV, he still knew how to conduct himself as king.

Richard may have arrived on the throne by evidently ruthless and unscrupulous means, but as a king he demonstrated above all a belief in fairness, and in his pursuit of that ideal he became, at least for a while, the champion of the commonfolk. Within months of taking the throne, he established the Court of Requests,

1484	1484	1484	1484
Portuguese explorer Diego Cano discovers the mouth of Africa's Congo River.	Dutch painter Hieronymus Bosch paints his masterpiece, *The Garden of Earthly Delights*.	Kyoto's Silver Pavilion is completed fro Japan's eighth Ashikaga shogun Yoshimasa near the Gold Pavilion completed in 1397.	The tea ceremony has been introduced by Japan's Yoshimasa. It will remain for centuries as a cherished part of Japanese culture.

in which anyone who had a grievance but could not afford legal representation could get a fair hearing. Shortly after that, he wrote into law the principle of bail, so that at least some suspected criminals could remain free until tried and convicted. He also lifted all restrictions on what could and could not be printed, and had the law codes translated from French into English. If the domestic measures he took serve as any indication, Richard was a conscientious and principled king.

But things went wrong. In April 1484, his only son Edward died at the age of eight. Within a year, his wife Anne died of consumption. Richard was stricken with grief, and only more so when rumors circulated that he had actually poisoned Anne, who could have no more children, so that he could produce an heir with a second wife. He did appear to consider marrying his niece, Elizabeth of York, but the time never arrived when he might pursue that question.

Elizabeth Woodville, Queen Consort of Edward IV and mother of the Princes in the Tower. She conspired with Lady Margaret Beaufort to bring down Richard III.

THE PRINCES IN THE TOWER

The rumors about the death of his wife Anne reflected the poisoned political atmosphere during the Wars of the Roses. It was largely a conflict among the nobility, and rumor and innuendo could have devastating effect within that culture, at once rarefied and violent. As opposition to Richard galvanized, he found himself unable to escape the most damning rumor of all: that he had ordered the deaths of Edward and Richard, the so-called Princes in the Tower.

And the rumor was very likely true. Once the princes had entered the Tower under Richard's "protection," they never again emerged. For a while, they were glimpsed within its precincts, sometimes even playing, but after July 1483, they vanished. When rumors began to circulate that Richard had ordered them killed, he proved unwilling—or, more likely, unable—to produce the boys and prove they were alive. Years later, during the reign of Henry VII, James Tyrell, a knight in Richard's service, confessed under torture that he had smothered the princes on Richard's orders and buried them near a staircase in the Tower grounds. In 1674, workmen there would dig up a box containing the bones of two children, of the approximate ages of the boys. There has, however, been no positive identification of those partial remains.

Rival theories abound, including ones that charge the Duke of Buckingham or even Henry VII with the murders, or go so far as to suggest that Richard quietly had the boys smuggled into exile, but by far the most likely scenario is that Richard had the princes killed. In doing so, he was being scarcely more ruthless than his brother Edward, who, to ensure his own security on the throne, had ordered the murder in the Tower of the pious, hapless Henry VI.

THE FINAL STRUGGLE

Once Richard had scattered the Woodvilles and eliminated other claimants to the throne, only one real rival remained: Henry Tudor, who could claim descent from Edward III's son John of Gaunt. Richard knew that Tudor was the focus of the schemes against him. In 1484, he nearly succeeded in having his rival captured in Brittany and sent back to England, but Tudor was on his guard and escaped Richard's grasp. In late 1483, an agreement had been quietly reached between two former enemies who now shared a common grief: Elizabeth Woodville and Margaret Beaufort, the mother of Henry Tudor. Henry would marry Elizabeth's daughter, Elizabeth of York. Such was their hatred of Richard that they would look past their years of enmity as Lancastrians and Yorkists.

1484	1484	1484
William Caxton prints his English translation of *Aesop's Fables*, credited to Aesop, a slave and story-teller believed to have lived in Ancient Greece between 620 and 560 BC.	Hungary's Matthias Corvinus expels the Holy Roman Emperor Frederick III from Vienna and Frederick becomes an imperial mendicant.	The Portuguese establish a base at the mouth of the Congo River.

The Battle of Bosworth, where Richard died after key allies held themselves apart from the fighting.

A POSSIBLE ALTERNATIVE SUSPECT

Henry Stafford, the 2nd Duke of Buckingham, occupies a darkly ambiguous position in the history of Richard III. In 1980, a manuscript was discovered referring to him as responsible for the murder of the Princes in the Tower. It is unclear whether that means he advised Richard to have them killed or undertook the deed without the king's knowledge. With the princes dead, Buckingham's claim to the throne would equal Henry Tudor's. It may be that Buckingham turned on Richard because he was shocked by the murders; it may also be that he was responsible for the murders, and that had he not been captured and executed in 1483 he would have challenged Henry Tudor for the throne.

1485 had begun grimly for Richard, with his wife's death and the storm of malicious rumors that followed. A solar eclipse on the day of her death was interpreted as a sign of his guilt. He had lost much of his standing with the nobility and the people. To some extent his people skills may have been to blame as well; it seems that even when he was highly respected he was not personally liked, and he surely suffered in comparison to his outgoing brother Edward. To make things worse, plague had struck London. If the notes found in his Book of Hours suggest anything, Richard brooded over his losses and his prospects.

When, in August, Richard received word that Henry Tudor had landed in Wales, however, he took decisive action, assembling a sizeable army and marching to meet the enemy. On August 21, he left Leicester, riding a white horse and wearing his battle crown. The following day, the two armies met at Bosworth. Richard was the last of the House of York, Henry the only claimant from the House of Lancaster. Both sides entered the fight knowing that by evening the conflict between their houses would be settled for good.

Richard was an experienced and capable military leader, and had with him his redoubtable ally John Howard, Duke of Norfolk; Henry Tudor had no experience as a soldier, so he gave command of his forces to John de Vere, the Earl of Oxford, a formidable commander, and remained with his bodyguards just behind his troops. Richard arranged his forces atop Ambion Hill, and had the troops of his ally Henry Percy of Northumberland hold back for use as reinforcements. Nearby stood the forces of Thomas, Lord Stanley, who occupied an ambiguous position in the conflict and was present to see where he might throw his weight behind the winning side. To keep Stanley, who had earned a reputation for self-serving alliances, from supporting the Lancastrians, Richard had brought Stanley's son with him as insurance. Regardless, Stanley remained aloof, declining to enter the fray.

1485
Peter Arbues, Inquisitor of Aragon in Spain, is fatally assaulted while praying in the cathedral in Zaragosa.

1485
Japanese peasants and lesser samurai of Yamashiro province, fed up with the chaos of the aristocratic Onin Wars, organize and rebel, eventually establishing their own provincial government.

1485
In southern India, Praudha Raya, the last of the Sangama Dynasty's rulers, is overthrown by his general Saluva Narasimha Deva Raya, inaugurating the Saluva Dynasty.

THE BATTLE OF BOSWORTH

The fighting began with the Lancastrians advancing in a compact formation. After a shower of arrows and other missiles, the two sides locked in close combat. Though Richard's army was larger, they began to lose ground. But when Richard signaled for Northumberland's reserves to enter the fray, they remained where they were. Historians disagree as to whether Percy deliberately withheld his troops in a betrayal of Richard or whether the battle had developed in a way that made it impossible for him to get his forces where Richard needed them.

In the distance, Richard apparently spotted Henry Tudor and some of his command riding toward the Stanley contingent, probably to persuade Stanley to enter the battle on his side. Shouting "Treason!", Richard decided to wager everything on an audacious attack, leading some of his knights in a furious charge at Tudor. And he almost managed to kill his enemy. According to contemporary accounts, Richard first slew Tudor's standard-bearer and then unhorsed one of his best knights before getting within a few feet of Tudor himself. In the ensuing melee, Richard's horse was either killed beneath him or bogged down in marshy ground. Declining offers from his knights to take their horses, he

fought on until, at some point, his helmet was removed. His exposed head received several blows, at least one of which was almost instantly fatal. As he fell, Welsh soldiers hacked at his body. Once word of his death spread, his forces collapsed, and Henry Tudor won the Battle of Bosworth and the throne of England.

That last, desperate charge earned Richard lasting respect for his bravery and fighting prowess, but it cost him his life. His savagely mutilated body was stripped of its armor, strapped to a horse, and taken into Leicester, where it lay in the open for two days, putrefying, as proof that he was dead. Then Henry Tudor allowed it to be buried unceremoniously at Greyfriars church in Leicester.

With Richard's death, an era ended. As a member of the cadet House of York, he was the last of the Plantagenet kings. Henry Tudor, who defeated and succeeded him, would found the most storied dynasty of them all, one that would take the English monarchy from the Middle

Two scenes from the 2012 excavation of Greyfriars monastery in Leicester, where Richard's remains were found beneath a parking lot.

1485	1485	1485
The conquistador Hernán Cortés is born in Medellín, Spain. He will go on to overthrow the Aztec Empire in 1521 and establish the colony of New Spain in what is now Mexico.	In Russia, Ivan III of Moscow successfully annexes the Grand Duchy of Tver, enabling him to become the first Russian ruler to pronounce himself Tsar of all Russia.	The Portuguese explorer Diego Cão sails up the Congo River after hearing rumors of fabulous kingdoms in the center of Africa.

RICHARD'S LEGACY OF SUPPORTERS

Thanks largely to Tudor-era depictions, Richard III has long been seen as an archetypal arch-villain. But the Richard III Society, founded in 1924, is devoted to rehabilitating the king's reputation. And several books, perhaps most famously Josephine Tey's The Daughter of Time, have argued that Richard is innocent of the murder of the Princes in the Tower. Most historians, however, agree that Richard is the most likely suspect in the crime.

Ages into the Renaissance. To legitimize their rule, the Tudors would advance and perpetuate an image of Richard as a monstrous tyrant, almost absurdly evil, and the Tudor myth would hold sway for centuries. In reality, Richard was no more and no less ruthless and destructive than many of his peers and rivals; he was a man of his time, and his time was unstable and violent. Had he won the day at Bosworth and enjoyed a longer rule, he would surely be remembered differently.

AN UNEXPECTED CODA

In 2012, a team of researchers received permission to excavate beneath a parking lot in the city of Leicester. They had calculated that, underneath, they would find the remains of Greyfriars monastery, the place where Richard had reportedly been buried, but which had been largely destroyed in the 16th century.

Among their goals was to recover the remains of Richard.

Early in their dig, near where they would expect Richard's body to have been interred, they found the largely intact skeleton of a man with mortal head wounds and severe scoliosis. After a series of tests, including DNA analysis using descendants of Richard's sister, it was determined conclusively that the remains were those of Richard. He had been buried in a crude grave, without a coffin, and possibly with his hands tied before him. His skeleton showed not only the wounds that killed him, but also the marks of subsequent mutilation.

The momentous discovery of the remains of Richard III, the last King of England killed in battle, made headlines around the world and reignited discussion about his life and legacy. Scientists were able to reconstruct his facial features, finding that he looked much like his image in period portraits, but was healthy and strong despite the scoliosis that would have made one shoulder higher than the other.

Richard III, so long an object of contempt and vilification, suddenly seemed all too human. Though there were calls to inter his remains in Westminster Abbey, authorities decided to bury them in a formal funeral in Leicester Cathedral. Even as the discovery of Richard's remains reopened debate about his place in history, it was as if a ghost that had haunted England for centuries was finally put to rest.

A 2013 reconstruction of the head of Richard III. The facial structure is based on his recently unearthed remains, the hair and hat on period portraits.

1485	1485	1485
At the Battle of Bosworth, Richard III fights fiercely but is killed in action against the victorious forces of Henry Tudor.	First outbreak of a disease known as the English Sweat occurs in London. Symptoms included high fever, profuse sweating, and sudden death. Later outbreaks came in 1502, 1507, 1517, and 1528, sometimes spreading to Europe. The disease has not be identified by modern doctors.	Catherine of Aragon, future first wife of Henry VIII, is born in Spain

The House of Tudor

After the Wars of the Roses had effectively culled the nobility of England, Henry Tudor was there to pick up the pieces, and he founded the dynasty that brought England into the modern era. Though it only lasted a little over a century, the Tudor dynasty transformed England completely. Henry VIII, brilliant as he was brash, made England a Protestant nation; his daughter Elizabeth I would keep it so, however ruthlessly, and in the process guide the nation through several dangerous decades to secure its place as a major European power. Under the Tudors, British culture blossomed spectacularly. It was the age of William Shakespeare and Francis Bacon. Here was Britain's Renaissance.

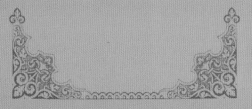

HENRY VII ✣ Remaker of the Monarchy

House Tudor
Born January 28, 1457
Died April 21, 1509
Reigned 1485–1509
Consort Elizabeth of York (died 1503);
Children Eight, including Henry VIII
Successor Henry VIII

Henry VII was an unlikely founder of England's most storied dynasty, but he proved a capable and forward-thinking monarch. In the wake of the Wars of the Roses, he fended off multiple challenges to his rule and left his heirs a legacy of shrewd diplomacy, tight-fisted control of the nobility, and enormous royal wealth.

When Richard III was unhorsed and slain at Bosworth, his adversary, Henry Tudor, found himself the last man standing in the Wars of the Roses. His unlikely bid for the throne had been engineered by two queens who had once been enemies in that conflict: his mother, Margaret Beaufort, of the Lancastrian faction, and Elizabeth Woodville, widow of Edward IV of the House of York. When, in January 1486, Henry married Elizabeth of York, daughter of Edward IV, the red and white roses of Lancaster and York merged into the Tudor rose, a symbol of reconciliation and new beginnings.

FROM FUGITIVE TO KING
Before launching his swift and effective campaign against Richard, Henry had spent 15 years in exile in Brittany. As the senior surviving Lancastrian male with any claim to the throne and therefore a target of Yorkist enmity, he had been spirited across the Channel at his mother's behest. During the reign of Edward IV, whose force of personality and accumulation of personal wealth followed the monarchic ideal of Sir John Fortescue, the York ascendancy appeared complete; but Edward's sudden death, and the political missteps of Richard, created an opening where none had seemed possible. At the age of 28, Henry landed in Wales, bringing with him a small French force that was soon supplemented by enthusiastic Welshmen.

After the swift and decisive carnage at

Bosworth, Henry took the throne of an England whose nobility had spent three decades thinning its own ranks. But his position was far from secure. The exchequer had been quickly drained after the death of Edward, stripping the Crown of the wealth Edward had used to subdue the "over-mighty" lords whose scheming had fueled the Wars of the Roses. Henry's chief task was therefore to bring a frayed kingdom under control. One of his first moves, at once fiscal and political, was to declare himself king retroactively to the day before Bosworth, allowing him to take possession of all of Richard's personal holdings. Henry also had the sense to extend olive branches to various Yorkists.

History was partly on his side. The Hundred Years' War may have invited disorder and violence in England and helped precipitate the Wars of the Roses, but it had also forged a strong sense of English national identity. The Tudor rose

> IN GOVERNMENT HE WAS SHREWD AND PRUDENT, SO THAT NO ONE DARED TO GET THE BETTER OF HIM THROUGH DECEIT OR GUILE
>
> *POLYDORE VERGIL*

Margaret of York, known after marriage as Margaret of Burgundy. The sister of Edward IV and Richard III, she was an implacable enemy of Henry VII, supporting the bids of both Lambert Simnel and Perkin Warbeck to usurp the English throne.

1492	1493	1495	1496	
Columbus discovers the New World, opening a tremendous new source of wealth and rivalry among the European powers.	Pope Alexander VI divides the New World between Spain and Portugal.	The world's first dry dock is built at Portsmouth by command of King Henry VII for the use of the English Royal Navy.	Bartholomew Columbus, brother of Christopher, founds a colony at Santo Domingo, which is still inhabited and thus the oldest European settlement in the Americas.	**Opposite** Henry VII, whose ability to seize the advantage and retain it against all his enemies established the Tudor dynasty. He laid the groundwork for the powerful kingship of his son Henry VIII.

The Crown Imperial, symbol of Tudor ambition, remained a potent symbol more than a century after its creation. In this portrait of the Stuart ruler Charles I and his family, it rests on the table at the king's right hand.

seemed to promise a return to order and continuity after the twists and turns of dynastic fortune that had characterized the past three decades. Henry himself appears to have had grand ambitions, which came to be symbolized by the new Crown Imperial, a 7 lb affair of gold and jewels, incorporating both the Cross of St. George and the Fleur-de-lis in an impressive show of regalia. But three brief forays into France led not to conquest but to the Treaty of Etaples in 1492, by which the French bought him off with the promise of an annual tribute of £12,500. Henry had neither the money nor the political support for another protracted expedition against an increasingly centralized and imperious France. That insecurity may have contributed to his character as a ruler: meticulous, reserved, and difficult to read.

FORGING ALLIANCES

One of Henry VII's most successful enterprises was the forging of new alliances. By arranging for his daughter Margaret to marry James IV of Scotland and his heir Arthur to wed Catherine of Aragon, daughter of Ferdinand and Isabella of Spain, Henry enhanced England's international stature and erected a bulwark of allegiances against France. In the shifting sands of European diplomacy, such alliances could only be temporary, but they bought England time to build economic, military, and diplomatic power. Henry's Tudor successors would take advantage of their nation's newfound prominence.

EARLY CHALLENGES TO HENRY'S RULE

In his first years as king, Henry faced two revivals of the Yorkist cause. They were late flare-ups of Yorkist ambition and resentment, but they were also occasioned partly by the political posturing of Henry's mother, whose high-handedness alienated her York in-laws. The Stafford and Lovell Rebellion of Easter 1486, a quixotic uprising by Yorkist Worcestershire nobles, never got off the ground. A more threatening attempt came the following year, when some remaining Yorkists, led by John de la Pole, Earl of Lincoln, propped up a ten-year-old boy named Lambert Simnel as the alleged son of Edward's brother the Duke of Clarence and therefore rightful heir to the throne. The result was a brief flashback to the Wars of the Roses, a bloody, three-hour battle at Stoke Field that left the Yorkist leaders dead and Lambert Simnel captive. In a justly famous stroke of political savvy, Henry spared Simnel's life, condemning him instead to a job in the royal kitchens.

THE PERKIN WARBECK CONSPIRACY

In 1497, a third attempted coup nearly cost Henry his throne. It centered on a pretender named Perkin Warbeck. Warbeck, a figure who remains mysterious to this day but was most likely a well-educated young Fleming, claimed to be Richard of Shrewsbury, the younger of the Princes in the Tower. For years, and with Henry's full knowledge, he had been marshaling support from abroad for his claim, finding it first with Edward IV's sister Margaret of Burgundy and then, more significantly, with James IV of Scotland, who was only too glad to find some pretext for badgering the English.

Warbeck's play for the throne proved costly and destabilizing. A brief Scottish invasion necessitated a £120,000 grant from Parliament to marshal the royal army and head north in response, only to have the Scots withdraw. The resulting taxes triggered unrest in Cornwall. Henry marched south and defeated a Cornish army in June 1497, only to have the indefatigable Warbeck take advantage of Cornish resentment three

1497
John Cabot sails to what is now Canada, financed by Henry. England will eventually establish settlements on the eastern coast of North America.

1498
Portuguese mariner Vasco da Gama reaches India after sailing round the south of Africa and effectively frees Europe from dependence on Venetian middlemen in the spice trade.

1498
Christopher Colombus makes a third voyage to the New World, this time with six ships, and discovers Trinidad.

1498
Leonard da Vinci completes The Last Supper, one of the pinnacles of Renaissance art.

months later, raising an army several thousand strong. He took flight at the approach of royal forces, however, and was captured as a fugitive, to be executed at Tyburn two years later.

NEW DIRECTIONS IN FOREIGN POLICY

Following the Perkin Warbeck conflict, Henry arranged a truce with Scotland in 1502, the so-called Treaty of Perpetual Peace, cementing it by the marriage of his daughter Margaret to James IV. The move demonstrated how Henry and his Privy Council recognized the changing dynamics of Europe. France and Spain were coalescing into unified, wealthy, and powerful states, and England was no longer the terror of Crécy and Poitiers. The best course of action would be to court Spain and isolate France. Accordingly, Henry sought to weaken the Auld Alliance of Scotland and France, and then arranged for the marriage of Prince Arthur, his eldest son, to Catherine of Aragon.

Henry also sought to enrich the royal coffers, and England as a whole, through economic diplomacy, some of which made even more lucrative the already profitable cloth trade with the continent. Margaret of Burgundy's support of Perkin Warbeck invited consequences, and Henry provided them in the form of a trade embargo, which included expelling Flemish merchants from London and forcing the Company of Merchant Adventurers of London to relocate its continental base from Antwerp to Calais. Though the embargo temporarily weakened the English cloth trade, it hurt Burgundy's economy enough to bring about a general agreement, the Intercursus Magnus, privileging English traders and requiring Margaret to acknowledge the Tudor ascendancy.

THE MISER KING

Henry's attention to the royal accounts evolved into an obsession. During the Hundred Years' War, regular infusions of plunder and ransom from France had periodically restocked the royal coffers; now that continental expeditions were no longer viable, revenue would have to be generated domestically. Mindful that

his position was not entirely secure and that Cornwall had risen in rebellion over taxes, Henry devised a range of strategies to bring money into the exchequer. Taxes did play a role. In the 1490s, Henry's Lord Chancellor, Archbishop John Morton of Canterbury, enforced a strict tax code, invoking what came to be known as Morton's Fork, the principle that those who were wealthy could afford to contribute to the royal coffers while those of modest means had demonstrated the fiscal discipline to manage in spite of taxes. Further, Henry transformed the legal system into a revenue generator, requiring large bonds from noblemen, which they would forfeit if they rebelled, and often punishing infractions through fines rather than imprisonment. Justices of the Peace, further empowered by Henry in 1495, increased in number and influence, and Henry relied at least as heavily on legal counsel as on ecclesiastical advice. In order to process important cases quickly and decisively, he revived the Court of Star Chamber, in which members of the Privy Council made rapid and often ruthless legal determinations in defense of royal prerogatives.

In 1502, personal disaster struck. In April of that year, Arthur succumbed to illness. Then, early in 1503, Elizabeth died in childbirth. Henry was grief-stricken; even those close to him were surprised at how evidently attached he was to his wife. The two losses contributed to the increasing isolation and acquisitiveness of his later years—as if he wanted to retreat from the world and control what was within his power. By his death, he was the wealthiest English ruler since the Normans, but he had come to be viewed as a miser, a cold and controlling monarch who had imposed inhuman authority over the realm. When his second son, Prince Henry, was crowned Henry VIII, the kingdom rejoiced. But Henry VIII and his successors would benefit from the tight-fisted policies of their dynasty's founder. He had stabilized royal authority, left the kingdom's coffers flush, and charted a patient and deliberate diplomatic course for England.

Perkin Warbeck, who claimed to be Richard of Shrewsbury. His fraudulent attempt on the throne at first cost Henry dearly but then proved advantageous diplomatically.

1499	1503	1503	1503	1504
Cannons are first used on ships at the First Battle of Lepanto, between the Turks and the Venetians.	Leonardo da Vinci begins his great mural The Battle of Anghiari for Florence's Palazzo della Signoria.	England's Canterbury Cathedral is completed after 436 years of construction.	France's Louis XII abandons claims to Naples following the breakup of his alliance with Ferdinand of Aragon.	Michelangelo completes his David in Florence; it becomes one of the most widely admired renderings of the human figure.

HENRY VIII ✠ Reshaper of England

House Tudor

Born June 28, 1491

Died January 28, 1547

Reigned 1509–1547

Consort Catherine of Aragon (divorced 1533), Anne Boleyn (died 1536), Jane Seymour (died 1537), Anne of Cleves (divorced 1540), Catherine Howard (died 1542), Catherine Parr; Children: Mary I, Elizabeth I, Edward VI

Successor Edward VI

Cardinal Thomas Wolsey, Henry's foremost advisor for the first half of his reign, and the architect of many of his policies.

Apart from William the Conqueror, no ruler changed England more than Henry VIII. A prodigiously talented, larger-than-life figure to his contemporaries as well as to posterity, he reigned over a nation facing the epochal changes of the Renaissance and the Reformation. At once conservative and audacious, great-spirited and cruel, he impressed his personality on his kingdom like no other monarch in English history.

Henry was not born or raised to be a king. As the second son of Henry VII, he was not expected to inherit the throne, and he spent his childhood happily with his mother and sisters, receiving a world-class education without being trained in the stern disciplines of kingship. But when he was ten, his older brother Arthur died, and suddenly Henry was pulled into his father's world of duties, calculations, and politics.

From an early age, Henry demonstrated extraordinary intelligence and talent. He became fluent in Latin and French, became a capable musician and composer and a passable poet, and instinctively knew how to present himself. He was also fine-figured and athletic, and enjoyed vigorous pursuits. No less a luminary than the great Renaissance humanist Erasmus, on meeting the eight-year-old Henry, marveled at his ability and his confidence. Here was a boy with an enormous appetite for life, and the capacity to achieve greatness.

When he abruptly became heir to the throne in 1502, Henry's life changed completely. His father had become a controlling, irascible, somewhat fearful monarch, and sought to protect Henry as his single greatest asset. Henry found himself escorted everywhere by bodyguards, kept from sports he loved because they might cause injury, and isolated from his former friends and family. The king occasionally attacked Henry physically in fits of temper. When

Henry VII died in 1509, it must have seemed to the prince that he could finally live and breathe again, with the vast resources of a united and financially healthy kingdom behind him.

NO PRINCE IN THE WORLD MORE FAVOURETH HIS SUBJECTS THAN I DO YOU

HENRY VIII

THE YEARS OF AMBITION

Above all, young King Henry was ambitious. Tall, handsome, charismatic, and outgoing, he reminded many observers of Edward IV, but his real hero was Henry V, and he intended to become not just a good king but the greatest in Europe. To that end, he surrounded himself with the most magnificent court possible, and lavished resources on palaces, horses, weapons, and tournaments in which he participated. In obedience to his father's wishes, but also, it seems, out of genuine affection, he married his brother Arthur's widow, Catherine of Aragon, cementing an alliance with Spain.

But he also showed early signs of a ruthlessness that would come to the fore later in his reign. Two days after his coronation, he ordered the executions for treason of two of his

1509	1513	1513	1516	
Desiderius Erasmus, the Dutch humanist, writes The Praise of Folly. Though Erasmus is a devout Catholic, the book satirically derides much of the religiosity he sees in the Europe of his day.	Vasco de Balboa claims the Pacific Ocean for the King of Spain.	Spanish explorer Vasco Núñez de Balboa climbs a mountain in central America and becomes the first European to see the Pacific Ocean.	With the death of Ferdinand II, Spain becomes part of the Habsburg Empire under Charles V.	**Opposite** Henry VIII, in one of the many portraits emphasizing the outsized personality of this powerful, imperious ruler, the best-known of all English kings.

father's most hated advisors, Edmund Dudley and Sir Richard Empson, who were the architects of some of the late king's most extortive fiscal policies. Their violent removal was the result of maneuvering by a man who became one of Henry's closest advisors, William Warham, Archbishop of Canterbury. To his credit, Warham also reaffirmed the principle, largely cast aside in the previous reign, that taxation require the consent of Parliament. But though the executions of Dudley and Empson were hailed at the time, in retrospect they reveal a willingness on Henry's part to resort quickly to extreme measures when faced with domestic difficulties.

Henry's chief advisor, however, was not Warham, but Thomas Wolsey, a commoner who had risen by talent and tenacity to the position of royal chaplain, and gradually eclipsed the counselors Henry had inherited from his father. In 1511, he gained a seat on the privy council. Within four years he had been appointed Archbishop of York, Lord Chancellor, and Cardinal. Wolsey's meteoric rise had much to do with his extraordinary talent and political acumen—he was expert at becoming the loudest and most persuasive voice in any meeting—but it also reflected the consonance of his and the king's personalities. Both men enjoyed living on a grand scale, and both entertained bold ambitions for England on the international stage.

Francis I, King of France. Like Henry a young and dynamic ruler, he proved a formidable rival, as did the similarly ambitious Holy Roman Emperor Charles V.

It was largely Wolsey who orchestrated Henry's 1513 invasion of France. Henry had deliberately insulted the French ambassador shortly after taking the throne, straining the already tense relations between the two regimes. When, in 1511, Pope Julius II appealed for support against Louis XII of France, who had threatened to remove him, Wolsey and Henry spotted the perfect opening for an invasion. Joining the Holy Alliance against France, they organized a massive and well-funded expedition. In recognition of their efforts, the Pope granted Henry the title of Most Christian King.

THE INVASION OF FRANCE

The invasion was a brilliant success in terms of Henry's image, both internationally and domestically. He rode at the front of his troops, clad in conspicuous royal armor and cloak even when under fire, and relished the hard work of campaigning. Two French cities fell rather apathetically to his sieges, and he won a victory in the field at the Battle of the Spurs, in August 1513, so called because the French forces retreated so quickly. In real terms, little was accomplished, but Henry had gained enormous symbolic capital. He was not only a defender of the Catholic faith, but also a warrior king in the grand tradition of Edward III and Henry V. In the resulting treaty, negotiated largely by Wolsey, Louis agreed to wed Henry's sister Mary, securing a tenuous but lasting peace. At home, things had gone equally well. The Scots, invoking their Auld Alliance with France, invaded England during Henry's absence, but he had prepared for that contingency, and Thomas Howard, Earl of Surrey, crushed an undisciplined Scottish army and killed their king at the Battle of Flodden in September.

But things soon changed on the continent. Louis of France died within months of marrying Mary, who then secretly married Henry's friend Charles Brandon, Duke of Suffolk—a decision that temporarily enraged the king by taking away the possibility of another diplomatic marriage. More importantly, the new French king, Francis I, was every bit the match of Henry. Young, talented, and ambitious, he presented a rivalry that could easily get out of hand. Similarly the new, even younger Holy Roman Emperor, Charles V, was a star in his own right. Europe was dominated not by Henry, but by these other two potentates, with Henry as the man in the middle—a position that offered influence and prestige, but not the outright dominance Henry craved.

1516	**1517**	**1519**	**1519**	
Bavaria introduces the Reinheitsgebot law to control the purity of beer, which remains in force.	Francis I invites Leonardo da Vinci to France. Leonardo brings with him the Mona Lisa, which becomes the property of France on the artist's death.	Hernan Cortes and his conquistadors conquer the Aztec Empire, bringing untold wealth to the coffers of Spain.	Spanish soldier and explorer Hernan Cortes lands in Mexico. By the end of the year he and his men have marched to Tenochtitlan to meet Montezuma, ruler of the Aztec Empire.	

The Field of the Cloth of Gold, the spectacular and carefully orchestrated summit between French and English kings and nobility in 1520. Though it did little to ease the unavoidable conflicts between the two nations, it was a magnificent gesture.

For the next few years, Henry sought every opportunity to launch another glorious invasion of France. Wolsey, wary of the potential costs in every sense, found a way to sublimate that urge. In 1520, he arranged an international conference in the north of France, in which English and French nobles would meet, feast, hold tournaments, and invest in a magnificent peace rather than glorious but draining war. Known as the Field of the Cloth of Gold for the extent of the finery on display, it was in effect a summit meeting between Henry and Francis, and for a while it worked, sustaining a peace until Charles V declared war on France the following year, and Henry sided with the Holy Roman Emperor. But Charles never backed Henry's bids for France with concrete support, and Henry was forced to let go of his ambitions.

Other changes were unfolding on the continent. In 1517 Martin Luther nailed his Ninety-five Theses (which protested against clerical abuses) to a church door in Wittenberg, and the Protestant Reformation, so long in germinating, began to bear fruit. Scandinavia would soon turn to Lutheranism, and the upheaval would completely transform the hitherto predictable, and often useful, role of papal authority in such matters as royal marriage and succession. Henry was aghast at Lutheranism, and even wrote a book in 1521 titled Assertio Septem Sacramentorum (A Defense of the Seven Sacraments), denouncing the reformers and emphatically asserting the authority of the papacy.

ROYAL RIVALS

Henry VIII was continually frustrated by his position relative to the more powerful rulers of France and the Holy Roman Empire. At the Field of the Cloth of Gold in 1520, his frustration took a different turn when he challenged Francis I of France to a friendly wrestling match and lost. Though the two rulers were often at odds militarily, they maintained a surprisingly candid private correspondence, exchanging news, congratulations, and even advice and support. Their shared status as kings, along with the burdens of that position, enabled them to have a distinctive bond in spite of their frequent adversarial positions.

1520	1520	1521
Battle of Otumpa. Spanish adventurer Hernan Cortes with local allies defeats the main Aztec army.	King Christian II of Denmark invades Sweden promising a free pardon to any opponents who recognize him as lawful sovereign. After his victory he breaks his promise and executes over 400 Swedish nobles and clergy, an event known as the Stockholm Bloodbath.	Cuauhtémoc, ruler of the Aztec Empire, surrenders to Hernan Cortes. He is later executed and his empire taken over by Spain.

THE BREAK WITH ROME

It was the changing religious situation on the continent that would help precipitate Henry's most momentous decisions as king. By 1525, Catherine of Aragon was 40 years old, past her childbearing years, and she and Henry had failed to produce a male heir. Further, Henry had become deeply enamored of Anne Boleyn, an educated, intelligent, and seductive lady in waiting whose sister had once been one of the king's mistresses. Anne, however, refused Henry's advances, sparring with him and insisting that she would only be his lover if she were also his wife. The combination of frustration with Catherine and attraction to the much younger Anne proved too much for Henry to tolerate.

The only solution was to extricate himself from his marriage to Catherine. This would be no easy task, since it would require papal approval, but Henry had an argument, in that the Book of Leviticus stipulates that it is unlawful to marry one's brother's wife. Since Henry had done so in marrying Arthur's widow, he stood a fair chance of getting an annulment. But Catherine, confronted with the decision in 1527, refused to cooperate. Wolsey was placed in the uncomfortable position of arranging the annulment without the queen's support.

THE FALL OF WOLSEY

But there was a gigantic obstacle, and it was not simply ecclesiastical. Catherine's nephew was none other than Charles V, the Holy Roman Emperor, and Charles had taken Rome and imprisoned Pope Clement VII. The Reformation and the rise of the Renaissance princes had made the papacy weak, and Clement was in no position to counter the wishes of his captor. Wolsey's negotiations dragged on until, in 1528, the Cardinal was able to arrange an ecclesiastical trial on English soil, run by Wolsey and a papal legate. But the papal legate stalled the proceedings, and once again Wolsey proved helpless in the face of the pope's submission to Charles.

Both Henry and Anne had lost their patience. Anne went so far as to accuse Wolsey of treasonously delaying the annulment in defiance of the king's wishes. In 1529, Wolsey was stripped of all his titles save Archbishop of York, and sent off ignominiously to Yorkshire. The next year, he was summoned to London to face charges of treason; mercifully, he died of illness on the journey. He would not be the

The ruins of Fountains Abbey in Yorkshire. Once a flourishing center of prayer and learning, it was dismantled in 1539 during the dissolution of the monasteries.

1521	**1524**	**1526**
Martin Luther refuses to recant and is excommunicated, beginning the Reformation in earnest.	Explorer Giovanni da Verrazzano enters what will later be named New York Bay and becomes the first European to see Manhattan.	The Battle of Mohacs sees Turkish Caliph Suleiman the Magnificent defeat and kill King Louis II of Hungary, after which most of Hungary and adjacent lands fall to Turkish rule.

Anne Boleyn, Henry's second wife, an alluring and intelligent woman who could be said to have brought about the English Reformation, but who eventually fell victim to Henry's impatience for a male heir and the accusations of her enemies.

last of Henry's talented advisors to lose his king's favor and suffer disastrous consequences.

In Thomas Cranmer, a Cambridge theologian, Henry found a formidable voice in favor of his divorce. As the pope continued to temporize, a bitter intellectual battle unfolded across the universities of Europe. Cambridge, and then Oxford, came around to the king's position, which evolved to include the principle that anointed kings are invested with spiritual as well as temporal powers. In 1531, Henry formally charged the English Church with exceeding its authority. Ultimately, he extracted a document that acknowledged the king as having charge of the Church of England "as far as the law of Christ would allow"—an ambiguous phrase that proved only the beginning. When the clergy retracted their support, Henry effectively accused them of treason.

By the end of 1532, Anne was pregnant. Henry appointed Cranmer Archbishop of Canterbury. Cranmer arranged a pro forma hearing and declared the king's marriage to Catherine null and void. The announcement was met with general shock and outrage. The pope excommunicated Henry and Anne. Henry bulled his way forward, and in 1534, Parliament passed the Act of Supremacy and the Act of Succession, making him supreme head of the English Church and establishing Anne's daughter Elizabeth as his sole heir.

Henry's bold decision had led him to unprecedented power as an English king, and he had accomplished his feat with the assistance of Parliament. It was a case of the right man at the right time: Henry was a strong-willed, popular monarch, and the Church had been weakened by religious upheaval and power politics. To some extent, Anne Boleyn's own Protestant leanings, which reflected a growing anti-papal sentiment in England, affected Henry's thinking as well.

But Henry's transformation of English society had also cost him. His popularity fell, and he became a much more ambiguous figure in the eyes of his people. Infamously, the single-mindedness with which he had pursued a divorce from Catherine had led him to destroy some of his closest and most capable advisors. The most famous of these was Sir Thomas More, Henry's onetime personal secretary, who had succeeded Wolsey as Lord Chancellor. The author of Utopia, More was one of the greatest scholars in Europe, a friend of Erasmus and a gifted administrator. But when Henry attempted to enforce the Act of Succession by requiring oaths of support, More refused to cooperate. Another of Henry's counselors, Thomas Cromwell, attempted to sway him, and though he was put on trial for treason, More refused to acknowledge that the King of England could displace the pope in matters of the spirit. His subsequent execution in July 1535 shocked Europe, and made him a martyr and eventually a saint.

1526	1527	1530	1532
Central Asian monarch Babur invades northern India, occupies Delhi and founds the Mughal dynasty that will rule most of India until the 19th century.	Gustavus I appropriates the assets of the Catholic Church in Sweden.	The Knights Hospitaller are given Malta as a base by Holy Roman Emperor Charles V.	Nicolaus Copernicus completes work on his book *De Revolutionibus Orbium Coelestium*, which states that the Earth orbits around the Sun. He circulates copies privately to trusted friends and colleagues but refuses to publish it for fear of the reaction it might provoke.

Hampton Court Palace. Built by Cardinal Wolsey, it later became a favorite residence of Henry.

A NEW KIND OF KING

For the remainder of his reign, Henry held nearly absolute power. In 1536 in a move of breathtaking cynicism and audacity, he began the Dissolution of the Monasteries, lining the royal coffers with their considerably wealth while eliminating them as possible bases of dissent. Henry's extravagant ambitions, and his indulgences—he built more than 50 castles during his reign, as well as maintaining an opulent court and engaging in foreign adventures—had squandered the enormous fortune left by his father. Of the hundreds of monasteries in England, many were wealthy, and now that he was head of the English church, Henry helped himself to their assets. In a five-year campaign of systematic desecration and destruction, monks were evicted from their dwellings, and monasteries great and small became the property of the crown. Many were razed so that every bit of precious materials could be used to line the royal coffers.

THE PILGRIMAGE OF GRACE

In 1536, appalled by Henry's actions, a rebellion took shape among northern nobility, commoners, and uprooted monks. Calling themselves the Pilgrimage of Grace, they marched south with surprising discipline, under a banner of the Five Wounds of Christ, demanding that Henry reverse his religious stance. Though they far outnumbered Henry's troops, they allowed themselves to be convinced that not the king but his counselors were behind the dissolution of the monasteries, and dispersed. A year later, Henry exacted revenge, arresting and executing large numbers of rebels; even monks and priests were hanged, drawn, and quartered.

And Henry's ruthlessness did not stop there. That same year, Anne Boleyn was executed on dubious charges of treason, though everyone knew her real offense was having failed to produce a male heir. In fact, she had lost one, suffering a miscarriage when she heard the news that Henry had been gravely injured in a jousting accident. The severe injuries, which included a blow to the head that left him unconscious for some time and a leg wound that never healed properly, may have lay behind his increasingly impulsive behavior in his later years. But it is nearly as likely, given his earlier conduct, that Henry's later reign was simply a study in unchecked narcissism.

Henry's third wife, Jane Seymour, was his favorite, for the straightforward reasons that she was more compliant than Anne Boleyn and managed in 1537 to produce a male heir, Prince Edward. But Jane died from postnatal complications within days, and after a period of mourning Henry turned his attention back to foreign adventures. In his final play for France, he once more conspired with Charles V, now more inclined to work with Henry since Catherine of Aragon had died the year before. Yet again, the promised support failed to materialize, and Henry was forced to settle for monetary tributes instead of the throne of France. Casting around for a fourth wife, he sought a dynastic match, and agreed to marry Anne, daughter of the Duke of Cleves, a worthwhile ally against Catholic aggression. In person, he found Anne utterly unattractive, and when he demanded an

1532

Francisco Pizarro conquers the Incan Empire with fewer than 200 men, expanding Spain's lands in the New World and securing more fabulous wealth.

1535

Sir Thomas More is executed for refusing to acknowledge King Henry VIII as head of the Church in England.

1536

The Incas under Manco Inca Yupanqui rebel against Spanish rule, setting up an independent state in the remote forests of lowland Peru near Vilacampa.

annulment in the summer of 1540, she complied without complaint. For her cooperation she was richly rewarded.

But the architect of that marriage, Henry's advisor Thomas Cromwell, suffered for its failure. Cromwell was the last of Henry's great counselors, tenacious and inventive in arranging the break from Rome, but he had no shortage of enemies eager to make the most of his failure in arranging a dynastic marriage. Henry had him arrested for treason and executed in 1540, a decision for which he would later express regret.

Henry's next marriage was a disaster in a different sense. Catherine Howard, presented to Henry by her uncle, the Duke of Norfolk, was a vivacious young woman in Anne of Cleves's retinue, and when Henry married her shortly after the annulment of his marriage to Anne he was altogether happier. The happiness did not last; Catherine, likely bored and even repelled by her aging, increasingly ill and overweight new husband, began having affairs. Thomas Cranmer was placed in charge of an investigation, and the corroborating evidence was found. Though she could conceivably have avoided execution by claiming a prior marriage contract, she refused. A bill designed to retroactively define her actions as treason was passed by Parliament, and she was duly beheaded in February 1542.

Only with Catherine Parr, whom he married in 1543, did Henry seem to find lasting satisfaction. It seems that, having been burned by letting his desires dictate his choices, he opted for easygoing companionship, and, apart from some conflict over her avowed Protestantism, the mature Catherine provided that. More importantly, she also engineered Henry's reconciliation with his daughters Mary and Elizabeth, who were eventually established in line to inherit the throne behind Prince Edward. It would prove a fateful decision.

AN AVID COLLECTOR

Henry VIII enjoyed building collections of things he valued, in particular weapons and horses. He owned thousands of pieces of arms and armor, and often showed them off to visitors. His stables were stocked with superb horses, which he often rode at tournaments in his younger years. Both collections reflected an ideal that Henry, despite his later infirmities, never entirely abandoned: that of the soldier king, surrounded by chivalric pageantry and victorious in battle. Henry himself had few military adventures, but his early invasion of France allowed him to live out some of his Arthurian fantasies.

DEATH AND LEGACY

On January 28, 1547, Henry died in Whitehall Palace. His final years had been plagued with declining health, and he had continued to spend his resources so lavishly that, despite the wealth reaped from the Dissolution of the Monasteries, he died in debt.

But he died having forever transformed England. The break from Rome both isolated the nation and endowed it with a more distinctive identity and an altogether different relationship to the continental powers, France and Spain. The Dissolution of the Monasteries had weakened the Church, much of whose former lands had now been taken over by the nobility. Henry had also recognized that, as a Protestant nation, England would need to defend itself, and had laid the foundations for the maritime power that would become its hallmark for centuries. He left his nation, poised at the threshold of a new era, to his nine-year-old son Edward, but it would ultimately come under the sway of his two very different daughters.

1541	1540		1542	1543
John Calvin establishes a strict Protestant rule in Geneva.	Waltham Abbey, the last monastic house in England, is closed down by order of King Henry VIII as part of his reformation of the Church in England.		Spanish Explorer Hernando de Soto becomes the first European to see the Mississippi River.	Copernicus first publishes his theory that the earth revolves around the sun.

BIRTH OF BRITISH NAVAL POWER

B"ritannia rule the waves," goes the classic tune, and it touches on one of the great glories of British history. The Royal Navy is the most storied of all maritime forces, and the rise of the British Empire is inseparable from Britain's domination of the seas. Though first formally named the Royal Navy in 1661, the British Navy has roots going back to Anglo-Saxon times—but it was under Henry VIII that it began to take shape as a prime expression of growing English power and reach.

It was Alfred the Great who first launched an English navy of any note. The Viking raiders had the advantage of swift, shallow-keeled, and Alfred eventually commissioned ships of his own, built to his specifications, as a counterweight. In 896, he launched a small fleet of perhaps a dozen vessels, much larger than Viking longships. Although too cumbersome to run down the Viking ships, they did serve as something of a deterrent.

Though other kings, most notably Edward the Confessor and Richard I, took steps to establish a system of naval readiness, it was not until the Hundred Years' War that the first major naval engagement took place: the Battle of Sluys in 1340, in which Edward III personally led a fleet of some 200 ships against a like number of French and Genoese vessels intended for an invasion of England. The French fleet was defeated and England had control of the Channel. Later in the war, Henry V would use well over a thousand ships and boats to ferry his army to France before Agincourt.

THE TUDOR FOUNDATION

Only with Henry VII did the idea of a power-projection navy take root. Henry was keenly aware of the economic and military importance of controlling the Channel, and began assembling a modest standing fleet, which was called the Navy Royal. In the process, he built the first dry dock on the Thames, in 1495. By the time of his death, he managed to have seven warships built.

It was Henry VIII who took that slender foundation and built it into something altogether new. Not only did he more than triple the number of warships in the first few years of his reign; in 1514, he launched the *Henry Grace à Dieu*, the largest warship on earth and the first to carry guns as its primary armament. Though its guns were not sufficiently heavy to sink a ship—their primary purpose was to kill sailors and soldiers on the enemy deck—the fact that *Henry Grace à Dieu* could inflict significant damage without ever coming into grappling range permanently changed naval warfare. Boarding would gradually give way to cannon fire, which would become more devastating as sturdier ships were built to accommodate heavy guns.

Henry issued a Royal Charter establishing Trinity House, which built and maintained navigational aids and coastal signals, from lighthouses to beacons. He also established the Naval Board to manage the growing fleet, and built the first of the naval yards at Portsmouth.

Sir Francis Drake, the most accomplished of Elizabeth I's "Sea Dogs." He not only raided Spanish ports and shipping but also circumnavigated the globe and served as second-in-command in the fight against the Spanish Armada in 1588.

THE MARY ROSE

The Mary Rose, launched in 1511, was one of the most impressive ships in Henry's navy. In 1545, in a minor action against the French, it suddenly heeled over, taking on water and sinking. Of nearly 700 crew, only about 30 survived. It may be that extensive retooling and expanding of the ship over time had made it unseaworthy, but the cause of the wreck remains unclear. In 1971, the wreckage was found, and in 1982 a massive salvage operation brought it to the surface. It was a goldmine of archeological evidence. The hull of the Mary Rose, along with many other artifacts, is preserved at Portsmouth, where a new museum opened in 2013.

According to contemporary documents, by Henry's death the standing navy consisted of between 40 and 60 ships of various sizes and armaments—a significant fleet, though it was still supplemented by merchant vessels in wartime.

Though it was Henry's vision that would ultimately make possible the defeat of the Spanish Armada in 1588, his daughter Elizabeth also saw the strategic value of a strong standing navy. She supported such "Sea Dogs" as Francis Drake and John Hawkins in their lucrative raids on Spanish shipping, and under her watch the shipyards at Portsmouth introduced a range of innovations, from fully rigged ships to dreadnoughts that carried massive cannon capable of firing devastating broadsides, though that tactic is not known to have been used before the 17th century.

The development of new technology for ships in the 15th and 16th centuries also made possible the voyages of exploration that launched the British Empire. Innovations in merchant and military shipbuilding benefited both endeavors, and British seamanship gradually became the gold standard of sail. To this day, the Royal Navy remains one of the most formidable fighting forces in the world.

EDWARD VI ✠ A Kingship Cut Short

House Tudor
Born October 12, 1537
Died July 6, 1553
Reigned 1547–1553
Consort None
Children None
Successor Lady Jane Grey

A Tudor-era painting showing Edward VI receiving power from his father Henry VIII, with the pope seemingly being crushed beneath the weight of the young monarch. Under Edward's reign, a more radical version of Protestantism was advanced than his father had envisioned.

> IF HE LIVES, HE WILL BE THE WONDER AND THE TERROR OF THE WORLD
>
> *JOHN HOOPER, BISHOP OF GLOUCESTER*

dward VI inherited the throne at nine years old, and died aged just 15. It was a short reign, but it was nonetheless important. Under Edward, England became a definitively Protestant nation—a change that, despite the efforts of his sister and eventual successor Mary, would never be reversed.

Henry VIII had made arrangements for a privy council of 16 executors to guide his son until he reached his majority. However, it did not take long for Edward Seymour, Earl of Hertford, to maneuver himself into the role of Lord Protector. After gaining titles provided for by Henry's will, he bought off other executors and secured letters from Edward giving him complete control over the privy council. He was now Duke of Somerset, and the de facto ruler of England.

RADICAL REFORMS

Somerset's tenure as Lord Protector was a disaster. Henry VIII had left England mired in debt, with a debased coinage, and the fencing in of farmlands had led to the displacement and destitution of many of the rural poor. Somerset was ill-equipped to deal with these problems. Even worse, his aggressive pursuit of a more extreme form of Protestantism than Henry would have countenanced proved culturally disruptive. With the support of Cranmer as well as the young king, he encouraged a campaign in which sacred images were removed or destroyed, traditional Mass at an exalted altar replaced with Holy Communion at a plain table, and Cranmer's Book of Common Prayer imposed throughout the realm. It was too extreme and too abrupt a change, and it sparked widespread unrest.

In 1549, another power play unfolded when John Dudley, Earl of Warwick and subsequently Duke of Northumberland, engineered the incompetent Somerset's removal and eventual execution. With the council under his control, England's affairs gradually stabilized, but the radical religious reformation continued. Throughout, Edward remained present at many council meetings, but it is unlikely that he had much real say in any significant decisions. A story goes that, at one meeting, the young king made a graphic statement of his frustration; slowly plucking and then dismembering one of his favorite falcons in front of the council, he declared that they were plucking him, but that eventually he would dismember them.

AN EARLY DEATH

In 1552, after bouts of measles and smallpox, Edward became seriously ill, probably with either tuberculosis or pneumonia. He gradually weakened, and it was clear he would not last long.

In what may have been his only kingly act, Edward took measures to ensure that the radical Protestantism advanced during his reign would not be curbed or undone by his Catholic sister Mary. In his Devise for the Succession, drafted in his hand on his deathbed, he altered the succession so that the throne would go to his Protestant cousin, Lady Jane Grey, daughter-in-law of Northumberland.

Edward may have been a largely ineffectual king, but under his rule England underwent a wrenching change into a radical Protestantism. The pendulum would soon swing the other way.

1547	1549	1550	1551	
Ivan IV becomes Tsar of Russia. Though he proves an effective ruler in some ways, his evident paranoia and seeming bouts of madness result in his being known as Ivan the Terrible.	Brazil becomes a Portuguese province. The race to colonize the New World will soon expand to include France and England as well as Portugal and Spain.	The shipment of African slaves to the New World begins. Slavery will be a source of wealth, and eventually of violence, as the history of the New World unfolds.	In France, the works of John Calvin and Martin Luther are banned. In the subsequent wave of persecution, thousands of Protestants are killed.	**Opposite** At the age of six Edward VI began a rigorous education under some of England's finest scholars. Significantly, his education was decidedly Protestant—more so than his father would have preferred.

LADY JANE GREY ✥ The Nine Days' Queen

House Tudor

Born Born: 1537

Died February 12, 1554

Reigned July 10–19, 1553

Consort Lord Guildford Dudley

Children Nonel

Successor Mary I

John Dudley, 1st Duke of Northumberland. It was his scheming that placed Lady Jane Grey on the throne. Both of them were executed.

An 1833 painting by Paul Delaroche of the execution of Lady Jane Grey. It evokes how she has endured in English history as the innocent victim of others' ambitions.

A bruptly named Queen of England as part of a vain effort to bar the accession of the Catholic Mary Tudor, Lady Jane Grey was a pawn in the schemes of Edward VI and the Duke of Northumberland. Within two weeks of being proclaimed Queen, she was beheaded in the Tower.

Jane was the daughter of Henry Grey, Duke of Suffolk, first cousin once removed to Edward VI. She was raised a Protestant, and given an excellent education for the time. On May 21, 1553, she married Guildford Dudley, son of the Duke of Northumberland who was effectively regent to Edward VI.

A SUDDEN ELEVATION

When Jane married Dudley, Edward VI lay dying. Like Jane, the young king was a devout Protestant, and his chief concern was how the succession would affect his recent religious reforms. His father's 1544 Act of Succession had restored Edward's older half-sisters Mary and Elizabeth to legitimacy, and Mary, a Catholic, stood to inherit the throne. On his deathbed, Edward wrote his Devise for the Succession, stipulating that Lady Jane rather than Mary should inherit the throne. It was an utterly untenable move as any such change in the succession would have to be approved by Parliament. A powerful king could force it through, but Edward was in no such position. Nonetheless, on July 10, 1553, days after Edward's death, Jane was proclaimed Queen.

The announcement sparked disbelief and outrage throughout England, even among many Protestants. Mary was almost universally seen as the rightful heir, and many regarded Jane's elevation as little more than a bid for continued power by her father-in-law. Avoiding Northumberland's clutches, Mary retreated to East Anglia and raised an army, declaring herself the true Queen.

Northumberland set out to capture Mary, but as soon as he was out of London the privy council threw their support behind Mary, and locked Jane and her husband in the Tower.

Northumberland was arrested, Mary entered London in triumph, and she was announced Queen of England on July 19. On August 22, Northumberland was beheaded for treason.

A SAD END

On November 13, a trial convicted Jane and Guildford of treason. Jane was deemed a usurper, having signed several letters as "Jane the Queen." Though both were sentenced to death, Mary's first inclination was to regard them as mere pawns and let them live. But events took a darker turn. When Mary announced her plans to marry the arch-Catholic Philip of Spain, a group of Protestant nobles led by Thomas Wyatt determined to rebel against her and place her half-sister Elizabeth, a Protestant, on the throne. The rebels briefly seemed to pose a genuine threat to Mary, but Wyatt overplayed his hand, demanding that he be given control of the Tower of London, and that the Queen be turned over to him. At that, many of the people of London rallied against him, and the revolt was suppressed.

Among the rebels was Jane's father, the Duke of Suffolk. In joining the rebellion, he doomed not only himself but Jane as well. Her execution was scheduled for February 9, 1554, but postponed to give Jane a chance to convert to Catholicism. She declined, and on the morning of February 12 first Guildford and then Jane were beheaded. Jane reportedly saw Guildford's body pass her cell window before being led out to Tower Green herself. On the scaffold, she famously blindfolded herself and then had trouble finding the block. The execution was swift. At the age of 16, Lady Jane Grey entered into English lore, a sad victim of political and religious intrigue, but also, for many, a Protestant martyr.

Opposite Portrait of Lady Jane Grey.

LA~ye

MARY I ✚ The Failed Reactionary

House Tudor
Born February 18, 1516
Died November 17, 1558
Reigned 1553–1558
Consort Philip II of Spain
Children None
Successor Elizabeth I

Known to history as "Bloody Mary," Mary Tudor attempted single-handedly to wrest England back into the arms of the Roman Catholic Church. She was not without support in that effort, but she so mismanaged it that, by the end of her brief and tumultuous reign, England was ready to accept the moderately Protestant, if ruthlessly enforced, settlement advanced by her half-sister and successor, the illustrious Elizabeth I.

Philip II of Spain. Mary's choice of husband provoked a furious backlash in Protestant England.

Mary Tudor was Henry VIII's daughter by his first wife, Catherine of Aragon, and she remained very much her mother's daughter. Growing up amid the intrigues and sudden realignments of her father's court, Mary endured disconcerting reversals of fortune which led her to cling all the more devoutly to her Roman Catholic faith.

In her youth, Mary was by all accounts an attractive, fresh-faced girl who excelled at her studies, gaining fluency in Latin, Greek, French, Italian, and Spanish. Her chief tutor, Juan Luis Vives, also encouraged her more ascetic tendencies, teaching her to resist the urges of the flesh and beware of the company of men. Under his guidance and her mother's, Mary also gained the fierce sense of Spanish dignity. King Henry was proud of her, having called her from a young age "the pearl of the realm," and had her raised in Ludlow Castle as Princess of Wales. But Henry's favor did not last. When Catherine proved unable to produce a male heir, Henry's attention turned to the captivating and imperious Anne Boleyn. When, in a momentous change for

England, Henry broke with Rome so he could have his marriage to Catherine annulled and wed Anne, Mary found herself cast aside along with her mother. At the age of 17, she went from being Henry's darling daughter to being the lonely, disinherited vestige of a forsaken marriage. When Anne gave birth to a daughter, Elizabeth in 1533, the newborn became a princess, and Mary simply Lady Mary. It was a humiliating, devastating reversal. For years, Mary lived in what she regarded as mortal peril, racked with period illnesses and subject to elimination at any time by her capricious father or his ruthless ministers. In fact, she was in no real danger, for the simple reason that her status as cousin, through her mother, of the powerful Holy Roman Emperor Charles V protected her.

When Anne Boleyn went to the block in May 1536, Mary's fortunes rose and Elizabeth's fell. Such were the vagaries of Henry's rule. But only with Henry's final marriage, to Catherine Parr, did Mary recover her onetime status as heir to the throne. By that time, Henry had secured his male heir, the young Prince Edward, and Catherine Parr was able to reconcile the king to both his estranged daughters. In 1544, Mary and Elizabeth, in that order, were established behind Edward in line for the throne. Edward's six-year rule proved dismaying to Mary. Though she was a devout Catholic, she had reconciled herself to her father's moderate form

I KNOW THIS QUEEN, SO GOOD, SO EASILY INFLUENCED, INEXPERT IN WORLDLY AFFAIRS AND A NOVICE ALL ROUND

SIMON RENARD, AMBASSADOR OF EMPEROR CHARLES V

1555
The Peace of Augsburg allows each prince within the Holy Roman Empire to decide for himself and his realm between Catholicism and Lutheranism.

1555
The Sultanate of Adal which has dominated the Horn of Africa for nearly two centuries suddenly collapses into chaos.

1555
After an exhausting siege, the Republic of Siena surrenders to the combined armies of Florence and the Holy Roman Empire—effectively Spain. The Spanish cede Siena to the Grand Duchy of Tuscany."

Opposite Mary I, who utterly lacked the political skills to advance her ambitious agenda of bringing England back into the Roman Catholic fold.

Thomas Cranmer, Archbishop of Canterbury. Cranmer's execution at the stake in 1556 was the most infamous of the martyrdoms under Mary's persecution of Protestants.

of Protestantism, which retained nearly all the core Catholic doctrines. Under Edward's reign, propelled by Archbishop Thomas Cranmer and the Duke of Somerset, a far more radical Protestantism was enforced across England. Relics and holy images, altars and rites, were removed or destroyed in favor of the austere practices of a "purer" Protestantism. Mary became a symbol for the old Church, which still commanded the reverence of many English.

When Edward died aged only 15 in 1553, Mary was next in line for the throne. But, in an audacious attempt to bar her way and preserve the Protestant agenda, Edward wrote on his deathbed that not Mary but his Protestant cousin Lady Jane Grey should inherit the throne. To Mary's relief, both the commons and the nobility rejected the move, and Mary was announced as Queen of England in July 1553. She was 37 years old.

A MARRIAGE AND A BACKLASH

Mary's sense of herself as queen was molded by her Catholic faith—to an extent that she proved incapable of grasping the ambiguities and complexities of her position. In her mind, God had given her the task of restoring England to the Catholic fold, and that mission became the overriding priority of her reign.

At first, she moved slowly and deliberately, appointing Catholic bishops, restoring churches, and encouraging a general movement back to Catholicism. But she also thought in terms of preserving a Catholic England beyond her death, and her search for a suitable husband settled on Prince Philip of Spain, the only son of Charles V and a similarly devout Catholic. She recounted to her ministers that she wept and prayed for days over her decision, and felt that God had steered her to Philip.

Mary's decision reflected her inability to read the political landscape, for she could scarcely have made a less popular choice. Protestants rejected Philip's militant Catholicism, and Catholics resisted the notion that England might become a mere colony of the mighty Habsburg Empire, which had been hostile for decades. A rebellion, led chiefly by Sir Thomas Wyatt the younger, marched on London, and very nearly toppled her before being crushed. Rather than reconsider her decision, Mary only hardened her position further. On July 25, 1554, she and Philip were married in Winchester Cathedral.

In November 1554, Cardinal Pole officially absolved England of its spiritual errors and welcomed it back into the Catholic fold. For Mary, it was a sign that she could begin vigorously enforcing what she had hitherto effected by gentler means. In short, Protestants would be treated as heretics, and burned. Over the next three years, she earned the nickname "Bloody Mary," as hundreds of Protestant dissidents were burned at the stake amid general persecution. In her zeal, Mary would not recognize how far, and how irrevocably, England had already changed. Even Philip's advisors, among them Catholic clerics, found Mary's relentless reign of terror offensive and counterproductive, but she would not be deterred.

Throughout the burnings, Protestant propaganda made martyrs of the victims—especially Bishops Ridley and Latimer—and John Foxe's graphic accounts, compiled in what became known as Foxe's Book of Martyrs, become enormously popular in England. One execution in particular undermined

1555	1556	1556	1556
Pope Paul VI establishes the Roman Ghetto, a Jewish ghetto which will remain under papal control until 1870..	*De Re Metallica* by Bohemian physician-mine owner Georgius Agricola is the world's first textbook on mining and metallurgy.	The great Shaanxi Earthquake strikes China killing an estimated 860,000 people, making this the deadliest earthquake in history.	After the abdication of Charles V, there are now two Habsburg Empires, Spanish and Austrian.

A stained-glass depiction of the Anglican bishops Thomas Cranmer, Hugh Latimer, and Nicholas Ridley, burned at the stake in Oxford during Mary's reign.

Mary's credibility: the burning at the stake of Archbishop Thomas Cranmer in March 1556. Under Henry and then Edward, Cranmer had presided over the shift into first a moderate and then a more radical form of Protestantism, and he had shown in pursuing those policies the same sort of insensitive and disruptive zeal that Mary had brought to her Catholic campaign. But the brutality of Mary's crackdown went far beyond anything Cranmer had supported.

When Cranmer was arrested, he was forced to watch the burnings of Ridley and Latimer outside Balliol College in Oxford. Horrified, he recanted his Protestantism. But what should have been a huge symbolic victory for Mary turned to bitter defeat when she insisted that he burn in spite of his cooperation, for just before his execution Cranmer dramatically retracted his recantation and affirmed his Protestantism. As the fires rose about him, he thrust his right hand, which had signed the recantation, into the fire to burn first. Resistance was further galvanized.

DELUSION, DECLINE, AND DEATH

Mary's union with Philip of Spain proved a crushing disappointment. Though she convinced herself that she was in love with him, he was merely kind to her, and wedded bliss was not an option. But in September of 1555, Mary began to show all the signs of pregnancy.

It was the fulfillment of her greatest hope: that she would preserve Catholic England through her own line. As the months went by, however, doubts began to emerge. By June, no baby had arrived, and then Mary's swollen belly simply collapsed. There had been no baby. It had been a phantom pregnancy, perhaps engendered by her obsessive desire for an heir.

Dissent is one threat to a ruler, but ridicule can be worse, and in the wake of her false pregnancy Mary became the butt of countless jokes. An exasperated and embarrassed Philip left England for Spain, and Parliament began to offer more resistance to Mary's initiatives. The loss of Calais, England's last holding on the continent, in an ill-advised military adventure undertaken at Philip's behest proved badly demoralizing, and a string of wet years that led to widespread famine only deepened the sense of failure that began to weigh down Mary's later reign.

Philip visited England again in 1557, and shortly after Mary convinced herself yet again that she was pregnant. As the due date of March 1558 approached, however, her symptoms revealed themselves to be not pregnancy but deadly illness, most likely ovarian or uterine cancer. On her deathbed, she resigned herself to having failed in her divine mission, and confirmed that the throne, according to the Act of Succession, should go to her half-sister Elizabeth. Still convinced that Philip was her great love, she sent him a ring. On November 17, she died, and the reign of Elizabeth I began.

From the start, Mary was a ruler whose time had passed. Her rigidly devout brand of Catholicism no longer fit into English culture, and her naïve incomprehension of political realities, though it might have proved harmless in a medieval queen consort, was downright destructive in a Renaissance monarch. Between her and Edward VI before her, England had been wrenched violently between two religious extremes; it was left to Elizabeth I, the last remaining child of Henry VIII, to secure some kind of balance.

BLOODY MARY

After England was welcomed back into the Catholic fold in 1554, Mary embarked on a campaign of persecution that shocked even Catholic ambassadors from the continent. Mary's obsessive pursuit of heretics was inseparable from her sense of herself as having been protected by God all her life, and ordained to cure England of its spiritual ills. Mary's fanaticism only strengthened the more extreme of the Protestants, leaving England deeply divided as her half-sister Elizabeth inherited the throne. Mary's delusional sense of a divine mission was also reflected in her phantom pregnancy, which made her the laughing stock of the country.

1557	1557	1557	1557
Portugal's Joao III (the Pious) dies on his 55th birthday after having instituted the Inquisition. He is succeeded by his grandson Sebastian.	Sao Paulo is founded by the Portuguese in Brazil.	Tsar Ivan the Terrible conquers Astrakhan, taking control of the Volga River. His subsequent use of the title 'Tsar of all the Russias' indicates the scale and diversity of the lands under his control.	The Portuguese, extending their reach toward East Asia, establish a trading colony on the island of Macao.

ELIZABETH I ✦ The Virgin Queen

House Tudor
Born September 7, 1533
Died March 24, 1603
Reigned 1558–1603
Consort None
Children None
Successor James I

rguably the most beloved monarch in English history, Elizabeth I reigned over a tremendous flowering of English culture. During more than 40 years on the throne, threatened from without and within England, she nonetheless managed to sustain a period of stability and confidence that gave rise to legendary exploits, victories, and cultural achievements.

The daughter of Henry VIII by his second wife, the captivating and intelligent Anne Boleyn, Elizabeth grew up enduring the same volatile fortunes as her older half-sister Mary, going in and out of favor according to her father's whims. In 1536, less than three years after Elizabeth was born, her mother was executed on trumped-up charges of treason, and for some time the young princess was marginalized. But as a child Elizabeth had excellent guardians to whom she remained fiercely loyal; she stayed close to her governess, Catherine Ashley, until the older woman's death years after Elizabeth took the throne.

From an early age, Elizabeth marked herself out as exceptionally bright—over the course of her life she reportedly gained fluency in at least seven languages—and she received a superb education, primarily under the tutelage of the great humanist scholar Roger Ascham. She seems to have taken great pains to remain on good terms with as many of her family members as possible, and when Catherine

Parr, Henry's sixth and last wife, managed to reconcile Henry to his daughters, the result was the 1544 Act of Succession, restoring both Mary and Elizabeth to the line of succession after the future Edward VI.

Under the six-year reign of Edward VI, Elizabeth was second in line to the throne, and therefore somewhat clear of court intrigues. She continued her studies. A portrait of her at the age of 14, around the time of her father's death and Edward's accession, suggests a modest, restrained, watchful young woman; fittingly enough, one of her mottos would be video et taceo—I see, and say nothing. But she could not avoid scandal when Thomas Seymour, Catherine Parr's new husband and the brother of Edward's Lord Protector, was found by his wife embracing young Elizabeth. Though it seems to have been known and accepted in the household that the two engaged in some innocent roughhousing, the incident was questionable, and Elizabeth was sent away in disgrace. Seymour would eventually be executed for scheming against his brother, but Elizabeth withstood questioning and was spared. From that point on, conscious that she would always risk being seen as very much the daughter of her allegedly wanton and scheming mother, Elizabeth conducted herself with even more restraint.

When Edward died in 1553 and Mary took the throne, Elizabeth found herself in the precarious position she would later describe as "second person." Mary, who had never liked her

A bookbinding embroidered by Princess Elizabeth at the age of 11 and given to her stepmother, Catherine (Katherine) Parr. As the daughter of Henry VIII, Elizabeth received a superb education, which she used to powerful effect as queen.

> ## I KNOW I HAVE THE BODY BUT OF A WEAK AND FEEBLE WOMAN, BUT I HAVE THE HEART AND STOMACH OF A KING, AND OF A KING OF ENGLAND TOO
>
> *ELIZABETH I*

1564

William Shakespeare and Christopher Marlowe, gigantic figures in the Elizabethan literary renaissance, are born.

1567

Mary, Queen of Scots, is forced to give up the throne to her infant son, James VI. On Elizabeth's death in 1603, he will become James I of England.

1569

German cartographer Gerardus Mercator first uses Mercator's projection in drawing a world map. It soon becomes the standard projection used on charts and maps.

Opposite Elizabeth I, the Virgin Queen, whose reign saw England blossom culturally and gain a new position of strength as a Protestant power in Europe.

William Cecil, Lord Burghley.
Elizabeth's foremost advisor,
he remained by her side for
more than 30 years.

queen's prosecutors could only throw up their hands. From then on, throughout Mary's reign, Elizabeth lived on a knife's edge, mostly under a kind of tacit house imprisonment at Hatfield Palace in Hertfordshire.

On November 17, 1558, an ill and dejected Mary died, abiding by the Act of Succession and leaving the throne to Elizabeth. When the news reached Elizabeth, she had already been quietly laying the groundwork for her reign, but as she recalled it many years later, she fell to her knees and thanked God, as much for her life as for the crown.

A CONFIDENT YOUNG QUEEN

From the start of her reign, Elizabeth was both popular and extraordinarily confident. She had the enviable position of succeeding a naïve, repressive, failed, and dismally unpopular queen, and she took full advantage. Though she established early and explicitly that she would seek out and rely on the best counselors she could find, she astonished visiting ambassadors with her forceful sense of command, so utterly different from Mary, yet so reminiscent of their father. But Elizabeth knew that she needed a strong, capable council, and in assembling one she demonstrated a remarkable ability both to identify talent and to manage the people who had it.

The queen's foremost counselor was one of the finest in English history: William Cecil, Lord Burghley. Thirteen years her senior, Burghley served Elizabeth as her Secretary of State and Lord High Treasurer, but his true task was to be an advising partner to a queen who knew her own mind but knew she needed a shrewd and experienced interlocutor when making decisions. Elizabeth, generally skittish of binding commitments and wary of unforeseen consequences, relied on Burghley's more decisive temperament. He would write her long memoranda, detailing the pros and cons of every decision, and after some discussion the queen would make up her mind, more often than not in accord with Burghley's. The two of them formed perhaps the most effective ruling partnership England has ever known.

half-sister, was determined to bring England back within the Catholic fold, and Elizabeth's Protestantism posed a threat. Not only would Elizabeth surely undo Mary's work if she succeeded her to the throne; she became the rallying point for Protestant resistance against the queen's Catholic agenda. When Sir Thomas Wyatt launched a revolt in 1554 after Mary announced her plans to wed the ultra-Catholic Philip of Spain, Elizabeth barely escaped with her life. Mary was sure her half-sister had been part of the plot, but Elizabeth so coolly and evasively handled her interrogation that the

1571	1572	1572
At the Battle of Lepanto, Spanish and Venetian galleys defeat the Turkish navy. It is the last large-scale use of galleys as military ships.	In the St. Bartholomew's Day Massacre, thousands of French Protestants, known as Huguenots, are killed.	The last remaining independent Inca state, Vilcabamba, is conquered by Spanish conquistadores.

MARY, QUEEN OF SCOTS

From the start of Elizabeth's reign, one person posed the most dangerous threat by far: Mary, Queen of Scots, a young cousin who had a legitimate claim to the English throne and already had become the great hope of militant Catholics. Mary's mother and regent, Mary of Guise, maintained a powerful French presence in Edinburgh, but was having trouble repressing a rising Protestant faction led by the so-called Lords of the Congregation. Elizabeth encouraged the Protestant dissidents, and

eventually ordered an English force to support them in a siege of Leith near Edinburgh, where the French forces were based. The expedition did not go well, but in 1560 Mary of Guise died, clearing the way for the Treaty of Edinburgh, in which both England and France pledged to withdraw their forces from Scotland. What had been a tactical defeat became a strategic victory, for once the French withdrew the gradual conversion of Scotland to Protestantism, spearheaded by Calvinist reformer John Knox, would unfold, and England and Scotland would remain in détente for the remainder of Elizabeth's reign.

THE ELIZABETHAN SETTLEMENT

The most pressing issue for Elizabeth, however, was not the French presence in Scotland; it was the presence of religious strife in England. The disorienting back-and-forth from Henry VIII's moderate Protestantism to the militant Protestantism of Edward VI and Archbishop Cranmer, and then to the fiercely repressive Catholicism of Mary, had left the population at odds. The potential for factional violence, even outright rebellion, was high, and Elizabeth would have to find a way to pacify the country as best she could.

It is not entirely clear what Elizabeth herself believed, but the evidence suggests that she adhered to a moderate form of Protestantism reminiscent of her father's. In any case, that middle way was what she sought for England, and it would take all her shrewdness and tenacity to achieve something close to it. Lord Burghley was a more hard-line Protestant in the Cranmer mold, and Parliament was divided, the House of Lords mostly Catholic and the Commons predominantly Protestant. The queen found herself in the difficult position of having to outmaneuver nearly everyone, including her chief counselor.

The first step was to reaffirm the Acts of Supremacy. Shortly after her coronation, Elizabeth advanced a Reformation Bill, one that promoted a more rigid Protestantism than

Robert Dudley, Earl of Leicester. If anyone could be termed the love of Elizabeth's life, it was he. On her accession, she appointed him Master of Horse, and she kept his letters to the end of her life.

1575	1576	1577	
The Raid of the Redeswire is the last armed conflict between England and Scotland, though only a few hundred men were involved.	The first theater in London, called The Theatre, is built by James Burbage. Burbage's son Richard will become the principal actor in William Shakespeare's troupe.	English mariner Francis Drake leaves England with a small fleet of ships that he will take into the Pacific to plunder Spanish colonies and ships. It is the start of an unofficial naval war between England and Spain while those kingdoms remain officially at peace.	

she likely preferred and probably reflected Burghley's influence. It met strong opposition in the House of Lords and ultimately had to be scrapped. Soon after, the queen had Parliament take up the same issues divided across two bills, the first of which restored much the same principle of Supremacy that Henry VIII had established. The bill passed without much difficulty, though Elizabeth had to accept the title of Governor rather than Head of the English Church. Much more problematic was the passage of her next measure, the Act of Uniformity, which required attendance at Sunday services of the Church of England, and mandated that those services use a revised, more radically Protestant Book of Common Prayer. It also, however, backed away from rigid enforcement of Protestant sacramental theology, removed aggressively anti-papal rhetoric from the liturgy, and abolished harsh punishments against Catholics. After a great deal of wrangling, during which Elizabeth and Parliament's more radical Protestants forged an alliance of convenience, the Act of Uniformity passed by only three votes in 1558.

But Elizabeth was not done crafting the

COUNSELOR AS CHARACTER?

William Cecil, Lord Burghley, was not only a great and esteemed statesman; he was also known for his willingness to sacrifice principles to serve the ends of the state. Some scholars believe that the character of Polonius, the chief minister in William Shakespeare's play Hamlet, is partly modeled on Burghley. Though the vain and manipulative Polonius ultimately dies at the hand of Prince Hamlet, he does offer some sensible worldly wisdom to his son Laertes. Burghley was such a powerful presence in and around court that it is not out of the question that Shakespeare, who was patronized by nobles and performed before Elizabeth, would have been familiar with Burghley's personality and reputation.

Church of England she envisioned, one that might accommodate a greater number of people inclined toward Catholicism. The following year, she issued the Royal Injunctions, a series of supplementary regulations allowing for more ritual continuity with the traditions of the old Catholic Church. In the end, neither the Catholics nor the Protestants were satisfied—the surest indicator that the queen had in fact found a middle way.

THE ELIZABETHAN SETTLEMENT
But the Elizabethan Settlement, as it was later known, came at a tremendous cost. England was once more an isolated Protestant nation facing the hostility of Catholic France and Spain, both of which could cast themselves as defenders of the true faith in any conflict with England. In 1569, a Catholic uprising in the north of England was put down brutally, with hundreds of executions. A year later, Pope Pius VI declared Elizabeth a heretic, unfit for the throne, and relieved her subjects of all obedience to her. It

Mapledurham, an estate in Oxfordshire. Like many great homes of Catholics and Catholic sympathizers in Elizabethan times, it contains many secret passages and rooms to conceal fugitive priests, and steep staircases to control visitors' lines of sight.

1580	1582	1586	1587
Michel de Montaigne publishes his Essais, a book that will exercise a huge influence over European literature and thought.	The Gregorian Calendar is introduced, though at first only Catholic countries adopt it. It corrects a discrepancy between the Julian Calendar of Julius Caesar and the actual movement of the Earth, which amounted to 3 days every 400 years.	Toyotomi Hideyoshi, the second great unifier of Japan, is acknowledged as supreme authority by the imperial court. His reforms begin a process of rigid class stratification that will shape Japan for the next three centuries.	Virginia Dare becomes the first English child born in America, but her colony, on Roanoke Island, soon vanishes.

Francis Walsingham, Elizabeth's spymaster. Walsingham, a devout Protestant, ran an intricate network of spies and informants, and his agents succeeded in uncovering countless conspiracies.

was an invitation to regicide, and the start of a bitter and often bloody struggle against Catholic intrigues and offensives.

THE PROBLEM OF SUCCESSION

As soon as she became Queen of England, Elizabeth faced expectations that she should find a husband and ensure the peaceful continuation of her line. But though she entertained, or at least seemed to entertain, a number of suitors, she refused to marry. Perhaps she was all too aware of the disastrous consequences of her predecessor Mary's marriage. It could be that she valued the prospect of marriage as a diplomatic tool too much to relinquish it. Another factor might be that if she could not marry whomsoever she wished, she would not marry at all. And if there was any love of Elizabeth's life, it was the companion of her youth, Robert Dudley, Earl of Leicester, whom she could not marry for a number of reasons.

Elizabeth's refusal to marry would, in the long run, become one of her most loved qualities; she would be known as the Virgin Queen, venerated almost as a kind of secular substitute for the lost Virgin Mary of Catholic tradition. But from a pragmatic standpoint it was a gigantic problem, because the person with by far the strongest claim to succession was Mary, Queen of Scots, who returned from France to Scotland in 1561 and made no secret of her desire for the English throne. Mary became the focal point of Catholic hopes; nearly every Catholic conspiracy Elizabeth would face

for the next 25 years would involve deposing or assassinating the Virgin Queen and placing Mary on the throne.

In 1566, Parliament took matters into its own hands, attempting to force Elizabeth to name a successor. Her response was devastating. She summoned dozens of Lords and Commons to Whitehall, and proceeded to give them a withering speech in which she refused to place anyone in the position she had once held, that of "second person." She also pointed out that many of those present, Commons and Lords alike, had been party to plots against her at one time or another, and she would prefer not to order the execution of anyone. It was a display of mastery unseen since her father's days; she had made it clear that anyone who attempted to force her hand on the issues of marriage or succession might, in a phrase she was known to use, be made shorter by a head.

But the problem of Mary, Queen of Scots would not go away. In fact, it came much closer to home. For all her beauty and charm, Mary had a gift for poor decisions, and her tenure in Scotland was an unqualified disaster. She lurched from scandal to scandal, ultimately becoming so reviled that, in 1568, she was forced to flee Scotland and seek Elizabeth's protection. Mary's arrival in England posed a terrible dilemma. Elizabeth and her council did not want Mary either restored to the Scottish throne or sent to brew up trouble in France. So they imprisoned her, under the guise of protecting her. For the next 19 years, Mary was kept in a series of guarded castles in the English countryside.

With Mary's arrival in England, the pace and subtlety of Catholic plots against Elizabeth—most of which involved Jesuits and others trained at seminaries in France and sent to England in secret—dramatically increased. Catholic nobles housed the priests in secret rooms, usually just for the purpose of performing Mass, but sometimes to nurture conspiracies. In response, Elizabeth's regime closed ranks. In 1584, her privy council drew up the Bond of Association, in which they and

Mary, Queen of Scots. Though Elizabeth would have preferred otherwise, Mary's apparent collusion in the Babington Plot of 1586 led to her execution.

hundreds of other signatories pledged that if Elizabeth were assassinated, they would take extreme vengeance, and use any means necessary to prevent the beneficiary of such a conspiracy from taking the throne. It was a measure of the loyalty Elizabeth commanded, and the enmity Mary had incurred.

THE DEATH OF MARY

Less symbolic but far more effective was Elizabeth's secret service, headed by the brilliant Francis Walsingham. Walsingham was something like Burghley's dark double, a similarly devout Protestant who ran extensive spy networks, organized ingenious sting operations, and ordered the extraction of confessions and information by often brutal means.

In 1586, Walsingham brought off a brilliant sting operation, planting a mole in a Catholic conspiracy in London. The Babington Plot, as it came to be called, was only one of the many conspiracies to assassinate Elizabeth and crown Mary, but in this case it was turned into a weapon against Mary. One of the participants was turned, and he and Robert Poley, one of Walsingham's most dangerous spies, arranged for the plotters to open a line of communication with Mary. Then they waited, and in due course a coded message came from Mary encouraging the plotters to accomplish their mission.

It was enough to damn her. Elizabeth was

left with little choice, and she signed Mary's death warrant. But she also stipulated that the execution not go forward without her further express direction. Burghley and Walsingham decided not to wait, and on February 8, 1587, Mary was beheaded at Fotheringhay Castle. So feckless in life, she was magnificent in death, facing the axe with uncommon dignity. On hearing of the execution, Elizabeth was livid, or at least appeared to be. But the single greatest threat to her life had been removed.

INTERNATIONAL TROUBLES AND TRIUMPHS

Elizabeth may have had troubles enough in England, but she also faced perils abroad. France and Spain were both avowed enemies, and much wealthier and more powerful than England. Spain in particular, its coffers lined with the gold of the New World, had the resources to invade the British Isles at any time.

Elizabeth pursued a cautious and deliberate foreign policy, to the point of maddening some of her more aggressively minded advisors and military leaders, such as Burghley and Sir Walter Raleigh. But her refusal to take major risks, though it made breakthroughs and decisive victories nearly impossible, kept England from being drawn into costly and hazardous conflicts. Elizabeth refused to commit many resources to the Protestant Low Countries, which endured a perpetual state of siege from the Catholic powers. She did, however, encourage exploration, including Sir Francis Drake's circumnavigation of the globe, and she commissioned privateers to waylay Spanish ships and steal their wealth for England.

In 1588, Spain finally launched the invasion fleet the English had long expected. The Spanish Armada, consisting of 22 warships and more than 100 converted merchant ships, was to pick up a large invasion force in France and cross the Channel. The English ships, outgunned but not outnumbered and far more maneuverable than the Spanish fleet, engaged the Armada in a series of skirmishes that cost the Spaniards

ELIZABETH'S NEMESIS TO THE END

Mary, Queen of Scots proved a problem in death as well as life. When she faced the block in 1587, however, she did so with a calculated dignity that maximized her status as a Catholic martyr. Wearing a petticoat of crimson, the color of martyrdom, she forgave her executioners and held a crucifix in her hands as she waited for the axe to fall. It was a bad job; the executioner needed three swings to completely sever Mary's head from her body, and when he held it up her hair was revealed to be a wig. But Mary had partly succeeded in controlling the narrative of her death.

1591

The Rialto Bridge in Venice is completed, the first bridge ever built across the Grand Canal.

1591

The Songhai Empire of West Africa collapses into more than a dozen warring states after being defeated by Judar Pasha of Morocco at the Battle of Tondibi.

1592

Japan invades the Korean peninsula, starting a seven year war that will see China side with the Koreans, leading to a stalemate.

Perhaps no event in Elizabeth's reign so captured the imagination of England as the defeat of the Spanish Armada in 1588. Though it owed much to good fortune, it signaled the start of a new era of English sea power.

descended into petty factionalism. In 1601, one of the queen's favorites, Robert Devereux, Earl of Essex, even attempted a coup, only to be sent to the block by a distraught Elizabeth. Fiscal troubles and more stringent measures against Catholics eroded her popularity. The Protestants divided into hostile camps.

But England continued to undergo a remarkable cultural flowering. Under Elizabeth's reign, some of England's greatest poets and dramatists—William Shakespeare, Edmund Spenser, Christopher Marlowe, and Sir Philip Sidney, among many others—carved out their careers. Universities flourished, as did geographical exploration. The literature, the art, the music, and even the language of the period reveal an England bursting with confidence and creativity, conscious of its new role as a rising power.

valuable time and resources. Ultimately, the English, under Lord Howard, Sir Francis Drake, and Sir John Hawkins, arrived at the tactic of remaining too far from the Spanish boats for boarding but close enough to fire cannon. It was a revolutionary shift in naval strategy, and it worked. The Armada was forced to withdraw, and on its voyage home suffered from devastating gales. Only half its ships returned to Spain.

It was an intoxicating victory for the English. During the campaign, Elizabeth had traveled to Tilbury to address the thousands of troops gathered there in anticipation of the Spanish invasion. Her speech became an iconic message of English pride and patriotism.

LATER REIGN
The defeat of the Armada was perhaps the pinnacle of Elizabeth's reign. She was growing older, many of her closest friends and counselors had died, and in her final decade the court

THE QUESTION OF SUCCESSION
As Elizabeth declined, the question of succession arose with renewed urgency. Her new Secretary of State was Robert Cecil, son of Lord Burghley and every bit as capable. In a careful process of discreet negotiation and quiet encouragement, he orchestrated the succession so smoothly that almost no one, in the event, questioned it. When Elizabeth breathed her last on March 24, 1603, she was succeeded by James VI of Scotland, son of Mary, Queen of Scots. The storied Tudor dynasty gave way to the Stuarts, and James VI, now James I, would lead England and Scotland together into a century of even greater upheaval and transformation than the last.

1593	1595	1597	1598
The Ottoman Turks invade Croatia, triggering the Long War between Habsburgs and Ottomans that would last to 1603 and end with the borders roughly where they had begun.	First known performance of a Shakespeare play: Richard II.	Christianity is banned in Japan.	The Edict of Nantes secures the rights of French Protestants.

MARY, QUEEN OF SCOTS

Mary Stuart, Queen of Scots, is one of the most romantic and scandalous figures in British history. From her accession as Queen of Scotland at only six days old to her beheading at the age of 44, she was both a political pawn and a feckless schemer who nonetheless became an iconic figure. To her detractors, Mary was destructive; to her admirers, she was tragic.

Born in 1542 at Linlithgow Castle in Scotland, Mary was the daughter of James V and his French wife Mary of Guise. Her father, already on his deathbed with a fever when she was born, died six days later. The running of the kingdom was given over to a regency, and within months of her birth, Mary was already a political chesspiece. Henry VIII of England arranged that she eventually marry his son, the future Edward VI, but the Scots reneged on the agreement, and Mary spent her childhood and adolescence in France, having been betrothed to Francis, the son and heir of King Henry II.

Mary as a teenager (above), living in France. Mary was happy and popular in the French court. She was by all accounts bright, charming, and quite beautiful: tall and slender, with auburn hair, hazel eyes, and flawless skin. It was during her time in France that she changed her name from the Scots Stewart to the more French spelling of Stuart.

Mary with her second husband, Lord Darnley, an increasingly problematic narcissist who was eventually murdered, possibly with Mary's complicity.

Her marriage to Francis was apparently successful, and when he inherited the throne at the age of 15 she became Queen of France and Scotland. But Francis died of an infection barely a year later, leaving Mary in an uncertain position. Her half-sister Elizabeth had acceded to the English throne in 1558, according to the directives of Henry VIII. Catholics, however, considered the Protestant Elizabeth illegitimate, the product of a sinful marriage, and Mary, who had her own impressive claim to the English throne, was once more a political pawn.

SCANDAL IN BRITAIN

A widow at only 18, Mary returned to a Scotland she did not know, and immediately began to show a penchant for poor decisions. She asked to be made heir to Elizabeth and was declined, for the obvious reason that such a move would make Elizabeth an even more attractive target for Catholic conspiracies. Then she made the first of two disastrous marriages, wedding her cousin Henry Stuart, Lord Darnley, an Englishman and a Catholic to boot. The marriage enraged both Elizabeth and Protestant Scots, leading briefly to open rebellion. Darnley, clearly something of a narcissist, became imperious and demanding. When Mary became pregnant, he accused her private secretary, David Rizzio, of fathering the child, and murdered him before Mary's eyes.

Once Mary had given birth to a son in June 1566, her situation was even more precarious, and Darnley had become intolerable. In February 1567, he was murdered in Edinburgh. Mary had been seeing much of James Hepburn, the Earl of Bothwell, the prime suspect in Darnley's murder. Pressed to put Bothwell on trial, Mary arranged a hasty acquittal then married him. Before, she had been politically reckless; now she was a scandal. In short order, she was imprisoned, made to abdicate in favor of her infant son, and forced to seek the dubious protection of Elizabeth.

A SORRY END IN ENGLAND

By 1568, aged 26, Mary had managed to descend from being Queen of France and Scotland to being a fugitive at the mercy of her half-sister. She must have expected Elizabeth to restore her to the Scottish throne, but Elizabeth instead had her moved from castle to castle in what passed for protective custody. Catholic unrest finally convinced Elizabeth that Mary should be kept imprisoned, however comfortably.

In her captivity, Mary became the focus of a series of plots against Elizabeth. But Elizabeth had an extensive and capable security apparatus,

THE BABINGTON PLOT

Elizabeth may have been keenly aware of the threat posed by Mary, but she was hesitant to act on it. Elizabeth's spymaster, Francis Walsingham, had no doubts at all, but he needed proof of Mary's actual involvement in an assassination plot. The opportunity came in 1585, when Gilbert Gifford, a Catholic conspirator, was "turned" under interrogation and became a double agent. Walsingham's spies worked with Gifford to uncover and manipulate what became the Babington Plot, centered on a young Catholic nobleman named Thomas Babington. Gifford arranged for the plotters to communicate with Mary by coded messages, hidden in wine casks, which Walsingham intercepted. On July 17, 1586, Mary wrote a message approving the murder of Elizabeth. It was what Walsingham had been waiting for, and it sent Mary to the block.

and in 1586 Mary fell victim to a sting, caught sending secret messages approving a plot to kill Elizabeth. After much hand-wringing, Elizabeth rather vaguely gave permission for Mary to be executed. Afterward, she would pretend to have been disobeyed.

Nothing in Mary's life became her like the leaving it. She wore a petticoat of crimson, the color of martyrdom, and conducted herself with queenly grace and gravity. But it was a messy beheading, requiring three blows of the axe, and when the executioner lifted Mary's severed head her long auburn tresses were revealed to be a wig, covering short gray hair. The once beautiful queen who had seemingly sought out misfortune met a very sorry end indeed.

The House of Stuart

The death of the childless Elizabeth I brought her cousin James VI of Scotland to the English throne as James I. Not only did James's coronation begin forging a union of Scotland and England that would be consummated generations later; it also brought back to the fore the religious conflicts that Elizabeth had worked so hard to keep in check. Those clashes would provide the backdrop for an increasingly violent debate about the limits of kingly power—a struggle that would culminate in the English Civil War, the beheading of Charles I, and the dictatorship of Oliver Cromwell. The Restoration of James II, and then the bloodless coup known as the Glorious Revolution, demonstrated an evolving sense among the British about what they expected from their monarchs and their parliaments.

JAMES I ✤ King of the Union

House Stuart

Born June 19, 1566

Died March 27, 1625

Reigned 1603–1625

Consort Anne of Denmark

Children Three, including Charles I of England and Elizabeth of Bohemia

Successor Charles I

For centuries, James I suffered in the shadow of his illustrious predecessor Elizabeth I, but more recently history has been kinder to the first of the Stuart kings of England. He ruled over a continuing cultural efflorescence, oversaw the earliest beginnings of the British Empire, and, despite his contentious dealings with Parliament, kept England on a steady keel for decades.

It is easy to overlook the fact that no English monarch ascended the throne with more experience than James I; after all, he had already been King of Scotland for more than 35 years when, in 1603, Elizabeth's death delivered him the English crown as well. But James's experience was both a positive and a negative: he understood the business of kingship and was inured to the squabbling of courtiers, but he also had rather absolutist notions of kingship that led to serious clashes with Parliament.

EARLY LIFE

James was born on June 19, 1566, the son of Mary, Queen of Scots and her husband at the time, Henry Stuart, Lord Darnley. He could scarcely have arrived in a more precarious royal environment. The Scottish court was rife with more and deadlier intrigues than its English counterpart. Mary, vilified for her scandalous behavior and even implicated in his father's subsequent murder—she quickly married the prime suspect—was forced to flee Scotland when James was scarcely a year old. The infant king grew up surrounded by feuding factions, sponsored by four regents of varying ability, two of whom died violently. As a result, he bore some similarities to his cousin Elizabeth, in that he became a guarded, watchful young man, alert to hidden agendas. Also like Elizabeth, James was exceptionally bright and a superb student; he mastered French and Latin by the

age of eight, and would go on to author several respected books in the course of his life. Though he loved hunting, he disliked violence, and earned the scorn of some of his nobles for being a scholar but not a warrior.

Religious strife was an ongoing crisis in Scotland as in England. James's mother had been a staunch Catholic—her Catholicism would pose problems for Elizabeth until 1587, when Mary would finally be executed for participating in a plot to assassinate the queen—but James had been educated as a Protestant, and his most effective regents, the Earls of Moray and Morton, championed the Protestant cause. The struggle was an often underhanded affair. At one point, when James displayed extraordinary favoritism toward the French-born and Catholic Esmé Stewart, Sieur d'Aubigny, the king was actually abducted by Protestants and held captive until he agreed to banish Stewart. The implication was that the two were lovers. They may have been, but that did not keep the king from having several children with Anne of Denmark, whom he married in 1590.

In 1583, at the age of 17, James announced his coming of age and threw off the influence of

The heraldic badge of James as King of both England and Scotland. The Union of Crowns, as it was called, is symbolized by the fusion of the English rose with the Scottish thistle.

THE WISEST FOOL IN CHRISTENDOM

HENRY IV OF FRANCE

1606	1606	1606	1607	
Dutch sailors make landfall in northern Australia, not suspecting that they have found a continent.	Dutch sea captain Willem Janszoon makes the first confirmed sighting of Australia by a European.	The English colony of Virginia is granted its first Charter.	The Flight of the Earls. Irish Catholic nationalists the earl of Tyrone and earl of Tyrconnell flee Ireland to avoid arrest by the English.	**Opposite** James I of England, King of both England and Scotland and first of the Stuart monarchs. During his reign, he faced conspiracies reminiscent of those directed at Elizabeth, most famously the Gunpowder Plot.

his regents and courtiers. For the next 20 years, he would engage in a cagey and sometimes combative campaign to secure his power over a fractious Scotland. Above all, that meant finding a religious settlement. Like Elizabeth, he took the middle way, incensing both Catholics and hard-line Protestants. Gradually, by skillfully applying his administrative powers and playing the two factions against each other, he engineered a stable settlement in which the king's authority was the last word. He even wrote a book on it in 1599, the Basilikon Doron, in which he asserted the divine right of kings; that absolutist vision of the monarchy would eventually bring trouble to him and catastrophe to his successor, Charles I.

James had one glaring weakness as a king: he was careless with finances, and constantly left himself and his kingdom in need of money. That flaw would come to haunt him as King of England, where Parliament held most of the purse strings and he would have to negotiate for funding. But his experience bringing an unruly kingdom under control—he had suppressed rebellions, negotiated settlements, resisted foreign intrigues, and even survived assassination attempts—prepared him for the prize he had awaited since 1586, when an understanding first arose that he might succeed Elizabeth. In 1603, when the word came, he said farewell to the Scots, promising that he would return often. In reality, he would only go back once. Traveling south through the lush English countryside, entertained lavishly by nobles and welcomed heartily by crowds, he was seduced by the wealth and glamour of England, and in England he remained.

Arbella Stuart, a cousin of James and of Elizabeth who reported to James a scheme to remove him from the throne and crown her. Despite this, she was later imprisoned for marrying without James's permission, and died of illness in the Tower.

A KING IN TRANSITION

James met no overt resistance in taking the English throne, but his accession engendered two parallel plots to overthrow him and replace him with his cousin, Arbella Stuart. One was financed by Spain, and involved Sir Walter Raleigh. Elizabeth's formidable security apparatus was still in place, however, and both plots were quickly unraveled. Raleigh would spend 13 years in the Tower before being executed, and James would order the banishment from England of all Catholic clergy. It was all the more impressive then, that within a year of taking the throne James managed to negotiate peace with Spain.

The abrupt encounter of a Scottish king, schooled in a different sense of the monarchy and speaking in an unfamiliar accent, with an English court and Parliament accustomed to their own procedures, made for a somewhat rocky start to the new king's reign. James tried almost immediately to unite Scotland and England not merely under one crown but also through a single Parliament; to James's consternation, the Scots were lukewarm at best, and the English flatly rejected the move. Nonetheless, in 1604 James proclaimed himself King of Great Britain, the first ruler to use the title.

But James, in concert with Elizabeth's Secretary of State Robert Cecil, had agreed to ensure continuity by maintaining the former queen's privy council more or less intact. While that decision exasperated those hoping for more radical change, it allowed James to begin adjusting, not wholly successfully, to the English way of doing things. Only gradually did he incorporate his own selections, including a handful of Scottish nobles, into the council.

DECIDING RELIGION

The religious situation in England posed a different problem from that in Scotland, in that the Elizabethan Settlement, which enforced a moderate Protestantism while retaining a number of ritual elements from Roman Catholicism, had held steady enough under Elizabeth's long reign to have taken firm root. James had resolved to be lenient with Catholics—he said privately that he would not trouble them if they only outwardly conformed,

1607–08	1608	1608
The English settle the colony of Jamestown, and French trappers establish Quebec, sowing the seeds of a fierce rivalry between England and France for control of North America.	Paraguay is founded by Jesuits in South America.	The English East India Company ship Hector arrives at Surat after a 17-month voyage and becomes the first Compay ship to reach India.

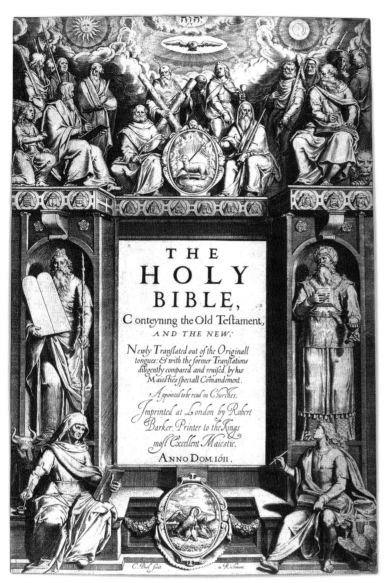

An early edition of the Authorized, or King James, Version of the Bible. Completed under James's auspices in 1611, it became one of the most important and influential texts in English history.

baptisms, and the problematic use of such terms as Absolution and Confirmation. James sided largely against the Puritans—he had dealt with them enough in Scotland to have formed a rather low opinion of them as working to undermine royal authority—but he was able to hold a moderate line. Above all, he resisted attempts to transfer governance of the Church from the bishops to presbyteries or similar assemblies. With the curt utterance, "No bishop, no king," James affirmed the monarch and his appointed bishops as governors of the Church.

The most important outcome of the Hampton Court Conference, however, arose from the Protestants' insistence that ordinary believers should have access to scripture without intermediaries. There was also some debate about the accuracy and theological import of earlier translations of the Bible. In response, James commissioned a new English translation. For the next seven years, 47 scholars worked steadily from all the available sources to produce a translation consistent with the moderate theology of the current settlement. The result, known as the Authorized Version because it was authorized for distribution throughout England, became one of the most important texts in English history. Not only did it serve as the core of Anglican worship for centuries; it also became an icon of English prose, and the literary ears of generations of English and American churchgoers were partly conditioned by its rhythms. Known also as the King James Version or King James Bible, it still holds pride of place as perhaps the most literary and most often quoted of translations.

THE GUNPOWDER PLOT

In confirming the Elizabethan settlement, the Hampton Court Conference discouraged the more militant Catholics, and James's peace with Spain led some of extremists to believe they had to take matters into their own hands. By 1604 more radical plots had begun to take shape. The most dangerous—and surely the most famous

and tolerated a discreet Catholicism even on his privy council—and the plots against his accession did not deter him.

In January 1604, he convened a conference at Hampton Court to address a list of grievances from hard-line Protestants, known as Puritans, who wanted to expunge the remaining Catholic elements from the Church of England. Debate centered on such issues as who could perform

1609	1610	1610
A Catholic League organized under the leadership of Bavaria's Duke Maximilian mobilizes its forces to oppose the Protestant Union organized last year by the Palatinate elector Frederick IV.	A combined Polish-Lithuanian army decisively defeats Russian and Swedish forces at the Battle of Klushino, paving the way for a brief Polish occupation of Moscow.	Siderius Nuncius by Galileo Galilei creates a sensation with talk of the unevenness of the moon's surface as observed by Galileo through his spyglass.

The Monteagle Letter, sent anonymously to Baron Monteagle shortly before the House of Lords was to be blown up in the Gunpowder Plot. It allowed James and his allies to disrupt the plot, an occasion for national celebration.

plot ever hatched against an English monarch—was the so-called Gunpowder Plot, an attempt to blow up Parliament while the king and his retinue were present, demolishing the English government at one blow and paving the way for a Catholic rebellion.

The mastermind of the plot was Robert Catesby, a militant Catholic who had also participated in the Earl of Essex's failed attempt to overthrow Elizabeth in 1601. He recruited a circle of co-conspirators, and, after purchasing a property near the House of Lords, began the slow and laborious process of digging a tunnel to its large undercroft. A huge amount of gunpowder—36 barrels, all told—was acquired on the black market, stored in a conspirator's home in Lambeth, and gradually rowed across

the Thames to be stored in the property. Henry Garnet, the chief Jesuit in England, was apprised of the plot; in a fateful decision, he privately discouraged it, even writing to Rome to ask for a papal ban on violent sedition in England, but he did not betray it.

A TERRIBLE BLOW

On October 26, 1605, a few days before Parliament was to convene, Lord Monteagle received an anonymous letter warning him that a "terrible blow" would strike Parliament, and that he should retire to the country and avoid the session. The letter was passed on, eventually to James. The king, possibly recalling his father's murder by explosion, determined that the letter suggested something similar, and ordered that the House of Lords be searched top to bottom the night before Parliament, so as to catch the conspirators. Shortly before midnight on November 4, Guy Fawkes was found guarding the 36 barrels of gunpowder, with matches and a fuse. He was presented to the king after dawn, and with his arrest and torture began a manhunt in which most of the conspirators were either gunned down or captured and

REMEMBERING THE FIFTH OF NOVEMBER

On November 5, 1605, Guy Fawkes was brought before King James, having been apprehended the night before while waiting to light the fuse that would lead to the explosion of Parliament. The next year, Parliament declared the 5th of November a day of national celebration. The official holiday was discontinued in 1859, but it remains in the form of Bonfire Night. The Gunpowder Plot gained a new and different kind of notoriety in the 1980s, with the publication of the graphic novel V for Vendetta. The film adaptation, released in 2005, made famous a Guy Fawkes mask, which is worn by a heroic rebel who succeeds in blowing up a totalitarian Parliament.

1610	1611	1611	1613
Henry IV of France, a religiously tolerant ruler, is assassinated, ensuring more religious strife in France.	Galileo demonstrates the powers of the telescope to Catholic officials. They are unimpressed by his theories.	The Authorized King James Version of the Bible is published in England.	Algonquian princess Pocahontas converts to Christianity and takes the name "Rebecca."

eventually executed. Henry Garnet, despite his protestations of innocence, was condemned to be hanged, drawn, and quartered.

The discovery and breakup of the Gunpowder Plot proved both traumatic and exhilarating to England. As a simulation performed in 2005 indicated, had the gunpowder been successfully set off it would have killed everyone in the building. To many at the time, it seemed that divine providence had protected James and Parliament, but Catholics would suffer heightened restrictions in the years that followed. In January 1606, Parliament passed an act inaugurating an annual commemoration of the event, and to this day Bonfire Night, which often involves the burning of Guy Fawkes

in effigy, takes place every November 5. The Gunpowder Plot backfired badly, in that it not only made the situation of Catholics in England more precarious, but also forged a bond between James and the people that would ensure the king's popularity for years, despite the clashes over policy that would characterize much of his subsequent reign.

JAMES AND PARLIAMENT

The Gunpowder Plot may have heightened James's popular support, but it did little to change the contentious relationship between king and Parliament. From the start, James disliked the degree of control, especially fiscal control, the English Parliament held over policy. In 1604, after his bid to unite England and Scotland under one Parliament was rejected, he called them "fools," and prorogued, or discontinued, the session. Subsequent Parliaments fared no better.

The real issues were money and manners. James was an extravagant king; from the start of his reign he treated the English treasury as his personal bank account, lavishing money on his favorites and decking out himself and his court in the most expensive materials possible. To many of his English courtiers, he seemed an uncouth Scotsman, a ruffian who had stumbled into a fortune. To an extent they were right; James had coarse manners and cared little for the more refined culture of the English court. Where Elizabeth had been imperious, and enjoyed sophisticated entertainment, James was broad and familiar, and preferred either hunting or watching the sorts of masques that English courtiers found tacky. He also drank too much, and encouraged others to do the same. It was all the more galling that much of the wealth of England was going to Scottish relations and favorites. Foreign ambassadors reported home that James presided over an altogether undignified court.

James responded to all this with indifference. Further, he continued to hold Parliament in contempt. He found it humiliating that he had to

Robert Cecil, Earl of Salisbury and Secretary of State to Elizabeth I and then James I. It was Cecil who engineered the smooth succession from Elizabeth to James, and then handled much of the business of government until his death in 1612.

SERO, SED SERIO

1616

In England, the traditional figure of Father Winter is renamed Father Christmas for a pageant organized by Ben Johnson for King James I.

1618

The Defenestration of Prague. Angry Protestant noblemen hurl representatives of Catholic emperor Ferdinand II out of a window—an event that leads to the Thirty Years War.

1619

The Dutch and British East India Companies agree to join forces against the Spanish and Portuguese presence in East Asia.

secure its permission for taxes, and insisted on using his royal prerogative to order taxes without Parliamentary approval. In 1610, he declared that his right to tax independently of Parliament was above question. Robert Cecil, now Earl of Salisbury, sought to resolve the impasse with what he called the Great Contract, in which the king would give up a range of his feudal rights in order to receive a first installment of £600,000, followed by annual supplements of £200,000. While it was unclear how this would resolve the situation if James failed to bring his spending under control, both sides rejected it, and James yet again dismissed Parliament.

AVOIDING FOREIGN CONFLICTS

In 1614, Parliament again refused James's requests for more funds, and he dissolved the session after only nine weeks. From that point on, the king ignored Parliament as much as possible, attempting to fund his lavish reign through selling titles and letting business managers handle his finances.

One potential source of income would be the dowry of a wealthy princess, and to that end James pursued lofty matches for his son Charles, heir to the throne. But the king was also wary of foreign entanglements. In this, he was much like his predecessor Elizabeth, and, much as she did, he used the prospect of marriage as a way of defusing, or simply deferring, conflicts that might otherwise flare up into war.

His first piece of diplomacy by marriage was the union of his daughter Elizabeth to Frederick, the Elector Palatine, which took place in 1613. The marriage was intended to forge a pan-European Protestant alliance, but when, several years later, Frederick became King of Bohemia and found himself at war with the Catholic Habsburg Empire, James had neither the resources nor the inclination to wade into and expand a war with the great Catholic powers. Still, the marriage proved important, for it was from Elizabeth's descendants that the next English dynasty, the House of Hanover, would eventually come.

THE SPANISH MATCH

The most successful instance of James's marriage diplomacy came to be known as the Spanish Match. As long as England remained Protestant, Spain was its most powerful enemy. Spain was already, if imperceptibly, in decline as a global power, but it still had tremendous wealth from its lands in the New World and considerable, if somewhat reduced, military might. Accordingly, James offered the prospect of a marriage between Prince Charles and the Infanta Maria Anna of Spain. It was a contentious policy at home—Catholic sympathizers supported it, while Protestants protested bitterly—but the marriage never happened. For nearly ten years, James dragged out the negotiations; as long as the marriage remained possible, Spain would not declare war on England.

In 1621, however, with the arrival of Frederick's war against Habsburg Austria, James summoned Parliament to rather half-heartedly request funding for a campaign in support of his son-in-law. The resulting Parliament was a circus, with James demanding money, and Parliament insisting that James declare outright war on Spain. In the ensuing bickering, James dissolved Parliament yet again.

Matters came to a head in 1623, when Charles, now in his twenties and beginning to wrest control from his declining father, traveled to Spain to sort out the marriage. The trip went badly, and on his return Charles, along with

George Villiers, 1st Duke of Buckingham, James's favorite late in his reign and a questionable influence on Prince Charles as well.

1619	1619	1619	1620
The Dutch and British East India Companies agree to join forces against the Spanish and Portuguese presence in East Asia.	The basics of modern mathematics are established by the French mathematician-philosopher René Descartes, aged 22, who applies algebra to geometry and formulates analytic geometry.	*Harmonice Mundi* by Johannes Kepler demonstrates that the planets move not in circles but in ellipses. His work is condemned as heretical.	The Mayflower carries Puritan colonists to North America, where they will found the Plymouth colony and establish Puritanism as one of the foundational worldviews of the eventual United States.

ENGLAND IN THE NEW WORLD

Under James I, England began establishing colonies in the New World, entering into a rivalry with France and Spain that would continue for generations. Jamestown, the first English settlement, was founded in 1607 in what is now the Commonwealth of Virginia. In 1620, Puritans would establish Plymouth Colony in what is now the State of Massachusetts, followed a few years later by the Massachusetts Bay Colony. Jamestown was a mercantile colony, the others predominantly religious settlements; those two impulses, often but not always conflicting, would determine much of the character of the future United States of America.

Frederick V, Elector Palatine and husband of James's daughter Elizabeth. James initially planned to marry his daughter to the Louis XIII of France, but his advisors counseled against it.

A dual portrait of Frederick V and Elizabeth Stuart. Their marriage would eventually lead to the House of Hanover taking the English throne.

the king's favorite the Duke of Buckingham, declared that England should form an alliance with France and declare war on Spain. The resulting Parliament of 1624 seemed to support Charles's initiative, but James, ever cautious, refused to go through with such a rash policy.

DECLINE AND LEGACY

The obvious disarray of James's late reign had many causes. In his last decade, James's faculties declined noticeably; he was frequently ill, and his formerly agile mind lost much of its sharpness. Further, James had relied heavily on Robert Cecil, so that when Cecil died in 1612 a resurgent factionalism began to unravel the machinery of government that had carried over from Elizabeth's reign. Then there was the matter of James's ongoing carelessness with money and lack of decorum at court. He never ceased playing favorites, and as he grew older his favorites gained more power.

In James's later years, no one held more sway than George Villiers, the Duke of Buckingham. He was an immensely handsome and charming courtier. Despite his dismal record of carelessly planned expeditions and his relentless self-aggrandizement, he commanded the affection of James with an ease that proved embarrassing to the court. As James declined, Buckingham fell in with Charles, and he would maintain his influence into the younger Stuart's reign. It was Buckingham who accompanied Charles on his 1623 trip to Spain and encouraged his subsequent reversal of allegiance, and he would prove a destructive influence on the young monarch.

In his final years, James retired into a relatively passive, enclosed existence, spending most of his time away from London. Though he was personally extravagant, he had never cared for the large-scale grandeurs and ceremonies of the kingship, and he gradually slipped into senility. On March 27, 1625, he died. He had battled with Parliament and failed to seek, much less achieve, grand international ambitions, but he had kept the kingdom peaceful and steady, and he was remembered fondly as a king who, at a minimum, had done England no harm.

Fredericus Rex Bohemie.

Michel van Iochom ex:

Elisabetha Regina Bohemia

B Monornet fc

1621	1621	1621	1621
Spain's Philip III dies, aged 42, after a 23-year reign. He is succeeded by his 15-year-old son who will reign until 1665 as Philip IV.	The Tamblot Uprising in the Philippines is inspired by a pagan revival against Christianity. It will be violently put down by 1622.	The English settlers of Plymouth Colony sign a peace treaty with Massasoit of the Wampanoags.	The first Thanksgiving, a feast shared between English settlers and Native Americans, takes place in Massachusetts.

CHARLES I ✠ Last of the Absolutists

House Stuart
Born November 19, 1600
Died January 30, 1649
Reigned 1625–1649
Consort Henrietta Maria of France
Children Seven, including Charles II and James II
Successor Charles II (after the Interregnum)

Charles I is most famous for having been beheaded at the order of Parliament in 1649, after civil war rocked Britain. The path that led him to the scaffold, however, was long and torturous, full of missed opportunities and misplaced loyalties. Whatever his other failings may have been, above all Charles was simply on the wrong side of history; he wanted the sort of monarchy whose time had passed.

Charles I was not, by any measure, born to be a king. His older brother Henry, hale and charismatic, stood to inherit the throne. Charles could scarcely have been more different: born with a frail constitution and weak feet and ankles, he spent his first three years in Scotland, cared for by the wife of a nobleman; only when he demonstrated that he could walk a fair distance unaided was he allowed, in July 1604, to travel to London and join his father's court. Over time, Charles overcame most of his physical handicaps, growing to a height of 5 ft 4 in (163 cm), but the emotional insecurities that accompanied his early infirmities never left him. Charles was socially awkward, often stammered, and adopted a haughty and imperious persona to make up for his sense of personal weakness. In 1612, however, Henry fell ill and died, probably of typhoid, and Charles, who had

idolized his brother, found himself the crown prince. At court, he eventually fell into the orbit of the magnetic George Villiers, eight years his senior and King James's favorite. In the final years of James's reign, Villiers was showered with titles, ultimately becoming the Duke of Buckingham and the most titled peer in the realm. In 1623, the two of them set off for Spain, hoping to conclude the Spanish Match, a dynastic marriage between Charles and the Spanish infanta. It was a diplomatically and domestically touchy situation: the Spanish made unreasonable demands, including that Charles convert to Catholicism, and many of the English were apprehensive about a dynastic union with a Catholic power. The trip went badly. Charles could make little headway in negotiations, and Buckingham was apparently undiplomatic enough to inspire angry letters from Spain to England asking James to punish his favorite.

On returning from their fruitless voyage, Charles and Buckingham found James so physically and mentally declined that he proved tractable to their agenda. Buckingham in particular began forcefully advocating war with Spain. In 1624, James called Parliament to ask for financing for a continental campaign on behalf of Protestants; he also asked Parliament to approve a different dynastic match for Charles, this one with the French princess Henrietta Maria. After taxing negotiations,

> THERE ARE THREE THINGS I WILL NOT PART WITH—THE CHURCH, MY CROWN, AND MY FRIENDS; AND YOU WILL HAVE MUCH ADO TO GET THEM FROM ME
>
> *CHARLES I*

1625
The Dutch settle the island of Manhattan, which they will soon buy from its inhabitants for inexpensive trade goods and name New Amsterdam. It will eventually be sold to the English and renamed New York.

1626
The Treaty of Paris ends the second Huguenot rebellion in France, in which Protestants engage in armed resistance to the increasingly oppressive Catholic regime of Louis XIII.

1627
Louis XIII and Cardinal Richelieu commence the siege of La Rochelle, the third-largest city in France and the stronghold of the Huguenots. The city will surrender the next year.

Opposite Charles I, whose refusal to change with the times and accept the demands of an increasingly powerful Parliament, coupled with rising religious strife, led to the English Civil War and his beheading.

Queen Henrietta Maria. She was a strong-willed and peremptory queen, and exerted enormous influence on her husband—some of which seriously jeopardized his position.

it was agreed that Henrietta Maria and her entourage could practice Catholicism, but such freedoms would extend no further. Still the idea of Charles's marriage to a Catholic princess sparked fears that she would prove the thin end of a Catholic wedge in England. The marriage was first sealed by proxy in Paris; by the time Charles and Henrietta had a formal wedding in June 1625, Charles had already been King of England for nearly three months.

And Charles very much enjoyed the prerogatives of kingship. His extravagantly ritualized coronation was shaped by his conviction that as King of England he was divinely sanctioned and protected. He proved as lavish a spender as his father, accumulating over the course of his reign what may be the greatest art collection of any ruler in European history. And he believed he should have absolute power.

FOREIGN MISADVENTURES
AND FIRST TROUBLES WITH PARLIAMENT

When James became king in 1625, the conflict that would come to be known as the Thirty Years' War was already well under way. The war was a prolonged catastrophe in central Europe, where in some places up to three-quarters of the population would die from violence, famine, and disease. Though it had begun as a religious conflict—James's son-in-law Frederick V, Elector Palatine and King of Bohemia, was the first leader of the Protestant forces—it gained other subtexts as it unfolded. Spain and France, both Catholic, opposed each other throughout

the war, making it partly a struggle between the Habsburg and Bourbon dynasties. Britain's position as an island insulated it from much of the conflict, but Charles, with Buckingham's active encouragement, had resolved to enter the war on the Protestant side. Parliament balked at the enormous cost of such involvement, even presenting the alternative of a raid on Spanish shipping to secure New World riches as financing, but Charles insisted on having Buckingham lead a continental expedition. Parliament agreed to finance the efforts, but on a shoestring budget.

America receives a Royal Charter. Its Puritan founders, along with those of the Plymouth Colony, set the cultural tone for the region still known as New England.

THE DOWNFALL OF BUCKINGHAM

Before long, England was mired in armed conflicts with both France and Spain. In 1626, identifying Buckingham as the chief mismanager of both conflicts, Parliament began impeachment proceedings against him; Charles simply dismissed Parliament. In 1628, Buckingham's French campaign appalled Parliament further by assisting the French regime in its repression of Protestant Huguenots; then Buckingham reversed course and began defending the Huguenot stronghold of La Rochelle, managing to lose more than half his small army and only bringing more violence upon the Huguenots. To make matters worse, Charles had supplemented Parliament's meager financing through a "Free Gift" program that was really a kind of extorted loan from the populace of England, with prison sentences for those who refused to pay. On August 23, 1628, Buckingham was stabbed to death in Portsmouth by a disgruntled officer while trying to mount another campaign. By the time of his murder, Buckingham had become the emblem of Charles's irresponsible and high-handed waste of England's money and manpower. By and large, he was not missed.

When Charles summoned Parliament in 1628,

1628	1629	1630	1631	1632
William Harvey publishes his theory about the circulation of the blood, a pivotal advance in the understanding of human physiology.	The Massachusetts Bay Colony in America receives a Royal Charter. Its Puritan founders, along with those of the Plymouth Colony, set the cultural tone for the region still known as New England.	A Dutch fleet captures Recife, establishing a Dutch colony in Brazil.	Mughal Emperor Shah Jahan, grief-stricken over the death of his wife Mumtaz, orders the construction of the Taj Mahal, which will begin in 1632 and take 20 years.	Swedish King Gustavus Adolphus, leader of Protestant forces in the Thirty Years' War, is killed while leading his troops to victory in the Battle of Lützen.

the conflict grew sharper. Parliament, channeling broad anger over the "Free Gift" and increases in customs duties, introduced a Petition of Right, insisting that the King agree that he could not raise taxes without Parliamentary consent, imprison subjects without due process, impose martial law, or force private citizens to board soldiers. Charles pretended to accede to those demands, but in reality he despised the very idea of a king having to work with or through a Parliament, and he had no compunction about simply reneging on any agreement he made. When Parliament resumed in early 1629, things became so heated that a resolution was read in Parliament that anyone who paid the tonnage and poundage customs duties Charles levied was an enemy of England. Charles angrily dissolved Parliament and imprisoned some of its leaders. Then, after negotiating peace with France and Spain, he resolved to rule without ever calling Parliament again.

BISHOP, SCHOLAR, MARTYR

William Laud, Archbishop of Canterbury, might have enjoyed a very different fate had he served under a different king. He was a firm believer in the Anglicanism of Henry VIII, with its emphasis on the efficacy of the sacraments and the importance of the Book of Common Prayer. His sharp tongue and refusal to compromise made him many enemies, and ultimately cost him his life. But Laud was more than a zealous Anglican; he was a broad scholar. As Chancellor of Oxford University, he established the Chair in Arabic, and acquired many Arabic manuscripts. His death in 1645 is commemorated in the Anglican and Episcopal churches.

THE SLIDE TOWARD CIVIL WAR

The next 11 years of Charles's reign became known as the Personal Rule. Charles refused to summon Parliament, and raised revenue through extraordinary application of antiquated taxes and laws. In some ways, it resembled the legalistic hoarding with which Henry VII built his enormous personal fortune—the difference being that Charles spent as much as he brought in. The most egregious extension of royal revenue-gathering power was the Ship Tax, which was designed only to be levied in wartime, and only on coastal areas, as a way to support naval forces. Charles's lawyers argued that the Ship Tax could be used in peacetime, and across the entire nation, and the royal court upheld that view. The resulting tax, initiated in 1634, generated some £200,000 per year in revenue, and an enormous amount of ill will toward the king in the bargain.

But the conflicts between Charles and Parliament over taxation and personal rights soon gave way to a more profound and violent difference over religion. Though Charles had married a Catholic princess, he had been raised Protestant and remained Protestant—but his faith differed markedly from that of many Protestants in England and Scotland. Charles believed in a sacramental, High Church sort of Anglican practice, but much of England had become dominated by a far more stripped-down, anti-sacramental form of worship, Puritan in the extreme, and resistant to the authority of bishops. Further, some Protestants felt that Charles's affinity for Arminianism—a form of Protestantism that rejected the Calvinist doctrine of predestination—made him something close to a heretic, or a Catholic in disguise. It was a combustible situation, and Charles would have done well to leave it alone. But he didn't. In 1633, he appointed William Laud to be Archbishop of Canterbury. Laud began a campaign to suppress and marginalize Puritanism, using extraordinary legal force to compel churches across England to use the old Book of Common Prayer and placing the sacraments back at the heart of the liturgy.

1633	1635	1636	1637	1638
Galileo is placed on trial by the Inquisition and forced to recant his heliocentric theory of the cosmos. He will spend most of the rest of his life under house arrest.	France, seeking more southerly colonies in the New World, colonizes Martinique and Guadalupe.	By consensus, the settlers of the Massachusetts Bay Colony establish New College, which will eventually become Harvard University.	Speculation in tulip bulbs has led to the Tulip Mania in Holland, a meteoric rise in the price of bulbs. The price collapses, leading to financial ruin for many investors.	Resistance to Archbishop Laud's staunchly Anglican policies leads to the signing of the Scottish Covenant in Edinburgh. The Covenanters take control of the Scottish government.

Laud's efforts met with significant resistance, but the situation might have remained salvageable had Charles not sought to impose the same sort of reforms in Scotland—and do it without so much as alerting either the Scottish Parliament or the General Assembly of the Scottish Church. In 1637, he ordered distributed in Scottish churches a new Book of Common Prayer closely modeled on that of the Church of England. The Scots were predominantly strict Calvinists, and many found the new order of liturgy so offensive that on its introduction in the summer of that year riots broke out in churches all over Scotland. Resistance organized swiftly, forming a coherent movement called the Covenanters, named after the covenant of God with the chosen people in the Bible.

Thomas Wentworth, Earl of Strafford. Attempting to further Charles's aims ended in Strafford's execution for high treason after a vendetta by John Pym. Allowing Strafford's execution was reportedly Charles's greatest regret.

THE BISHOPS' WARS

In two conflicts that came to be known as the Bishops' Wars because the king favored church government by bishops rather than the Scottish preference for elders, Charles sent armies to Scotland in 1639 and then 1640 to assert royal authority. The first time, neither side wanted a fight, and a settlement was quickly reached. The following year, Charles decided to call Parliament for the first time in 11 years and request money for the campaign. In April 1640, Parliament convened. Over the past decade its leaders had done their homework, and with the militant and shrewd leadership of a Puritan MP named John Pym, the Commons placed before Charles a list of grievances and demanded that they be addressed before any further business was conducted. Charles angrily dissolved the Parliament—called the Short Parliament because it only lasted from April 13 to May 5.

In November 1640, Charles summoned Parliament once more, and things turned out even worse. Among others, the Earl of Strafford, who had been recalled from a post in Ireland to strengthen Charles's hand against Parliament, was impeached for high treason. The impeachment failed, but the implacable Pym transferred the charges into a bill of attainder. Strafford, imprisoned, wrote to Charles freeing him from all promises of protection should Parliament insist on a capital sentence. Reluctantly, Charles agreed to Strafford's execution, which occurred in May of 1641. Parliament dragged on, passing acts that required the king to summon it at least once every three years, and ultimately one establishing that Parliament could only be dissolved through an internal vote—hence the name that has since accompanied this period: the Long Parliament.

The conflict in Parliament soon precipitated violence elsewhere. In October 1641, Ireland descended into religious strife, the Catholics claiming to act on behalf of the king.

But then Pym and his associates overplayed their hand, calling a vote in the Commons on

1639	1640	1642	1643
Rembrandt van Rijn has earned enough from his painting to buy a house in Amsterdam, which is now the heart of the Rembrandt House Museum.	The first known European coffee house opens for business in Venice. Coffee houses will spread rapidly and become centers of business and debate in the coming century.	Sieur de Maisonneuve founds the settlement that will become Montreal, Quebec. French and English ambitions in the New World are developing in close proximity.	At the age of five, Louis XIV becomes King of France. He will grow into an extraordinarily powerful, absolutist monarch and rule until 1715.

A contemporary illustration of Charles's beheading outside Whitehall in 1649. For the next 11 years, England would go without a king.

The Great Remonstrances, a withering series of charges and complaints against Charles and his government that barely passed with a simple majority. But then Charles made a poor move of his own. On January 4, 1642, egged on by Henrietta Maria, he personally entered Parliament with an armed escort and demanded that Pym and a handful of other MPs be turned over to face charges of conspiring with the Scots against the king. The charges may well have been true, but the violent entry into Parliament was disastrous politically for Charles, who looked like the tyrant the more radical elements in Parliament claimed him to be. A week later, Charles left London, readying for armed conflict. Nobles and commoners began choosing sides. On August 22, 1642, Charles raised the royal military standard in Nottingham, and moved his base to Oxford. War had come.

CIVIL WAR

Parliament raised its own army, and soon enough the Royalist and Parliamentary forces, eventually known as the Cavaliers and the

Roundheads respectively (the Parliamentary forces for their distinctive helmets), were engaging in a series of inconclusive battles. In June 1645, however, Parliament's New Model Army, partly led by Oliver Cromwell, crushed the Royalist forces at Naseby in Northamptonshire. From then, it was only a matter of time. Charles was forced to seek refuge with the Scots. After some negotiations, they turned him over to Parliament, and the Royalists and Parliamentarians reached a truce in which Charles remained under house arrest.

War seemed to have been contained. But in 1647, Charles struck a deal with the Scots that if they restored his power he would grant them three years without any royal interference in their church affairs. So began what became known as the Second Civil War, a more ruthless affair than the first. It culminated in August 1648 with the Battle of Preston in Lancashire, where Cromwell's army decimated the invading Scots.

Furious at Charles's scheming, in December of 1648 the army took control of Parliament, locking everyone out but a radical contingent of Puritans. Called the Rump Parliament, this faction tried Charles for high treason. He was convicted and sentenced to death. It was, in effect, a military coup, and Cromwell stood behind it.

Charles may have ruled badly, but he died well. On January 30, 1649, he was brought to a scaffold outside the Palace of Whitehall. On his travels through the country as a prisoner, he had been cheered by throngs of commoners, for most of England was decidedly uncomfortable with the notion of putting an anointed king on trial, much less executing him. For his part, Charles was ready. After a short, defiant speech, he calmly put his head on the block. It was severed in one blow.

For the next 11 years, England would have no king; for several of them, it would have Cromwell as Lord Protector. But Charles's queen and his sons Charles and James had escaped to the continent. When England decided to renew the kingship, they would be on hand to assume it.

1644	1645	1647	1649	1648
English poet and Puritan John Milton publishes Areopagitica, a forceful and elegant argument against censorship.	Miyamoto Musashi, the greatest swordsman in Japanese history, dies quietly in spiritual retirement after writing his classic Book of Five Rings.	In America, the General Assembly of the colony of Rhode Island passes legislation separating church and state. Such separation will eventually become central to the founding of the United States.	Several months after Charles's death, Oliver Cromwell begins his conquest of Ireland.	Amid the chaos of the English Civil War, George Fox, founder of the Religious Society of Friends, more commonly known as the Quakers, travels England preaching.

OLIVER CROMWELL

I f ever there was an uncrowned King of England, Oliver Cromwell was that man. After establishing himself as a compelling leader during the Civil War, he eventually became Lord Protector of England—king in all but name. His son Richard, who somewhat reluctantly inherited that position after his father's death, followed a different path, to a different fate.

Oliver Cromwell was born in 1599 to minor gentry in Cambridgeshire. His family was not wealthy enough to allow him a leisured life; after his father's death in 1617, he had to withdraw from Cambridge University without taking a degree. In 1620, he married and began raising a family.

FROM PARLIAMENTARIAN TO SOLDIER
In 1640, Cromwell represented Cambridge in what would become known as the Short Parliament; he held the same position in the Long Parliament that followed, gaining some stature over the course of the contentious negotiations. When civil war broke out in 1642, Cromwell distinguished himself by leading successful charges and showing exemplary leadership.

By 1644, Cromwell was Lieutenant General of horse in the army of the Earl of Manchester, and he distinguished himself again at the Battle of Marston Moor, leading ferocious charges that broke Royalist lines. But Cromwell also offended the sensibilities of some of his commanders, making trusted commoners his officers rather than appointing gentlemen. For Cromwell, leadership was about merit, and merit was about Christian character, as he understood it.

In 1645, Parliament approved an overhaul of its military forces. Cromwell masterminded many of the reforms, and his New Model Army, in which he served as second-in-command to Sir Thomas Fairfax, became a disciplined,

streamlined machine. Beginning with the pivotal Battle of Naseby that year, the New Model Army steamrolled Royalist troops in several encounters; in 1646, Charles I surrendered.

FROM SOLDIER TO LORD PROTECTOR
Though fiercely devout, Cromwell was in fact more moderate in his political views than many of his fellow Protestants; at one point during Charles's captivity, Cromwell even attempted to negotiate a mutually satisfactory settlement that would keep the king on the throne. But when Charles escaped and a second round of civil war began, Cromwell's position hardened. He helped bring about Charles's defeat with a devastating massacre of Scottish Royalists at Preston in 1648. After Charles's capture, Cromwell became one of the most prominent advocates of the king's execution, which took place in January 1649.

After Charles's death, Parliament declared a republic: the Commonwealth of England.

Statue of Oliver Cromwell with his sword and his bible at Westminster, London, sculpted by Hamo Thornycroft. At some point during the late 1620s Cromwell seems to have undergone a religious crisis. His subsequent letters reveal a man devoutly Puritan, convinced that he has been saved through grace alone, and determined to live a godly life.

Charles Landseer's 1851 painting of Oliver Cromwell at the Battle of Naseby in 1645, where he cemented his reputation as a brave and decisive military leader.

Richard Cromwell, Oliver's third son and his successor as Lord Protector. The portrait suggests the lack of forcefulness that led to his resignation. Royalist propagandists and satirists would refer to him as "Tumbledown Dick."

Cromwell became its undisputed military leader. Having developed formidable tactical skills, he embarked on a series of ruthless campaigns against Irish and Scottish Royalists. In Ireland, where massacres on both sides had resulted in bloody-minded religious conflict, he suppressed Catholicism with unsparing, sometimes brutal, efficiency. While his individual responsibility for some of the resulting atrocities is uncertain, to this day he is one of the most reviled figures in Irish history. Scotland fared better, being less Catholic. At Dunbar he decimated a much larger Royalist army, and when Charles II attempted to invade England from Scotland, Cromwell's army crushed Charles's forces at Worcester, nearly capturing Charles himself.

After Parliament proved unable to reach agreement on a form of government, in 1653 its leaders turned to Cromwell, investing him as Lord Protector of England—in effect, dictator. Despite his ruthless military campaigning, or perhaps because of it, he made his first objective national reconciliation and healing. In an effort to restore order and prosperity, he refused to make radical, leveling reforms, invited Jews back to England for the first time in over three centuries, and promoted an agenda of moral reform. In 1657, he was offered the crown, but refused it, saying "I would not build Jericho again."

The End of the Interregnum

In 1658, at the age of 59, Cromwell died of an infection; after a magnificent funeral, he was interred in Westminster Abbey. His son,

Richard, succeeded him, but he had no taste for public service and lacked the absolute loyalty of the military that had always underpinned his father's regime. In May of 1659, unable to manage the various factions in the government, he resigned and went into voluntary exile. After years of traveling Europe under assumed names, he returned to England in around 1680 and lived out his days in relative anonymity. After the Restoration, Oliver Cromwell's body—or what was believed to be his body—was exhumed, beheaded, and publicly displayed, along with those of other chief advocates of Charles I's execution. To this day, this complex man—fervent reformer and political pragmatist, ruthless general and advocate of tolerance—remains a much-debated figure in British history.

CROMWELL'S HEAD

On January 30, 1661, 12 years to the day after the beheading of Charles I, Royalists exhumed Oliver Cromwell's body, along with those of other Parliamentarians who had argued for the king's execution, and beheaded it at Tyburn. Cromwell's head was left on a spike atop Westminster Hall, where it remained for at least ten years before either falling to the ground or being removed. Afterward, it passed through several people's hands, eventually becoming known as the Wilkinson Head after a family who owned it for some time. It was studied several times in the early to middle 20th century, with examiners generally finding no reason to doubt its authenticity. In 1960, it was finally re-interred—not in Westminster Abbey, but somewhere within Sidney Sussex College, which Cromwell had attended while at Cambridge. Its exact location is a closely guarded secret.

CHARLES II ✚ The Merry Monarch

House Stuart
Born May 29, 1630
Died February 6, 1685
Reigned 1660–1685
Consort Catherine of Braganza
Children None legitimate, but more than a dozen illegitimate including James Scott, Duke of Monmouth
Successor James II

Charles II, first ruler of the restored monarchy, was very nearly the antithesis of the Puritan ideal: a charming hedonist with a laissez-faire approach to governance. He was often neglectful as a king, but he commanded great popular affection, and was in some ways the right man for the moment in British history.

When Charles was born in 1630, his mother, Queen Henrietta Maria, was somewhat put off by the evidently Mediterranean appearance he had derived from the Medici strain in his family. But, unlike his father, who had been weak and sickly as a child, young Charles was vigorous and strong. He grew to be a tall, athletic, outgoing teenager. When the Civil War erupted, he accompanied his father on campaigns at the age of 14; perhaps more importantly, he spent a good amount of time among career soldiers, enjoying their ribald humor and their penchants for gambling and chasing women.

As the Civil War turned against his father, Charles retreated with his mother and brothers to the continent, first in France, where his cousin Louis XIV was a boy-king, and then in the Low Countries, where his sister was married to William II of Orange. After the execution of Charles I in January 1649, young Charles did find support in Scotland, where he was named King of Great Britain, though barred from entering Scotland unless he agreed to promote Presbyterianism, the Protestantism of Scotland, universally. Eventually, Charles agreed, and in 1650 he advanced into England with a Scottish army, intent on regaining the throne for the House of Stuart. At the Battle of Dunbar, Oliver Cromwell's New Model Army defeated Charles's force, and Charles was forced back into Scotland, where, on New Year's Day 1651, he was formally crowned King of Scotland. It was indeed a formality, as he had no real power; the Covenanters, the elders of the Scottish Kirk (Church), controlled Scotland.

In the late summer of 1651, Charles made one more effort to invade England at the head of a Scottish army. He marched south, hoping to inspire widespread resistance to the Parliamentary regime, but though people often cheered him they had little interest in fighting for him. When battle came, at Worcester on September 3, Charles's forces lost again, and this time Charles fled the field in fear for his life.

For the next 40 days, Charles lived an outlaw existence as a Parliamentary manhunt, complete with posters describing his appearance, spread across England. At one point shortly after the defeat at Worcester, he and an advisor spent a day hiding in a large oak tree at Boscobel House in Shropshire while Parliamentary soldiers combed the area, passing beneath Charles. The tree became famously known as the Royal Oak.

> WE HAVE A PRETTY WITTY KING,
> AND WHOSE WORD NO MAN RELIES ON,
> HE NEVER SAID A FOOLISH THING,
> AND NEVER DID A WISE ONE

JOHN WILMOT, EARL OF ROCHESTER

Opposite Charles II, a hedonistic king but also a sagacious and tactful politician, nonetheless could not escape controversy toward the end of his reign.

1660
The old Cockpit Theatre reopens in London, inaugurating a rebirth of English drama and comedy. For the first time, women will be allowed to work as stage actors.

1661
With the death of Cardinal Mazarin, France's Louis XIV begins to rule on his own, rapidly demonstrating the talent and ambition to become the dominant European monarch.

1662
The Royal Society of London for Improving Natural Knowledge, or the Royal Society for short, is established as the first European organization for the advancement of scientific knowledge.

On another occasion, a fugitive and incognito Charles actually insulted himself as part of his disguise. Eventually, he was able to make his way across the Channel to safety, arriving in mid-October. Charles's familiarity with the manners of soldiers, and his easy charm with people of all backgrounds, doubtless aided him in his escape.

THE RESTORATION

For the next nine years, Charles would languish in exile on the continent, living a dissipated existence based on the generosity of royal relations in France and the Low Countries. In 1660, however, Oliver Cromwell had been dead for two years, and his son Richard had resigned as Lord Protector. England was in a crisis of governance, and Charles realized that, perhaps, his time had come.

General George Monck, the Governor of Scotland, had realized much the same thing: that England was having a governmental identity crisis that carried the risk of renewed Civil War and possible anarchy. He marched on London, took over Parliament, and demanded a new round of Parliamentary elections. When they happened, the result was a rather balanced legislative body, divided between Anglicans and Calvinists, Royalists and Parliamentarians. Compromise seemed possible.

Monck and Charles corresponded, and on April 4, 1660, Charles's carefully composed Declaration of Breda was read aloud in the new Parliament. In the Declaration, Charles voiced respect for Parliament, promised unconditional amnesty for nearly all his father's enemies—excepting those who masterminded the former king's trial and execution—and outlined a policy of religious

General George Monck, who intervened with Parliament to effect the Restoration of the Monarchy.

tolerance. Parliament—known subsequently as the Convention Parliament, because it was not summoned by a king but summoned a king—voted to restore the monarchy, and on May 29, 1660, his 30th birthday, Charles triumphantly entered London. In December the Convention Parliament dissolved, and on April 23, 1661, Charles was formally crowned in Westminster Abbey, to tremendous popular acclaim. England had decided that, whatever limits it might place upon their power, it would not go without its kings and queens. A year after his coronation, Charles married Catherine of the Portuguese House of Braganza.

EARLY COMPROMISES AND CRISES

After Charles's coronation, a new Parliament formed. Dominated by Royalists, it became known as the Cavalier Parliament. This was less advantageous to Charles than one might think; his moderate and tolerant stance on matters of religion proved difficult to sustain in the face of an Anglican voting bloc that advanced legislation promoting Anglicanism above Calvinism and Catholicism. From 1661–1665, Charles would somewhat reluctantly accede to a series of acts designed to promote and entrench the Church of England. Associated with Edward Hyde, Earl of Clarendon and Charles's Lord Chancellor, who promoted some of the measures, they became known as the Clarendon Code. The measures were strict; they included oaths of allegiance to the Church from municipal office-holders, bans on religious gatherings of more than five people apart from Anglican worship, and mandatory use of the Book of Common Prayer in the liturgy. Religious tensions remained—they would surface in a particularly malign form later in Charles's reign—but other matters soon took center stage. The first was a war on the Dutch, who were now a formidable mercantile power and had gained control over much of the Channel. A naval victory at Lowestoft in 1665 was a promising start, and England gained permanent control of the Dutch colony of New

1663	1664	1665	1666	1667
Using a primitive microscope, Robert Hooke discovers that cork is made of tiny divisions, which he calls cells.	Dutch Governor Peter Stuyvesant cedes control of the Dutch colony of New Amsterdam to the English. In honor of James Stuart, Duke of York, it will be renamed New York.	Jan Vermeer paints A Lady Writing a Letter, probably in his home in Delft. Though Vermeer was mostly forgotten shortly after his death, he is now regarded as one of the greatest Dutch painters.	The Annus Mirabilis of Sir Isaac Newton, who makes a number of discoveries, including those related to optics, motion, and gravitation.	John Milton, blind and living in poverty, sells the copyright to Paradise Lost, which is published to great acclaim.

St. Paul's Cathedral as redesigned by Sir Christopher Wren after the Great Fire of 1666. It remains one of the iconic buildings of London, and the site of many celebrated events.

The huge area gutted by the Great Fire of London. Though in some ways the fire allowed for a renovation of the city's infrastructure, it also cost a staggering sum.

Amsterdam—renamed New York. But in 1667 the Dutch fleet audaciously sailed up the Thames, burned a large portion of the English fleet, and sailed off with Charles's flagship. The Treaty of Breda, closing the conflict, was soon signed. Blame for the war—especially for the embarrassing episode on the Thames—fell on Lord Clarendon, who fled into exile rather than face impeachment for high treason.

But another reason for concluding the war involved crises within London itself. In 1665, a wave of plague swept through the city. It was the last outbreak of the bubonic plague in England and fell well short of the devastation of the Black Death, but close to 80,000 people succumbed to it, roughly one in six Londoners. As the plague wound down, a second disaster struck: over three days in September of 1666, a fire in a bakery erupted into a massive conflagration that devastated London, destroying over 13,000 homes and many other buildings. Ninety churches were destroyed, including St. Paul's Cathedral. Charles and his brother James took an active role in trying to contain the fire. The Great Fire of London was a catastrophe, but it was also a chance for renewal. Many plans to remake London as a grand capital were proposed, but the difficulty of determining ownership of much of the land prevented such proposals from ever being realized. With the participation of such architects as Sir Christopher Wren and Nicholas Hawksmoor, however, St. Paul's and many other churches and edifices were rebuilt in a new, classical style.

Silver linings aside, the fire was costly. Hundreds of thousands of Londoners were displaced, and the price of recovery would cost in the order of £10 million. Though spread over decades, it was still an enormous sum for an already strained treasury. Charles's lavish spending did not help matters. Known as the Merry Monarch, he oversaw a court that could scarcely be less puritanical; hedonism in all its forms flourished, as if both court and country made up for lost years of entertainment and indulgence. Theater returned, now with women playing the female roles, which had formerly been reserved for boys. One of the most famous actresses of the era, the famously beautiful and witty Nell Gwynn, became as a teenager one of Charles's many mistresses.

THE RESURGENCE OF RELIGIOUS STRIFE

In 1670, Charles made a secret but fateful decision. Though after the Treaty of Breda England had stood with the Protestant Dutch against the Catholic French, Charles covertly reversed course. He signed the Treaty of Dover, in which, in exchange for an annual stipend from France, Charles promised to return to the Catholic Church when he felt the time was right, at which point Louis XIV would supply him with an army to suppress any resistance. Charles refrained from converting, but his brother

1668	1669	1670	1671	1672
The British East India Company takes control of Bombay. British conquest of India, culminating in the Raj, begins with such mercantile empire-building.	In Italy, Mount Etna erupts, destroying towns and killing tens of thousands of people.	English activity in the Caribbean escalates. England takes possession of Jamaica, and the enterprising pirate Henry Morgan captures Panama.	Colonel Thomas Blood, an Anglo-Irish soldier, attempts to steal the Crown Jewels and nearly succeeds. In a decision that remains puzzling, Charles not only pardons him but gives him land and a stipend.	In Florida, Spain begins construction of the Castillo de San Marcos to protect its settlement of St. Augustine. The fort still stands, and St. Augustine is the oldest continuously inhabited colonial settlement in North America.

A MISTRESS OF MANY TALENTS

Nell Gwynn became one of the greatest actresses of the Restoration and the most storied of Charles's mistresses. Though her origins are unclear, she appears to have worked in a London brothel run by her mother before becoming an actress. Beautiful, but also brilliantly witty, she captivated audiences and eventually became Charles's favorite. One tale recounts her intervening when her coachman fought with a bystander who called Nell a whore; Nell remarked, "I am a whore. Find something else to fight about." Nell died in 1687, at the age of 37, leaving a legacy to the prisoners of Newgate Prison. She remains a somewhat ironic Cinderella figure in English popular imagination.

James made no secret of his own Catholicism. In March 1672 Charles advanced the Declaration of Indulgence, lifting the restrictions of the Clarendon Code from Catholics as well as dissenting Protestants; then he declared war with France on the Dutch. Parliament refused to finance war against the Dutch, and forced Charles not only to drop the Declaration of Indulgence but also to sign a Test Act excluding Catholics from public office. In 1677, Charles placated the opposition by marrying his niece Mary to William III of Orange, a Protestant match. The marriage would prove momentous in the years to come.

Titus Oates, disgraced priest and instigator of the Popish Plot fraud. Parliament's susceptibility to his scheming resulted in a slew of arrests and executions before he was eventually punished.

THE POPISH PLOT

In 1678, religious tensions—especially anti-Catholic sentiment—reasserted itself. First, Charles's back-door dealings with France came back to haunt him. An incensed Parliament sought to impeach Lord Danby, the Lord High Treasurer, for high treason for having contributed to the negotiations.

Though the impeachment stalled between the two houses of Parliament, Charles agreed to confine Danby in the Tower of London. But anxiety about Catholic designs on England escalated. Charles dissolved the Cavalier Parliament, only to have it replaced by another, more hostile one. And this Parliament fell victim to one of the most irrational episodes in English history: the Popish Plot.

Anti-Catholic feeling had been growing in England since the Great Fire, which was wrongly held by many to have been the result of a Catholic plot. It did not help that Robert Hubert, a watchmaker of questionable soundness of mind, was executed after confessing to having set the fire as part of a Catholic conspiracy, only to have his story revealed as false after his death. But in 1678, Titus Oates, a disreputable Anglican priest, along with his friend Israel Tonge, circulated a document in which Oates testified that he had extensive information on a Jesuit plot to kill Charles and forcibly convert England back to Catholicism. The document was pure fiction, but it caught the imagination of enough well placed people to come to Charles's attention. He personally interrogated Oates, caught him out as a liar, and had him arrested.

But Parliament ordered Oates's release, and gave him altogether more credibility. Oates would ultimately make more than 80 accusations, moving from commoners to peers and even accusing the personal physician of Queen Catherine of plotting to kill Charles. This may have been patently absurd, but in the overheated environment of the time Parliament made him the star witness in a series of absurd trials and executions that went on for years.

1673	1674	1675	1677	1678	1680
French Jesuit and explorer Jacques Marquette explores the Great Lakes and the Mississippi River for France.	The French Royal Academy holds the first Salon to showcase paintings by graduates of the École des Beaux-Arts. It is the beginning of the Academic tradition in French painting.	Gottfried Leibniz records in his notebooks his first use of integral calculus.	Jules Hardouin Mansart begins work on the Place Vendome in Paris, an icon of Baroque public architecture.	John Bunyan publishes The Pilgrim's Progress, a work of devotional literature that will have broad and deep influence among Protestant readers for centuries.	In America, the Pueblo Indians revolt against Spanish colonial rule and capture Santa Fe.

Oates was given an apartment in Whitehall and a stipend; many of his targets were executed. By 1681, however, it had become clear to all but the most jaundiced observers that Oates was a liar. Judges began throwing out convictions. Oates was evicted from his lodgings at Whitehall, and Charles promptly had him imprisoned for perjury. Since perjury was not punishable by death, Oates was publicly and brutally flogged.

But by then the anti-Catholic forces in Parliament had forced yet another crisis. Though Charles had fathered many illegitimate children, he and Catherine had never managed to have a child. This left Charles's openly and devoutly Catholic brother James heir to the throne. In 1679, under the leadership of Anthony Ashley Cooper, Earl of Shaftesbury,

Anthony Ashley Cooper, Earl of Shaftesbury. His introduction of the Exclusion Bill polarized Parliament into two parties: the Tories and the Whigs.

Parliament introduced the Exclusion Bill. It was the ultimate Test Act; it barred Catholics from inheriting the throne. Since this was clearly designed to prevent James's accession, Charles stalled the process by dissolving Parliament several times between 1679 and 1682. The two opposing sides took names that would become defining terms in English politics for generations: supporters of the Exclusion Act were called Whigs; the opposition became known as Tories.

In 1683, however, a very real plot to assassinate both Charles and James came to light—and it was a Whig conspiracy. A group of Whig extremists based at Rye House in Hertfordshire resolved to gun down the king and his heir as they passed en route back to London from the races at Newmarket. Fortunately for Charles and James, a fire in Newmarket changed their plans, and the plot failed to come off. Between the exposure of the Popish Plot as a fraud and the discovery of the Rye House Plot, the anti-Catholic forces lost credibility, and the Exclusion Act was dropped. Shaftesbury and others were forced into exile to avoid impeachment for treason.

A MUCH-MOURNED MONARCH

On the morning of February 2, 1685, James suffered a sudden fit, perhaps a stroke, and it was clear that the end had come. Four days later, after saying his farewells, he entered the Catholic Church and died in Whitehall Palace. His brother James, a man of very different inclinations, succeeded him.

On his death, Charles was widely mourned. Though his court was famously decadent and by temperament he was far more a politician than a ruler, he had maintained his personal appeal, and he had a well-earned reputation for being genuinely gracious to peers and commoners alike. He had also patronized the arts and sciences, ensuring a new flowering of both. His very aversion to conflict, along with his easygoing tolerance, helped ensure that England did not slide back into sectarian warfare.

1681	1682	1683:	1684	1685
William Penn, a wealthy Quaker, receives a Royal Charter for land that will become the colony of Pennsylvania.	Peter the Great becomes Tsar of Russia. The gifted, forward-thinking monarch will bring Russia into closer contact with Western Europe.	A huge Ottoman Turk army lays siege to Vienna. Forces led by Jan III Sobieski of Poland successfully repulse the invasion, in a battle involving a cavalry charge of 20,000 troops, the largest in history.	The Chinese regime gives the British East India Company permission to build a trading post in Canton.	Louis XIV passes the so-called "Code Noir," permitting slavery throughout the French colonies.

JAMES II ✠ The Last Catholic King

House Stuart

Born October 14, 1633

Died September 16, 1701;

Reigned 1685–1688

Consort Mary of Modena

Children Seven, including Mary II of England and Queen Anne of Great Britain

Successor William III of Orange and Mary II.

James II brought to the throne not only a devout Catholic faith but also a desire for religious tolerance and an affinity for the sort of authoritarian kingship modeled by Louis XIV in France. He pursued those ideals with single-minded purpose, but England did not share them, and in due course simply replaced James.

James II, the second son of Charles I, was an object of suspicion and antipathy to many when he took the throne after his brother Charles II's death in February 1685, but he had also earned praise in the course of his earlier life. Unlike his older brother, he remained in the Royalist stronghold of Oxford through most of the Civil War. Captured in 1646, he was confined to St. James's Palace until, in 1648, he successfully escaped and made his way to the continent. There, he served under the brilliant generals the Vicomte de Turenne and Louis de Condé in the French civil war known as the Fronde, acquitting himself well in battle. He and Charles differed on how to navigate the shifting alliances of continental conflicts, but shortly after Spain and France made peace in 1659, Charles was invited to return to England as king, and James accompanied him.

But while serving with French and Spanish soldiers, James had been exposed to Catholicism, and his sympathy with Catholics marked him as a questionable figure in the minds of many English Protestants. His marriage to a commoner—

Anne Hyde, the daughter of Charles's Lord Chancellor—met with disapproval on dynastic grounds but also removed the possibility of his making dynastic Catholic marriage. By 1669, however, James had converted, though for political reasons he kept his practice covert. During Charles's reign, James served as Lord High Admiral, demonstrating a real capacity for leadership and strategy on the seas. He commanded the victory over the Dutch at Lowestoft in the Second Dutch War, and oversaw the construction of new coastal defenses after the embarrassing Dutch raid on the Medway, in which they torched many English ships and made off with Charles's flagship. In 1666, Charles placed James in charge of containing the Great Fire of London; though by the time James took over the fire was beyond control, he received high praise for his efforts.

But whatever good feelings James had generated largely evaporated when, after Parliament passed the Test Act in 1673, he stepped down as Lord High Admiral rather than repudiate Catholicism. His conversion was now in the open. Two years earlier, his wife Anne had died, and now he married the Catholic Mary of Modena. Charles disapproved of the match and insisted that James and Mary's children be raised Protestant, but there was little he could do to stem the tide of disapproval. Even James's marriage of his daughter Mary to William III of Orange, a Protestant prince, failed to help.

> # THIS GOOD PRINCE HAS ALL THE WEAKNESSES OF HIS FATHER WITHOUT HIS STRENGTH
>
> JOHN MAITLAND, EARL OF LAUDERDALE

1685	1685	1686	
The composers Johann Sebastian Bach and Georg Friedrich Handel are born in Germany.	After 87 years of religious tolerance, the revocation of France's Edict of Nantes forbids the practice of any religion but Catholicism and forbids Huguenots to emigrate. Half a million people will emigrate to Protestant countries.	New York City is granted a colonial charter. It will quickly become one of the most important cities in the American colonies.	**Opposite** James II, last of the Stuart kings, a devout Catholic who badly misread the politics of religion in England and ultimately lost the throne to a Protestant newcomer.

Misgivings about James only intensified as it became clear, after a series of failed pregnancies, that Charles's queen, Catherine of Braganza, would likely never give birth to an heir, leaving James the heir presumptive. In 1679, a group of MPs led by the Earl of Shaftesbury introduced the Exclusion Bill, which would bar any Catholic from taking the throne. It was clearly designed to remove James from consideration as king; James withdrew into voluntary exile before returning to Scotland. Dissolving a series of Parliaments, Charles temporized, and eventually public opinion broke in favor of James. The debate over the Exclusion Act divided most of Parliament into two groups: the Whigs, who supported the measure, and the Tories, who rejected it. Those two labels would go on to define much of English politics in the next centuries.

A BRIEF AND TROUBLED REIGN

On Charles's death in early 1685, James took the throne in a smooth and swift succession, retaining many of his brother's advisors. But within months he had to face two anti-Catholic uprisings. The first, in Scotland, was tiny and easily suppressed; the second, involving his father's illegitimate son James Scott, Duke of Monmouth, posed more of a threat. But Monmouth, who had sailed from the continent with only three ships and about 80 men, only managed to draw about 3,000 in total. James had a small standing army, but he managed to organize a compact force against Monmouth. On July 6, 1685, the two armies collided at Sedgemoor in Somerset, in what would be the last such clash of armies on English soil. Monmouth was defeated and captured. His execution nine days later was infamously difficult; it took several blows of the axe to separate Monmouth's head from his body.

But it was not from the Whigs that James would encounter the gravest opposition; it was the Tories who would eventually bring him down. Though they had backed him against the Act of Exclusion, they fully expected him to abide by the settlement in which the king fully supported the Church of England. They were mistaken. And events abroad would color

James Scott, illegitimate son of Charles II and Duke of Monmouth. His rebellion in 1685 was quickly put down, but it boded ill for James's reign.

The execution of the Duke of Monmouth, a gory affair that involved several swings of the axe.

the situation in England in ways that would aggravate tensions to breaking point.

In October 1685, Louis XIV revoked the Edict of Nantes, which had extended rights to French Protestants since 1598. It was a catastrophe for French Huguenots and a bracing shock to English Protestants. James expressed disapproval of the persecutions that followed in France, but he also organized a standing army of 20,000 soldiers, with a number of Catholics among its officers. It looked to many Protestants like the makings of Catholic coercion visited upon them by an English king. When James summoned Parliament in November, he immediately alienated them, having one MP arrested for disrespectful language and pre-emptively rejecting the removal of any Catholics from his army or other positions, regardless of the Test Act. He then handpicked a panel of judges to rule that the king was not obligated to enforce any of Parliament's laws, but could use his power of dispensing to make exceptions at will. A further affront came when he forced Catholic appointments on Oxford colleges. It was becoming distressingly clear that James, like Louis, was bent on restoring a wholly Catholic order.

In early 1688, James began instructing his underlings to purge from public office anyone they could identify as opposed to giving Catholics complete freedom of religion. In April, he introduced his Declaration of Indulgence, a carefully crafted edict using the power of dispensing to revoke restrictions on Catholics and Protestant Dissenters. But when he demanded that bishops read the Declaration from the pulpit, many, including the Archbishop of Canterbury, refused. In a move that can only be described as politically obtuse, James had several bishops arrested for seditious libel. That was exactly what they had been hoping for. In an early display of civil disobedience, they accepted imprisonment in the Tower, thereby becoming heroes in the popular imagination and precipitating a trial involving public argument over the power of dispensing. In the end, the bishops were declared not guilty. It was a

1686	1686	1686	1687
The League of Augsburg allies a formidable array of European powers against France's Louis XIV.	A brief conflict in which the Mughal Empire defeats the forces of the British East India Company begins the move toward a more aggressive stance by the British in India.	Cordon Bleu cookery has its origins in the Institut de Saint-Louis, founded by Mme. de Maintenon for 250 daughters of impoverished nobility.	Sir Isaac Newton publishes his *Principia Mathematica*. The book, which explains the laws of gravity and mechanics, effects a revolution in human understanding of the natural world.

A portrait of James's queen, Mary of Modena, with their son James, who many years later would seek the throne for himself, becoming known as the Old Pretender.

resounding rejection of James's bid for more power, and the beginning of the end of his reign.

A CHANGE OF RULE

The breaking point came in June, when Mary of Modena gave birth to a son. Despite a number of witnesses to the birth, rumors swirled, encouraged by James's Protestant daughters Mary and Anne, that the child was a changeling. The real issue was that a male heir meant the very real prospect of decades of pro-Catholic rule, and the Protestants would have none of that. Many of the Whigs and Tories, united in their anxiety, formally invited Mary and William of Orange to take the throne.

William had seen the moment coming and prepared a large invasion force. When his enemy Louis XIV turned his designs to Germany that year, William was free to launch his armada for England. On November 5, William landed in Devon, where, in a stroke of modernist strategy,

he set a printing press brought for the purpose to produce reams of propaganda. Princess Anne fled London to join William, as did James's best military commander, Lord Churchill. Pitched from overweening confidence to abject despair, James abandoned the cause, and with it his throne. He clearly suffered a complete breakdown. On December 11, after reportedly tossing the Great Seal into the Thames, he managed to get himself captured by a fisherman while trying to escape to the continent. After being brought back to London by some of his own soldiers, he was eventually detained by William's forces. On December 23, doubtless under orders, they looked the other way so James could finally make good his escape. He would never set foot in England again. William entered London as co-ruler with James's daughter Mary. Not a shot had been fired. It became known as the Glorious Revolution. When James made one attempt to regain power, landing in Ireland in 1689, his forces were defeated by William at the Battle of the Boyne. James resolved to give up seeking power.

James was received in France by Louis XIV, who accorded his cousin a palace and a stipend to support a comfortable existence. In his retirement, he lived the life of a Catholic renunciate, dying quietly in 1701. James was in many ways paradoxical: a crusader for religious tolerance as a means of gradually bringing England back to Catholicism; an accomplished soldier who fell apart at the crucial moment when he might have defended his throne; a high-handed, vain monarch who finally chose the life of a penitent. England had little to thank him for, except perhaps his choice to flee the country rather than spill more English blood.

LOUIS XIV

Louis XIV, the most powerful ruler of France, spent much of his 72-year reign attempting to bring Europe under French hegemony. An autocratic monarch known as the Sun King, he famously remarked, "L'état, c'est moi" ("I am the state"). He built the magnificent palace of Versailles, and lived in breathtaking splendor while prosecuting territorial and religious conflicts across Europe. He was James's cousin, but saw all alliances in terms of French advantage. Though he ruled France with absolute authority, he also squandered much of its resources, beginning the downward slide that would eventually lead to the French Revolution.

1687	1687	1688	1688
Russian forces fail dismally in their first attempt to take Crimea during the Russo-Turkish war, never even reaching their destination.	The Second Battle of Mohacs gives Charles of Lorraine a victory over the Ottoman Turks. The diet of Pressburg confers hereditary succession to the Hungarian throne upon the male line of Austria.	The Quakers of Germantown, Pennsylvania produce the first known anti-slavery tract in America.	Edward Lloyd opens a coffeehouse in London that becomes a popular venue for conducting business. It will eventually evolve into Lloyd's of London.

WILLIAM III & MARY II ✠ Advent of a New Monarchy

WILLIAM III
House Orange
Born November 4, 1650
Died March 8, 1702
Reigned 1688–1702
Queen Mary II
Children None
Successor Queen Anne

MARY II
House Stuart
Born April 30, 1662
Died December 28, 1694
Reigned 1688–1694
King Mary II
Children None
Successor William III

illiam III and Mary II came to power in the Glorious Revolution, a bloodless Protestant coup against the determinedly Catholic James II; their accession as co-rulers ensured that England would remain a Protestant nation. Though Mary was much loved, William, who functioned as ruler before and after Mary's death, lacked personal charm and met with a great deal of criticism. Regardless, the two of them ensured stability and continuity at a crucial time.

William III of Orange was literally born to rule. His father died a week before William was born, in late 1650, making him stadtholder, or chief executive, of the Principality of Orange. The Dutch system did not have kings, but rather politically appointed leaders. This form of government, so different from the absolute monarchy of France, would prove important to William's later rule in England.

As a child, William was a political chesspiece, his destiny uncertain. His mother, Mary Stuart, the daughter of Charles I, paid her son little attention. As heir to the House of Orange and nephew to Charles I, he was a threat to some established Dutch leaders. William was short and asthmatic, but extraordinarily focused and strong-willed, and he learned quickly how to fend for himself in a politically charged environment.

Across the Channel, Mary was born 12 years after William to James Stuart, brother of Charles II and eventually his successor. She also saw little of her parents, having been raised by a governess at Richmond Palace. Though Mary's

parents converted to Catholicism around 1688, Charles had decreed that James's daughters be raised as Anglicans. Two years after her mother died in 1671, Mary's father remarried Mary of Modena, an Italian princess only four years older than Mary, and a devout Catholic.

While Mary enjoyed a privileged and relatively staid childhood in England, William proved himself on the field of battle. Johan de Witt had placed him as a ward of the state to better control the young heir to the House of Orange, but as William grew older he began to shift for himself. In 1671, as war with the French and English loomed, he was appointed provisional Captain-General of the Dutch States Army. The following year, the young leader of the House of Orange would be severely tested.

The year 1672 saw the Low Countries invaded by the full force of Louis XIV's absolutist France and its allies. In June, after a dogged but unsuccessful defensive campaign against superior forces, William was forced to withdraw into Holland, and in a last defensive measure the Dutch opened their dikes. This defense, known as the Dutch Water Line, had been designed in the previous century to create the option of a gigantic moat around the Dutch heartland. In this case, it created a stalemate. At this point, William was the acknowledged leader of the Dutch; he was named stadtholder

> THE LIBERTIES OF ENGLAND AND
> THE PROTESTANT RELIGION
> I WILL MAINTAIN
>
> *WILLIAM III*

1689	1692	1694	Opposite
The Jacobite Rising of '89 sees several Highland clans of Scotland rebel in support of exiled King James VII of Scotland. They are led by the charismatic Viscount John of Dundee.	The Salem Witch Trials, a wave of mass hysteria in which 19 people are hanged for witchcraft and scores imprisoned, take place in the Massachusetts Bay Colony in America.	The Bank of England is founded. It is the first central state bank in the modern sense of the word and later forms the model for all such banks.	A period illustration of the coronation of William and Mary. It conveys some of the jubilation that led to their accession being called the Glorious Revolution.

by multiple territories, and spent the next year harassing Louis's forces as best he could. Fortunately, the Dutch navy had greater success, and an uneasy peace was negotiated in 1678.

A MARRIAGE AND A CORONATION

The year before, in a mutually advantageous move, Charles II and William had agreed that William should wed Mary. Mary reportedly wept for a day or more on hearing the news, but acquiesced to the match. It took a while for the newlyweds to warm to each other, but they eventually did. Mary's open and vivacious personality compensated for the dour seriousness that so often characterized William, and she became unexpectedly popular among the Dutch.

By 1688, Mary's father, who had become James II in 1685, had aroused so much opposition in England with his pro-Catholic agenda that the throne seemed within William and Mary's grasp. For William, this meant a unified Anglo-Dutch front against the ambitions of Louis XIV. For Mary, it meant a return to England and the life of a sovereign. When the invitation from Protestant leaders came in early July of that year, William had already prepared an invasion force. Shortly after its arrival in England in November 1688, James attempted to flee for the continent. William, unwilling to evoke memories of the beheading of Charles I, allowed James to escape.

William took the reins of government that month, and in January summoned a Convention Parliament. After some negotiations, Parliament determined that James had abdicated the throne, and appointed William and Mary as joint rulers, each continuing to reign in the event of the other's death. In April, Scotland followed suit. William and Mary were crowned on April 11, 1689 in Westminster Abbey. The bloodless transition came to be known as the Glorious Revolution.

A DIFFICULT BUT DECISIVE REIGN

Though William and Mary were joint sovereigns,

Mary deferred to William whenever he was in England. This was the case during the Convention Parliament of 1689, and during this Parliament foundations were laid for a very different sort of monarchy than England had so far experienced. The political situation was ideal for such a change: William needed to remain on good terms with Parliament to fund his wars against France, and Parliament was eager to curb the royal prerogative. Unlike James II, who had modeled himself on the imperious kingship of Louis XIV, William came from the more corporate and consensus-driven Dutch model of government, and was more open to such measures.

Two major reforms thus came almost immediately. The first was the Act of Toleration, which extended religious freedom to dissenting Protestants; William would have preferred a more comprehensive reform, but he accepted that step. Second, and far more important, was the Bill of Rights, which passed in December 1689. Reflecting the political thought of the philosopher John Locke, it was an extraordinary string of reforms, stipulating no taxation without the express permission of Parliament, no royal interference in legal processes, no standing army in peacetime without Parliamentary approval, no retribution for petitions to the monarch, no cruel and unusual punishment, and absolute freedom of speech in Parliamentary debate. The Bill of Rights remains a cornerstone of British law to this day. From its passage forward, Parliament became the real center of gravity in British government.

But there still remained resistance to the accession of William and Mary, especially in Ireland and Scotland. In 1689, James II landed in Ireland with a force of French soldiers, and William ordered his army to repel the Jacobite forces and subdue Ireland. When progress toward those ends came too slowly, he personally took command of the army and defeated James's forces at the Battle of the Boyne in July of that year. Though the battle left relatively few casualties, it resulted in James abandoning his designs on the throne and

A half-crown from the reign of William and Mary. The establishment of the Bank of England in 1694 led to an influx of revenue that financed, among other things, a massive expansion of the British navy.

1696	1697	1698	1699	1700
With the death of his half-brother Ivan IV, Peter the Great becomes sole ruler of Russia, accelerating his process of Westernizing the nation.	The new St. Paul's Cathedral, redesigned by Sir Christopher Wren after the Great Fire of London in 1666, is opened.	As part of the Darien scheme, Scottish settlers embark for Panama to form the colony of Caledonia. The attempt will prove a disastrous failure, both in the New World and, financially, in Scotland.	The first steam engine is presented to the Royal Society by inventor Thomas Savery. The design is flawed, but it paves the way for the introduction of steam power in the coming century.	Records indicate that around this time Bartolmeo Cristofori, Keeper of the Instruments for Ferdinando de'Medici, invented the piano.

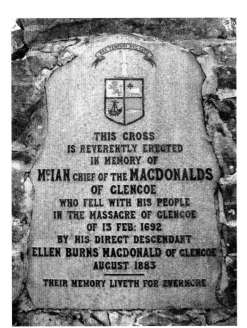

Glencoe in Scotland, where, with William's permission, scores of members of the MacDonald clan, including women and children, were killed or left to die of exposure in 1692. William probably did not know the real nature of the planned atrocity when he sanctioned it.

returning to permanent exile in France.

In Scotland, William fared worse—not because of any military defeat, but because of an atrocity. He had extended an amnesty to any Scottish clans willing to pledge support to his rule before January 1, 1692. When the chief of the MacDonalds of Glencoe, delayed by circumstances beyond his control, failed to sign the oath soon enough, his enemies persuaded William to authorize a raid on Glencoe. William was told that his agents were breaking up a gang of brigands; in reality, the Campbell clan, enemies of the MacDonalds, massacred everyone at Glencoe. William's reputation never fully recovered from the incident.

William divided his time between England and the continent, where the power and aggression of France had actually precipitated an alliance between the Vatican and Protestant countries. The costly war dragged on until 1697, when a tenuous peace was reached. But one other far-reaching change occurred as a result of the war: in 1694, William authorized the establishment of the Bank of England to finance his campaigns. This introduction of a Dutch financial model would ensure a higher degree of financial stability and accountability from that time forward.

But William remained unpopular. He could occasionally draw support from the Tories or the Whigs, but he had no people skills and could be curt and peremptory in manner. His expensive wars on the continent served the larger purpose of containing French power, but drew little admiration from the English, and though his navy asserted itself with victories over the French, William could claim no comparable successes on land. Mary, a conscientious, reflective, and altogether more gracious ruler in William's absence, was far more popular, and when she died of smallpox in 1694 William was not only grief-stricken but saddled alone with the rule of England. Opposition mounted, and several times he considered abdicating the throne. William and Mary had no children, and in 1700, Anne's son William, heir presumptive, died. Fearing another crisis of succession, Parliament passed the 1701 Act of Settlement, redirecting the succession to Anne and then to Sophia of Hanover, granddaughter of James I, ensuring a Protestant monarch.

In February 1702, William's horse stumbled beneath him; William broke his collarbone in the fall. He soon succumbed to an infection, and on March 8 he died. An unpopular if not a hated king, he was given a hasty burial late at night, which few attended. The chief architect of the continental alliance against Catholic France, the king who had preserved England as a Protestant nation, went largely unmourned.

PHILOSOPHER OF HUMAN RIGHTS

John Locke (1632–1704) was one of the most important thinkers of the Enlightenment. His writings ranged across a number of disciplines, but he is best known for his theory of the mind as a tabula rasa, or blank slate, inscribed only by experience, and for his ideas about the social contract. The latter became foundational for both the English Bill of Rights and the American Declaration of Independence. Locke's work remains important in multiple areas of philosophy.

1701 In Britain, Jethro Tull invents a machine to place seeds in holes drilled in the soil. This seed drill starts the agricultural revolution that massively increases the amount of food that can be grown.

1701 In Japan, the feudal lord Asano Naganori is ordered to commit suicide. The sentence is suspicious, and 47 of Asano's samurai begin plotting revenge. Their successful plot becomes one of the most loved and retold stories of Japanese history.

1702 In March, the Daily Courant, the first English-language daily newspaper, begins publication in London.

QUEEN ANNE The Dutiful Monarch

House Stuart
Born February 6, 1665
Died August 1, 1714
Reigned 1702–1714
Consort George of Denmark;
Children None
Successor George I

Queen Anne, the last of the Stuart monarchs, came to the throne at the age of 37 but with little preparation. She won the affection of her subjects, however, by taking on her duties with a deep sense of obligation—and by ruling over the advent of Great Britain as the most powerful nation in Europe.

Anne was born in 1665, the second daughter of James Stuart, who would in 1685 succeed his brother Charles II as King of England, and his first wife, Anne Hyde. Along with her older sister Mary, Anne was raised largely apart from her parents, and, according to Charles's directive, as an Anglican. Her mother's death in 1671, and then the public revelation of her father's conversion to Catholicism in 1673, further separated her from James. Anne lacked the vivacity and charm of her sister, and from an early age demonstrated a kind of dull but dogged character, given to intense personal loyalties.

The first and most important of those loyalties was to her childhood friend Sarah Jennings, who would later marry John Churchill, James's brilliant military commander. Their friendship, easy and intimate, conformed to the pattern of leader and sidekick—but Sarah had an outgoing, witty personality that Anne appreciated. Though Anne far outranked Sarah, privately the two girls, and then women, treated each other as peers. Anne also wrote often to her sister after Mary's marriage to William of Orange and subsequent relocation

to the Low Countries. In 1683, Anne entered an arranged marriage to Prince George of Denmark; it was by all evidence a good match, and Sarah Churchill became a personal attendant, or lady of the bedchamber, to Anne, ensuring that they could continue to spend time together.

After the Glorious Revolution in 1688, tensions arose between Anne and Mary that revealed something of Anne's temperament. Mary disliked the Churchills, regarding them as overambitious and unscrupulous, but Anne stuck with them, continuing her close friendship with Sarah, even after John Churchill was disgraced and dismissed in 1692 for borderline insubordination—he had undermined William's Dutch commanders. It was clear that, for Anne, personal loyalty trumped political expediency. But Mary's opinion of Sarah was not far wrong; Sarah became an effective political operator, even helping secure Anne a Parliamentary allowance large enough to make her even more independent of her sister.

After Mary's death in 1694, William never remarried, and it gradually became clear that Anne would succeed him. Given that she had no children—despite more than 15 pregnancies, she had given birth only three times, and all three children had died of illnesses—in 1701 Parliament passed the Act of Settlement, such that the throne would pass to the Protestant House of Hanover assuming Anne had no surviving children. James was still alive in France, along with his son James Francis Stuart,

Sarah Churchill, Duchess of Marlborough, childhood friend and close advisor to Anne. The two women eventually fell out over Sarah's overpowering and aggressive attitude toward Anne.

> SHE MEANT WELL AND WAS NOT A FOOL, BUT NOBODY CAN MAINTAIN THAT SHE WAS WISE, NOR ENTERTAINING IN CONVERSATION
>
> *SARAH CHURCHILL, DUCHESS OF MARLBOROUGH*

1702
In America, the French establish a fort in what is now Mobile, Alabama, making it the capital of French Louisiana.

1703
Peter the Great founds the city of St. Petersburg in Russia. It will eventually become the imperial capital of the nation.

1704
English naval forces capture Gibraltar from Spain. England will never relinquish control of the island.

1705
Isaac Newton, whose theories have already transformed European thought, is knighted by Queen Anne.

Opposite In her modesty and devotion to duty Anne helped solidify the new form of government that had taken shape under William and Mary.

and Parliament was determined to ensure a Protestant succession.

QUEEN OF A RISING ENGLAND

In March 1702, William died from complications of a riding accident; on March 8, Anne became Queen of England. Anne had not been raised with the sophisticated education she might have received had it been obvious in her early years that she might one day take the throne, so she had to rely on her instincts—and on the advice of the politically inclined Sarah Churchill—to navigate the labyrinth of royal power. Anne was 37, and her health was already beginning to suffer; she was overweight and suffered from debilitating gout and other ailments. At her coronation, her gout was so severe that she had to be carried in a chair. But her first speech in Parliament was a success, for the simple reason that she knew to emphasize her native Englishness after the much-resented Dutch origins and sensibility of William. It helped also that Anne had one political gift: a well-trained and mellifluous speaking voice.

In actuality, apart from her poor health and lack of education, Anne was almost ideally positioned as a monarch. She was native English, moderate and cautious by nature, and committed both to the Anglican Church in which she was raised and the continental struggle against the formidable power of France. Though she tended to gravitate toward the Tories, the Whigs found reasons to appreciate her.

The opportunity to confront France came quickly in the form of the War of the Spanish Succession, which would be the defining event of Anne's reign. The Spanish king, Charles II, was soon to die without issue, and one of his possible heirs was the Dauphin of France, Louis XIV's son Louis. Though Spain had weakened considerably since the magisterial heights of its power a century before, it still owned extensive lands, and the prospect of an already powerful and aggressive France encompassing those resources was unacceptable.

But Anne had Europe's trump card: John Churchill, who had been elevated to Duke of Marlborough and named Captain-General of England's army shortly after Anne's accession. The greatest general England has ever produced, and perhaps its only true military genius, Marlborough quickly expanded and modernized the English army, and by 1703 had driven the French from the Dutch Republic. His crowning victory came the next year, with the Battle of Blenheim. On August 13, 1704, in a masterful display of strategy and skill, Allied forces led by Marlborough and Eugene of Savoy inflicted a massive defeat on French forces led by Marshal Tallard. At the day's end, half the French army, including Tallard and other commanders, were killed or captured. It was the greatest English-led military victory since Agincourt, and it marked the arrival of England as a modern, formidable European power.

But despite further successes under the gifted Marlborough, the war dragged on, and

John Churchill, Duke of Marlborough. Anne's Captain-General, he was a brilliant military strategist and surely the greatest general Britain has ever produced. When Anne declared war on France in May 1702, Louis XIV reportedly joked about women waging war. He had no idea what he was in for.

1707

Charles XII of Sweden invades Russia. His subsequent defeat at Poltava marks the decline of the Swedish Empire and the rise of Russian power in Europe.

1708

Johann Sebastian Bach is named chamber musician and organist to the Weimar Court.

1709

The Great Frost of 1709, a three-month spell of the coldest weather in centuries, freezes the Atlantic coast and results in tens of thousands of deaths.

FROM A VICTORY TO A PALACE

No battle showcased the Duke of Marlborough's genius more than Blenheim. The overwhelming victory signaled England's arrival as a dominant power in Europe. As a reward, Queen Anne had a palace—the only non-royal home designated as such—built for Marlborough not far from Oxford. The Duke named it after the battle that earned him the reward. Built between 1705 and 1725, Blenheim Palace is a magnificent edifice, but its construction became fraught with political maneuvering and cost overruns. Still, it became the home of the Churchill family for the next three centuries. Now, it is one of the most popular tourist destinations in England.

Parliament and the people began to chafe under the continuous expense and loss of life. After a crushing victory at Oudenarde in 1708, Louis was prepared to sue for peace, but the terms given him were so objectionable that he fought on, the French rallying around what had become a matter of national pride, and the English casualties at the 1709 Battle of Malplaquet were so severe that the war seemed not worth prosecuting. A peace would not be negotiated, however, until after Anne's death.

DOMESTIC TROUBLES

As the war on the continent played itself out, Anne was forced to confront domestic troubles. The Scots, dissatisfied with the Act of Settlement, passed their own Act of Security in 1703; it not only opened the door to James Francis Stuart, but also stipulated that any new King of Scotland who was also King of England would have to accord full trading rights to Scotland, including England's rapidly growing colonies in America. Parliament retorted with the Alien Act of 1705, which threatened to curtail trade with Scotland unless Scotland united completely with England. As it turned out, however, the two positions were not so far apart. In 1706, after only three days of negotiations, it was agreed that England and Scotland would unite. With the Acts of Union in 1707, England and Scotland formally became Great Britain, one state with one Parliament.

Anne, for whom personal loyalties had always mattered most, had more immediate political problems. Sarah Churchill, whom Anne had given the prominent posts of Groom of the Stole and Keeper of the Privy Purse, became a relentless partisan for the Whig cause, and as time went by increasingly tried to impose her agenda on Anne. The queen, often incapacitated by gout or other infirmities, found herself browbeaten, and on one occasion Sarah was witnessed treating Anne disrespectfully in public. Eventually they fell out, and Anne found another, more modest friend in a different lady of the bedchamber, Abigail Masham. The Churchills made unseemly attempts to have Parliament remove Sarah's rival from her position, but at this point Anne was uncharacteristically decisive. In 1711, she elevated a number of new peers to the House of Lords to ensure Parliamentary approval of the proposed Peace of Utrecht, the beginning of the end of the war with France and, immediately after, both Churchills were removed from their posts.

But Anne did not have much longer to live. Her husband had died in 1708, and she was increasingly lonely and depressed. Her health was failing as well. After a series of serious illnesses, she succumbed on August 1, 1714. According to the Act of Settlement, she was succeeded by George of the House of Hanover, who became George I.

Anne was not a great monarch, but under her rule England had become a major power, and in London's thriving tea- and coffee-house culture new ideas and ambitions were being entertained. The coming century would see enormous transformations.

Blenheim Palace, named by the Duke of Marlborough after his greatest victory.

1710	1711		1712	1713	1714
Beijing is now the largest city in the world.	Alexander Pope publishes An Essay on Criticism, a poem that defines and encapsulates the classical and witty fashions of the era.		With the Treaty of Aargau, Switzerland resolves its religious settlement, keeping the nation Protestant but preserving the rights of Catholics.	The Treaties of Utrecht end the War of the Spanish Succession. France gives over to Britain parts of what is now Canada.	Parliament offers a substantial cash reward to anyone who can solve the navigational problem of longitude, a persistent problem for global exploration.

The House of Hanover

When George I came from Hanover to assume the British throne in 1714, he spoke scarcely a word of English—yet the House of Hanover eventually became one of the most distinctly English royal families, in both loyalty and style. Under the Hanovers, with their modest view of the royal prerogative, England succeeded in evolving into a modern, democratic state, while at the same time building the largest and wealthiest empire of the era. And the Hanoverian kings and queens were far more colorful figures than we tend to remember: their scandalous affairs, father-son quarrels, and personal eccentricities make for fascinating stories. Under the Hanoverians, the throne gave way almost completely to Parliament as the center of political power; to their credit, they accepted the inevitable.

GEORGE I ✦ Inaugurator of a New Dynasty

House Hanover
Born May 28, 1660
Died June 11, 1727
Reigned 1714–1727
Consort Sophia Dorothea of Celle
Children Five, two legitimate, including George II
Successor George II

James Francis Stuart, known as the Pretender (and later the Old Pretender), son of James II and initiator of an ineffectual rebellion in Scotland against Hanoverian rule.

George I was a paradoxical ruler. Though scandalously autocratic and even cruel as a man, as a king he was moderate, responsible, and steady. Still, he never won the affection of his subjects, largely because he did not seek it. Private, uncommunicative, and distant to the end, he set a good course for the Hanoverian dynasty but died an unloved king.

Like his predecessor Queen Anne, George was already well into adulthood when he inherited the English throne at the age of 54; unlike Anne, he was highly trained and experienced in statecraft. He had already served in leading positions in Hanover, and had fought alongside Marlborough in the War of the Spanish Succession. Further, he understood the sort of government he was coming to head, and tempered his authoritarianism in order to work with Parliament and rule, insofar as possible, through consensus and moderation.

He arrived in England, however, with a somewhat tainted reputation as a man. In 1682, George had married his cousin Sophia Dorothea of Celle, an attractive and lively woman. The next year, she bore him a son, George Augustus, but things eventually soured. All indications are that George held a deep, abiding disrespect for women, and his mistreatment of his wife may have contributed to her having an affair with a Swedish nobleman, Count von Königsmarck. In 1694,

Königsmarck was murdered—according to some, at George's behest—and soon after the marriage was dissolved. George kept Sophia Dorothea under house arrest in her native Celle for the remaining three decades of her life; it was a cruel decision, and it left a permanent rift between George and their son George Augustus.

A KING WITH CLEAR PREFERENCES

After Anne's death in 1714, George took his time arriving in England, allowing himself to be feted on the continent first. When he did reach London, the reception was decidedly mixed. Crowds were more curious than jubilant, and George, who cared little for public displays, did nothing to spark celebration. He spoke little English, extended few pleasantries, and brought with him an entourage of Germans and two ferociously loyal Turkish bodyguards who may have known him better than anyone else. If William of Orange was a foreigner, George of Hanover was an alien.

His reception in Parliament was mixed as well, and he anticipated as much, having kept tabs for years on the British political scene through representatives in London. Many of the Tories had reservations about the Hanoverian succession, some even preferring the possible return of James Francis Stuart, son of the late abdicated James II. George made it clear from the start that he favored

> IF THE AMBITION OF THOSE ABOUT HIM HAD NOT BEEN GREATER THAN HIS OWN, WE SHOULD NEVER HAVE SEEN HIM IN ENGLAND
>
> *LADY MARY WORTLEY MONTAGU*

Opposite George I, first of the Hanoverian kings, who much preferred his native Hanover to England but who set crucial precedents with his willingness to negotiate and compromise with Parliament.

1714	1715	1717	1717
The Ottoman Empire declares war on Venice, the latest contest for control of the Mediterranean.	Nine fully laden treasure ships returning to Spain sink in a storm after leaving Cuba. The disaster is symbolic of the waning fortunes of once-mighty Spain.	After a month-long siege, the forces of Eugene of Savoy take the city of Belgrade from the Ottoman Empire.	A Frenchman named Francois-Marie Arouet is imprisoned in the Bastille for writing satirical verse against the Regent of France. When he is released, he will take the pen-name Voltaire.

Robert Walpole, the talented and gregarious Whig politician who became effectively the first Prime Minister of Britain.

the Whigs, even though they were the party advocating Parliamentary power over royal prerogative. In 1715, the Whigs took control of Parliament. One of the Whig leaders, Robert Walpole, so well understood George, and so well managed the machinery of government, that he successfully navigated the twists and turns of George's entire reign.

But 1715 also saw a challenge to Hanoverian rule. James Francis Stuart, assisted by disgruntled Tories and Scots and supported by France, made arrangements to come to Scotland and challenge George's accession by force. The prospect of the Stuart heir making a bid for the throne distressed the Whig majority, and even a number of Tories, but George, a veteran of religious and dynastic wars of much greater scale, simply ordered an army north once James had arrived in Scotland. James, known by his detractors as the Pretender, proved an ineffective one, failing to generate much enthusiasm and fleeing Scotland before any meaningful conflict could ensue. The death of Louis XIV that September cemented James's fate; the new French regime sought peace with England, and James spent the rest of his life in exile.

The following year, the simmering resentment between George and his son came to a public boil when the king returned to Hanover for an extended visit, refusing to let George Augustus serve as regent. By this time, George had made his distaste for England clear, and he had become the butt of both ridicule and contempt through much of the country. George Augustus and his vivacious wife Caroline, however, were immensely popular. Whether or not they genuinely loved England, they certainly took pains to create the impression that they did, and they set up a household in Leicester House that made the court of King George, such as it was, look downright dour in comparison. When George returned, he brought with him the composer Georg Friedrich Handel, who went on to compose a series of pieces that might be called the score to Georgian Britain.

FINANCIAL TROUBLES

Soon, George found himself confronting more serious troubles outside the family. In imitating the Dutch financial model, England had not only introduced a national bank but also embarked on trading in securities. It was new territory, fraught with pitfalls, and in 1720 England fell into one.

The South Sea Company, established in 1711, was a kind of shadow Bank of England, founded by Tories as a mechanism for managing the national debt while making a tidy profit. The essential mechanism was that loans to the government were converted into Company shares, which could then be sold on the market. But in 1719, after it purchased the princely sum of £30,000 of national debut, such hype began surrounding the Company that a fever of speculation took hold, and nearly everyone with sufficient assets, including the king, who was technically governor of the Company, wanted in. By the summer of 1720 shares were being sold that had no assets backing them up. It was a charade, and the upward spiral of speculation soon crashed into reality. The financial losses of the South Sea Bubble, as it was called, ruined an untold number of fortunes. Though records show he took a financial hit as well, George, as governor of the Company, took the blame.

But there was one beneficiary: Robert Walpole. Somehow, he had either steered

1717	1718	1719	1720	1720
First known attack by the pirate Edward Teach, who would later gain fame by his nickname Blackbeard.	The War of the Quadruple Alliance begins on the continent when France declares war on Spain. Britain joins on the side of France.	Daniel Defoe publishes *Robinson Crusoe*, a narrative whose popularity helps inaugurate the tradition of the English novel.	Edmond Halley, discoverer of Halley's Comet, is appointed Astronomer Royal.	Jonathan Swift begins writing *Gulliver's Travels*, perhaps the most famous satire in British literature.

Francis Atterbury, Bishop of Rochester and inflammatory opponent of the House of Hanover. His Jacobite intrigues eventually let to his being arrested and exiled for life.

clear of the speculation or simply missed the boat, but when public outrage resulted in a purge of Whig leaders seen as connected to the scandal, he was the sole one left standing. One prominent MP, Lord Stanhope, died after a heated debate in Parliament, evidently from the stress of the crisis. For all intents and purposes, the government was Walpole's. In power if not in title—he was officially Chancellor of the Exchequer—England had its first Prime Minister. Walpole masterfully contrived to minimize the fiscal damage, and for the remainder of George's reign was the true head of Britain's government.

Walpole was a large man with an expansive and canny personality. Born in Norfolk, educated at Eton and Cambridge, and gifted with both impressive rhetorical skill and nearly unerring political instincts, he nonetheless retained an unpretentious style, earning the nickname "the fat old Squire of Norfolk." His rise to power had everything to do with his ability to control the political center; though a dedicated Whig, he understood how to compromise, and did his best to curb the overzealous tendencies of his fellow Whigs. He also knew that a great deal of political power still came from the favor of the king. It was Walpole who, after the public breach between George and George Augustus,

persuaded them to at least appear to get along—an accomplishment that demonstrated his formidable people skills. With Walpole, the government largely remained on an even keel.

None of this mattered very much to George, who had little interest in the domestic affairs of England. He spent a fair amount of time in Hanover, looking after his homeland's interests and enjoying a purely German milieu. In 1722, however, a plot against the king's life was uncovered. Called the Atterbury plot after one of its ringleaders, Francis Atterbury, Bishop of Rochester, it would likely have proved ineffectual. But the interesting aspect of the plot was its consequences: no one was executed. Even Atterbury was merely stripped of titles and assets and sent into permanent exile. The influence of Parliament as the new seat of power meant that plots against the king, even murderous ones, no longer seemed apocalyptic. In fact, they no longer seemed to have much point.

DECLINE AND DEATH

Over the course of the 1720s, George declined markedly. He was growing old, and he yearned more and more for the Hanover of his youth. It was on a trip there in 1727 that he grew suddenly ill and died. Such was the low estimation of the British for George that he was not even brought back to England for burial, but interred in Hanover. He surely would have preferred that final resting place.

But as much as George had alienated his English subjects, he had also ruled with a judicious sense of the limits of royal power, and under his relatively benign rule English culture flourished. His was the age of Samuel Johnson, Jonathan Swift, and Alexander Pope. Politically, George's reign helped set the foundations of a new and modern Britain, one in which men of talent and ambition, and sometimes genius, could rise through the ranks of Parliament and steer the nation. It would be such men, not the kings and queens, who would build the British Empire.

WHIGS AND TORIES

The term Whig comes from the Scots word whiggamor, or cattle driver, and became used as a form of derision for those Members of Parliament who so opposed rule by a Roman Catholic monarch that they supported the Exclusion Bill. It eventually became a badge of honor for those who advanced the bill. Their opponents, the Tories, were so called in reference to the Irish word for an outlaw, because many Catholics in Ireland supported a Catholic monarchy—as did quite a few of the Tories. Though the names were linked to a specific issue, they also invoked wider principles, and over time they stuck. The two parties would dominate British politics for generations.

1721	1722	1723	1724
Peter the Great is proclaimed Emperor of All the Russias, signaling the arrival of a Russian Empire that will become a major force in Europe.	Jean-Philippe Rameau publishes his Treatise on Harmony, a seminal work in music theory, in the same year that Bach composes The Well-Tempered Clavier.	Louis XV of France attains his majority. He will rule until 1774, a period of decline leading to the French Revolution 15 years after his death.	King Philip V of Spain abdicates in favor of his son Louis I. Within the year, Louis will die of smallpox, forcing his father to return to the throne.

GEORGE II ✦ Figurehead and Fighter

House Hanover

Born November 9, 1683

Died October 25, 1760;

Reigned 1727–1760

Consort Caroline of Ansbach

Children Eight, including Frederick, Prince of Wales

Successor George III

The reign of George II saw England continue to expand as a military and mercantile power. Though he was often curt and personally difficult, George, like his father, understood the changing nature of British kingship, and under his rule the establishment of Parliament as the true center of power was largely completed. George was the last of England's soldier kings, and if his reign lacked vision it provided the stability and continuity a rapidly growing Britain needed.

Queen Caroline, George's consort and a canny political operator as well. She knew how to sway her husband, and her partnership with Prime Minister Robert Walpole proved highly effective until her untimely death in 1737.

George was born in Hanover—the last English king to be born abroad—but he took to England far more enthusiastically than his father, at least at first. While George I made clear from his first day as king that he would prefer to be in Hanover, young George waded into London life, earning his father's jealousy with his outgoing, open-handed style. Alongside George, who was known as George Augustus, was his alluring wife Caroline, whom he had married in 1705. By the time he inherited the throne in 1727, he and Caroline had four children, including two sons, Frederick and William.

It was at William's christening in 1717 that George and his father had a nasty and public falling out after George had a peer participate in the ceremony whom he knew William disliked. As a result, George and Caroline were expelled from St. James's Palace, and they set up a thriving, culturally and politically active household in Leicester House. Their popularity, especially among his political opponents, only made King George envious. Robert Walpole, the Prime Minister (though the office did not formally exist until much later), managed to heal the breach superficially, but the mutual dislike of father and son persisted to the end.

It is all the more ironic, then—or perhaps predictable—that by the time he took the throne at the age of 43, George had become as cantankerous as the father he had despised. He was a captious stickler for protocol, and began scorning England and rhapsodizing about Hanover in much the same tones that George I had made all too familiar.

HIS CHARACTER WOULD NOT AFFORD SUBJECT FOR EPIC POETRY, BUT WILL LOOK WELL IN THE SOBER PAGES OF HISTORY

ELIZABETH MONTAGU

HANOVERIAN FAMILY DYSFUNCTION

When George became king in 1727, he was at first inclined to dismiss Walpole, who he felt had manipulated him into a forced

1729

Jonathan Swift publishes A Modest Proposal, a brief and brilliant satire criticizing British treatment of the Irish.

1731

The Treaty of Vienna pits France and Spain on one side against Britain and Austria on the other.

1732

In London the Covent Garden Theatre Royal, now the Royal Opera House, is officially opened.

1734

In the War of the Polish Succession, Russian forces capture the city of Gdansk after a six-month siege.

Opposite George II, who made few friends as king but let superior men in Parliament make major decisions, reigned over the accelerating rise of Britain as a European and global power.

reconciliation with his father so as to gain more political power. But he soon found that Walpole was indispensable, partly because the Prime Minister had made a valuable ally: Queen Caroline. Flirtatious and politically savvy, she knew how to handle her obstreperous husband, and soon enough Walpole figured out that the way to work with George II was to approach him through his queen. Caroline, conscious of her position as the keeper of the keys to George's mind, became a de facto minister alongside Walpole, as the two of them conspired to convince the king that Walpole's Whig agenda was in fact not so bad. Like his father, George was more interested in continental than domestic affairs, so Walpole had a free hand in running the government.

Another reason Walpole had such power was that George was distracted with family conflicts, which seem to have been a Hanoverian trademark. The central problem was the perpetuation of a pattern of abusive behavior between fathers and sons. One would think that

George II at the Battle of Dettingen. His undeniable courage leading troops into combat at the age of 60 resurrected his reputation among his subjects.

George, having been so controlled and belittled by his father, would be kinder to his eldest son Frederick, Prince of Wales; in fact, he resented that his father had treated Frederick kindly, and took out his anger on the prince. Frederick, in turn, became a more extreme version of George in his youth, socializing constantly, drinking too much, and accruing gambling debts. Tensions between the two men escalated; when George was on trips to Hanover, he refused to let Frederick have a hand in government while he was gone.

But a more dire event eclipsed the family squabbling when, in November of that year, Caroline died. As difficult as he could be, George loved his queen, and was so distraught that when, on her deathbed, she asked him to remarry, he refused. "No! I shall have mistresses," he replied—as odd as it may sound to modern ears, it was an honest profession of love. But Caroline's death also had political repercussions, in that without her Walpole was deprived of his ability to sway the king. Once George had recovered from grieving, he was eager to wade into continental affairs—especially the conflicts involving Hanover. Before the queen's death, Walpole had been able to avert such involvements, preferring to nurture Britain's economy and stabilize its finances. Soon enough, Walpole would find himself and Britain dragged into war.

WAR ABROAD AND AT HOME

In 1731, a Spanish coastal patrol sent a party to board the British merchant ship Rebecca off the shores of Florida. Though the Spaniards were allowed to do this according to a treaty negotiated in 1713, tensions often ran high. In the confrontation that followed this boarding, the British captain, Robert Jenkins, had an ear cut off by a Spanish officer, who was convinced, possibly correctly, that the Rebecca was involved in smuggling. Even worse, the Spanish officer promised to do the same to King George.

It was a compelling story, and in 1738 it made for incendiary political theater when Jenkins was brought to testify about the incident before

1735	1737	1738		1740	1741
The Qianlong Emperor takes the Chinese throne. In his long rule, he will prove a remarkable patron and preserver of the arts.	An earthquake in Calcutta, India, kills an estimated 300,000—the second-largest earthquake toll in history.	The conversion of John Wesley marks the beginning of the Methodist movement.		Frederick II of Prussia invades Silesia, starting the War of the Austrian Succession.	The New York Slave Rebellion begins with a number of fires, apparently started by slaves.

BONNIE PRINCE CHARLIE

Tall, handsome, and charismatic at the age of 24, Charles Edward Stuart inspired loyalty among many Scots in a way that the unimpressive James Stuart had failed to do. But Bonnie Prince Charlie, as he was called, was no military leader, and proved too callow to handle adversity with the poise of a king. After his defeat at Culloden, he fled Scotland disguised as a serving woman. In exile, he sank into alcoholism and lived a shiftless life. When, in 1759, he was interviewed by the French foreign minister about a possible invasion of England, Charles proved so lackluster that the French sent him away.

like a whirlpool best avoided, but in the elections of 1741, actively opposed by Prince Frederick and others, he proved unable to maintain tight control over Parliament, and he stepped down. The new administration committed to the war, and a delighted George headed off to the continent, the last English king to lead an army into battle.

Even at the age of 60, George clearly savored the rigors of campaign life; he wrote letters about the pleasure of sleeping on hard ground under an open sky. In June 1743, at the Battle of Dettingen, the king threw himself into the action, ignoring a hail of musket balls and cannon shot around him as he exhorted his troops to battle. When he returned to England, he was a hero. But though the public loved their feisty old soldier king, they soon tired of a war that did not seem to serve British interests.

In 1745, France, looking to make trouble in Britain, supported one last attempt to place a Stuart back on the throne. Charles Edward Stuart, known as Bonnie Prince Charlie, was a dashing young courtier with tremendous charisma. When he landed in Scotland in 1745, he quickly stirred up patriotic sentiment in the Highlands and soon had control of Edinburgh. In September of that year, his forces defeated an English army at Prestonpans and began marching toward London. But no English support for the Stuart cause materialized. Still, with English troops largely occupied on the continent, there was little to stop Bonnie Prince Charlie from marching all the way to London. But stop he did, and then he turned about and headed back to Scotland, for reasons that remain unclear. He was pursued by a highly trained army under George's second son William, Duke of Cumberland. At Culloden, near Inverness, in April 1746, Cumberland's troops, using a formation designed to defeat Scottish tactics, won a crushing victory. Bonnie Prince Charlie, after months on the run, returned to exile on the continent. Cumberland ravaged the Highlands as punishment. The Stuart cause was effectively ended.

But the public was still dissatisfied with

Parliament. Accounts differ as to whether or not he produced the severed ear, but Jenkins proved a one-man argument for war with Spain. George eagerly complied. Though it would not be called the War of Jenkins' Ear for over a hundred years, it was the beginning of a series of engagements on the continent that would transform George's image as a king and make Britain the most powerful nation on earth.

In 1740, after Britain had already declared war on Spain, the Holy Roman Emperor Charles VI died without a male heir, leaving his realms to his daughter, Maria Theresa. France and Prussia seized the opportunity to cut down the weakening House of Habsburg by declaring that it was unlawful for a female to inherit the Habsburg throne. Once again, Europe was convulsed by rivalries among its great houses. The resulting War of the Austrian Succession looked to Walpole

1742	1743	1745	1746	1747
Handel's Messiah is first performed in Dublin in April.	George II is the last English king to lead his troops into battle at Dettingen.	In Russia, Catherine the Great marries Peter III. She will eventually take over as Empress, and rule over a brilliant age of Russian modernization and expansion.	Samuel Johnson agrees to compile the first-ever systematic dictionary of the English language.	James Lind discovers that citrus fruits somehow prevent scurvy. Subsequent supplies of fruit to British sailors lead to their being called Limeys.

the cost and stress of a continental war. The resulting reshuffle in Parliament left George with one of the most distasteful decisions of his reign. A group of young Whig politicians called the Young Patriots had begun agitating against Walpole years before, and they asserted themselves so forcefully during the War of the Austrian Succession that Walpole's protégé Henry Pelham, briefly appointed Prime Minister, proved unable to control Parliament and resigned. George's handpicked replacements, Lords Bath and Carteret, also failed to form a governing coalition. Out of the Young Patriots, one extraordinarily gifted leader had emerged, a man who had opposed many of George's foreign policies as more pro-Hanoverian than pro-British, a man George despised: William Pitt, known to history as William Pitt the Elder. Grudgingly, in 1746, George assented to Pitt's becoming part of the cabinet. It was the greatest stroke of good fortune in George's reign. William Pitt the Elder would become one of the greatest ministers in British history.

A GLOBAL POWER

In 1748 the War of the Austrian Succession came to an end with the Treaty of Aix-la-Chappelle. But any hopes that such a peace would last were shortlived, as alliances were simply reshuffled. Maria Theresa of Austria, disenchanted with Britain and eager to win land from Prussia, pivoted away and leagued her nation with France and Russia. Britain responded by allying itself with Prussia. Militarily, it was a strong partnership: Prussia, under Frederick II, had Europe's finest army, and Britain had its largest navy.

When the next European war, called the Seven Years' War, erupted in 1756, it had already begun in the New World. In North America, British and French colonists had begun to vie for land, especially the Ohio territory. A young officer named George Washington was experiencing his first taste of battle there. The English were also verging on war with the

William Pitt the Elder, architect of Britain's strategy in the Seven Years' War and one of the greatest British statesmen.

French in India, and the Caribbean was a hive of imperialist conflict. This was the first European war that would extend around the world, and William Pitt saw the implications. What he understood most presciently was what we now call globalization. If the European powers were vying for colonies all over the world, wars would seldom be fought in Europe alone, and if national wealth was the source of lasting power, then controlling resource-rich colonies was the way forward. If you could take them from your enemies, so much the better.

George resented Pitt, but there was little he could do about him, and Pitt had a strategic vision that extended beyond Europe and well into the future. His strategy in the war was at once pragmatic and brilliant: the Prussians, under the superb generalship of Frederick II, would hold the field on the continent, and the British would use their navy to bleed France at the edges of its empire. The gradual hemorrhaging of French assets would lead to victory.

The war began badly, with the French taking the island of Minorca in the Mediterranean. After a spell of Parliamentary instability, Pitt entered a coalition government with the Duke of Newcastle as Prime Minister and himself as Secretary of State, so he could prosecute the war. Pitt's two-pronged strategy was given time to take effect. At the heart of Pitt's thinking was the strength of the British navy. It was not just the size of the fleet; it was also the technological sophistication with which ships were being designed and built at the vast naval dockyards. British warships were superior to the French in nearly every way, down to how their crews were quartered and fed. It was the greatest power-projection navy the world had ever seen.

On the continent, Frederick waged a steady war of attrition, holding out against the superior numbers of his enemies and even managing some striking victories. Meanwhile, the British navy blockaded French ports and supported a string of successes on multiple continents. Most dramatic was the 1759 capture of Quebec by General James Wolfe, who was killed at the

1748	1748	1751	1753	1755	1757
The ruins of Pompeii are discovered.	Bach begins composing his Mass in B Minor, one of his last and greatest works.	The first edition of the French Encyclopedia, edited by Denis Diderot, compiles and enshrines the knowledge and attitudes that will characterize the Enlightenment.	With the Jewish Naturalization Act, Parliament extends citizenship to Jews.	A massive earthquake strikes Lisbon, Portugal, killing scores of thousands.	At the Battle of Plassey in India, Robert Clive's army of 3,000 men defeats an Indian army of 50,000.

The death of General James Wolfe in 1759, as painted by Benjamin West. Wolfe's successful siege of Quebec meant that Britain would eventually control all of what is now Canada.

climax of the battle but whose successful siege ultimately ensured British control of Canada. French plans to invade England that year were scuttled by two crushing defeats at the hands of the British navy.

George benefited from the morale-boosting success of British forces around the globe, but he was growing old. Blind in one eye and losing his hearing, he nonetheless held to his passion for protocol and his old grudges, but he and his Whig ministers had developed a working rapport. Prince Frederick had died in 1751, leaving a son as heir to the throne, so a smooth succession was assured. On October 25, 1760, at the age of 77, George died suddenly and indecorously, collapsing from an aneurysm while using his chamberpot. Though he had never been fully accepted as an English king, he was widely and sincerely mourned.

George's rule was in many ways similar to that of his father. He had so little interest in British internal affairs that his Prime Ministers became, for all intents and purposes, domestic heads of state. By the time of the Seven Years' War, Pitt was steering foreign policy as well. On one occasion, George said, "Ministers are kings in this country." And he was largely right. George may have lamented the waning power of the Crown, but he accepted it, and thereby ensured a kind of stability that England had never known, one founded not on the personality of a monarch but on the continuity of process.

Whatever one may think of George's personality, it is hard to argue with the results of his holding the throne. He and his ministers left Britain superbly positioned for his grandson, who would go on to a long and eventful reign of his own.

1758

Halley's comet appears to the naked eye for the first time since Edmond Halley discovered it in 1705.

1759

Voltaire publishes Candide, his classic picaresque satire. Its irreverence for a range of human beliefs and institutions results in its being widely banned.

1760

Lord Granby famously loses his hat and wig leading a heroic cavalry charge at the Battle of Warburg, a Hanoverian victory in the Seven Years' War.

BONNIE PRINCE CHARLIE

harles Edward Stuart (1720–1788), known as the Young Pretender or, more commonly, Bonnie Prince Charlie, is one of the most mythologized figures in Scottish history. The grandson of James II and eldest son of James Francis Edward Stuart (the Old Pretender), he was the last of the Stuart line to contest the throne of England. His 1745 campaign, which ended with his narrow escape to the continent, has become the stuff of legend, but his life afterward was anything but heroic.

Charles was born in Rome, where his father was living in comfortable exile at the Palazzo Muti after his own failed attempt to take the English throne in 1715. Raised in luxury and very well educated, Charles was imbued with a belief in the divine right of kings—a Stuart dogma—and a sense that the family must recover what it had lost in 1688 in the Glorious Revolution.

Charles was raised to restore the Stuart monarchy. At the age of 14, he was taken to study warfare in the field, observing the siege of Gaeta by Spanish troops during the War of the Spanish Succession. In 1743, his father named him Prince Regent, effectively placing on Charles's shoulders the task of regaining the throne. The following year, a scheme for Charles to lead a French invasion was aborted when a storm threw off the timing of the crossing, alerting the British fleet to the operation.

FROM PRETENDER TO FUGITIVE

In 1745, Charles embarked on a different path to the English throne, one that placed him on friendly British soil, among potential soldiers. The English forces of George II were mostly on the continent, embroiled in the War of the Austrian Succession, and had suffered heavy losses in the Battle of Fontenoy. In July, French ships dropped him with seven companions at Eriskay in the Outer Hebrides. From there, Charles could cross to the mainland and drum up forces from among the Highland clans, most of whom supported the Stuart cause. By Loch Shiel in the northwest of Scotland, he raised his father's banner and began to march on Edinburgh. By the time he arrived, he had a small army of about 2,000 highlanders.

Edinburgh opened its gates to Charles after only token resistance. Only the garrison of the city's impressive castle refused to surrender. The only English field army in Scotland was an inexperienced, poorly trained force of some 2,300 troops under Sir John Cope. The two small armies met near Prestonpans, just east of Edinburgh, on September 20. The battle was over in minutes, as the English troops collapsed in the face of charging highlanders.

The immediate effect of the victory at Prestonpans was to spark a bit more enthusiasm for the Jacobite cause among a Scottish population that had been mostly lukewarm. Charles's army swelled to over 5,000 men. Marching south, the Jacobite forces took Carlisle and made for London. Frustrated by the lack of enthusiasm they encountered on their march, and given misinformation about English troops blocking the way to London, Charles's military advisors held a council at Derby, and decided to withdraw back to Scotland. A large English army led by George Augustus, the Duke of Cumberland, set out in pursuit.

Charles insisted on fighting a defensive campaign, and retreated further into the Highlands. Cumberland waited out the winter, training his troops and being reinforced with 5,000 Hessians. Though Charles's advisors advocated a guerrilla campaign, he chose otherwise. On April 16, at Culloden Moor near Inverness, the armies met in the last pitched battle on British soil. After a failed charge by the highlanders, Cumberland's force routed the Scots in less than an hour. Charles fled the field with the some of his officers, issuing an order that every man must shift for himself.

TOP: Charles Edward Stuart as a young man, before his 1745 campaign to restore the Stuart dynasty.

ABOVE: A period depiction of the Battle of Culloden by the Swiss painter David Morier. In reality, the highlanders were better armed than the painting suggests; many had French muskets.

ESCAPE AND DISILLUSIONMENT

In the aftermath of Culloden, with a bounty of £30,000 on his head, Charles had to run for his life. Though legends suggest that the highlanders refused to give up any information on his whereabouts, in reality he constantly risked betrayal and capture. But he had enough allies that he managed to elude his pursuers. Eventually, he was returned to the continent by a French ship. The Stuart cause was lost.

Bonnie Prince Charlie's later life was a study in disillusionment and dissolution. Unable to cope with the failure of his campaign, he declined into alcoholism and depression, living an ineffectual existence until his death in 1788.

FLORA MACDONALD

Flora MacDonald was 24 years old when Bonnie Prince Charlie, fleeing English troops, came to the island of Benbecula in the Outer Hebrides where she lived. She famously disguised Charles as her Irish maid and succeeded in taking him by boat to Skye. MacDonald was later arrested for aiding the prince and imprisoned briefly in the Tower of London. In 1774, she emigrated to the American colonies, but later returned to live in Skye until her death in 1790. She remains an icon of loyalty and courage.

GEGORGE III ✠ From Steadiness to Madness

House Hanover
Born June 4, 1738
Died January 29, 1820
Reigned 1760–1820
Consort Charlotte of Mecklenburg-Strelitz
Children Fifteen, including George IV and William IV
Successor George IV

George III was the first of the Hanoverians born in Britain. England was his home and his foremost priority, and he doggedly worked at his kingly responsibilities for as long as he could through his 60 years of rule. Though he made costly mistakes, and in his later years declined into such poor mental health that a regency was instituted for the final decade of his reign, George gained the affection and admiration of his subjects. With his stolid, earnest sense of rectitude, he turned the kingship into a symbol of British values.

George entered life uncertainly, born two months prematurely on June 4, 1738. In those times, such a birth almost surely meant that he wouldn't survive infancy, but he did, perhaps indicating the stubbornness that would sometimes characterize his conduct as king. As the child of Prince Frederick, who was estranged from George II, young George was exceptionally well schooled in preparation for eventual kingship, even studying science systematically—the first English king so educated—and becoming an accomplished musician. He was a well-behaved and earnest child, not particularly outgoing, but when his father died unexpectedly in 1751, George was thrust into the role of heir apparent.

The stolid decency for which George would become famous during his reign appears to have marked his early adulthood. This was partly because his mother, the Dowager Princess of Wales, and his tutor, Lord Bute, kept him on a tight leash, but George seems to have needed little correction. Apart from one dalliance—it remains unclear how serious—with Hannah Lightfoot, a commoner, he appears to have kept his impulses in check. And George was a romantic. He first fell in love, at the age of 21, with Lady Sarah Lennox, one of the famed Lennox sisters who would go on to chart more or less scandalous courses through the Hanoverian aristocracy. But she did not meet with royal approval, and George was forced to move on. He saw his relinquishment of Sarah as the first of his dutiful choices as a future king. That future arrived the following year, when George II died and Prince George became King George III.

LEARNING THE KINGSHIP

While his careful and disciplined upbringing had instilled George with a firm sense of integrity and a solid education, it had left him somewhat sheltered, and when he took the throne on October 25, 1760, he was overwhelmed by the complexity and ambiguity of Parliamentary politics and the welter of issues before the government. The Seven Years' War was still under way, without any resolution in sight, and he had not found a wife.

The question of George's marriage was quickly resolved. After casting around, George settled on Princess Charlotte of Mecklenburg-

BORN AND EDUCATED IN THIS COUNTRY, I GLORY IN THE NAME OF BRITAIN

GEORGE III

1762	1766	1768	1770	
Jean-Jacques Rousseau publishes his seminal works The Social Contract and Émile in France. They will form part of the foundation of coming revolutionary and Romantic movements.	Sweden introduces Europe's first legislation ensuring freedom of the press.	Captain James Cook sails from England on the HMS Endeavor for his first voyage of discovery. It will take three years, during which he will map much of the coasts of Australia and New Zealand.	A famine in Bengal claims close to 10 million lives, the worst natural disaster in recorded history.	**Opposite** George III, whose native decency made him very popular, despite the loss of the American colonies and his later descent into mental illness.

Queen Charlotte. A good match for George, she was also a respected patron of the arts. George and Charlotte had 15 children, 13 of whom lived to adulthood.

Strelitz. It was purely an arranged marriage; the bride and groom met on their wedding day. But it proved to be a happy match. George, not merely out of rectitude but from sincere affection for his queen, never took a mistress, and the couple produced no fewer than 15 children.

The issues of war and Parliamentary leadership proved far more refractory. In 1759, the war had gone all Britain's way, with the capture of Quebec and two major naval victories that eliminated any threat of a French invasion. But the effort and expense of a global war were taking their toll: England's finances were dwindling, and food shortages led to unrest in London. George, who cared little for Hanover and hence for protracted campaigns on the continent, and cared even less for Prime Minister Thomas Pelham and Secretary of State William Pitt, maneuvered the Whigs out of power for the first time in decades, bringing in a Tory government under Lord Bute. Bute had no interest in furthering the war, and weathered fierce opposition, including libelous attacks, to bring it to a negotiated conclusion in 1763.

But by then, the damage was done on both sides. France was drained and humiliated. Britain had impoverished itself in the short term, but in the long term had positioned itself for fabulous wealth from a global array of colonies. India belonged to Britain, as did all of North America east of the Mississippi River. In an effort to encourage complete colonization of the coastal regions and put relations with Native Americans on a stable footing, the Royal Proclamation of 1763 barred further settlement beyond the Appalachian mountain range. The American colonists were not happy with the arrangement. It would be neither the first nor the most momentous conflict between the American colonies and their mother country.

CONFLICTS WITH THE AMERICAN COLONIES

In 1763, the 13 British colonies in North America had a population approaching two million people, and they sprawled across an area much larger than England. They also encompassed a remarkable range of origins. Some, like Massachusetts (Puritans), Pennsylvania (Quakers), and Maryland (Catholics), had been founded mainly by and for religious dissenters, while others were built around mercantile ventures. There was no unified colonial government, and the colonies were often beset with rivalries. America was not a tamed and largely manicured land like England; it was bigger, wilder, more extreme, and more dangerous. Something akin to national pride was developing among its settlers. And its patrician class had nurtured a rising generation of highly educated, confident, and philosophically minded leaders.

In Britain, the chief concern after the Seven Years' War was the enormous deficit the conflict had accrued: well over £100 million. Revenue would need to be harvested, and since the colonies had directly benefited from the war effort and still had British troops protecting them, the thinking went that the colonists should share the costs. In early 1765, Parliament passed the Stamp Act, imposing a tax on paper used for many daily transactions. It seemed a simple enough proposition, but it ignited fierce protest from the colonies and from merchants who did business there. The essential protest was not against taxation itself, but against the fact that the colonies were being taxed without representation in Parliament. "No taxation without representation," a rallying cry all too reminiscent of Britain's 1688 Bill of Rights, gained currency in Boston, New York, Philadelphia, and other cities. Assemblies in the colonies, starting with

1772	1773	1776	1779	1780
Austria, Russia, and Prussia partition Poland, dividing it among themselves in order to maintain their balance of power.	Pugachev's Rebellion in Russia, a movement absorbing Cossacks, peasants, and others, gains considerable momentum before being suppressed under Catherine the Great.	In London, Adam Smith publishes The Wealth of Nations, perhaps the most influential text in the history of economics.	On his third voyage of discovery, Captain James Cook is killed by Hawaiians in the Sandwich Islands.	The Marquis de La Fayette sails from France to America, offering French support and his own generalship to the Americans fighting British rule.

EDMUND BURKE & HUMAN RIGHTS

Edmund Burke had already distinguished himself as a philosopher before entering Parliament, and his brilliance as a thinker and orator discerned him as a leader among the Whigs. Perhaps due to his Irish heritage, Burke was keenly sensitive to the plight of the exploited and the need for guarantees of rights. He argued passionately for compromise with the American colonies, and orchestrated the unsuccessful prosecution of Warren Hastings, Governor-General of Bengal, for alleged misconduct. When the French Revolution occurred, Burke saw the potential for terrorism and tyranny and decried the destruction he anticipated. The resulting book, Reflections on the French Revolution, became extremely influential.

William Pitt repealed the Stamp Act soon after it was passed. Beginning in 1767, Chancellor of the Exchequer Charles Townshend sponsored a series of measures designed to enforce taxation on the colonies, using the revenue to pay the royal governors of the colonies and thus remove the power of the purse from colonial assemblies. When agitation continued into 1768 troops were sent to Boston to ensure public order. In 1770, a public confrontation in Boston led to violence in which five colonists were shot by British soldiers.

The Boston Tea Party (as it was later called), a theatrical political protest in 1773 against taxation of the American colonies without their being represented in Parliament.

Virginia, drafted resolutions defying the tax, and in Massachusetts, which would become the epicenter of radical resistance, there were public demonstrations.

Had he been blessed with a strong and capable Prime Minister, George might have attended more thoughtfully to these ominous rumblings. But Lord Bute was completely ineffective, and a government under Lord Rockingham and

By this time, George had found a Prime Minister whose approach to the colonies approximated his own: Lord North. In 1770, North repealed many of the Townshend duties, but kept in place a tax on tea, largely as a symbolic gesture to affirm Parliament's absolute right to tax the colonies.

George was not the right king for this situation; nor was North the right Prime Minister. The dogged rectitude that served the king so well in some situations steered him wrong in the case of the colonies. It was but a small step from a strong sense of propriety to a rigid paternalism, and both George and North were determined to bring the colonies to heel rather than negotiate. In 1773, North developed and George approved the Tea Act, which had the threefold purpose of ensuring the sale of surplus tea from the East India Company, reducing smuggling into the colonies, and getting the colonists to agree in practice if not principle to paying taxes, as the tea would include a modest duty. But positions had hardened, and in December of that year a group of radical colonists boarded ships in

1783	1785	1786	1788
The Montgolfier brothers present the first public demonstration of their hot air balloon in France.	Napoleon Bonaparte receives a commission as a lieutenant in the French artillery, the beginning of his military career.	Sir William Jones documents the similarities among Sanskrit, Latin, and Greek and asserts, correctly, their shared origin in an Indo-European language.	In Vienna, Wolfgang Amadeus Mozart completes his final symphony, later known as the Jupiter Symphony.

Boston harbor and threw hundreds of tea chests overboard. It was a manifestly criminal act, and though it did not reflect the sentiments of most colonists, it brought harsher punitive measures from North's government.

Prominent statesmen argued in Parliament that Britain was at risk of alienating the American colonies so thoroughly that they would be lost altogether. Both William Pitt and Edmund Burke gave striking speeches arguing that a punitive mentality would leave the colonists feeling as though they would have to choose between Britain and freedom. But North, with George's approval, plowed forward with the Coercive Acts, meant to make an example of Massachusetts. The measures proved a disastrous miscalculation. In 1775, in the towns of Lexington and Concord, the conflict erupted into open rebellion, as a colonial militia engaged in battle with a contingent of British soldiers.

In July 1776, representatives from all 13 colonies met in Philadelphia as the Continental Congress. On July 2, they voted to declare the colonies' independence from Great Britain, and assigned Thomas Jefferson to draft a formal declaration. The resulting Declaration of Independence, steeped in Lockean and Whig rhetoric, labeled George a tyrant, effectively making him more than Parliament the object of resistance.

For the next several years, American rebels would wage a fluid, largely indecisive war on British troops sent to assert control over the colonies. Though many colonists favored remaining part of the British Empire, the die had been cast. A number of prominent citizens had knowingly laid themselves open to charges of high treason, and the propaganda machine of the radical opposition continued churning. More importantly, the leaders of the rebellion, including Jefferson, John Adams, Benjamin Franklin, and most prominently George Washington, proved talented and resourceful. As the conflict dragged on inconclusively, it became clear on the continent that Britain,

master of the world after the Seven Years' War, was vulnerable.

In 1780, riots broke out in London, partly a flare-up of anti-Catholic feeling, but more an expression of deep discontent over the economic costs of the war. Eager to avenge their humiliation in 1763, the French had invested heavily in making life more difficult for the English, throwing their support to the colonists and launching offensives elsewhere to further drain English resources; the Spanish and Dutch soon followed suit. With an infusion of mainly French naval support and other assistance, the colonial forces began to sustain their successes, culminating in 1781 with the surrender of Lord Cornwallis's forces at Yorktown, in Virginia. In 1783, with the Treaty of Paris, the colonies were granted independence. It was a humiliating failure, all the more galling because, in retrospect, it had been so avoidable. Lord North's government fell to a no-confidence vote, and another period of Parliamentary instability ensued.

ILLNESS AND GLORY

But there was a silver lining to the defeat. France had managed to dislodge a portion of the British Empire, but at great cost to itself and relatively little to Britain, for trade with the former colonies resumed quickly and began reinvigorating the British economy. In 1783, William Pitt the Younger was able to form a government, becoming Prime Minister at only 24 years old. It was a victory for George, who had clashed with a rapid series of ineffective regimes after the fall of North's government. Pitt presided over a period of reform and rising prosperity. He used a range of means, including income tax, to reduce the national debt, and with the India Act of 1784 brought India under government oversight rather than the exclusive control of the East India Company. He also ended Britain's international isolation by forming an alliance with Prussia and the Dutch Republic.

Through these years, George became immensely popular. His clear sense of decency

Lord Frederick North, Prime Minister during the American War of Independence. North largely shared George's punitive attitude to the colonies, a stance that only ensured their loss.

1789	1790	1791	1794
The French Revolution begins in earnest with the fall of the Bastille.	George Washington, first President of the United States, has his first year in office.	The Observer, the world's first Sunday newspaper, begins publication in London. 1792: Captain George Vancouver claims the region of Puget Sound, in what is now the State of Washington, for England.	The Thermidorian Reaction ends the Reign of Terror in the French Revolution. Maximilien Robespierre, the last of the leaders of the Terror, is executed.

William Pitt the Younger, son of William Pitt the Elder and a gifted Prime Minister in his own right. He masterfully handled the British recovery from the American War of Independence, and led the nation into the early Napoleonic Wars.

His gentleness and understanding won him even more affection. But soon George would be afflicted with his own psychological crisis. In 1788, he fell victim to an extended bout of mental and physical illness, in which he babbled incoherently for hours and seemed incapable of comprehending clearly what was going on around him. The treatments he received, which accorded with the era's crude understanding of mental health, scarcely helped. It appears that George suffered from porphyria, a hereditary blood disorder. While he was incapacitated, Parliament negotiated over how to arrange for a regency under Prince George, the king's eldest son. Before a regency bill could pass, however, the king recovered, ensuring the continuation of his reign and Pitt's successful government.

No sooner did George recover and resume his duties, though under the careful eyes of observers, than a new crisis arose: the French Revolution. With the fall of the Bastille in 1789, European affairs changed utterly. At first, the European powers were paralyzed by the shocking overthrow of the French royalty, but then came a period of retrenchment and conflict. In England, sympathizers with the French Revolution were often branded traitors, and Parliament passed a series of measures to muzzle would-be reformers, even suspending the writ of habeas corpus. In early 1793, Louis XVI was beheaded and the French regime, the Directory, was on the march, conscripting huge numbers of troops to engage in war on multiple fronts. For the next ten years, Britain would once more be locked in battle with France.

Britain had a relatively small standing army, and contributed to the war with its navy. Over the course of the next decade, two great military leaders emerged: for the British, Admiral Horatio Nelson; for the French Napoleon Bonaparte. The two would never, because of their differing commands, meet in battle, but between them they would eventually decide Britain's fate in relation to a transformed and aggressive France. Napoleon proved as charismatic as he was brilliant, and after he defeated multiple armies on the continent set

and moral purpose, which contrasted with the often scandalous behavior of his brothers, especially the philandering Prince Henry, made him a symbol of British values—a crucial and lasting change in the role of the monarchy. In 1786 he was attacked by a mentally unstable woman while alighting from his carriage; on the spot, he declared that she was mad and should be treated humanely, not punished.

1796	1799	1803	1804	1805
The Dutch cede control of Ceylon (Sri Lanka) to the British.	Napoleon executes a coup d'etat in France, establishing the Consulate, of which he is First Consul.	With the Louisiana Purchase of French territories from Napoleon, the United States doubles its size.	Napoleon crowns himself Emperor of France.	Two of the most pivotal battles in the Napoleonic Wars take place: Trafalgar, in which Nelson's fleet decimates the combined French and Spanish fleets, preventing an invasion of England; and Austerlitz, in which Napoleon's triumph utterly defeats Austria and ends the Holy Roman Empire.

George Delacroix's famous painting Liberty Leading the People, which, though painted in commemoration of the Revolution of 1830, has also come to symbolize the aspirations of 1789.

out in 1798 for Egypt. It seems that the Directory were happy to let him pursue his increasingly outsized ambitions far from Paris. But while he won territory on land, Nelson decimated his fleet that August in the Battle of the Nile.

George remained a popular figurehead in the ongoing conflict. When Napoleon instigated a coup and became First Consul in 1799, his successes on the continent had compelled so many other countries into peace that Britain, protected by the Channel, stood alone against his increasingly imperial ambitions. In 1800, there was a pause in the conflict; Pitt took advantage of it to orchestrate what became the 1801 Act of Union, which added

Ireland to Great Britain to create the United Kingdom. Folded in with those negotiations were Pitt's efforts to establish greater religious freedom for Catholics, which George opposed on the grounds that he was the defender of Protestantism. The stress of the dispute plunged George into another round of mental instability, and, without the king supporting him, Pitt lost the premiership to Henry Addington, who rolled back some of Pitt's reforms and made peace with France in 1802.

George knew better than to expect a lasting peace with Napoleon, and waited for war to resume. It took less than a year, at which point George was able, with broad public support, to reinstate Pitt. Napoleon was known to be preparing for an invasion of England, and patriotic fervor ran high. In 1803, George himself inspected volunteer troops in London, a spectacle that drew throngs of spectators. But the next year George suffered another spell of mental collapse, and once more Pitt was ousted and had to wait for the king's recovery to resume running the government. Napoleon's invasion never came, because on October 21,

NAPOLEON

Napoleon Bonaparte has become such a commonly known figure that it is hard for us to comprehend what he meant in his own time. One of history's greatest military geniuses and ruthlessly successful in imposing his own rule, he was a terrifying figure to much of Europe. Some were even convinced he was the Antichrist evoked in the biblical Book of Revelation. Napoleon's armies, well drilled, well equipped, and led by superb generals, were among the most effective Europe had ever seen. In the end, he was defeated as much by his own grand ambitions as any collection of enemies; his invasion of Russia in 1812 turned into a disaster when a combination of scorched-earth Russian tactics and brutal winter weather wiped out most of his Grande Armée. From that point on, he no longer seemed invincible.

1805, Nelson led a daring attack on the combined French and Spanish fleets at Trafalgar, and crushed them. The victory cost Nelson his life, making him one of England's greatest heroes in death, and news of the battle led to jubilation throughout Britain. The celebratory mood dampened two months later, when Napoleon's great victory at Austerlitz destroyed what remained of the Holy Roman Empire and left him master of continental Europe.

1806	1807	1808	1810
The British take control of the Cape Colony in what will eventually become South Africa.	The British navy firebombs the port of Copenhagen to prevent the Danish navy from being given over to Napoleon. Thousands of civilians are killed.	In Weimar, Johann Wolfgang von Goethe publishes the first part of his drama Faust, a hugely influential work.	The Hindoostanee Coffee House, the first Indian restaurant in Britain, opens in London. It remains in business for about a year.

In 1806, Pitt died, and George entered into a period of protracted struggle with Parliament. Though Trafalgar had ensured that Napoleon would not invade England, he still terrorized the continent, and differences over how to sustain British military manpower and ensure financial stability dominated government debate.

A LONG TWILIGHT

By 1809, George was 71 years old, and his health was failing. He was enormously popular; his iconic status as the stolid custodian of British values preserved him in the public's estimation, as did his unpretentious manner, and his Royal Jubilee that year was festive. But in 1810 he suffered another bout of mental debility, one that effectively ended his reign. In November, his youngest daughter Amelia, whom he adored, died of complications of tuberculosis. It was a devastating blow for the entire family. One of her parting gestures was to have a ring made from a lock of her hair and given to her father after her death. George descended into desperate weeping and delusional chatter. He would never entirely recover.

In 1811, Prince George took over as Regent, and the king was confined to Windsor Castle. There he would spend his final few years, nearly blind, his hair growing long, occasionally playing the harpsichord. When Queen Charlotte died in 1818, he did not understand what had happened. He died in 1820, having been King of England for over 59 years—the longest reign yet. Prince George stepped from Regent to King.

George would inspire both scorn and admiration in future historians. On the one hand, he made costly mistakes, especially regarding the American colonies; on the other, he established the monarchy as a repository of values rather than trying to reassert it as a political force, and in supporting William Pitt the Younger as Prime Minister he ensured that the ablest man led Britain through a disorienting and dangerous time. He patronized science, becoming known as "Farmer George" for his interest in agriculture and letting scholars have open access to the royal library. Under his reign, English literature flourished. And, unlike his two immediate predecessors, he loved England deeply, and never left it.

The Battle of Trafalgar. Lord Horatio Nelson lost his life in the course of this, his greatest victory, which ended Napoleon's hopes of invading England.

1812	1815	1816	1819
Napoleon invades Russia, only to retreat from Moscow having lost nearly his entire army to attrition. Tchaikovsky's famous 1812 Overture celebrates the Russian victory.	Napoleon returns from his first exile for the Hundred Days, which culminate in his defeat at Waterloo.	The Elgin Marbles, from the Parthenon in Athens, are purchased from Lord Elgin by the British government for display in the British Museum.	Simon Bolivar proclaims the Republic of Gran Colombia, as Latin America begins to free itself from Spanish and Portuguese rule.

GEORGE IV ✛ The Dandy King

House Hanover
Born August 12, 1762
Died June 26, 1830
Reigned 1820–1830
Consort Caroline of Brunswick
Children Princess Charlotte of Wales
Successor William IV

George IV was only King of England for ten years, but he functioned as king for nearly twice as long. During his decade as Regent for the mentally ill and declining George III, he became famous—and infamous—for his personal style and his poor behavior. As king, he fared no better, his conduct too often beneath the standard set by his father, but his imperial vision for Britain had far-reaching cultural effects.

Born in 1762 at St. James's Palace, George IV was a healthy, bright, outgoing child who showed every promise of becoming an excellent king. But this was not to last. As George came of age, he followed the Hanoverian custom of reacting against his father's influence; in his case, that meant resisting the strong sense of moral rectitude George III embodied and hoped to instill in his children.

At the age of 18, Prince George was given his own household, and immediately threw himself into extravagant behavior of all kinds. His ability to spend money was staggering; all through his life he accrued massive personal debts. Equally excessive was his appetite for women, which was tinged with a romanticism that only made matters worse. Rather than simply taking mistresses with an eye to the customary boundaries of those relationships, he threw himself into them with a childish lack of discretion. At the age of 17, he thought himself in love with Perdita Robinson, an actress. When the relationship ended, the king was forced to pay Robinson thousands of pounds to retrieve George's embarrassingly explicit love letters.

Three years later, George became smitten with Maria Fitzherbert. A commoner who was several years older than the prince, twice divorced, and Roman Catholic to boot, she could scarcely have been less acceptable as a partner, but George nonetheless contracted to marry her in 1785. The marriage was legally void, as it was made without the king's permission, but Fitzherbert considered herself George's wife, and they remained committed to each other, on and off, for more than 20 years. The king and Parliament tacitly agreed to keep the indiscretion private.

More public was George's financial recklessness. The king was famously unpretentious and frugal; George seemed to have no regard for those virtues, surrounding himself with hedonistic friends, who called him "Prinny," and lavishing money on everything from food and drink to clothes to traveling. The king was in favor of leaving George to the consequences of his behavior, refusing him money and forcing him to move in with Fitzherbert for a time. Parliament, however, keen to avoid more embarrassment about that relationship and stocked with well-placed Whig allies who were happy to assist George in spite of the king, arranged to pay his enormous debts.

In 1788, George III succumbed to his first attack of the mental illness that would

> # THERE NEVER WAS AN INDIVIDUAL LESS REGRETTED BY HIS FELLOW CREATURES THAN THIS DECEASED KING
>
> *THE TIMES OF LONDON*

1820	**1821**	**1822**	**1823**	
The participants in the Cato Street conspiracy, an attempt to assassinate the British cabinet, are the last men to be sentenced to decapitation in Britain.	Following a year of rebellion, Mexico wins its independence from Spain.	Percy Bysshe Shelley, the great Romantic poet, drowns in a storm while sailing off the coast of Italy.	President James Monroe of the United States establishes the Monroe Doctrine, stating that the United States will regard any European attempt to recolonize land in the western hemisphere as an act of hostility.	**Opposite** George IV, whose shameless self-indulgence and laissez-faire approach to kingship made him deeply unpopular, but whose sense of style had far-reaching effects.

Queen Caroline, consort to George IV. There was perhaps no more miserable marriage in the history of the British monarchy.

eventually overtake him completely. For two months, Parliament debated how best to arrange for a regency, which would be assumed by the prince. Before a final bill could be passed, the king recovered, and George was spared the responsibilities of rule. The crisis might have encouraged him to curb his appetites and look toward his eventual role as king, but George, though bright and sophisticated, was not reflective. He continued living extravagantly and running up debts.

A MARRIAGE OF INCONVENIENCE

In an effort to bring the prince under control and ensure some dynastic continuity, King George determined to block all financial support for his son until the wayward prince found a suitable wife. And the king had just the candidate in mind: George's cousin Princess Caroline of Brunswick. The two were married in April 1795. Their marriage holds the dubious distinction of being surely the worst royal match in British history. On meeting her, George called for a glass of brandy. Not only did the two feel no physical attraction to each other, they intensely disliked each other. George had already grown corpulent, and Caroline was coarse-mannered and somewhat lacking in personal hygiene. They managed to conceive a child, Princess Charlotte, on their wedding night or the night after, and never shared a bed again. As soon as Charlotte was born, George altered his will to leave her mother nothing.

The fact that Caroline became far more popular than George is less a testament to her virtues than an indictment of his vices. In 1797, she permanently moved into her own household, where she almost certainly took lovers, but George's luxurious lifestyle, offensive to many

Beau Brummell, an icon of fashion during the Regency. After years of defining men's style, he eventually ran up unmanageable debts and died in a Paris asylum, impoverished and stricken with syphilis.

during times of war and hardship, allowed Caroline to look like a discarded wife.

THE REGENCY

In 1810, the king descended into his final breakdown, and a year later George became Prince Regent. In that role, George was less assertive than his father on most issues, often allowing Parliament to run the country without much in the way of royal consultation. He did, early on, make somewhat contradictory decisions about the premiership, but they did not go well, and as war with Napoleon intensified he left matters in far more capable hands than his own.

But George did concern himself with less consequential issues. Though he was scorned for his irresponsible behavior, he was also widely admired for his impeccable taste. Not only did he have an eye for art and interior decoration; he transformed English dress and manners. When he stopped wearing wigs in favor of styling his natural hair, wigs faded from the scene. One of his boon companions, Beau Brummell, became the archetypal dandy, a charismatic if inconsequential man whose sense of personal style trumped all other considerations. Brummell dispensed with the traditional breeches and stockings in favor of sober but impeccably tailored suits of the finest fabrics, with flawless knotted cravats, and spent hours each day bathing and grooming himself. Singlehandedly, he permanently changed how Englishmen dress.

George also oversaw significant changes in London. He was keenly aware that other European capitals, especially Paris and Vienna, were far more grand than London. He commissioned architect John Nash to redesign portions of the city to look more imperial; the results, including Regent's Park and Regent Street, made central London a far more impressive place to visit. George also had the Brighton Pavilion built in an ornate, Asiatic style. The exoticism of the Pavilion reflected the orientalist aesthetic that had taken hold at the time. George's orientalism, however, extended to his personal habits; like many well-heeled

1824	1825	1826		1826	1827
In Vienna, Ludwig van Beethoven's Ninth Symphony, considered by many his greatest work, is first performed.	In Russia, young officers rise up in the Decembrist revolt. Their attempt to establish a representative government is crushed by Tsar Nicholas I.	The Spanish Inquisition imposes its last penalties on those deemed to be heretics.		Former Presidents of the United States and bitter rivals Thomas Jefferson and John Adams both die on the 50th anniversary of the Declaration of Independence.	In Algeria, the Ottoman ruler strikes the French consul with his fly-whisk, occasioning a conflict that will lead to French colonization of Algeria.

men of his time, he had begun taking laudanum, a form of opium, recreationally, and very likely became addicted to it.

AN UNPOPULAR KING

In 1820, the king died, and at 57 years old Prince George became King George IV. It was a difficult time in Britain: the Napoleonic Wars had ended in triumph, but had cost the nation dearly, and the accelerating industrial revolution was degrading the condition of the working classes. The previous year, a large protest in Manchester had been violently dispersed by the military in what became known as the Peterloo Massacre. Nonetheless, George resolved to have the most opulent and expensive coronation in British history.

His plans for the event were upended by Caroline's involvement. She had been paid off to live outside England since 1814, and had accumulated a reputation abroad nearly as tainted as her husband's. George's contempt for her ran so deep that when their daughter Charlotte died in childbirth in 1817, he had not even notified Caroline. When it became clear that Caroline was planning to return to England and enjoy the perks of being Queen, George tried to drive through Parliament the Pains and Penalties Bill, which would void their marriage. The bill had no real chance of passage, and it was such a flagrant politicization of an essentially private dispute that George's popularity plummeted further, and Caroline's rose. Nonetheless, he barred her from his coronation. When she made a scene at Westminster trying to enter by multiple doors, she lost her credibility. The day after, she became ill, and three months later, in August 1821, she died.

The following year, George visited Scotland, the first English ruler to do so since Richard II. The three-week visit, orchestrated by the novelist and playwright Sir Walter Scott, was a public-relations success, and the resulting enthusiasm for "clan tartans" and other items of Scottish nostalgia, many of which were simply invented for the occasion, has never entirely abated. Once more, George's sense of style proved politically useful, as his visit knitted Scotland and England more tightly together.

The major political struggle of George's reign involved the question of rights for Catholics. Like his father, George regarded himself as the guardian of Protestantism, and steadfastly refused to sign any Catholic relief bill until 1829, when, after much wrangling, the Duke of Wellington, who had gone from winning Waterloo to serving as Prime Minister, finally persuaded George to sign off on the Catholic Relief Act.

Apart from that controversy, George did little to alter the course of Parliamentary rule. As the decade wore on, his excesses took a toll on his health: he was obese, frequently ill, and mentally unstable, and lived in relative retirement at Windsor. On June 26, 1830, he died in his bed. He was little mourned, and the throne passed to his brother, William IV.

SIR WALTER SCOTT'S SCOTLAND

Before visiting Scotland in 1822, George had been taken with the writings of Sir Walter Scott, some of which, such as the novel Waverley, romanticized earlier Highland life. George even had Scott to dinner. Scott carefully orchestrated the king's visit, even dictating the dress of any attendees at formal events. At the center of the fuss were tartan kilts. When Scott stipulated that attendees at the Highland Ball wear traditional kilts, Scottish aristocrats scrambled to get them, and many of the so-called clan patterns were invented to accommodate their needs. But Scott's efforts were largely successful: the romantic vision of Scotland he conjured for George's visit wed Scottish nationalism to a larger sense of British unity.

1828	1829	1830	1830
The Ottoman Empire closes the Dardanelles to Russian ships, precipitating the Russo-Turkish War of 1828–29, as a result of which Russia gains territory around the Black Sea.	The Metropolitan Police are established in London to maintain order in areas outside the City of London, which has its own police force.	The state of Belgium breaks away from the Netherlands and is recognized as an independent country.	The Liverpool and Manchester Railway opens, the first railway linking two cities carrying paying passengers on a regular timetable operated by steam locomotives.

WILLIAM IV ✠ The Sailor King

House Hanover
Born August 21, 1765
Died June 20, 1837
Reigned 1830–1837
Consort Adelaide of Saxe-Meiningen
Children Princesses Charlotte and Elizabeth of Clarence, both dead in infancy, also ten illegitimate children
Successor Victoria

William IV was one of the most unpretentious monarchs ever to take the English throne. Though he regarded himself as something of a caretaker, holding the reins of the kingdom until his niece Victoria was of age to take them, on his watch some of the most momentous reforms in British history took place. His common touch, born of an early career in the Royal Navy, made him both approachable to commoners and sensible in his responses to the events that unfolded during his reign.

Dorothea Jordan, the actress with whom William cohabitated for 20 years. They had ten children before parting ways in 1811.

William was known as the "Sailor King" for good reason. The third son of George III, he was groomed not for the throne but for a life of service. When William was 13 and a lackluster student who was already showing signs of his brothers' debauchery, King George had him enlist in the Royal Navy. George thought the discipline of naval life would do William some good, and in certain ways he was right. William had his own tutor with him, but otherwise he lived the life of an ordinary midshipman, with a range of regular duties but also with periods of shore leave in which he lived as raucously as his shipmates. On one occasion he was arrested for participating in a drunken brawl, and he certainly had his share of sexual adventures.

William rose quickly through the ranks, and not simply because of his royal status. By 1786, he was Captain of the HMS Pegasus and a good friend of Admiral Horatio Nelson, who thought highly of him as a naval officer. Within two years he was a Rear Admiral, and in 1789 his father created him Duke of Clarence, giving him a seat in the House of Lords. When he mustered out of the navy in 1790, he thought to devote himself more to politics, and when war broke out with Revolutionary France in 1793 he at first opposed it before asking for a naval command, which was never granted. Only in 1811, when he was given the symbolic position of Admiral of the Fleet, did he once more get a taste of naval life. In that position he would serve with distinction as an administrator, eliminating flogging for all but the most grave offenses and establishing more regular and efficient reporting on the seagoing condition of ships. He would hold the position until 1828, when his craving for life at sea led him to lead a handful of ships out to sea for no apparent purpose, at which point he was asked to resign.

In his private life, William proved much more staid than his extravagant brothers. From 1791 until 1811, he lived in happy domesticity with Dorothea Jordan, an Irish actress; the two of them had ten children. They lived in modest but spacious lodgings at Bushy Wood, which King George had granted them, and William's London residence, Clarence House, was a model of restraint. But William's debts nonetheless took a toll, and after the relationship ended

> I HAVE MY VIEW OF THINGS, AND I TELL THEM TO MY MINISTERS. IF THEY DO NOT ADOPT THEM, I CANNOT HELP IT. I HAVE DONE MY DUTY.
>
> *WILLIAM IV*

1830
In the USA, Joseph Smith publishes the Book of Mormon, thus founding the Church of Jesus Christ of Latter Day Saints, known informally as the Mormons.

1831
Belgium becomes independent of the Netherlands.

1831
A widespread cholera pandemic reaches London, where thousands eventually die as a result. Public fear of the disease reaches such a pitch that it becomes known as "King Cholera."

Opposite William IV, whose unpretentious, pragmatic approach to the realities of British politics allowed for major reforms and confirmed the dominance of Parliament as the arena of political decision-making.

he pursued a wife who could provide more financial stability. The quest took on more urgency after the untimely death in 1817 of George IV's daughter Charlotte. William settled on Princess Adelaide of Saxe-Meiningen, only 26 years old to William's 52 when she married him in 1818. Though none of William and Adelaide's children survived infancy, the union nevertheless proved a happy one. Adelaide was content to take charge of William's large brood of illegitimate children, and there is no record of William's taking any mistresses after his marriage. Marriage to Adelaide also domesticated William, so that his rougher edges from life at sea gradually smoothed away.

During the Regency and then the reign of George IV, William took part in Parliamentary debates, arguing, on the basis of what he had seen during his naval expeditions in the Caribbean, against the abolition of slavery, but also vocally supporting relief for Catholics. Though he gravitated toward the Whigs, he maintained his independence as a thinker and as a voter, his opinions largely based on his life experience rather than his education. As George IV's reign wore on, it became clear that the king's health was failing, largely due to his indulgent lifestyle, and that William would succeed him. When George died in 1830, William became king at the age of 64. He was the oldest ruler ever to take the English throne.

KINGSHIP AND REFORM

William took to the kingship as he might to the captaincy of a ship: with a strong sense of duty but very little tolerance for ceremony. He was often undignified and even eccentric in his public remarks, but his ministers, who had spent years dealing with the negligence of George IV, found him responsive and industrious. And he needed those qualities, because a political crisis erupted just as he took the throne.

Britain was in a state of wrenching transition. Victory in the Napoleonic Wars had proved costly, and subsequent bad harvests as well as the disorienting effects of the Industrial Revolution

had led to a sense that the government was broken and needed fixing. Radicalism of the French sort played almost no role in popular unrest; unlike pre-revolutionary France, Britain had enjoyed a degree of representative government for over a century. But Parliament was organized according to an antiquated map of Britain. Major cities and expanding industrial centers had no representation, while "rotten boroughs," often comprised of very few inhabitants, still elected Members of Parliament. Further, those rotten boroughs were often under the control of aristocrats who could effectively determine the vote. Pressure for reform had reached boiling point.

In 1830, the Whigs were riding the crest of public discontent, and the Duke of Wellington, the Tory Prime Minister, could not sustain his government. A new government was formed under Earl Grey, who is best known now for his namesake style of tea despite the fact that he initiated some of the most important reforms in British history. In 1831, Earl Grey attempted to pass a reform bill that would update and overhaul the system of Parliamentary representation, but he could not get it past the Commons. Grey suggested that William dissolve Parliament, and when the opposition threatened to block that action, William acted decisively. Demanding his carriage, he went immediately to Westminster, unceremoniously put on his crown, and dismissed Parliament, forcing new elections, which the pro-reform Whigs won handily.

In September of that year, William was formally crowned—if the word "formal" applies to the stripped down, inexpensive ceremony on which he insisted, and which cost one-eighth as much as George IV's imperial affair. In fact, he only assented to a coronation at all because too many in Parliament insisted on it.

After the coronation, the battle over reform resumed, and late that year a bill passed the Commons but was rejected by the Lords. It was a stalemate. Riots erupted throughout the country, but the Lords refused to budge. When Grey asked William to create enough new peers to stack the

Charles, Earl Grey, under whose premiership the Reform Act of 1832 modernized and expanded the electoral process.

1834

The Spanish Inquisition, in continuous operation since the 15th century, is shut down by Royal Decree.

1835

Texas declares itself independent of Mexico. Ten years later it will become the 28th of the United States, precipitating the U.S.-Mexican War."

1835

Charles Darwin reaches the Galapagos Islands aboard the HMS Beagle. What he finds there will contribute to his theory of natural selection.

A MODEST, BELOVED QUEEN

Adelaide was 26 years younger than William, and outlived him by a dozen years. From the first, her mild and modest demeanor won her public affection, and her painful misfortunes with her children—she had multiple miscarriages, and her two daughters did not survive infancy—gained her their sympathy as well. After William's death, Adelaide lived a modest life, residing at Witley Court in Worcestershire, where many people sought to meet her. When she died in 1849, she was given the quiet and simple funeral she requested, and interred alongside William in the Royal Vault at Windsor Castle.

opposition with a flood of new peerages. The writing was on the wall. The opposition chose to abstain, and the Reform Act of 1832 passed. It was a tectonic shift in British government, eliminating rotten boroughs, granting representation to new industrial cities, and enfranchising hundreds of thousands more voters.

Other reforms soon followed. The next year saw a new Factory Act limiting the use of child labor as well as the Abolition Act, outlawing slavery in British colonies. In 1834, the Poor Law Amendment Act attempted to clean up an outdated and inefficient system of relief for the poor. William did not always agree with the reforms, but he acknowledged in principle their necessity, and only once, in an unsuccessful attempt to block the rise to power of the radical Lord John Russell, did the king dismiss a cabinet; it was the last time in British history that a monarch made such a move.

CONTROLLING THE SUCCESSION

As William grew older and his health began to decline, the problem of succession loomed. The difficulty lay not in who would succeed—it was clear that his niece Victoria would take the throne—but in when she would succeed. In 1836, Victoria was 17 years old and therefore had not reached her majority. If William died within the year, Victoria's mother, the manipulative Duchess of Kent, along with her ambitious private secretary John Conroy, would have effective control of the government.

At a dinner that year, William declared his resolve to remain alive until Victoria reached her majority, to ensure that the Duchess of Kent would have no say in the young queen's reign. Victoria burst into tears at the blunt announcement, even though she had already resolved to distance herself from her mother.

William just managed to meet this last challenge. On June 20, 1837, he died peacefully in his bed at Windsor Castle, attended by Adelaide. A month earlier, Victoria had reached her majority, and she inherited the throne as a fully empowered monarch.

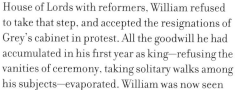

The Slavery Abolition Act of 1833 outlawed slavery throughout nearly all the British Empire. This period illustration shows the celebratory response to the legislation.

House of Lords with reformers, William refused to take that step, and accepted the resignations of Grey's cabinet in protest. All the goodwill he had accumulated in his first year as king—refusing the vanities of ceremony, taking solitary walks among his subjects—evaporated. William was now seen as an obstacle to reform.

William might have, like his father George III with the American colonies, dug in his heels. But his life experience had taught him compromise, and he recalled Grey's government and gave the opposition among the Lords two options: they could abstain from voting, or they could place him in a position in which he would have to override their

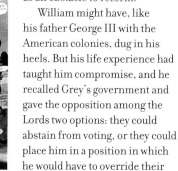

1836	1837	1837
In America, the Republic of Texas wins its independence from Mexico.	Louis Daguerre invents the daguerreotype, opening the age of photography.	Samuel Morse patents the telegraph, which will rapidly transform communication.

QUEEN VICTORIA ✦ Ruler of an Empire

House Hanover
Born May 24, 1819
Died January 22, 1901
Reigned 1837–1901
Consort Albert of Saxe-Coburg-Gotha
Children Nine, including Edward VII
Successor Edward VII.

Queen Victoria, last monarch of the House of Hanover, ruled for 63 years—the longest reign in British history. Her long tenure on the throne saw a remarkable evolution: Britain mastered a vast global empire, and Victoria weathered personal loss and political difficulties to become one of the best-loved of Britain's monarchs. Her descendants would go on to inherit thrones all across Europe.

Alexandrina Victoria, known as Drina in her childhood, was literally born to take the throne. In 1817, when George IV's daughter Charlotte died, the Hanoverian line was in danger of dying out. The king's brothers scrambled to produce heirs, and the only one to do so was Prince Edward, a vain and dissipated man who married Princess Victoria of Saxe-Coburg-Saalfeld, sister of Charlotte's widower Leopold. Victoria was born on May 24, 1819 at Kensington Palace.

But her childhood was anything but happy. Her father died a few months after she was born, and her mother, the Duchess of Kent, grew close to John Conroy, who had formerly served Prince Edward. The two adults, who may well have been lovers, conspired to isolate and control Victoria, keeping her away from her Hanoverian relations and attempting to make her dependent on Conroy's guidance. Strict punishments, including being left alone on a staircase with her hands bound, were inflicted whenever Victoria resisted her mother and Conroy's authority. She was instructed only in disciplines her mother considered appropriate for a woman, such as languages, art, and music. But Victoria's governess, Baroness Lehzen, instilled a strong sense of duty and independence in her young charge, and Victoria quietly awaited the day when she could throw off the corrosive control of her mother and Conroy.

That day came in 1837, when Victoria turned 18. Within a month, King William, who had declared the previous year that he was determined to stay alive long enough to ensure that Victoria would inherit the throne without the Duchess having any regency powers, passed away, and Victoria became Queen of the United Kingdom of Great Britain and Ireland.

AN ASSERTIVE YOUNG QUEEN

When Victoria assumed the throne, she wasted no time banishing her mother and Conroy to the hinterlands of her life. She had prepared carefully for her new role—at the age of 11, discovering that she was likely to become Queen, she had said, "I will be good"—and she displayed astonishing poise from the start. At her first meeting with her council, she gave a clear, confident speech and displayed such a winning combination of modesty and assertiveness that her ministers were elated. This was a monarch capable beyond her years.

The honeymoon would not last. To begin with, despite the reforms enacted during William IV's reign, the monarchy remained

> ## WE ARE NOT INTERESTED IN THE POSSIBILITIES OF DEFEAT; THEY DO NOT EXIST
>
> *QUEEN VICTORIA*

Opposite Queen Victoria, under whose long reign the British Empire dominated the globe, and who served as personification of conservative British values.

1841
British forces occupy Hong Kong during the First Opium War. With few interludes, Britain will maintain control of Hong Kong until 1997.

1842
Forces of the British East India Company, under the command of Sir William Elphinstone, are wiped out in a long retreat from Kabul in Afghanistan. Only one Englishman survives.

1843
Charles Dickens's A Christmas Carol is first published. It not only offers a seasonal fable but also highlights the plight of London's poor.

William Lamb, Lord Melbourne. As Victoria's first Prime Minister, he patiently tutored her in politics.

Victoria, Albert, and their children as portrayed in 1846. Victoria and Albert had one of the happiest and most successful of all royal marriages until his premature death in 1861.

unpopular. Victoria, painfully aware of the degree to which she had been controlled as a child, both delighted in her new freedom to schedule and attend parties and balls but also relied heavily on the counsel of her Prime Minister, Lord Melbourne. Melbourne, who had lost a daughter, regarded the young queen as a kind of ward, and Victoria treated him as a father. They spent hours every day going over the intricacies of Parliamentary process and domestic and foreign policy. Rumors even arose that the Queen might marry her Prime Minister, four decades her senior, though there was no basis for such speculation.

Things turned dire when Victoria accused one of her Ladies in Waiting, Flora Hastings, of a scandalous pregnancy by none other than John Conroy. Hastings did have a swelling belly, but the accusation was a rash decision by the young queen, who associated Hastings with the miseries of childhood. An eventual examination revealed Hastings to be a virgin, and she soon died of the real cause of her swollen belly, a tumor. Victoria came across as heartless and vindictive, and her popularity plummeted.

When Melbourne resigned in 1839 over a failed bill, Robert Peel took over as Prime Minister, and immediately he and Victoria clashed. Many of the Queen's Ladies of the Bedchamber were the wives of prominent Whigs, the party Victoria favored, and Tories insisted that Victoria show no sign of favoritism to a party opposed to the current government. When they requested that she replace her Ladies of the Bedchamber, she flatly refused, and in the ensuing conflict Melbourne regained the premiership.

It was clear, however, that Victoria needed to marry. Some considered her too difficult to manage and hoped that a husband would calm her down; others saw a husband as the surest way to rid her of any possible influence by her mother. And Victoria's future husband had already been decided: her cousin Prince Albert of Saxe-Coburg-Gotha, who had previously been introduced to Victoria by her uncle Leopold of Belgium.

VICTORIA AND ALBERT

Victoria first met Albert in 1837, when both were 17 years old. Though he did not make a strong impression the first time they met, Leopold arranged another visit in October of 1839. This time, Victoria was smitten. Albert was not a robustly healthy young man, but he had a romantic beauty, and lofty ideals to go with it. He had also had a difficult childhood himself, and in some way the two young royals must have responded to each other's need for affection. During that second visit, Victoria, as required by protocol, proposed to Albert. They were married on February 10, 1840, both 20 years old.

The marriage was an extraordinary success. For Victoria, the cerebral but affectionate Albert was both a mentor and an emotional support; for Albert, Victoria was a loyal and passionate partner. Though they fought occasionally—most notably over Albert's successful insistence that Baroness Lehzen be dismissed in order to create a gentler household for the family—they formed an enduring partnership, working side by side at adjoining desks. Victoria would have had

1845	1848	1852	1855	1857
The Great Famine begins in Ireland. It will last until 1852. Around a million people will die, and as many will emigrate from Ireland.	Revolutions erupt across continental Europe and even in Latin America. Nearly all ultimately fail, demoralizing and radicalizing opposition in the coming decade.	In France, Louis-Napoleon Bonaparte declares a new French Empire and titles himself Napoleon III.	In central Africa, missionary and explorer David Livingstone becomes the first European to set eyes on Victoria Falls, the world's largest waterfall.	The Indian Rebellion erupts against the British East India Company. It spells the end of the Mughal Empire and of the British East India Company, as India is placed under the direct control of the Crown.

THE CRYSTAL PALACE

The Crystal Palace, the centerpiece and exhibition hall of the Great Exhibition of 1851, was itself a feat of engineering. The latest technology for making large sheets of sufficiently strong plate glass allowed for a dazzling sense of light and space within the building. It immediately became a symbol of human progress and utopian aspirations across Europe. After the Exhibition ended, the Palace was disassembled and rebuilt in South London, on Penge Common. In 1936 the Crystal Palace was destroyed in a fire, but it gave its name to that neighborhood of London, and many of the institutions based there.

The earliest known photograph of Victoria, which dates from around 1844. With her is her eldest daughter, Victoria, the Princess Royal.

Albert crowned King if it had been permissible, and she took his advice on nearly every aspect of rule. Gradually, he took over a number of administrative functions of the monarchy.

At the time of the wedding, Victoria was deeply unpopular; she and Albert survived multiple botched assassination attempts. Though he was seen as rigid and aloof, Albert gradually transformed Victoria's image, mostly because he changed the monarchy itself. He was an idealistic, reform-minded royal, determined to bring Britain into the modern era, and he also recognized that the monarchy should serve as a moral beacon to the nation and the empire.

In 1841, Robert Peel again replaced Melbourne as Prime Minister, and Albert began to assert more publicly the idealism that would guide his decisions. In 1843, he became president of the Royal Society for the Encouragement of Arts, Manufactures and Commerce—the Royal Society of Arts, for short—and used it to advance British agricultural and manufacturing techniques. At first tacitly and then openly, he supported Peel's moves to cut back on child labor and improve working conditions. As Britain woke up to the fact that it had a somewhat progressive monarchy, Victoria and Albert became more popular, and their clear sense of moral rectitude endeared them to the increasingly powerful middle class.

In 1848, while revolutions swept across the continent, Albert spoke eloquently for reform. His position as president of the Society for the Improvement of the Conditions of the Labouring Classes made his position clear. England remained free of the continental unrest, though some of Albert's relations suffered and even lost their positions. Victoria, who was less committed to reform than Albert, also agonized over the revolutions. From 1843 onward, she had pursued a policy of active mutual support among European sovereigns, encouraging royal visits. Britain saw relatively few demonstrations inspired by the revolutions, but Victoria and Albert felt it prudent to withdraw to Osborne House, their estate on the Isle of Wight, for some time.

Albert's drive to modernize the monarchy and Britain came to fruition with the Great Exhibition of 1851. Years in the making, it was a showcase of industry, designed to foreground Britain's pre-eminence as a manufacturing nation. Albert had faced stiff opposition to his

1861	1862	1865		1868
The American Civil War begins with the bombardment of Fort Sumter, in Charleston Harbor, by Confederate forces. It will last until 1865 and cost several hundred thousand lives.	Otto von Bismarck, Minister President of Prussia, delivers his famous "Blood and Iron" speech, announcing his intention of building a strong nation by force of arms.	The American Civil War ends. Shortly after, Abraham Lincoln is assassinated by actor John Wilkes Booth.		The 15-year-old emperor Meiji declares himself to have full powers in Japan. The Meiji Restoration will result in rapid modernization of Japan, which had been closed to foreigners for centuries under the Tokugawa Shogunate.

proposal; many thought it would lead to riots, or to hostile activity from foreign visitors. In the event, it was a stupendous success, not only paying for itself but generating £180,000 in profit, which Victoria and Albert steered toward cultural institutions, most famously the Victoria and Albert Museum. The centerpiece of the exhibition was the Crystal Palace, a sort of gigantic solarium made of only glass and cast iron, extending over nearly a million square feet of Hyde Park. It became the symbol of Britain as a progressive industrial power.

Over the next several years, foreign affairs dominated Victoria's rule. The Crimean War, a conflict with Russia that Albert had hoped to avoid, would unfold between 1853 and 1856. Though Britain would lose far fewer troops than its ally France, the war revealed how much the British army needed modernization. No sooner was the Crimean War concluded than troubles

erupted in India. In 1857, long-simmering tensions among the Sepoys, Indian soldiers of the British East India Company, erupted into violence with the introduction of new rifles whose paper cartridges were coated with beef or pork fat—the former unacceptable to Hindus, the latter to Muslims. In the ensuing rebellion, thousands died and both sides committed atrocities. In 1858, the Government of India Act dissolved the British East India Company, placing India under the direct rule of the Crown through the India Office. Victoria insisted that the Act include explicit reference to religious toleration. It was the beginning of the British Raj.

EMERGING FROM THE DARK

1861 would prove to be the most trying year of Victoria's life. That March, her mother died. Though Albert had worked hard to heal the breach between them, Victoria the Duchess had remained largely estranged over the years. She was present at her mother's death, and afterward sorted through the private papers left behind. Concluding that her mother had in fact loved her, and that Conroy and Baroness Lehzen were to blame for the breach that had continued for so long, Victoria was sunk in grief.

Albert gamely took over most of the royal duties. Since 1859, he had suffered from chronic stomach troubles, and the strain of handling Victoria's responsibilities as well as his own took a toll. British government was far more complex than even a generation before, and an attentive sovereign, though not holding the reins of power, had a great deal of administrative work to do. Also draining were the allegations that their son Albert Edward, known as Bertie, was engaging in licentious behavior at Cambridge. Despite his illness, and in foul weather, Albert took a carriage to Cambridge that November to confront Bertie. On his return, he grew even more ill, and in December it became clear that he would not survive. Doctors diagnosed typhoid, but given the extended nature of his illness it was more

The Albert Memorial, in Hyde Park across from the Royal Albert Hall. The magnificent monument both commemorates Albert and celebrates empire.

1871

For two months, Paris is under the control of the Paris Commune, a revolutionary government, before it is brutally suppressed by the military.

1873

In Paris, the young poet Arthur Rimbaud publishes Une saison en enfer (A Season in Hell), a difficult and extravagant poem that exercises a huge influence on the literature of the coming decades.

1876

Alexander Graham Bell is issued a patent for his new invention, the telephone.

1878

Bulgaria wins its independence from the Ottoman Empire, which is rapidly fading.

John Brown, the faithful servant and companion to Victoria in the years between Albert's death in 1861 and his own in 1883.

came to rely heavily on John Brown, a Scottish servant who became her closest friend. His evident importance to her was such that even her daughters joked about the possibility of a romantic relationship, and she became known as Mrs. Brown. Though no clear evidence has surfaced to suggest that the relationship was anything other than purely platonic, Victoria was tainted with the possibility of scandal, and her children, especially Bertie, resented Brown's position. Victoria resisted all calls to remove or demote him, and he would remain her most devoted servant and companion until his death in 1883, after which Victoria had a statue in his honor erected at Balmoral Castle.

Though she remained in seclusion throughout the 1860s, Victoria still functioned as Queen. In 1866, she was persuaded to attend the opening of Parliament, but she did so dressed in mourning clothes and wearing a veil, and did not give the customary speech. The next year, she signed off on the Reform Act of 1867, which enfranchised all male householders in Britain, effectively giving voting rights to all working class men and doubling the size of the electorate. The Act was advanced by a confluence of forces: widespread and sometimes huge demonstrations, anxiety about potential class violence, and not least the rivalry between two of the great statesmen of the age, the Liberal William Ewart Gladstone and Conservative Benjamin Disraeli, who so challenged each other on the bill that, somewhat ironically, it became more and more expansive.

In 1871, events outside Britain drew Victoria out of seclusion. Napoleon III, a monarch with whom Victoria and Albert had been on good terms, was captured by the Prussians, and in his absence the French Commune declared a republic. Soon enough, the republican ideal found its way to England, and Victoria realized she would have to make a case for her own existence as Queen. That year, she opened Parliament, wearing a small crown fitted to her widow's cap, and opened the Royal Albert Hall as well as attending her daughter Princess

likely a chronic inflammatory or autoimmune disorder. On December 14, at the age of 42, Albert died.

The entire country grieved. Victoria, already mourning her mother's death, was devastated. She descended into a deep depression, resolving to dress in black for the rest of her life and almost completely withdrawing from public life. It was precisely the wrong decision, but Victoria's highly emotional temperament drove her, and despite the encouragement of those around her she became known as the Widow of Windsor. Together, Albert and Victoria had begun to restore the esteem of the monarchy; now it receded again, as her grief was seen as obsessive and self-absorbed.

The next ten years were effectively a lost decade for the Queen. In her seclusion, she

1879	1881	1882	1885	1887
Zulu forces, under a solar eclipse, destroy an invading British force at Isandlwana in what is now South Africa.	Tsar Alexander II of Russia is killed when bombs thrown by radicals explode near his carriage. Ironically, he had been about to introduce representative government to Russia.	The Triple Alliance is formed among Germany, Austria-Hungary, and Italy. It will hold until the start of the First World War in 1914.	King Leopold II of Belgium establishes the Congo Free State. While pretending to advocate humane practices, he in fact enforces ruthless exploitation of the local populations in pursuit of personal wealth.	Construction begins on the Eiffel Tower in Paris. It will serve as the gateway to the World's Fair of 1889.

Victoria in old age, when she had become a maternal figure and a symbol of the British Empire.

piece of political spectacle calculated to revive affection for the monarchy, and it worked.

EMPRESS VICTORIA

In 1874, Gladstone, whom Victoria had never liked, fell from office, and Disraeli took over as Prime Minister. Where Gladstone had been stiff and professorial, Disraeli intuited that Victoria would respond far better to charm than to exhortations, and he set about forming a more relaxed and flattering relationship with her. It worked. The supreme expression of Disraeli's flattery came in 1876, when he advanced a bill to have Victoria crowned Empress of India. In a sense, it was purely a semantic move—Victoria was to be the equal of the Russian Emperor— but the word struck a nerve in many MPs, and Gladstone fervently opposed the bill. It passed, however, and Disraeli went forward with an aggressive vision of Britain as an imperial power. He secured the Suez Canal, maneuvered against the Russian Empire in Central Asia in what Rudyard Kipling would eventually call the Great Game, and humiliated Russia by finessing the terms of the Congress of Berlin, which minimized Russian influence in the Balkans.

Disraeli retired after losing the elections of 1880 and died the following year, but his imperial vision would govern British foreign policy through the rest of Victoria's reign. He believed in realpolitik, the hard-nosed business of sacrificing higher ideals to the more fundamental business of advancing Britain's material interests, and he proved very effective in that capacity. Victoria supported him wholeheartedly. When Khartoum fell to Sudanese rebels in 1885, leading to the death of General Charles George Gordon, the Queen publicly rebuked Gladstone, who had returned as Prime Minister, for not hastening troops to relieve what had been a ten-month siege. It was a questionable charge, as Gordon had disobeyed orders to evacuate the city and the region, but it cost Gladstone his position for a year and demonstrated that Victoria was wholly committed to the imperial enterprise.

Louise's wedding. But doubts remained, and late that year a Liberal MP called for the abolition of the monarchy.

It took near-disaster to revive Victoria's fortunes. Shortly after the Parliamentary speech against the monarchy, Bertie fell desperately ill with typhoid, exactly ten years after his father's death. All of Britain was captivated by the crisis. On December 14, the anniversary of his father's death, Bertie rallied, and then he recovered. Gladstone, the Prime Minister at the time, persuaded Victoria to hold a national day of celebration for the prince's recovery. It was a

1888	1890	1891	1892	1894
Kaiser Wilhelm II is crowned in Germany. By the start of the First World War, he will have squandered most of his power.	Tchaikovsky's ballet Sleeping Beauty premiers in St. Petersburg.	The London-Paris telephone system is inaugurated, another step in the acceleration of communication through technology.	Ellis Island in New York harbor begins processing the admission of immigrants to the United States.	French Captain Alfred Dreyfus, a Jew, is falsely accused of espionage. He will be imprisoned on Devil's Island. His case sparks years of controversy before he is cleared of all charges in 1906.

THE GREAT GAME

The imperial agenda devised by Disraeli and supported by Victoria led Britain into increasing conflict with the Russian Empire, especially in Central Asia. The term the Great Game, which originated earlier but became famous from its use by Rudyard Kipling in his 1901 novel Kim, was the decades-long chess match between Britain and Russia for control of Central Asia. Afghanistan was the centerpiece of the struggle, as Britain hoped to fend off any possible Russian incursions into India. The Great Game wound down in 1907, as Russia and Britain opted to join forces in resistance to German ambitions.

IMPERIAL LEGACY

By 1897, Victoria was already being seen in terms of her legacy, which was gigantic. Not only did she rule over the wealthiest and most populous empire in history; her nine children would go on to have 42 grandchildren, tying the English monarchy by blood to royal families all over the continent and earning her the nickname "the grandmother of Europe." For her Diamond Jubilee that year, she invited the dignitaries of all British dominions, and a parade of troops from all over the empire saluted her where she sat in an open carriage, too weary to step down to the street. An outdoor service of thanksgiving at St. Paul's Cathedral culminated the festivities. Many of Europe's royals, so many of them relations, attended as well.

In her remaining years, Victoria would confront new losses. The Second Boer War began in 1899, and the ruthless tactics on both sides led to high casualties. The conflict was so unpopular on the continent that in 1900 Victoria was advised to visit Ireland instead—an ironic turn, given that Victoria had steadfastly opposed any move toward Irish home rule. That same year, her second son, Alfred, died.

As the new century began, Victoria accepted her infirmity. She was nearly blind from cataracts, easily exhausted, and afflicted with a range of ailments, but she remained good-humored and still fulfilled her duties as sovereign. After spending Christmas of 1900 at Osborne House, as was her custom, she rapidly faded. On January 22, 1901, with her heir Bertie and her grandson Kaiser Wilhelm II at her bedside, she died peacefully.

Victoria left detailed instructions for her funeral, which was to be, in sharp contrast with her dress since Albert's death, white instead of black. She was buried in her wedding dress, with mementos of family, friends, and faithful servants placed in the coffin. Among them was a dressing gown of Albert's, along with a plaster cast of his hand; also included were a lock of John Brown's hair, several of his letters, a photograph of him, and, on her right hand, a ring that had belonged to his mother. Flowers were arranged to conceal the photograph of Brown. Two days after her funeral on February 2, she was interred alongside Albert in the mausoleum she had had built for the purpose in Windsor Great Park.

It is difficult to compare monarchs from different eras—Victoria never held anywhere near the power of Elizabeth I, for instance—but there is no denying the importance of Victoria's reign, the longest to date of any British sovereign. She did not hold the levers of power, and for much of her reign she largely withdrew from the public eye, but she nonetheless became a potent symbol of a nation and an age. Her unglamorous steadiness and decency, and her maternal demeanor in her older years, firmly established the monarchy as a symbolic force for continuity and stability in a world fraught with increasingly rapid change. When she died, an era ended.

Benjamin Disraeli, Victoria's favorite among the Prime Ministers to serve during her long reign.

1895	1897	1898	1900	1901
Oscar Wilde, after losing a libel suit against the Marquess of Queensbury, is convicted of sodomy and indecency and sentenced to two years in Reading Gaol.	At the Battle of Saragarhi, 21 Sikhs of the Sikh Regiment in India hold off 10,000 tribesmen for hours, fighting to the death to buy valuable time for nearby forts. They are all decorated posthumously.	The explosion and sinking of the USS Maine in Havana harbor precipitates the Spanish-American war.	The Boxer Rebellion in China attempts to expel all foreigners. It collapses when Western forces arrive and take over Beijing.	The Commonwealth of Australia is officially formed, with Edmund Barton as its first Prime Minister.

THE SUN NEVER SETS

Though the phrase "the empire on which the sun never sets" was first used to describe Spanish dominions, it eventually became a catchphrase for the British Empire, which at its peak, around 1922, covered over 13 million square miles (33 million km2) and included more than 450 million people.

Though England might be said to have had imperial dominions in France under the Plantagenet kings, the history of the British Empire more properly begins in 1497, with John Cabot's discovery of Newfoundland. Nearly a century later, in 1583, Humphrey Gilbert claimed the island for Elizabeth I. It was the heady era of imperial competition for the vast resources of the New World, a game that had first been won by Spain but would be played in North America chiefly between England and France. The first permanent English settlement came in 1607, with the establishment of Jamestown in what is now the State of Virginia.

The Netherlands had already begun to establish a far-reaching mercantile presence, and the British followed their model. Jamestown was a commercial venture of the sort that would come to define the empire. It was followed within the next few decades by colonies in the West Indies. Joint-stock companies, such as the British East India and the Hudson's Bay companies, were granted monopolies on trade in India and what is now Canada, bringing direct conflict with French ambitions.

As Spain's fortunes began to wane, France emerged once more as the main rival to English power. The War of the Spanish Succession demonstrated Britain's increasing might, and the Seven Years' War led to significant expansion of overseas English territories: Canada was ceded to the British, and the East India Company, using its own armies against those of French proxies, managed to extend its control deep into India.

With the loss of its American colonies after their war of independence, Britain pivoted to the Pacific. In 1770, William Cook had claimed Australia (he called it New South Wales) for Britain, and in 1788 the first shiploads of convicts arrived at the penal colony of Botany Bay. As Australia's resources were tapped, its then-capital of Melbourne became fabulously wealthy, and more and more fortune-seekers settled the continent.

THE APEX OF EMPIRE
By the turn of the 20th century, the British Empire was near its peak. It became a complex array of Dominions (self-governing realms largely populated by people of British descent), Crown Colonies (controlled by British governors), and Protectorates (British-controlled, but with a semblance of self-rule). Territories in Africa further swelled its land area. Its most prized piece, "the jewel in the crown," was the Indian Empire, which had been brought under direct rule of the Crown in 1858. The entire Empire was connected by steamships and a system of coaling stations above the sea and an unrivaled system of telegraph cables below.

The British Empire, the largest the world has ever known, was the product not of systematic conquest so much as mercantile ambitions. With its peerless navy and enterprising explorers and traders, Britain gradually gained control of territories around the world. The Queen Victoria Memorial Building (above), in Calcutta, is testament to the might of the British Empire in India.

Mahatma Gandhi's (right) nonviolent protest movement was crucial to the eventual independence of India.

DECLINE AND TRANSITION

The Empire reached its greatest extent in the aftermath of World War I, when the victorious allies divided among themselves various chunks of the German and Ottoman empires. But ensuing years saw the increasing dominance of the United States and other new global powers, and independence movements gained momentum in India and elsewhere. British lawmakers and citizens where already rethinking how to address these changes when World War II wreaked its devastation. Britain emerged from the war victorious but bankrupt, and a gradual dissolution of the Empire began.

Over the next 20 years, it shrank to a tiny fraction of its former size, as first India and then a series of Dominions, Colonies, Protectorates, and Mandated Territories gained their independence. For the most part, the transitions themselves involved little violence, and efforts were made to ensure the continued rule of law. But empire, as the English novelist Joseph Conrad wrote, "is not a pretty thing." Its subjugations and traumas and arbitrary boundaries, engendered local and regional conflicts that in many cases persist to this day.

CECIL RHODES: THE FACE OF EMPIRE

Perhaps no single man better embodies the unsavory aspects of late British imperialism than Cecil Rhodes (1853–1902): South African colonist, politician, diamond magnate, and tireless advocate of empire. He arrived in South Africa at the age of 17, and within 20 years controlled nearly all the world's diamond supply. By 1890, he was Prime Minister of the Cape Colony, from which post he not only initiated ruthlessly exploitative policies but also sparked the Second Boer War. Later, with his British South Africa Company, he took control of vast territories that came to be called Rhodesia (now mostly Zimbabwe). A confirmed and vocal racist, Rhodes believed that the Anglo-Saxon and German peoples were inherently superior and entitled to impose their supremacy on Africans and others. At the same time, he endowed universities and established the Rhodes Scholarship.

The House of Windsor

When George V changed his family name from Saxe-Coburg and Gotha to Windsor during the First World War, he was making an unequivocal statement: the royal family is English through and through, and it has a vocation to serve Britain rather than rule it. That Windsor sensibility—the monarchy as cultural symbol rather than political authority— has weathered two world wars, the loss of the empire, and such crises as the abdication of Edward VIII and the untimely death of Princess Diana of Wales. George VI embodied the Windsor ideals of service and tradition, and his daughter Elizabeth II has, with varying success, sought to do the same.

EDWARD VII ✠ The Peacemaker King

House Saxe-Coburg
and Gotha

Born November 9, 1841

Died May 6, 1910

Reigned 1901-1910

Consort Alexandra of
Denmark

Children Seven, Including
George V and Queen Maud
of Norway

Successor George V

When Edward VII took the throne at the death of his mother Victoria, he was 59 years old, and had been heir-apparent for the longest stretch in British history. Though in his younger years he had shown great charm but little discipline, Edward proved a capable and self-aware monarch, admired particularly for his extraordinary common touch and his diplomatic ability.

Prince Albert Edward, the eldest son and second child of Victoria and Albert, was hardly promising as a child. His parents, with their strict sense of duty and propriety, set him on a course of rigorous education and training for the monarchy, and expected him to apply himself with dedication. But Prince Albert, known as Bertie, did not live up to their expectations.

Bertie proved to be a difficult child, inattentive and lackluster in his studies, stubborn in his attitude to authority, and entirely too inclined to indulge his appetites. None of this boded well for a future monarch, but in some ways it was predictable. Victoria and Albert were affectionate but also controlling parents; it may be that both of them, having had difficult childhoods, were too determined to raise Bertie carefully. He may also have inherited a measure of his mother's emotionally charged temperament. Whatever the cause, he was a difficult child, and elicited his father's near-continual disappointment.

But Bertie had one thing going for him: charisma. Though he was not conventionally handsome—he had a weak chin and a rather doughy face as a young man—he took such evident pleasure in life, and was so free and easy in manner, that even people inclined to look askance at his waywardness liked him nonetheless. In 1860, at the age of 19, he embarked on the first-ever tour of the United States by an heir to the British throne. The United States was a rapidly

HE HAD A TREMENDOUS ZEST FOR PLEASURE BUT HE ALSO HAD A REAL SENSE OF DUTY

J. B. PRIESTLEY

growing country at the time, but it was also racked with internal controversy over such issues as slavery and states' rights; the year after Bertie's visit it would descend into a bitter and devastating civil war. But Bertie's visit was a gigantic success. The prince, so garrulous and easygoing, charmed his American hosts. He met with statesmen and poets, and basked in the attention of the public as he was feted in a series of cities. It was a foretaste of kingship, though that particular form of celebrity would elude him for another 40 years.

THE PLAYBOY PRINCE

Like some of his predecessors, young Albert Edward displayed in full the moral hazard of being heir-apparent for many years. As he matured, attending Oxford and then Cambridge, where he became a passable if not brilliant student, his pleasures became more scandalous. Though he could not, as first in line to the throne, pursue an active military career, after returning from his triumphant American tour, he trained with British troops in Ireland.

1901	1902	1903	
Eleven years after his death, Vincent van Gogh's paintings suddenly become famous as a result of a show in Paris.	The Second Boer War ends with the Treaty of Vereeniging, incorporating what will become the Union of South Africa into the British Empire.	The Wright brothers launch their first powered flight in Kitty Hawk, North Carolina.	

Opposite Edward VII, whose charisma and zest for life, made him popular despite his vices, which had darkened his reputation in his younger years.

Alexandra of Denmark, Edward's Queen Consort. The two had a successful marriage, and she seems to have genuinely tolerated his many dalliances.

While there, he took his first known mistress, an erstwhile actress and camp follower named Nellie Clifden. Had Bertie left her in Ireland, the affair might have blown over, but rumors soon circulated that he had brought her back to England. Albert, ever the high-minded father, traveled to Cambridge in 1861 to reprimand Bertie despite feeling unwell; within weeks he died. Though Albert's death was likely due to a chronic condition—he had been ill for a couple of years—the official diagnosis was typhoid, and Victoria blamed Albert's fatal decline on the stress of Bertie's scandalous behavior.

After his father's death, Bertie was sent out on a tour of the Mediterranean, but he was also propelled into marriage. Fortunately, the bride, who had been chosen by Albert and Victoria, proved a good match. Alexandra of Denmark was an attractive young woman, and though Denmark's tensions with Prussia, where Victoria's relations held the throne, were a bit of a sticking point, Alexandra and Bertie had liked each other well enough in a couple of arranged

meetings, and no one more suitable could be found. In early March of 1863, Alexandra took a royal yacht from Denmark to England, and that month she and Bertie were married.

Marriage, however, did little to curb the appetites of the young prince. Though he and Alexandra got on well and soon began having children, Bertie became an icon of aristocratic hedonism. He took mistresses—some of them, such as Lillie Langtry, became famous. He bred racehorses, indulged in far too much food, alcohol, and tobacco, and went to theaters with other high-living young men. Even among his friends, he was known to be capricious, with quicksilver changes of mood and a mean streak that occasionally surprised even those closest to him. Throughout Europe, a new decadence was just beginning to make itself felt, and the prince was its harbinger in England.

None of this made him popular. In the 1860s, with Albert gone and Victoria in seclusion, it fell to Bertie to be the public face of the monarchy, and he did not do the Crown much honor. Through his twenties, his hedonism flew in the face of the strict sense of propriety Victoria and Albert had sought to model for the nation.

But in 1871, ten years to the month after his father's death, Bertie nearly died of typhoid, and Britain was caught up in the intimate drama of Victoria's son and the heir-apparent fighting for his life against a deadly disease. When Bertie recovered, celebrations were held across the country. Prime Minister William Gladstone used the occasion to bring Victoria some way out of her seclusion and restore some luster to the monarchy.

Apart from one notable scandal in 1890, when he was caught gambling illegally and covering up for an acquaintance's cheating at baccarat, for the next 30 years, Albert Edward's self-indulgent behavior would come to be accepted by the nation. His mistresses, his racehorses, his hunting tweeds, his appetites, all were accepted as inalienable aspects of the man, whose geniality compensated for his

A MODERN KING

Edward came of age in a time of rapid transition, and he often combined the old and the new. Though he restored many of the ceremonial functions that had been neglected under Victoria, he also enjoyed riding in his fleet of automobiles rather than in carriages, often at high speed. He was known for treating people from all walks of life with the same easygoing dignity. Like his predecessor George IV, he became a fashion icon, popularizing such new looks as Homburg hats and sporty tweeds, and black tie rather than white tie and tails for formal dinners. In this respect, his zest for life allowed him not only to embrace change but also to use the iconic status of royalty to transform standards of taste and decorum.

1904	1905	1906	1907
Britain and France enter into the Entente Cordiale, formally becoming allies and paving the way for the Triple Entente with Russia.	Mass strikes and military unrest lead to an abortive revolution in Russia, which is put down by Tsarist forces.	In India, satyagraha, Sanskrit for "insisting on truth," becomes the word describing nonviolent resistance to British rule.	In Finland, parliamentary elections are the first in the world to have female candidates for office and universal suffrage.

Alice Keppel, Edward's last mistress. She became such an accepted fixture in his life that she was allowed by Queen Alexandra to visit the king on his deathbed.

vices. He had George IV's sense of style but a more generous spirit. There was something egalitarian in his zest for life; on a tour of India in 1875, he struck onlookers by his insistence on engaging personally with Anglo-Indians and Indians alike. He took genuine pleasure in attending public functions and performing ceremonial duties. Despite all this, Victoria left him out of matters of state until the very last years of her reign; she simply did not trust Bertie to be discreet in such things.

A DECADE AS KING

On January 22, 1901, Victoria died after 63 years on the throne. Her last utterance was "Bertie." At the age of 59, Bertie was at last King of the United Kingdom. The next day, he announced that he would rule not as Albert I but as Edward VII, so as to preserve the royal name Albert for his father. Three weeks later, he opened Parliament in the traditional manner, splendidly dressed and giving a ceremonial speech. Though his and Alexandra's coronation had to be postponed when he needed emergency surgery for acute appendicitis and was eventually scaled back, it was still a glittering affair that recalled more of the majesty of monarchy than the widow's weeds and staid, maternal manner Victoria had projected for most of her reign.

King Edward wasted no time putting his own stamp on the monarchy, clearing out and

redecorating both Windsor Palace and Buckingham Palace in a brighter, more opulent style. He collected automobiles, often going out for drives, and his patronage of the arts included founding the Order of Merit. He had extraordinary success as a breeder of racehorses, winning the Derby three times. Though he still indulged in his huge appetites for food, drink, and tobacco, and carried on with mistresses—one of his late paramours, Alice Keppel, was treated almost like a member of the family—he appeared no longer as a young, scandalous decadent but rather as a dignified, tweedy nobleman who happened to perform a highly symbolic and ceremonial role in British society.

And he was little more than that. Edward took relatively little interest in governing, and he had no direction over Parliament. What he could do was use his position and his personal charm to be a sort of unofficial diplomat, especially in Europe. Edward spent long holidays every year in France and Germany. In 1903, his state visit to Paris was every bit as successful as his youthful tour of America; speaking fluent French and lavishing praise on French culture, he played a small and symbolic but meaningful role in warming Anglo-French relations in a time when international isolation would have been perilous to Britain. His skill as an unofficial diplomat earned him the nickname Peacemaker. Such symbolic clout was little compared to the powers enjoyed by earlier monarchs, but it sufficed for Edward.

On May 6, 1910, after the onset of bronchitis, the king suffered a series of heart attacks. He was on his deathbed when his son and heir George brought him news that one of his horses had won a race that day. "I am glad," said Edward. Those were his last words.

Edward's son George, who had only become heir-apparent after the death of his older brother Albert Victor, known as Eddy, in 1892, was grief-stricken, calling the late king "the best of fathers." He may not have been the best of kings, but he did far better than many had expected.

Edward VII's extraordinary common touch earned him wide affection, making his funeral an occasion of genuine public mourning. At right, the funeral cortege. Above, his lying in state.

1908	1909	1910
Henry Ford produces the first Model T, making automobiles more affordable for American consumers.	In a precursor to the Armenian Genocide of 1915–16, Ottoman forces slaughter thousands of Armenians.	The four colonies of South African are merged into the Union of South Africa, a dominion of the British Empire. It will remain so until 1961, when it becomes the Republic of South Africa.

GEORGE V ✛ The People's King

House Windsor
Born June 3, 1885
Died January 20, 1936
Reigned 1910-1936
Consort Mary of Teck
Children Six, including Edward VIII and George VI
Successor Edward VIII

George V well understood the position and power of the modern monarchy, and his modest but serious style of kingship helped carry Britain through a series of crises in his quarter-century on the throne. Through political reform, world war, and global economic crisis, George's steady, unpretentious style and willingness to work as a mediator gained him the abiding affection of the British people.

George was born on June 3, 1865, in Marlborough House, the London home of his parents, at the time the Prince and Princess of Wales. He was not originally expected to take the throne; as the second son of the heir-apparent, he stood behind his father and his older brother Albert Victor, known in the family as Eddy, in the line of succession. George and Eddy were raised in a relatively relaxed manner of which their grandmother Queen Victoria disapproved; while they pursued outdoor sports with enthusiasm, they were allowed to be indifferent students. Eddy was a particularly difficult case, in that he seldom showed much interest in anything productive unless George was there to spur him on.

When George was only 12 years old, his father placed him and his brother in the Royal Navy to learn the practical discipline of military service. Eddy would presumably become king and therefore could not risk the hazards of a long naval career, but George could look forward to more extended service. From the start, George had to hold his own against his fellow cadets, many of whom were taller and stronger than he, but he rose to the challenge. In 1879, George and Albert Victor embarked on their first tour of duty, sailing around the world and generally living the ordinary life of a sailor apart from the presence of their private tutor. After their return to England, Albert Victor went to Cambridge, but George returned to active service, remaining in the Royal Navy until his last tour of duty in 1891–92. George became fond of the steady, predictable rhythms and responsibilities of shipboard life.

BECOMING HEIR

While George flourished in his burgeoning naval career, Eddy never found his way, and his sometimes embarrassing behavior was kept quiet by the royal family. In 1891, Victoria decided that the only way to settle him down was to fix him in a marriage. A suitable bride, Princess Victoria Mary of Teck, known to intimates as May, was found, and the relatively apathetic Eddy agreed to the match. But in 1891 Eddy died of pneumonia. As grief-stricken as his parents and grandmother were, on some level they surely understood that the more capable and trustworthy prince would now inherit the throne. George, who had already had one young love undone when his cousin Marie of Edinburgh had declined a marriage proposal, grew close to May in the aftermath of Eddy's

> # I MAY BE UNINSPIRING, BUT I'LL BE DAMNED IF I'M ALIEN
>
> *GEORGE V*

Opposite George V, whose ability to confront change and crisis with a combination of moral rectitude and political flexibility enhanced the monarchy's status as both unifying symbol and custodian of values.

1911
With the resignation of Porfirio Diaz, the Mexican Revolution succeeds in changing the regime.

1912
The passenger liner RMS Titanic, the world's largest ship, strikes an iceberg and sinks, with a loss of over 1,500 lives.

1913
The premiere of Igor Stravinsky's The Rite of Spring, performed in Paris by Sergei Diaghilev's Ballets Russes, leads to rioting.

1914
After the assassination in Sarajevo of Austrian Archduke Franz Ferdinand, Europe slides into World War I.

York Cottage, the comparatively modest home where George and May lived before his accession.

much of it as a sailor, but on a subsequent visit to India in 1905 he developed a particular attachment, publicly expressing his opposition to racism and suggesting that Indians play a more prominent role in their own governance. In what had become another, healthier pattern among the royals, George's service in the navy, which had exposed him to much of the world, had instilled an egalitarian streak in his otherwise aristocratic worldview. He saw himself as an ordinary man destined to inherit a position he would prefer not to take.

death. In July of 1893, the two of them married. George was 28, May 26.

Now that George was likely to inherit the throne, he had to give up his naval career. Instead of living the opulent life of a prince and princess, he and May, now the Duke and Duchess of York, opted to pursue a modest, quiet existence, settling in York Cottage, a relatively small estate house in Sandringham. George's fondness for routine and for the outdoors governed his life there. He became an avid stamp collector and an accomplished shooter—probably the best marksman in British royal history. He and May had an apparently happy, scandal-free marriage that produced five sons and one daughter.

As a father, however, George was controlling and overbearing. He browbeat his children over the slightest deviation from his high and narrow expectations. It was as if the old Hanoverian pattern of toxic relations between fathers and sons, suspended in the case of George and his father, returned with a vengeance in his attitude toward his children. His eldest son, Edward, known to close family and friends as David, was charismatic and worldly, and clashed often and fiercely with his austerely minded father. David's younger brother Bertie developed a stammer that would plague him for much of his life. George's parenting style surely contributed to the eventual crisis of his son's abdication of the throne.

In 1901, George and May went on a tour of the British Empire. George had already seen

A KING AMID CRISES

On May 6, 1910, Edward VII died, and George became George V, King of the United Kingdom and the British Dominions. He was distraught over his father's death—the two of them had understood each other well—and one of his first acts as king was to follow through on his father's wish to have the Accession Declaration, which George would have to recite at his coronation, changed to eliminate its antiquated anti-Catholic rhetoric. The Prime Minister, Herbert Asquith, agreed, and the Declaration was abbreviated by more than half its length. The change was a symbolic gesture, both of tolerance and of respect for Edward VII's legacy.

But part of what George inherited when he accepted the crown was a seething controversy in Parliament. Since gaining control of the Commons in 1906, the Liberal party had advanced a number of social reforms, including old age pensions, that had disquieted the more conservative members of the House of Lords. In 1909, spurred on by the "terrible twins," Chancellor of the Exchequer David Lloyd George and President of the Board of Trade Winston Churchill, the Liberals announced what they called the People's Budget. It introduced new taxes on the wealthy, including a tax on land values, to finance a social and economic safety net for the poor. For the first time in 200 years, the Lords violated what had become a tradition

1915		1916	1917	1918
A German U-Boat sinks the RMS Lusitania, with the loss of about 1,200 lives.		The Battle of the Somme begins in northern France with an Allied offensive. By its end, the battle will cost over a million casualties.	With the abdication of Tsar Nicholas II of Russia, the Russian Empire comes to an end. The Russian Revolution will eventually lead to the authoritarian rule of Vladimir Lenin.	On November 11, an armistice brings World War I to an end after appalling loss of life on all sides.

WEARING THE CROWNS

Unlike his father Edward VII, George V detested pomp and ceremony; it made him intensely uncomfortable to be at the center of royal spectacles of any kind. But his sense of duty was such that, if he were required to perform such offices, he would do them to the fullest. He therefore decided that he should wear the crown, because the people would expect their monarch to look the part. From 1913 on, he wore the Imperial State Crown, recently embellished with the massive Cullinan II diamond from South Africa. The heavy, poorly fitted crown gave him headaches, but he wore it nonetheless. This commitment to enduring discomfort to fulfill a symbolic role for Britain became a hallmark of the House of Windsor.

of accepting any budgets put forward by the Commons: they threw out the People's Budget, demanding that the Liberals demonstrate that they had sufficient popular support for the budget by winning an election. The Liberals were able to hold their majority, but only with the help of the Irish Nationalists, who tied their support of the bill to Liberal support of Irish Home Rule. After some negotiations, a modified budget passed both Houses in April 1910. But resentments still simmered, and late that year came to a boil.

David Lloyd George and Winston Churchill, called the Terrible Twins by their political opponents, were largely responsible for the controversial reforms at the start of George V's reign.

SUPREMACY OF TH E COMMONS

The Liberals, incensed by the Lords' opposition, advanced a further bill explicitly eliminating the right of the Lords to reject financial bills forwarded by the Commons. George had tried to let the conflict be resolved within Parliament—his own private secretaries disagreed over the right course of action—but when the standoff showed no sign of abating, he quietly began urging the Lords to back down. Only when George reluctantly agreed that he would create more than 400 new Liberal peers to ensure passage of the bill did the Lords concede. The bill, passed as the Act of Parliament 1911, which eliminated the right of the Lords to veto nearly any bill from the Commons, formally established the supremacy of the House of Commons in British government.

This sort of political wrangling exasperated George, and in its aftermath he and May, now known as Queen Mary, set off to tour the Dominions. In India, they laid the first stone of New Delhi; George hunted big game in Nepal. It was a welcome respite, but the crises were only beginning. The year 1912 brought two more blows to British morale, the sinking of the Titanic and the death of the famed polar explorer Robert Scott, who had lost his race to the South Pole to the Norwegian Roald Amundsen.

SUFFRAGETTES

Domestically, the movement for women's suffrage had gained momentum among the educated classes, and was becoming more and more militant in the face of the sometimes brutal tactics used to suppress it. In 1913, a young Northumbrian suffragette named Emily Davison ventured onto the track at the Epsom Derby and blocked the king's horse, which ran her down; she died of her injuries a few days later. Though her intentions were unclear, the publicity was enormous. These and other incidents frayed George's nerves, as did malicious rumors that he was a heavy drinker and a bigamist, neither of which was remotely true. But though aristocrats belittled his lack of sophistication, George's unpretentious manner and simple tastes seemed a mark of solidarity with his subjects, and they grew fond of him.

THE GREAT WAR

Those misfortunes paled in comparison to the catastrophe that would soon strike. On June 28, 1914, Archduke Franz Ferdinand of Austria was assassinated in Sarajevo by a Serbian student.

1919		1920	1921	1922
Walter Gropius founds the Bauhaus, or "School of Building," in Weimar, Germany, giving rise to one of the most influential design aesthetics of the century.		Civil War in Ireland escalates, as both the Black and Tans (members of the new Royal Irish Constabulary) and the Irish Republican Army commit atrocities.	In Germany, Adolf Hitler becomes chairman of the Nazi (National Socialist) party.	With the publication of T. S. Eliot's The Waste Land and James Joyce's Ulysses, the movement known as Modernism takes firm and controversial hold of the literary scene.

The devastation of the Western Front in World War I. It was because anti-German feeling ran so high that George changed the royal family's name from Saxe-Coburg and Gotha to Windsor.

John, George's the youngest son, suffered from epilepsy, and died at the age of 13.

Austria exploited the situation to declare war and annex Serbia. Soon, Germany, Russia, and France were drawn into the fray by their various alliances. When German troops entered Belgium, England, bound by the 1839 Treaty of London, found itself in the same situation. World War I had begun. Over the next four years, six million British men would serve in the war, and one in eight would not return alive. Many of the best and brightest of Europe's rising generation would simply disappear.

The royal family did not remain entirely aloof from the hardships of war. George's sons David and Bertie served in the military, and George and Mary observed the same rationing as other Britons, and made several visits to British forces on sea and land; in one visit to France, George fractured his pelvis when his horse fell on him. At home, the war emboldened those opposed to the very existence of the British monarchy, not least because George was first cousin to Kaiser Wilhelm of Germany. With that in mind, George officially changed the name of the royal family from Saxe-Coburg and Gotha to Windsor; a more distinctively English name can scarcely be imagined. As stress took its toll on the king, his beard turned white, and depression often settled over him. When the Russian Revolution took place in 1917 and the family of his cousin Tsar Nicholas II asked for sanctuary in England, anti-monarchical feeling was so high that George turned them down. When they were subsequently murdered, he felt partly responsible.

In January of 1919, just two months after the end of the war, George and Mary's son John died at the age of 13. He had suffered from epilepsy since the age of four, and in the year before his death his condition had worsened, but his end was sudden, and it further darkened the king's spirits. After the war, George was in the unthinkable position of being the only monarch

1923	1924	1925	1926
After the dissolution of the Ottoman Empire, Turkey becomes a republic, with Kemal Atatürk as its president.	In the Soviet Union, Vladimir Lenin dies and is buried in a mausoleum. Josef Stalin maneuvers to take power.	Benito Mussolini announces that he is now dictator of Italy, starting a Fascist regime that will last into World War II.	Hirohito becomes Emperor of Japan, inaugurating the Showa era. He will serve as Emperor until his death in 1989.

An armored car patrols mostly desolate streets in Ireland during the Irish Civil War, to which George sought resolution.

Paul Whiteman and his jazz band. The arrival of the Jazz Age and its relaxed mores was one of many changes George faced.

the Representation of the People Act had given the vote to all men over 21 and all women over 30, tripling the size of the electorate at a stroke. George was in many ways still a Victorian, conservative in his outlook and dismayed by the relaxed morals and fashions that followed the traumatic war years. It was the Jazz Age. In 1920, Paul Whiteman brought his jazz orchestra to England; at the same time, the advent of the gramophone made it possible for jazz to become a kind of perpetual soundtrack to the lives of young Britons. Movies also took hold of public imagination. The British Broadcasting Company was formed to make use of public airwaves. George looked askance at most of this, but he found the political situation far more troubling.

By 1921, some two million British workers were unemployed and restive. Their eye on the Russian Revolution, many royals, peers, and Conservatives feared the rise of organized labor in Britain. The Labour party, formed in 1900 but newly popular after the war, began to show real political muscle in the 1920s. George was a royal and as far as possible lived the life, however modest, of a country gentleman, and he had little liking for the Labour agenda—but he also understood that change was inevitable, and that the only way to manage it was to work with it rather than against it. Instead of reflexively opposing the rise of the Labour party, he actively engaged it, even appointing the first Labour Prime Minister, Ramsay MacDonald, when the opportunity arose in 1924. To be sure, part of his motivation was to domesticate the political left, to neutralize its more radical tendencies; in this, George was extraordinarily successful. He took pains to emphasize his ordinariness, and positioned himself as a king who empathized with the lives and concerns of the working class. And the empathy was sincere: in 1926 he even

in Europe whose empire had not merely survived the war but actually expanded in its aftermath. Of the other rulers, some were dead, others—including his cousin Kaiser Wilhelm—living out their lives in informal exile, and still others sorting among the pieces of their fragmented realms. Civil war had erupted in Ireland, and George, horrified at the reprisals and counter-reprisals involved, did what he could to encourage a negotiated peace, which finally arrived with the partition of Ireland in 1922.

MONARCHY WITH A SOCIAL CONSCIENCE

In the wake of the Great War, manners and mores changed in Britain as they did elsewhere. Women, who had proved so redoubtable in the war effort, began to achieve the gains so many activists had sought. In early 1918,

1927

Leon Trotsky is expelled from the Soviet Union. Josef Stalin assumes complete control.

1928

In Paris, the Kellogg-Briand Pact, theoretically outlawing war as an instrument of policy, is signed.

1929

In October, the inflated United States stock market crashes, initiating what will become a global economic depression.

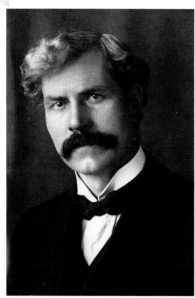

Ramsay MacDonald, the first Labour Prime Minister, whose unlikely political alliance with George V led to the National Government of the 1930s.

defended striking workers against the retaliatory urgings of some Conservatives.

That same year, George chaired an Imperial Conference in which, through the Balfour Declaration, the British Dominions were granted an unprecedented level of self-determination; in time, their Prime Ministers were no longer even considered representatives of the British government. In 1931, the Statute of Westminster formalized the legislative independence of the Dominions. The Empire had begun to transform into a Commonwealth.

But between those two events, another disaster had struck in the form of the global economic crash of 1929. Britain was devastated: its budget was revealed as so imbalanced that there was a run on the pound, and unemployment soared. George actively promoted the idea of a National Government formed from all political parties and entrusted with navigating Britain's way out of the economic crisis. In 1931, Labour leader Ramsay MacDonald formed such a government, which in various permutations would hold power for the rest of the decade. At first the National Government failed to reach any consensus, but over time it managed to function, and gradually the British economy began to recover.

The king, ever aware of the symbolic power of the Crown, took personal measures to reinforce a sense of national solidarity in the face of the Great Depression. He voluntarily took a cut in his annual allowance from the Civil List, and revived the medieval custom of personally handing out "Maundy Money" to the needy just before Easter. At the urging of his advisors, in 1932 he delivered a Christmas radio address—an innovation that immediately became a royal custom. George little understood how much hearing the king's voice over the airwaves humanized him in the minds of his subjects; in actuality, the radio addresses made him hugely popular.

THE FINAL YEARS

In 1935, George celebrated his silver jubilee. In his 25 years on the throne, he had seen Britain through a World War, an economic catastrophe, and a round of enormous changes in the United Kingdom and the Empire as a whole. His modesty and unpretentiousness, as well as his evident approachability, had so endeared him to Britons that he was floored by the outpouring of enthusiasm and affection he encountered everywhere he went.

But all was not well with the royal family.

Edward, Prince of Wales. A lively and charismatic figure, he was made an international celebrity by newsreels and by his personal charm, but George rightly held grave doubts about his capacity as a future king.

1930		1931	1932
Mahatma Gandhi leads the Salt March, a major nonviolent protest, in India. It is followed by a declaration of independence by the Indian National Council.		Catastrophic flooding in central China leads to untold deaths, in possibly the worst natural disaster in recorded history.	Aldous Huxley publishes the farsighted novel Brave New World, which captures the period's growing anxiety about the human costs of technological progress.

THE ORDER OF THE BRITISH EMPIRE

Of the many ways in which George V brought the monarchy closer to the general populace, one of the most enduring was the establishment of the Order of the British Empire. While other, older chivalric orders were limited by number of members and social class, the Order of the British Empire was conceived as a broad, inclusive way of recognizing excellence and commitment in any citizen of the Empire. The first investiture was held not in a palace but in a soccer stadium. Since then, OBE's, as they are called, have been given to a range of British subjects, honoring all sorts of accomplishments. The images of King George and Queen Mary were eventually placed on the OBE medal.

At the time of the economic crash in late 1929, George had only recently recovered from a life-threatening bout of blood poisoning from which it took him several months to regain his strength. For a while his prognosis had been doubtful, and all eyes had turned to his heir-apparent, David, more properly known as Edward, Prince of Wales.

As George's eldest son, David had borne the brunt of his father's most overbearing conduct as a parent, and as he matured he had acted out in ways that created grave doubts about his capacity to occupy the throne responsibly. Though charming and cultured, he displayed little tolerance for ceremony or, more disconcertingly, for the standards of conduct now expected of the royal family. He embarked on a series of affairs with married women, which he took no real care to conceal, and preferred to spend his time socializing with hedonistic friends at Fort Belvedere, his haven in Windsor Park. George never stopped hectoring David about his conduct; David never ceased to resist his father and go his own way.

Sandringham House. George V remarked that it was his favorite place on earth, and it was here that he died.

George had no illusions about his children. David he knew to be fundamentally weak, unable and unwilling to curb his passions and impulses. The king much preferred his second son, Bertie, and Bertie's young daughter Elizabeth, whom he called Lilibet. On one occasion he was heard to say that he hoped the throne would go to Bertie and then to Lilibet—a wish that would come true, as Bertie would eventually become George VI and Lilibet Elizabeth II.

By 1936, the last of the great changes to unfold during George's rule had been accomplished in the form of Home Rule for India. But the king saw other changes brewing, and many of them distressed him. Above all, he was concerned about the rise of Nazi Germany, which he recognized early as a destructive force, even predicting that Hitler would start another European war. His anxiety about the German threat was exacerbated by David's evident enthusiasm for Fascism, which would only become more of an embarrassment as the decade progressed. His assessment of his heir-apparent's character was that David wouldn't last a year as king without disgracing himself—yet another instance in which George's instinctive reading of human situations proved accurate.

In January of 1936, George retired to his room in Sandringham House, complaining of a bad cold. It was the beginning of the end. For the past year he had needed supplementary oxygen to alleviate respiratory problems from his lifelong smoking habit; now he was old, tired, and ready to depart. On the night of January 20, his physician administered an injection of morphine and cocaine to bring the king's life to a quiet end. He was widely mourned.

In many ways, George V set the standard for the House of Windsor. His unpretentious devotion to the monarchy as a vocation, his combination of gentility and ordinariness, and his sense of the symbolic and mediating role played by the king all shaped the reigns of subsequent Windsor monarchs.

1933	1934	1935	1935
Adolf Hitler becomes Chancellor of Germany; within a year he will be Führer, or head of state.	Japanese forces invade and conquer Manchuria, which they rename Manchukuo.	President Franklin Roosevelt signs into law the Social Security Act, establishing an economic "safety net" in American society.	Radar (then called Radio Direction Finding) is invented in the UK.

EDWARD VIII ✠ A Throne Lost for Love

House Windsor

Born June 23, 1894

Died May 28, 1972

Reigned January 20-December 11, 1936

Consort None (later married Wallis Simpson)

Children None

Successor George VI

dward VIII is famous—or infamous—for having abdicated the throne in order to marry an American divorcée. Edward may have been a royal, but he was also a product of his times, and embodied some of the changes rapidly altering the social and political landscape.

Edward, known to family and close friends as David, was born at White Lodge on the edge of London. As David matured, he became increasingly resistant to discipline and impatient with royal duties. But he also had an engaging manner and a zest for life that made him enormously charismatic. When war erupted in 1914 he was eager to join the fighting. Even though his wish was categorically rejected, he made trips to the front lines whenever possible, and on one occasion a German shell hit his car, killing its driver, moments after the prince had exited the vehicle. His conduct made him immensely popular among the troops.

Even his investiture as Prince of Wales in 1910 seemed ridiculous to the young heir to the throne.

THE CELEBRITY PRINCE

After the war, he became very much the man about town, taking married mistresses and turning up in posh London clubs, drinking and dancing and even playing the drums with jazz bands. His seemingly effortless style and charisma made him an icon of the new, postwar mentality of the young. He was a prince for the Jazz Age, a celebrity rather than a symbol.

None of this endeared him to his father, but the prince was so attractive a personality that, in the eyes of a public that knew little about his deeper indiscretions, his attitude simply seemed free and outgoing. Inseparable from this glamorous image was his appearance on film. Through the 1920s, George sent his son on a series of goodwill trips around the world, the sort of public performances at which David excelled. The resulting newsreels, seen around the world, made him the equivalent of a movie star.

As the 1930s approached and King George began to grow old, the royal family and political leaders grew more concerned about David's fitness for the throne. He increasingly enclosed himself in a private world of luxury, and showed no concern for the ceremonial and symbolic responsibilities of kingship. The king predicted

Edward with Wallis Simpson, the woman for whom he gave up the throne. Known as the Duke and Duchess of Windsor, the two lived a life of mostly aimless luxury after his abdication in 1936.

that David would ruin himself within a year of taking the throne; it was a prescient remark.

David then fell hopelessly in love with Wallis Simpson. Though not conventionally beautiful, Simpson had a forceful and witty personality, and she treated the prince with a rather domineering irreverence that seemed inextricable from his attachment to her. Friends noted that he never seemed so happy and at ease as when in her presence. By 1935, as George approached the last months of his life, it became clear that David intended to marry Simpson as soon as she could divorce her second husband.

But marrying a twice-divorced woman was out of the question for a British king. As head of the Church of England, the king had to embody at least some of its rules, one of which at the time was that divorced people could not remarry while their former spouses still lived.

On January 20, 1936, George died, and David became King Edward VIII. Once Simpson's second divorce was granted in October, he privately broached the issue of marrying her. The prospect met stiff opposition, not only from the Conservative-led government but from the leaders of the Dominions, most of whom also rejected the idea of a morganatic marriage in which Simpson would be his wife but not queen. Though Edward had his supporters, including Winston Churchill, the choice was clear: he could cause an even more dire crisis by insisting on his kingship and the marriage, or he could give one of them up.

On December 10, he signed his abdication papers. His brother Bertie took the throne as George VI. The following evening, the former king announced his abdication in a speech on the BBC. From then until his death in 1972, he and Wallis Simpson would remain together, living a luxurious but rootless existence and mostly spurned by the royal family.

Opposite Edward VIII, whose iconic status as a man of style endures, despite the objectionable aspects of his character.

GEORGE VI ✠ The Reluctant King Makes Good

House Windsor

Born December 14, 1895

Died February 6, 1952

Reigned 1936-1952

Consort Elizabeth Bowes-Lyon

Children Elizabeth II, Margaret

Successor Elizabeth II

George VI never expected to become king, and shortly after he took the throne in the wake of the abdication of his brother Edward VIII, he confronted one of the gravest crises in all of British history: World War II. Seldom has a British monarch so splendidly risen to a potentially overwhelming challenge. George's decency, steadfastness, and genuine commitment to the common good made him one of the best-loved of British kings.

Albert Frederick Arthur George, known as Bertie to his family, was born in 1895 at York Cottage, the relatively modest home of his father, the future King George V, and Queen Mary. Growing up, he was very much in the shadow of his more outgoing, charismatic brother Edward, known intimately as David. While both sons suffered from the authoritarian parenting style of their father, they reacted in different ways. David grew increasingly rebellious and self-absorbed. Bertie, though a good athlete and happiest outdoors, seemed weaker and less self-willed. He was given to a stammer that reflected his tremendous anxiety, easily grew upset, and had to wear leg braces for years to correct a case of knock-knees. It is one of the most intriguing ironies in the history of British royalty that, in the long run, Bertie would prove far stronger and more kingly than David. In 1909, Bertie was enrolled in the Royal Naval

College, Osborne, where he was treated like any other cadet. The next year, his father became King George V, but Bertie did not distinguish himself at Osborne, coming in last in his class in 1911. Regardless, he was moved on to the next level of the College, at Dartmouth, and from there began the naval career that would in many ways make him as a man.

By the time the Great War began, Bertie was already a seasoned midshipman, having sailed around the Atlantic on a couple of vessels; his crewmates referred to him as Mr. Johnson. During the war, he became a turret officer, and received high marks from his superiors for his conduct aboard the HMS Collingwood during the large if inconclusive naval battle at Jutland. Though he missed much further action due to chronic illness, in 1918 he became the first British royal to be certified as a pilot, and served as a staff officer at bases of the fledgling Royal Air Force.

IF THE 'GREATNESS' OF A KING CAN BE MEASURED BY THE EXTENT TO WHICH HIS QUALITIES RESPONDED TO THE NEEDS OF A NATION AT A GIVEN MOMENT IN HISTORY, THEN GEORGE VI WAS A GREAT KING, AND PERHAPS A VERY GREAT KING.

RENÉ MASSIGLI, FRENCH AMBASSADOR TO THE COURT OF ST. JAMES

1936

At the Berlin Olympics, meant by Hitler to showcase German supremacy, African American athlete Jesse Owens dominates.

1937

In the Spanish Civil War, the Basque town of Guernica is bombed by German and Italian planes, sparking international outrage and inspiring Picasso's commemorative painting.

1938

In the Munich Agreement, Nazi Germany is allowed to annex the Sudetenland from Czechoslovakia. It is the last gesture of appeasement before war.

Opposite George VI, whose profound decency and steadiness in the midst of crisis made him one of the most loved of British monarchs.

Queen Elizabeth, formerly Lady Elizabeth Bowes-Lyon. She was a remarkably effective Queen Consort and the object of lasting adoration among the public.

lasted until World War II. Bertie became known as the Industrial Prince for his commitment to these causes. It was a far less glamorous identity than the movie-star celebrity enjoyed by his brother David, but it gave Bertie a sense of purpose.

AN EXTRAORDINARY WIFE

Partly because he was not expected to take the throne, but also because his parents bowed to the inexorable current of social change, Bertie was allowed a relatively free hand when it came to marriage. No longer required, like his predecessors, to marry a royal, he fell abjectly in love with a peer's daughter, Elizabeth Bowes-Lyon, who had first been introduced to his brother David but who had captivated Bertie. Twice she rejected his proposals, unwilling to commit herself to the narrow behavioral expectations of a member of the royal family. But on the third attempt, she said yes, and the two of them were married on April 26, 1923.

Seldom has a British king made so fortunate a marriage. Elizabeth, known after her marriage as Her Royal Highness the Duchess of York, not only proved an indefatigably supportive spouse but became the best-loved member of the House of Windsor. Even at their wedding at Westminster Abbey, she displayed a remarkable instinct for just the right response to any situation, laying her bouquet at the Tomb of the Unknown Warrior in a gesture that instantly became a tradition at royal weddings. Elizabeth became known as the Smiling Duchess, because she radiated an unfailing graciousness and human warmth that made her nearly impossible to dislike.

Her support to Bertie led to his overcoming the greatest lingering weakness from his childhood: his stammer, which tended to reassert itself in all its mortifying acuteness when he was called upon to speak in public. In 1925, she supported him as he began working with Lionel Logue, a forward-thinking speech therapist from Australia who gradually helped Bertie come to terms with his stammer and largely master it—a process mythologized in the Oscar-winning 2010 film The King's Speech.

After the war, Bertie spent a year at Cambridge before being created Duke of York—a title of which he was very proud—and beginning to undertake the royal duties of a spare prince, which included tours of the country that made him keenly conscious of the conditions of the working class. As a result, he became President of the Industrial Welfare Society; pursuing better health and working conditions for labor became a lasting interest. In 1921, he established the Duke of York camps, where every year 200 boys, half from elite public schools and half from industrial firms, lived and played together for a week, led by the Duke himself; it was a farsighted attempt to break down some of the class barriers of British society, and it

1939
On September 1, Germany invades Poland, starting the World War II.

1940
The year of the Battle of Britain, in which the Royal Air Force successfully fends off the German Luftwaffe, preventing German forces from invading Britain.

1941
After a surprise attack by the Japanese on Pearl Harbor, the United States enters World War II.

1942
By the year's end, several extermination camps for Jews and other "undesirables" have been put in operation in territories under German control.

George and Elizabeth on a royal tour in 1939. They proved a formidable team during the crisis of the Second World War.

Queen Elizabeth with Eleanor Roosevelt. The hugely popular Queen Consort had considerable diplomatic skills.

PROPELLED INTO KINGSHIP

When George V died in early 1936 and David took the throne as Edward VIII, Bertie little anticipated the firestorm that would soon follow. Though the brothers were close in some ways, David kept Bertie out of his deliberations about possibly marrying the soon-to-be twice divorced American Wallis Simpson. When Edward was faced with the choice of precipitating a government crisis, giving up Simpson, or abdicating the throne, he chose the last. His decision brought home to Bertie all the latent feelings of anxiety and insecurity that had haunted him since childhood; on hearing the news, he wept. Not only was he being thrust into a position for which he hadn't prepared; he was taking the throne as the result of a crisis in the monarchy, and replacing his popular, charismatic brother.

On May 12, 1937, Bertie was crowned King George VI. Having prepared assiduously with Lionel Logue, he was ready to recite the Accession Declaration without any stammer. It was a symbolic change, and it took root. Though he had not been trained for the special responsibilities of kingship and had difficult grasping some of the political subtleties that came with the throne, he put enormous effort into doing the job well. This was partly the result of his naval training, but also an extension of the idea of royal responsibility that George V had pioneered: that the monarch must be a kind of elite and symbolically charged public servant.

Unexpectedly, George took to kingship well. Within weeks, as he began to settle into its rhythms and responsibilities, a great deal of his shyness and hesitancy melted away. Though he still needed to work with Lionel Logue on making speeches, the sense of purpose and dignity that went with the crown brought out the best in George's character. Like his father, he seemed a living embodiment of traditional English values.

Also like his father—and unlike his brother, the former king—George was deeply concerned about the aggression of Nazi Germany. But having

When the Duke and Duchess toured various parts of the Dominions in the 1920s, she buoyed his confidence and made a tremendous impression of her own. On one occasion, when a stray dog wandered into an event in Fiji where Elizabeth was greeting a line of guests, she shook the dog's paw.

Back in Britain, Bertie and Elizabeth developed a happy home life. They had two

daughters, Elizabeth (known as Lilibet) and Margaret; Bertie referred to the family as "us four." Since he was still not expected ever to take the throne, he did not prepare for the business of kingship and instead pursued his regular duties, especially his continuing interest in working conditions. He also enjoyed his favorite pastimes of shooting, tennis, gardening, and meteorology.

1943	1944	1945		1946
Allied forces invade Italy in the wake of the collapse of Italy's Fascist regime, originally under Benito Mussolini.	In the largest amphibious invasion in history, Allied forces cross the English Channel from England and invade France.	World War II ends with the surrender of Germany in May and Japan in August. Japan's surrender is precipitated by the dropping of two atomic bombs on Hiroshima and Nagasaki.		The first meeting of the United Nations is held in Westminster, London.

George and Elizabeth on the steps of the United States Capitol during their 1939 tour of North America. They proved as popular abroad as within Britain.

George and Elizabeth visiting a bombed neighborhood in London during the Blitz. Their steadfastness and solidarity during the war proved inspiring.

lived through, and fought in, World War I, George was for avoiding another major European conflict if at all possible. When, in 1938, Prime Minister Neville Chamberlain arranged the Munich Accords, proclaiming "peace in our time," George took the politically clumsy action of having Chamberlain appear on the royal balcony at Buckingham Palace—for all intents and purposes, an irregular endorsement of a political policy. But when war broke out the next year, George was quick to marshal support for the war effort from around the Empire with a radio address.

In fact, George and Elizabeth had already prepared for the coming war, touring Canada and the United States in the previous year to build support on that side of the Atlantic. The trip had been a huge success, and George and Elizabeth forged a lasting bond with United States President Franklin Roosevelt and his wife Eleanor.

A KING IN WARTIME

Soon enough, the Blitz began. German bombs began falling on London, mainly on the East End where industrial works and docks could be crippled, but also elsewhere in the capital. Though it would have been easy for George and his family to retreat to the country, they resolved to stay in London, enduring the same risks and practicing the same rationing as everyone else. Though they spent most nights in the relative safety of Windsor Castle, every day was spent in Buckingham Palace and going out in support of the war effort. The king and queen visited neighborhoods hit by bombs, inspecting the damage, and Londoners took heart from the sense of solidarity those visits inspired. In September 1940, bombs fell in the quadrangle by Buckingham Palace, only some 30 yards from where George and Elizabeth were sitting. Elizabeth famously said she was glad the palace had been bombed, as she could now look the East End in the face.

In putting their symbolic weight behind the war effort, and in support of a beleaguered London, the king and queen endeared themselves to the people. Their visits were not mere formalities or photo opportunities; they both talked with whoever happened to be there, commiserating with those who had lost homes or businesses or even loved ones. When word circulated that George had himself marked the bathtubs in Buckingham Palace with the low maximum fill lines required by rationing, the sense of common cause grew deeper. Yet much that George did remained unknown. In his spare time, he used his own tools at Windsor to manufacture weapons parts, and rather than order new collars and cuffs, whenever possible he had them made from fabric cut from elsewhere in his wardrobe.

George even built an extraordinary relationship with Churchill. Though the two had not seen eye-to-eye early in the king's reign, they came to respect each other enormously. Churchill had been among the supporters of Edward VIII in the abdication crisis, and at first he felt the lesser man had taken the throne, but

1946	1947	1948	1949	
In a speech at Westminster College, Winston Churchill openly accuses the Soviet Union of lowering an Iron Curtain across Europe in order to expand its sphere of influence. The Cold War has begun	Jackie Robinson becomes the first African American to play Major League Baseball.	Mahatma Gandhi, whose work of nonviolent resistance did so much to ensure Indian independence, is assassinated by a Hindu nationalist.	The People's Republic of China is officially announced, under the leadership of Communist Party Chairman Mao Zedong.	

Winston Churchill waves from the balcony of Buckingham Palace on V-E Day, 1945. George invited him to join the royal family for that public celebration of Germany's surrender.

as he got to know George—and as the former king's Nazi sympathies became known—he realized that Britain had come out much better off with George. Every Tuesday, the two of them would have lunch and discuss frankly and openly the conduct of the war.

No less important to the war effort was Queen Elizabeth, whose winsome combination of elegance, graciousness, humor, and candor made her as much a symbol of a united Britain as her husband was. Hitler, acknowledging her remarkable power to lift the spirits of the British, even called her the most dangerous woman in Europe.

When victory came in Europe in May of 1945, enormous crowds gathered near the palace, and roared when George and Elizabeth appeared on the balcony, this time with a triumphant Winston Churchill.

ELIZABETH, QUEEN MOTHER

Though George died in 1952, his queen Elizabeth lived on as the most beloved member of the House of Windsor. On her husband's death, she at first sought a quiet retirement in Scotland, but Winston Churchill convinced her to return to England and take up a new role as matriarch of the royal family. When not making public appearances and going on goodwill tours, the Queen Mother took care of her grandchildren when Elizabeth II was away, bred horses, and engaged in other hobbies. In March of 2002, the Queen Mother died peacefully in her sleep at Windsor, her sole surviving daughter Elizabeth by her side.

THE FINAL YEARS

After the war, George and Elizabeth remained popular, though many wrenching changes came to Britain. Churchill did not last, and a Labour government under Clement Attlee came to power, but George's concern for and familiarity with the conditions of the working class allowed him to work well with Attlee. Still, the war left a great deal of hardship in its wake, and it had aged George. He suffered from arteriosclerosis, and his health was not improved by the strain of discovering in captured German documents how deep his brother Edward's Nazi sympathies had gone—deep enough that George had the papers destroyed. He found himself confronted by a new world of altered power relations—the Cold War, the Korean War, and the accelerating dissolution of the Empire. In 1947, the British withdrew from India, now partitioned into India and Pakistan. That same year, despite his failing health, the king toured South Africa and Rhodesia.

When he could, George retreated more and more to the country, donning tweeds and shooting, or engaging in other relaxing pursuits. But his health continued to decline. In 1948, he had surgery for blocked arteries in his legs; in 1951, he had part of a lung removed due to cancer. Though the extent of his illness was kept from him, he did not have long to live. In the wee hours of February 6, 1952, he died peacefully in his sleep. When the news broke the next morning, traffic stopped all over Britain, and people got out of their cars to pay their respects to the king who had led them through the war. His death notice in the Daily Mirror read, "This was, by any standards, anywhere, a good man."

A statue of George VI, built to commemorate a century of British Colonial rule in Hong Kong, stands in the Hong Kong Zoological and Botanical Gardens.

1950	1951	1952	1952
North Korean troops cross the 38th parallel into South Korea, starting the Korean War.	J. D. Salinger publishes *The Catcher in the Rye*, capturing for posterity the predicament of an alienated teenager in affluent postwar America.	The world's first transistor hearing aid transforms life for millions of the hard of hearing.	Eva Perón, recently named "Spiritual Leader of the Nation" in Argentina, dies of cancer at the age of 33. Despite never holding office, she is given a state funeral.

THE WINDSORS AND THE TWO WORLD WARS

A 1917 PUNCH CARTOON OF GEORGE V ridding himself of German connections. His change of the royal family's name from Saxe-Coburg and Gotha to Windsor asserted their Englishness.

By the turn of the century, the House of Saxe-Coburg and Gotha held a largely symbolic role as the kings and queens of Britain. But symbols are powerful things, and amid the trauma of two world wars the royal family became an emblem of patriotism, steadfastness, and solidarity. Their success in playing that role contributed importantly to British morale, especially on the home front.

World War I arose from a complete breakdown in diplomacy—a somewhat ironic fact since it had been diplomacy that built the complex and binding networks of alliances that drew most of Europe into the conflict. A different sort of interconnectedness posed problems for George V. Not only was he of German extraction; he was cousin to both Kaiser Wilhelm and Tsar Nicholas II of Russia. With the massive mobilization of British forces, the king became a figurehead for the war effort. But his German background also made him a polarizing figure. Kaiser Wilhelm was depicted in British propaganda as the personification of aggression, the Hun.

HOUSE OF WINDSOR

The irony was that George was thoroughly English, in temperament and in personal identity—perhaps the most "English" of English kings in centuries. Accordingly, in 1917 he addressed the situation by inscribing Englishness into the family record. He changed the royal family's name to the House of Windsor. He had relatives in England Anglicize their German titles; most famously, the Battenbergs became the Mountbattens. He also restricted the royal titles of Prince and Princess, and formally cut off any relations who fought on the German side.

The Windsors' approach to the war effort reflected both George V's proud sense of his Englishness and his belief that the monarchy was inseparable from public service.

Prince Edward and Prince Albert's involvement as soldiers may have been limited—the former by government restriction and the latter by illness—but their commitment, especially that of Edward, earned them popularity. George's daughter, Princess Mary, showed enterprise of her own during the war. Not only did she undertake hospital visits to wounded soldiers with the Queen; like other women of various social classes, she trained to become a nurse and served in hospitals herself. She also initiated a program that raised over £150,000 to distribute Christmas gifts to soldiers on the front lines.

KING GEORGE V in 1928

A DIFFERENT KIND OF HOME FRONT

When World War II erupted in 1939, George VI found himself facing an altogether different, even more pitiless brand of warfare, and a far more trying home front. By this time, any misgivings about the German background of the Windsors were long past, and George and his queen Elizabeth were free to support the war effort without reservation. The fact that

THE DUKE AND DUCHESS OF WINDSOR meet Adolf Hitler in 1937, against the wishes of the British government. The Duke made it clear that he had fascist sympathies, and he had to be carefully monitored during the war.

GEORGE VI AND ELIZABETH visiting a bomb site in London during the Blitz. Their willingness to share the dangers of Londoners during this time, however marginally, boosted civilian morale and made the king and queen very popular.

England was under direct attack during the Blitz, and for a while faced the prospect of a German invasion, meant that the royals had to cultivate a deeper sense of solidarity with the people of London especially.

George had earlier supported Neville Chamberlain's policy of appeasement, but once the fighting began he threw himself behind the war effort. His BBC speech on September 3, 1939, two days after the German invasion of Poland, transformed him in the public eye from an awkward, stammering prince into a steadfast leader. Though he and Winston Churchill were wary of each other at first, they became partners and even friends; once a week, the Prime Minister and the king would discuss the war freely over lunch.

Though they kept their daughters at Windsor Castle during the war, George and Elizabeth often stayed at Buckingham Palace, symbolically participating in the dangers endured by other Londoners. Bombs fell on the palace grounds no fewer than nine times, on one occasion in a courtyard very near a room where the king and queen were sitting. George and Elizabeth also participated in rationing. Their visits to bomb-ravaged areas of London, where they met with citizens and consoled victims, made them immensely popular; Elizabeth's popularity was such that Hitler referred to her as the most dangerous woman in Europe.

The role of the Windsors in the war was not all positive. The former Edward VIII, now the Duke of Windsor, had visited Germany and given Nazi salutes in 1937. During the war, he gave an interview suggesting that Britain was doomed to defeat, at which point he was summoned by Churchill to return to England on pain of a court martial. The Duke was installed as Governor of the Bahamas, out of the way of the war effort, though he continued to be monitored. After the war, George had some of his brother's private papers destroyed, likely because their contents were damning. Some historians have speculated that Hitler wanted to install Edward as a puppet king after the hoped-for conquest of Britain, and George believed that his brother may have encouraged the targeting of Buckingham Palace for bombing.

PRINCESS ELIZABETH, in keeping with the Windsors' commitment to the war effort in the Second World War, served as a member of the Auxiliary Territorial Service.

THE GEORGE CROSS

As a way of supporting the war effort, George established the George Cross, awarded for "acts of the greatest heroism or of the most conspicuous courage in circumstances of extreme danger." Second only to the Victoria Cross, which is specifically awarded for courage under fire, the George Cross was intended primarily for civilians, at the time for those who showed exceptional courage on the home front. In 1942, the entire Island Fortress of Malta received the medal for heroic resistance against a German siege; the George Cross now appears on the Maltese flag. Since its establishment, over 400 medals have been awarded.

ELIZABETH II ✚ A Queen Confronts Modernity

House Windsor

Born April 21, 1926

Reigned 1952–Present

Consort Prince Philip, Duke of Edinburgh

Children Princes Charles, Andrew, and Edward, and Princess Anne

Successor Charles, Prince of Wales

hen Elizabeth II celebrated her Diamond Jubilee in 2012, Britain gazed back over six decades of extraordinary change. Through all those transformations, the Queen has been a stalwart if somewhat reserved monarch. Given the upheavals within the royal family and the vicissitudes of public opinion, her steadiness has been her greatest asset. Poised to become the longest-serving monarch in British history, Elizabeth is perhaps more popular now than ever, and the House of Windsor is adapting to the realities of a very different world from that of her accession in 1952.

Elizabeth was born in London on April 21, 1926, the first of the two daughters of Prince Albert, the Duke of York, and his wife Elizabeth. Given that Albert's older brother was the heir-apparent, it was unlikely that Elizabeth would ever take the throne, even though she was third in the line of succession. As children, she and her younger sister Margaret were half of what their father referred to as "us four"—a close-knit family with an affectionate and relatively relaxed home life. But the girls lived a sheltered existence, involving little contact with what lay beyond the borders of the various royal residences; the rest of Britain, and the world, surely remained an abstraction. Elizabeth and Margaret were privately educated by their governess, Marion Crawford, without the special rigor that would have been invoked had Elizabeth been expected to become queen. As

it was, the young princess developed a lifelong fondness for horses and dogs. She also had a close relationship with her grandfather, King George V, whom she called "Grandpa England." Elizabeth herself was known as Lilibet.

But when Elizabeth was ten years old, her prospects changed completely. Her uncle, Edward VIII, abdicated rather than give up the prospect of marrying the American divorcée Wallis Simpson, and Prince Albert took the throne as King George VI. Suddenly, Elizabeth was the heir presumptive, and she had to prepare as best she could for the responsibilities she would face as queen. She had always been a thoughtful, responsible, well-behaved child—even Winston Churchill had noted her essential seriousness when she was still very young—but even her subsequent tutoring in constitutional matters could not

> I DECLARE BEFORE YOU ALL THAT MY WHOLE LIFE, WHETHER IT BE LONG OR SHORT, SHALL BE DEVOTED TO YOUR SERVICE AND THE SERVICE OF OUR GREAT IMPERIAL FAMILY TO WHICH WE ALL BELONG.
>
> *ELIZABETH II*

Opposite Elizabeth II has served as Queen for over six decades, weathering scandal, national hardships, wars, and family crises, and achieving her greatest popularity in her later years.

1952
The Mau Mau uprising against British rule in Kenya begins. Historians are divided over whether the unsuccessful revolt hastened or delayed Kenyan independence.

1953
In Cambridge, James Watson and Francis Crick announce their discovery of the structure of the DNA molecule, making possible huge advances in the study of genetics.

1955
In the wake of the defeat of the French in Indochina, the first American military advisors are sent to South Vietnam, the beginning of an involvement that will lead to the Vietnam War.

Elizabeth (far left) in her Women's Auxiliary uniform, on the balcony at Buckingham Palace with her family and Winston Churchill on VE Day, 1945. Elizabeth and her sister Margaret would later mingle with the celebrating crowds.

The 1953 Coronation Portrait of Elizabeth and Philip. Though they seemed to struggle as a couple in the 1950s, by the decade's end many difficulties were apparently settled.

Always dutiful, the young queen was nonetheless accused by some of seeming out of touch with most of the British people.

make up for the years of rigorous primary education she had already missed. But Elizabeth was nothing if not assiduous in doing what she could to ready herself. Her deep sense of personal responsibility would shape her understanding of what it means to be Queen.

When World War II erupted, Elizabeth played a role in the royal family's support of the war effort, spending most of her time near London at Windsor Castle. In 1940, at the age of 14, she broadcast a speech on the BBC to the children of Britain. In 1945, she was allowed to serve the nation more directly, as a cadet in the Women's Auxiliary Territorial Service, where she learned how to drive and repair automobiles. At the war's end, on May 8, 1945, all of Britain celebrated VE (Victory in Europe) Day; Churchill appeared on the balcony of Buckingham Palace with the royal family, and Elizabeth and Margaret ventured incognito into the jubilant crowds filling the streets of London.

BECOMING QUEEN

Another pivotal event, this one more personal, had taken place for Elizabeth during the war. In 1939, during a visit to the Royal Naval College at Dartmouth, the 13-year-old princess found herself taken with her dashing and athletic cousin Philip, an exiled prince of Greece who had just finished school and enlisted in the Navy. Through the war, during which Philip distinguished himself in active duty in both the European and Pacific theaters, the two of them exchanged letters. Afterward, they resolved to marry.

It was certainly a love match: Philip was an exiled prince, with relatively little to his name and, to make matters worse, very close German relations. Despite some murmuring both within and without royal circles, Philip asked for King George's blessing and received it, and Elizabeth and he were wed on November 20, 1947 in Westminster Abbey. Beforehand, it had been arranged that Philip would renounce his continental titles, adopt British citizenship, and accept the title of Duke of Edinburgh.

Within a year, Elizabeth had given birth to a son, Prince Charles; two years after came Princess Anne. Elizabeth also began a practice of touring the Commonwealth and the world that would eventually make her the most widely traveled monarch in history. It was on one of these trips, in February 1952, that she received word her father had died. Philip broke the news, and Elizabeth returned to England immediately. Once a dutiful young princess, she would now shoulder the responsibilities of being Queen.

Elizabeth's coronation, on June 2, 1953, marked a momentous shift in the public perception of the British monarchy for one

1956	1957	1960	1963	1965
Egyptian president Gamal Abdel Nasser nationalizes the Suez Canal. Britain, France, and Israel move to take control of the canal by force, precipitating the Suez Crisis, which brings the world to the brink of another global war.	The Soviet Union successfully launches Sputnik 1, the first orbital satellite, precipitating the Space Race.	Israeli intelligence agents hunt down, capture, and smuggle out of Argentina Nazi war criminal Adolf Eichmann, who will be put on trial in Israel.	President John F. Kennedy is assassinated in Dallas, Texas. His death is a national trauma for the United States.	Winston Churchill dies in London. His death is seen as the end of an era of British statesmanship, and his state funeral in January is the largest in history.

ROYALTY IN THE INFORMATION AGE

Elizabeth's reign has been the first to unfold entirely through the era of television and into the internet age. The resulting media coverage of the royal family has included coronations, weddings, and funerals as well as miscellaneous functions and a great deal of gossip. Elizabeth at first resisted the idea of having her coronation televised, but she has adapted to the realities of television and newer media in recent years, in spite of its sometimes intrusive and sensational coverage of events involving the House of Windsor. Now, the British Monarchy even has its own official website, part of which is devoted to news and information about the Queen.

overwhelming reason: it was televised. Millions of people across the globe watched the ceremony from their homes or other gathering-places. The crown and scepter, the royal robes, the Coronation Oath, and the splendor of the setting, formerly far beyond the experience of ordinary Britons and others around the world, were suddenly accessible to all. As a result, a new fascination with the monarchy, born of actually seeing the pomp of the coronation, caught hold. It gave Elizabeth, at the age of 27, the aura of a fairytale queen who would usher in a new golden age reminiscent of the first Elizabeth. Time magazine named her Woman of the Year for 1952.

But Elizabeth was not that sort of monarch. Though poised, disciplined, and dedicated, she was not a visionary, nor was she blessed

Princess Margaret, whose star-crossed romance with RAF Group Captain Peter Townsend, a divorcé, foreshadowed later romantic and marital issues in the royal family.

with the star quality that might have held up to the glare of this new public attention. Her natural seriousness worked against her. Dressing conservatively, growing increasingly reserved and distant, and attending more to goodwill tours around the Commonwealth than to her image at home, Elizabeth soon proved

something of a disappointment. It would have been difficult for nearly anyone to fulfill the outsized expectations her televised coronation had inspired, but Elizabeth, it seemed, was determined not to live up to them. Her idea of the monarchy was derived from her father and grandfather: it was a serious business of symbolic leadership and public service, and to succumb to the temptations of celebrity would cheapen it.

Further, the lead up to Elizabeth's coronation had been beset by controversy within the royal family. In the months preceding the ceremony, Margaret had informed Elizabeth of her desire to marry Peter Townsend, an officer in the Royal Air Force who had served as equerry to George VI and stayed on in that role for Elizabeth. Unfortunately, Townsend was 16 years older than Margaret and divorced, with two sons from his previous marriage, and his former wife was still alive; canon law of the Church of England forbade such marriages. Hoping that Margaret would change her mind, Elizabeth asked her to wait until after the coronation to settle the issue. But the marriage proved impossible, and Margaret broke off the relationship. She would marry a different man, Mark Phillips, a few years later, and eventually divorce him. Margaret's marital drama signaled how changing times were affecting the royal family, not just in their public presentation but in their individual emotional lives; it also foreshadowed the bitter and destructive marital conflicts that would later haunt Elizabeth's children.

QUEEN OF A CHANGING REALM
When Elizabeth embarked on an extended tour of the Commonwealth in 1953–54, the British Empire was already largely a figment of history. Britain's economy was still struggling, and its share of foreign trade plummeting. Though she remained the focus of tremendous attention—it is estimated that around three in four Australians set eyes on her during her first visit there—Elizabeth struggled to find the right approach in a postwar world.

Part of the difficulty may have been personal

1966	1968	1969	1972
England wins its first and only World Cup, when the tournament is hosted in England.	Popular demonstrations erupt around the world. In the United States, protests for Civil Rights and against the Vietnam War escalate; in France, student demonstrations, linked with a general strike, threaten to topple the government.	With the successful landing of Apollo 11, the first human beings land on the moon. Astronaut Neil Armstrong is the first to set foot on lunar soil.	Eleven Israeli athletes, along with six others, are killed in a terrorist attack at the Munich Olympics.

Harold Macmillan, the largely successful Tory Prime Minister whom Elizabeth appointed in 1955. He remained outspoken and full of ideas until his death in 1986.

The Queen at her Silver Jubilee in 1977. At the time, she was widely regarded as out of touch but still popular. The next 20 years of her reign would see her popularity, and that of the monarchy, go into a steep decline.

as well as public. Philip, ever outspoken and inclined to modernize the monarchy where possible, chafed under the staid protocols and mores of the royal family. As a confident, energetic, capable man who had distinguished himself in military service, he found it difficult to serve as a consort, not even being allowed to extend his family name of Mountbatten to his and Elizabeth's children. Rumors swirled that the two of them fought often, that he acted out by behaving badly, and even that he was having affairs. Her very vulnerability in the face of these rumors may have encouraged Elizabeth to become more remote, more turned in on herself and on her work. By the end of the 1950s she and Philip seemed to have weathered the early storms of their marriage, and Philip had finally been accorded the title of Prince, but a certain amount of damage had been done.

In 1956, party politics forced their way into Elizabeth's reign. The Suez Crisis, in which Britain and France attempted to take control of the Suez Canal from the Egyptian government of Gamal Abdel Nasser, led to the resignation of Conservative Prime Minister Anthony Eden. Since the Conservative Party had no established means of replacing him, it

had fallen to Elizabeth to choose his successor. Relying on the advice of Eden, Churchill, and a small number of other Tory politicians, she named Harold MacMillan. This display of the monarch stepping into party politics, even when invited to do so, was regarded as unseemly by many Britons, and led to widespread criticism of Elizabeth and of the monarchy as a whole.

The criticism came to a head in 1957, when Lord Altrincham publicly accused the Queen of being "out of touch." The swiftness and savagery of the criticism he received—he was even physically attacked by a disgruntled citizen—attested to the fact that his comments had struck a nerve. From that point on, Elizabeth worked harder to appear approachable. Though she continued tirelessly to engage in predictably bland public ceremonies, tours, and speeches, she also began regularly undertaking royal walkabouts, in which she would move among the public, greeting and chatting with members of the crowd.

But Elizabeth was in a double-bind. As the 1950s gave way to the 1960s and beyond, the royal family was expected somehow to embody "timeless" British values of home, family, integrity, and service while also avoiding the perception that they were mired in an old-fashioned, class-driven, narrow-minded way of life. It was perhaps an untenable position, at least for Elizabeth, and she erred on the side of tradition rather than innovation. If the festive public reception of her Silver Jubilee in 1977 were any indication, she remained popular, but there were already rumblings of a new contempt for the monarchy. That same year, the Sex Pistols' song "God Save the Queen," a wickedly ironic take on the national anthem, reached the top of some singles charts while proclaiming that Elizabeth was "not a human being" and that there was "no future for England's dreaming." It was a sign of things to come.

The Queen's status made her a target not only for criticism but also for violence. More than once she faced violent demonstrations in countries where the wounds of Empire were still

1974	1977	1980		1982
In the wake of the Watergate scandal, Richard Nixon resigns as President of the United States. He is replaced by his Vice-President, Gerald Ford.	The movie Star Wars is released; the enormous popularity of this movie and its successors makes it a touchstone of popular culture for decades.	John Lennon is shot and killed by a mentally unstable fan, Mark David Chapman, in New York City.	ENGLISH HERITAGE JOHN LENNON 1940–1980 Musician and Songwriter lived here in 1968	Argentine forces invade and occupy the Falkland Islands, precipitating a war with the United Kingdom. Prince Andrew flies a helicopter in the conflict, which the UK wins.

A stamp commemorating the 1973 wedding of Princess Anne to Lt. Mark Phillips. The couple's troubled marriage and eventual divorce in 1992 formed part of what Elizabeth would call her "annus horribilis."

Prince Andrew and Sarah Ferguson, Duke and Duchess of York. The breakup of their marriage, and the Duchess's subsequent behavior, made for scores of tabloid headlines.

keenly felt. In 1974, an attempted kidnapping led to shots being fired at Elizabeth's daughter Princess Anne. In 1979, Lord Mountbatten, Prince Philip's uncle and onetime guardian, was assassinated by members of the Irish Republican Army, and two years later a gunman fired six blanks at the Queen herself. Most famously, in 1982, a mentally unstable man by the name of Michael Fagan penetrated Buckingham Palace security one night and made his way to Elizabeth's bedroom, where she was sleeping.

All these events received wide television coverage. As the mass media caught on to the profitability of news and gossip about the royal family, the line between monarchy and celebrity, once only crossed by those who, like Edward VIII, chose to do so, became increasingly blurred, and at times even obliterated. As the monarchy came to seem more and more antiquated as an institution, it took on a kind of voyeuristic fascination, with editors and reporters scrambling to provide their readers with vivid and sometimes salacious details of royal life.

A DECADE OF CRISES

As the 1980s ended, the monarchy as an institution came under mounting criticism. The government of Conservative Prime Minister Margaret Thatcher, who put her stamp on the decade, advanced economic policies that, to many, seemed to cut away the safety nets built up by British Society over the preceding decades; amid widespread strikes and bitter debates over questions of social and economic justice, the luxurious and seemingly leisured life of the royal family came to represent the arrogance and complacency of the upper classes. Elizabeth did little to dispel that sentiment. Though rumors persisted that she disliked both Thatcher and her policies, nothing in the Queen's public conduct suggested any real engagement with the problems facing the vast majority of Britons.

The 1990s brought a series of heavy blows. In 1992—the year Elizabeth would refer to as her annus horribilis—the monarchy came under heavy criticism when, after a fire at Windsor Castle, it was revealed that the building and its contents had not been insured and that repairs would be paid for from the public purse. As a result, the Queen began to pay income tax. Then her radio speech for the 40th anniversary of her accession was leaked to the Sun days in advance. But those setbacks shrunk in comparison to the highly public collapse that same year of the marriages of Prince Charles, Prince Andrew, and Princes Anne. Anne divorced her husband of 20 years when it surfaced that she had become enamored of another man, Timothy Laurence, whom she subsequently wed. That divorce might have attracted a good deal more censure had not other, more spectacular marital scandals erupted.

In 1986, Andrew, the Duke of York, had married Sarah Ferguson, a vivacious redhead known popularly as Fergie. At first, she seemed a breath of fresh air in the royal household, but her indecorous behavior—including appearances on television game shows—grew increasingly embarrassing. By 1991 she was

1984	1986	1988	1989
Prime Minister Indira Gandhi of India is assassinated by two of her Sikh bodyguards, leading to widespread anti-Sikh violence in India. She is succeeded by Rajiv Gandhi.	A nuclear reactor at Chernobyl, in the Ukrainian Soviet Republic, suffers a catastrophic meltdown, killing thousands in the most serious non-wartime nuclear catastrophe in history.	Iran and Iraq agree to end their several-years' war, in which over a million lives have been lost.	A wave of revolutions, many of them bloodless, sweep the former East Bloc as the Soviet Union collapses. The fall of the Berlin Wall becomes the symbolic centerpiece of the transformations in Europe.

Diana, Princess of Wales. Called after her death "the people's princess" by Prime Minister Tony Blair, she personified the increasingly blurred distinction between royalty and celebrity.

seen consorting with various well-heeled men while Andrew was away on military duty. In the spring of 1992 the couple announced their separation; later that year, photographs surfaced of Fergie enjoying topless sunbathing alongside an American financier. Though she and Andrew would not formally divorce until 1996, the damage was largely done. Fergie had turned the royal family into a tabloid spectacle, and the resulting feeding frenzy would continue for years.

If the divorce of Andrew and Fergie played out as farce, the breakup of Charles and his wife, Princess Diana of Wales, proved far more traumatic. They had married in 1981, after a long courtship in which Charles had actually waffled over whether or not to propose. In the public imagination, however, the romance of Charles and Diana was hugely mythologized, and the sugar-coated narrative was consummated with the worldwide telecast of their magnificent wedding. Though Charles had always been seen as diffident and awkward if well-meaning,

the attractive and photogenic Diana looked and acted every inch a fairytale princess. In retrospect, it is clear that she played the part so well because she naively believed in the fairytale.

But the life of the royal family is no fairytale, and Diana quickly proved too emotionally fragile for the pressures of life amid the monarchy. The rigid decorum, tedium, and sheer exhaustion of being Princess of Wales made her feel controlled and boxed in. Further, she and Charles had little in common. Even more damaging was the realization that her husband did not love her; Charles had for many years been in love with Camilla Parker-Bowles, who was herself married. As the Prince and Princess's marriage came undone, both engaged in affairs—he with Parker-Bowles, she with her riding instructor, James Hewitt, and others. In 1992, the situation was sensationalized with the publication of Diana: Her True Story, a biography initiated by Diana that chronicled her profound, even suicidal unhappiness during her marriage and laid bare her affair with Hewitt.

From there, the conflict spiraled into a media war. At first, Diana won overwhelming sympathy: she was far more charismatic, and she had gained great popularity through her extensive charity work and her extraordinary common touch. In 1996, she and Charles formally divorced. By then, Diana's embrace of celebrity had begun to catch up with her: though she remained popular, her increasingly racy lifestyle cost her moral credibility. When she died in an automobile accident in Paris in 1997, however, the outpouring of grief was enormous. Though much of it had to do with the charisma of Diana and the shock of her death, there was also a sense that the dream of an ideal monarchy had died with her. "Goodbye, England's rose," sang her friend Sir Elton John at her televised funeral.

RISING FROM THE ASHES

After Diana's death, it seemed that the royal family might have permanently lost all its luster. But after the turn of the millennium, a number of events converged to salvage the monarchy.

A QUESTION OF SUCCESSION

Elizabeth has held the throne for so long that two generations of the royal family have come of age during her reign. In the late 1990s, after the death of Diana, speculation arose that the Queen might pass over the unpopular Charles in the succession and hand the throne to his eldest son, William. Since then, William's coming of age, marriage, and establishment as an enormously popular prince have kept those rumors alive but such a change in the succession is unlikely. The House of Windsor, especially under Elizabeth, has been very traditionally minded about such things, and Charles has become much more liked and even admired in the past decade. It is almost certain that England's next monarch, assuming he takes this name, will be King Charles III.

1998	2000	2001	2003
Hugo Chavez is elected President of Venezuela. The former military man will rule until his death in 2013 as an avowed resistor of American hegemony; political opponents are harassed and suppressed.	Amid other millenarian beliefs, widespread anxiety about "Y2K" problems among computers failing to adjust to the turn of the millennium prove unfounded, as most issues are resolved through simple software updates.	On September 11, Al Queda terrorists hijack three planes in the United States, flying two of them into the New York World Trade Center Towers, which catch fire and collapse, killing thousands.	United States forces, assisted by some allies, invade Iraq. The war and occupation drag on for several years at tremendous cost to the Iraqi people and, to a lesser but debilitating extent, to the United States as well.

The wedding of Prince William and Catherine Middleton in 2011. The enormous popularity of William and Kate bodes well for the future of the monarchy.

Elizabeth at her Diamond Jubilee in 2012. After six decades on the throne and many vicissitudes, she is perhaps more popular now than ever before.

The sons of Charles and Diana, Princes William and Harry, proved engaging and sympathetic figures despite their occasional misbehavior. Charles gained considerable public esteem through his charity program the Prince's Trust as well as his environmental initiatives; where he once seemed eccentric and awkward, he is now admired for his progressive attitudes and civic activism. His eventual marriage to Camilla Parker-Bowles, now styled the Duchess of Cornwall, actually met with widespread public approval.

Elizabeth herself is now perhaps more popular than ever. Her Golden Jubilee in 2002, though shadowed by the deaths of the Queen Mother and Princess Margaret, was surprisingly successful. The 2006 film The Queen, in which Dame Helen Mirren gave a sympathetic and convincing performance as Elizabeth confronting the crisis of Diana's death, did much to humanize the royal family in the public eye. The film arrived at a turning point in the public's view of the monarchy. Over the course of Elizabeth's reign, the pendulum of public opinion had swung from regarding the royal family as stodgy and aloof to viewing them as fodder for often malicious gossip; now

it had centered in such a way that they were seen as generally admirable, if fallible, human beings. Elizabeth herself had come to personify a distinct set of values: dedication, loyalty, dignity, and endurance.

In April 2011, Prince William, second in line to the throne behind his father Charles, married Catherine Middleton, a commoner, in Westminster Abbey; viewers around the globe may well have numbered over a billion. Styled the Duke and Duchess of Cambridge, though more commonly known as William and Kate, the couple have proved hugely popular, and news of Kate's first pregnancy the next year created a wave of excitement. In 2012, the Queen's Diamond Jubilee was a globally televised extravaganza, the London rains failing to dampen the spirits of scores of thousands of celebrants.

If anything, the future of Britain's monarchy seems far more promising now than at any time in the previous century. Without doubt, opinions will continue to vary, and public esteem for the royal family will ebb and flow, but for the foreseeable future—partly because of Elizabeth's steady if unostentatious conduct as Queen—Britain, and the world, would like the monarchy to remain.

Prince William and his wife Catherine with their first child— Prince George is third in line to the throne.

2005	2007	2008	2010
Pope John Paul II, a hugely influential international figure who contributed to the collapse of the East Bloc, dies in Rome. Millions of pilgrims flock to Rome to commemorate his papacy.	Former Pakistani Prime Minister Benazir Bhutto is assassinated while campaigning to regain office. Though an affiliate group of Al Queda takes responsibility, it remains unclear how far the conspiracy extended.	Barack Obama, a Democrat, is elected the first President of the United States of African-American descent.	In North Africa and the Middle East, a series of popular uprisings known as the "Arab Spring" begin. They will bring down established regimes in Egypt, Libya, and Tunisia, and force reforms in other states. The resulting elections tilt political power in some of these countries toward Islamist parties.

Royal Documents

Though historical analysis offers insights into the lives of Britain's monarchs, primary texts—from statutes and edicts to private letters—provide a sense of history not just as a narrative but as a living, present event.

Some of the documents are important codes of laws, which trace the evolution of civil society in Britain. Others are more personal in nature. The inventory of Henry I's household displays a great deal about the life of a Norman king, while the letters from Henry VIII to Anne Boleyn reveal the personal drama of a monarch committed to a politically hazardous relationship. Elizabeth I's speech at Tilbury is the expression of a confident queen expecting to face the defining crisis of her reign; Elizabeth II's *"Annus Horribilis"* address presents a modern queen facing a very different form of test. In each case, the personality of the ruler comes through with unmistakable clarity and force.

FROM THE LAWS OF ALFRED (C. 885–899)

THIS EXCERPT FROM KING ALFRED'S LEGAL CODE DEMONSTRATES
BOTH HIS STABILIZING INFLUENCE AND THE ANGLO-SAXON
CHARACTER OF THE NATION HE RULED.

Int. 28.1 If anyone entrust property to his friend, if he steal it himself, let him repay two-fold. If he knows not who stole it, let him clear himself, that he committed no fraud there. If it then were livestock, and he says that an army took it, or that it killed itself, and he has witness, he need not pay for it. If then he have no witness, and he (the owner) will not believe him, let him bring an oath.

Int. 30.2 The women who are in the habit of receiving wizards and sorcerers and magicians, thou shalt not suffer to live.

Int. 40.3 Do not thou heed the word of the false man, to obey therefore, nor consent to his judgments, nor say any witness after him.

Int. 41. Do not thou turn thyself to the folly and unjust will of the people in their speech and clamour, against thy right (judgment), and do not yield for them to the teaching of the most foolish.

Int. 43.4 Judge thou very fairly. Do not judge one judgment for the rich and another for the poor; nor one for the one more dear and another for the one more hateful.

Int. 49.6. A man can think on this one sentence alone, that he judges each one rightly; he has need of no other law-books. Let him bethink him that he judge to no man what he would not that he judged to him, if he were giving the judgment on him.

Int. 49.7. Afterwards when it came about that many peoples had received the faith of Christ, many synods were assembled throughout all the earth, and likewise throughout the English people, after they had received the faith of Christ, of holy bishops and also of other distinguished wise men; they then established, for that mercy which Christ taught, that secular lords might with their permission receive without sin compensation in

money for almost every misdeed at the first offence, which compensation they then fixed; only for treachery to a lord they dared not declare any mercy, because Almighty God adjudged none for those who scorned him, nor did Christ, the Son of God, adjudge any for him who gave him over to death; and he charged (everyone) to love his lord as himself.

Int. 49.8. They then in many synods fixed the compensations for many human misdeeds, and they wrote them in many synod-books, here one law, there another.

Int. 49.9. Then I, King Alfred, collected these together and ordered to be written many of them which our forefathers observed, those which I liked; and many of those which I did not like I rejected with the advice of my councillors, and ordered them to be differently observed. For I dared not presume to set in writing at all many of my own, because it was unknown to me what would please those who should come after us. But those which I found, which seemed to me most just, either in the time of my kinsman, King Ine, or of Offa, king of the Mercians,1 or of Ethelbert, who first among the English received baptism, I collected herein, and omitted the others.

Int. 49.10. Then I, Alfred, king of the West Saxons, showed these to all my councillors, and they then said that they were all pleased to observe them.

1. First we direct, what is most necessary, that each man keep carefully his oath and pledge.

1.1. If anyone is wrongfully compelled to either of these, (to promise) treachery against his lord or any illegal aid, then it is better to leave it unfulfilled than to perform it.

1.2. (If, however, he pledges what it is right for him to perform,) and leaves it
unfulfilled, let him with humility give his weapons and his possessions into his friends' keeping and be 40 days in

prison at a king's estate; let him endure there what penance the bishop prescribes for him, and his kinsmen are to feed him if he has no food himself.

1.3. If he has no kinsmen and has not the food, the king's reeve is to feed him.

1.4. If he has to be forced thither, and will not go otherwise, and he is bound, he is to forfeit his weapons and his possessions.

1.5. If he is killed, he is to lie unpaid for.

1.6. If he escapes before the end of the period, and he is caught, he is to be 40 days in prison, as he should have been before.

1.7. If he gets clear, he is to be outlawed, and to be excommunicated from all the churches of Christ.

1.8. If, however, there is secular surety for him, he is to pay for the breach of surety as the law directs him, and for the breach of pledge as his confessor prescribes for him.

2. If anyone for any guilt flees to any one of the monastic houses to which the king's food-rent belongs, or to some other privileged community which is worthy of honour, he is to have a respite of three days to protect himself, unless he wishes to be reconciled.

2.1. If during that respite he is molested with slaying or binding or wounding, each of those (who did it) is to make amends according to the legal custom, both with wergild and with fine, and to pay to the community 120 shillings as compensation for the breach of sanctuary, and is to have forfeited his own (claim against the culprit).

3. If anyone violates the king's surety, he is to pay compensation for the charge as the law directs him, and for the breach of the surety with five pounds of pure pennies. The breach of the archbishop's surety or of his protection is to be compensated with three pounds; the breach of the surety or protection of another bishop or an ealdorman is to be compensated with two pounds.

4. If anyone plots against the king's life, directly or by harbouring his exiles or his men, he is liable to forfeit his life and all that he owns.

4.1. If he wishes to clear himself, he is to do it by (an oath equivalent to) the king's wergild.

4.2. Thus also we determine concerning all ranks, both *ceorl* and noble: he who plots against his lord's life is to be liable to forfeit his life and all that he owns, or to clear himself by his lord's wergild.

5. Also we determine this sanctuary for every church which a bishop has consecrated: if a man exposed to a vendetta reaches it running or riding, no one is to drag him out for seven days, if he can live in spite of hunger, unless he himself fights (his way) out. If however anyone does so, he is liable to (pay for breach of) the king's protection and of the church's sanctuary — more, if he seizes more from there.

5.1. If the community have more need of their church, he is to be kept in another building, and it is to have no more doors than the church.

5.2. The head of that church is to take care that no one give him food during that period.

5.3. If he himself will hand out his weapons to his foes, they are to keep him for 30 days, and send notice about him to his kinsmen.

5.4. Further sanctuary of the church: if any man has recourse to the church on account of any crime which has not been discovered, and there confesses himself in God's name, it is to be half remitted.

5.5. Whoever steals on Sunday or at Christmas or Easter or on the Holy Thursday in Rogation days; each of those we wish to be compensated doubly, as in the Lenten fast.

6. If anyone steals anything in church, he is to pay the simple compensation and the fine normally belonging to that simple compensation, and the hand with which he did it is to be struck off.

6.1. And if he wishes to redeem the hand, and that is allowed to him, he is to pay in proportion to his wergild.

7. If anyone fights or draws his weapon in the king's hall, and he is captured, it is to be at the king's judgment, whether he will grant him death or life.

7.1. If he escapes, and is afterwards captured, he shall always pay for himself with his wergild, and compensate for the crime, with wergild as with fine, according to what he has done.

8. If anyone brings a nun out of a nunnery without the permission of the king or the bishop, he is to pay 120 shillings, half to the king and half to the bishop and the lord of the church which has the nun.

8.1. If she outlives him who brought her out, she is to have nothing of his inheritance.

8.2. If she bears a child, it is not to have any of that inheritance, any more than the mother.

8.3. If her child is killed, the share of the maternal kindred is to be paid to the king; the paternal kindred are to be given their share.

9. If a woman with child is slain when she is bearing the child, the woman is to be paid for with full payment, and the child at half payment according to the wergild of the father's kin.

9.1. The fine is always to be 60 shillings until the simple compensation rises to 30 shillings; when the simple compensation has risen to that, the fine is afterwards to be 120 shillings.

9.2. Formerly, (the fine) for the stealer of gold, the stealer of stud-horses, the stealer of bees, and many fines, were greater than others; now all are alike, except for the stealer of a man: 120 shillings.

10. If anyone lies with the wife of a man of a twelve-hundred wergild, he is to pay to the husband 120 shillings; to a man of a six-hundred wergild 100 shillings is to be paid; to a man of the *ceorl* class 40 shillings is to be paid.

12. If a man burns or fells the wood of another, without permission, he is to pay for each large tree with five shillings, and afterwards for each, no matter how many there are, with fivepence; and 30 shillings as a fine.

13. If at a common task a man unintentionally kills another (by letting a tree fall on him) the tree is to be given to the kinsmen, and they are to have it from that estate within 30 days, or else he who owns the wood is to have the right to it.

14. If anyone is born dumb, or deaf, so that he cannot deny sins or confess them, the father is to pay compensation for his misdeeds.

15. If anyone fights or draws a weapon in the presence of

the archbishop, he is to pay 150 shillings compensation; if this happens in the presence of another bishop or of an ealdorman, he is to pay 100 shillings compensation.

16. If anyone steals a cow or a brood-mare and drives off a foal or a calf, he is to pay a shilling compensation (for the latter), and for the mothers according to their value.

17. If anyone entrusts to another one of his helpless dependants, and he dies during that time of fostering, he who reared him is to clear himself of guilt, if anyone accuses him of any.

18. If anyone in lewd fashion seizes a nun either by her clothes or her breast without her leave, the compensation is to be double that we have established for a lay person.

18.1. If a betrothed maiden commits fornication, if she is of *ceorl* birth, 60 shillings compensation is to be paid to the surety; and it is to be paid in livestock, cattle (only), and one is not to include in it any slave.

18.2. If she is a woman of a six-hundred wergild, 100 shillings are to be given to the surety.

18.3. If she is a woman of a twelve-hundred wergild, 120 shillings are to be paid to the surety.

19. If anyone lends his weapon to another that he may kill a man with it, they may, if they wish, join to pay the wergild.

19.1. If they do not join, he who lent the weapon is to pay a third part of the wergild and a third part of the fine.

19.2. If he wishes to clear himself, that in making the loan he was aware of no evil intent, he may do so.

19.3. If a sword-polisher receives another man's weapon to polish it, or a smith a man's tool, they both are to give it back unstained, just as either of them had received it; unless either of them had stipulated that he need not be liable to compensation for it.

20. If anyone entrusts property to another man's monk, without the permission of the monk's lord, and it is lost to him, he who owned it before is to bear its loss.

21. If a priest slays another man, he is to be handed over, and all of the (minster) property which he bought for himself, and the bishop is to unfrock him, when he is to be delivered up out of the minster, unless the lord is

willing to settle the wergild on his behalf.

22. If anyone brings up a charge in a public meeting before the king's reeve, and afterwards wishes to withdraw it, he is to make the accusation against a more likely person, if he can; if he cannot, he is to forfeit his compensation.

23. If a dog rends or bites a man to death, (the owner) is to pay six shillings at the first offence; if he gives it food, he is to pay on a second occasion 12 shillings, on a third 30 shillings.

23.1. If in any of these misdeeds the dog is destroyed, nevertheless this compensation is still to be paid.

23.2. If the dog commits more offences, and the owner retains it, he is to pay compensation for such wounds as the dog inflicts, according to the full wergild.

24. If a neat wounds a man, (the owner) is to hand over the neat, or to make terms.

25. If anyone rapes a *ceorl*'s slave-woman, he is to pay five shillings compensation to the *ceorl*, and 60 shillings fine.

25.1. If a slave rape a slave-woman, he is to pay by suffering castration.

26 (29). If anyone with a band of men kills an innocent man of a two-hundred wergild, he who admits the slaying is to pay the wergild and the fine, and each man who was in that expedition is to pay 30 shillings as compensation for being in that band.

27 (30). If it is a man of a six-hundred wergild, each man (is to pay) 60 shillings as compensation for being in that band, and the slayer the wergild and full fine.

28 (31). If he is a man of a twelve-hundred wergild, each of them (is to pay) 120 shillings, and the slayer the wergild and the fine.

28.1 (31.1). If a band of men does this and afterwards wishes to deny it on oath, they are all to be accused; and then they are all collectively to pay the wergild, and all one fine, as is accordant to the wergild.

29 (26). If anyone rapes a girl not of age, that is to be the same compensation as for an adult.

30 (27). If a man without paternal kinsmen fights and kills a man, and if then he has maternal kinsmen, those are to pay a third share of the wergild, (and the associates a third; for the third part) he is to flee.

30.1 (27.1). If he has no maternal kinsmen, the associates are to pay half, and for half he is to flee.

31 (28). If anyone kills a man so placed, if he has no kinsmen, he is to pay half to the king, half to the associates.

32. If anyone is guilty of public slander, and it is proved against him, it is to be compensated for with no lighter penalty than the cutting off of his tongue, with the proviso that it be redeemed at no cheaper rate than it is valued in proportion to the wergild.

33. If anyone charges another about a pledge sworn by God, and wishes to accuse him that he did not carry out any of those (promises) which he gave him, he (the plaintiff) is to pronounce the preliminary oath in four churches, and the other, if he wishes to clear himself, is to do it in twelve churches.

34. Moreover, it is prescribed for traders: they are to bring before the king's reeve in a public meeting the men whom they take up into the country with them, and it is to be established how many of them there are to be; and they are to take with them men whom they can afterwards bring to justice at a public meeting; and whenever it may be necessary for them to have more men out with them on their journey, it is always to be announced, as often as it is necessary for them, to the king's reeve in the witness of the meeting. 35. If anyone binds an innocent *ceorl*, he is to pay him ten shillings compensation.

35.1. If anyone scourges him, he is to pay him 20 shillings compensation. 35.2. If he places him in the stocks,1 he is to pay him 30 shillings compensation. 35.3. If in insult he disfigures him by cutting his hair, he is to pay him 10 shillings compensation.

35.4. If, without binding him, he cuts his hair like a priest's, he is to pay him 30 shillings compensation.

35.5. If he cuts off his beard, he is to pay him 20 shillings compensation.

35.6. If he binds him and then cuts his hair like a priest's, he is to pay him 60 shillings compensation.

36. Moreover, it is established: if anyone has a spear over his shoulder, and a man is
transfixed on it, the wergild is to be paid without the fine.

36.1. If he is transfixed before his eyes, he is to pay the wergild; if anyone accuses him of intention in this act, he is to clear himself in proportion to the fine, and by that (oath) do away with the fine,

36.2. If the point is higher than the butt end of the shaft. If they are both level, the point and the butt end, that is to be (considered) without risk.

37. If anyone from one district wishes to seek a lord in another district, he is to do so with the witness of the ealdorman, in whose shire he previously served.

37.1. If he do it without his witness, he who accepts him as his man is to pay 120 shillings compensation; he is, however, to divide it, half to the king in the shire in which the man served previously, half in that into which he has come.

37.2. If he has committed any wrong where he was before, he who now receives him as his man is to pay compensation for it, and 120 shillings to the king as fine.

38. If anyone fights in a meeting in the presence of the king's ealdorman, he is to pay wergild and fine, as it is the law, and before that, 120 shillings to the ealdorman as a fine. 38.1. If he disturbs a public meeting by drawing a weapon, (he is to pay) 120 shillings
to the ealdorman as a fine.

38.2. If any of this takes place in the presence of the deputy of the king's ealdorman,
or of the king's priest, 30 shillings (is to be paid) as a fine.

39. If anyone fights in the house of a *ceorl*, he is to pay six shillings compensation to
the *ceorl*.

39.1. If he draws a weapon and does not fight, it is to be half as much.

39.2. If either of these things happens to a man of a six-hundred wergild, it is to
amount to three-fold the compensation to a *ceorl*; (if) to a man of a twelve-hundred wergild, to double that of the man of the six-hundred wergild.

40. Forcible entry into the king's residence shall be 120 shillings; into the archbishop's, 90 shillings; into another bishop's or an ealdorman's, 60 shillings; into that of a man of a twelve-hundred wergild, 30 shillings; into that of a man of a six-hundred wergild, 15 shillings; forcible entry into a *ceorl*'s enclosure, five shillings.

40.1. If any of this happens when the army has been called out, or in the Lenten fast, the compensations are to be doubled.

40.2. If anyone openly neglects the rules of the Church in Lent without permission, he is to pay 120 shillings compensation.

41. The man who holds bookland, which his kinsmen left to him —then we establish that he may not alienate it from his kindred if there is a document or witness (to show) that he was prohibited from doing so by those men who acquired it in the beginning and by those who gave it to him; and that is then to be declaredı in the witness of the king and of the bishop, in the presence of his kinsmen.

42. Moreover we command: that the man who knows his opponent to be dwelling at home is not to fight before he asks justice for himself.

42.1. If he has sufficient power to surround his opponent and besiege him there in his house, he is to keep him seven days inside and not fight against him, if he will remain inside; and then after seven days, if he will surrender and give up his weapons, he is to keep him unharmed for 30 days, and send notice about him to his kinsmen and his friends.

42.2. If he, however, reaches a church, it is then to be (dealt with) according to the privilege of the church, as we have said above.

42.3. If he (the attacker) has not sufficient power to besiege him in his house, he is to ride to the ealdorman and ask him for support; if he will not give him support, he is to ride to the king, before having recourse to fighting.

42.4. Likewise, if a man run across his opponent, and did not previously know him to be at home, if he will give up his weapons, he is to be kept for 30 days and his friends informed; if he will not give up his weapons, then he may fight against him. If he is willing to surrender, and to give up his weapons, and after that anyone fights against him, he (who does) is to pay wergild or compensation for wounds according to what he has done, and a fine, and is to have forfeited (the right to avenge) his kinsman.

42.5. Moreover we declare that a man may fight on behalf of his lord, if the lord is being attacked, without incurring a vendetta. Similarly the lord may fight on behalf of his man.

42.6. In the same way, a man may fight on behalf of his born kinsman, if he is being wrongfully attacked, except against his lord; that we do not allow.

42.7. And a man may fight without incurring a vendetta if he finds another man with his wedded wife, within closed doors or under the same blanket, or with his legitimate daughter or his legitimate sister, or with his mother who was given as a lawful wife to his father.

43. These days are to be given to all free men, but not to slaves or unfree labourers: 12 days at Christmas, and the day on which Christ overcame the devil, and the anniversary of St Gregory, and seven days at Easter and seven days after, and one day at the feast of St Peter and St Paul, and in harvesttime the whole week before the feast of St Mary, and one day at the feast of All Saints. And the four Wednesdays in the four Ember weeks are to be given to all slaves, to sell to whomsoever they choose anything of what anyone has given them in God's name, or of what they can earn in any of their leisure moments.

FROM THE LAWS OF WILLIAM THE CONQUEROR

FROM A LATER MANUSCRIPT, INCLUDING LAWS ESTABLISHED THROUGHOUT WILLIAM'S REIGN.

Here is set down what William, king of the English, established in consultation with his magnates after the conquest of England:

1. First that above all things he wishes one God to be revered throughout his whole realm, one faith in Christ to be kept ever inviolate, and peace and security to be preserved between English and Normans.

2. We decree also that every freeman shall affirm by oath and compact that he will be loyal to King William both within and without England, that he will preserve with him his lands and honour with all fidelity and defend him against all his enemies.

3. I will, moreover, that all the men whom I have brought with me, or who have come after me, shall be protected by my peace and shall dwell in quiet. And if any one of them shall be slain, let the lord of his murderer seize him within five days, if he can; but if he cannot, let him begin to pay me 46 marks of silver so long as his substance avails. And when his substance is exhausted, let the whole hundred in which the murder took place pay what remains in common.

4. And let every Frenchman who, in the time of King Edward, my kinsman, was a sharer in the customs of the English, pay what they call "scot and lot", according to the laws of the English. This decree was ordained in the city of Gloucester.

5. We forbid also that any live cattle shall be bought or sold for money except within cities, and this shall be done before three faithful witnesses; nor even anything old without surety and warrant. But if anyone shall do otherwise, let him pay once, and afterwards a second time for a fine.

6. It was also decreed there that if a Frenchman shall charge an Englishman with perjury or murder or theft or homicide or "ran", as the English call open rapine which cannot be denied, the Englishman may defend himself, as

he shall prefer, either by the ordeal of hot iron 3 or by wager of battle. But if the Englishman be infirm, let him find another who will take his place. If one of them shall be vanquished, he shall pay a fine of 40 shillings to the king. If an Englishman shall charge a Frenchman and be unwilling to prove his accusation either by ordeal or by wager of battle, I will, nevertheless, that the Frenchman shall acquit himself by a valid oath.

7. This also I command and will, that all shall have and hold the law of King Edward in respect of their lands and all their possessions, with the addition of those decrees I have ordained for the welfare of the English people.

8. Every man who wishes to be considered a freeman shall be in pledge 1 so that his surety shall hold him and hand him over to justice if he shall offend in any way. And if any such shall escape, let his sureties see to it that they pay forthwith what is charged against him, and let them clear themselves of any complicity in his escape. Let recourse

be had to the hundred and shire courts as our predecessors decreed. And those who ought of right to come and are unwilling to appear, shall be summoned once; and if for the second time they refuse to come, one ox shall be taken from them, and they shall be summoned a third time. And if they do not come the third time, a second ox shall be taken from them. But if they do not come at the fourth summons, the man who was unwilling to come shall forfeit from his goods the amount of the charge against him — "ceapgeld" as it is called — and in addition to this a fine to the king.

9. I prohibit the sale of any man by another outside the country on pain of a fine to be paid in full to me.

10. I also forbid that anyone shall be slain or hanged for any fault, but let his eyes be put out and let him be castrated. And this command shall not be violated under pain of a fine in full to me.

THE CORONATION CHARTER OF HENRY I (5 AUGUST 1100)

THIS CHARTER, APPARENTLY DISTRIBUTED THROUGHOUT ENGLAND, REPRESENTS HENRY'S ATTEMPT TO ENSURE BROAD SUPPORT FOR HIS KINGSHIP.

Henry, king of the English, to Samson the bishop, and Urse of Abbetot, and to all his barons and faithful vassals, both French and English, in Worcestershire, greeting.

1. Know that by the mercy of God and by the common counsel of the barons of the whole kingdom of England I have been crowned king of this realm. And because the kingdom has been oppressed by unjust exactions, I now, being moved by reverence towards God and by the love I bear you all, make free the Church of God; so that I will neither sell nor lease its property; nor on the death of an archbishop or a bishop or an abbot will I take anything from the demesne of the Church or from its vassals during

the period which elapses before a successor is installed. I abolish all the evil customs by which the kingdom of England has been unjustly oppressed. Some of those evil customs are here set forth.

2. If any of my barons or of my earls or of any other of my tenants shall die, his heir shall not redeem his land as he was wont to do in the time of my brother, but he shall henceforth redeem it by means of a just and lawful "relief". Similarly the men of my barons shall redeem their lands from their lords by means of a just and lawful "relief".

3. If any of my barons or of my tenants shall wish to give in marriage his daughter or his sister or his niece or his cousin, he shall consult me about the matter; but I will

neither seek payment for my consent, nor will I refuse my permission, unless he wishes to give her in marriage to one of my enemies. And if, on the death of one of my barons or of one of my tenants, a daughter should be his heir, I will dispose of her in marriage and of her lands according to the counsel given me by my barons. And if the wife of one of my tenants shall survive her husband and be without children, she shall have her dower and her marriage portion, and I will not give her in marriage unless she herself consents.

4. If a widow survives with children under age, she shall have her dower and her marriage portion, so long as she keeps her body chaste; and I will not give her in marriage except with her consent. And the guardian of the land, and of the children, shall be either the widow or another of their relations, as may seem more proper. And I order that my barons shall act likewise towards the sons and daughters and widows of their men.

5. I utterly forbid that the common mintage, 3 which has been taken from the towns and shires, shall henceforth be levied, since it was not so levied in the time of King Edward. If any moneyer or other person be taken with false money in his possession, let true justice be visited upon him.

6. I forgive all pleas and all debts which were owing to my brother, except my own proper dues, and except those things which were agreed to belong to the inheritance of others, or to concern the property which justly belonged to others. And if anyone had promised anything for his heritage, I remit it, and I also remit all "reliefs" which were promised for direct inheritance.

7. If any of my barons or of my men, being ill, shall give away or bequeath his movable property, I will allow that it shall be bestowed according to his desires. But if, prevented either by violence or through sickness, he shall die intestate as far as concerns his movable property, his widow or his children or his relatives or one of his true men shall make such division for the sake of his soul, as may seem best to them.

8. If any of my barons or of my men shall incur a forfeit,

he shall not be compelled to pledge his movable property to an unlimited amount, as was done in the time of my father and my brother; but he shall only make payment according to the extent of his legal forfeiture, as was done before the time of my father and in the time of my earlier predecessors. Nevertheless, if he be convicted of breach of faith or of crime, he shall suffer such penalty as is just.

9. I remit all murder-fines which were incurred before the day on which I was crowned king; and such murder-fines as shall now be incurred shall be paid justly according to the law of King Edward.

10. By the common counsel of my barons I have retained the forests in my own hands as my father did before me.

11. The knights, who in return for their estates perform military service equipped with a hauberk of mail, shall hold their demesne lands quit of all gelds and all work; I make this concession as my own free gift in order that, being thus relieved of so great a burden, they may furnish themselves so well with horses and arms that they may be properly equipped and prepared to discharge my service and to defend my kingdom.

12. I establish a firm peace in all my kingdom, and I order that this peace shall henceforth be kept.

13. I restore to you the law of King Edward together with such emendations to it as my father made with the counsel of his barons.

14. If since the death of my brother, King William, anyone shall have seized any of my property, or the property of any other man, let him speedily return the whole of it. If he does this no penalty will be exacted, but if he retains any part of it he shall, when discovered, pay a heavy penalty to me.

Witness: Maurice, bishop of London; William, bishop-elect of Winchester; 2 Gerard, bishop of Hereford; Henry the earl; 3 Simon the earl; 4 Walter Giffard; Robert of Montfort-sur-Risle; Roger Bigot; Eudo the steward; Robert, son of Haimo; and Robert Malet.

At Westminster when I was crowned.

Farewell.

THE ESTABLISHMENT OF THE KING'S HOUSEHOLD (C. 1135)

COMPILED AT THE END OF THE REIGN OF HENRY I, THIS DOCUMENT REVEALS SOME OF THE WORKINGS OF THE NORMAN ROYAL HOUSEHOLD.

THIS IS THE ESTABLISHMENT OF THE KING'S HOUSEHOLD.

The chancellor shall receive 5 shillings a day, and 1 lord's simnel loaf, and 2 salted simnel loaves, and 1 sextary of clear wine, and 1 sextary of ordinary wine, and 1 fat wax candle and 40 pieces of candle.

The master of the writing office used at first to receive 10 pence a day and 1 salted simnel loaf, and half a sextary of ordinary wine, and 1 fat wax candle and 12 pieces of candle; but King Henry increased the allowance of Robert "of the Seal" 1 to the extent that on the day when that king died, Robert was receiving 2 shillings and 1 sextary of ordinary wine and 1 salted simnel loaf, and 1 small wax candle and 24 pieces of candle.

The chaplain in charge of the chapel and of the relics shall have the provision of two men; and the four servants of the chapel shall each receive double food, and for each of the two packhorses assigned to the chapel they shall have an allowance of a penny a day, and also a penny a month for shoeing. For their service of the chapel they shall have 2 wax candles on Wednesday, and 2 on Saturday; and 30 pieces of candle; and 1 gallon of clear wine for mass; and 1 sextary of ordinary wine on Maundy Thursday for the washing of the altar; and on Easter day 1 sextary of clear wine for Communion, and 1 of ordinary wine.

CONCERNING THE STEWARDS

The steward shall receive the same as the chancellor if they live outside the king's household; but if they live within the king's household, they shall receive

each day 3 shillings and 6 pence, and 2 salted simnel loaves, and 1 sextary of ordinary wine and a candle.

The clerk of the issue of bread and wine shall receive 2 shillings a day and 1 salted simnel loaf and 1 sextary of ordinary wine and 1 small candle and 24 pieces of candle.

CONCERNING THE DISPENSERS

The master-dispenser of bread who is permanently in office shall receive 2 shillings and 10 pence each day, if he lives outside the king's household, and 1 salted simnel loaf, and 1 sextary of ordinary wine and 1 small wax candle and 24 pieces of candle; but if he lives within the king's household he shall receive 2 shillings and half a sextary of ordinary wine and 1 candle.

CONCERNING THE DISPENSERS WHO SERVE BY TURN

If they live outside the king's household they shall receive 19 pence daily and 1 salted simnel loaf, and 1 sextary of ordinary wine and 1 fat wax candle and 20 pieces of candle. If they live within the king's household they shall receive 10 pence and half a sextary of ordinary wine and a candle.

CONCERNING THE NAPERERS

The naperer shall receive the customary allowance of food. He shall have 3 halfpence a day for his man and 1 penny a day for his packhorse, and 1 penny a month for its shoeing.

The usher of issues shall have the same except for the

payments in respect of the packhorse.

The counter of bread shall have the customary food.

CONCERNING THE FOUR BAKERS WHO SERVE IN PAIRS BY TURN

The two who serve in the king's house shall live in the king's household; and the two that are travelling ahead shall have 40 pence to procure a bushel of Rouen out of which they must render 40 lord's simnel loaves and 140 salted simnel loaves and 260 ordinary loaves from the bakery. They shall receive a lord's simnel loaf for four men; a salted simnel loaf for two; a baker's loaf for one.

CONCERNING THE WAFERER

The waferer shall have the customary allowance of food and 3 halfpence a day for his man.

The keeper of the tables shall receive the same together with a packhorse and its allowances.

The bearer of the alms-dish shall live in the king's household.

CONCERNING THE DISPENSERS OF THE LARDER

The master-dispenser of the larder shall receive the same allowance as the master- dispenser of bread and wine. Similarly, the dispensers of the larder who serve by turn shall receive the same allowance as the dispensers of bread and wine who serve by turn.

The larderers who serve by turn shall receive the customary food, and they shall have 3 halfpence a day for their man. The usher of the larder likewise. The slaughtermen shall similarly have the customary food.

CONCERNING THE COOKS

The cook of the king's kitchen shall live in the king's household, and he shall receive 3 halfpence a day for his man. The usher of the same kitchen shall have the customary food and 3 halfpence a day for his man. The keeper of the vessels shall live in the king's household and shall receive 3 halfpence a day for his man, and also a packhorse with its allowances. The scullion 3 of the same kitchen shall have the customary food. The cook for the king's private household and the dispenser likewise. Ralph "de Marchia", who before his death was cook to the king (Henry I), lived in the king's household and received 3 halfpence for his man.

CONCERNING THE GREAT KITCHEN

Oinus Pochard shall have the customary food and 3 halfpence a day for his man. Two cooks shall likewise have the customary food and 3 halfpence a day for their man. The servants of the same kitchen shall have the customary food. The usher of the turnspit shall have the customary food and 3 halfpence a day for his man. The turnspit likewise. The keeper of the dishes receives the same and also a packhorse with its allowances. The carter of the great kitchen shall have double food and a just allowance for his horse. The carter of the larder likewise. The servant who takes in the beasts killed in the chase shall live in the king's household and shall receive 3 halfpence a day for his man.

CONCERNING THE BUTLERY

The master-butler shall be as the steward, and they shall both have the same allowance. The master-dispenser of the butlery shall be as the master-dispenser of bread and wine. The dispensers of the butlery who serve by turn shall be as the dispensers of issue except that they shall have one candle more, for they have 1 small wax candle and 24 pieces of candle. The usher of the cutlery shall have the customary food and 3 halfpence a day for his man. The keepers of the wine barrels shall live in the king's household, and each one of them shall receive 3 halfpence a day for his man. The keeper of the wine-butts shall have the customary food and 3 pence for his man, and half a sextary of ordinary wine and 12 pieces of candle. The cellarman shall have the customary food, but Sereius shall have besides this 3 halfpence a day for his man, and 2 packhorses with their allowances.

CONCERNING THE KEEPERS OF THE CUPS

Four serve together in turn, of whom two shall live in the household, and each one shall have for his man 3 halfpence a day. The other two shall have the customary food and likewise 3 halfpence a day for their men.

CONCERNING THE FRUITERERS

The fruiterer shall live in the king's household and shall receive 3 pence a day for his men. The carter shall have the customary food and an allowance for his horses. The master-chamberlain is the equal of the steward in his allowance. The treasurer shall be as the master-chamberlain if he is at the court and is serving in the treasury. William Mauduit shall have 14 pence a day and shall live always in the king's household, and he shall have 1 fat wax candle and 12 pieces of candle, and 3 packhorses with their allowance. The porter of the king's bed shall live in the king's household and shall receive 3 halfpence a day for his man, and 1 packhorse with its allowances. The chamberlain who is on duty shall receive 2 shillings a day and 1 salted simnel loaf and 1 sextary of ordinary wine and 1 small wax candle and 24 pieces of candle. The chamberlain of the candle shall receive 8 pence a day and half a sextary of ordinary wine. The king's cutter shall live in the king's household, and shall receive 3 halfpence a day for his man. The chamberlains who do not receive an allowance shall live in the king's household if they wish. The ewerer shall have double the customary food, and when the king goes on a journey he shall receive a penny a day for drying the king's clothes, and when the king takes a bath he shall have

4 pence except on the three feasts of the year. About the wages of the washerwoman there is some doubt. The constables have their allowances as do the stewards. William, son of Odo, shall have 1 lord's simnel loaf and 1 sextary of clear wine and 1 wax candle and 24 pieces of candle. Henry "de la Pomerai", if he lives outside the king's household, shall have 2 shillings a day and 1 salted simnel loaf and 1 sextary of ordinary wine, and 1 small wax candle and 24 pieces of candle. If he lives within the household, he shall have 14 pence, and half a sextary of ordinary wine and a candle at discretion. Roger "d'Oilly" likewise.

CONCERNING THE MARSHALSHIP

The master-marshal, to wit, John, has similar payment; and he shall also have tallies for the gifts and allowances which are made from the treasury of the king and from his chamber; and he shall have tallies against all the king's officials as a witness to all these things. The four marshals who serve the men of the king's household — clerks and knights and serjeants — when they go billeting, or when they stay outside the king's household on the king's business, shall have 8 pence each day, and a gallon of ordinary wine, and 12 pieces of candle. When they live within the household they shall have 3 pence a day for their man and a candle. But if any of the marshals be sent on the king's business he shall only have 8 pence a day. The serjeants of the marshals, when they are sent on the king's business, shall each have 3 pence a day, but not when they are living in the king's household. The ushers, if they are knights, shall live in the king's household, and they shall have 3 halfpence a day for each of their men, and 8 pieces of candle. Gilbert Goodman and Rannulf shall live in the king's household, and shall have 3 halfpence a day for their men. The other ushers, who are not knights, shall live in the king's household without further allowances. The watchmen shall have double food and 3 halfpence for their men, and 4 candles; and besides this each one of them shall receive in the morning 2 loaves and a tray of meat, and a measure of beer. The stoker of the fire shall live always within the king's household, and from Michaelmas until Easter he shall have 4 pence a day for the fire. The usher of the chamber shall receive, on each day that the king travels, 4 pence for the king's bed. The keeper of the tents shall live in the king's household, and when the tents have to be carried, he shall receive an allowance for a man and a packhorse.

Each one of the horn-blowers shall have 3 pence a day. And there are twenty servants each of whom receives 1 penny a day. Each keeper of the greyhounds shall have 3 pence a day, and 2 pence for his men, and a halfpenny a day for each greyhound. The keeper of the kennels shall have 8 pence a day. The knights-huntsmen shall each receive 8 pence a day. The hunt-servants shall each receive 5 pence. The leader of the bloodhound shall receive 1 penny a day and 1 halfpenny for the bloodhound. The keeper of the running hounds shall receive 3 pence a day. The huntsmen of the stag- hunt shall each receive 3 pence a day; and there shall be 1 penny for each four of the greater staghounds, and 1 penny for each six of the lesser staghounds. Two men each receiving 1 penny a day shall attend to the greater staghounds, and two men each receiving 1 penny a day shall attend to the lesser staghounds. Each one of the keepers of the small hounds shall receive 3 pence a day. The huntsmen of the wolf-hunt shall have 20 pence a day for horses and men and dogs, and they are required to maintain 24 running hounds and 8 greyhounds; and they shall have 6 pounds a year wherewith to buy horses; but they themselves say it ought to be 8 pounds. The bowman who carries the king's bow shall have 5 pence a day, and the other bowmen likewise. Bernard, Ralph "le Robeur", and their fellows shall each have 3 pence a day.

CHARTER OF HENRY II ADDRESSED GENERALLY (19 DECEMBER 1154)

IN THIS CHARTER, RELEASED UPON HIS CORONATION, HENRY II REASSURES THE ENGLISH THAT HE WILL RETAIN THE POLICIES OF HIS GRANDFATHER HENRY I.

Henry (by the grace of God), king of the English, duke of the men of Normandy and Aquitaine, and count of the Angevins to all his earls, barons and liegemen, both French and English, greeting. Know that for the honour of God and holy Church, and for the common restoration of my whole realm, I have granted and restored, and by this present charter confirmed, to God and to holy Church, and to all my earls, barons and vassals all concessions, gifts, liberties and free customs, which King Henry, my grandfather, granted and conceded to them. Likewise all evil customs, which he abolished and relaxed, I also grant to be relaxed and abolished in my name and in that of my heirs. Wherefore I will, and firmly command, that holy Church and all my earls, barons and vassals shall have and hold all these customs, gifts, liberties and freedom from pecuniary exactions, freely and unmolested, fully, rightly and in peace from me and my heirs for themselves and their heirs, as freely and peaceably and fully in everything as King Henry, my grandfather, granted and conceded to them and confirmed by his charter.

Witness: Richard of Lucé.

At Westminster.

THE ASSIZE OF CLARENDON (1166)

THIS DOCUMENTS SOME OF THE MAJOR ADMINISTRATIVE LEGAL REFORMS PASSED DURING THE REIGN OF HENRY II.

Here begins the assize of Clarendon made by King Henry II with the assent of the archbishops, bishops, abbots, earls and barons of all England,

1. In the first place the aforesaid King Henry, on the advice of all his barons, for the preservation of peace, and for the maintenance of justice, has decreed that inquiry shall be made throughout the several counties and throughout the several hundreds through twelve of the more lawful men of the hundred and through four of the more lawful men of each vill upon oath that they will speak the truth, whether there be in their hundred or vill any man accused or notoriously suspect of being a robber or murderer or thief, or any who is a receiver of robbers or murderers or thieves, since the lord king has been king. And let the justices inquire into this among themselves and the sheriffs among themselves.

2. And let anyone, who shall be found, on the oath of the aforesaid, accused or notoriously suspect of having been a robber or murderer or thief, or a receiver of them, since the lord king has been king, be taken and put to the ordeal of water, and let him swear that he has not been a robber or murderer or thief, or receiver of them, since the lord king has been king, to the value of 5 shillings, so far as he knows.

3. And if the lord of the man, who has been arrested, or his steward or his vassals shall claim him by pledge within the third day following his capture, let him be released on bail with his chattels until he himself shall stand his trial.

4. And when a robber or murderer or thief or receiver of them has been arrested through the aforesaid oath, if the justices are not about to come speedily enough into the county where they have been taken, let the sheriffs send word to the nearest justice by some well-informed person that they have arrested such men, and the justices shall send back word to the sheriffs informing them where they desire the men to be brought before them; and let the sheriffs

bring them before the justices. And together with them let the sheriffs bring from the hundred and the vill, where they have been arrested, two lawful men to bear the record of the county and of the hundred as to why they have been taken, and there before the justice let them stand trial.

5. And in the case of those who have been arrested through the aforesaid oath of this assize, let no man have court or justice or chattels save the lord king in his court in the presence of his justices; and the lord king shall have all their chattels. But in the case of those who have been arrested otherwise than by this oath let it be as is customary and due.

6. And let the sheriffs, who have arrested them, bring them before the justice without any other summons than that they have from him. And when robbers or murderers or thieves, or receivers of them, who have been arrested through the oath or otherwise, are handed over to the sheriffs, let them receive them immediately and without delay. And in the several counties where there are no gaols, let such be made in a borough or some castle of the king at the king's expense and from his wood, if one shall be near, or from some neighbouring wood at the oversight of the king's servants, to the end that in them the sheriffs may be able to guard those who shall be arrested by the officials accustomed to do this, or by their servants.

8. Moreover, the lord king wills that all shall come to the county courts to take this oath, so that none shall remain behind on account of any franchise which he has, or any court or soke, which he may have, but that they shall come to take this oath.

9. And let there be no one within his castle or without, nor even in the honour of Wallingford, who shall forbid the sheriffs to enter into his court or his land to take the view of frankpledge and to see that all are under pledges; and let them be sent before the sheriffs under free pledge.

10. And in cities or boroughs let no one hold men or receive

them into his house or on his land or in his soke, whom he will not take in hand to produce before the justice, should they be required; or else let them be in frankpledge.

11. And let there be none in a city or a borough or a castle or without it, nor even in the honour of Wallingford, who shall forbid the sheriffs to enter into their land or their soke to arrest those who have been accused or are notoriously suspect of being robbers or murderers or thieves or receivers of them, or outlaws, or persons charged concerning the forest; but the king commands that they shall aid the sheriffs to capture them.

12. And if anyone shall be taken in possession of the spoils of robbery or theft, if he be of evil repute and bears an evil testimony from the public and has no warrant, let him have no law. And if he has not been notoriously suspect on account of the goods in his possession, let him go to the ordeal of water.

13. And if anyone shall confess to robbery or murder or theft, or to harbouring those who have committed them, in the presence of the lawful men or in the hundred court, and afterwards he wish to deny it, let him not have his law.

14. Moreover, the lord king wills that those who shall be tried by the law and absolved by the law, if they have been of ill repute and openly and disgracefully spoken of by the testimony of many and that of the lawful men, shall abjure the king's lands, so that within eight days they shall cross the sea, unless the wind detains them; and with the first wind they shall have afterwards they shall cross the sea, and they shall not return to England again except by the mercy of the lord king; and both now, and if they return, let them be outlawed; and on their return let them be seized as outlaws.

15. And if the lord king forbids that any vagabond, that is, a wanderer or unknown person, shall be given shelter anywhere except in a borough, and even there he shall not be given shelter longer than one night, unless he become sick there, or his horse, so that he can show an evident excuse.

16. And if he shall remain there longer than one night, let him be arrested and held until his lord shall come to give surety for him, or until he himself shall procure safe pledges; and let him likewise be arrested who gave him shelter.

17. And if any sheriff shall send word to another sheriff that men have fled from his county into another county, on account of robbery or murder or theft or the harbouring of them, or on account of outlawry or of a charge concerning the king's forest, let him (the second sheriff) arrest them; and even if he knows of himself or through others that such men have fled into his county, let him arrest them and guard them until he has taken safe pledges for them.

18. And let all the sheriffs cause a record to be made of all fugitives who have fled from their counties; and let them do this before the county courts and carry the names of those written therein before the justices, when next they come to them, so that these men may be sought throughout England, and their chattels may be seized for the needs of the king.

19. And the lord king wills that from the time the sheriffs shall receive the summons of the itinerant justices to present themselves before them, together with the men of the county, they shall assemble them and make inquiry for all who have newly come into their counties since this assize; and they shall send them away under pledge to attend before the justices, or they shall keep them in custody until the justices come to them, and then they shall present them before the justices.

20. Moreover, the lord king forbids monks or canons or any religious house to receive any men of the lower orders as a monk or a canon or a brother, until it be known of what reputation he is, unless he shall be sick unto death.

21. Moreover, the lord king forbids anyone in all England to receive in his land or his soke or in a house under him any one of that sect of renegades who were branded and excommunicated at Oxford. And if anyone shall so receive them, he himself shall be at the mercy of the lord king, and the house in which they have dwelt shall be carried outside the village and burnt. And each sheriff shall swear an oath that he will observe this, and shall cause all his officers to swear this, and also the stewards of the barons and all knights and freeholders of the counties.

22. And the lord king wills that this assize shall be kept in his realm so long as it shall please him.

THE ASSIZE OF ARMS (1181)

THIS DOCUMENT OFFERS A WINDOW ON HOW ARMIES WERE MANNED AND EQUIPPED IN THE ERA OF HENRY II.

1. Let every holder of a knight's fee have a hauberk, a helmet, a shield and a lance. And let every knight have as many hauberks, helmets, shields and lances, as he has knight's fees in his demesne.

2. Also, let every free layman, who holds chattels or rent to the value of 16 marks, have a hauberk, a helmet, a shield and a lance. Also, let every free layman who holds chattels or rent worth 10 marks have an "aubergel" and a headpiece of iron, and a lance.

3. Also, let all burgesses and the whole body of freemen have quilted doublets and a headpiece of iron, and a lance.

4. Moreover, let each and every one of them swear that before the feast of St Hilary he will possess these arms and will bear allegiance to the lord king, Henry, namely the son of the empress Maud, and that he will bear these arms in his service according to his order and in allegiance to the lord king and his realm. And let none of those who hold these arms sell them or pledge them or offer them, or in any other way alienate them; neither let a lord in any way deprive his men of them either by forfeiture or by gift, or as surety or in any other manner.

5. If anyone bearing these arms shall have died, let his arms remain for his heir. But if the heir should not be of age to use the arms, should the need arise, let him who has him in ward likewise have the custody of his arms, and let him find a man who can use them in the service of the lord king, until the heir be of age to bear arms, and then let him have them.

6. Let every burgess who has more arms than he ought to have according to this assize, sell them or give them away or otherwise bestow them on such a man as will retain them for the service of the lord king of England. And let none of them keep more arms than he ought to have according to this assize.

7. Item, let no Jew keep in his possession a hauberk or an "aubergel", but let him sell them or give them away or otherwise dispose of them that they may remain in the king's service.

8. Item, let no one carry arms out of England except by order of the lord king; neither let anyone sell arms to anyone who will carry them out of England.

9. Item, let the justices cause oaths to be sworn by lawful knights and other free and lawful men of the hundreds or boroughs, as many as they deem fit, who shall have chattels of such value as makes it necessary for him to have a hauberk, an "aubergel", a lance and a shield, according as has been said, namely that, one by one, they will give the names of all in their hundreds and neighbourhoods and boroughs who have 16 marks either in chattels or rent, and likewise of those who have 10 marks. And afterwards let the justices cause to be enrolled all those who have sworn on oath and others, who have this amount of chattels or rents, and also what arms they ought to possess according to the value of their chattels or rents, and afterwards, in their presence and in the hearing of them as a body, let the justices cause this assize concerning the bearing of arms to be read, and let them swear on oath that they will have these arms according to the aforesaid value of chattels and rents and that they will hold them in the service of the lord king in accordance with the said assize at the command and allegiance of the lord king, Henry, and of his realm. If indeed it should happen that any of those who ought to possess these arms are not present in the county at the time the justices shall be in that county, let the justices appoint him a time in another county to come before them. And if he shall not have come to them in any county through which they shall pass, and shall not have been in this land, let a time be appointed him at Westminster in the octave of Michaelmas there to take his oath, as he values his life and all his possessions. And let

order be given him to have arms according as he ought to have before the feast of St Hilary.

10. Item, let the justices cause it to be announced throughout all the counties through which they shall pass, that those who have not these arms, according as has been said, the lord king will seize their persons, but will on no account take from them their land or their chattels.

11. Item, let no one swear concerning lawful and free men who has not 16 marks or 10 marks in chattels.

12. Item, let the justices command throughout all the counties that no one, as he values his life and his possessions, may buy or sell any ship with intent to take it out of England, or may export timber or cause it to be exported out of England. And the king commands that none shall be accepted for the oath of arms except a free man.

THE ASSIZE OF THE FOREST (1184)

THIS, HENRY II'S FORMULATION OF LAWS REGULATING THE FOREST, OR THE KING'S PRESERVES, REPRESENTS A VITAL PART OF ENGLISH LAW IN MEDIEVAL TIMES.

This is the assize of the lord king, Henry, son of Maud, concerning the forest, and concerning his deer in England; it was made at Woodstock with the advice and assent of the archbishops, bishops, barons, earls, and magnates of England.

1. First he forbids that anyone shall transgress against him in regard to his hunting-rights or his forests in any respect; and he wills that no trust shall be put in the fact that hitherto he has had mercy for the sake of their chattels upon those who have offended against him in regard to his hunting-rights and his forests. For if anyone shall offend against him hereafter and be convicted thereof, he wills that full justice be exacted from the offender as was done in the time of King Henry, his grandfather.

2. Item, he forbids that anyone shall have bows or arrows or hounds or harriers in his forests unless he shall have as his guarantor the king or some other person who can legally act as his guarantor.

3. Item, he forbids anyone to give or sell anything to the wasting or destruction of his own woods which lie within the forest of King Henry: he graciously allows them to take from their woods what they need, but this is to be done without wasting and at the oversight of the king's forester.

4. Item, he has commanded that all who have woods within the bounds of the royal forest shall install suitable foresters in their woods; for these let those to whom the woods belong act as sureties, or let them find such suitable sureties as can give redress if the foresters shall transgress in anything which pertains to the lord king. And those who have woods without the bounds of the forest visitation but in which the venison of the lord king is covered by the king's peace, shall have no forester, unless they have sworn to the assize of the lord king, and to keep the peace of his hunt and to provide someone as keeper of his wood.

5. Item, the lord king has commanded that his foresters shall have a care to the forest of the knights and others who have woods within the bounds of the royal forest, in order that the woods be not destroyed; for, if in spite of this, the woods shall be destroyed, let those whose woods have been destroyed know full well that reparation will be exacted from their persons or their lands, and not from another.

6. Item, the lord king has commanded that all his foresters shall swear to maintain his assize of the forest, as he made it, according to their ability, and that they will not molest knights or other worthy men on account of anything which the lord king has granted them in respect of their woods.

7. Item, the king has commanded that in any county in which he has venison, twelve knights shall be appointed to guard his venison and his "vert" together with the forest; and that four knights shall be appointed to pasture cattle in his woods and to receive and protect his right of pannage. Also the king forbids anyone to graze cattle in his own woods, if they lie within the bounds of the forest, before the king's woods have been pastured; and the pasturing of cattle in the woods of the lord king begins fifteen days before Michaelmas and lasts until fifteen days after Michaelmas.

8. And the king has commanded that if his forester shall have demesne woods of the lord king in his custody, and those woods shall be destroyed, and he cannot show any just cause why the woods were destroyed, the person of the forester himself and not something else shall be seized.

9. Item, the king forbids that any clerk shall transgress either in regard to his venison or to his forests; he has given strict orders to his foresters that if they find any such trespassing there, they shall not hesitate to lay hands upon them and to arrest them and to secure their persons, and the king himself will give them his full warrant.

10. Item, the king has commanded that his "assarts", both new and old, shall be inspected, and likewise both "purprestures" and the wastes of the forest; and that each shall be set down in writing by itself.

11. Item, the king has commanded that the archbishops, bishops, earls, barons, knights, freeholders and all men shall heed the summons of his master-forester to come and hear the pleas of the lord king concerning his forests and to transact his other business in the county court, if they would avoid falling into the mercy of the lord king.

12. At Woodstock the king commanded that safe pledges shall be taken from any who shall be guilty of one transgression in respect of the forest, and likewise if he shall trespass a second time; but if he shall transgress a third time, for this third offence no other pledges shall be taken from him nor anything else, except the very person of the transgressor.

13. Item, the king has commanded that every male attaining the age of twelve years and dwelling within the jurisdictions of the hunt, shall swear to keep the king's peace, and likewise the clerks who hold lands in lay fee there.

14. Item, the king has commanded that the mutilation of dogs shall be carried out wherever his wild animals have their lairs and were wont to do so.

15. Item, the king has commanded that no tanner or bleacher of hides shall dwell in his forests outside of a borough.

16. Item, the king has commanded that none shall hereafter in any wise hunt wild animals by night with a view to their capture, either within the forest or without, wheresoever the animals frequent or have their lairs or were wont to do so, under pain of imprisonment for one year and the payment of a fine or ransom at his pleasure. And no one, under the same penalty, shall place any obstruction whether alive or dead in the path of his beasts in his forests and woods or in other places disafforested by himself or his predecessors.

THE MAGNA CARTA 1215

THE GREAT CHARTER WHICH ATTEMPTED TO LIMIT THE POWERS OF THE KING AND PRESERVE THOSE OF THE BARONS.

John, by the grace of God, king of England, lord of Ireland, duke of Normandy and Aquitaine, and count of Anjou, to the archbishops, bishops, abbots, earls, barons, justiciars, foresters, sheriffs, stewards, servants, and to all his bailiffs and faithful subjects, greeting. Know that we, out of reverence for God and for the salvation of our soul and those of all our ancestors and heirs, for the honour of God and the exaltation of holy church, and for the reform of our realm, on the advice of our venerable fathers, Stephen, archbishop of Canterbury, primate of all England and cardinal of the holy Roman church, Henry archbishop of Dublin, William of London, Peter of Winchester, Jocelyn of Bath and Glastonbury, Hugh of Lincoln, Walter of Worcester, William of Coventry and Benedict of Rochester, bishops, of master Pandulf, subdeacon and member of the household of the lord pope, of brother Aymeric, master of the order of Knights Templar in England, and of the noble men William Marshal earl of Pembroke, William earl of Salisbury, William earl of Warenne, William earl of Arundel, Alan of Galloway constable of Scotland, Warin fitz Gerold, Peter fitz Herbert, Hubert de Burgh seneschal of Poitou, Hugh de Neville, Matthew fitz Herbert, Thomas Basset, Alan Basset, Philip de Aubeney, Robert of Ropsley, John Marshal, John fitz Hugh, and others, our faithful subjects:

(1) In the first place have granted to God, and by this our present charter confirmed for us and our heirs for ever that the English church shall be free, and shall have its rights undiminished and its liberties unimpaired; and it is our will that it be thus observed; which is evident from the fact that, before the quarrel between us and our barons began, we willingly and spontaneously granted and by our charter confirmed the freedom of elections which is reckoned most important and very essential to the English church, and obtained confirmation of it from the lord pope Innocent

III; the which we will observe and we wish our heirs to observe it in good faith for ever. We have also granted to all free men of our kingdom, for ourselves and our heirs for ever, all the liberties written below, to be had and held by them and their heirs of us and our heirs.

(2) If any of our earls or barons or others holding of us in chief by knight service dies, and at his death his heir be of full age and owe relief he shall have his inheritance on payment of the old relief, namely the heir or heirs of an earl; £100 for a whole earl's barony, the heir or heirs of a baron £100 for a whole barony, the heir or heirs of a knight 100s, at most, for a whole knight's fee; and he who owes less shall give less according to the ancient usage of fiefs.

(3) If, however, the heir of any such be under age and a ward, he shall have his inheritance when he comes of age without paying relief and without making fine.

(4) The guardian of the land of such an heir who is under age shall take from the land of the heir no more than reasonable revenues, reasonable customary dues and reasonable services, and that without destruction and waste of men or goods; and if we commit the wardship of the land of any such to a sheriff, or to any other who is answerable to us for its revenues, and he destroys or wastes what he has wardship of, we will take compensation from him and the land shall be committed to two lawful and discreet men of that fief, who shall be answerable for the revenues to us or to him to whom we have assigned them; and if we give or sell to anyone the wardship of any such land and he causes destruction or waste therein, he shall lose that wardship, and it shall be transferred to two lawful and discreet men of that fief, who shall similarly be answerable to us as is aforesaid.

(5) Moreover, so long as he has the wardship of the land, the guardian shall keep in repair the houses, parks,

preserves, ponds, mills and other things pertaining to the land out of the revenues from it; and he shall restore to the heir when he comes of age his land fully stocked with ploughs and the means of husbandry according to what the season of husbandry requires and the revenues of the land can reasonably bear.

(6) Heirs shall be married without disparagement, yet so that before the marriage is contracted those nearest in blood to the heir shall have notice.

(7) A widow shall have her marriage portion and inheritance forthwith and with-out difficulty after the death of her husband; nor shall she pay anything to have her dower or her marriage portion or the inheritance which she and her husband held on the day of her husband's death; and she may remain in her husband's house for forty days after his death, within which time her dower shall be assigned to her.

(8) No widow shall be forced to marry so long as she wishes to live without a husband, provided that she gives security not to marry without our consent if she holds of us, or without the consent of her lord of whom she holds, if she holds of another.

(9) Neither we nor our bailiffs will seize for any debt any land or rent, so long as the chattels of the debtor are sufficient to repay the debt; nor will those who have gone surety for the debtor be distrained so long as the principal debtor is himself able to pay the debt; and if the principal debtor fails to pay the debt, having nothing where-with to pay it, then shall the sureties answer for the debt; and they shall, if they wish, have the lands and rents of the debtor until they are reimbursed for the debt which they have paid for him, unless the principal debtor can show that he has discharged his obligation in the matter to the said sureties.

(10) If anyone who has borrowed from the Jews any sum, great or small, dies before it is repaid, the debt shall not bear interest as long as the heir is under age, of whom-soever he holds; and if the debt falls into our hands, we will not take anything except the principal mentioned in the bond.

(11) And if anyone dies indebted to the Jews, his wife shall have her dower and pay nothing of that debt; and if the dead man leaves children who are under age, they shall be provided with necessaries befitting the holding of the deceased; and the debt shall be paid out of the residue, reserving, however, service due to lords of the land; debts owing to others than Jews shall be dealt with in like manner.

(12) No scutage or aid shall be imposed in our kingdom unless by common counsel of our kingdom, except for ransoming our person, for making our eldest son a knight, and for once marrying our eldest daughter; and for these only a reasonable aid shall be levied. Be it done in like manner concerning aids from the city of London.

(13) And the city of London shall have all its ancient liberties and free customs as well by land as by water. Furthermore, we will and grant that all other cities, boroughs, towns, and ports shall have all their liberties and free customs.

(14) And to obtain the common counsel of the kingdom about the assessing of an aid (except in the three cases aforesaid) or of a scutage, we will cause to be summoned the archbishops, bishops, abbots, earls and greater barons, individually by our letters — and, in addition, we will cause to be summoned generally through our sheriffs and bailiffs all those holding of us in chief — for a fixed date, namely, after the expiry of at least forty days, and to a fixed place; and in all letters of such summons we will specify the reason for the summons. And when the summons has thus been made, the business shall proceed on the day appointed, according to the counsel of those present, though not all have come who were summoned.

(15) We will not in future grant any one the right to take an aid from his free men, except for ransoming his person, for making his eldest son a knight and for once marrying his eldest daughter, and for these only a reasonable aid shall be levied.

(16) No one shall be compelled to do greater service for a knight's fee or for any other free holding than is due from it.

(17) Common pleas shall not follow our court, but shall be held in some fixed place.

(18) Recognitions of *novel disseisin*, of *mort d'ancester*, and of *darrein presentment*, shall not be held elsewhere than in the counties to which they relate, and in this manner — we, or, if we should be out of the realm, our chief justiciar, will send two justices through each county four times a year, who, with four knights of each county chosen by the county, shall hold the said assizes in the county and on the day and in the place of meeting of the county court.

(19) And if the said assizes cannot all be held on the day of the county court, there shall stay behind as many of the knights and freeholders who were present at the county court on that day as are necessary for the sufficient making of judgments, according to the amount of business to be done.

(20) A free man shall not be amerced for a trivial offence except in accordance with the degree of the offence, and for a grave offence he shall be amerced in accordance with its gravity, yet saving his way of living; and a merchant in the same way, saving his stock-in-trade; and a villein shall be amerced in the same way, saving his means of livelihood — if they have fallen into our mercy: and none of the aforesaid amercements shall be imposed except by the oath of good men of the neighbourhood.

(21) Earls and barons shall not be amerced except by their peers, and only in accordance with the degree of the offence.

(22) No clerk shall be amerced in respect of his lay holding except after the manner of the others aforesaid and not according to the amount of his ecclesiastical benefice.

(23) No vill or individual shall be compelled to make bridges at river banks, except those who from of old are legally bound to do so.

(24) No sheriff, constable, coroners, or others of our bailiffs, shall hold pleas of our crown.

(25) All counties, hundreds, wapentakes and trithings shall be at the old rents with- out any additional payment, except our demesne manors.

(26) If anyone holding a lay fief of us dies and our sheriff or bailiff shows our letters patent of summons for a debt that the deceased owed us, it shall be lawful for our sheriff or bailiff to attach and make a list of chattels of the deceased found upon the lay fief to the value of that debt under the supervision of law-worthy men, provided that none of the chattels shall be removed until the debt which is manifest has been paid to us in full; and the residue shall be left to the executors for carrying out the will of the deceased. And if nothing is owing to us from him, all the chattels shall accrue to the deceased, saving to his wife and children their reasonable shares.

(27) If any free man dies without leaving a will, his chattels shall be distributed by his nearest kinsfolk and friends under the supervision of the church, saving to every one the debts which the deceased owed him.

(28) No constable or other bailiff of ours shall take anyone's corn or other chattels unless he pays on the spot in cash for them or can delay payment by arrangement with the seller.

(29) No constable shall compel any knight to give money instead of castle-guard if he is willing to do the guard himself or through another good man, if for some good reason he cannot do it himself; and if we lead or send him on military service, he shall be excused guard in proportion to the time that because of us he has been on service.

(30) No sheriff, or bailiff of ours, or anyone else shall take the horses or carts of any free man for transport work save with the agreement of that freeman.

(31) Neither we nor our bailiffs will take, for castles or other works of ours, timber which is not ours, except with the agreement of him whose timber it is.

(32) We will not hold for more than a year and a day the lands of those convicted of felony, and then the lands shall be handed over to the lords of the fiefs.

(33) Henceforth all fish-weirs shall be cleared completely from the Thames and the Medway and throughout all England, except along the sea coast.

(34) The writ called *Praecipe* shall not in future be issued to anyone in respect of any holding whereby a free man may lose his court.

(35) Let there be one measure for wine throughout our kingdom, and one measure for ale, and one measure for corn, namely "the London quarter"; and one width for cloths whether dyed, russet or halberget, namely two ells within the selvedges. Let it be the same with weights as with measures.

(36) Nothing shall be given or taken in future for the writ of inquisition of life or limbs: instead it shall be granted free of charge and not refused.

(37) If anyone holds of us by fee-farm, by socage, or by burgage, and holds land of another by knight service, we will not, by reason of that fee-farm, socage, or burgage, have the wardship of his heir or of land of his that is of the fief of the other; nor will we have custody of the fee-farm, socage, or burgage, unless such fee-farm owes knight service. We will not have custody of anyone's heir or land which he holds of another by knight service by reason of any petty serjeanty which he holds of us by the service of rendering to us knives or arrows or the like.

(38) No bailiff shall in future put anyone to trial upon his own bare word, without reliable witnesses produced for this purpose.

(39) No free man shall be arrested or imprisoned or disseised or outlawed or exiled or in any way victimised, neither will we attack him or send anyone to attack him, except by the lawful judgment of his peers or by the law of the land.

(40) To no one will we sell, to no one will we refuse or delay right or justice.

(41) All merchants shall be able to go out of and come into England safely and securely and stay and travel throughout England, as well by land as by water, for buying and selling by the ancient and right customs free from all evil tolls, except in time of war and if they are of the land that is at war with us. And if such are found in our land at the beginning of a war, they shall be attached, without injury to their persons or goods, until we, or our chief justiciar, know how merchants of our land are treated who were found in the land at war with us when war broke out; and if ours are safe there, the others shall be safe in our land.

(42) It shall be lawful in future for anyone, without prejudicing the allegiance due to us, to leave our kingdom and return safely and securely by land and water, save, in the public interest, for a short period in time of war — except for those imprisoned or outlawed in accordance with the law of the kingdom and natives of a land that is at war with us and merchants (who shall be treated as aforesaid).

(43) If anyone who holds of some escheat such as the honour of Wallingford, Nottingham, Boulogne, Lancaster, or of other escheats which are in our hands and are baronies dies, his heir shall give no other relief and do no other service to us than he would have done to the baron if that barony had been in the baron's hands; and we will hold it in the same manner in which the baron held it.

(44) Men who live outside the forest need not henceforth come before our justices of the forest upon a general summons, unless they are impleaded or are sureties for any person or persons who are attached for forest offences.

(45) We will not make justices, constables, sheriffs or bailiffs save of such as know the law of the kingdom and mean to observe it well.

(46) All barons who have founded abbeys for which they have charters of the kings of England or ancient tenure shall have the custody of them during vacancies, as they ought to have.

(47) All forests that have been made forest in our time shall be immediately dis-afforested; and so be it done with river-banks that have been made preserves by us in our time.

(48) All evil customs connected with forests and warrens, foresters and warreners, sheriffs and their officials, river-banks and their wardens shall immediately be inquired into in each county by twelve sworn knights of the same county who are to be chosen by good men of the same county, and within forty days of the completion of the inquiry shall be utterly abolished by them so as never to be restored, provided that we, or our justiciar if we are not in England, know of it first.

(49) We will immediately return all hostages and charters given to us by Englishmen, as security for peace or faithful service.

(50) We will remove completely from office the relations

of Gerard de Athée so that in future they shall have no office in England, namely Engelard de Cigogné, Peter and Guy and Andrew de Chanceaux, Guy de Cigogné, Geoffrey de Martigny and his brothers, Philip Marc and his brothers and his nephew Geoffrey, and all their following.

(51) As soon as peace is restored, we will remove from the kingdom all foreign knights, cross-bowmen, serjeants, and mercenaries, who have come with horses and arms to the detriment of the kingdom.

(52) If anyone has been disseised of or kept out of his lands, castles, franchises or his right by us without the legal judgment of his peers, we will immediately restore them to him: and if a dispute arises over this, then let it be decided by the judgment of the twenty-five barons who are mentioned below in the clause for securing the peace: for all the things, however, which anyone has been disseised or kept out of without the lawful judgment of his peers by king Henry, our father, or by king Richard, our brother, which we have in our hand or are held by others, to whom we are bound to warrant them, we will have the usual period of respite of crusaders, excepting those things about which a plea was started or an inquest made by our command before we took the cross; when however we return from our pilgrimage, or if by any chance we do not go on it, we will at once do full justice therein.

(53) We will have the same respite, and in the same manner, in the doing of justice in the matter of the disafforesting or retaining of the forests which Henry our father or Richard our brother afforested, and in the matter of the wardship of lands which are of the fief of another, wardships of which sort we have hitherto had by reason of a fief which anyone held of us by knight service, and in the matter of abbeys founded on the fief of another, not on a fief of our own, in which the lord of the fief claims he has a right; and when we have returned, or if we do not set out on our pilgrimage, we will at once do full justice to those who complain of these things.

(54) No one shall be arrested or imprisoned upon the appeal of a woman for the death of anyone except her husband.

(55) All fines made with us unjustly and against the law

of the land, and all amercements imposed unjustly and against the law of the land, shall be entirely remitted, or else let them be settled by the judgment of the twenty-five barons who are mentioned below in the clause for securing the peace, or by the judgment of the majority of the same, along with the aforesaid Stephen, archbishop of Canterbury, if he can be present, and such others as he may wish to associate with himself for this purpose, and if he cannot be present the business shall nevertheless proceed without him, provided that if any one or more of the aforesaid twenty-five barons are in a like suit, they shall be removed from the judgment of the case in question, and others chosen, sworn and put in their place by the rest of the same twenty-five for this case only.

(56) If we have disseised or kept out. Welshmen from lands or liberties or other things without the legal judgment of their peers in England or in Wales, they shall be immediately restored to them; and if a dispute arises over this, then let it be decided in the March by the judgment of their peers — for holdings in England according to the law of England, for holdings in Wales according to the law of Wales, and for holdings in the March according to the law of the March. Welshmen shall do the same to us and ours.

(57) For all the things, however, which any Welshman was disseised of or kept out of without the lawful judgment of his peers by king Henry, our father, or king Richard, our brother, which we have in our hand or which are held by others, to whom we are bound to warrant them, we will have the usual period of respite of crusaders, excepting those things about which a plea was started or an inquest made by our command before we took the cross; when however we return, or if by any chance we do not set out on our pilgrimage, we will at once do full justice to them in accordance with the laws of the Welsh and the foresaid regions.

(58) We will give back at once the son of Llywelyn and all the hostages from Wales and the charters that were handed over to us as security for peace.

(59) We will act toward Alexander, king of the Scots,

concerning the return of his sisters and hostages and concerning his franchises and his right in the same manner in which we act towards our other barons of England, unless it ought to be otherwise by the charters which we have from William his father, formerly king of the Scots, and this shall be determined by the judgment of his peers in our court.

(60) All these aforesaid customs and liberties which we have granted to be observed in our kingdom as far as it pertains to us towards our men, all of our kingdom, clerks as well as laymen, shall observe as far as it pertains to them towards their men.

(61) Since, moreover, for God and the betterment of our kingdom and for the better allaying of the discord that has arisen between us and our barons we have granted all these things aforesaid, wishing them to enjoy the use of them unimpaired and unshaken for ever, we give and grant them the under-written security, namely, that the barons shall choose any twenty-five barons of the kingdom they wish, who must with all their might observe, hold and cause to be observed, the peace and liberties which we have granted and confirmed to them by this present charters of ours, so that if we, or our justiciar, or our bailiffs or any one of our servants offend in any way against anyone or transgress any of the articles of the peace or the security and the offence be notified to four of the aforesaid twenty-five barons, those four barons shall come to us, or to our justiciar if we are out of the kingdom, and, laying the transgression before us, shall petition us to have that transgression corrected without delay. And if we do not correct the transgression, or if we are out of the kingdom, if our justiciar does not correct it, within forty days, reckoning from the time it was brought to our notice or to that of our justiciar if we were out of the kingdom, the aforesaid four barons shall refer that case to the rest of the twenty-five barons and those twenty-five barons together with the community of the whole land shall distrain and distress us in every way they can, namely, by seizing castles, lands, possessions, and in such other ways as they can, saving our person and the persons of our queen and

our children, until, in their opinion, amends have been made; and when amends have been made, they shall obey us as they did before. And let anyone in the land who wishes take an oath to obey the orders of the said twenty-five barons for the execution of all the aforesaid matters, and with them to distress us as much as he can, and we publicly and freely give anyone leave to take the oath who wishes to take it and we will never prohibit anyone from taking it. Indeed, all those in the land who are unwilling of themselves and of their own accord to take an oath to the twenty-five barons to help them to distrain and distress us, we will make them take the oath as aforesaid at our command. And if any of the twenty-five barons dies or leaves the country or is in any other way prevented from carrying out the things aforesaid, the rest of the aforesaid twenty-five barons shall choose as they think fit another one in his place, and he shall take the oath like the rest. In all matters the execution of which is committed to these twenty-five barons, if it should happen that these twenty-five are present yet disagree among themselves about anything, or if some of those summoned will not or cannot be present, that shall be held as fixed and established which the majority of those present ordained or commanded, exactly as if all the twenty-five had consented to it; and the said twenty-five shall swear that they will faithfully observe all the things aforesaid and will do all they can to get them observed. And we will procure nothing from anyone, either personally or through anyone else, whereby any of these concessions and liberties might be revoked or diminished; and if any such thing is procured, let it be void and null, and we will never use it either personally or through another.

(62) And we have fully remitted and pardoned to everyone all the ill-will, indignation and rancour that have arisen between us and our men, clergy and laity, from the time of the quarrel. Furthermore, we have fully remitted to all, clergy and laity, and as far as pertains to us have completely forgiven, all trespasses occasioned by the same quarrel between Easter in the sixteenth year of our reign and the restoration of peace. And, besides, we have

caused to be made for them letters testimonial patent of the lord Stephen archbishop of Canterbury, of the lord Henry archbishop of Dublin and of the aforementioned bishops and of master Pandulf about this security and the aforementioned concessions.

(63) Wherefore we wish and firmly enjoin that the English church shall be free, and that the men in our kingdom shall have and hold all the aforesaid liberties, rights and concessions well and peacefully, freely and quietly, fully and completely, for themselves and their heirs from us and our heirs, in all matters and in all places for ever, as is aforesaid. An oath, moreover, has been taken, as well on our part as on the part of the barons, that all these things aforesaid shall be observed in good faith and without evil disposition. Witness the above-mentioned and many others. Given by our hand in the meadow which is called Runnymede between Windsor and Staines on the fifteenth day of June, in the seventeenth year of our reign.

THE PROVISIONS OF OXFORD (1258)

THIS DESCRIPTION OF THE PROVISIONS OF OXFORD REVEALS HOW
THE BARONS CURTAILED, AT LEAST TEMPORARILY, THE POWER OF HENRY III.

THE PROVISION
made at Oxford

It was provided that from each county there are to be chosen four discreet and law-worthy knights, who on every day when the county is held are to meet to hear all complaints of any trespasses and injuries whatsoever inflicted upon any persons whatsoever by sheriffs, bailiffs, or whatsoever others, and to make the attachments arising out of the said complaints pending the first coming of the chief justiciar to those parts. In such wise that they take sufficient sureties from the plaintiff that he will proceed with the suit and likewise from him who is complained of that he will appear and submit to the law before the said justiciar at his first coming. And the aforesaid four knights are to have all the aforesaid complaints with their attachments enrolled in proper order and sequence, namely arranged according to hundred and each hundred separately. So that the aforesaid justiciar on his first coming can hear and determine the aforesaid complaints one by one from each hundred. And they are to let the sheriff know that they are summoning before the said justiciar at his next coming for days and places which he will make known to them, all his hundredors and bailiffs. So that every hundredor shall produce all plaintiffs and defendants of his bailiwick in the order in which the said justiciar shall think fit to take the pleas of that hundred; and enough men of such a sort — as well knights as other free and law-worthy men — from his bailiwick that the truth of the matter may be the better found, in such a way that all are not troubled at one and the same time, but as many appear as can have their cases heard and determined in one day. Also it was provided that no regard is to be had for any knight of the aforesaid counties because of exemption by a charter of the lord king from being put on juries or assizes, nor is he to be quit in respect of this provision made in this wise for the common benefit of the whole kingdom.

THOSE CHOSEN FROM
the lord king's side

The lord bishop of London. The lord bishop elect of Winchester. The lord H(enry), son of the king of Germany. The lord J(ohn), earl Warenne. The lord Guy de Lusignan. The lord W(illiam) de Valence. The lord J(ohn), earl of Warwick. The lord John Mansel. Brother J(ohn) of Darlington. The abbot of Westminster. The lord H(enry) of Hengham.

THOSE CHOSEN FROM
the side of the earls and barons

The lord bishop of Worcester. The lord Simon, earl of Leicester. The lord Richard, earl of Gloucester. The lord Humphrey, earl of Hereford. The lord Roger the marshal. The lord Roger of Mortimer. The lord J(ohn) fitz Geoffrey. The lord Hugh Bigod. The lord Richard de Grey. The lord W(illiam) Bardolf. The lord P(eter) of Montfort. The lord Hugh the Dispenser.

And if it should happen that of necessity any one of those cannot be present, the rest of them are to choose whom they will for the other one needed in place of the absentee to proceed with the business.

THIS THE COMMUNITY
of England swore at Oxford

We, so and so, make known to all people that we have sworn on the holy gospels, and are held together by this oath, and promise in good faith, that each one of us and all of us together will help each other, both ourselves and those belonging to us, against all people, doing right and taking nothing that we cannot take without doing wrong, saving faith to the king and the crown. And we promise upon the same oath that none of us will ever take anything of land or movables whereby this oath can be disturbed or in any way impaired. And if any one acts contrary to this, we will hold him as a mortal enemy.

THIS IS THE OATH
of the twenty-four

Each one swore on the holy gospels that he for the glory of God and in loyalty to the king and for the benefit of the kingdom will ordain and treat with the aforesaid sworn persons upon the reform and improvement of the condition of the kingdom. And that he will not fail for gift or for promise, for love or for hatred, for fear of any one, for gain or for loss, loyally to act according to

the tenour of the letter that the king has given on this and his son likewise.

THIS THE CHIEF JUSTICIAR
of England swore

He swears that he will well and loyally according to his power do what belongs to the justiciar's office of dispensing justice to all men for the profit of the king and the kingdom, in accordance with the provision made and to be made by the twenty-four, and by the king's council and the magnates of the land, who will swear to help and support him in these things.

THIS THE CHANCELLOR
of England swore

That he will not seal any writ except a writ of course without the order of the king and of the councillors who are present. Nor will he seal a gift of a great wardship or of a large sum of money or of escheats without the assent of the full council or of the greater part of it. And that he will not seal anything that is contrary to what has been and will be ordained by the twenty-four or by the greater part of them. And that he will not take any reward otherwise than is agreed for others. And he will be given a companion in the way that the council will provide.

THIS IS THE OATH
that the keepers of the castles took

That they will keep the king's castles loyally and in good faith for the use of the king and his heirs. And that they will give them up to the king or his heirs and to no other and (do it) through his council and in no other way, that is to say, through men of standing in the land elected to his council or through the greater part of them. And this form above written is to last full twelve years. And thenceforward they shall not be prevented by this establishment and this oath from being able to give them up freely to the king or his heirs.

THESE ARE THOSE WHO
are sworn of the king's council

The archbishop of Canterbury, the bishop of Worcester, the earl of Leicester, the earl of Gloucester, the Earl Marshal, Peter of Savoy, the count of Aumale, the earl of Warwick, the earl of Hereford, John Mansel, John fitz Geoffrey, Peter of Montfort, Richard de Grey, Roger of Mortimer, James of Audley.

The king's twelve have chosen from the twelve of the community: the earl Roger the marshal, Hugh Bigod. And the party for the community has chosen from the twelve who are of the king's side: the earl of Warwick, John Mansel.

And these four have power to choose the council of the king, and when they have chosen, they shall show them to the twenty-four and what the greater part of these agree on shall hold good.

THESE ARE THE TWELVE
who are chosen by the barons to treat in three parliaments a year with the king's council for all the community of the land about the common business

The bishop of London, the earl of Winchester, the earl of Hereford, Philip Basset, John de Balliol, John de Verdun, John de Grey, Roger de Sumery, Roger de Mohaut, Hugh the Dispenser, Thomas de Gresley, Giles d'Argentein.

THESE ARE THE TWENTY-FOUR
who are appointed by the community to treat of an aid for the king

The bishop of Worcester, the bishop of London, the bishop of Salisbury, the earl of Leicester, the earl of Gloucester, the Earl Marshal, Peter of Savoy, the earl of Hereford, the count of Aumale, the earl of Winchester, the earl of Oxford, John fitz Geoffrey, John de Grey, John de Balliol, Roger of Mortimer, Roger de Mohaut, Roger de Sumery, Peter of Montfort, Thomas de Gresley, Fulk of Kerdiston, Giles d'Argentein, John Kyriel, Philip Basset, Giles of Erdinton.

And if any of these cannot be there, or will not, those who are there are to have the power of choosing another in his place.

OF THE CONDITION
of holy church

It is to be remembered that the condition of holy church is to be amended by the twenty-four chosen to reform the condition of the kingdom of England, when they see place and time, in accordance with the power they have in that regard by the letter of the king of England.

OF THE CHIEF JUSTICIAR

Furthermore that a justiciar be appointed, one or two, and what power he is to have, and that he is not to be for more than a year. So that at the end of the year he answer before the king and his council for his time and before the one who is to succeed him.

OF THE TREASURER,
and of the exchequer

Likewise of the treasurer. Except that he is to render account at the end of the year. And other good men are to be put at the exchequer in accordance with the ordinance of the aforesaid twenty-four. And there all the issues of the land are to come and no part of them elsewhere. And what is seen to need amendment is to be amended.

OF THE CHANCELLOR

Likewise of the chancellor. So that at the end of

the year he answer for his time. And that he seal not out of course by the will of the king alone; but do it through the councillors who are with the king.

OF THE POWER OF THE
justiciar and of the bailiffs

~ The chief justiciar has power to amend the wrongs committed by all other justices and by bailiffs, and earls and barons and all other men, in accordance with the law and right of the land. And writs are to be pleaded according to the law of the land, and in proper places. And that the justiciar take nothing unless it be a present of bread and wine and such things, that is to say food and drink, as one has been accustomed to bring to the tables of men of quality for the day. And this same thing is to be understood of all the councillors of the king and of all his bailiffs. And that no bailiff because of a plea or of his office take any reward by his own hand or through another person in any way. And if he is convicted, that he be condemned to make fine, and he who gives also. And so it is necessary for the king to give to his justiciar and to his people who serve him, so that they have no need to take anything from anyone else.

OF SHERIFFS

~ Sheriffs are to be provided, loyal people and good men and landholders; so that in each county a vavassour of the same county be sheriff, to treat the people of the county well, loyally and justly. And that he take no reward, and that he is not to be sheriff for more than a year at a time. And that in the year he render his accounts at the exchequer and answer for his term. And that the king grant him of his own according to his estimate of how he can keep the county rightly. And that he take no reward, neither he nor his bailiffs. And if they are convicted, they are to be condemned to make fine.
It is to be remembered that such amendment is to be applied to the Jewry and to the wardens of the Jewry that the oath relating thereto may be kept.

OF ESCHEATORS

~ Good escheators are to be appointed. And that they take nothing of the goods of the dead from such lands as ought to be in the king's hand. But that the executors have free administration of the goods as soon as they have satisfied the king if they owe him a debt. And this in accordance with the form of the charter of liberty. And that enquiry be made into wrongs done by escheators in the past, and that amendment be made of such and such. Neither tallage nor other thing is to be taken save as it ought to be according to the charter of liberty.
The charter of liberty is to be kept firmly.

OF THE EXCHANGE OF LONDON

~ It is to be remembered about amending the exchange of London and about the city of London and all the other cities of the king that have gone to shame and destruction through tallages and other oppressions.

OF THE HOUSEHOLD
of the king and of the queen

~ It is to be remembered to amend the households of the king and queen.

OF THE PARLIAMENTS,
when they shall be held in the year and how

~ It is to be remembered that the twenty-four have ordained that there are to be three parliaments a year. The first on the octave of Michaelmas. The second, the morrow of Candlemas. The third, the first day of June, that is to say, three weeks before St John's day. To these three parliaments shall come the chosen councillors of the king, even if they are not summoned, to view the state of the kingdom and to treat of the common business of the kingdom and of the king likewise. And at other times they are to meet when there is need, on a summons of the king. And it is to be remembered that the community is to choose twelve good men who shall come to the parliaments and at other times, when there is need, when the king or his council shall summon them to treat of the common business of the king and of the kingdom. And that the community are to hold as established what these twelve shall do. And this is to be done to spare the community expense.

Fifteen are to be named by these four, that is to say by the earl Marshal, the earl of Warwick, Hugh Bigod and John Mansel, who have been chosen by the twenty-four to name the aforesaid fifteen who are to be of the king's council. And they are to be confirmed by the aforesaid twenty-four or by the greater part of them. And they are to have authority to advise the king in good faith on the government of the kingdom and on all things pertaining to the king or the kingdom. And (authority) to amend and redress all the things they see need to be redressed and amended. And (authority) over the chief justiciar, and over all other people. And if they cannot all be present, what the majority does shall be firm and established.

THE STATUTE OF WESTMINSTER (1275)

THIS MAGNIFICENT CODIFICATION AND INTEGRATION OF ENGLISH LAWS WAS ONE FOUNDATIONAL EDWARD I'S HIGHLY SUCCESSFUL REIGN. SOME PARTS OF IT ARE ACTUALLY STILL IN FORCE AS LAW IN THE UNITED KINGDOM.

These are the establishments of king Edward, son of king Henry, made at Westminster at his first parliament general after his coronation after the Close of Easter in the 3rd year of his reign, by his council and by the assent of archbishops, bishops, abbots, priors, earls, barons and the community of the land thereto summoned. Because our lord the king greatly wills and desires to set to rights the state of his kingdom in the things in which there is need of amendment, and this for the common profit of holy church and the kingdom; and because the state of holy church has been ill-managed and the prelates and religious of the land burdened in many ways and the people otherwise treated, and the peace less kept, than ought to be, and the laws abused and malefactors less punished than they ought to be and for that people are less afraid to do wrong, The king has ordained and established the things underwritten, which he intends to be profitable and suitable for the whole kingdom,

(c. 1) First the king wills and commands that the peace of holy church and of the land be well kept and maintained in all points, and that common justice be done to all, as well to the poor as to the rich, without regard for anyone. Because abbeys and houses of religion have been overburdened and badly affected by the coming of the great and of others who had means enough to entertain themselves and the religious have as a result been so reduced and impoverished that they could not support themselves or the burden of their accustomed charity, it is for this reason provided that no one come to eat, lodge or lie in a house of religion of anyone's patronage other than their own at the cost of the house, if he is not specially invited or requested beforehand by the ruler of the house, and that no one henceforth come to lie in a house of religion at his own cost against the will of the house. And by these statutes the king does not intend that the grace of hospitality should be withheld from the needy or that patrons of houses should be able by their coming to overburden and ruin. It is likewise provided that no one, great or small, on the strength of relationship, special friendship or other connection or on any other pretext, shall course in another's park, or fish in another's pond or stay on another's manor, or in the house of a prelate, man of religion or any other against the will and leave of the lord or his bailiff, whether at the cost of the lord thereof or at his own. And if he comes, willy nilly the lord or his bailiff, he shall cause no lock, door, window or any sort of fastening to be opened or broken by himself or anyone else, and shall take no sort of provisions or anything else, by making a show of purchasing or otherwise. And that no one cause the corn to be threshed or the corn or any sort of provisions or other goods taken of any prelate, man of religion, parson or any other, clerk or lay, by making a show of purchasing or otherwise, against the will or leave of the owner or the custodian, be it within a market town or without. And that no one take horses, oxen, wagons, carts, ships or boats for transport without the goodwill or the leave of the owner, and if he does it with his consent, then he shall immediately pay according to the covenant made between them. And they who contravene the aforesaid statutes and are convicted of this shall be committed to the king's prison and after that shall make fine according to the quantity and the kind of the trespass, as the king or his court shall think fit. And be it known that if those against whom the trespass is committed wish to sue, the damage they have suffered shall be awarded and restored to them twofold, and they that have committed the trespass shall be punished in the aforementioned way; and if no one wishes to sue, the king shall have the suit as in respect of a thing committed against his orders and against his peace. And the king will have enquiry made year by year, as he thinks fit, what people have committed such trespass, and those who are indicted in such inquests shall be attached and distrained by the great distress to come on a certain day within the space of a month into the king's court where it pleases him; and if they do not come on that day, let them be distrained again by the same distress to come on a certain day within six weeks; and if they then do not come they shall be judged as convicted and render double damages, at the king's suit, to those who have suffered the damage, and shall be severely punished according to the nature of the trespass. And the king forbids and commands that no one shall henceforth hurt, damage

or oppress any man of religion, person of holy church or anyone else because they have denied lodging or food to anybody or because someone complains in the king's court of feeling aggrieved in any of the things aforesaid, and if anyone does so and is convicted of it, he shall incur the aforesaid penalty. And it is provided that the aforesaid points shall bind as well our counsellors, justices of the forest and our other justices as other people. And so that the aforesaid points shall be maintained and kept, the king forbids, on pain of his grievous forfeiture, any prelate, abbot, man of religion, or bailiff or anyone of them or of anyone else to receive any man contrary to the aforesaid way of doing. And that no one send men, horses or dogs to stay at a house or manor of a man of religion or any other man, and that no one receive them; and he who does, shall, because it is contrary to the prohibition and command of the king, be severely punished. It is further provided that sheriffs shall not lodge in any place with more than five or six horses, or burden people of religion or others by often coming or lying at their houses or their manors.

(c. 2) It is likewise provided that when a clerk is taken on an accusation of felony and is claimed by the ordinary, he is to be handed over to him in accordance with the privilege of holy church, on such peril as pertains thereto, according to the customs used before now; and the king admonishes the prelates and enjoins them on the faith they owe him and for the common profit and the peace of the land that those who are indicted of such accusation by solemn inquest of men of standing made in the king's court they shall in no wise release without due purgation, so that the king will have no need to apply any other remedy thereto.

(c. 3) It is likewise provided that nothing from now on shall be demanded or taken or levied for the escape of a thief or a felon, until it is adjudged by justices in eyre; and he who does otherwise shall pay back what he has received to him or them who have paid it and the like amount to the king.

(c. 4) On wreck of the sea it is agreed that when a man, a dog or a cat escapes alive from a ship, neither the ship nor the boat nor anything that was in them shall be adjudged wreck, but the things shall be saved and kept, by view of the sheriff, the coroner or the king's bailiffs, in the hands of the people of the vill where the goods are found, so that if anyone sue for these goods within a year and a day and can prove that they are his or his lord's, or were lost when in his keeping, they shall be restored to him without delay; and if not, they shall remain the property of the king and be appraised by the sheriff and the coroner and given to the township to answer before the justices for wreck belonging to the king. And where wreck belongs to someone other than the king, he shall have it in like manner. And he who acts otherwise and is attainted of it, shall be sentenced to prison and make fine at the will of the king, and shall render damages also. And if a bailiff does it and is disavowed by the lord, and the lord has appropriated nothing for himself, the bailiff shall answer if he has the means, and if he has not the means the lord shall hand over the person of the bailiff to the king.

(c. 5) Because elections ought to be free the king forbids on pain of his heavy penalty any man, great or otherwise, to interfere by force of arms or by malicious conduct with the making of a free election.

(c. 6) And that no city, borough or vill, nor any man, is to be amerced without reasonable cause and in accordance with the degree of the offence, that is in the case of a freeman saving his way of living, a merchant, his stock-in-trade, a villein, saving his means of livelihood, and this by their peers.

(c. 7) On prises taken by constables or castellans from people other than those of the vills where the castles are situated, it is provided that no constable or castellan shall from now on take any sort of prise from any man other than a man from the vill where his castle is situated, and it is to be paid for or an agreement made within forty days, unless it is an ancient prise due to the king or the castle or the lord of the castle,

(c. 8) And that nothing is to be taken for *beaupleader*, as was formerly forbidden in the time of king Henry, father of the present king.

(c. 9) And because the peace of the land has been weakly kept until now for lack of good pursuit being made of felons in due manner, and especially because of liberties where felons are received, it is provided that all shall ordinarily be ready and apparalled, at the command and summons of the sheriffs or at the cry of the countryside, to pursue and arrest felons when need arises, as well within liberties as without; and the king will act severely towards those who do not do this and are convicted of it. And if default is found in the lord of a liberty, the king will take over the liberty; and if the default is in the bailiff he shall have one year's imprisonment and then be heavily fined, and if he has not the means he is to have two years' imprisonment. And if a sheriff or other bailiff, within liberties or without, for reward or on request or because of any sort of relationship, conceal or consent to or procure concealment of felonies committed in their bailiwicks, or pretend to arrest or to attach wrongdoers when in reality they could, or otherwise pretend to perform their office as any sort of favour to the wrongdoers, and are convicted of it, they shall have one year's imprisonment and then be heavily fined, and if they have no means they shall have four years' imprisonment.

(c. 10) Because of late unimportant and inexperienced people are commonly chosen for the office of coroner and there is need for substantial, lawful and experienced men to take up this office, it is provided that in every county men that are sufficient shall be chosen to be coroners from the most lawful and experienced knights who shall best know, watch over and be able to attend to this office and who will attach and present pleas of the crown according to law, and the sheriffs shall have counter-rolls with the coroners as well of appeals as of inquests, attachments and other things belonging to the office, and that no coroner shall demand or take anything from any one for doing his office on pain of the king's grievous forfeiture.

(c. 11) And because many accused of homicide, and guilty of the same, are by favourable inquests taken by sheriffs and by the king's writ called *odio et atia* replevied until the eyre of the justices itinerant, it is provided that these inquests shall from now on be taken by men of standing chosen by oath, of whom two at least shall be knights who are not connected with the prisoners by any relationship and are not otherwise suspect.

(c. 12) It is likewise provided that known felons and

those who are manifestly of bad repute and will not put themselves upon inquests for felonies that men accuse them of at the king's suit before justices, shall be remanded to a prison strong and hard1 as men who refuse to submit to the common law of the land. But this is not to be understood as applying to prisoners who are taken upon slight suspicion,

(c. 13) And the king forbids anyone to rape, or take by force a damsel under age,2 either with her consent or without it, or a married woman or a damsel of age or any other woman against her will; and if anyone does so the king will, at the suit of him who will sue within forty days, do common justice therein; and if no one begins his suit within forty days the king will sue in the matter; and those whom he finds guilty shall have two years' imprisonment and then shall make fine at the will of the king, and if they have not the means from which to be fined at the king's pleasure they are to be punished by longer imprisonment, according to what the offence demands.

(c. 14) Because it has been the practice in some counties to outlaw people appealed of commandment, force, aid and receipt during the period that one is in the process of outlawing him who is appealed of the deed, it is provided and granted by the king that no one is to be outlawed because of appeal of commandment, force, aid or receipt until the one appealed of the deed is convicted, so that there may be one uniform law for this throughout the land; but he who appeals shall not because of this omit to make his appeal of them at the next county as well as of those appealed of the deed, but the exigent shall wait in their case until those appealed of the deed have been attainted by outlawry or otherwise.

(c. 15) Because sheriffs and others have arrested and kept in prison people accused of felonies and have many times released on bail people who were not replevisable3 and have kept in prison those who were replevisable, for the sake of making a profit out of the one lot and of harassing the other; and because up to now it has not been determined with certainty who were replevisable and who not (except those who were arrested for homicide or at the command of the king or of his justices or for forest offences), it

is provided and commanded by the king that prisoners previously outlawed, those who have abjured the land, approvers, all who are taken with the mainour,1 those who have broken the king's prison, common and notorious thieves, those appealed by approvers as long as the approver is alive (if they are not of good repute), those arrested for arson feloniously done or for counterfeiting money or forging the king's seal, persons excommunicate arrested at the request of the bishop, those arrested for manifest crime and those arrested for treason touching the king himself are to be in no wise replevisable by the common- law writ or without writ. But those indicted for larceny by inquests of sheriffs and bailiffs taken in the course of their office, either on slight suspicion or for petty larceny amounting to not more than twelve pence in value (provided that he has not been accused of larceny before, or accused of the harbouring of felons or inciting, supporting or helping) as also those accused of some other offence for which one ought not to lose life or limb, and a man appealed by an approver after the death of the approver if he is not a common thief, shall henceforth be released by sufficient surety (for which the sheriff shall be answerable) and this without any payment. And if sheriffs or others release on bail anyone who is not replevisable, if he be sheriff, constable or other bailiff of fee who has the keeping of the prisoners, and is convicted of this, let him lose the fee and the bailiwick for ever. And if an undersheriff, constable, or bailiff of him who has this fee for keeping the prisoners has done this without his lord's wish, let him or any other bailiff who is not of fee be imprisoned for three years and make fine at the king's pleasure. And if any one detains prisoners who are replevisable after the prisoner has offered sufficient surety he shall be liable to heavy amercement by the king. And if he exacts payment for releasing him he shall restore double the amount to the prisoner and also be liable to heavy amercement by the king.

(c. 16) In view of the fact that some people seize and cause to be seized the beasts of another and drive them out of the county in which they were seized, it is provided that no one shall do it and if anyone does he is to make heavy

fine in accordance with the provisions of the statutes of
Marlborough made in the time of king Henry, father of
the king who now is. And those are to be treated in the
same way who seize beasts and levy distress in the fee of
another and they are to be more heavily punished if the
nature of the offence requires it.

(c. 17) It is likewise provided that, if any from now on
seize the beasts of another and has them driven to a castle
or a fort and keeps them there within the enclosure of
the castle or the fort against gage and pledge after they
have been solemnly demanded by the sheriff or other
bailiff of the king at the suit of the plaintiff, the sheriff
or the bailiff taking with him the posse of his county or
his bailiwick is to go and try to get release of the beasts
from him who seized them or from his lord or from any
other men whatever of his lord who may be found where
the beasts were driven, and if release of the beasts is then
forcibly prevented or if no man is found who will answer
for the lord of him who seized the beasts and release them,
then after the lord of him who seized the beasts has been
warned by the sheriff or bailiff if he is in the district or
near enough to be properly warned by him who seized the
beasts or by another of his men if he was not in the district
when the seizure was made to cause the beasts to be released,
if he does not straightway have them released the king for
the despite and for the trespass will have the castle or fort
razed beyond rebuilding and all the loss that the plaintiff
has suffered in respect of his beasts or because of hindrance
to his husbandry or in any other way since the first demand
for the beasts was made by the sheriff or bailiff shall be
restored to him twofold by him who seized the beasts if he
has sufficient means and if he has not, then by the lord—
whenever and however release is made after the sheriff or
bailiff has come to effect the release, that is to say that
where the sheriff ought to make return of the king's writ to
the bailiff of the lord of the castle or fort or to another to
whom the return of the king's writ in this matter belongs,
if after receiving it the bailiff of this liberty does not make
the release the sheriff is without delay to discharge his office
as aforesaid and with the aforesaid penalty. And release is

to be made in the same way by attachment of plaint made
without writ and with the same penalty. And this is to be
understood everywhere where the king's writ runs. And if
it is in the marches of Wales or elsewhere where the king's
writ does not run, the king, who is their sovereign lord,
will do right therein to those who wish to complain.

(c. 18) Because the common fine and amercement of the
whole county injustices' eyres for false judgment or for other
offence is badly assessed by sheriffs and barrators in the
counties so that the total amount is increased many times and
the portions are assessed otherwise than they ought to be to
the damage of the people and are often paid to the sheriffs
and barrators who do not acquit the payers, it is provided,
and the king's will, that from now on injustices' eyres this
amount shall be assessed before them before their departure
by the oath of knights and other good men on all those who
ought to contribute to it, and the justices shall cause the
portions to be put down in their estreats, which they will
deliver to the exchequer, and not the total amount,

(c. 19) As regards sheriffs, and others who answer personally
at the exchequer, who have received debts due to king
Henry, the father of the present king, or the debts of the
king himself up to now and have not given the debtors
quittance at the exchequer, it is provided that the king shall
send good men through every county to hear all those who
wish to complain of this and to determine the business so
that those who can show that they have paid shall be forever
quit, whether the sheriffs or others are dead or alive, by a
certain form that is to be given to them; and those (sheriffs
and others) who have acted so (i.e. not acquitted the debtor)
shall, if they are alive, be severely punished, and if they
are dead their heirs shall answer and be charged with the
debt. And the king commands that sheriffs and the others
aforesaid shall henceforth lawfully acquit debtors at the next
accounting after they have received payment of the debt and
then the debt shall be allowed at the exchequer so that it
shall not in future appear in the summons. And if a sheriff
does otherwise and is found guilty of it, he shall pay the
plaintiff treble the amount he has received and make fine at
the king's pleasure; and let each sheriff take good care to have

a receiver such as he is prepared to answer for, because the king will proceed against sheriffs and their heirs for the full amount. And if anyone else who answers personally at the exchequer does other wise let him pay the plaintiff threefold and make fine in like manner. And that sheriffs make tallies for all those who pay them their debt to the king, and that they cause the summons of the exchequer to be shown to all debtors who care to ask to see it without denying anyone and without anything being given; and the king will take severe measures against him who does not do so.

(c. 20) It is provided concerning wrongdoers in parks and preserves that if anyone is convicted thereof at the suit of the plaintiff there shall be awarded appropriate and heavy damages according to the nature of the offence and three years imprisonment, from which he shall be ransomed, at the king's will, if he has the wherewithal to make fine, and then he shall find good security that he will not misbehave in future. And if he has not wherewith to make fine he shall after the three years imprisonment find the same security. And if he cannot find the security he shall abjure the realm. And if anyone accused of wrongdoing takes to flight and has neither land nor tenement by which he can be distrained, he is to be called county by county as soon as the king has discovered this by lawful inquest and if no one is forthcoming, let him be outlawed. And it is provided that if no one has sued within a year and a day of the wrong being done, the king shall have the suit, and those whom he finds guilty of it by lawful inquest shall be punished in the same way in all respects as is said above. And if any such malefactor is convicted of having taken domesticated animals or anything else in parks by way of robbery while coming, staying, or returning he is to be dealt with at common law as one convicted of open robbery and larceny, as well at the suit of the king as of another.

(c. 21) As regards lands of heirs under age who are in the wardship of their lord, it is provided that the guardians shall keep and maintain them without causing destruction of anything; and that with regard to wardships of this kind it be done in all respects as is contained in the great charter of liberties of king Henry, father of the present king, and

be it so done from now on; and archbishoprics, bishoprics, abbeys, churches and dignities are to be kept in the same way in times of vacancy,

(c. 22) Concerning heirs under age married without the agreement of their guardians before the age of fourteen years, be it done according to what is contained in the provision of Merton. And of those who are married without the agreement of their guardians after they have reached fourteen years, the guardian is to have twice the value of the marriage according to the tenor of the same provision. In addition, those who have withheld the marriage are to render the full value of the marriage to the guardian for the offence; and the king is nonetheless to receive satisfaction in accordance with this same provision from him who has withheld it.[1]

Concerning female heirs who attained the age of fourteen and the lord to whom their marriage belongs will not marry them but out of desire to retain the land wishes to keep them unmarried, it is provided that the lord can not on the pretext of the marriage have or hold the land of these female heirs more than two years beyond the term of the aforesaid fourteen years. And if the lord does not marry them within these two years, then they shall have an action to recover their inheritance freely, without giving anything for the wardship or for the marriage. And if they, of malice or by evil counsel, refuse to be married by their chief lord where they would not be disparaged, then the lord may hold the land and the inheritance until the age when a male attains his majority, namely the age of twenty-one and beyond that until he has received the value of the marriage.

(c. 23) It is likewise provided that no stranger who is of this kingdom is to be distrained in a city, borough, vill, fair or market for what he is neither debtor nor pledge for, and he who does this is to be severely punished and the distress is to be released without delay by the bailiffs of the place or by the other, the king's, bailiffs if need be.

(c. 24) It is likewise provided that no escheator, sheriff or other bailiff of the king is to disseise any man of his freehold or of anything touching his freehold on the strength of his office without special warrant or instruction or definite authority appertaining to his office, and if any does this, it is to be at the discretion of the disseised whether the king *ex officio* has the wrong amended on his complaint1 or whether he sues at common law by writ of *novel disseisin*. And he who is convicted of this shall pay double damages to the plaintiff himself and shall be liable to heavy amercement by the king.

(c. 25) No royal official shall maintain, personally or through another, pleas, suits or business in the king's court concerning lands, tenements or any other thing, in consideration of receiving part thereof, or other advantage by agreement made between them,2 and he who does is to be punished at the king's pleasure,

(c. 26) And that no sheriff or other royal official is to accept a consideration for discharging his office, but is to be paid by what he receives from the king, and he who does shall give back twice as much and be punished at the king's pleasure,

(c. 27) And that no clerk of a justice, escheator or of one conducting an inquiry is to accept anything for delivering chapiters,3 except only clerks of justices in eyre and that two shillings from every wapentake, hundred or vill which answers by twelve or by six according to what used to be done. And he who does otherwise shall give back three times what he has taken and shall be suspended from his master's service for one year.

(c. 28) And that no clerk of the king or of his justices shall henceforth accept presentation to any church, about which there is an action or dispute in the king's court, without the special permission of the king; and the king forbids this on pain of dismissal from his service. And that no clerk of a justice or a sheriff shall maintain parties to quarrels or business in the king's court, or commit any fraud for the purpose of delaying or obstructing common justice; and if any does, he shall be punished with the penalty just mentioned or with a heavier one if the offence requires it.

(c. 29) It is likewise provided that if any serjeant-pleader or other commit any sort of deceit or collusion in the king's court or be a party to deceiving the court in order to delude the court or a party and is convicted of this, then he shall be imprisoned for a year and a day and be heard in court no more after that pleading for anybody. And if it be someone other than a pleader, he shall in like manner be imprisoned for a year and a day at least. And if the offence calls for a greater penalty, let him be at the king's pleasure.

(c. 30) Because many people complain that serjeant-criers at fee and other marshals of the justices in eyre unlawfully take money from those who recover seisin of land or who win their suits, from fines levied, from jurors, townships, prisoners and from others attached upon pleas of the crown, otherwise than they ought to do in many ways, and because there are more of them than ought to be, whereby people are badly oppressed, the king forbids such things to be done henceforth; and if any serjeant at fee does it his office is to be taken into the king's hands, and if justices' marshals do it they are to be severely punished at the king's pleasure, and both are to give back to all plaintiffs threefold what they took.

(c. 31) With regard to those who take excessive tolls contrary to the common usage of the realm in a market town, it is provided that if anyone does it in a town belonging to the king himself which is let at fee farm the king will take the franchise of the market into his own hands. And if it is someone else's town and this is done by the lord of the town, the king will act in the same way. And if it is done by a bailiff without orders from his lord, the bailiff shall give back to the plaintiff as much for the excessive prise as he would have taken from him if he had avoided paying his toll and in addition be imprisoned for forty days. With regard to citizens and burgesses to whom the king or his father has granted murage to enclose their town and who take such murage otherwise than it was granted to them and are convicted of this, it is provided that they shall lose this favour forever and be liable to heavy amercement by the king.

(c. 32) As to those who take victuals or anything else for the king's use on credit either for the provisioning of a castle or for another reason, and when they have received payment therefor at the exchequer, in the wardrobe or elsewhere, withhold it from the creditors, to their great loss and the king's discredit, it is provided, in the case of those who have lands and tenements, that it be immediately levied from their lands and their chattels and paid to the creditors together with the damages they have sustained and they are to make fine for their trespass; and if they have no lands or tenements, they are to be in prison at the king's pleasure. As regards those who accept part of the king's debts or accept other rewards from the king's creditors for getting them payment of these same debts, it is provided that they are to give back double what they received and be heavily punished at the king's pleasure. As to those who take more horses or carts for doing the king's carrying than are needed and accept a reward for releasing horses or carts, it is provided that if anyone belonging to the court does it, he shall be severely punished by the marshals, and if it be done out of court by someone of the court or by someone else who is convicted of it, he shall give back threefold and be in the king's prison for forty days.

(c. 33) It is provided that no sheriff shall allow a barrator to maintain suits in the county court, or stewards of magnates or anyone else, if he is not appointed attorney of his lord to perform suit, nor to render judgments of the county court or pronounce judgments if he is not specially prayed and requested to do this by all the suitors and attornies of the suitors who are there that day; and if any does the king will proceed severely against both the sheriff and him.

(c. 34) Because many have often invented and told lying tales, as a result of which there has often been discord or the intention of discord between the king and his people, or some magnates of his kingdom, it is forbidden, because of the damage that has been and that could still be, for anyone henceforward to be so bold as to utter or repeat false news or fabrications whence any discord, or intention of discord, or slander could arise between the king and his people or the magnates of his kingdom; and he who does is to be taken and kept in prison until he has declared in court who started the talk.

(c. 35) With regard to magnates and their bailiffs and others (except the king's officers to whom special authority has been given to do this) who on somebody's complaint or on their own authority attach others with their chattels who are passing through their dominion to answer before them concerning contracts, covenants and trespasses made outside their power and jurisdiction, whereas they (the attached) hold nothing either of them or within the liberty where their authority is, to the prejudice of the king and the crown and the damage of the people, it is provided that from now on no one is to do it; and if anyone does he shall pay him who is attached double the amount of his damages and be liable to heavy amercement by the king,

(c. 36) Because reasonable aid for making sons knights or for marrying daughters has never yet been defined,2 nor when it ought to be taken, nor at what time, whereby some levied excessive aid sooner than seemed necessary, at which the people felt aggrieved, it is provided that from now on for a whole knight's fee only 20s is to be paid, and for 20 librates of land held in socage 20s and for more, more and for less, less according to the assessment. And that no one can levy such aid for making his son a knight until his son is fifteen years old, or for marrying his daughter until she is seven years old, and there shall be mention made of this in the king's writ drawn up for the purpose when he wishes to claim it. And if it happens that the father, after he has levied such an aid from his tenants, dies before he has married his daughter, the father's executors are to be bound to the daughter for as much as the father received by way of aid and if the father's goods do not suffice, the heir is to be bound to the daughter for it.

(c. 37) It is likewise provided and agreed that if any man is attainted by recognition of assize of *novel disseisin* of disseisin committed in the time of the present king with robbery of any kind of goods or movables, the judgment is to be that the plaintiff shall recover his seisin and his damages as well in respect of the goods and movables aforesaid as in respect of the rest, and the disseisor shall make fine whether he is present or not, provided that if he is present he is first to be sentenced to prison. And the same is to be done in the case of disseisin by force and arms, although robbery is not committed.

(c. 38) Because some people in the land have less fear than they ought of swearing a false oath, whereby many people are disinherited and lose their right, it is provided that from now on the king will *ex officio* grant attaints on inquests in pleas of land or franchise (or anything) concerning a free tenement when it seems to him that there is need.

(c. 39) And because a long time has passed since the writs named below were limited, it is provided that in reckoning descent on a writ of right no one is to be given a hearing to claim seisin by an ancestor of his farther back than the time of king Richard, uncle of king Henry, the father of the present king; and that the writ of *novel disseisin* and that of purpartie which is called *nuper obiit* are to have the limitation "since the first crossing of king Henry, father of our lord the king who now is, to Gascony", and the writs of *mort d'ancestor, cosinage, ael* and entry, and the writ of *neifty* are to have the limitation "from the coronation of king Henry", and not before. Except that all writs purchased at once or purchased between now and a year after St John's day are to be pleaded from the time they used previously to be pleaded from.

(c. 40) And because many people are hindered from obtaining their right by false vouching to warranty, it is provided that in possessory writs (especially such as writs of *mort d'ancestor, cosinage, ael, nuper obiit*, intrusion and other like writs, whereby lands or tenements are claimed which ought to descend, revert, remain or escheat by the death of an ancestor or of another), if the tenant vouches to warranty and the demandant counterpleads it and is willing to aver, by the assize or by the country or otherwise as the king's court shall award, that the tenant, or his ancestor whose heir he is, was the first to enter after the death of him from whose seisin he (the demandant) claims, the demandant's averment is to be received if the tenant will abide thereupon; if he will not, he is to be driven to make another answer if he has not his warrantor present willing to warrant him voluntarily and enter immediately upon the defence, saving to the demandant his exceptions against him (if he wishes to vouch further) as he had before against the first tenant. Again, in all kinds of writs of entry which mention degrees it is provided that no one henceforth shall vouch out of the line. In other writs of entry where no mention is made

of degrees (which writs are not to be maintained save where the aforesaid writs in the degrees cannot lie nor rightfully have place) and in writ of right, it is provided that, if the tenant vouches to warranty and the demandant wishes to counterplead it and is ready to aver by the country that neither he who is vouched nor his ancestors ever had seisin of the land or the tenement demanded whether in fee or in service by the hand of the tenant or of his ancestors since the time of him upon whose seisin the demandant bases his claim until the time when the writ was purchased and the plea moved so that he could not aver that the tenant or his ancestor was his feoffee, the demandant's averment is to be received if the tenant will abide thereupon; if he will not, the tenant is to be driven to make another answer if he has not his warrantor present willing to warrant him voluntarily and enter immediately upon the defence, saving to the demandant his exceptions against him as he had before against the first tenant. And the aforesaid exception is to have place in writ of *mort d'ancestor* and the other writs before named, as well as in writs that concern right. And if the tenant has perchance a charter of warranty from another man besides so that he is not obliged in any of the aforesaid cases to warrant voluntarily, his recovery is saved to him by a writ of warranty of charter from the king's chancery when he wishes to purchase it, but the plea is not to be held up because of this.

(c. 41) Concerning the oath of champions it is provided—because it seldom happens that a demandant's champion is not perjured, in that he swears that he or his father saw the seisin of his lord or of his lord's ancestry and that his father enjoined him to have it vindicated—that the demandant's champion is not henceforth to be compelled to swear this; but the oath is to be kept in all its other points,

(c. 42) Because in writs of assizes and of attaints and of juries *utrum*, the jurors are often harassed by tenants' excuses for non-appearance, it is provided that from the time that he (a tenant) has once appeared in court he cannot after that make excuse, but, if he will, is to appoint an attorney to sue for him; if he will not, the assize or the jury is to be taken because of his default.

(c. 43) Because demandants are oftentimes hindered from obtaining their right because there are many parcener-tenants, of whom one cannot answer without the other, or because there are many tenants jointly enfeoffed where none knows his several and these tenants often fourch by essoin, so that each of them has an excuse for non-appearance, it is provided that from now on these tenants are not to have essoin except on one day and no more than one sole tenant, so that in future they can fourch only with one essoin.

(c. 44) Because many people have themselves falsely essoined on the ground of being overseas when they were in England on the day of the summons, it is provided that from now on this essoin is not to be allowed at all if the demandant challenges it and is ready to aver that he was in England on the day the summons was made and for three weeks after, but is to be adjourned in this way: that, if the demandant on such and such a day prosecutes the averment by the country or as the king's court shall award and it is found that the tenant was within the four seasi the day he was summoned and for three weeks after so that he could have reasonable notice of the summons, the essoin is to be turned into a default—and this, be it understood, only before justices.

(c. 45) With regard to delays in all kinds of writs connected with attachments, it is provided that if the tenant or the defendant defaults after the attachment has been proved, the grand distress is to be awarded immediately and if the sheriff does not make sufficient return on the day he is to be heavily amerced. And if he returns that he has made execution in due fashion and delivered the issues to the sureties, the sheriff is then to be ordered to have the issues brought before the justices on another day; and if he who is attached comes to remedy his defaults, he is to have the issues, and if he does not come the king is to have them. And the justices of the king's pleas shall have them delivered into the wardrobe, the justices of the bench at Westminster shall have them delivered into the exchequer; and the justices in eyre to the sheriff of the shire where the pleadings are,2 both of that shire and of other shires, and he is to be charged with this in the summons by the roll of the justices,

(c. 46) It is likewise provided, and ordered by the king, that justices of the king's bench and justices of the bench at Westminster are from now on to plead to the end pleas started on one day before broaching or beginning the following day's pleas, except that essoins are to be entered, judged and allowed. And no one because of this is to presume not to come on the day which has been given him.

(c. 47) It is likewise provided that if any one from now on purchases a writ of *novel disseisin* and if he whom the writ proceeds against as principal disseisor dies before the assize is passed, the plaintiff is to have his writ of entry founded *sur disseisin* against the heir or against the heirs of the disseisor, of whatever age they are; in the same way let the heir or the heirs of the disseised have their writ of entry against the disseisors, of whatever age they are, if perchance the disseised dies before he has made his purchase of the writ; so that because of the nonage of the heirs of either of the parties the writ shall not be abated or the plea delayed, but as much as can be done without offending the law it shall be speeded up to make lively suit after the disseisin. In like manner this article is to be observed with regard to prelates, religious, and others to whom lands or tenements may come in any way after the death of another person. And if the parties in pleading proceed to an inquest and it passes against an heir who is under age, and especially against the heir of the disseised, in that case he shall have an attaint as an act of royal grace.

(c. 48) If a guardian who is the immediate lord enfeoff any man with land which is of the inheritance of a child who is under age and in his wardship, to the disinheritance of the heir, it is provided that the heir is to have his recovery immediately by writ of *novel disseisin* against his guardian and against the tenant; and the seisin is to be handed over by the justices, if it is recovered, to the next friend to whom the inheritance cannot descend to improve for the child's benefit and to answer to the heir for the issues when he comes of age; and the guardian is to lose for life wardship of the thing recovered and all the rest of the inheritance that he holds in the heir's name. And if a guardian other than the immediate lord does it, he is to lose the wardship of the whole and is to be liable to severe punishment from the king. And if the child is moved away or disturbed by the guardian or by the feoffee or by another with the result that he cannot sue for his assize, one of his next friends who is willing to do so may sue on his behalf and shall be admitted.

(c. 49) In a writ of dower in which the woman has nothing, the writ is not henceforth to be abated by the exception of the tenant that she has received her dower from another man before her writ was purchased, unless he can show that she had received part of the dower from himself and in the same vill before her writ was purchased,

(c. 50) And because the king does these things in honour of God and of holy church and for the common good and the relief of those who are oppressed, he does not wish them to turn at another time to his prejudice or that of the crown, but that the rights that belong to him should be saved to him in all points.

(c. 51) And because it would be very much a Christian act2 to do right to all and at all times, it would be useful for assizes of *novel disseisin, mort d'ancestor* and *darrein presentment,* with the assent of the prelates, to be taken in Advent, on Septuagesima and in Lent as indeed is done with inquests; and the king asks this of the bishops.

Here ends the statute of the lord king Edward made at Westminster on the morrow of the Close of Easter in the third year of his reign, after his coronation.

ARTICLES AGAINST PIERS GAVESTON PRESENTED BY THE EARL OF LINCOLN TO THE KING (1308)

THIS DOCUMENTS THE ULTIMATELY SUCCESSFUL ATTEMPT BY A NUMBER OF BARONS TO BRING DOWN PIERS GAVESTON, THE BOON COMPANION OF EDWARD II.

THE FIRST UNDERTAKING
and the ordinance presented by the earl of Lincoln to the king

Homage and the oath of allegiance are more in respect of the crown than in respect of the king's person and are more closely related to the crown than to the king's person; and this is evident because, before the right to the crown has descended to the person, no allegiance is due to him. And, therefore, if it should befall that the king is not guided by reason, then, in order that the dignity of the crown may be preserved the lieges are bound by the oath made to the crown to reinstate the king in the dignity of the crown or else they would not have kept their oath. The next question is how the king should be reinstated, whether by an action at law or by constraint. It is not, however, possible by recourse to the law to obtain redress, because there would be no other judges than the royal judges, in which case, if the king's will was not accordant with right reason, the only result would be that error would be maintained and confirmed. Hence, in order that the oath may be saved, when the king will not right a wrong and remove that which is hurtful to the people at large and prejudicial to the crown, and is so adjudged by the people, it behoves that the evil must be removed by constraint, for the king is bound by his oath to govern his people, and his lieges are bound to govern with him and in support of him.

As regards the person who is talked about, the people ought to judge him as one not to be suffered because he disinherits the crown and, as far as he is able, impoverishes it. By his counsel he withdraws the king from the counsel of his realm and puts discord between the king and his people, and he draws to himself the allegiance of men by as stringent an oath as does the king, thereby making himself the peer of the king and so enfeebling the crown, for by means of the property of the crown he has gathered to himself and put under his control the power of the crown, so that by his evil deeds it lies solely with him to determine whether the crown should be destroyed and he himself made sovereign of the realm, in treason towards his liege lord and the crown, contrary to his fealty.

Since the lord king has undertaken to maintain him against all men on every point, entirely without regard to right reason, as behoves the king, he cannot be judged or attainted by an action brought according to law, and therefore, seeing that he is a robber of the people and a traitor to his liege lord and his realm, the people rate him as a man attainted and judged, and pray the king that, since he is bound by his coronation oath to keep the laws that the people shall choose, he will accept and execute the award of the people.

MANIFESTO DECLARING EDWARD III'S REASONS FOR WAR WITH FRANCE (1337)

THIS DOCUMENT, CIRCULATED THROUGHOUT ENGLAND, SIGNALED THE START OF THE HUNDRED YEARS' WAR.

SCHEDULE TO BE READ BY VARIOUS MAGNATES AND ROYAL officials commissioned to explain the king's business to meetings to be held in all the shires.

These are the offers made to the King of France by the King of England, to avoid war.

First, the King of England sent to the King of France various solemn messages, begging him to return to him the lands which he is withholding from him, arbitrarily and against reason, in the Duchy of Guienne; but to these requests the King of France did nothing, until, at last, he promised that, if the King of England would come in his own person, he would do him justice, grace, and favour.

Trusting in this promise, the King of England crossed secretly into France and came to him, humbly requesting the delivery of his lands, offering and doing to the king as much as he ought and more; but the King of France always put him off with words and negotiations, and did nothing for him in fact; and moreover, during the negotiations, wrongfully drew to himself, more and more, the rights of the King of England in the Duchy.

Also, the King of England, seeing the hardness of the King of France, in order to have his goodwill, and that which he wrongfully detains, held out to him the great offers written below, i.e. when one was refused, he put forward another.

First, the marriage of his eldest son, now Duke of Cornwall, with the daughter of the king of France, without taking anything for the marriage.

Item, the marriage of his sister, now Countess of Guelders, with his son, together with a very great sum of money.

Item, the marriage of his brother, the Earl of Cornwall, whom God absolve, with any lady of the blood royal.

Item, to make recompense for the inconvenience, he offered him as much money as he could reasonably demand.

Item, because the King of England was given to understand that the King of France wished to undertake a crusade to the Holy Land, and wished to have the king of England

Schedule to be read by various magnates and royal officials commissioned to explain the king's business to meetings to be held in all the shires.

These are the offers made to the King of France by the King of England, to avoid war.

In his company, and therefore he wished to show him grace and favour, the King of England, so that no hindrance of the crusade could be alleged against him, offered to the King of France to go with a large force with him in the crusade; so that, however, before he set off, the French king should make him full restitution of all his lands.

Item, then he offered to go with him on the said crusade, on condition that before he went, the French king should restore half, or a certain part of the lands.

Item, afterwards he made him larger offers, that he would go with the French king if he would make such restitution on his return from the Holy Land.

Item, then to stop the malice of the King of France, who was striving to blame the prevention of the said crusade on the King of England, he professed his readiness to go on the crusade with him, provided that on his return the King of France would do justice towards him.

But the King of France, who was striving by all the means that he could to undo the King of England and his people, so that he could keep what he wrongfully withheld, and conquer more from him, would accept none of these offers; but, seeking his opportunities, busied himself in aid and maintenance of the Scots, the enemies of the King of England, attempting to delay him by the Scottish war, so that he would have no power to pursue his rights elsewhere.

Item, then, in courtesy to the King of France, and at the request of his messages, the King of England granted to the Scots respite of war and truces, in hope of peace negotiations; but during this truce the Scots killed the Earl of Athol and others, and captured several great men of the King of England's allegiance, and besieged and captured castles and other places belonging to the king and his men.

THE STATUTE OF TREASONS (1352)

A FIRM BUT JUDICIOUS STATUTE FROM THE REIGN OF EDWARD III, INCLUDING THE CUSTOMARY PHRASE 'AID AND COMFORT'.

Also whereas there have been divers opinions before this time as to what cases should be adjudged treason and what not; the king at the request of the lords and of the commons has made the following declaration, that is to say: When a man attempts or plots the death of our lord the king, or of our lady his queen or of their eldest son and heir; or if a man violates the king's wife or the king's eldest unmarried daughter, or the wife of the king's eldest son and heir: or if a man levies war against our lord the king in his realm, or adheres to the king's enemies, giving to them aid and comfort in his realm or elsewhere, and of this shall be attainted and proved of open deed by men of their rank; and if a man counterfeit the king's great or privy seal or his money...and if a man slay the chancellor, treasurer, or the king's justices of the one bench or the other, justices in eyre, or justices of assize, and any other justices assigned to hear and determine, being in their places, doing their offices. And it is to be understood that in the cases rehearsed above, (anything) ought to be judged treason which extends to our lord the king and his royal majesty; and of such treason the forfaiture of the escheats belongs to our sovereign lord the king....

And moreover there is another kind of treason, that is to say, when a servant slays his master, or a wife her husband, or when a secular cleric or a religious kills his prelate, to whom he owes faith and obedience; and in such kinds of treason the escheats ought to pertain to every lord of his own fee.

And as many other similar cases of treason may happen in time to come, which a man cannot think nor declare at the present time, it is agreed that if any other case, supposed treason, which is not specified above, should come before any justices, the justices shall wait, without passing sentence of treason, till the case be shown and declared before the king and his parliament, whether it ought to be judged treason or some other felony.

AN ACCOUNT OF THE DEPOSITION OF RICHARD II (1399)

KING RICHARD WAS DEPOSED IN 1399 AND REPLACED BY HENRY IV.

The record and process of the renunciation of King Richard, the Second after the Conquest, and of the acceptance of the same renunciation, together with the deposition of King Richard, follow hereafter. Memorandum that on Monday, the feast of St Michael the Archangel, in the 23rd year of King Richard II, the lords spiritual and temporal and other notable persons (16 names follow) deputed for the following act, came into the presence of the said king Richard, being within the Tower of London, at nine o'clock. And the Earl of Northumberland recited before the king on behalf of the aforesaid deputation, how the same king at Conway in North Wales, being still at liberty, promised to the lord Thomas Archbishop of Canterbury and to the Earl of Northumberland that he was willing to cede and renounce the crown of England and France and his royal majesty, because of the inability and insufficiency to which the same king confessed, and to do this in the best manner and form which could be done as might be best devised by the counsel of experienced men. The king in the presence of the lords and others named above benignly replied that he was willing to give effect to what he had formerly promised; he desired however to have speech with Henry of Lancaster and the arch-bishop (Arundel) his kinsmen, before he fulfilled his promise. He asked for a copy of the resignation to be made by him to be given to him, so that he might in the mean-time deliberate on it; this copy was given to him, and the lords and the others returned to their lodgings. Afterwards on the same day after dinner the king greatly desiring the arrival of the Duke of Lancaster, who tarried for a long time, at last the Duke, the lords and persons named above and also the Archbishop of Canterbury, came into the king's presence in the Tower, the lords Roos, Willoughby, and Abergavenny and many others being present. And after the king had spoken apart with the duke and the archbishop, looking from one to the other with a cheerful countenance, as it seemed to the bystanders, at last the king, calling all those present to him, declared publicly in their presence, that he was ready to make the renunciation and resignation according to his promise. And although, to save the labour of such a lengthy reading, he might, as he was told, have had the resignation and renunciation, which was drawn up in a certain parchment schedule, read by a deputy, the king willingly, as it seemed, and with a cheerful countenance, holding the same schedule in his hand, said that he would read it himself, and he did read it distinctly. And he absolved his lieges and made renunciation and cession, and swore this...and he signed it with his own hand, as is more fully contained in the schedule, of which the tenor follows in these words....

And immediately he added to the aforesaid renunciation and cession, in his own words, that if it were in his power the Duke of Lancaster should succeed him in the realm. But because this was in no wise in his power, as he said, he asked the Arch-bishop of York and Bishop of Hereford, whom he appointed as his proctors to declare and intimate his renunciation and cession to all the estates of the realm, to declare his intention and wish in this matter to the people. And as a token of his intention and wish in this matter, he took off his finger the gold ring with his signet, and put it on the duke's finger, desiring the same, as he affirmed, to be known to all the estates of the realm. And when this was done, all said farewell to him and left the Tower to return to their lodgings.

On the morrow, Tuesday, the feast of St Jerome, in the great hall at Westminster, in the place honourably prepared for holding parliament, the Archbishops of Canterbury and York and the Duke of Lancaster, and other dukes, and lords both spiritual and temporal, whose names are written below, and a great multitude of the people of the realm being gathered there on account of parliament, the Duke of Lancaster occupying his usual and proper place, and the royal throne, solemnly prepared with cloth of gold being vacant, without any president, the Archbishop of York and the Bishop of Hereford according to the king's injunction publicly declared the cession and renunciation to have been made by him, with the delivery of the seal, and the royal signature, and they caused the cession and renunciation to be read, first in Latin and then in English. And at once the Archbishop of Canterbury, to whom pertains by reason of the dignity and prerogative of the metropolitan church of Canterbury to have the first voice amongst the prelates and magnates of the realm, asked the estate of the people then present, whether they wished to accept the renunciation and cession for their interests and the good of the realm. The estates and people considering, for the reasons specified by the king himself in his renunciation and cession, that it would be very expedient, each one singly, and then in common with the people, unanimously and cordially gave his consent. After this acceptance it was publicly set forth that besides the cession and renunciation which had been accepted, it would in many ways be expedient and advantageous for the kingdom, to avoid all scruple and evil suspicion, that

the many crimes and defects frequently committed by the king in the bad government of the realm — on account of which, as he himself had asserted in his abdication, he was worthy to be deposed — should by means of articles which had been drawn up in writing be publicly read, that they might be declared to the people. And so a large part of these articles was then publicly read, of which article the tenor is as follows:

(Then follows a copy of the coronation oath of Richard II. After this comes the heading "Here follow the indictments against the king concerning his deposition".)

1. In the first place the king is indicted on account of his evil rule, that is, he has given the goods and possessions which belong to the crown to unworthy persons and otherwise dissipated them indiscreetly, and therefore has imposed collections and other grave and insupportable burdens on his people without cause. And he has perpetrated innumerable other evils. By his assent and command certain prelates and other lords temporal were chosen and assigned by the whole parliament to govern the realm; and they faithfully laboured with their whole strength for the just government of the realm. Nevertheless the king made a conventicle with his accomplices and proposed to accuse of high treason the lords spiritual and temporal who were occupied for the good of the realm; and in order to strengthen his evil design he violently forced the justices of the realm by fear of death and torture of body to destroy the said lords.

2. Also the king caused the greater part of his justices to come before him and his adherents secretly at Shrewsbury, and he induced, made and compelled them to reply singly to certain questions put to them on behalf of the king, touching the laws of the realm. This was contrary to their wishes, and other than what they would have replied if they had been free and not under compulsion. By colour of these replies the king proposed to proceed later to the destruction of the Duke of Gloucester, the Earls of Arundel and Warwick and other lords, against whom the king was extremely indignant because they wished the king to be under good rule. But with divine help and the

resistance and power of the said lords opposing him, the king could not bring his scheme into effect.

3. (Instead of satisfying the grievances of the appellant lords in parliament, the king incited Robert de Vere to raise an army against them, thus causing many deaths and other evils in the realm.)

4. (Although the king in full parliament and with its assent pardoned the Duke of Gloucester and the Earls of Arundel and Warwick, and for years acted in a friendly way towards them, nevertheless he carried venom in his heart, and when the opportunity came he had the Duke of Gloucester murdered, the Earl of Arundel beheaded and the Earl of Warwick and Lord Cobham sentenced to perpetual imprisonment.)

5. (At the time when Gloucester, Arundel and Warwick were condemned, the king, in order to fulfil his harmful designs on others, caused a great multitude of malefactors to be raised in the county of Chester. These ruffians caused many injuries to the king's subjects, as murders, beatings, woundings, robberies, rapes and other excesses, for none of which would the king give justice to plaintiffs.)

6. (Although the king made proclamation when he arrested Gloucester, Arundel and Warwick, that he did not intend to proceed against any of their households, nevertheless many of the households of these lords were compelled by fear of death to make fines and redemptions as if they were traitors.)

7. Also, after many of these people had made fines and redemptions, they sought from the king letters patent of general pardon, concerning the above; but they could secure no advantage from these letters of pardon until they had paid new fines and redemptions to save their lives; by this they were much impoverished. On account of this the royal name and estate were brought into great disrepute.

8 (Also, in the parliament of Shrewsbury the king secured the appointment of a commission to decide certain petitions.) By colour of this concession the persons thus deputed proceeded with other matters touching generally that parliament — and this at the will of the king, in derogation of the estate of parliament, and a great damage to the whole realm, and a pernicious example. And in order that those persons might seem to have a certain colour and authority for such deeds, the king caused the rolls of parliament to be deleted and changed to suit his purposes, against the intention of the commission.

9. (Contrary to his coronation oath he had denied justice to Henry duke of Lancaster.)

10. Also, although the crown of England and the rights of the crown, and the same realm, have been so free for all time past that neither the lord high pontiff nor anyone else outside the kingdom ought to intermeddle with the same, yet the king, in order to strengthen his erroneous statutes, begged the lord pope to confirm the statutes ordained in the last parliament. On which the king sought for apostolic letters, in which grave censures were threatened against all who presumed to contravene the statutes in any way....

11. (When the Duke of Lancaster had been about to do battle with the Duke of Norfolk, the king had stopped the fight and had sentenced the Duke of Lancaster to ten years of exile, against all justice, the laws and customs of the realm and military rights.)

12. (He had revoked the letters patent which he had granted to the duke of Lancaster, allowing him to inherit his estates by attorney and to defer homage.)

13. (He had interfered with the ordinary course of election of sheriffs, in order to appoint those who, he knew, would not resist his will.)

14. (He had borrowed money from various lords and others of the realm, promising to repay the money at a certain term, and had failed to do so.)

15. (He imposed very heavy burdens of taxation on his subjects in nearly every year of his reign, to their great impoverishment, and used the income thus obtained, not for the benefit of the realm of England, but for his own ostentation, pomp and vainglory.)

16. Also, the king refused to keep and defend the just laws and customs of the realm, but according to the whim of his desire he wanted to do whatever appealed to his wishes. Sometimes — and often when the laws of the realm had been

declared and expressed to him by the justices and others of his council and he should have done justice to those who sought it according to those laws — he said expressly, with harsh and determined looks, that the laws were in his own mouth, sometimes he said that they were in his breast, and that he alone could change or establish the laws of his realm. And deceived by this idea, he would not allow justice to be done to many of his lieges, but compelled very many persons to desist from suing for common justice by threats and fear.

17. Also, after certain statutes were established in his parliament, which should always bind until they should be especially repealed by the authority of another parliament the king, desiring to enjoy such liberty that no statutes should bind him... subtly procured that such a petition should be put forward in parliament on behalf of the community of the realm, and to be granted to him in general, that he might be as free as any of his predecessors were before him. By colour of this petition and concession the king frequently did and ordered many things contrary to such statutes which had never been repealed, acting expressly and knowingly against his oath made in his coronation.

18. (He continued his favourite sheriffs in office for two or three years instead of only the legal one year.)

19. Also, although by statute and custom of the realm, upon the summons of parliament the people of each shire ought to be free to choose and depute knights for the shire to be present in parliament to set forth their grievances, and sue for remedy as might seem to them expedient; yet the king, that he might be the more free to carry out in parliament his rash designs, directed his mandates frequently to his sheriffs, to see that certain persons nominated by himself should come to parliament as knights of the shire. The knights thus favourable to him he could induce, as he frequently did, sometimes by fear and various threats, sometimes by gifts, to agree to measures prejudicial to the realm and extremely burdensome to the people; and especially he induced them to concede to the king the subsidy of wools for the term of his life, and another subsidy for a term of years, oppressing his people too much.

20. (The king caused the sheriffs to swear more than their accustomed oath, and especially to promise to obey all his mandates under the great and privy seals and also letters under the signet. And the sheriffs were to arrest any of their bailiffs whom they heard speaking in public or in private to the discredit or slander of the king, and cause them to be imprisoned at the king's pleasure.)

21. Also, the king, wishing to crush the people under his feet and craftily acquire their goods, that he might have a superabundance of riches, induced the people of seventeen shires to make their submission to the king as traitors, by letters under their seals; by colour of which he obtained great sums of money conceded by the clergy and people of the shires, to be taken at the king's pleasure. And although to please the people the king caused those forced letters to be restored to them, yet the king caused the proctors of the people, who had full powers conceded to them to bind themselves and their heirs to the king, to give undertakings to him under their seals in the name of the people. Thus he deceived his people, and craftily extorted their goods from them.

22. (He extorted large sums of money from abbots and priors for his expedition to Ireland.)

23. Also, in many great councils of the king, when the lords of the realm, the justices, and others were charged faithfully to counsel the king in matters touching the estate of himself and the realm, often the lords, justices and others when they were giving their advice according to their discretion were suddenly and sharply rebuked and censured by him, so that they did not dare to speak the truth about the state of the king and the kingdom in giving their advice.

24. (The king took the treasures and crown jewels to Ireland without the consent of the estates of the realm. He also falsified the records of the realm.)

25. (The king was so variable and dissimulating in his words and writings, especially to popes and rulers outside the realm, that no one could trust him.)

26. Also, although the lands and tenements, goods and chattels of every freeman, according to the laws of the

realm used through all past times, ought not to be seized unless they have been lawfully forfeited; nevertheless the king, proposing and determining to undo such laws, declared and affirmed in the presence of very many lords and others of the community of the realm that the lives of every one of his lieges and their lands, tenements, goods, and chattels are his at his pleasure, without any forfeiture; which is entirely against the laws and customs of the realm.

27. (Contrary to Clause 39 of Magna Carta of 1215 many persons were accused before the constable and marshal of England and were forced to defend themselves by trial by battle, regardless of their age or strength.)

28. (By his letters, directed to every shire of the realm, the king made his lieges take certain oaths which might be turned to their destruction and confirm such oaths with their seals.)

29. (The king hindered legitimate processes in ecclesiastical courts, contrary to Magna Carta, by the issue of writs of prohibition.)

30. (He exiled Archbishop Arundel, against the laws of the realm.)

31. (The king left money in his will to his successor, provided he should uphold all the enactments and judgements of the parliament begun on 17 September 1397 at Westminster and continued at Shrewsbury, and all the ordinances, etc., made at Coventry and Westminster in September 1398 and March 1399, and all ordinances and judgements which might be made in future by authority of the same parliament.)

32. (At King's Langley, in the presence of the Dukes of Lancaster and York and many others, the king solemnly swore on the Host that he forgave the Duke of Gloucester for all past offences and would never proceed against him for them; yet afterwards he had the duke cruelly murdered for these offences.)

33. (When the Speaker of the Commons accused Archbishop Arundel in parliament, the king did not allow him to speak in his defence, but craftily told him to go away to his lodging to prepare his defence, and said that meanwhile the king would look after his interests. By these means the king kept him away for five days or more, and during this period got him condemned in his absence to exile and forfeiture of all his goods.)

It seemed to all the estates who were interrogated thereupon, singly and in common, that those accusations of crime and defaults were sufficient and notorious enough for the deposition of the king; and they also considered his confession of inadequacy and other matters contained in the renunciation and cession, publicly announced; whereupon all the estates unanimously agreed that there was abundant reason for proceeding to deposition, for the greater security and tranquillity of the realm and the good of the kingdom. Therefore the estates and communities unanimously and cordially constituted and publicly deputed certain commissioners, i.e. the Bishop of St Asaph, the Abbot of Glastonbury, the Earl of Gloucester, Lord Berkeley, Sir Thomas Erpingham, Sir Thomas Grey, and William Thirnyng, Justice, to carry out this sentence of deposition and to depose King Richard from all his royal dignity, majesty, and honour, on behalf of, in the name of, and by authority of, all the estates, as has been observed in similar cases by the ancient custom of the realm. And soon the commissioners assuming the burden of the commission, and sitting before the royal seat as a tribunal, had some discussion on these matters and reduced the sentence of deposition to writing; and by the wish and authority of the commission the sentence was read and recited by the Bishop of St Asaph in these words....

And at once, it being manifest from the foregoing transactions and by reason of them that the realm of England with its appurtenances was vacant, Henry Duke of Lancaster, rising in his place, and standing erect so that he might be seen by the people, and humbly making the sign of the cross on his forehead and his breast, and invoking the name of Christ, claimed the realm of England, vacant as aforesaid, along with the crown and all its members and appurtenances, in his mother tongue in the following words:

In the name of the Father, Son, and Holy Ghost, I, Henry of Lancaster, challenge this realm of England and the crown with all its members and appurtenances, as I am descended by right line of the blood coming from the good lord King Henry III, and through that right that God of his grace has sent me, with the help of my kindred and my friends to recover it; the which realm was on the point of being undone for default of governance and undoing of good laws. (The duke then showed Richard's signet to the assembly, whereupon the arch-bishop led him by the right hand to the throne. In front of it Henry knelt and prayed a while, after which both archbishops seated him on the throne, amid great applause. Archbishop Arundel then preached a sermon on the text "Vir dominabitur populo" (1 Samuel ix, 17).)

When this sermon was finished, the lord king Henry, in order to set at rest the minds of his subjects declared publicly in these words: —

Sires, I thank God and you lords spiritual and temporal and all the estates of the land; and let you know that it is not my will that any man should think that by way of conquest I would disinherit any man of his heritage, franchise, or other rights that he ought to have, nor put him out of what he has and has had by the good laws and customs of the realm; except those persons who have been against the good purpose and the common profit of the realm.

... And afterwards on the Wednesday next following the said proctors deputed as aforesaid, came to Richard lately king within the Tower and lord William Thirnyng, justice, on behalf of himself and his...fellow proctors and all the estates and people aforesaid...notified the...sentence of deposition to the same Richard, and renounced homage and fealty to him...in these words:

Sire, it is well known to you that there was a parliament summoned of all the estates of the realm to be at Westminster and to begin on the Tuesday, the morrow of the feast of St Michael the Archangel (30 September), that was yesterday, and because of this summons all the estates of the land were gathered there and made these same persons who have come here to you now their proctors and given them full authority and power and charged them to say the words that we shall say to you in their name and on their behalf; that is to say, the Bishop of St Asaph for archbishops and bishops, the Abbot of Glastonbury for abbots and priors, and all other men of holy church, secular and regular; the Earl of Gloucester for dukes and earls; Lord Berkeley for barons and bannerets; Sir Thomas Erpingham, chamberlain, for all the bachelors and commons of this land of the South, Sir Thomas Grey for all the bachelors and commons of the North; and my colleague John Markham and me, to come with them for all these estates. And so, sire, these words and the doing that we shall say to you are not only our words but the words and doings of all the estates of this land and our charge and in their name.

And he answered and said that he knew well that we would not speak but as we were charged.

(Sir William Thirning then recounted the previous stages of the deposition — Richard's abdication on Monday, Michaelmas Day, in the Tower, the reading of this renunciation to the estates and people at Westminster, the reading of the thirtythree articles of default of governance, and the declaration of deposition.)

And we, the proctors of all these estates and people, as we are charged by them, and by their authority given to us, and in their name, yield you up, for all the estates and people aforesaid, liege homage and fealty, and all allegiance and all other bonds, charges, and services which belong to it. And none of all these estates and people from this time forward shall bear you faith, nor do you obedience as to their king. And he answered and said, that he looked not thereafter; but he said, that after all this he hoped that his cousin would be a good lord to him.

On Monday, the day of St Edward, King and Confessor, King Henry was crowned at Westminster, with all the solemnity and honour that was fitting; and certain lords and others did severally their services to king Henry according to their tenures, in the accustomed manner at the time of such a coronation.

FROM THE FINAL DEMANDS OF HENRY V, AS PRESENTED TO THE KING OF FRANCE (1415)

THIS DOCUMENTS WHAT WAS ESSENTIALLY A DECLARATION OF WAR, LEADING TO HENRY'S FABLED VICTORY AT AGINCOURT.

We sought, first, from his cousin of France the crown and kingdom of France, with all the rights and appurtenances belonging to it, to be effectually restored and handed over to our dread lord the king. And after a short interval, because it truly seemed to us that the commissaries and deputies of our kinsman of France would not accept this proposal at all, for the good of the negotiation and speedier conclusion of it, under certain protests we condescended to other proposals. We sought that at the least there might be restored to our aforesaid most dread lord other rights, inheritances, and lordships belonging to him in addition to the crown of France, and detained on behalf of his kinsman, that is:

The homage, superiority and lordship of the duchy of Normandy

The homage, superiority, and lordship of the duchy of Touraine, and of the county of Anjou and Maine

The superiority and homage of the duchy of Brittany

The superiority and homage of the county and country of Flanders. And all that part of Aquitaine which the aforesaid kinsman of France and others on his behalf, detains at present. And all other duchies, counties, lordships, towns, estates, etc., which by the treaty of peace between Edward late king of England and John then his brother of France, of good memory, were assigned to the aforesaid Edward.... And moreover...we demand all the castles, towns, strongholds, lordships, etc. between the waters of the Somme and Gravelines.

And that our most dread lord and his heirs may have and hold all the foregoing freely and quietly as a neighbour, without any superiority or appeal to be claimed from him or his heirs on behalf of the said kinsman of France or his heirs in any way whatsoever....

We demanded...half of the county of Provence with the castles and lordships of Beaufort and Nogent to be effectively delivered to our lord the king, to belong to him by hereditary right. We, the aforesaid ambassadors, demanded 1,600,000 crowns, of which two shall be worth an English noble, which ought to have been paid to the aforesaid former King Edward, for the ransom of John, lately his brother of France of excellent memory, which yet remain unpaid, to be effectively handed over to our lord King Henry And we demanded for the dowry of the aforesaid Lady Catherine in the event of her being joined in marriage by the favour of God to our most dread lord the king, 2,000,000 crowns, of which two shall always be worth one English noble.

NEGOTIATIONS FOR THE MARRIAGE OF PRINCE HENRY AND CATHERINE OF ARAGON (1503)

THIS DOCUMENT OFFERS A GLIMPSE OF THE COMPLICATED DEALINGS THAT
WENT INTO DYNASTIC MARRIAGES—IN THIS CASE, THE MARRIAGE OF
THE FUTURE HENRY VIII TO CATHERINE OF ARAGON, WIDOW OF HENRY'S
OLDER BROTHER ARTHUR AND THE FIRST OF HENRY'S SIX WIVES.

1. Ferdinand and Isabella, as well as Henry VII promise to employ all their influence with the Court of Rome, in order to obtain the dispensation of the Pope necessary for the marriage of the Princess Katharine with Henry, Prince of Wales. The Papal dispensation is required, because the said Princess Katharine had on a former occasion contracted a marriage with the late Prince Arthur, brother of the present Prince of Wales, whereby she became related to Henry, Prince of Wales, in the first degree of affinity, and because her marriage with Prince Arthur was solemnized according to the rites of the Catholic Church, and afterwards consummated.

2. If the aforesaid dispensation be obtained, Ferdinand and Isabella on the one side, and Henry VII on the other, promise that a marriage per verba de praesenti shall be contracted within two months after this treaty shall have been ratified by both the contracting parties.

3. When the Princess Katharine contracted her marriage with Prince Arthur, Ferdinand and Isabella promised to give her a marriage portion of 200,000 scudos, each scudo being worth 4s. 2d. of English money. Of this sum 100,000 scudos were paid into the hands of King Henry VII at the time when the said marriage was solemnized. Ferdinand and Isabella renounce in their name and in the name of the Princess Katharine, all right to demand restitution of this payment.

4. Ferdinand and Isabella promise Henry VII to pay, on the marriage of their daughter to Henry, Prince of Wales, a marriage portion of 200,000 scudos, each scudo being worth 4s. 2d. of English money. Henry VII on the other hand, confesses that he has already received one half of the said 200,000 scudos. The remaining 100,000 scudos are to be paid in the following manner; viz. 65,000 scudos in coined gold, 15,000 scudos in plate, and vessels of gold and silver, according to the valuation of silversmiths in London, 20,000 scudos in jewels, pearls, ornaments etc. of the Princess of Wales, according to their prices in London, which is to be fixed by sworn valuers. All these payments are to be made in London, within ten days before or after the solemnization of the marriage. The marriage to be solemnized as soon as Prince Henry shall have completed the fourteenth year of his age, and as soon as Ferdinand and Isabella, or their successors, can show that the whole marriage portion is in London, ready for delivery. Ferdinand and Isabella pledge their and their subjects' fortunes as security for the punctual execution of this clause of the treaty.

5. Prince Arthur had settled on the Princess of Wales her dowry, consisting of lands, manors etc, the revenues of which amount to the third part of the revenues of Wales, Cornwall, and Chester. She is to give back, within ten days before or after the solemnization of her new marriage, all documents and title deeds respecting this dowry; and Prince Henry will endow her on the day of the solemnization of the marriage with a new dowry as great and as well secured as her first dowry was. Henry VII promises to ratify the constitution of the new dowry within one month after the solemnization of the marriage. The Princess Katharine renounces all other claims on the revenues of Wales, Cornwall and Chester, and promises to be content with her dowry.

6. In case the Princess Katharine become Queen of England, she is to have, besides her dowry as Princess of Wales, a dowry as Queen, consisting of the third part of all the revenues of the Crown of England. She is to hold both dowries for life.

7. The right of succession to the Crown of Spain is reserved to the Princess Katharine.

8. If the Princess Katharine become Queen of England, she is to enjoy, during the lifetime of her royal husband, all the privileges and revenues that other Queens of England have enjoyed before her. Henry VII pledges the whole of his fortune and the fortunes of his subjects as security for the punctual fulfilment of his obligation.

9. If Henry, Prince of Wales, should die before his father, and leave a son or sons born of the Princess Katharine, during her marriage with him, Henry VII promises to create such sons or the first born son, Prince of Wales, and to do all in his power to secure to the said son the succession to the throne after his death.

10. Both contracting parties promise to ratify this treaty within six months after the date of its conclusion.

LETTERS OF HENRY VIII TO ANNE BOLEYN (C. 1527)

MANY OF HENRY'S LETTERS TO ANNE BOLEYN, WRITTEN DURING THEIR COURTSHIP, WERE PRESERVED, THOUGH NOT PUBLISHED UNTIL 1714. THEY OFFER A FASCINATING WINDOW ON A STORIED HISTORY.

MY MISTRESS AND FRIEND.

I and my heart put ourselves in your hands, begging you to have them suitors for your good favour, and that your affection for them should not grow less through absence. For it would be a great pity to increase their sorrow since absence does it sufficiently, and more than ever I could have thought possible reminding us of a point in astronomy, which is, that the longer the days are the farther off is the sun, and yet the more fierce. So it is with our love, for by absence we are parted, yet nevertheless it keeps its fervour, at least on my side, and I hope on yours also: assuring you that on my side the ennui of absence is already too much for me: and when I think of the increase of what I must needs suffer it would be well nigh unbearable for me were it not for the firm hope I have of your steadfast affection for me. So, to remind you of that sometimes, and as I cannot be with you in person, I am sending you the nearest possible thing to that, namely, my picture set in a bracelet, with the whole device which you already know. Wishing myself in their place when it shall please you. This by the hand of
Your loyal servant and friend
H.Rex.

TO MY MISTRESS.

Because the time seems to me very long since I have heard of your good health and of you, the great affection I have for you urges me to send this messenger to you to be better informed of your health and wishes: and because, since I parted from you, I have been told that the opinion in which I left you is now completely changed, and that you are unwilling to come to court, neither with madam your mother nor in any other way. If this report is true I cannot enough marvel at it, seeing that I have since made certain I have never offended you. And it seems to me a very small return for the great love I have for you to be kept apart both from the presence and the person of the woman whom I most esteem in the world. And if you love me with as great affection as I hope I am sure that this estrangement of our two selves must be a little vexing to you, though not so much to the mistress as to the servant. Consider well, my mistress, that your absence grieves me greatly, hoping that it is not your will that it should be so. But if I knew for certain that you wished it of your own will I could not do other than deplore my ill fortune while putting from me little by little my mad infatuation.

And so, for lack of time, I make an end of my rude letter begging you to believe what the bearer will tell you on my behalf.
Written with the hand of your entire servant
H.Rex.

The reasonable request of your last letter with the pleasure also that I take to know them true causeth me to send you now these news: the legate which we most desired arrived at Paris on Sunday or Monday last past so that I trust by the next Monday to hear of his arrival at Calais, and then I trust within a while after to enjoy that which I have so long longed for to God's pleasure and our both comfort: no more to you at this present mine own darling for lack of time but that I would you were in my arms or I in yours for I think it long since I kissed you. Written after the killing of an hart at a xj. of the clock minding with God's grace tomorrow mightily timely to kill another: by the hand of him which I trust shortly shall be yours.
Henry R.

The approach of the time I have so long awaited rejoices me so much that it seems already here. Nevertheless, the complete fulfilment cannot be until the two persons meet, which meeting is more desired on my side than anything on earth: for what joy in this world can be so great as having the company of the one who is one's dearest friend: knowing also that her choice is also the same, which thought gives me great pleasure. Judge then what her presence will do, whose absence has given me such pangs as neither tongue nor pen can express, and that never anything but that can remedy. Begging you, my mistress, to tell my lord your father, on my behalf, that I beg him to put forward by two days the time appointed so as to be in court, before the old date or at least on the day arranged, for otherwise I shall think that he will not serve the lovers' turn as he said he would, nor come up to my expectations. No more now for lack of time, hoping quite soon to tell you by word of mouth the rest of the pangs I have suffered through your absence. Written by the hand of the secretary who wishes himself at this time with you privately, and who is and ever will be
Your loyal and most assured servant
(H. seeks no other R.)

THE ACT OF SUPREMACY (1534)

THE STATUTE THAT ESTABLISHED HENRY VIII AS SUPREME HEAD
OF THE ENGLISH CHURCH – PART OF THE PIVOTAL BREAK FROM ROME.

Albeit the King's Majesty justly and rightfully is and oweth to be the supreme head of the Church of England, and so is recognized by the clergy of this realm in their Convocations; yet nevertheless for corroboration and confirmation thereof, and for increase of virtue in Christ's religion within this realm of England, and to repress and extirp all errors, heresies, and other enormities and abuses heretofore used in the same, Be it enacted... that the King our sovereign lord, his heirs and successors kings of this realm, shall be taken, accepted, and reputed the only supreme head in earth of the Church of England called Anglicana Ecclesia, and shall have and enjoy annexed and united to the imperial crown of this realm as well the title and style thereof, as all honours, dignities, pre-eminences, jurisdictions, privileges, authorities, immunities, profits, and commodities, to the said dignity of supreme head of the same Church belonging and appertaining: And that our said sovereign lord, his heirs and successors kings of this realm, shall have full power and authority from time to time to visit, repress, redress, reform, order, correct, restrain, and amend all such errors, heresies, abuses, offences, contempts, and enormities, whatsoever they be, which by any manner spiritual authority or jurisdiction ought or may lawfully be reformed, repressed, ordered, redressed, corrected, restrained, or amended, most to the pleasure of Almighty God, the increase of virtue in Christ's religion, and for the conservancy of the peace, unity and tranquillity of this realm: any usage, custom, foreign laws foreign authority, prescription or any other thing or things to the contrary hereof notwithstanding.

THE ACT OF SUPREMACY (1559)

ALONG WITH THE ACT OF UNIFORMITY OF THE SAME YEAR, THIS LAW ESTABLISHED WHAT HAS COME TO BE KNOWN AS THE ELIZABETHAN RELIGIOUS SETTLEMENT. IT REASSERTS, AFTER THE RULE OF MARY I, THE INDEPENDENCE OF THE CHURCH OF ENGLAND FROM THE AUTHORITY OF ROME.

Most humbly beseech your most excellent majesty, your faithful and obedient subjects, the Lords spiritual and temporal, and the Commons, in this your present Parliament assembled, that where in time of the reign of your most dear father, of worthy memory, King Henry VIII, divers good laws and statutes were made and established, as well for the utter extinguishment and putting away of all usurped and foreign powers and authorities out of this your realm, and other your highness's dominions and countries, as also for the restoring and uniting to the imperial crown of this realm the ancient jurisdictions, authorities, superiorities, and preeminences to the same of right belonging and appertaining, by reason whereof we, your most humble and obedient subjects, from the five-and-twentieth year of the reign of your said dear father, were continually kept in good order, and were disburdened of divers great and intolerable charges and exactions before that time unlawfully taken and exacted by such foreign power and authority as before that was usurped, until such time as all the said good laws and statutes, by one Act of Parliament made in the first and second years of the reigns of the late King Philip and Queen Mary, your highness's sister, intituled an Act repealing all statutes, articles, and provisions made against the See Apostolic of Rome since the twentieth year of King Henry VIII, and also for the establishment of all spiritual and ecclesiastical possessions and hereditaments conveyed to the laity, were all clearly repealed and made void, as by the same Act of repeal more at large does and may appear; by reason of which Act of repeal, your said humble subjects were eftsoons brought under an usurped foreign power and authority, and do yet remain in that bondage, to the intolerable charges of your loving subjects, if some redress, by the authority of this your High Court of Parliament, with the assent of your highness, be not had and provided:

May it therefore please your highness, for the repressing of the said usurped foreign power and the restoring of the rites, jurisdictions, and preeminences appertaining to the imperial crown of this your realm, that it may be enacted by the authority of this present Parliament, that the said Act made in the said first and second years of the reigns of the said late King Philip and Queen Mary, and all and every branch, clauses, and articles therein contained (other than such branches, clauses, and sentences as hereafter shall be excepted) may, from the last day of this session of Parliament, by authority of this present Parliament, be repealed, and shall from thenceforth be utterly void and of none effect.

And that also for the reviving of divers of the said good laws and statutes made in the time of your said dear father, it may also please your highness, that one Act and statute made in the twenty-third year of the reign of the said late King Henry VIII, intituled, An Act that no person shall be cited out of the diocese wherein he or she dwells, except in certain cases;

And one other Act made in the twenty-fourth year of the reign of the said late King, intituled, An Act that appeals in such cases as have been used to be pursued to the see of Rome shall not be from henceforth had nor used, but within this realm;

And one other Act made in the twenty-fifth year of the said late King, concerning restraint of payment of annates and firstfruits of archbishoprics and bishoprics to the see of Rome;

And one other Act in the said twenty-fifth year, intituled, An Act concerning the submission of the clergy to the king's majesty;

And also one Act made in the said twenty-fifth year, intituled, An Act restraining the payment of annates or firstfruits to the Bishop of Rome, and of the electing and consecrating of archbishops and bishops within this realm;

And one other Act made in the said twenty-fifth year, intituled, An Act concerning the exoneration of the king's subjects from exactions and impositions heretofore paid to the see of Rome, and for having licences and dispensations within this realm, without suing further for the same;

And one other Act made in the twenty-sixth year of the said late king, intituled, An Act for nomination and consecration of suffragans within this realm;

And also one other Act made in the twenty-eighth year of the reign of the said late king, intituled, An Act for the release of such as have obtained pretended licences and dispensations from the see of Rome;

And all and every branches, words, and sentences in the said several Acts and statutes contained, by authority of this present Parliament, from and at all times after the last day of this session of Parliament, shall be revived, and shall stand and be in full force and strength, to all intents, constructions, and purposes.

And that the branches, sentences, and words of the said several Acts, and every of them, from thenceforth shall and may be judged, deemed, and taken to extend to your highness, your heirs and successors, as fully and largely as ever the same Acts, or any of them, did extend to the said late King Henry VIII, your highness's father.

And that it may also please your highness, that it may be enacted by the authority of this present Parliament, that so much of one Act or statute made in the thirty-second year of the reign of your said dear father King Henry VIII, intituled, An Act concerning precontracts of marriages, and touching degrees of consanguinity, as in the time of the late King Edward VI, your highness's most dear brother, by one other Act or statute, was not repealed; and also one Act made in the thirty-seventh year of the reign of the said late King Henry VIII, intituled, An Act that doctors of the civil law, being married, may exercise ecclesiastical jurisdiction; and all and every branches and articles in the said two Acts last mentioned, and not repealed in the time of the said late King Edward VI, may from henceforth likewise stand and be revived, and remain in their full force and strength, to all intents and purposes; anything contained in the said Act of repeal before mentioned, or any other matter or cause to the contrary notwithstanding.

And that it may also please your highness, that it may be further enacted by the authority aforesaid, that all other laws and statutes, and the branches and clauses of any Act or statute, repealed and made void by the said Act of repeal, made in the time of the said late King Philip and Queen Mary, and not in this present Act specially mentioned and revived, shall stand, remain, and be repealed and void, in such like manner and form as they were before the making of this Act; anything herein contained to the contrary notwithstanding.

And that it may also please your highness, that it may be enacted by the authority aforesaid, that one Act and statute made in the first year of the reign of the late King Edward VI, your majesty's most dear brother, intituled, An Act against such persons as shall unreverently speak against the Sacrament of the Body and Blood of Christ, commonly called the Sacrament of the altar, and for the receiving thereof under both kinds, and all and every branches, clauses, and sentences therein contained, shall and may likewise, from the last day of this session of Parliament, be revived, and from thenceforth shall and may stand, remain, and be in full force, strength, and effect, to all intents, constructions, and purposes, in such like manner and form as the same was at any time in the first year of the reign of the said late King Edward VI; any law, statute, or other matter to the contrary in any wise notwithstanding.

And that also it may please your highness, that it may be further established and enacted by the authority aforesaid, that one Act and statute made in the first and second years of the said late King Philip and Queen Mary, intituled, An Act for the reviving of three statutes made for the punishment of heresies, and also the said three statutes mentioned in the said Act, and by the same Act revived, and all and every branches, articles, clauses, and sentences contained in the said several Acts and statutes, and every of them, shall be from the last day of this session of Parliament deemed and remain utterly repealed, void, and of none effect, to all intents and purposes; anything in the said several Acts or any of them contained, or any other matter or cause to the contrary notwithstanding.

And to the intent that all usurped and foreign power and authority, spiritual and temporal, may for ever be clearly extinguished, and never to be used or obeyed within this realm, or any other your majesty's dominions or coun-tries, may it please your highness that it may be further enacted by the authority aforesaid, that no foreign prince, person, prelate, state, or potentate, spiritual or temporal, shall at any time after the last day of this session of Parliament, use, enjoy, or exercise any manner of power, jurisdicdiction, superiority, authority, preeminence or privilege, spiritual or ecclesiastical, within this realm, or within any other your majesty's dominions or countries that now be, or hereafter shall be, but from thenceforth the same shall be clearly abolished out of this realm, and all other your highness's dominions for ever; any statute, ordinance, custom, constitutions, or any other matter or cause whatsoever to the contrary in any wise notwithstanding.

And that also it may likewise please your highness, that it may be established and enacted by the authority aforesaid, that such jurisdictions, privileges, superiorities, and preeminences, spiritual and ecclesiastical, as by any spiritual or ecclesiastical power or authority have heretofore been, or may lawfully be exercised or used for the visitation of the ecclesiastical state and persons, and for reformation, order, and correction of the same, and of all manner of errors, heresies, schisms, abuses, offences, contempts, and enormities, shall for ever, by authority of this present Parliament, be united and annexed to the imperial crown of this realm.

And that your highness, your heirs and successors, kings or queens of this realm, shall have full power and authority by virtue of this Act, by letters patent under the great seal of England, to assign, name, and authorize, when and as often as your highness, your heirs or successors, shall think meet and convenient, and for such and so long time as shall please your highness, your heirs or successors, such person or persons being natural-born subjects to your highness, your heirs or successors, as your majesty, your heirs or successors, shall think meet, to exercise, use, occupy, and execute under your highness, your heirs and successors, all manner of jurisdictions, privileges, and preeminences, in any wise touching or concerning any spiritual or ecclesiastical jurisdiction, within these your realms of England and Ireland, or any other your highness's dominions or countries; and to visit, reform, redress, order, correct, and amend all such errors, heresies, schisms, abuses, offences, contempts, and enormities whatsoever, which by any manner spiritual or ecclesiastical power, authority, or jurisdiction, can or may lawfully be reformed, ordered, redressed, corrected, restrained, or amended, to the pleasure of Almighty God, the increase of virtue, and the conservation of the peace and unity of this realm, and that such person or persons so to be named, assigned, authorized, and appointed by your highness, your heirs or successors, after the said letters patent to him or them made and delivered, as is aforesaid, shall have full power and authority, by virtue of this Act, and of the said letters patent, under your highness, your heirs and successors, to exercise, use, and execute all the premises, according to the tenor and effect of the said letters patent; any matter or cause to the contrary in any wise notwithstanding.

And for the better observation and maintenance of this Act, may it please your highness that it may be further enacted by the authority aforesaid, that all and every archbishop, bishop, and all and every other ecclesiastical person, and other ecclesiastical officer and minister; of what estate, dignity, preeminence, or degree soever he or they be or shall be, and all and every temporal judge, justice, mayor, and other lay or temporal officer and minister, and every other person having your highness's fee or wages, within this realm, or any your highness's dominions, shall make, take, and receive a corporal oath upon the evangelist, before such person or persons as shall please your highness, your heirs or successors, under the great seal of England to assign and name, to accept and to take the same according to the tenor and effect hereafter following, that is to say: I, A. B., do utterly testify and declare in my conscience, that the queen's highness is the only supreme governor of this realm, and of all other her highness's dominions and countries, as well in all spiritual or ecclesiastical things or causes, as temporal, and that no foreign prince, person, prelate, state or potentate, has, or ought to have, any jurisdiction, power, superiority, preeminence, or authority ecclesiastical or spiritual, within this realm; and therefore I do utterly renounce and forsake all foreign jurisdictions, powers, superiorities, and authorities, and do promise that from henceforth I shall bear faith and true allegiance to the queen's highness, her heirs and lawful successors, and to my power shall assist and defend all jurisdictions, pre-eminences, privileges, and authorities granted or belonging to the queen's highness, her heirs and successors, or united and annexed to the imperial crown of this realm. So help me God, and by the contents of this book.'

And that it may be also enacted, that if any such archbishop, bishop, or other ecclesiastical officer or minister, or any of the said temporal judges, justiciaries, or other lay officer or minister, shall peremptorily or obstinately refuse to take or receive the said oath, that then he so refusing shall forfeit and lose, only during his life, all and every ecclesiastical and spiritual promotion, benefice, and office, and every temporal and lay promotion and office, which he has solely at the time of such refusal made; and that the whole title, interest, and incumbency, in every such promotion, benefice, and other office, as against such person only so refusing, during his life, shall clearly cease and be void, as though the party so refusing were dead.

And that also all and every such person and persons so refusing to take the said oath, shall immediately after such refusal be from thenceforth, during his life, disabled to retain or exercise any office or other promotion which he, at the time of such refusal, has jointly, or in common, with any other person or persons.

And that all and every person and persons, that at any time hereafter shall be preferred, promoted, or collated to any archbishopric or bishopric, or to any other spiritual or ecclesiastical benefice, promotion, dignity, office, or ministry, or that shall be by your highness, your heirs or successors, preferred or promoted to any temporal or lay office, ministry, or service within this realm, or in any your highness's dominions, before he or they shall take upon him or them to receive, use, exercise, supply, or occupy any such archbishopric, bishopric, promotion, dignity, office, ministry, or service, shall likewise make, take, and receive the said corporal oath before mentioned, upon the evangelist, before such persons as have or shall have authority to admit any such person to any such office, ministry, or service, or else before such person or persons as by your highness, your heirs or successors, by commission under the great seal of England, shall be named, assigned, or appointed to minister the said oath.

And that it may likewise be further enacted by the authority aforesaid, that if any such person or persons, as at any time hereafter shall be promoted, preferred, or collated to any such promotion spiritual or ecclesiastical, benefice, office, or ministry, or that by your highness, your heirs or successors, shall be promoted or preferred to any temporal or lay office, ministry, or service, shall and do peremptorily and obstinately refuse to take the same oath so to him to be offered; that then he or they so refusing shall presently be judged disabled in the law to receive, take, or have the same promotion spiritual or ecclesiastical, the same temporal office, ministry, or service within this realm, or any other your highness's dominions, to all intents, constructions, and purposes.

And that it may be further enacted by the authority aforesaid, that all and every person and persons temporal, suing livery or ouster le main out of the hands of your highness, your heirs or successors, before his or their livery or ouster le main sued forth and allowed, and every temporal person or persons doing any homage to your highness, your heirs or successors, or that shall be received into service with your highness, your heirs or successors, shall make, take, and receive the said corporal oath before mentioned, before the lord chancellor of England, or the lord keeper of the great seal for the time being, or before such person or persons as by your highness, your heirs or successors, shall be named and appointed to accept or receive the same.

And that also all and every person and persons taking orders, and all and every other person and persons which shall be promoted or preferred to any degree of learning in any university within this your realm or dominions, before he shall receive or take any such orders, or be preferred to any such degree of learning, shall make, take, and receive the said oath by this Act set forth and declared as is aforesaid, before his or their ordinary, commissary, chancellor or vice-chancellor, or their sufficient deputies in the said university.

Provided always, and that it may be further enacted by the authority aforesaid, that if any person, having any estate of inheritance in any temporal office or offices, shall hereafter obstinately and peremptorily refuse to accept and take the said oath as is aforesaid, and after, at any time during his life, shall willingly require to take and receive the said oath, and so do take and accept the same oath before any person or persons that shall have lawful authority to minister the same; that then every such person, immediately after he has so received the same oath, shall

be vested, deemed, and judged in like estate and possession of the said office, as he was before the said refusal, and shall and may use and exercise the said office in such manner and form as he should or might have done before such refusal, anything in this Act contained to the contrary in any wise notwithstanding.

And for the more sure observation of this Act, and the utter extinguishment of all foreign and usurped power and authority, may it please your highness, that it may be further enacted by the authority aforesaid, that if any person or persons dwelling or inhabiting within this your realm, or in any other your highness's realms or dominions, of what estate, dignity, or degree soever he or they be, after the end of thirty days next after the determination of this session of this present Parliament, shall by writing, printing, teaching, preaching, express words, deed or act, advisedly, maliciously, and directly affirm, hold, stand with, set forth, maintain, or defend the authority, preeminence, power or jurisdiction, spiritual or ecclesiastical, of any foreign prince, prelate, person, state, or potentate whatsoever, heretofore claimed, used, or usurped within this realm, or any dominion or country being within or under the power, dominion, or obeisance of your highness, or shall advisedly, maliciously, and directly put in ure or execute anything for the extolling, advancement, setting forth, maintenance, or defence of any such pretended or usurped jurisdiction, power, preeminence, or authority, or any part thereof; that then every such person and persons so doing and offending, their abettors, aiders, procurers, and counsellors, being thereof lawfully convicted and attainted, according to the due order and course of the common laws of this realm, for his or their first offence shall forfeit and lose unto your highness, your heirs and successors, all his and their goods and chattels, as well real as personal.

And if any such person so convicted or attainted shall not have or be worth of his proper goods and chattels to the value of twenty pounds, at the time of his conviction or attainder, that then every such person so convicted and attainted, over and besides the forfeiture of all his said goods and chattels, shall have and suffer imprisonment by the space of one whole year, without bail or mainprize. And that also all and every the benefices, prebends, and other ecclesiastical promotions and dignities whatsoever, of every spiritual person so offending, and being attainted, shall immediately after such attainder be utterly void to all intents and purposes, as though the incumbent thereof were dead; and that the patron and donor of every such benefice, prebend, spiritual promotion and dignity, shall and may lawfully present unto the same, or give the same, in such manner and form as if the said incumbent were dead.

And if any such offender or offenders, after such conviction or attainder, do eftsoons commit or do the said offences, or any of them, in manner and form aforesaid, and be thereof duly convicted and attainted, as is aforesaid; that then every such offender and offenders shall for the same second offence incur into the dangers, penalties, and forfeitures ordained and provided by the statute of Provision and Praemunire, made in the sixteenth year of the reign of King Richard II.

And if any such offender or offenders, at any time after the said second conviction and attainder, do the third time commit and do the said offences, or any of them, in manner and form aforesaid, and be thereof duly convicted and attainted, as is aforesaid; that then every such offence or offences shall be deemed and adjudged high treason, and that the offender and offenders therein, being thereof lawfully convicted and attainted, according to the laws of this realm, shall suffer pains of death, and other penalties, forfeitures, and losses, as in cases of high treason by the laws of this realm.

And also that it may likewise please your highness, that it may be enacted by the authority aforesaid, that no manner of person or persons shall be molested or impeached for any of the offences aforesaid committed or perpetrated only by preaching, teaching, or words, unless he or they be thereof lawfully indicted within the space of one half-year next after his or their offences so committed; and in case any person or persons shall fortune to be imprisoned for any of the said offences committed by preaching,

teaching, or words only, and be not thereof indicted within the space of one half-year next after his or their such offence so committed and done, that then the said person so imprisoned shall be set at liberty, and be no longer detained in prison for any such cause or offence.

Provided always, and be it enacted by the authority aforesaid, that this Act, or anything therein contained, shall not in any wise extend to repeal any clause, matter, or sentence contained or specified in the said Act of repeal made in the said first and second years of the reigns of the said late King Philip and Queen Mary, as does in any wise touch or concern any matter or case of Praemunire, or that does make or ordain any matter or cause to be within the case of Praemunire; but that the same, for so much only as touches or concerns any case or matter of Praemunire, shall stand and remain in such force and effect as the same was before the making of this Act, anything in this Act contained to the contrary in any wise notwithstanding.

Provided also, and be it enacted by the authority aforesaid, that this Act, or anything therein contained, shall not in any wise extend or be prejudicial to any person or persons for any offence or offences committed or done, or hereafter to be committed or done, contrary to the tenor and effect of any Act or statute now revived by this Act, before the end of thirty days next after the end of the session of this present Parliament; anything in this Act contained or any other matter or cause to the contrary notwithstanding.

And if it happen that any peer of this realm shall fortune to be indicted of and for any offence that is revived or made Praemunire or treason by this Act, that then he so being indicted shall have his trial by his peers, in such like manner and form as in other cases of treason has been used.

Provided always, and be it enacted as is aforesaid, that no manner of order, Act, or determination, for any matter of religion or cause ecclesiastical, had or made by the authority of this present Parliament, shall be accepted, deemed, interpreted, or adjudged at any time hereafter, to be any error, heresy, schism, or schismatical opinion; any order, decree, sentence, constitution, or law, whatsoever the same be, to the contrary notwithstanding.

Provided always, and be it enacted by the authority aforesaid, that such person or persons to whom your highness, your heirs or successors, shall hereafter, by letters patent, under the great seal of England, give authority to have or execute any jurisdiction, power, or authority spiritual, or to visit, reform, order, or correct any errors, heresies, schisms, abuses, or enormities by virtue of this Act, shall not in any wise have authority or power to order, determine, or adjudge any matter or cause to be heresy, but only such as heretofore have been determined, ordered, or adjudged to be heresy, by the authority of the canonical Scriptures, or by the first four general Councils, or any of them, or by any other general Council wherein the same was declared heresy by the express and plain words of the said canonical Scriptures, or such as hereafter shall be ordered, judged, or determined to be heresy by the High Court of Parliament of this realm, with the assent of the clergy in their Convocation; anything in this Act contained to the contrary notwithstanding.

And be it further enacted by the authority aforesaid, that no person or persons shall be hereafter indicted or arraigned for any the offences made, ordained, revived, or adjudged by this Act, unless there be two sufficient witnesses, or more, to testify and declare the said offences whereof he shall be indicted or arraigned; and that the said witnesses, or so many of them as shall be living and within this realm at the time of the arraignment of such person so indicted, shall be brought forth in person, face to face, before the party so arraigned, and there shall testify and declare what they can say against the party so arraigned, if he require the same.

Provided also, and be it further enacted by the authority aforesaid, that if any person or persons shall hereafter happen to give any relief, aid, or comfort, or in any wise be aiding, helping, or comforting to the person or persons of any that shall hereafter happen to be an offender in any matter or case of Praemunire or treason, revived or made by this Act, that then such relief, aid, or comfort given shall not be judged or taken to be any offence, unless there be two sufficient witnesses at the least, that can and

will openly testify and declare that the person or persons that so gave such relief, aid, or comfort had notice and knowledge of such offence committed and done by the said offender, at the time of such relief, aid, or comfort so to him given or ministered; anything in this Act contained, or any other matter or cause to the contrary in any wise notwithstanding.

And where one pretended sentence has heretofore been given in the Consistory in Paul's before certain judges delegate, by the authority legatine of the late Cardinal Pole, by reason of a foreign usurped power and authority, against Richard Chetwood, Esq., and Agnes his wife, by the name of Agnes Woodhall, at the suit of Charles Tyrril, gentleman, in a cause of matrimony solemnized between the said Richard and Agnes, as by the same pretended sentence more plainly doth appear, from which sentence the said Richard and Agnes have appealed to the Court of Rome, which appeal does there remain, and yet is not determined: may it therefore please your highness, that it may be enacted by the authority aforesaid, that if sentence in the said appeal shall happen to be given at the said Court of Rome for and in the behalf of the said Richard and Agnes, for the reversing of the said pretensed sentence, before the end of threescore days next after the end of this session of this present Parliament, that then the same shall be judged and taken to be good and effectual in the law, and shall and may be used, pleaded, and allowed in any court or place within this realm; anything in this Act or any other Act or statute contained to the contrary notwithstanding.

And if no sentence shall be given at the Court of Rome in the said appeal for the reversing of the said pretended sentence before the end of the said threescore days, that then it shall and may be lawful for the said Richard and Agnes, and either of them, at any time hereafter, to commence, take, sue, and prosecute their said appeal from the said pretended sentence, and for the reversing of the said pretended sentence, within this realm, in such like manner and form as was used to be pursued, or might have been pursued, within this realm, at any time since the twenty-fourth year of the reign of the said late King Henry VIII, upon any sentences given in the court or courts of any archbishop within this realm.

And that such appeal as so hereafter shall be taken or pursued by the said Richard Chetwood and Agnes, or either of them, and the sentence that herein or thereupon shall hereafter be given, shall be judged to be good and effectual in the law to all intents and purposes; any law, custom, usage, canon, constitution, or any other matter or cause to the contrary notwithstanding.

Provided also, and be it enacted by the authority aforesaid, that where there is the like appeal now depending in the said Court of Rome between one Robert Harcourt, merchant of the staple, and Elizabeth Harcourt, otherwise called Elizabeth Robins, of the one part, and Anthony Fydell, merchant-stranger, on the other part, that the said Robert, Elizabeth, and Anthony, and every of them, shall and may, for the prosecuting and trying of their said appeal, have and enjoy the like remedy, benefit, and advantage, in like manner and form as the said Richard and Agnes, or any of them, has, may, or ought to have and enjoy; this Act or anything therein contained to the contrary in any wise notwithstanding.

THE ACT OF UNIFORMITY (1559)

THIS, THE SECOND KEY DOCUMENT OF THE ELIZABETHAN RELIGIOUS SETTLEMENT, MANDATED THE USE OF THE BOOK OF COMMON PRAYER AND REQUIRED, ON PAIN OF A FINE, WEEKLY ATTENDANCE AT CHURCH OF ENGLAND SERVICES.

Where at the death of our late sovereign lord King Edward VI there remained one uniform order of common service and prayer, and of the administration of sacraments, rites, and ceremonies in the Church of England, which was set forth in one book, intituled: The Book of Common Prayer, and Administration of Sacraments, and other rites and ceremonies in the Church of England; authorized by Act of Parliament holden in the fifth and sixth years of our said late sovereign lord King Edward VI, intituled: An Act for the uniformity of common prayer, and administration of the sacraments; the which was repealed and taken away by Act of Parliament in the first year of the reign of our late sovereign lady Queen Mary, to the great decay of the due honour of God, and discomfort to the professors of the truth of Christ's religion:

Be it therefore enacted by the authority of this present Parliament, that the said statute of repeal, and everything therein contained, only concerning the said book, and the service, administration of sacraments, rites, and ceremonies contained or appointed in or by the said book, shall be void and of none effect, from and after the feast of the Nativity of St. John Baptist next coming; and that the said book, with the order of service, and of the administration of sacraments, rites, and ceremonies, with the alterations and additions therein added and appointed by this statute, shall stand and be, from and after the said feast of the Nativity of St. John Baptist, in full force and effect, according to the tenor and effect of this statute; anything in the aforesaid statute of repeal to the contrary notwithstanding.

And further be it enacted by the queen's highness, with the assent of the Lords (sic) and Commons in this present Parliament assembled, and by authority of the same, that all and singular ministers in any cathedral or parish church, or other place within this realm of England, Wales, and the marches of the same, or other the queen's dominions, shall from and after the feast of the Nativity of St. John Baptist next coming be bounden to say and use the Matins, Evensong, celebration of the Lord's

Supper and administration of each of the sacraments, and all their common and open prayer, in such order and form as is mentioned in the said book, so authorized by Parliament in the said fifth and sixth years of the reign of King Edward VI, with one alteration or addition of certain lessons to be used on every Sunday in the year, and the form of the Litany altered and corrected, and two sentences only added in the delivery of the sacrament to the communicants, and none other or otherwise.

And that if any manner of parson, vicar, or other whatsoever minister, that ought or should sing or say common prayer mentioned in the said book, or minister the sacraments, from and after the feast of the nativity of St. John Baptist next coming, refuse to use the said common prayers, or to minister the sacraments in such cathedral or parish church, or other places as he should use to minister the same, in such order and form as they be mentioned and set forth in the said book, or shall wilfully or obstinately standing in the same, use any other rite, ceremony, order, form, or manner of celebrating of the Lord's Supper, openly or privily, or Matins, Evensong, administration of the sacraments, or other open prayers, than is mentioned and set forth in the said book (open prayer in and throughout this Act, is meant that prayer which is for other to come unto, or hear, either in common churches or private chapels or oratories, commonly called the service of the Church), or shall preach, declare, or speak anything in the derogation or depraving of the said book, or anything therein contained, or of any part thereof, and shall be thereof lawfully convicted, according to the laws of this realm, by verdict of twelve men, or by his own confession, or by the notorious evidence of the fact, shall lose and forfeit to the queen's highness, her heirs and successors, for his first offence, the profit of all his spiritual benefices or promotions coming or arising in one whole year next after his conviction; and also that the person so convicted shall for the same offence suffer imprisonment by the space of six months, without bail or mainprize.

And if any such person once convicted of any offence concerning the premises, shall after his first conviction eftsoons offend, and be thereof, in form aforesaid, lawfully convicted, that then the same person shall for his second offence suffer imprisonment by the space of one whole year, and also shall therefore be deprived, ipso facto, of all his spiritual promotions; and that it shall be lawful to all patrons or donors of all and singular the same spiritual promotions, or of any of them, to present or collate to the same, as though the person and persons so offending were dead.

And that if any such person or persons, after he shall be twice convicted in form aforesaid, shall offend against any of the premises the third time, and shall be thereof, in form aforesaid, lawfully convicted, that then the person so offending and convicted the third time, shall be deprived, ipso facto, of all his spiritual promotions, and also shall suffer imprisonment during his life.

And if the person that shall offend, and be convicted in form aforesaid, concerning any of the premises, shall not be beneficed, nor have any spiritual promotion, that then the same person so offending and convicted shall for the first offence suffer imprisonment during one whole year next after his said conviction, without bail or mainprize. And if any such person, not having any spiritual promotion, after his first conviction shall eftsoons offend in anything concerning the premises, and shall be, in form aforesaid, thereof lawfully convicted, that then the same person shall for his second offence suffer imprisonment during his life.

And it is ordained and enacted by the authority aforesaid, that if any person or persons whatsoever, after the said feast of the Nativity of St. John Baptist next coming, shall in any interludes, plays, songs, rhymes, or by other open words, declare or speak anything in the derogation, depraving, or despising of the same book, or of anything therein contained, or any part thereof, or shall, by open fact, deed, or by open threatenings, compel or cause, or otherwise procure or maintain, any parson, vicar, or other minister in any cathedral or parish church, or in chapel, or in any other place, to sing or say any common or open prayer, or to minister any sacrament otherwise, or in any other manner and form, than is mentioned in the said book; or that by any of the said means shall unlawfully interrupt or let any parson, vicar, or other minister in any cathedral or parish church, chapel, or any other place, to sing or say common and open prayer, or to minister the sacraments or any of them, in such manner and form as is mentioned in the said book; that then every such person, being thereof lawfully convicted in form abovesaid, shall forfeit to the queen our sovereign lady, her heirs and successors, for the first offence a hundred marks.

And if any person or persons, being once convicted of any such offence, eftsoons offend against any of the last recited offences, and shall, in form aforesaid, be thereof lawfully convicted, that then the same person so offending and convicted shall, for the second offence, forfeit to the queen our sovereign lady, her heirs and successors, four hundred marks.

And if any person, after he, in form aforesaid, shall have been twice convicted of any offence concerning any of the last recited offences, shall offend the third time, and be thereof, in form abovesaid, lawfully convicted, that then every person so offending and convicted shall for his third offence forfeit to our sovereign lady the queen all his goods and chattels, and shall suffer imprisonment during his life.

And if any person or persons, that for his first offence concerning the premises shall be convicted, in form aforesaid, do not pay the sum to be paid by virtue of his conviction, in such manner and form as the same ought to be paid, within six weeks next after his conviction; that then every person so convicted, and so not paying the same, shall for the same first offence, instead of the said sum, suffer imprisonment by the space of six months, without bail or mainprize. And if any person or persons, that for his second offence concerning the premises shall be convicted in form aforesaid, do not pay the said sum to be paid by virtue of his conviction and this statute, in such manner and form as the same ought to be paid, within six weeks next after his said second conviction; that then every person so convicted, and not so paying the same, shall,

for the same second offence, in the stead of the said sum, suffer imprisonment during twelve months, without bail or mainprize.

And that from and after the said feast of the Nativity of St. John Baptist next coming, all and every person and persons inhabiting within this realm, or any other the queen's majesty's dominions, shall diligently and faithfully, having no lawful or reasonable excuse to be absent, endeavour themselves to resort to their parish church or chapel accustomed, or upon reasonable let thereof, to some usual place where common prayer and such service of God shall be used in such time of let, upon every Sunday and other days ordained and used to be kept as holy days, and then and there to abide orderly and soberly during the time of the common prayer, preachings, or other service of God there to be used and ministered; upon pain of punishment by the censures of the Church, and also upon pain that every person so offending shall forfeit for every such offence twelve pence, to be levied by the churchwardens of the parish where such offence shall be done, to the use of the poor of the same parish, of the goods, lands, and tenements of such offender, by way of distress.

And for due execution hereof, the queen's most excellent majesty, the Lords temporal (sic), and all the Commons, in this present Parliament assembled, do in God's name earnestly require and charge all the archbishops, bishops, and other ordinaries, that they shall endeavour themselves to the uttermost of their knowledges, that the due and true execution hereof may be had throughout their dioceses and charges, as they will answer before God, for such evils and plagues wherewith Almighty God may justly punish His people for neglecting this good and wholesome law.

And for their authority in this behalf, be it further enacted by the authority aforesaid, that all and singular the same archbishops, bishops, and all other their officers exercising ecclesiastical jurisdiction, as well in place exempt as not exempt, within their dioceses, shall have full power and authority by this Act to reform, correct, and punish by censures of the Church, all and singular persons which shall offend within any their jurisdictions or dioceses, after the said feast of the Nativity of St. John Baptist next coming, against this Act and statute; any other law, statute, privilege, liberty, or provision heretofore made, had, or suffered to the contrary notwithstanding.

And it is ordained and enacted by the authority aforesaid, that all and every justices of oyer and terminer, or justices of assize, shall have full power and authority in every of their open and general sessions, to inquire, hear, and determine all and all manner of offences that shall be committed or done contrary to any article contained in this present Act, within the limits of the commission to them directed, and to make process for the execution of the same, as they may do against any person being indicted before them of trespass, or lawfully convicted thereof.

Provided always, and be it enacted by the authority aforesaid, that all and every archbishop and bishop shall or may, at all time and times, at his liberty and pleasure, join and associate himself, by virtue of this Act, to the said justices of oyer and terminer, or to the said justices of assize, at every of the said open and general sessions to be holden in any place within his diocese, for and to the inquiry, hearing, and determining of the offences aforesaid.

Provided also, and be it enacted by the authority aforesaid, that the books concerning the said services shall, at the cost and charges of the parishioners of every parish and cathedral church, be attained and gotten before the said feast of the Nativity of St. John Baptist next following; and that all such parishes and cathedral churches, or other places where the said books shall be attained and gotten before the said feast of the Nativity of St. John Baptist, shall, within three weeks next after the said books so attained and gotten, use the said service, and put the same in use according to this Act.

And be it further enacted by the authority aforesaid, that no person or persons shall be at any time hereafter impeached or otherwise molested of or for any the offences above mentioned, hereafter to be committed or done contrary to this Act, unless he or they so offending be thereof indicted at the next general sessions to be holden before any such justices of oyer and terminer or justices of assize, next after any offence committed or done contrary to the tenor of this Act.

Provided always, and be it ordained and enacted by the authority aforesaid, that all and singular lords of the Parliament, for the third offence above mentioned, shall be tried by their peers.

Provided also, and be it ordained and enacted by the authority aforesaid, that the mayor of London, and all other mayors, bailiffs, and other head officers of all and singular cities, boroughs, and towns corporate within this realm, Wales, and the marches of the same, to the which justices of assize do not commonly repair, shall have full power and authority by virtue of this Act to inquire, hear, and determine the offences abovesaid, and every of them, yearly within fifteen days after the feasts of Easter and St. Michael the Archangel, in like manner and form as justices of assize and oyer and terminer may do.

Provided always, and be it ordained and enacted by the authority aforesaid, that all and singular archbishops and bishops, and every their chancellors, commissaries, archdeacons, and other ordinaries, having any peculiar ecclesiastical jurisdiction. shall have full power and authority by virtue of this Act, as well to inquire in their visitation, synods, and elsewhere within their jurisdiction at any other time and place, to take occasions (sic) and informations of all and every the things above mentioned, done, committed, or perpetrated within the limits of their jurisdictions and authority, and to punish the same by admonition, excommunication, sequestration, or deprivation, and other censures and processes, in like form as heretofore has been used in like cases by the queen's ecclesiastical laws.

Provided always, and be it enacted, that whatsoever person offending in the premises shall, for the offence, first receive punishment of the ordinary, having a testimonial thereof under the said ordinary's seal, shall not for the same offence eftsoons be convicted before the justices: and likewise receiving, for the said offence, first punishment by the justices, he shall not for the same offence eftsoons receive punishment of the ordinary; anything contained in this

Act to the contrary notwithstanding.

Provided always, and be it enacted, that such ornaments of the church, and of the ministers thereof, shall be retained and be in use, as was in the Church of England, by authority of Parliament, in the second year of the reign of King Edward VI, until other order shall be therein taken by the authority of the queen's majesty, with the advice of her commissioners appointed and authorized, under the great seal of England, for causes ecclesiastical, or of the metropolitan of this realm.

And also, that if there shall happen any contempt or irreverence to be used in the ceremonies or rites of the Church, by the misusing of the orders appointed in this book, the queen's majesty may, by the like advice of the said commissioners or metropolitan, ordain and publish such further ceremonies or rites, as may be most for the advancement of God's glory, the edifying of His Church, and the due reverence of Christ's holy mysteries and sacraments.

And be it further enacted by the authority aforesaid, that all laws, statutes, and ordinances, wherein or whereby any other service, administration of sacraments or common prayer, is limited, established, or set forth to be used within this realm, or any other the queen's dominions or countries, shall from henceforth be utterly void and of none effect.

ELIZABETH I'S SPEECH TO THE TROOPS AT TILBURY (1588)

ELIZABETH'S CONCISE, POWERFUL SPEECH SHORTLY BEFORE THE ARRIVAL OF THE SPANISH ARMADA REMAINS A CLASSIC OF ROYAL ORATORY.

MY LOVING PEOPLE

We have been persuaded by some that are careful of our safety, to take heed how we commit our selves to armed multitudes, for fear of treachery; but I assure you I do not desire to live to distrust my faithful and loving people. Let tyrants fear. I have always so behaved myself that, under God, I have placed my chiefest strength and safeguard in the loyal hearts and good-will of my subjects; and therefore I am come amongst you, as you see, at this time, not for my recreation and disport, but being resolved, in the midst and heat of the battle, to live and die amongst you all; to lay down for my God, and for my kingdom, and my people, my honour and my blood, even in the dust. I know I have the body of a weak, feeble woman; but I have the heart and stomach of a king, and of a king of England too, and think foul scorn that Parma or Spain, or any prince of Europe, should dare to invade the borders of my realm; to which rather than any dishonour shall grow by me, I myself will take up arms, I myself will be your general, judge, and rewarder of every one of your virtues in the field.

I know already, for your forwardness you have deserved rewards and crowns; and We do assure you on a word of a prince, they shall be duly paid. In the mean time, my lieutenant general shall be in my stead, than whom never prince commanded a more noble or worthy subject; not doubting but by your obedience to my general, by your concord in the camp, and your valour in the field, we shall shortly have a famous victory over these enemies of my God, of my kingdom, and of my people.

ELIZABETH I'S "GOLDEN SPEECH" TO REPRESENTATIVES OF PARLIAMENT (1601)

AN ACCOUNT OF A SPEECH GIVEN TO MEMBERS OF PARLIAMENT THAT LATER BECAME KNOWN AS ELIZABETH'S FAREWELL.

MR SPEAKER,

We have heard your declaration and perceive your care of our estate. I do assure you there is no prince that loves his subjects better, or whose love can countervail our love. There is no jewel, be it of never so rich a price, which I set before this jewel: I mean your love. For I do esteem it more than any treasure or riches; for that we know how to prize, but love and thanks I count invaluable. And, though God hath raised me high, yet this I count the glory of my Crown, that I have reigned with your loves. This makes me that I do not so much rejoice that God hath made me to be a Queen, as to be a Queen over so thankful a people. Therefore I have cause to wish nothing more than to content the subject and that is a duty which I owe. Neither do I desire to live longer days than I may see your prosperity and that is my only desire. And as I am that person still yet, under God, hath delivered you and so I trust by the almighty power of God that I shall be his instrument to preserve you from every peril, dishonour, shame, tyranny and oppression, partly by means of your intended helps which we take very acceptably because it manifesteth the largeness of your good loves and loyalties unto your sovereign.

Of myself I must say this: I never was any greedy, scraping grasper, nor a strait fast-holding Prince, nor yet a waster. My heart was never set on any worldly goods. What you bestow on me, I will not hoard it up, but receive it to bestow on you again. Therefore render unto them I beseech you Mr Speaker, such thanks as you imagine my heart yieldeth, but my tongue cannot express. Mr Speaker, I would wish you and the rest to stand up for I shall yet trouble you with longer speech. Mr Speaker, you give me thanks but I doubt me I have greater cause to give you

thanks, than you me, and I charge you to thank them of the Lower House from me. For had I not received a knowledge from you, I might have fallen into the lapse of an error, only for lack of true information.

Since I was Queen, yet did I never put my pen to any grant, but that upon pretext and semblance made unto me, it was both good and beneficial to the subject in general though a private profit to some of my ancient servants, who had deserved well at my hands. But the contrary being found by experience, I am exceedingly beholden to such subjects as would move the same at first. And I am not so simple to suppose but that there be some of the Lower House whom these grievances never touched. I think they spake out of zeal to their countries and not out of spleen or malevolent affection as being parties grieved. That my grants should be grievous to my people and oppressions to be privileged under colour of our patents, our kingly dignity shall not suffer it. Yea, when I heard it, I could give no rest unto my thoughts until I had reformed it. Shall they, think you, escape unpunished that have oppressed you, and have been respectless of their duty and regardless our honour? No, I assure you, Mr Speaker, were it not more for conscience' sake than for any glory or increase of love that I desire, these errors, troubles, vexations and oppressions done by these varlets and lewd persons not worthy of the name of subjects should not escape without condign punishment. But I perceive they dealt with me like physicians who, ministering a drug, make it more acceptable by giving it a good aromatical savour, or when they give pills do gild them all over. I have ever used to set the Last Judgement Day before mine eyes and so to rule as I shall be judged to answer before a higher judge, and now if my kingly bounties have been abused and my grants turned to the hurt of my people contrary to my will and meaning, and if any in authority under me have neglected or perverted what I have committed to them, I hope God will not lay their culps and offenses in my charge. I know the title of a King is a glorious title, but assure yourself that the shining glory of princely authority hath not so dazzled the eyes of our understanding, but that we well know and remember that we also are to yield an account of our actions before the great judge. To be a king and wear a crown is a thing more glorious to them that see it than it is pleasant to them that bear it. For myself I was never so much enticed with the glorious name of a King or royal authority of a Queen as delighted that God hath made me his instrument to maintain his truth and glory and to defend his kingdom as I said from peril, dishonour, tyranny and oppression.

There will never Queen sit in my seat with more zeal to my country, care to my subjects and that will sooner with willingness venture her life for your good and safety than myself. For it is my desire to live nor reign no longer than my life and reign shall be for your good. And though you have had, and may have, many princes more mighty and wise sitting in this seat, yet you never had nor shall have, any that will be more careful and loving.

'For I, oh Lord, what am I, whom practices and perils past should not fear? Or what can I do? That I should speak for any glory, God forbid.' And turning to the Speaker and her councilors she said, 'And I pray to you Mr Comptroller, Mr Secretary and you of my Council, that before these gentlemen go into their countries, you bring them all to kiss my hand.'

FROM AN ACT FOR THE BETTER DISCOVERING AND REPRESSING OF POPISH RECUSANTS (1606)

THIS OATH OF ALLEGIANCE WAS ESTABLISHED BY JAMES I IN THE WAKE OF THE GUNPOWDER PLOT.

I, A.B. do truly and sincerely acknowledge, profess, testify, and declare in my conscience before God and the world, that our Sovereign Lord King James, is lawful and rightful King of this realm, and of all other in his Majesties Dominions and Countries; And that the Pope neither of himself, nor by any authorities of the Church or See of Rome, or by any means with any other hath any power or authority to depose the King, or to dispose any of his Majesty's kingdoms, or dominions, or to authorize any foreign prince to invade or annoy him, or his countries, or to discharge any of his Subjects of their allegiance and obedience to his Majesty, or to give any license or leave to any of them to bear arms, raise tumult, or to offer any violence, or hurt to his Majesty's royal person, state, or government, or to any of his Majesty's subjects within his Majesty's dominions.

Also, I do swear from my heart that, notwithstanding any declaration or sentence of excommunication or deposition made or granted, or to be made or granted by the Pope or his successors, or by any authority derived, or pretended to be derived from him, or his See against the King, his heirs or successors, or any absolution of the said subjects from their obedience: I will bear faith and true allegiance to his Majesty, his heirs and successors, and him or them will defend to the uttermost of my power, against all conspiracies and attempts whatsoever, which shall be made against his or their persons, their crown and dignity, by reason or color of any such sentence or declaration or otherwise, and will doe my best endeavor to disclose and make known unto his Majesty, his heirs and successors, all treasons and traitorous conspiracies, which I shall know or hear of to be against him or any of them:

And I do further swear, that I do from my heart abhor, detest and abjure, as impious and heretical, this damnable doctrine and position, that princes which be excommunicated or deprived by the Pope, may be deposed or murdered by their subjects, or any whatsoever. And I do believe and in conscience am resolved, that neither the Pope nor any person whatsoever, hath power to absolve me of this oath, or any part thereof, which I acknowledge by good and full authority to bee lawfully ministered unto me, and do renounce all pardons and dispensations to the contrary: And all these things I do plainly and sincerely acknowledge and swear, according to these express words by me spoken, and according to the plain and common sense and understanding of the same words, without any Equivocation, or mental evasion, or secret reservation whatsoever: And I doe make this recognition and acknowledgement heartily, willingly, and truly, upon the true faith of a Christian: So help me God.

THE PETITION OF RIGHT (1628)

A MILESTONE IN THE LEGAL HISTORY OF BRITAIN, THIS PETITION SUCCESSFULLY CHALLENGED SOME OF THE ARBITRARY IMPOSITIONS OF CHARLES I.

TO THE KING'S
Most Excellent Majesty,

Humbly show unto our Sovereign Lord the King, the Lords Spiritual and Temporal, and Commons in Parliament assembles, that whereas it is declared and enacted by a statute made in the time of the reign of King Edward I, commonly called Statutum de Tallagio non concedendo, that no tallage or aid shall be laid or levied by the king or his heirs in this realm, without the good will and assent of the archbishops, bishops, earls, barons, knights, burgesses, and other the freemen of the commonalty of this realm; and by authority of parliament holden in the five-and-twentieth year of the reign of King Edward III, it is declared and enacted, that from thenceforth no person should be compelled to make any loans to the king against his will, because such loans were against reason and the franchise of the land; and by other laws of this realm it is provided, that none should be charged by any charge or imposition called a benevolence, nor by such like charge; by which statutes before mentioned, and other the good laws and statutes of this realm, your subjects have inherited this freedom, that they should not be compelled to contribute to any tax, tallage, aid, or other like charge not set by common consent, in parliament.

Yet nevertheless of late divers commissions directed to sundry commissioners in several counties, with instructions, have issued; by means whereof your people have been in divers places assembled, and required to lend certain sums of money unto your Majesty, and many of them, upon their refusal so to do, have had an oath administered unto them not warrantable by the laws or statutes of this realm, and have been constrained to become bound and make appearance and give utterance before your Privy Council and in other places, and others of them have been therefore imprisoned, confined, and sundry other ways molested and disquieted; and divers other charges have been laid and levied upon your people in several counties by lord lieutenants, deputy lieutenants, commissioners for musters, justices of peace and others, by command or direction from your Majesty, or your Privy Council, against the laws and free custom of the realm.

And whereas also by the statute called 'The Great Charter of the Liberties of England,' it is declared and enacted, that no freeman may be taken or imprisoned or be disseised of his freehold or liberties, or his free customs, or be outlawed or exiled, or in any manner destroyed, but by the lawful judgment of his peers, or by the law of the land. And in the eight-and-twentieth year of the reign of King Edward III, it was declared and enacted by authority of parliament, that no man, of what estate or condition that he be, should be put out of his land or tenements, nor taken, nor imprisoned, nor disinherited nor put to death without being brought to answer by due process of law. Nevertheless, against the tenor of the said statutes, and other the good laws and statutes of your realm to that end provided, divers of your subjects have of late been imprisoned without any cause showed; and when for their deliverance they were brought before your justices by your Majesty's writs of habeas corpus, there to undergo and receive as the court should order, and their keepers commanded to certify the causes of their detainer, no cause was certified, but that they were detained by your Majesty's special command, signified by the lords of your Privy Council, and yet were returned back to several prisons, without being charged with anything to which they might make answer according to the law.

And whereas of late great companies of soldiers and mariners have been dispersed into divers counties of the realm, and the inhabitants against their wills have been compelled to receive them into their houses, and there to suffer them to sojourn against the laws and customs of this realm, and to the great grievance and vexation of the people.

And whereas also by authority of parliament, in the five-and-twentieth year of the reign of King Edward III, it is declared and enacted, that no man shall be forejudged of life or limb against the form of the Great Charter and the law of the land; and by the said Great Charter and other the laws and statutes of this your realm, no man ought to be adjudged to death but by the laws established in this your realm, either by the customs of the same realm, or by acts of parliament: and whereas no offender of what kind soever is exempted from the proceedings to be used, and punishments to be inflicted by the laws and statutes of this your realm; nevertheless of late time divers commissions under your Majesty's great seal have issued forth, by which certain persons have been assigned and

appointed commissioners with power and authority to proceed within the land, according to the justice of martial law, against such soldiers or mariners, or other dissolute persons joining with them, as should commit any murder, robbery, felony, mutiny, or other outrage or misdemeanor whatsoever, and by such summary course and order as is agreeable to martial law, and is used in armies in time of war, to proceed to the trial and condemnation of such offenders, and them to cause to be executed and put to death according to the law martial.

By pretext whereof some of your Majesty's subjects have been by some of the said commissioners put to death, when and where, if by the laws and statutes of the land they had deserved death, by the same laws and statutes also they might, and by no other ought to have been judged and executed. And also sundry grievous offenders, by color thereof claiming an exemption, have escaped the punishments due to them by the laws and statutes of this your realm, by reason that divers of your officers and ministers of justice have unjustly refused or forborne to proceed against such offenders according to the same laws and statutes, upon pretense that the said offenders were punishable only by martial law, and by authority of such commissions as aforesaid; which commissions, and all other of like nature, are wholly and directly contrary to the said laws and statutes of this your realm.

They do therefore humbly pray your most excellent Majesty, that no man hereafter be compelled to make or yield any gift, loan, benevolence, tax, or such like charge, without common consent by act of parliament; and that none be called to make answer, or take such oath, or to give attendance, or be confined, or otherwise molested or disquieted concerning the same or for refusal thereof; and that no freeman, in any such manner as is before mentioned, be imprisoned or detained; and that your Majesty would be pleased to remove the said soldiers and mariners, and that your people may not be so burdened in time to come; and that the aforesaid commissions, for proceeding by martial law, may be revoked and annulled; and that hereafter no commissions of like nature may issue forth to any person or persons whatsoever to be executed as aforesaid, lest by color of them any of your Majesty's subjects be destroyed or put to death contrary to the laws and franchise of the land.

All which they most humbly pray of your most excellent Majesty as their rights and liberties, according to the laws and statutes of this realm; and that your Majesty would also vouchsafe to declare, that the awards, doings, and proceedings, to the prejudice of your people in any of the premises, shall not be drawn hereafter into consequence or example; and that your Majesty would be also graciously pleased, for the further comfort and safety of your people, to declare your royal will and pleasure, that in the things aforesaid all your officers and ministers shall serve you according to the laws and statutes of this realm, as they tender the honor of your Majesty, and the prosperity of this kingdom.

(Which Petition being read the 2nd of June 1628, the King's answer was thus delivered unto it.

The King willeth that right be done according to the laws and customs of the realm; and that the statutes be put in due execution, that his subjects may have no cause to complain of any wrong or oppressions, contrary to their just rights and liberties, to the preservation whereof he holds himself as well obliged as of his prerogative.

On 7 June the answer was given in the accustomed form *Soit droit fait comme il est desire.*)

THE DECLARATION OF BREDA (1660)

WITH THIS DECLARATION, CHARLES II SECURED THE RESTORATION OF THE MONARCHY.

CHARLES R. Charles, by the grace of God, king of England, Scotland, France and Ireland, Defender of the Faith, &c., to all our loving subjects, of what degree or quality soever, greeting. If the general distraction and confusion which is spread over the whole kingdom doth not awaken all men to a desire and longing that those wounds which have so many years together been kept bleeding may be bound up, all we can say will be to no purpose. However, after this long silence we have thought it our duty to declare how much we desire to contribute thereunto, and that as we can never give over the hope in good time to obtain the possession of that right which God and nature hath made our due, so we do make it our daily suit to the Divine Providence that he will, in compassion to us and our subjects after so long misery and sufferings, remit and put us into a quiet and peaceable possession of that our right, with as little blood and damage to our people as is possible. Nor do we desire more to enjoy what is ours than that all our subjects may enjoy what by law is theirs, by a full and entire administration of justice throughout the land, and by extending our mercy where it is wanted and deserved. And to the end that the fear of punishment may not engage any, conscious to themselves of what is past, to a perseverance in guilt for the future, by opposing the quiet and happiness of their country in the restoration both of king, peers and people to their just, ancient and fundamental rights, we do by these presents declare that we do grant a free and general pardon, which we are ready upon demand to pass under our great seal of England, to all our subjects, of what degree or quality soever, who within forty days after the publishing hereof shall lay hold upon this our grace and favour, and shall by any public act declare their doing so, and that they return to the loyalty and obedience of good subjects (excepting only such persons as shall hereafter be excepted by Parliament). Those only excepted, let all our loving subjects, how faulty soever, rely upon the word of a king, solemnly given by this present declaration, that no crime whatsoever committed against us or our royal father before the publication of this shall ever rise in judgment or be brought in question against any of them, to the least endamagement of them, either in their lives, liberties or estates, or (as far forth as lies in our power) so much as to the prejudice of their reputations by any reproach or term of distinction from the rest of our best subjects ; we desiring and ordaining that henceforward all notes of discord, separation and difference of parties be utterly abolished among all our subjects, whom we invite and conjure to a perfect union among themselves, under our protection, for the re- settlement of our just rights and theirs in a free Parliament, by which, upon the word of a king, we will be advised.

And because the passion and uncharitableness of the times have produced several opinions in religion, by which men are engaged in parties and animosities against each other, which, when they shall hereafter unite in a freedom of conversation, will be composed or better understood, we do declare a liberty to tender consciences, and that no man shall be disquieted or called in question for differences of opinion in matter of religion which do not disturb the peace of the kingdom; and that we shall be ready to consent to such an Act of Parliament as upon mature deliberation shall be offered to us for the full

granting that indulgence.

And because, in the continued distractions of so many years and so many and great revolutions, many grants and purchases of estates have been made to and by many officers, soldiers and others, who are now possessed of the same and who may be liable to actions at law upon several titles, we are likewise willing that all such differences, and all things relating to such grants, sales and purchases, shall be determined in Parliament, which can best provide for the just satisfaction of all men who are concerned.

And we do further declare that we will be ready to consent to any Act or Acts of Parliament to the purposes aforesaid, and for the full satisfaction of all arrears due to the officers and soldiers of the army under the command of General Monck, and that they shall be received into our service upon as good pay and conditions as they now enjoy.

Given under our sign manual and privy signet, at our court at Breda, this 4/14 day of April 1660, in the twelfth year of our reign.

THE EXCLUSION BILL (1680)

THIS ATTEMPT TO BAR THE SUCCESSION FROM THE ROMAN CATHOLIC DUKE OF YORK, EVENTUALLY JAMES II, GAVE RISE TO THE RIVALRY OF THE TORY AND WHIG PARTIES.

AN ACT FOR SECURING
of the Protestant religion by disabling James, Duke of York, to inherit the imperial crown of England and Ireland and the dominions and territories thereunto belonging

Whereas James, duke of York, is notoriously known to have been perverted from the Protestant to the popish religion, whereby not only great encouragement hath been given to the popish party to enter into and carry on most devilish and horrid plots and conspiracies for the

destruction of his Majesty's sacred person and government, and for the extirpation of the true Protestant religion, but also, if the said duke should succeed to the imperial crown of this realm, nothing is more manifest than that a total change of religion within these kingdoms would ensue, for the prevention whereof be it therefore enacted... that the said James, duke of York, shall be and is by authority of this present Parliament excluded and made for ever incapable to inherit, possess or enjoy the imperial crown of this realm and of the kingdom of Ireland and the dominions and territories to them or either of them belonging, or to have, exercise or enjoy any dominion, power, jurisdiction or authority within the same kingdoms, dominions or any of them.

And be it further enacted...that if the said James, duke of York, shall at any time hereafter challenge, claim or attempt to possess or enjoy, or shall take upon him to use or exercise any dominion, power, authority or jurisdiction within the said kingdoms, dominions or any of them as king or chief magistrate of the same, that then he the said James, duke of York, for every such offence shall be deemed and adjudged guilty of high treason, and shall suffer the pains, penalties and forfeitures as in cases of high treason. And further, that if any person or persons whatsoever shall assist, aid, maintain, abet or willingly adhere unto the said James, duke of York, in such his challenge, claim or attempt, or shall of themselves attempt or endeavour to put or bring the said James, duke of York, into the possession or exercise of any regal power, jurisdiction or authority within the kingdoms or dominions aforesaid, or shall by writing or preaching advisedly publish, maintain or declare that he hath any right, title or authority to exercise the office of king or chief magistrate of the kingdoms and dominions aforesaid, that then every such person shall be deemed and adjudged guilty of high treason, and shall suffer and undergo the pains, penalties and forfeitures aforesaid.

And be it further enacted...that if the said James, duke of York, shall at any time from and after the fifth day of November in the year of our Lord God one thousand six hundred and eighty return or come into or within any of the kingdoms or dominions aforesaid, that then he, the said James, duke of York, shall be deemed and adjudged guilty of high treason, and shall suffer the pains, penalties and forfeitures as in cases of high treason; and further, that if any person or persons whatsoever shall be aiding or assisting unto such return of the said James, duke of York, that then every such person shall be deemed and adjudged guilty of high treason, and shall suffer as in cases of high treason.

And be it further enacted...that the said James, duke of York, or any other person being guilty of any of the treasons aforesaid, shall not be capable of or receive benefit by any pardon otherwise than by Act of Parliament....

And be it further enacted and declared, and it is hereby enacted and declared, that it shall and may be lawful to and for all magistrates, officers and other subjects whatsoever of the kingdoms and dominions aforesaid, and they are hereby enjoined and required, to apprehend and secure the said James, duke of York, and every other person offending in any of the premises, and with him or them in case of resistance to fight, and him or them by force to subdue, for all which actings and for so doing they are and shall be by virtue of this Act saved harmless and indemnified.

Provided, and be it hereby declared, that nothing in this Act contained shall be construed, deemed or adjudged to disable any person from inheriting or enjoying the imperial crown of the realms and dominions aforesaid (other than the said James, duke of York), but that in case the said James, duke of York, shall survive his now Majesty and the heirs of his Majesty's body, the said imperial crown shall descend to and be enjoyed by such person and persons successively during the lifetime of the said James, duke of York, as should have inherited and enjoyed the same in case the said James, duke of York, were naturally dead, anything in this Act contained to the contrary notwithstanding.

And be it enacted...that during the life of the said James, duke of York, this Act shall be given in charge at every assizes and general sessions of the peace within the kingdoms, dominions and territories aforesaid, and also shall be openly read in every cathedral, collegiate church, parish church and chapel within the aforesaid kingdoms, dominions and territories by the several and respective parsons, vicars, curates and readers thereof, who are hereby required, immediately after divine service in the forenoon, to read the same twice in every year, that is to say on the five and twentieth day of December and upon Easter Day, during the life of the said James, duke of York.

SIR WILLIAM PETTY'S LIST OF THE POWERS OF THE KING OF ENGLAND (1685)

THIS ACCOUNT OF THE ROYAL POWERS PROVIDES A WINDOW
ON THE RESTORATION MONARCHY.

THE POWERS OF THE KING OF ENGLAND
10 December 1685

1. The king has a prerogative which lawyers must expound.

2. The king makes peers in Parliament, who are perpetual legislators, as also the last and highest judicature of England and Ireland, and have great privileges and immunities for themselves and servants.

3. The king is the fountain of honour, titles and precedencies, and of all the powers which the Lord Marshal and heralds exercise,

4. The king makes bishops, and they priests and deacons and clerks of the convocation, and has also all the power which the Pope had formerly. Bishops make chancellors and other officers of the spiritual courts, have power to excommunicate, &c.

5. The king makes the chancellors of the universities, makes heads and fellows in several colleges, and is also visitor in some cases.

6. The king has the power of coinage, and can give the name, matter, fineness, character and shape to all species of money, and can cry money up and down by his proclamation, which some extend to this, viz., that if A. lend B. 100/, weighing 29 pounds of sterling silver, if the king by his proclamation declare that one ounce of silver shall be afterwards called one hundred pounds, that then, B. paying to A. the said ounce of silver, the debt is answered.

7. The king makes sheriffs, and they juries upon life and estate, limb and liberty, as also jailers, bailiffs and executioners of all sorts.

8. The king makes a Chancellor, or chief judge in equity, who stops proceedings in other courts of law, &c. The Chancellor makes justices of the peace, and they high and petty constables and sessions of peace, &c,

9. The king makes judges durante beneplacito. They set fines and punish at their own discretion in several cases. They govern proceedings at law, declare and interpret the law, reprieve, &c, ; and the king can suspend the law, pardon or prosecute,

10. The king can give charters for boroughs to Parliament; appoint electors and judges of elections; prorogue, adjourn and dissolve Parliaments from time to time and from place to place; disapprove the Speaker, &c,

11. The king appoints his lieutenants to command the grand standing militia, can press any man to serve his allies beyond seas as soldiers, can equip and appoint what number of ships and seamen he pleases, and their wages, and pari ratione a mercenary army to serve at land, as also guards for his person of several sorts.

12. The king has some revenue by common law and prerogative, and can by his judges interpret statutes concerning the branches and the collection there of.

13. The king has great power over forests and mines, colonies, monopolies.

14. The king can do no wrong, and his coming to the Crown clears him from all punishments, &c., due before, and obedience to him after coronation excuses from

15. The king, by ceasing or forbearing to administer the several powers above named, can do what harm he pleases to his subjects.

PROCLAMATION OF THE DUKE OF MONMOUTH ON TAKING THE TITLE OF KING (1685)

WHEN JAMES II TOOK THE THRONE, HE ALREADY SUFFERED FROM A LACK
OF BROAD SUPPORT, AS THIS PROCLAMATION REVEALS.

JAMES R.

Whereas upon our first landing at Lyme in our county of Dorset on Thursday the 11th day of this instant month of June, we did publish a declaration in the name of ourself, by the name of James, duke of Monmouth, and the noblemen, gentlemen and others now in arms for defence and vindication of the Protestant religion, and of the laws, rights and privileges of England, from the invasion made upon them, and for delivering the kingdom from the usurpation and tyranny of James, duke of York; wherein amongst other things therein contained we did declare that out of the love we bear to the English "nation, whose welfare and settlement we did infinitely prefer to whatever might concern ourselves, we would not at present insist upon our title, but leave the determination thereof to the authority of a Parliament legally chosen and acting with freedom; since which it hath pleased Almighty God to succeed and prosper us hitherto in a very eminent manner, and also disposed the hearts of our loving subjects that from all parts of the country they flock in unanimously for the defence of our person and of the righteous cause we are engaged in; by which we have been enabled to march from Lyme aforesaid unto our good town of Taunton to the terror and amazement of all our enemies round about us: and whereas as well during our said march as since our coming to Taunton aforesaid all our loving subjects have with warm and repeated solicitations importuned us to exert and take upon us our sovereign and royal authority of king as well as of the power of a general, that we might thereby be enabled to make

use of the laws and statutes of the realm in conjunction with our arms for their safety and preservation; and have likewise earnestly implored us for their own sakes not to defer the execution of our kingly office to so late a period as is mentioned in the said declaration, for that it will in all probability render the progress of our arms more slow, and thereby give our enemies a longer season to harass and impoverish our kingdom: we could not but with great reluctancy incline to consent to anything that might seem to be a departure from our said declaration, and thereby raise any diffidence amongst the sober and virtuous, or give occasion to wicked and malicious men to arraign the sincerity of our intentions; but as the said clause in the said declaration was inserted under this prospect, to convince the world that we postponed all things to the safety and welfare of our people, and that we consulted not so much our own interest as their prosperity, being so convinced both from the circumstances of affairs and from united advice of all our loving people's petitions that it was absolutely necessary for their protection and defence that we should immediately insist upon our title to the crowns of England, Scotland, France and Ireland, and the dominions and territories thereunto belonging, as son and heir apparent to Charles the Second, king of England, our royal father lately deceased: we have therefore suffered ourselves to be prevailed upon, and have complied with the earnest importunities and necessities of our people, giving way to our being proclaimed king on the 20th day of this instant June at our town of Taunton aforesaid; which we hereby solemnly declare we have consented unto out of tenderness and for the interest of all our loving subjects, and not upon any motives arising from ourself.

And we do further declare and faithfully promise upon the word of a king that we will inviolably keep and perform all and every the articles, sentences and clauses specified and comprised in our said declaration for the good of our kingdom and benefit of all our loyal subjects; and that we will in our first Parliament pass into laws all methods therein contained for the relief, ease and safety of our people.

Given at our camp at Taunton,
the 21st day of June,
in the first year of our reign.

LETTER OF INVITATION TO WILLIAM OF ORANGE (1688)

THIS LETTER FROM PARLIAMENT TO THE DUTCH WILLIAM OF ORANGE PRECIPITATED THE BLOODLESS COUP KNOWN AS THE GLORIOUS REVOLUTION, ENDING THE STUART DYNASTY.

30 JUNE 1688

We have great satisfaction to find by 35 (Russell), and since by Monsieur Zuylestein, that your Highness is so ready and willing to give us such assistances as they have related to us. We have great reason to believe we shall be every day in a worse condition than we are, and less able to defend ourselves, and therefore we do earnestly wish we might be so happy as to find a remedy before it be too late for us to contribute to our own deliverance. But although these be our wishes, yet we will by no means put your Highness into any expectations which may misguide your own councils in this matter; so that the best advice we can give is to inform your Highness truly both of the state of things here at this time and of the difficulties which appear to us.

As to the first, the people are so generally dissatisfied with the present conduct of the government in relation to their religion, liberties and properties (all which have been greatly invaded), and they are in such expectation of their prospects being daily worse, that your Highness may be assured there are nineteen parts of twenty of the people throughout the kingdom who are desirous of a change, and who, we believe, would willingly contribute to it, if they had such a protection to countenance their rising as would secure them from being destroyed before they could get to be in a posture able to defend themselves. It is no less certain that much the greatest part of the nobility and gentry are as much dissatisfied, although it be not safe to speak to many of them beforehand; and there is no doubt but that some of the most considerable of them would venture themselves with your Highness at your first landing, whose interests would be able to draw great numbers to them whenever they could protect them and the raising and drawing men together. And if such a strength could be landed as were able to defend itself and them till they could be got together into some order, we make no question but that strength would quickly be increased to a number double to the army here, although their army should all remain firm to them; whereas we do upon very good grounds believe that their army then would be very much divided among themselves, many of the officers being so discontented that they continue in their service only for a subsistence (besides that some of their minds are known already), and very many of the common soldiers do daily shew such an aversion to the popish religion that there is the greatest probability imaginable of great numbers of deserters which would come from them should there be such an occasion; and amongst the seamen it is almost certain there is not one in ten who would do them any service in such a war. Besides all this, we do much doubt whether this present state of things will not yet be much changed to the worse before another year, by a great alteration which will probably be made both in the officers and soldiers of the army, and by such other changes as are not only to be expected from a packed Parliament, but what the meeting of any Parliament (in our present circumstances) may produce against those who will be looked upon as principal obstructers of their proceedings there, it being taken for granted that if things cannot then be carried to their wishes in a parliamentary way other measures will be put in execution by more violent means; and although such proceedings will then heighten the discontents, yet such courses will probably be taken at that time as will prevent all possible means of relieving ourselves.

These considerations make us of opinion that this is a season in which we may more probably contribute to our own safeties than hereafter (although we must own to your Highness there are some judgments differing from ours in this particular), insomuch that if the circumstances stand so with your Highness that you believe you can get here time enough, in a condition to give assistances this year sufficient for a relief under these circumstances which have been now represented, we who subscribe this will not fail to attend your Highness upon your landing and to do all that lies in our power to prepare others to be in as much readiness as such an action is capable of, where there is so much danger in communicating an affair of such a nature till it be near the time of its being made public. But, as we have already told your Highness, we must also lay our difficulties before your Highness, which are chiefly, that we know not what alarm your preparations for this expedition may give, or what notice it will be necessary for you to give the States beforehand, by either of which

means their intelligence or suspicions here may be such as may cause us to be secured before your landing. And we must presume to inform your Highness that your compliment upon the birth of the child (which not one in a thousand here believes to be the queen's) hath done you some injury, the false imposing of that upon the princess and the nation being not only an infinite exasperation of people's minds here, but being certainly one of the chief causes upon which the declaration of your entering the kingdom in a hostile manner must be founded on your part, although many other reasons are to be given on ours. If upon a due consideration of all these circumstances your Highness shall think fit to adventure upon the attempt, or at least to make such preparations for it as are necessary (which we wish you may), there must be no more time lost in letting us know your resolution concerning it, and in what time we may depend that all the preparations will be ready, as also whether your Highness does believe the preparations can be so managed as not to give them warning here, both to make them increase their force and to secure those they shall suspect would join with you. We need not say anything about ammunition, artillery, mortar pieces, spare arms, &c., because if you think fit to put anything in execution you will provide enough of these kinds, and will take care to bring some good engineers with you; and we have desired Mr.H(erbert) to consult you about all such matters, to whom we have communicated our thoughts in many particulars too tedious to have been written, and about which no certain resolutions can be taken till we have heard again from your Highness.

25. Shrewsbury.
24. Devonshire.
27. Danby.
29. Lumley.
31. Bishop of London.
35. Russell.
33. Sidney.

THE BILL OF RIGHTS (1689)

THIS MOMENTOUS PIECE OF LEGISLATION, A HALLMARK OF THE REIGN OF WILLIAM AND MARY, HAS BEEN SINCE ITS ESTABLISHMENT AN ANCHOR OF BRITISH GOVERNMENT.

AN ACT DECLARING
the rights and liberties of the subject and settling the succession of the Crown

Whereas the Lords Spiritual and Temporal and Commons assembled at Westminster, lawfully, fully and freely representing all the estates of the people of this realm, did upon the thirteenth day of February in the year of our Lord one thousand six hundred eighty- eightı present unto their Majesties, then called and known by the names and style of William and Mary, prince and princess of Orange, being present in their proper persons, a certain declaration in writing made by the said Lords and Commons in the words following, viz.:

Whereas the late King James the Second, by the assistance of divers evil counsellors, judges and ministers employed by him, did endeavour to subvert and extirpate the Protestant religion and the laws and liberties of this kingdom;

By assuming and exercising a power of dispensing with and suspending of laws and the execution of laws without consent of Parliament;

By committing and prosecuting divers worthy prelates for humbly petitioning to be excused from concurring to the said assumed power;

By issuing and causing to be executed a commission under the great seal for erecting a court called the Court of Commissioners for Ecclesiastical Causes;

By levying money for and to the use of the Crown by pretence of prerogative for other time and in other manner than the same was granted by Parliament;

By raising and keeping a standing army within this kingdom in time of peace without consent of Parliament, and quartering soldiers contrary to law;

By causing several good subjects being Protestants to be disarmed at the same time when papists were both armed and employed contrary to law;

By violating the freedom of election of members to serve in Parliament;

By prosecutions in the Court of King's Bench for matters and causes cognizable only in Parliament, and by divers other arbitrary and illegal courses;

And whereas of late years partial, corrupt and unqualified persons have been returned and served on juries in trials, and particularly divers jurors in trials for high treason which were not freeholders;

And excessive bail hath been required of persons committed in criminal cases to elude the benefit of the laws made for the liberty of the subjects;

And excessive fines have been imposed; And illegal and cruel punishments inflicted; And several grants and promises made of fines and forfeitures before any conviction or judgment against the persons upon whom the same were to be levied; All which are utterly and directly contrary to the known laws and statutes and freedom of this realm; And whereas the said late King James the Second having abdicated the government and the throne being thereby vacant, his Highness the prince of Orange (whom it hath pleased Almighty God to make the glorious instrument of delivering this kingdom from popery and arbitrary power) did (by the advice of the Lords Spiritual and Temporal and divers principal persons of the Commons) cause letters to be written to the Lords Spiritual and Temporal being Protestants, and other letters to the several counties, cities, universities, boroughs and cinque ports, for the choosing of such persons to represent them as were of right to be sent to Parliament, to meet and sit at Westminster upon the two and twentieth day of January in this year one thousand six hundred eighty and eight,ı in order to such an establishment as that their religion, laws and liberties might not again be in danger of being subverted, upon which letters elections having been accordingly made;

And thereupon the said Lords Spiritual and Temporal and Commons, pursuant to their respective letters and elections, being now assembled in a full and free representative of this nation, taking into their most serious consideration the best means for attaining the ends aforesaid, do in the first place (as their ancestors in like case have usually done) for the vindicating and asserting their ancient rights and liberties declare

That the pretended power of suspending of laws or the execution of laws by regal authority without consent of Parliament is illegal;

That the pretended power of dispensing with laws or the execution of laws by regal authority, as it hath been assumed and exercised of late, is illegal;

That the commission for erecting the late Court of Commissioners for Ecclesiastical Causes, and all other commissions and courts of like nature, are illegal and pernicious;

That levying money for or to the use of the Crown by pretence of prerogative, without grant of Parliament, for longer time, or in other manner than the same is or shall be granted, is illegal;

That it is the right of the subjects to petition the king, and all commitments and prosecutions for such petitioning are illegal;

That the raising or keeping a standing army within the kingdom in time of peace, unless it be with consent of Parliament, is against law;

That the subjects which are Protestants may have arms for their defence suitable to their conditions and as allowed by law;

That election of members of Parliament ought to be free;

That the freedom of speech and debates or proceedings in Parliament ought not to be impeached or questioned in any court or place out of Parliament;

That excessive bail ought not to be required, nor excessive fines imposed, nor cruel and unusual punishments inflicted;

That jurors ought to be duly impanelled and returned, and jurors which pass upon men in trials for high treason ought to be freeholders;

That all grants and promises of fines and forfeitures of particular persons before conviction are illegal and void;

And that for redress of all grievances, and for the amending, strengthening and preserving of the laws, Parliaments ought to be held frequently.

And they do claim, demand and insist upon all and singular the premises as their undoubted rights and liberties, and that no declarations, judgments, doings or proceedings to the prejudice of the people in any of the said premises ought in any wise to be drawn hereafter into consequence or example; to which demand of their rights they are particularly encouraged by the declaration of his Highness the prince of Orange as being the only means for obtaining a full redress and remedy therein. Having therefore an entire confidence that his said Highness the prince of Orange will perfect the deliverance so far advanced by him, and will still preserve them from the violation of their rights which they have here asserted, and from all other attempts upon their religion, rights and liberties, the said Lords Spiritual and Temporal and Commons assembled at Westminster do resolve that William and Mary, prince and princess of Orange, be and be declared king and queen of England, France and Ireland and the dominions thereunto belonging, to hold the crown and royal dignity of the said kingdoms and dominions to them, the said prince and princess, during their lives and the life of the survivor of them, and that the sole and full exercise of the regal power be only in and executed by the said prince of Orange in the names of the said prince and princess during their joint lives, and after their deceases the said crown and royal dignity of the said kingdoms and dominions to be to the heirs of the body of the said princess, and for default of such issue to the Princess Anne of Denmark and the heirs of her body, and for default of such issue to the heirs of the body of the said prince of Orange. And the Lords Spiritual and Temporal and Commons do pray the said prince and princess to accept the same accordingly.

And that the oaths hereafter mentioned be taken by all

persons of whom the oaths of allegiance and supremacy might be required by law, instead of them; and that the said oaths of allegiance and supremacy be abrogated.

I, A.B., do sincerely promise and swear that I will be faithful and bear true allegiance to their Majesties King William and Queen Mary. So help me God.

I, A.B., do swear that I do from my heart abhor, detest and abjure as impious and heretical this damnable doctrine and position, that princes excommunicated or deprived by the Pope or any authority of the see of Rome may be deposed or murdered by their subjects or any other whatsoever. And I do declare that no foreign prince, person, prelate, state or potentate hath or ought to have any jurisdiction, power, superiority, pre-eminence or authority, ecclesiastical or spiritual, within this realm. So help me God.

THE ACT OF SETTLEMENT (1701)

DESIGNED TO ENSURE A PROTESTANT MONARCH, THE ACT OF SETTLEMENT NOT ONLY BROUGHT THE HOUSE OF HANOVER TO THE THRONE OF BRITAIN; IT ALSO EVENTUALLY FORMED THE BASIS OF THE UNION OF PARLIAMENTS BETWEEN ENGLAND AND SCOTLAND.

AN ACT FOR THE FURTHER
limitation of the Crown and better securing the rights and liberties of the subject

Whereas in the first year of the reign of your Majesty and of our late most gracious Sovereign Lady Queen Mary (of blessed memory) an Act of Parliament was made, entituled, An Act for declaring the rights and liberties of the subject and for settling the succession of the crown, wherein it was (amongst other things) enacted, established and declared, that the crown and regal government of the kingdoms of England, France and Ireland and the dominions thereunto belonging should be and continue to your Majesty and the said late queen during the joint lives of your Majesty and the said queen and to the survivor, and that after the decease of your Majesty and of the said queen the said crown and regal government should be and remain to the heirs of the body of the said late queen, and for default of such issue to her Royal Highness the Princess Anne of Denmark and the heirs of her body, and for default of such issue to the heirs of the body of your Majesty; and it was thereby further enacted, that all and every person and persons that then were or afterwards should be reconciled to or shall hold communion with the see or Church of Rome, or should profess the popish religion or marry a papist, should be excluded, and are by that Act made forever incapable to inherit, possess or enjoy the crown and government of this realm and Ireland and the dominions thereunto belonging or any part of the same, or to have, use or exercise any regal power, authority or jurisdiction within the same, and in all and every such case and cases the people of these realms shall be and are thereby absolved of their allegiance; and that the said crown and government shall from time to time descend to and be enjoyed by such person or persons being Protestants as should have inherited and enjoyed the same in case the said person or persons so reconciled, holding communion, professing or marrying as aforesaid were naturally dead; after the making of which statute and the settlement therein contained your Majesty's good subjects, who were restored to the full and free possession and enjoyment of their religion, rights and liberties by the providence of God giving success to your Majesty's just undertakings and unwearied endeavours for that purpose, had no greater temporal felicity to hope or wish for than to see a royal progeny descending from your Majesty, to whom (under God) they owe their tranquillity, and whose ancestors have for many years been principal assertors of the reformed religion and the liberties of Europe, and from our said most gracious sovereign lady, whose memory will always be precious to the subjects of these realms; and it having since pleased Almighty God to take away our said sovereign lady and also the most hopeful Prince William, duke of Gloucester (the only surviving issue of her Royal Highness the Princess Anne of Denmark), to the unspeakable grief and sorrow of your Majesty and your said good subjects, who under such losses being sensibly put in mind that it standeth wholly in the pleasure of Almighty God to prolong the lives of your Majesty and of her Royal Highness, and to grant to your Majesty or to her Royal Highness such issue as may be inheritable to the crown and regal government aforesaid by the respective limitations in the said recited Act contained, do constantly implore the divine mercy for those blessings, and your Majesty's said subjects having daily experience of your royal care and concern for the present and future welfare of these kingdoms, and particularly recommending from your throne a further provision to be made for the succession of the crown in the Protestant line for the happiness of the nation and the security of our religion, and it being absolutely necessary for the safety, peace and quiet of this realm to obviate all doubts and contentions in the same by reason of any pretended titles to the crown, and to maintain a certainty in the succession thereof to which your subjects may safely have recourse for their protection in case the limitations in the said recited Act should determine: therefore for a further provision of the succession of the crown in the Protestant line, we your Majesty's most dutiful and loyal subjects the Lords Spiritual and Temporal and Commons in this present Parliament assembled do beseech your Majesty that it may be enacted and declared, and be it enacted and declared by the king's most excellent Majesty, by and with the advice and consent of the Lords Spiritual and Temporal and Commons in this present Parliament assembled and by the authority of the same, that the most excellent Princess Sophia, electress and duchess dowager of Hanover, daughter of the most excellent Princess Elizabeth, late queen of

Bohemia, daughter of our late Sovereign Lord King James the First of happy memory, be and is hereby declared to be the next in succession in the Protestant line to the imperial crown and dignity of the said realms of England, France and Ireland, with the dominions and territories thereunto belonging, after his Majesty and the Princess Anne of Denmark and in default of issue of the said Princess Anne and of his Majesty respectively, and that from and after the deceases of his said Majesty our now sovereign lord, and of her Royal Highness the Princess Anne of Denmark, and for default of issue of the said Princess Anne and of his Majesty respectively, the crown and regal government of the said kingdoms of England, France and Ireland and of the dominions thereunto belonging, with the royal state and dignity of the said realms, and all honours, styles, titles, regalities, prerogatives, powers, jurisdictions and authorities to the same belonging and appertaining, shall be, remain and continue to the said most excellent Princess Sophia and the heirs of her body being Protestants; and thereunto the said Lords Spiritual and Temporal and Commons shall and will in the name of all the people of this realm most humbly and faithfully submit themselves, their heirs and posterities, and do faithfully promise that after the deceases of his Majesty and her Royal Highness, and the failure of the heirs of their respective bodies, to stand to, maintain and defend the said Princess Sophia and the heirs of her body being Protestants, according to the limitation and succession of the crown in this Act specified and contained, to the utmost of their powers with their lives and estates against all persons whatsoever that shall attempt anything to the contrary.

II. Provided always, and it is hereby enacted, that all and every person and persons who shall or may take or inherit the said crown by virtue of the limitation of this present Act, and is, are or shall be reconciled to, or shall hold communion with, the see or Church of Rome, or shall profess the popish religion or shall marry a papist, shall be subject to such incapacities as in such case or cases are by the said recited Act provided, enacted and established; and that every king and queen of this realm who shall come to and succeed in the imperial crown of this kingdom by virtue of this Act shall have the coronation oath administered to him, her or them at their respective coronations, according to the Act of Parliament made in the first year of the reign of his Majesty and the said late Queen Mary, entituled, An Act for establishing the coronation oath,1 and shall make, subscribe and repeat the declaration in the Act first above recited, mentioned or referred to in the manner and form thereby prescribed.

III. And whereas it is requisite and necessary that some further provision be made for securing our religion, laws and liberties from and after the death of his Majesty and the Princess Anne of Denmark, and in default of issue of the body of the said princess and of his Majesty respectively, be it enacted by the king's most excellent Majesty, by and with the advice and consent of the Lords Spiritual and Temporal and Commons in Parliament assembled and by the authority of the same;

That whosoever shall hereafter come to the possession of this crown shall join in communion with the Church of England as by law established.

That in case the crown and imperial dignity of this realm shall hereafter come to any person not being a native of this kingdom of England this nation be not obliged to engage in any war for the defence of any dominions or territories which do not belong to the crown of England without the consent of Parliament.

That no person who shall hereafter come to the possession of this crown shall go out of the dominions of England, Scotland or Ireland without consent of Parliament.

That from and after the time that the further limitation by this Act shall take effect all matters and things relating to the well governing of this kingdom which are properly cognizable in the Privy Council by the laws and customs of this realm shall be transacted there, and all resolutions taken thereupon shall be signed by such of the Privy Council as shall advise and consent to the same.

That after the said limitation shall take effect as aforesaid no person born out of the kingdoms of England, Scotland or Ireland, or the dominions thereunto belonging (although he be naturalized or made a denizen, except such as are born of English parents), shall be capable to be of the Privy Council, or a member of either House of Parliament, or to enjoy any office or place of trust either civil or military, or to have any grant of lands, tenements or hereditaments from the crown to himself or to any other or others in trust for him.

That no person who has an office or place of profit under the king, or receives a pension from the crown, shall be capable of serving as a member of the House of Commons.

That after the said limitation shall take effect as aforesaid judges' commissions be made quam din se bene gesserint, and their salaries ascertained and established, but upon the address of both Houses of Parliament it may be lawful to remove them.

That no pardon under the great seal of England be pleadable to an impeachment by the Commons in Parliament.

IV. And whereas the laws of England are the birthright of the people thereof, and all the kings and queens who shall ascend the throne of this realm ought to administer the government of the same according to the said laws, and all their officers and ministers ought to serve them respectively according to the same, the said Lords Spiritual and Temporal and Commons do therefore further humbly pray that all the laws and statutes of this realm for securing the established religion and the rights and liberties of the people thereof, and all other laws and statutes of the same now in force, may be ratified and confirmed, and the same are by his Majesty, by and with the advice and consent of the said Lords Spiritual and Temporal and Commons, and by authority of the same, ratified and confirmed accordingly.

ROYAL MARRIAGES ACT (1772)

THIS ACT, WHICH REQUIRES MEMBERS OF THE ROYAL FAMILY TO GAIN THE MONARCH'S
PERMISSION FOR ANY PROPOSED MARRIAGE, WAS ESTABLISHED IN THE AFTERMATH
OF TWO HANOVERIAN PRINCES' MARRYING BELOW THEIR STATION.

MOST GRACIOUS SOVEREIGN

Whereas your Majesty, from your paternal affection to your own family, and from your royal concern for the future welfare of your people, and the honour and dignity of your crown, was graciously pleased to recommend to your parliament to take into serious consideration, whether it might not be wise and expedient to supply the defect of the laws now in being; and, by some new provision, more effectually to guard the descendants of His late majesty King George the Second, (other than the issue of princesses who have married, or may hereafter marry, into foreign families) from marrying without the approbation of your Majesty, your heirs, or successors, first had and obtained; we have taken this weighty matter into our serious consideration; and, being sensible that marriages in the royal family are of the highest importance to the state, and that therefore the Kings of this realm have ever been entrusted with the care and approbation thereof; and, being thoroughly convinced of the wisdom and expediency of what your Majesty has thought fit to recommend, upon this occasion, we, your Majesty's most dutiful and loyal subjects the lords spiritual and temporal, and commons, in this present parliament assembled, do humbly beseech your Majesty that it may be enacted: and be it enacted by the King's most excellent majesty, by and with the advice and consent of the lords spiritual and temporal, and commons, in this present parliament assembled, and by the authority of the same,

That no descendant of the body of his late majesty King George the Second, male or female, (other than the issue of princesses who have married, or may hereafter marry, into foreign families) shall be capable of contracting matrimony without the previous consent of his Majesty, his heirs, or successors, signified under the great seal, and declared in council, (which consent, to preserve the memory thereof is hereby directed to be set out in the licence and register of marriage, and to be entered in the books of the privy council); and that every marriage, or matrimonial contract, of any such descendant, without such consent first had and obtained, shall be null and void, to all intents and purposes whatsoever.

II. Provided always, and be it enacted by the authority aforesaid, That in case any such descendant of the body of his late majesty King George the Second, being above the age of twenty-five years, shall persist in his or her resolution to contract a marriage disapproved of or dissented from, by the King, his heirs, or successors; that then such descendant, upon giving notice to the King's privy council, which notice is hereby directed to be entered in the books thereof, may, at any time from the expiration of twelve calendar months after such notice given to the privy council as aforesaid, contract such marriage; and his or her marriage with the person before proposed, and rejected, may be duly solemnized, without the previous consent of his Majesty, his heirs, or successors; and such marriage shall be good, as if this act had never been made, unless both houses of parliament shall, before the expiration of the said twelve months, expressly declare their disapprobation of such intended marriage.

III. And be it further enacted by the authority aforesaid, That every person who shall knowingly or wilfully presume to solemnize, or to assist, or to be present at the celebration of any marriage with any such descendant, or at his or her making any matrimonial contract, without such consent as aforesaid first had and obtained, except in the case above-mentioned, shall, being duly convicted thereof incur and suffer the pains and penalties ordained and provided by the statute of provision and premunire made in the sixteenth year of the reign of Richard the Second.

FROM AN OFFICIAL COMMUNICATION
MADE TO THE RUSSIAN AMBASSADOR AT LONDON ON 19 JAN. 1805, EXPLANATORY OF THE VIEWS WHICH HIS MAJESTY AND THE EMPEROR OF RUSSIA FORMED FOR THE DELIVERANCE AND SECURITY OF EUROPE

THIS LETTER OFFERS A GLIMPSE INTO THE DELICATE AND DETAILED NEGOTIATIONS BEHIND THE ALLIANCE AGAINST NAPOLEON.

The result of the communications which have been made by Prince Czartoriski to his Majesty's Ambassador at St. Petersburg, and of the confidential explanations which have been received from your Excellency, has been laid before the King; and H.M. has seen with inexpressible satisfaction the wise, dignified and generous policy which the Emperor of Russia is disposed to adopt under the present calamitous situation of Europe. H.M. is also happy to perceive that the views and sentiments of the Emperor respecting the deliverance of Europe, and providing for its future tranquillity and safety, correspond so entirely with his own. He is therefore desirous of entering into the most explicit and unreserved explanations on every point connected with this great object, and of forming the closest union of councils, and concert of measures with his Imperial Majesty, in order, by their joint influence and exertions, to insure the co-operation and assistance of other Powers of the Continent, on a scale adequate to the magnitude and importance of an undertaking, on the success of which the future safety of Europe must depend.

For this purpose, the first step must be to fix as precisely as possible the distinct objects to which such a concert is to be directed.

These, according to the explanation given of the sentiments of the Emperor, in which H.M. entirely concurs, appear to be three:

1. To rescue from the dominion of France those countries which it has subjugated since the beginning of the Revolution, and to reduce France within its former limits, as they stood before that time.

2. To make such an arrangement with respect to the territories recovered from France, as may provide for their security and happiness, and may at the same rime constitute a more effectual barrier in future against encroachments on the part of France.

3. To form, at the restoration of peace, a general agreement and guarantee for the mutual protection and security of different Powers, and for re-establishing a general system of public law in Europe.

The first and second objects are stated generally, and in their broadest extent; but neither of them can be properly considered in detail without reference to the nature and extent of the means by which they may be accomplished. The first is certainly that to which, without any modification or exception, H.M.'s wishes, as well as those of the Emperor, would be preferably directed, and nothing short of it can completely satisfy the views which both Sovereigns form for the deliverance and security of Europe. Should it be possible to unite in concert with Great Britain and Russia, the two other great military Powers of the Continent, there seems little doubt that such a union offeree would enable them to accomplish all that is proposed. But if (as there is too much reason to imagine may be the case) it should be found impossible to engage Prussia in the Confederacy, it may be doubted whether such operations could be carried on in all the quarters of Europe, as would be necessary for the success of the whole of this project.

The second point of itself involves in it many important considerations. The views and sentiments by which H.M. and the Emperor of Russia are equally animated in endeavouring to establish this concert, are pure and disinterested.

The first view, therefore, with respect to any of the countries which may be recovered from France, must be to restore, as far as possible, their ancient rights, and provide for the internal happiness of their inhabitants; but in looking at this object, they must not lose sight of the general security of Europe, on which even that separate object must principally depend.

Pursuant to this principle, there can be no question that, whenever any of these countries are capable of being restored to their former independence, and of being placed in a situation in which they can protect it, such an arrangement must be most congenial to the policy and the feelings on which this system is founded: but there will be found to be other countries among those now under the dominion of France, to which these considerations cannot apply, where either the ancient relations of the country are so completely destroyed that they cannot be restored, or where independence would be merely nominal, and alike inconsistent with security for the country itself, or for Europe; happily the larger number is of the first description. Should the arms of the Allies be successful to the full extent of expelling France from all the dominions she has acquired since the Revolution, it would certainly be the first object, as has already been stated, to re-establish the republics of the United Provinces and Switzerland, the territories of the King of Sardinia, Tuscany, Modena (under the protection of Austria) and Naples. But the territories of Genoa, of the Italian Republic, including the three Legations, Parma and Placentia; and on the other side of Europe, the Austrian Netherlands, and the States which have been detached from the German Empire on the left bank of the Rhine, evidently belong to the second class. With respect to the territories enumerated in Italy, experience has shown how little disposition existed in some, and how little means in any, to resist the aggression or influence of France. The King of Spain was certainly too much a party to the system of which so large a part of Europe has been a victim, to entitle the former interests of his family in Italy to any consideration; nor does the past conduct of Genoa, or any of the other States, give them any claim, either of justice or liberality. It is also obvious that these separate petty sovereignties would never again have any solid existence in themselves, and would

only serve to weaken and impair the force which ought to be, as much as possible, concentrated in the hands of the chief Powers in Italy.

It is needless to dwell particularly on the state of the Netherlands. Events have put out of the question the restoration of them to the House of Austria; they are therefore necessarily open to new arrangements, and evidently can never exist separate and independent.

Nearly the same considerations apply to the Ecclesiastical Electorates and the other territories on the left bank of the Rhine, after their being once detached from the Empire, and the former possessors of them indemnified. There appears, therefore, to be no possible objection, on the strictest principles of justice and public morality, to making such a disposition with respect to any of these territories as may be most conducive to the general interests; and there is evidently no other mode of accomplishing the great and beneficent object of re-establishing (after so much misery and bloodshed) the safety and repose of Europe on a solid and permanent basis. It is fortunate too that such a plan of arrangements as is in itself essential to the end proposed, is also likely to contribute, in the greatest degree, to secure the means by which that great end can best be promoted.

It is evidently of the utmost importance, if not absolutely indispensable for this purpose, to secure the vigorous and effectual co-operation both of Austria and Prussia; but there is little reason to hope that either of those Powers, and especially Prussia, will be brought to embark in the common cause, without the prospect of obtaining some important acquisition to compensate for its exertions.

On the grounds which have been already stated, H.M. conceives that nothing could so much contribute to the general security as giving to Austria fresh means of resisting the views of France on the side of Italy, and placing Prussia in a similar situation with respect to the Low Countries; and the relative situations of the two Powers would naturally make those the quarters to which their views would respectively be directed.

In Italy, sound policy would require that the power and

influence of the King of Sardinia should be augmented, and that Austria should be replaced in a situation which may enable her to afford an immediate and effectual support to his dominions, in case of their being attacked. H.M. sees with satisfaction, from the secret and confidential communications recently received through your Excellency, that the views of the Court of Vienna are perfectly conformable to this general principle, and that the extension at which she aims, might not only safely be admitted, but might even be increased, with advantage to the general interest. In other respects H.M. entirely concurs in the outline of the arrangement which he understands the Emperor of Russia to be desirous of seeing effected in this quarter. H.M. considers it as absolutely necessary for the general security that Italy should be completely rescued both from the occupation and influence of France, and that no Powers should be left within it who are not likely to enter into a general system of defence for maintaining its independence. For this purpose it is essential that the countries now composing what is called the Italian Republic should be transferred to other Powers. In distributing these territories an increase of wealth and power should undoubtedly be given to the King of Sardinia; and it seems material that his possessions, as well as the Duchy of Tuscany (which it is proposed to restore to the Grand Duke) should be brought into immediate contact, or ready communication with those of Austria.

On this principle, the whole of the territories which now compose the Ligurian Republic might, it is conceived, be annexed to Piedmont.

Supposing the efforts of the Allies to have been completely successful, and the two objects already discussed to have been fully obtained, H.M. would nevertheless consider this salutary work as still imperfect if the restoration of peace were not accompanied by the most effectual measures for giving solidity and permanence to the system which shall thus have been established. Much will undoubtedly be effected for the future repose of Europe by these territorial arrangements, which will furnish a more effectual barrier than has before existed, against the ambition of France. But in order to render this security as complete as possible, it seems necessary, at the period of a general pacification, to form a Treaty to which all the principal Powers of Europe should be parties, by which their respective rights and possessions, as they shall then have been established, shall be fixed and recognised; and they should all bind themselves mutually to protect and support each other against any attempt to infringe them. It should re-establish a general and comprehensive system of public law in Europe, and provide, as far as possible, for repressive future attempts to disturb the general tranquillity; and above all, for restraining any projects of aggrandisement and ambition similar to those which have produced all the calamities inflicted on Europe since the disastrous era of the French Revolution.

FROM THE REGENCY ACT OF 1811

THE FAMOUS MADNESS OF KING GEORGE III LED TO THIS LEGISLATION, WHICH RESULTED IN GEORGE, PRINCE OF WALES AND LATER GEORGE IV, TAKING OVER ROYAL RESPONSIBILITIES.

Whereas by reason of the severe indisposition with which it hath pleased God to afflict the King's most excellent Majesty, the personal exercise of the royal authority by H.M., is for the present, so far interrupted, that it becomes necessary to make provision for assisting H.M. in the administration and exercise of the royal authority, and also for the care of his royal person during the continuance of H.M.'s indisposition, and for the resumption of the exercise of the royal authority by H.M.; Be it therefore enacted... That H.R.H.George Augustus Frederick, Prince of Wales shall have full power and authority, in the name and on the behalf of H.M., and under the style and title of "Regent of the United Kingdom of Great Britain and Ireland," to exercise and administer the royal power and authority to the Crown of the United Kingdom of Great Britain and Ireland belonging, and to use, execute and perform all authorities, prerogatives, acts of government and administration of the same, which lawfully belong to the King...to use, execute and perform; subject to such limitation, exceptions, regulations and restrictions, as are hereinafter specified and contained; and all and every act and acts which shall be done by the said Regent, in the name and on the behalf of H.M., by virtue and in pursuance of this Act, and according to the powers and authorities hereby vested in him, shall have the same force and effect to all intents and purposes as the like acts would have if done by H.M. himself, and shall to all intents and purposes be full and sufficient warrant to all persons acting under the authority thereof; and all persons shall yield obedience thereto, and carry the same into effect, in the same manner and for the same purposes as the same persons ought to yield obedience to and carry into effect the like acts done by H.M. himself; any Law, course of office, or other matter or thing to the contrary notwithstanding.

II. (Lays down the form of Signature of the Regent.)

III. When H.M. shall by the blessing of God be restored to such a state of health as to be capable of resuming the personal exercise of his royal authority, and shall have declared his royal will and pleasure thereupon, as hereinafter provided, all and every the powers and authorities given by this Act, for the exercise and administration of his royal power and authority, or for the care of H.M's Royal Person, shall cease and determine; and no act, matter, or thing,...shall, if done after such declaration of H.M.'s royal will and pleasure, be thenceforth valid or effectual.

IV. Provided always, that all persons holding any offices or places, or pensions during H.M.'s pleasure, at the time of such declaration, under any appointment or authority of the Regent, or her Majesty, under the provisions of this Act, shall continue to hold the same, and to use,

exercise, and enjoy all the powers, authorities, privileges and emoluments thereof, notwithstanding such declaration of the resumption of the royal authority by H.M., unless and until H.M.shall declare his royal will and pleasure to the contrary; and all orders, acts of government or administration of H.M.'s royal authority, made, issued or done by the said Regent, before such declaration, shall be and remain in full force and effect, until the same shall be countermanded by H.M.

V. Provided also, that no acts of regal power...which might lawfully be done or executed by the King's most excellent Majesty, personally exercising his royal authority, shall, during the continuance of the Regency by this Act established, be valid and effectual, unless done and executed in the name and on the behalf of H.M., by the authority of the said Regent, according to the provisions of this Act, and subject to the limitations, exceptions, regulations and restrictions hereinafter contained.

VI. (The Regent to take three oaths: (i) allegiance to the King; (ii) to execute duties according to this Act and for the welfare of King and people; (iii) to maintain the Presbyterian Church in Scotland.)

VII. (The Regent on taking the oaths to subscribe the declaration 30 Chas. II, c. 2, and produce a certificate of having taken the sacrament.)

VIII. Provided always, that until after the 1st day of February 1812, if Parliament shall be then assembled,...for six weeks...or if Parliament shall be then assembled, but shall not have been so sitting for six weeks, then until the expiration of six weeks after Parliament shall have been so assembled...or if Parliament shall not then be assembled, then until the expiration of six weeks after Parliament shall have been assembled...the Regent shall not have or exercise any power or authority to grant, in the name or on the behalf of H.M. any rank, title or dignity of the peerage, by letters patent, writ of summons, or any other manner whatever, or to summon any person to the House of Lords by any title to which such person shall be the heir apparent, or to determine the abeyance of any rank, title or dignity of peerage, which now is or hereafter shall be in abeyance, in favour of any of the coheirs thereof by writ of summons or otherwise.

IX. Provided also, that the said Regent shall not, until after the said 1st Feb. 1812, or the expiration of such six weeks as aforesaid, have power or authority to grant, in the name or on the behalf of H.M., any office or employment whatever, in reversion, or to grant for any longer term than during H.M.'s pleasure, any office, employment, salary or pension whatever, except such offices and employments in possession for the term of the natural life, or during the good behaviour of the grantee or grantees thereof respectively, as by law must be so granted: provided always, that nothing herein contained shall in any manner affect or extend to prevent or restrain the granting of any pensions under the provisions of.... (The Acts 39 Geo. III, c. no, 48 Geo. III, c. 145, 40 Geo. III (Ireland), c. 69.)

X. (Exempts pensions under 41 Geo. III, c. 96, 43 Geo. III, c. 160, 45 Geo. III, c. 72.)

XI. Nothing in this Act contained shall extend or be construed to extend to empower the said Regent, in the name and on the behalf of H.M., to give the royal assent to any Bill or Bills in Parliament, for repealing, changing, or in any respect varying the order and course of succession to the Crown of this realm, as the same stands now established....

XII. Provided also, that if his said R.H., George Augustus Frederick Prince of Wales shall not continue to be resident in the U.K. of Great Britain and Ireland, or shall at any time marry a Papist, then and in either of such cases, all the powers and authorities vested in his said R.H. by this Act, shall cease and determine.

XIII. The care of H.M.'s royal person, and the disposing, ordering and managing of all matters and things relating thereto, shall be, and the same are hereby vested in the Queen's most excellent Majesty, during the continuance of H.M.'s indisposition. ...(The section further provides for the King's Household being managed by the Queen, giving her the right to appoint to offices, except the Lord Chamberlain, the Gentlemen of the Bedchamber, the Equerries, the Captain of the Guard, and the Captain of the Band of Pensioners. She cannot dismiss those appointed by the King.)

XIV. (Officers of the Household may not make appointments for any longer term than during H.M.'s pleasure.)

XV. (Provides the Queen with a Council) XVI. (Members of Her Majesty's Council to take an oath.) XVII, XVIII, XIX. (Prescribe the duties of the Council concerning the King's health and his recovery.)

XX. (Deals with the summoning of the Privy Council should the King recover.)

XXI. If H.M., by the advice of six or more of such Privy Council so assembled,

shall signify his royal pleasure to resume the personal exercise of his royal authority, and to issue a Proclamation declaring the same, such Proclamation shall be issued accordingly, countersigned by the said six or more of the said Privy Council, and all the powers and authorities given by this Act shall from thenceforth cease and determine, and the personal exercise of the royal authority by H.M. shall be and be deemed to be resumed by H.M., and shall be exercised by H.M., to all intents and purposes, as if this Act had never been made.

XXII. (On the death of the Regent, or on his ceasing to be Regent under the provisions of this Act, a Proclamation to be issued by the Privy Council in the King's name; on the Queen's death, the Regent to issue a Proclamation.)... And in case the Parliament in being at the time of the issuing of any Proclamation declaring the death of the Regent or of her Majesty, or at the time of the issuing of any Proclamation for the resumption of the personal exercise of the royal authority by H.M., shall then be separated, by any adjournment or prorogation, such Parliament shall forthwith meet and sit.

XXIII-XXX. (Deal with the dissolution of Parliament; the death of the Queen; the issue of money from the Civil List to the Queen and Royal Family; the Keeper of the Queen's Privy Purse; the care of the King's estates; and authorizing the Regent to dispose of Droits of the Crown and of the Admiralty.)

NAPOLEON'S LETTER TO THE PRINCE REGENT (1815)

THIS BRIEF LETTER FROM NAPOLEON TO THE FUTURE GEORGE IV
REMAINS A FASCINATING ENTRY IN THE CHRONICLE OF THE NAPOLEONIC WARS.

Exposed to the factions which distract my country and to the enmity of the greatest Powers of Europe, I have ended my political career, and I come, like Themistocles, to throw myself upon the hospitality of the British people. I put myself under the protection of their laws, which I claim from your Royal Highness, as the most powerful, the most constant, and the most generous of my enemies.

Rochefort, 13 July 1815.

FROM A LETTER FROM BARON STOCKMAR TO PRINCE ALBERT (1854)

THIS PIECE OF POLITICAL COUNSEL TO PRINCE ALBERT, WHO HAD BEEN EMBROILED
IN POLITICAL CONTROVERSY, REVEALS THE PREDICAMENT OF THE IDEALISTIC PRINCE
CONSORT IN HIS EFFECTIVE ROLE AS PRIVATE SECRETARY TO QUEEN VICTORIA.

The old Tories, who, before the Reform Bill, were in power for fifty years, had a direct interest in upholding the prerogatives of the Crown, and they did uphold them manfully, although the Hanoverian Kings, by their immoral, politically exceptionable, dynastic or private wishes and interests, made the task anything but an easy one. As a race, these Tories have died out, and the race, which in the present day bears their name, are simply degenerate bastards. Our Whigs, again, are nothing but partly conscious, partly unconscious Republicans, who stand in the same relation to the Throne as the wolf does to the lamb. And these Whigs must have a natural inclination to push to extremity the constitutional fiction — which, although undoubtedly of old standing, is fraught with danger — that it is unconstitutional to introduce and make use of the name and person of the irresponsible Sovereign in the public debates on matters bearing on the Constitution. But if the English Crown permit a Whig Ministry to follow this rule in practice, without exception, you must not wonder, if in a little time you find the majority of the people impressed with the belief, that the King, in the view of the law, is nothing but a mandarin figure, which has to nod its head in assent, or shake it in denial, as his Minister pleases.

Now, in our time, since Reform, the extinction of the genuine Tories, and the growth of those politicians of the Aberdeen school, who treat the existing Constitution merely as a bridge to a Republic, it is of extreme importance, that this fiction should be countenanced only provisionally, and that no opportunity should be let slip of vindicating the legitimate position of the Crown. And this is not hard to do, and can never embarrass a Minister, where such straightforward loyal personages as the Queen and the Prince are concerned. For the most jealous and distrustful Liberalism, in any discussion about the definite interpretation of the law of Royal prerogative, must be satisfied, if this be placed no higher than a right on the part of the King to be the permanent President of his

Ministerial Council. Now the most stupid of Englishmen knows, that, up to the present hour at least, his country is always governed by only one party, and that consequently the Premier of the Cabinet for the time is and can be nothing else but the Chief of the Party then in power. Out of the very character of this Party Chief it ought to be demonstrable to the narrowest capacity, that every Premier, even were he a patriot of the most far-seeing views, and absolutely exempt from prejudice, must suffer from two drawbacks inherent in his office, which demand a constitutional corrective, and for which none can be sought or found, except in the true position of the Crown towards the Cabinet, and in the way it deals with it in the exercise of its prerogative. The first of these drawbacks consists in the temptation, to which the Premier is directly exposed by the obvious insecurity and brief duration of his tenure of office, to give to the personal, selfish, and transitory tendencies of the dominant majority precedence over the substantial interests of the country. The second arises from the instinctive struggle of party (without reference to whether, so far as the State is concerned, they are in the right or not), to strengthen their majority, and to weaken the minority by every possible official resource....

Prior to 1831, the centre of gravity of the combined forces of the State in their relation to each other had lain in the Upper House, where the Tories for sixty years had commanded the majority. Although the Oppositions of those days sometimes spoke "of an overgrown power in the Crown," nothing more was seriously meant by this than the identity of principle and interest which was assumed to exist between the Crown and the majority of the Upper House. This notion the dominant majority could afford to encourage, and in its own interest to protect a Crown, which was making itself every day more unpopular and weak by its folly and immorality.

The Reform Act, while it gave to the democratic element a preponderance in the Constitution over the aristocratic, removed its centre of gravity from the Upper to the Lower House, and thereby threw all political life into a state of feverish excitement and oscillation, which was very apt to have proved fatal to it. In this conjuncture the healing force of the self-adjusting principle was demonstrated, all the more that Peel proved himself an honest and skilful physician. By successfully allaying the dangerous excitement of the one organ, which had now gained the preponderance, it was for the first time brought into harmonious action with the others, and the dangers were averted, which most imminently threatened the entire fabric.

A happy change, which placed a moral Sovereign upon the throne, came powerfully and palpably in aid of the self-adjusting principle and of Peel's endeavours. Whether the Minister, whether the Upper House was ever consciously aware, what a safeguard for them against the wild power of democracy had grown up in the moral purity of the Queen, I do not know. The Ministry, however, could hardly fail to know, even although they did not openly acknowledge, how greatly the popularity of the throne operated to the advantage and security of their administration; and just as little could the Lords fail to be struck by the reflection, that, instead of the time when they had to support an unpopular Sovereign, another time had come, in which a popular Sovereign was able to support them, and disposed to do so, on the assumption, that the part which they were entitled to take in legislation would be performed with intelligence, with sympathetic feeling suited to the spirit of the age (zeitmässiger Humanität), with industry and with courage....

The feverish crisis into which the life of the Constitution has been thrown by the Reform, in consequence of the very material alterations of the reciprocal relations between the individual forces of the State which had previously existed, is not yet past; although the self-adjusting principle and Peel's statesmanship have averted serious danger, and brought about a healthier state of things... Still, much remains to be done. The task which is especially incumbent on the Minister, and is his foremost duty is manfully to defend the present well-deserved popularity of the Sovereign, while yours is to lend all the aid in your power towards the assumption by the Lords of their rightful position in the Legislature, and the fulfilment of their vocation as sagacious, liberally-minded, and honourable men....

QUEEN VICTORIA AND HER PRIME MINISTERS

THESE THREE LETTERS REVEAL THE MANNER IN WHICH VICTORIA DEALT WITH THREE OF HER POWERFUL PRIME MINISTERS: DERBY, GLADSTONE, AND DISRAELI.

LETTER TO LORD DERBY
(1869)

Balmoral, 7th June 1869.

The Queen writes to Lord Derby to-day upon a subject which causes her the deepest anxiety, and, she must add, considerable surprise.

She hears that it is proposed to throw out the Irish Church Bill by opposing the second reading.

The Queen has never concealed her opinion as to this measure — which remains unaltered; but, after the Dissolution last autumn, and the large majorities with which the Bill has been passed in the House of Commons, for the House of Lords to throw it out, and thus place itself in collision with the House of Commons, would be most dangerous, if not disastrous.

The Queen knows too well how loyal, and how devoted to her person and Throne, Lord Derby is; and she cannot therefore doubt, that he will pause before he concurs in pursuing a course fraught with such danger to the country and constitution.

If the House of Lords does not oppose the second reading, it will be in its power to make important and useful amendments, which it is hoped the House of Commons may be disposed to adopt.

This would raise the House of Lords in the country; but to put itself into collision with the other House would — above all at this moment when alas! the aristocracy is lowered by the conduct of so many who bear the oldest, proudest names — she must repeat it, lead to most disastrous results.

Most earnestly does the Queen appeal to Lord Derby to try and prevent this dangerous course from being pursued. She would ask him to show this letter in confidence to Lord Cairns.

LETTER TO WILLIAM GLADSTONE
(1869)

Osborne, 22nd July 1869.

The Queen has to thank Mr. Gladstone for all his letters received yesterday, as well as for the telegram, and the communication received this morning with a full account of the deliberations of the Cabinet. She was deeply grieved to see that the hopes of an amicable settlement between both Houses, which we had good reason to entertain on Monday, were all frustrated on Tuesday night. The Queen, however, rejoices to see that the most moderate counsels have prevailed in the Cabinet, and she still hopes that if a conciliatory spirit is shown in the House of Commons, and attempts to coerce and override the House of Lords are abstained from, that the House of Lords will also meet them in a spirit of conciliation, and then this most unhappy question may be settled this Session.

LETTER TO BENJAMIN DISRAELI
(March 13, 1873)

Buckingham Palace, March 13, 1873

Mr. Gladstone has just been here and has tendered his resignation and that of his colleagues in consequence of the vote of the House of Commons on Tuesday night — which the Queen has accepted. She therefore writes to Mr. Disraeli to ask him whether he will undertake to form a Government.

The Queen would like to see Mr. Disraeli at 6 or as soon after as possible.

She sends this letter by her private secretary, Colonel Ponsonby, who can be the bearer of any written or verbal answer from Mr. Disraeli.

Memorandum by Queen Victoria on an Interview with Disraeli
(March 13, 1873)

Buckingham Palace, March 13, 1873.

Mr. Disraeli came at a little after 5. After expressing my feeling for him in his sorrow and shaking hands with him, I said I had sent for him in consequence of last night's vote; and he asked whether I wished him to give a categorical answer, or to say a few words on the present state of affairs. I said I should willingly hear what he had to say.

He then went on to say that he had not expected the vote; he had thought, after Mr. Cardwell's speech, the Government would have a majority. That the Conservative party never was more compact or more united; that there was the most perfect understanding between him and all those who had served with him, and especially named Ld. Derby, Ld. Cairns, Mr. Hardy, and Sir S. Northcote. That he was perfectly able to form a Government at once, perfectly fit to carry on the administration of the country to my entire satisfaction; that he could command 280 votes; that since, as he said, "I had left your Majesty's immediate service, for I never consider myself out of your Majesty's service," the party had gained considerably, about thirty seats; that he had laboured to keep the party as much together and in as efficient a state as possible; but that it would be useless to attempt to carry on the Government with a minority in the House of Commons, and that he must therefore state his inability to undertake to form a Government in the present Parliament.

What was then to be done? I asked. "Mr. Gladstone ought to remain in and continue to carry on the Government." This, I said, I thought he very likely would object to, having declared his views so strongly on this measure. This was a mistake, Mr. Disraeli replied, and he ought never to have done so. That might be so or not, I said, but anyhow Mr. Gladstone did feel this, and did not ask for a dissolution, therefore I thought it doubtful whether he would consent to resume or continue in office, feeling he could not submit to this vote. "But he has condoned for it by his resignation and readiness to give up power," was the answer; that he should not throw up office merely for this vote; it would not be a good return to the present Parliament, which had supported him so warmly, and in which he had carried 3 great measures, for so he must call them, though he might not agree with them. I again asked him what I was to say to Mr. Gladstone, and he repeated that "I decline to form a Government in the present Parliament, and I do not ask for a dissolution."

Of course, he said, there were instances where a Sovereign had been left without a Government, and in such a case he would, of course, be ready to serve me. I said that I would at once let Mr. Gladstone know, but that I might have to call upon him again.

QUEEN VICTORIA'S PROCLAMATION AS EMPRESS OF INDIA (1876)

VICTORIA'S ADDITIONAL TITLE OF EMPRESS OF INDIA UNDERSCORED
THE SHEER SCALE AND WEALTH OF THE STILL-GROWING BRITISH EMPIRE.

BY THE QUEEN.
A Proclamation.

VICTORIA, R.

WHEREAS an Act has been passed in the present Session of Parliament, intituled "An Act to enable Her Most Gracious Majesty to make an Addition to the Royal Style and Titles at present appertaining to the Imperial Crown of the United Kingdom and its Dependencies," which Act recites that, by the Act for the Union of Great Britain and Ireland, it was provided that after such Union the Royal Style and Titles appertaining to the Imperial Crown of the United Kingdom and its Dependencies should be such as His Majesty by His Royal Proclamation under the Great Seal of the United Kingdom should be pleased to appoint: and which Act also recites that, by virtue of the said Act, and of a Royal Proclamation under the Great Seal, dated the 1st day of January, 1801, Our present Style and Titles are "Victoria, by the Grace of God, of the United Kingdom of Great Britain and Ireland, Queen, Defender of the Faith:" and which Act also recites that, by the Act for the better Government of India, it was enacted that the Government of India, theretofore vested in the East India Company in trust for Us, should become vested in Us, and that India should thenceforth be governed by Us and in Our name, and that it is expedient that there should be a recognition of the transfer of Government so made by means of an addition to be made to Our Style and Titles: And which Act, after the said recitals, enacts that it shall be lawful for Us, with a view to such recognition as aforesaid, of the transfer of the Government of India, by Our Royal Proclamation under the Great Seal of the United Kingdom, to make such addition to the Style

and Titles at present appertaining to the Imperial Crown of the United Kingdom and its Dependencies as to Us may seem meet; We have thought fit, by and with the advice of Our Privy Council, to appoint and declare, and We hereby, by and with the said advice, appoint and declare that henceforth, so far as conveniently may be, on all occasions and in all instruments wherein Our Style and Titles are used, save and except all Charters, Commissions, Letters Patent, Grants, Writs, Appointments, and other like instruments, not extending in their operation beyond the United Kingdom, the following addition shall be made to the Style and Titles at present appertaining to the Imperial Crown of the United Kingdom and its Dependencies; that is to say, in the Latin tongue in these words: "Indiæ Imperatrix." And in the English tongue in these words: "Empress of India." And Our will and pleasure further is, that the said addition shall not be made in the Commissions, Charters, Letters Patent, Grants, Writs, Appointments, and other like instruments, hereinbefore specially excepted. And Our will and pleasure further is, that all gold, silver, and copper moneys, now current and lawful moneys of the United Kingdom, and all gold, silver, and copper moneys which shall, on or after this day, be coined by Our authority with the like impressions, shall, notwithstanding such addition to Our Style and Titles, be deemed and taken to be current and lawful moneys of the said United Kingdom; and further that all moneys coined for and issued in any of the Dependencies of the said United Kingdom, and declared by Our Proclamation to be current and lawful money of such Dependencies, respectively bearing Our Style, or Titles, or any part or parts thereof, and all moneys which shall hereafter be coined and issued according to such Proclamation, shall, notwithstanding such addition, continue to be lawful and current money of such Dependencies respectively, until Our pleasure shall be further declared thereupon.

Given at Our Court at Windsor, the twenty-eighth day of April, one thousand eight hundred and seventy-six, in the thirty-ninth year of Our Reign.

GOD save the QUEEN.

THE ABDICATION SPEECH OF EDWARD VIII (DECEMBER 11, 1936)

EDWARD VIII'S CHOICE TO ABDICATE THE THRONE RATHER THAN FORGO MARRIAGE TO WALLIS SIMPSON PRECIPITATED A ROYAL CRISIS. HIS SPEECH, BROADCAST ON THE BBC, MEMORABLY ARTICULATED HIS DECISION.

At long last I am able to say a few words of my own. I have never wanted to withhold anything, but until now it has not been constitutionally possible for me to speak. A few hours ago I discharged my last duty as King and Emperor, and now that I have been succeeded by my brother, the Duke of York, my first words must be to declare my allegiance to him. This I do with all my heart. You all know the reasons which have impelled me to renounce the throne. But I want you to understand that in making up my mind I did not forget the country or the empire, which, as Prince of Wales and lately as King, I have for twenty-five years tried to serve.

But you must believe me when I tell you that I have found it impossible to carry the heavy burden of responsibility and to discharge my duties as King as I would wish to do without the help and support of the woman I love.

And I want you to know that the decision I have made has been mine and mine alone. This was a thing I had to judge entirely for myself. The other person most nearly concerned has tried up to the last to persuade me to take a different course.

I have made this, the most serious decision of my life, only upon the single thought of what would, in the end, be best for all.

This decision has been made less difficult to me by the sure knowledge that my brother, with his long training in the public affairs of this country and with his fine qualities, will be able to take my place forthwith without interruption or injury to the life and progress of the empire. And he has one matchless blessing, enjoyed by so many of you, and not bestowed on me — a happy home with his wife and children.

During these hard days I have been comforted by her majesty my mother and by my family. The ministers of the crown, and in particular, Mr. Baldwin, the Prime Minister, have always treated me with full consideration. There has never been any constitutional difference between me and them, and between me and Parliament. Bred in the constitutional tradition by my father, I should never have allowed any such issue to arise.

Ever since I was Prince of Wales, and later on when I occupied the throne, I have been treated with the greatest kindness by all classes of the people wherever I have lived or journeyed throughout the empire. For that I am very grateful.

I now quit altogether public affairs and I lay down my burden. It may be some time before I return to my native land, but I shall always follow the fortunes of the British race and empire with profound interest, and if at any time in the future I can be found of service to his majesty in a private station, I shall not fail.

And now, we all have a new King. I wish him and you, his people, happiness and prosperity with all my heart. God bless you all! God save the King!

GEORGE VI'S SPEECH ON THE START OF THE SECOND WORLD WAR (SEPTEMBER 3, 1939)

THIS BROADCAST, FAMOUS AS 'THE KING'S SPEECH', DEMONSTRATED THE MORAL LEADERSHIP GEORGE VI WOULD ENDEAVOR TO DISPLAY THROUGHOUT THE WAR.

In this grave hour, perhaps the most fateful in our history, I send to every household of my peoples, both at home and overseas, this message, spoken with the same depth of feeling for each one of you as if I were able to cross your threshold and speak to you myself.

For the second time in the lives of most of us we are at war. Over and over again we have tried to find a peaceful way out of the differences between ourselves and those who are now our enemies. But it has been in vain. We have been forced into a conflict. For we are called, with our allies, to meet the challenge of a principle which, if it were to prevail, would be fatal to any civilised order in the world.

It is the principle which permits a state, in the selfish pursuit of power, to disregard its treaties and its solemn pledges; which sanctions the use of force, or threat of force, against the sovereignty and independence of other states. Such a principle, stripped of all disguise, is surely the mere primitive doctrine that might is right; and if this principle were established throughout the world, the freedom of our own country and of the whole British Commonwealth of Nations would be in danger. But far more than this — the peoples of the world would be kept in the bondage of fear, and all hopes of settled peace and of the security of justice and liberty among nations would be ended.

This is the ultimate issue which confronts us. For the sake of all that we ourselves hold dear, and of the world's order and peace, it is unthinkable that we should refuse to meet the challenge.

It is to this high purpose that I now call my people at home and my peoples across the seas, who will make our cause their own. I ask them to stand calm, firm, and united in this time of trial. The task will be hard. There may be dark days ahead, and war can no longer be confined to the battlefield. But we can only do the right as we see the right, and reverently commit our cause to God. If one and all we keep resolutely faithful to it, ready for whatever service or sacrifice it may demand, then, with God's help, we shall prevail.

May He bless and keep us all.

PRINCESS ELIZABETH'S SPEECH TO THE CHILDREN OF THE COMMONWEALTH (OCTOBER 13, 1940)

IN THIS BBC BROADCAST, HER FIRST PUBLIC SPEECH, ELIZABETH PLAYED HER ROLE AS A VOICE OF STEADINESS AND PATRIOTISM DURING BRITAIN'S DARKEST STRETCH OF THE SECOND WORLD WAR.

In wishing you all 'good evening' I feel that I am speaking to friends and companions who have shared with my sister and myself many a happy Children's Hour. Thousands of you in this country have had to leave your homes and be separated from your fathers and mothers. My sister Margaret Rose and I feel so much for you as we know from experience what it means to be away from those we love most of all.

To you, living in new surroundings, we send a message of true sympathy and at the same time we would like to thank the kind people who have welcomed you to their homes in the country.

All of us children who are still at home think continually of our friends and relations who have gone overseas — who have travelled thousands of miles to find a wartime home and a kindly welcome in Canada, Australia, New Zealand, South Africa and the United States of America.

My sister and I feel we know quite a lot about these countries. Our father and mother have so often talked to us of their visits to different parts of the world. So it is not difficult for us to picture the sort of life you are all leading, and to think of all the new sights you must be seeing, and the adventures you must be having.

But I am sure that you, too, are often thinking of the Old Country. I know you won't forget us; it is just because we are not forgetting you that I want, on behalf of all the children at home, to send you our love and best wishes — to you and to your kind hosts as well.

Before I finish I can truthfully say to you all that we children at home are full of cheerfulness and courage. We are trying to do all we can to help our gallant sailors, soldiers and airmen, and we are trying, too, to bear our own share of the danger and sadness of war.

We know, everyone of us, that in the end all will be well; for God will care for us and give us victory and peace. And when peace comes, remember it will be for us, the children of today, to make the world of tomorrow a better and happier place.

My sister is by my side and we are both going to say goodnight to you.

Come on, Margaret.

Goodnight, children.

Goodnight, and good luck to you all.

GEORGE VI'S SPEECH ON THE END
OF THE WAR IN EUROPE (MAY 8, 1945)

BROADCAST AFTER THE SURRENDER OF NAZI GERMANY, THIS SPEECH DISPLAYS GEORGE'S AWARENESS OF THE ROYAL FAMILY'S ROLE AS NATIONAL ICONS OF SERVICE AND PATRIOTISM.

Today we give thanks to Almighty God for a great deliverance. Speaking from our Empire's oldest capital city, war-battered but never for one moment daunted or dismayed — speaking from London, I ask you to join with me in that act of thanksgiving.

Germany, the enemy who drove all Europe into war, has been finally overcome. In the Far East we have yet to deal with the Japanese, a determined and cruel foe. To this we shall turn with the utmost resolve and with all our resources. But at this hour, when the dreadful shadow of war has passed from our hearths and homes in these islands, we may at last make one pause for thanksgiving and then turn our thoughts to the tasks all over the world which peace in Europe brings with it.

Let us remember those who will not come back, their constancy and courage in battle, their sacrifice and endurance in the face of a merciless enemy: let us remember the men in all the Services and the women in all the Services who have laid down their lives. We have come to the end of our tribulation, and they are not with us at the moment of our rejoicing.

Then let us salute in proud gratitude the great host of the living who have brought us to victory. I cannot praise them to the measure of each one's service, for in a total war the efforts of all rise to the same noble height and all are devoted to the common purpose. Armed or unarmed, men and women, you have fought, striven, and endured to your utmost. No one knows that better than I do; and as your King I thank with a full heart those who bore arms so valiantly on land and sea, or in the air; and all civilians who, shouldering their many burdens, have carried them unflinchingly without complaint.

With those memories in our minds, let us think what it was that has upheld us through nearly six years of suffering and peril. The knowledge that everything was at stake: our freedom, our independence, our very existence as a people; but the knowledge also that in defending ourselves we were defending the liberties of the whole world; that our cause was the cause not of this nation only, not of this Empire and Commonwealth only, but of every land where freedom is cherished and law and liberty go hand in hand. In the darkest hours we knew that the enslaved and isolated peoples of Europe looked to us; their hopes were our hopes; their confidence confirmed our faith. We knew that, if we failed, the last remaining barrier against a world-wide tyranny would have fallen in ruins. But we did not fail.

We kept our faith with ourselves and with one another; we kept faith and unity with our great allies. That faith and unity have carried us to victory through dangers which at times seemed overwhelming.

So let us resolve to bring to the tasks which lie ahead the same high confidence in our mission. Much hard work awaits us, both in the restoration of our own country after the ravages of war and in helping to restore peace and sanity to a shattered world.

This comes upon us at a time when we have all given of our best. For five long years and more, heart and brain, nerve and muscle have been directed upon the overthrow of Nazi tyranny. Now we turn, fortified by success, to deal with our last remaining foe. The Queen and I know the ordeals which you have endured throughout the Commonwealth and Empire. We are proud to have shared some of these ordeals with you, and we know also that together we shall all face the future with stern resolve and prove that our reserves of will-power and vitality are inexhaustible.

There is great comfort in the thought that the years of darkness and danger in which the children of our country have grown up are over and, please God, for ever. We shall have failed, and the blood of our dearest will have flowed in vain, if the victory which they died to win does not lead to a lasting peace, founded on justice and established in good will. To that, then, let us turn our thoughts on this day of just triumph and proud sorrow; and then take up our work again, resolved as a people to do nothing unworthy of those who died for us and to make the world such a world as they would have desired, for their children and for ours.

This is the task to which now honour binds us. In the hour of danger we humbly committed our cause into the Hand of God, and He has been our Strength and Shield. Let us thank him for His mercies, and in this hour of Victory commit ourselves and our new task to the guidance of that same strong Hand.

QUEEN ELIZABETH II'S CORONATION OATH (JUNE 2, 1953)

THIS PRESENTATION OF THE CORONATION OATH IS TAKEN FROM THE ORDER OF SERVICE FOR THE CORONATION.

The Queen having returned to her Chair... the Archbishop standing before her shall administer the Coronation Oath, first asking the Queen,
Madam, is your Majesty willing to take the Oath?
And the Queen answering, I am willing.
The Archbishop shall minister these questions; and The Queen, having a book in her hands, shall answer each question severally as follows:
Archbishop. Will you solemnly promise and swear to govern the Peoples of the United Kingdom of Great Britain and Northern Ireland, Canada, Australia, New Zealand, the Union of South Africa, Pakistan, and Ceylon, and of your Possessions and the other Territories to any of them belonging or pertaining, according to their respective laws and customs?
Queen. I solemnly promise so to do.
Archbishop. Will you to your power cause Law and Justice, in Mercy, to be executed in all your judgements?
Queen. I will.
Archbishop. Will you to the utmost of your power maintain the Laws of God and the true profession of the Gospel? Will you to the utmost of your power maintain in the United Kingdom the Protestant Reformed Religion established by law? Will you maintain and preserve inviolably the settlement of the Church of England, and the doctrine, worship, discipline, and government thereof, as by law established in England? And will you preserve unto the Bishops and Clergy of England, and to the Churches there committed to their charge, all such rights and privileges, as by law do or shall appertain to them or any of them?
Queen. All this I promise to do.
Then the Queen arising out of her Chair, supported as before, the Sword of State being carried before her, shall go to the Altar, and make her solemn Oath in the sight of all the people to observe the premisses: laying her right hand upon the Holy Gospel in the great Bible (which was before carried in the procession and is now brought from the Altar by the Arch-bishop, and tendered to her as she kneels upon the steps), and saying these words:
The things which I have here before promised, I will perform and keep. So help me God.
Then the Queen shall kiss the Book and sign the Oath.
The Queen having thus taken her Oath shall return again to her Chair, and the Bible shall be delivered to the Dean of Westminster.

ELIZABETH II'S 'ANNUS HORRIBILIS' SPEECH (NOVEMBER 24, 1992)

THIS MEMORABLE SPEECH, IN WHICH ELIZABETH II DISCUSSES THE DIFFICULTIES
ARISING FROM HER CHILDREN'S MARRIAGES AND OTHER MISFORTUNES,
REMAINS EMBLEMATIC OF HER CHARACTER AS QUEEN.

My Lord Mayor,

Could I say, first, how delighted I am that the Lady Mayoress is here today.

This great hall has provided me with some of the most memorable events of my life. The hospitality of the City of London is famous around the world, but nowhere is it more appreciated than among the members of my family.

I am deeply grateful that you, my Lord Mayor, and the Corporation, have seen fit to mark the fortieth anniversary of my Accession with this splendid lunch, and by giving me a picture which I will greatly cherish.

Thank you also for inviting representatives of so many organisations with which I and my family have special connections, in some cases stretching back over several generations. To use an expression more common north of the Border, this is a real 'gathering of the clans'.

1992 is not a year on which I shall look back with undiluted pleasure. In the words of one of my more sympathetic correspondents, it has turned out to be an 'Annus Horribilis'. I suspect that I am not alone in thinking it so. Indeed, I suspect that there are very few people or institutions unaffected by these last months of worldwide turmoil and uncertainty. This generosity and whole-hearted kindness of the Corporation of the City to Prince Philip and me would be welcome at any time, but at this particular moment, in the aftermath of Friday's tragic fire at Windsor, it is especially so.

And, after this last weekend, we appreciate all the more what has been set before us today. Years of experience, however, have made us a bit more canny than the lady, less well versed than us in the splendours of City hospitality, who, when she was offered a balloon glass for her brandy, asked for 'only half a glass, please'.

It is possible to have too much of a good thing. A well-meaning Bishop was obviously doing his best when he told Queen Victoria, "Ma'am, we cannot pray too often, nor too fervently, for the Royal Family". The Queen's reply was: "Too fervently, no; too often, yes". I, like Queen Victoria, have always been a believer in that old maxim "moderation in all things".

I sometimes wonder how future generations will judge the events of this tumultuous year. I dare say that history will take a slightly more moderate view than that of some contemporary commentators. Distance is well-known to lend enchantment, even to the less attractive views. After all, it has the inestimable advantage of hindsight.

But it can also lend an extra dimension to judgement, giving it a leavening of moderation and compassion — even of wisdom — that is sometimes lacking in the reactions of those whose task it is in life to offer instant opinions on all things great and small.

No section of the community has all the virtues, neither does any have all the vices. I am quite sure that most people try to do their jobs as best they can, even if the result is not always entirely successful. He who has never failed to reach perfection has a right to be the harshest critic.

There can be no doubt, of course, that criticism is good for people and institutions that are part of public life. No institution — City, Monarchy, whatever — should expect to be free from the scrutiny of those who give it their loyalty and support, not to mention those who don't.

But we are all part of the same fabric of our national society and that scrutiny, by one part of another, can be just as effective if it is made with a touch of gentleness, good humour and understanding.

This sort of questioning can also act, and it should do so, as an effective engine for change. The City is a good example of the way the process of change can be incorporated into the stability and continuity of a great institution. I particularly admire, my Lord Mayor, the way in which the City has adapted so nimbly to what the Prayer Book calls "The changes and chances of this mortal life". You have set an example of how it is possible to remain effective and dynamic without losing those indefinable qualities, style and character. We only have to look around this great hall to see the truth of that.

Forty years is quite a long time. I am glad to have had the chance to witness, and to take part in, many dramatic changes in life in this country. But I am glad to say that the magnificent standard of hospitality given on so many occasions to the Sovereign by the Lord Mayor of London has not changed at all. It is an outward symbol of one other unchanging factor which I value above all — the loyalty given to me and to my family by so many people in this country, and the Commonwealth, throughout my reign.

You, my Lord Mayor, and all those whose prayers — fervent, I hope, but not too frequent — have sustained me through all these years, are friends indeed. Prince Philip and I give you all, wherever you may be, our most humble thanks.

And now I ask you to rise and drink the health of the Lord Mayor and Corporation of London.

ELIZABETH II'S BROADCAST ON THE DEATH OF PRINCESS DIANA OF WALES (SEPTEMBER 5, 1997)

IN THE AFTERMATH OF THE UNTIMELY DEATH OF DIANA, ELIZABETH EMERGED FROM PRIVATE GRIEVING TO GIVE THIS SPEECH OVER THE BBC.

Since last Sunday's dreadful news we have seen, throughout Britain and around the world, an overwhelming expression of sadness at Diana's death. We have all been trying in our different ways to cope. It is not easy to express a sense of loss, since the initial shock is often succeeded by a mixture of other feelings: disbelief, incomprehension, anger — and concern for those who remain. We have all felt those emotions in these last few days. So what I say to you now, as your Queen and as a grandmother, I say from my heart.

First, I want to pay tribute to Diana myself. She was an exceptional and gifted human being. In good times and bad, she never lost her capacity to smile and laugh, nor to inspire others with her warmth and kindness. I admired and respected her — for her energy and commitment to others, and especially for her devotion to her two boys. This week at Balmoral, we have all been trying to help William and Harry come to terms with the devastating loss that they and the rest of us have suffered.

No one who knew Diana will ever forget her. Millions of others who never met her, but felt they knew her, will remember her. I for one believe there are lessons to be drawn from her life and from the extraordinary and moving reaction to her death. I share in your determination to cherish her memory.

This is also an opportunity for me, on behalf of my family, and especially Prince Charles and William and Harry, to thank all of you who have brought flowers, sent messages and paid your respects in so many ways to a remarkable person. These acts of kindness have been a huge source of help and comfort.

Our thoughts are also with Diana's family and the families of those who died with her. I know that they too have drawn strength from what has happened since last weekend, as they seek to heal their sorrow and then to face the future without a loved one.

I hope that tomorrow we can all, wherever we are, join in expressing our grief at Diana's loss, and gratitude for her all-too-short life. It is a chance to show to the whole world the British nation united in grief and respect.

May those who died rest in peace and may we, each and every one of us, thank God for someone who made many, many people happy.

ELIZABETH II'S DIAMOND JUBILEE SPEECH (MARCH 20, 2012)

ELIZABETH II MARKED HER DIAMOND JUBILEE WITH THIS SPEECH IN WESTMINSTER. IT WAS A CONFIDENT STATEMENT OF HER PRINCIPLES AS QUEEN AND HER VISION OF BRITAIN.

My Lords and Members of the House of Commons, I am most grateful for your Loyal Addresses and the generous words of the Lord Speaker and Mr. Speaker. This great institution has been at the heart of the country and the lives of our people throughout its history. As Parliamentarians, you share with your forebears a fundamental role in the laws and decisions of your own age. Parliament has survived as an unshakeable cornerstone of our constitution and our way of life. History links monarchs and Parliament, a connecting thread from one period to the next. So, in an era when the regular, worthy rhythm of life is less eye-catching than doing something extraordinary, I am reassured that I am merely the second Sovereign to celebrate a Diamond Jubilee.

As today, it was my privilege to address you during my Silver and Golden Jubilees. Many of you were present ten years ago and some of you will recall the occasion in 1977. Since my Accession, I have been a regular visitor to the Palace of Westminster and, at the last count, have had the pleasurable duty of treating with twelve Prime Ministers. Over such a period, one can observe that the experience of venerable old age can be a mighty guide but not a prerequisite for success in public office. I am therefore very pleased to be addressing many younger Parliamentarians and also those bringing such a wide range of background and experience to your vital, national work.

During these years as your Queen, the support of my family has, across the generations, been beyond measure. Prince Philip is, I believe, well-known for declining compliments of any kind. But throughout he has been a constant strength and guide. He and I are very proud and grateful that The Prince of Wales and other members of our family are travelling on my behalf in this Diamond Jubilee year to visit all the Commonwealth Realms and a number of other Commonwealth countries.

These overseas tours are a reminder of our close affinity with the Commonwealth, encompassing about one-third of the world's population. My own association with the Commonwealth has taught me that the most important contact between nations is usually contact between its peoples. An organisation dedicated to certain values, the Commonwealth has flourished and grown by successfully promoting and protecting that contact.

At home, Prince Philip and I will be visiting towns and cities up and down the land. It is my sincere hope that the Diamond Jubilee will be an opportunity for people to come together in a spirit of neighbourliness and celebration of their own communities.

We also hope to celebrate the professional and voluntary service given by millions of people across the country who are working for the public good. They are a source of vital support to the welfare and wellbeing of others, often unseen or overlooked.

And as we reflect upon public service, let us again be mindful of the remarkable sacrifice and courage of our Armed Forces. Much may indeed have changed these past sixty years but the valour of those who risk their lives for the defence and freedom of us all remains undimmed. The happy relationship I have enjoyed with Parliament has extended well beyond the more than three and a half thousand Bills I have signed into law. I am therefore very touched by the magnificent gift before me, generously subscribed by many of you. Should this beautiful window cause just a little extra colour to shine down upon this ancient place, I should gladly settle for that. We are reminded here of our past, of the continuity of our national story and the virtues of resilience, ingenuity and tolerance which created it. I have been privileged to witness some of that history and, with the support of my family, rededicate myself to the service of our great country and its people now and in the years to come.

INDEX

D

ACKNOWLEDGMENTS

b: below, c: center, l: left, r: right, t: top

16bl Shutterstock/mountainpix | 17r Jim Champion | 17bl Shutterstock/Rob Wilson | 18c Mike Christie | 19bc gugganij | 21tr Secisek | 22cl Richard M Buck | 23bc JohnArmagh | 26 Soloist | 27br Shutterstock/Solodov Alexey | 28b ŁW | 30bl Andrew Dunn | 31 Shutterstock/steve estvanik | 32b Yale Center for British Art, Paul Mellon Collection | 32c Christine Matthews | 33c, 34-35 Myrabella | 36bl Shutterstock/Imladris | 36br PHGCOM | 37 Shutterstock/Georgios Kollidas | 38b Dan Koehl | 39c Myrabella | 39b Shutterstock/Claudio Divizia | 40t Auximines | 40br MaiDireLollo | 42l Shutterstock/peresanz | 43t Stephen Fulljames | 43br Urban | 44c Myrabella | 46b Nandhp | 49t Shutterstock/Kamira | 49br Stan Shebs | 50bl ChevronTango | 53 istockphoto/duncan1890 | 54tl Graham Horn | 54bl Prinz Wilbert | 55b Patricia Drury | 56b Shutterstock/ anshar | 57 Shutterstock/Georgios Kollidas | 60-61 The British Library | 66c The Walters Art Museum | 66b Shutterstock/Dmitriy Kurnyavko | 67tr Jim | 68b Shutterstock/Kiril Stanchev | 69 Touriste | 71 Shutterstock/ jennyt | 73b Damien Moore | 75t Elian | 77 Shutterstock/Georgios Kollidas | 78 Shutterstock/Darren Green | 80l Raimond Spekking / CC-BY-SA-3.0 | 82b Shutterstock/Bertl123 | 83 Val_McG | 87 Shutterstock/Georgios Kollidas | 89bl Shayno | 89t Jerry "Woody" | 90cl Bubobubo | 291bl The British Library | 91br Library of Congress | 95t Kim Traynor | 101br Shutterstock/Kenneth Dedeu | 105, 107br Shutterstock/Georgios Kollidas | 108t istockphoto/duncan1890 | 118 The British Library | 120 Shutterstock/Bocman1973 | 129 Shutterstock /Radek Sturgolewski | 132t Shutterstock/Sponner | 133b Shutterstock/NCG | 136 Aaron Logan | 137, 139, 143t Shutterstock/Georgios Kollidas | 144l RobinLeicester | 144r Sue Hutton | 155br El Comandante | 156c Klaus with K | 158t Andreas Tille | 159b JohnArmagh | 172b The lifted lorax | 174 Motmit | 176t Shutterstock/ BasPhoto | 182l Sodacan | 186b Shutterstock/QQ7 | 189t Bamundsen | 191 Shutterstock/Georgios Kollidas | 193 Mattana | 196 Shutterstock/Bertl123 | 201t Shutterstock/Dan Breckwoldt | 210 Jerry "Woody" | 211t Kim Traynor | 212b Heidas | 214c Magnus Manske | 224b Shutterstock/Georgios Kollidas | 229t camano10 | 236t Shutterstock/Oleg Golovnev | 236c Shutterstock/Neftali | 245br Shutterstock/Everett Collection | 249b Library of Congress/LC-DIG-ppmsca-19234 | 250c Diliff | 254-255 Shutterstock/JeremyRichards | 256-257 Shutterstock/dutourdumonde | 258 NASA | 260c Library of Congress/LC-USZ62-59503 | 261c Library of Congress/LC-DIG-ggbain-08204 | 261cb Library of Congress/LC-DIG-ggbain-08216 | 261b Ford Motor Company | 264t The Giant Puffin | 265b Tom Alt | 266b Library of Congress/LC-USZ62-70915 | 267t National Library of Ireland/HOG6 | 268tl Library of Congress/LC-DIG-ggbain-29588 | 268c The German Federal Archive | 269c Iain Robinson | 269b The German Federal Archive | 273 Library of Congress/LC-DIG-matpc-14736 | 275c Library of Congress/LC-USZ62-111580 | 275b NARA | 276t Library of Congress/ LC-DIG-hec-26818 | 277cl Richard Stone | 277cr NBG626 | 278c Library of Congress/LC-DIG-ggbain-35407 | 279br Acmthompson | 280 NASA/Bill Ingalls | 282tl USAAF | 284b Simon Harriyott | 285t Shutterstock/irisphoto1 | 286b Dan Marsh | 287t Robbie Dale | 288-289 Shutterstock/McCarthy's PhotoWorks

The publisher wishes to thank all of the photographers (known and unknown) whose images appear in this book. We apologize in advance for any omissions, or neglect, and will be pleased to make any corrections in future editions.